# NAVIGATING
## Tradition and Innovation
Essays Commemorating the Permanent Settlement of Hutterites in Manitoba

Kenny Wollmann, editor

2024

© 2024 Hutterian Brethren Book Centre
All rights reserved.

Cover image: Phil Hossack/Winnipeg Free Press.

**Softcover ISBN 978-1-927913-86-4**
**Hardcover ISBN 978-1-998141-06-7**

**Library and Archives Canada Cataloguing in Publication**
Title: Navigating tradition and innovation : essays commemorating the permanent settlement of Hutterites in Manitoba / Kenny Wollmann, editor.
Names: Wollmann, Kenny, editor. | Hutterian Brethren Book Centre, publisher.
Description: Includes bibliographical references and index.
Identifiers: Canadiana 20240289269 | ISBN 9781998141067 (hardcover) | ISBN 9781927913864 (softcover)
Subjects: LCSH: Hutterian Brethren—Manitoba—History. | LCSH: Christian communities—Manitoba—History. | LCSH: Manitoba—Church history.
Classification: LCC BX8129.H8 N38 2024 | DDC 289.77127—dc23

Box 40 • MacGregor, MB • R0H 0R0
p. 204-272-5132 • f. 204-252-2381 • e. orders@hbbookcentre.com

**Printed in Canada.**

Dedicated to

**Benjamin Maendel (1939–2018)**

and

**Paul Wollmann (1947–2021)**

of blessed memory

## Table of Contents

**Kenny Wollmann** | Introduction: "A Good Witness to the World?"...... I

**Astrid von Schlachta** | "May God Hold us in his Love and in the Covenant of his Peace Forever:" Jakob Huter—His Life and Thought..... 1

**James M. Stayer** | The Moravian Hutterites and the Beginning of Anabaptist History Writing: Kaspar Braitmichel, the First Historian of Anabaptism ..................................................................................25

**Bruce Wiebe** | "Despairing in Canada?" The Land Transactions of Hutterite Immigration to Manitoba......................................................45

**Leonard Gross** | *Community and Ethics*: Samuel Kleinsasser's Analysis and Interpretation of Schmiedeleut Faith and History ..........155

**Gerald J. Mast** | Navigating the Internet Question: Hutterite Leadership Practices and Schmiedeleut Smartphone Struggles ...........175

**Ian Kleinsasser** | Voices of Conflict: A Perspective of the 1992 Schmiedeleut Church Schism ...............................................................197

**Simon Evans and Peter Peller** | Beating the Squeeze: Adaptive Strategies on Hutterite Communities ...................................................261

**Cheryl Rockman-Greenberg, A. Micheil Innes, and J. Michael Charette** | Genetic Research with the Hutterites: Its Importance and Projections for the Future........................................307

**Jesse D. Hofer** | Building Capacity for Communal Conversation: *Gemeindeordnungen* and Discernment in the Hutterite World .............321

**Kenny Wollmann** | A Selected Bibliography ........................................347

# INTRODUCTION
## "A Good Witness to the World?"

"Group of People Reported Crossing the Manitoba-North Dakota Border." This hypothetical headline could just as easily have been written in 1918 as today. On June 7, 1918, forty-nine Hutterites from South Dakota crossed the U.S.-Canada border, fleeing conscription by the U.S. Army. This group was the first of several waves to permanently establish communities in Manitoba. The year 2018 marked the centennial of Hutterites in Manitoba, and this publication is an overdue attempt to commemorate this significant landmark. As such, this book offers an opportunity to reflect on the Hutterite legacy in this province. Today, there are almost 120 Hutterite communities scattered throughout the province, from Lac du Bonnet to Decker, from Piney to Fisher Branch. What has been their witness?

### A Micro-History

Beginning as it did in the flight from persecution, the story of Hutterites in Manitoba is a microcosm of the longer Hutterite story: a story of persecution, displacement, and intense internal struggle, all while attempting to live out a concrete vision of the kingdom of God. It is a story of a people who wandered through countries that today exist only in history textbooks.

Hutterites emerged in the Tyrol of sixteenth-century Europe (now part of modern-day Austria and Italy), as part of the radical wing of the larger Reformation movement. Because of persecution in the Tyrol region, no groups were able to practice community-of-goods—a Hutterite distinctive—despite a considerable contingent of community-minded Anabaptists living there. Persecution there and in other places led Hutterites to migrate through various regions in Europe, including Moravia (now part of Czechia), Hungary, Romania, and Ukraine. In the 1870s, facing economic hardship and the looming forces of Russification, most Hutterites moved to North America, settling in the Dakota Territory (present-day South Dakota and North Dakota).

In 1918, during World War I, anti-German sentiment and pressure to conform to American cultural norms, including military conscription, prompted the most recent Hutterite migration, this time over the border into Canada: the Schmiedeleut group to Manitoba, and the Darius- and Lehrerleut to Alberta. Amid political intrigue and outrage at an influx of German-speaking, pacifist immigrants, the vision of Canada's Minister of the Interior, Clifford Sifton, to settle the prairies continued to unfold.[1] By the end of 1918, six Hutterite communities had re-established themselves along the Assiniboine River in the Rural Municipality of Cartier.[2]

So much for the movement's temporal origins and history. The "founding narrative" of the Hutterite movement in the Hutterite *Chronicles*[3] begins with the biblical account of creation: God made the earth and filled it with creatures. Humanity, according to the narrative, was the crown of creation—but they failed to show him proper obedience. Before this failure, perfect *Gemeinschaft* (fellowship or community) had existed between the Creator and his creation. There was full *shalom*, i.e., neither enmity nor death. The *Chronicle* goes on to cite examples of how God has always worked out his purposes in earthly time through his chosen ones.[4] With this rhetorical move, Hutterites clearly articulated the conviction that community-of-goods and their shared lives are the initial and most perfect intention of God. Peter Riedemann reiterated in his *Confession of Faith* that "creation still testifies today that in the beginning God ordained that people should own nothing individually but should have all things in common."[5] The Hutterite tradition, at its best, has viewed its collective life as a foretaste of the *shalom* that God in Christ will one day reestablish in all of creation.

The human story of Hutterite history, as any living member can attest, is much more messy, precarious—and all too human.

---

1  Bruce Wiebe, "A Politically Risky Land Sale," *Preservings* 32 (2012), 35–38.
2  A "first word" on the one hundred years of Hutterite settlement in Manitoba is Ian Kleinsasser, *Blessings and Burdens: 100 Years of Hutterites in Manitoba* (MacGregor: Hutterian Brethren Book Centre, 2019).
3  The Hutterite Chronicles are vital primary sources documenting the historical, doctrinal, and communal life of Hutterites from the sixteenth century onwards. These meticulously maintained records offer detailed insights into religious beliefs, social and work regulations, and experiences, including martyrdom and migrations.
4  *The Chronicle of the Hutterian Brethren*, vol. 1, trans. Hutterian Brethren (Rifton: Plough Publishing House, 1987), 1–4.
5  Peter Riedemann, *Peter Riedeman's Hutterite Confession of Faith*, trans. John J. Friesen (Walden: Plough Publishing House, 2019), 119.

## Coming into Their Own: Oscillating between Tradition and Innovation

The story of Hutterites in Manitoba can be viewed through the classic historical lens of continuity and change. Another way of framing this is through the tension between the practice of tradition and the introduction of innovations.[6] For much of the twentieth century, Hutterite life was characterized by simplicity and asceticism, with firm guidelines for virtually every facet of life. Much of this was necessitated by the challenging economic and social circumstances associated with migrating from South Dakota to Manitoba. Through *Gemeindeordnungen*, the grapes of individuality were systematically crushed into the strong wine of communal living. Today, well into the twenty-first century, the emphases of the past—in significant portions of the Hutterite world—are no longer the normative factors in Hutterite life; the regulations that controlled life's minutiae have relaxed considerably. This shift from persecution to prosperity, from hardship to comfort and convenience, is the most consequential challenge that today's Hutterites must learn to navigate. Perhaps the most significant obstacle associated with this recent experience of prosperity is that most Hutterites would not even consider it a conundrum![7]

There is much to celebrate in the century of Hutterite settlement in Manitoba: overcoming significant financial odds and opposition from other settlers, suffering through the Great Depression and World War II, and navigating conscientious objector status, to say nothing of dealing with internal challenges such as the 1992 schism, the initial six communities having grown to almost 120—adding over one per year, on average.

As with all human endeavours, however, there is also much that bears thoughtful reflection or outright lament. Hutterites still have not produced an adequate number of trained professionals commensurate with our population; unlike our Anabaptist cousins, we have not established educational institutions, hospitals, or publishing houses, nor have we earnestly set out on the journey to come to terms with the painful legacy of settler colonialism.

---

6 In delivering the 2020 Jacob D. Maendel Lectures, Astrid von Schlachta effectively explored four earlier periods of Hutterite history through a similar lens. Astrid von Schlachta, *"Holding Fast to What is Good?" Tradition and Renewal in Hutterite History* (MacGregor: Hutterian Brethren Book Centre, 2020).

7 This notion was originally developed for a German publication commemorating the five-hundred-year anniversary of the Anabaptist movement. See Kenny Wollmann, "*Mit Bequemlichkeit und Annehmlichkeit zurechtkommen: Mündig leben als Hutterer im 21. Jahrhundert* [Coping with Comfort and Convenience: Living Maturely as Hutterites in the 21st Century]," *Gewagt! 500 Jahre Täuferbewegung, 1525-2025: Themenjahr 20 gewagt! mündig leben* (Frankfurt am Main, 2020), 63.

The Hutterite practice of community-of-goods, in some quarters of the American and Canadian context, has by and large become another version of the pursuit of the American Dream: comfort, convenience, and individualism as the highest human aspiration. Hutterite communities, far from living lives of simplicity and generosity, have been co-opted into the larger American project of consumption and a unique form of "collective individualism."[8]

Hutterites have always seen themselves as "alien citizens," which has sometimes meant that Hutterites have shown a lack of responsibility toward their national community; however, more recently the opposite—a overly-close identification with national causes at the expense of a counter-cultural Christian witness—has also become evident. As a result of this, Hutterites often struggle to find answers to the wrong questions.

Hutterites of the sixteenth century, for all their shortcomings, actively established an alternative society to address the problems they identified within mainstream society and religion. It is true that Hutterites of today have maintained many of these cultural artifacts (patterns and traditions) from another era. These artifacts, however, do not always result in a meaningful or helpful counter-cultural force that serves to further the kingdom of God.[9]

What will Hutterites of the twenty-first century accomplish? What will be celebrated or lamented at the bicentennial of permanent Hutterite settlement in Manitoba?

### Introducing *Navigating Tradition and Innovation*

In reading Hutterite history sources, it is possible to identify different visions of what it means to be faithful to the teachings of Jesus Christ. In the early era, Hutterite writers readily pointed out the shortcomings of the established church, opposed it at great price, and sought to find new ways to embody the Gospel. This resulted in a very small but growing group that did things differently from the surrounding society.

Later in Hutterite history, a different perspective emerged. Writers urged the faithful to avoid any innovation, to stay with what their

---

8   In his critique of Hutterites in the 1930s, German theologian and eventual Hutterite minister Eberhard Arnold diagnosed it as a "collective egoism." See *Brothers Unite: An Account of the Uniting of Eberhard Arnold and the Rhön Bruderhof With the Hutterian Church*, trans. Hutterian Brethren (Ulster Park: Plough Publishing House, 1988), 174.

9   My thoughts on this are in part shaped by the intense work of the Riedemann Arbeitskreis as we laboured to produce a history textbook. Lothar G. Korff, *Glauben und Geschichte: Die Hutterer in der Reformation des 16. Jahrhunderts* (unpublished manuscript, 2014).

forefathers had established, and to listen carefully to the counsel of the elders. They did this, too, in the name of Jesus. This was the approach during a time of inner decay in an attempt to preserve what good remained within the movement.

Since coming to Manitoba and permanently settling in 1918, Hutterites have vacillated between these two poles: preserving tradition versus implementing innovation. Several essays in this collection highlight the tension and conflict that has resulted from these divergent perspectives. On the one hand, being faithful has meant recognizing the value of the traditions that those before us have imparted and working to preserve and uphold those gifts. On the other hand, innovation and reform has been the great cry of those who wanted to reclaim the vitality of the early Hutterite movement and indeed of the early church. The cover illustration of this volume is evocative of this tension: A Hutterite woman in traditional dress simultaneously upholds tradition while challenging a taboo on hockey rinks and female participation in sport. The solitary figure suggests that the path of innovation is often a lonely one. This, while true, also obscures the fact that innovators are always standing on the shoulders of giants. Tradition and innovation are an indissoluble pair.

It is a truism to say that both perspectives—an openness to change, and a stewarding of tradition—are in and of themselves valid. It is also a truth—but one less commonly acknowledged—that both of these perspectives can result in less-than-desirable consequences: openness to change can result in a condition worse than what preceded the reform (Matthew 12:43–45), unfaithfulness, and a loss of identity. Refusal to change can lead to unfaithfulness of a different kind, to the "burying of talents" (Matthew 25:14–30), and the sacralization of an ungodly status quo. Within the church—from the early church onward—these differing perspectives can result in a great deal of tension and conflict. Perhaps one of the primary lessons Hutterites have had the opportunity to learn in the last century is that it is not so much what kind of conflict we have or what its content is, but that what truly defines a Christian church is how conflict is resolved and processed—metabolized in a way that strengthens the body of Christ.

Paul wrote the following words to a church divided about whether to hold on to Jewish traditions or to move beyond them:

> If your brother or sister is being injured by what you eat, you are no longer walking in love. Do not let what you eat cause the ruin of one for whom Christ died. […] Let us then pursue what makes for peace and for mutual edifica-

tion. Do not, for the sake of food, destroy the work of God (Romans 14:15, 19–20).

The body of Christ here is divided about whether to "ingest" or "abstain" from innovations. Paul's advice is to proceed in these matters in the way of love. This means seeing our theological opponent as "one for whom Christ died" rather than an enemy to be destroyed. The goal should not be to scandalize others, but to "pursue what makes for peace and for mutual edification" of the body of Christ. Whether we eat (innovate), or whether we abstain (maintain tradition), Paul calls us to do both for the glory of God, for the edification of Christ's body, and in view of the kingdom of God (Romans 14:6).

## History for the Sake of the Church; History as Redemptive

Shortly after the 1992 church schism among the Schmiedeleut, Leonard Gross, the doyen of Hutterite history at the time, wrote a letter to Hutterites encouraging reconciliation and suggesting a way forward. One of his suggestions included an internal self-analysis of leadership styles and structures in the church. Additionally, he pointed to the "redemptive element" of historical enquiry. Gross wrote:

> The writing of history can contain a redemptive element, by helping to bring together divergent groups who previously have not seen eye to eye. […] You as Western Hutterites as a whole have yet to get your heads together in organizing materials, and then writing, historically, your ongoing history from your own perspective.[10]

Disappointingly, but perhaps understandably given the upheaval of the time, this letter was largely ignored in Hutterite circles. I wasn't aware of its existence until Gross shared it with me and a colleague on a research trip to the Mennonite Historical Archives in Goshen, Indiana, in 2015. It is my hope that the seed planted by Leonard Gross can be seen germinating in this publication.

On the same study trip, I had the privilege of meeting the well-known Mennonite historian, writer, and filmmaker John Ruth. In a motley assembly of Anabaptists from various traditions, brought together by the indefatigable Old Order Mennonite historian and founder of the Muddy Creek Farm Library and Archives, Amos B. Hoover, we deliberated on the fissiparous tendencies of Anabaptists. We discussed various challenges and made light of the numerous reasons Anabaptists have banned each other or formed new communities: "At least we don't kill each other;" "Good

---

10  Leonard Gross to "the Dariusleut, the Lehrerleut, the Schmiedeleut," May 19, 1993.

wood splits, bad wood rots." Despite these moments of levity in our conversation, it was evident to all of us that such infighting was damaging not only to our communities but also to the larger mission of the universal church. John said it succinctly and profoundly: "We are not a good witness to the world." The hope for this volume is that it will help us evaluate and assess the Hutterite witness before a watching and waiting world.

History is messy and complicated precisely because life is messy and complicated. Good historical writing, on the other hand, is cogent and concise. This clarity in writing occasionally comes at the price of oversimplification. In addition to these challenges, there is the Anabaptist-Hutterite (and, indeed, human!) tendency to romanticize history, regarding it as a past where there was more faithfulness, cohesion, and peace within the church. Discerning readers of the essays in this book will quickly realize that real challenges were present at every stage of Hutterite history. (Discerning readers of the book of Acts will realize the same thing about the early Church.) At the same time, there are important glimpses of how God has actively moved through the vision of individual people, communities, and the faithful practices of the church.

If we are to grow and learn from the past, an essential starting point is a truthful—if awkward and painful—history. In his memoirs, the Hutterite chronicler Johannes Waldner articulates three reasons for the truthful telling of history. Waldner admits that he would "much rather have passed over these quarrels in silence." Schmiedeleut Hutterites reflecting on the sordid history of the 1992 schism understand the sentiment. Waldner continues:

> I have found it hard and distressing enough to revive for posterity the memories of these old faults and failures in the church, for perhaps as people died these things might have been forgotten. But my heart and conscience compelled me to write against my will, for the following reasons: First, in order to present the whole truth about our history and keep back nothing important that took place, both praiseworthy and unpraiseworthy acts are recorded, just as in Bible stories about the God-fearing people of old—patriarchs, kings, and prophets. Second, to serve as a warning, for while quarrels and divisions arise all too often among believers, no one should reject community and the sharing of a common life because of faults and weaknesses. [...] Third, to warn against any of us presuming to introduce a new practice he has invented himself and thereby

alter, disturb, and displace the old, well-proven order of the church.[11]

Waldner clearly stands more strongly on the side of tradition than of innovation, but his words about the purpose of history as a positive force within the life of the church ring true. A church that cannot tell the truth about itself, a church that fears the truth, is a church that operates within a purely human horizon, devoid of grace. The truthful historian in the service of the church recognizes that it is ultimately the work of God that brings the kingdom of God, not the fallible machinations of humanity.

**The Essays**

Because the Manitoba Hutterite centennial cannot be understood without reaching back to Hutterite roots, two essays on European Hutterianism rightly begin this volume. Leading scholars Astrid von Schlachta and James M. Stayer sketch the biographies and influence of Jakob Huter (Jacob Hutter) and Kaspar Braitmichel, essential figures in the Hutterite story.[12] I am thankful to John Roth for his English translation of Astrid von Schlachta's essay from the original German.

Against this helpful backdrop, the remaining seven essays deal with the primary theme of this publication: the North American—specifically the Manitoban—Hutterite experience. This set of essays begins—as the Hutterite experience in Manitoba did—with land transactions, in Bruce Wiebe's exhaustive forensic analysis of the first Hutterite land purchases. Combining a unique skill set and attention to detail with a determined pursuit of sources, Wiebe has managed to sketch out a history that has largely been lost in the Hutterite consciousness.

Wiebe's look at economic transactions is followed by a more theological piece from Leonard Gross that presents and contextualizes excerpts from a unique primary source: Samuel Kleinsasser's unpublished manuscript *Community and Ethics*. Written in the aftermath of the 1992 church division, this text was incisively written with enough to pique both parties in the Schmiedeleut conflict. Kleinsasser clearly had the ability to stand on his own feet and develop his own critical insights. Leaving the specific commentary on the 1992 Schmiedeleut division to the side, Gross has excerpted the theological vision that undergirds Kleinsasser's critiques. This text, in Gross's judgment, "may well be a first among Hutterites

---

11   *The Chronicle of the Hutterian Brethren*, vol. 2 (Ste. Agathe: Crystal Spring Colony, 1998), 494–95.
12   In the interval since von Schlachta completed this essay, the collected works of Huter have been released. See Emmy Barth Maendel and Jonathan Seiling, eds. and trans., *Jakob Hutter: His Life and Letters* (Walden: Plough Publishing House, 2024).

for the manner in which the author attempts to ferret out the primary [theological] motifs of the Hutterian Brethren."

The essay by Gerald J. Mast takes up the theme of tradition and innovation with regard to alternative approaches to internet and cellphone use among the Schmiedeleut I and Schmiedeleut II conferences. Both groups have sometimes had difficulty understanding each other, with polemics of legalism or liberal permissiveness being lobbed back and forth. Mast's sympathetic and insightful look at the approaches of both groups may help the discerning reader understand more traditional approaches to technology, and in the process aid us in discerning how to nurture healthy and responsible technology use in community.

With enviable access to essential primary sources—both textual and otherwise—Ian Kleinsasser presents an initial Schmiedeleut I perspective on the 1992 division. This is, of course, not *the* Schmiedeleut I perspective, but rather the attempt of one Hutterite historian earnestly seeking truth in a situation where it might be impossible to objectively find it. This essay represents the first internal attempt to move beyond chronicling these events—often from a particular partisan perspective—to doing historical work that is subject to critique, revision, and sustained dialogue. Kleinsasser also raises key questions for the church of today.

The essay by Simon Evans and Peter Peller explores the theme of tradition and innovation with respect to Hutterites and industry. Traditionally, Hutterites have flourished in the realm of agriculture and livestock production, but as new challenges emerged at the end of the twentieth century, some ventured into manufacturing. Evans and Peller provide an initial interprovincial survey of this development, including the evolution of some specific companies, and tease out preliminary observations on what this transition might mean for Hutterites. In doing so, they draw attention to a lively conversation that has already been taking place in Hutterite circles.

If innovation brings the risk of too much change, there are also dangers associated with a lack of change! Cheryl Rockman-Greenberg and her colleagues have been working with Hutterites in the area of genetic studies for decades. Their essay provides a historical survey of Hutterite genetic studies, pays tribute to past luminaries in the field, and highlights the unique challenges facing Hutterites in this aspect of their lives.

The final essay, fittingly from a Hutterite voice, is Jesse Hofer's theological reflections on developing effective communal conversations. Unlike most of the other contributions to this volume, this one is unapologetically aimed at internal readership. Hofer takes his cue from the 2018 letter to

Schmiedeleut I communities by Arnold Hofer and Samuel Waldner that aimed to begin the process of reconciliation between leaders and congregations wounded by the 1992 Schmiedeleut schism. Hofer sees in this letter the hopeful possibility of a different approach to communal conversations, one that involves the entire baptized body of Christ in collective discernment.

The volume concludes with a selected bibliography featuring publications of the last few decades in the area of Hutterite-Anabaptist studies, including internal publications from Hutterite printers and bookbinderies not released via traditional publishing channels.

## Conventions

### Jakob Huter/Hutter

The Hutterite eponym Jakob Hutter has his name variably spelled "Huter" or "Hutter." Most primary and many German sources use a single t, while there is usually a double t in English—indeed, Hutterite is always spelled with a double t. In this publication his name has intentionally not been unified, to signal an origin in a time when spelling conventions had not yet stabilized.

### Schmiedeleut Groups

In reference to the 1992 conference division that resulted in two Schmiedeleut groups, most publications use "Group One" and "Group Two" to identify the factions. This publication uses the more flexible combination of "Group I"/"Schmiedeleut I" and "Group II"/"Schmiedeleut II." The more pejorative "Oiler" and "Gibb" labels are left to the side.

### Colony or Community: What's in a Name?

In a broad sense, this book uses the term "community" rather than "colony." Exceptions occur when quoting other sources or making direct reference to official and legal names. The reasons for this editorial preference are multiple. First, "colony" evokes colonialism and the inherent problems associated with it. Additionally, it is a poor rendering of the German words *Gemeinschaft*, *Gemein*, *Gemeinde*, *Gma*, or *Haushaben* typically used in Hutterite chronicles, theological literature, correspondence, and hymnody.

The term "colony" dates back to settlement in Russia, when Hutterites—along with Mennonites, Lutherans, Catholics, Jews, and other Germanic groups—accepted the invitation of Catherine II in the second half of the eighteenth century to settle in her realm. These groups were granted various privileges that gave them considerable autonomy such as local self-governance with minimal interference and education that didn't include Russian language instruction. This arrangement enabled these groups to remain German cultural islands in a Russian sea. Their rights and privileges were guaranteed by the 1763 Manifesto and the 1764 Colonization Law. Adam Giesinger points out that these Germans "called themselves 'colonists,' not peasants, and considered themselves [...] culturally superior to the uncouth and ignorant native peasants."[13]

The term "colony" is therefore not so much a Hutterite label as it is one introduced by forces outside the tradition and eventually adopted by the majority. Additionally, it is an anachronism to refer to Hutterite communities predating the Russian era as "colonies." In this publication, therefore, at the risk of making a distinction without a difference, I attempt to provide a corrective to what I perceive as a misnomer.

## Personal Thanks

The vast majority of Hutterite historical work—both primary and secondary—has been done by non-Hutterites. These outside voices have been a gift to the Hutterite people, and the table of contents of this volume indicate many of the stalwart contributors of the last decades, as well as a few new ones. *Navigating Tradition and Innovation* also joins a small, but I hope growing, trend of trained researchers and historians from within the Hutterite tradition contributing to the broader academic conversation. These scholars write with an ecclesiological sensitivity that seeks to bring academia into the service of the church. This progress would not have been possible without the work of an earlier generation of Hutterite researchers like David Gross, John S. Hofer, Johnny Hofer, Paul S. Gross (1910–98), *Ältester* Jacob Kleinsasser (1922–2017), Dora Maendel, Mike "Gus" Maendel (1933–2020), Patricia McAdams (1935–2024), Tony Waldner, *Ältester* Elias Walter (1862–1938), and other storytellers and genealogy enthusiasts whose efforts are recorded in the collective memory of their people. They have preserved parts of the Hutterite story in an era when academic work was not always valued. Thanks be to God.

This book has been a long time coming. Along with the Jacob D. Maendel Lectures, it found its genesis in informal conversations surrounding the one-hundred-year anniversary of permanent Hutterite settlement in Manitoba.[14] I am thankful for the people who were part of those con-

---

13  Adam Giesinger, *From Catherine to Khrushchev: The Story of Russia's Germans* (Battleford: Marian Press, 1974), 48.
14  More information can be found on the series' website at www.jdmlectures.org.

versations, among them Jesse Hofer, Johnny Hofer, Ian Kleinsasser, Tom Waldner, and Tony Waldner.

I am indebted to Dan Epp-Tiessen, Paul Doerksen, John J. Friesen, Irma Fast Dueck, Brian Froese, Gerald Gerbrandt, Sheila Klassen-Wiebe, and Karl Koop, professors past and present at Canadian Mennonite University, for shaping my love and interest in Anabaptist history and theology, and providing an important witness that academic work can, and indeed must, serve the church.

The visionary efforts of the *Ältester* Jacob Kleinsasser (1922–2017), teachers Anna Maendel (1953–2022) and Dora Maendel, and minister Benjamin Maendel (1939–2018) laid the foundation that made my education possible. What I have been able to do was empowered by their vision, courage, and foresight, and I give thanks to God for them. I am also grateful for the opportunity to work alongside *Ältester* Arnold Hofer. His keen appreciation for Anabaptist history has inspired me and continues to give me hope.

I have been surrounded by, and stand in the presence of, an astonishing cloud of witnesses—some present, others who have passed on. *Deo gratias*.

Every book is the result of much labour and learning. It has been my privilege to work and learn alongside the writers. I find myself grateful for their im/patience and trust. Numerous people have contributed much to this volume from an editorial perspective; in particular I am grateful for the consummate skills of Maureen Epp, Brock Peters, Julian Waldner, and Lydia Wollmann.

Finally, this work would not have been possible without the multiplicities of gracious and loving action and support toward me by my family and Baker Hutterite Community. I particularly wish to acknowledge my wife, Sheri, who bore the brunt of the burden in caring for our twin daughters (whose arrival in 2016 contributed to the lengthy gestation of this volume) while I pursued my undergraduate degrees. I am deeply grateful to live life alongside Sheri, Kali and Hali, Olivia, and Sophia. When I consider what I hope my work here and elsewhere will accomplish, it is to leave behind a community, church, and world that has more *shalom* as a result, and that it might equip them to contribute in their own God-given way to the healing of all of God's creation. May it be so.

*Soli Deo gloria.*

Kenny Wollmann
July 2024

**Astrid von Schlachta** is the historian and director of the Mennonitische Forschungsstelle [Mennonite Research Centre] in Weierhof, Germany, and a lecturer at the University of Regensburg. For nearly her entire academic life, von Schlachta has been researching the Anabaptists, with particular emphasis on the Hutterites. Her dissertation concentrated on the Hutterites of the late sixteenth and early seventeenth centuries. Her most recent book, *Täufer: Von der Reformation ins 21. Jahrhundert* [Anabaptists: From the Reformation to the Twenty-first Century] was released in June 2020. Astrid von Schlachta is also president of the Mennonitische Geschichtsverein [Mennonite Historical Society, Germany] and the 500 Jahre Täuferbewegung 2025 Society, which is preparing to commemorate the 500th anniversary of the Anabaptist Movement in 2025.

# "May God Hold us in his Love and in the Covenant of his Peace Forever:"[1]
# Jakob Huter—His Life and Thought

## ASTRID VON SCHLACHTA

What mental image of Jakob Huter do we have in our imagination? That of a tireless missionary? An organizer who sought to ensure that Tyrolean Anabaptists had a secure and stable home in Moravia? A stalwart defender of his cause, who did not shrink from conflict and could "cut loose" with invective? A persecuted soul, who met a tragic end as martyr on the executioner's pyre in front of the Goldenes Dachl in Innsbruck? All of these images can be found in the sources. Together they form a composite picture of Jakob Huter, the human being.

At the time of Huter's birth around 1500 in the hamlet of Moos near St. Lorenzen in the Puster Valley, the Tyrol was already in the midst of a spiritual awakening. Glimmers of light were pushing back against what people sometimes describe as the "dark" Middle Ages. Indeed, a desire to reform the faith was evident well before the Reformation. Already in the fifteenth century a reform movement known as the *Devotio Moderna* (modern devotion) had found supporters within the Catholic Church who were dissatisfied with established forms of religiosity. This movement anticipated ideas that later found full expression in the Reformation: a conviction that faith should focus more on Jesus Christ and the Word of God, and an emphasis on a deep inner piety. In the Tyrol, the bishop of Brixen, Nikolaus von Kues (1401–64), was an especially devoted follower of the *Devotio Moderna*. He preached in German rather than Latin; he also

---

[1] These are the final words from the last letter Jakob Huter wrote, as quoted in Hans Georg Fischer, "Jakob Huter—sein Leben und Wirken: Ein Zeugnis evangelischer Frömmigkeit im 16. Jahrhundert" (Diss. Wien, 1949), 56.
This essay has been translated from German by John D. Roth.

attempted to reform the monasteries and sought to nurture a deeper piety among his parishioners. Yet despite all this openness to reform, there were also reports of numerous problems among Tyrolean priests. For example, church offices in the early sixteenth century were filled with priests who served multiple parishes or couldn't speak German. The spiritual care of ordinary people was not guaranteed. This growing dissatisfaction opened the people to new ideas—on the one hand to those of the Anabaptists, and on the other to those of the Reformation.[2]

Politically, the Tyrol belonged to the Habsburg monarchy. Beginning in 1521, Archduke Ferdinand I ruled over the region. According to the Hutterite *Chronicle*, he personally stood on the balcony under the Goldenes Dachl in Innsbruck and watched as Jacob Huter was burned at the stake. As the administrator of the Hereditary Lands of the Habsburgs, Ferdinand oversaw regional governors in the capital of every territory—Innsbruck in the case of the Tyrol—who were expected to rule according to his directives. These authorities always took a hard line in the persecution of the Anabaptists, whereas local officials lower in the bureaucracy occasionally protected them. At the local level, the web of personal relations was much tighter; indeed, families of local officials often included several members of the Anabaptist faith.[3]

While the government responded harshly to Anabaptists, it was somewhat milder in how it responded to Protestants. Although Catholic territorial princes were not willing to tolerate Protestants in a formal way, Protestant beliefs seemed to be somewhat less threatening and less likely to result in sedition and rebellion.

The situation was quite different with respect to Anabaptists. More than the principle of believers' baptism, authorities regarded Anabaptist teachings on nonresistance, their rejection of the oath, and their separatism with particular concern. This is fully understandable from the government's perspective. Territorial princes in the early modern era considered the feudal obligations of their subjects—above all, personal loyalty—to be of utmost importance. For their part, the territorial princes were expected to defend and protect their subjects. These were mutual obligations.

---

2   Cf. Rudolf Leeb, "Der Streit um den wahren Glauben: Reformation und Gegenreformation in Österreich," in *Geschichte des Christentums in Österreich: Von der Spätantike bis zur Gegenwart*, ed. Rudolf Leeb, et al. (Vienna: Überreuter, 2003), 145–279; Heinz Noflatscher, "Martin Luther und die Reformation in Tirol," *Österreich in Geschichte und Literatur* 42 (1998), 140–151.

3   For more on the development of various Anabaptist groups in the Tyrol, see Werner O. Packull, *Die Hutterer in Tirol: Frühes Täufertum in der Schweiz, Tirol und Mähren* (Innsbruck: Universitätsverlag Wagner, 1996) and *Verbrannte Visionen? Erinnerungsorte der Täufer in Tirol*, ed. Astrid von Schlachta, Ellinor Forster, and Giovanni Merola (Innsbruck: Innsbruck University Press, 2007).

According to contemporary understandings, loyalty to the prince included the obligation to bear arms in the event of war. The oath also played an important role in the sixteenth century, since it explicitly expressed a subject's trustworthiness. Every territorial prince demanded an act of fealty from his subjects at the beginning of his reign, a sworn oath of loyalty to the prince and his authority. Refusal to swear oaths could be interpreted as a rebellious act. Thus, Anabaptist convictions called into question several essential principles in the mutual relationship between the territorial prince and his subjects, principles that seemed to be critical elements for social and political stability.

## Jakob Huter—Personality and Biographical Details

Who was Jakob Huter? If one wanted to describe him in personal terms, one might turn to Hutterite reports such as those found in the "Great Chronicle" (*Grosses Geschichtsbuch*). On the other hand, numerous interrogations of his supporters also reveal an image of the Anabaptist preacher. It is striking that the Hutterite reports are actually very sparse in terms of Huter's personal details. To honour him as the source of a religious tradition or the founder of a community, or to regard his writings as particularly authoritative or even as confessional statements, was foreign to the Hutterites of the sixteenth century. The *Chronicle* describes Huter as someone committed to "peace, love, and unity."[4] Similar attributions can also be found in reports of the various debates and divisions. In connection with the discovery of the adultery committed by Simon Schützinger's wife, for example, the *Chronicle* notes that Huter was "a man richly gifted by God."[5]

What did he look like, this Jakob Huter? If we are going to focus on the life of a significant Anabaptist preacher and leader, then having an image of him in our minds would be helpful. Unfortunately, we are out of luck! Except for a few hints regarding his clothing, we have no information about Huter's physical appearance. To be sure, there is a portrait that appears regularly in books, but it does not originate in the sixteenth century. Whether or not Huter actually resembled the image created by the anonymous engraver, who probably lived in the seventeenth or eighteenth century, remains pure speculation.

However, several warrants for his arrest, issued by the authorities seeking information about Huter include a few bits of information regarding

---

4   *Das große Geschichtbuch der Hutterischen Brüder*, ed. Rudolf Wolkan (Cayley: Macmillan Colony, 1974), 79.
5   *Geschichtbuch*, 80; *The Chronicle of the Hutterian Brethren*, vol. I (Rifton: Plough Publishing House, 1987), 105.

his clothing. Thus, at one point he apparently wore a black overcoat with a cape—that is, a light, flowing outer garment, originally worn by knights, that had become a common style. In addition, he had a blue waistcoat, white pants, and a black hat. In another account, the Anabaptist Katharina Tagwerker testified that Huter had worn a leather-coloured coat that had creases in the front, as well as a black hat and white breech pants. At one point, it was said that he had a black beard; on another occasion, it was reported that he had a closely trimmed beard.[6] In any case, Huter likely dressed in a simple peasant style that was customary for the time.

More recently, a debate has emerged regarding the meaning of a passage in the arrest warrant of March 1532, where it reads that Huter carried a *hackl*, that is, an harquebus (*Hakenbüchse*) or portable gun supported by a tripod. Some of the sources refer explicitly to a *püchsen*—a long rifle. Anabaptist historians have debated over the meaning of this reference.[7] Were Huter's adversaries perhaps trying to vilify him by depicting him as someone ready to use violence? Or was he actually armed with the intention of defending himself while on his many travels? Or did the term *hackl* merely refer to a staff, which people commonly took with them on their travels? In this instance, the sources refuse to yield an answer as to what was actually meant by the term. Regardless, what we do know is that by 1532, non-resistance was already a significant principle for the Tyrolean Anabaptists. From that year we have a statement by Sigmund of Kiens, who formally testified that the leaders forbade them "to carry any weapon other than a staff." If authorities wanted to arrest them, he said, Anabaptists should not defend themselves.[8]

If we turn our focus away from outward appearances to the character of Jakob Huter, we find that his contemporaries described him as an articulate and charismatic man. The Anabaptist Michael Ebner, for example, characterized him as someone whose words were powerful and who spoke with the authority of God.[9] Huter's opponents depicted him in very similar terms, although they interpreted these qualities quite differently. Thus, the Anabaptist preacher Gabriel Ascherham described Huter, in the course of a conflict with his community, as an "arrogant and proud spirit."[10] Evidently, Huter did not shy away from conflict. He was a confident and strong-willed person, capable of a certain stubbornness and gifted with a

---

6  Grete Mecenseffy, ed., *Österreich*, 3. Teil, Quellen zur Geschichte der Täufer 14 (Gütersloh: Mohn Verlag, 1983), 37; Packull, *Hutterer in Tirol*, 37.
7  Mecenseffy, *Österreich*, 3. Teil, 37; Packull, *Hutterer in Tirol*, 198f.
8  Mecenseffy, *Österreich*, 3. Teil, 21.
9  Ibid., 22.
10  Packull, *Hutterer in Tirol*, 259; Christoph Andreas Fischer, *Der Hutterischen Widertauffer Taubenkobel* (Ingolstadt, 1607), 55.

talent for organization. He was well-spoken and could preach in an impassioned and convincing manner. These were all qualities useful for building up and leading a congregation. And these were also characteristics precisely suited for his role as an effective missioner and preacher of the Anabaptist faith in the Tyrol. For Robert Friedmann, Huter was a "charismatic leader with unique spiritual qualities, absolutely convinced that he had been called to serve as the bishop or shepherd of his flock." Huter regarded it as his task to instill in his congregation a solid eschatological vision of the Kingdom of God and to also make this known to the "world," which had not yet seen the "true light."[11]

We know relatively little about Jakob Huter's early years. He knew how to read and write, which implies that he had received a basic education—something relatively uncommon at the time. The name "Huter" likely derived not from his later occupation as a hat-maker, but rather from the farmstead where he grew up. The Pröslhof in Moos by St. Lorenzen was earlier known as "Hueterhof." That Huter's family name derived from a geographic location is further supported by the fact that Jakob's sister, Agnes, also used the name "Hueterin." She was also an Anabaptist, and was executed at the end of 1530 or early in 1531. Today it is equally correct to spell Jakob's family name as "Huter," "Hutter," or "Hueter"—since there were no fixed standards of spelling in the sixteenth century, people wrote the name as they understood it or however they thought was correct.

Jakob Huter learned the hat-making trade from his cousin Caspar Huter in Stegen close to Bruneck. Here he also encountered the Anabaptist faith. In the fall of 1526 a goatherd named Wölfl, a very early Anabaptist convert in the Tyrol, preached in the home of Caspar Huter. In a later interrogation, Caspar stated that Jakob had listened enthusiastically to Wölfl's sermon and was "receptive to it." Immediately, Jakob went to the marketplace in Bozen in order to get his hands on a New Testament. He then started to preach to him (i.e., Caspar) as well as to all of the household servants.[12] Caspar Huter added that he had forbidden his cousin to preach at his home, whereupon Jakob left the house a month later. Whether or not Caspar said this to protect Jakob remains unclear. But there is one more story related to Jakob's departure. In his formal statement to the authorities, Caspar claimed that he and Jakob had gambled with Jakob's savings. According to Caspar, everything proceeded in a fair manner. In the end he won the money, but Jakob was so plagued by his conscience that Caspar gave the winnings back to him. A second version of the story

---

11  Robert Friedmann, *Hutterite Studies: Celebrating the Life and Work of an Anabaptist Scholar*, ed. Harold Bender, 2nd ed. (MacGregor: Hutterian Brethren Book Centre, 2010), 205.
12  Mecenseffy, *Österreich*, 3. Teil, 314; Packull, *Hutterer in Tirol*, 226.

suggests that Caspar had attempted to rob Jakob of his wages and savings, whereupon Jakob became angry and left the home of his cousin.[13]

## Jakob Huter and His Theology

In order to gain a clearer understanding of Jakob Huter's theology and his inner perspectives we must heed his own words. Altogether eight letters by Huter, written between 1530 and 1535, have survived. These letters represent a small portion of the extensive correspondence exchanged within the Hutterite community during the sixteenth century. Likely more than 500 letters—or "epistles," as they were described at the time—written by missionaries and elders were sent back and forth between Moravia and the various regions in the Holy Roman Empire where Hutterite missionaries were travelling.[14] As we learn from a 1576 letter by Peter Walpot, if the letters reached the Hutterite communities in Moravia, they were read aloud to the congregation:

> To you, our dear brothers, Mathes and Paul, I want to let you know that we received your message in the week prior to Pentecost. We were delighted to receive your words of comfort. I read both of the letters to the community on the Monday of Pentecost and also requested that they should continue to be read for the comfort and admonition of the community. And so that we think of you in our prayer, just as you think of us. May the Lord be truly praised in this![15]

After the letter was read aloud, it was taken to the copy room of the Hutterite community and copied in very beautiful handwriting into large, heavy books. These books can still be found today in various archives and libraries, especially in eastern European countries. Through the centuries the books containing the copies were confiscated by government authorities or by Jesuits, who were attempting to bring Hutterites back into the Catholic fold. A reference from 1783 notes that Catholic priests took more than two wagonloads of books from the Hutterite communities in Lewär to Bratislava.[16]

---

13  Packull, *Hutterer in Tirol*, 226.
14  A portion of these letters are published in *Die Hutterischen Episteln*, 4 vols. (Elie: James Valley Book Centre, 1986–1991).
15  Peter Walpot in a letter to Mathes Binder and Paul Glock, in *Die Hutterischen Episteln*, vol. 3, 325.
16  Robert Friedmann, "Die Briefe der österreichischen Täufer," *Archiv für Reformationsgeschichte* 26 (1929), 41ff.

In their construction, many of the Hutterite letters—including those written by Jakob Huter—are reminiscent of the New Testament apostolic letters. They begin with a lengthy greeting to the recipient(s). Thus, in his last letter from the Tyrol to the community in Moravia in 1535, Huter began as follows:

> I, Jakob, a servant of God and apostle of Jesus Christ, and a servant of all of his elected saints here and there and throughout upper and lower Moravia, called to this task through the unfathomable grace and inexpressible mercy of God.

After many expressions of praise to God, Huter added that he had been appointed by God "to be a watchman, a shepherd, and caretaker of his holy people, of his elected, holy, Christian community."[17] Then followed words of encouragement to the persecuted congregation, admonitions to remain steadfast, laments over the circumstances that made an orderly congregational life so difficult, as well as reports on the situation in the Tyrol, or, as the case may be, in Moravia. The conclusion included greetings to family and friends along with words of blessing.

Jakob Huter repeatedly referred to his congregation as "elected" and "called." He understood himself to have been called by God to lead the congregation, to preach, and to travel throughout the land as a missionary. The following greeting, which he sent in 1535 from the Tyrol to Moravia, is illustrative of many of his letters:

> I, Jakob, a poor, suffering little worm of the Lord, yet still a servant and a caretaker, and, as I hope, your apostle and shepherd and your dear brother out of his great mercy, and your companion in the tribulations and in the patience of Jesus Christ and his little children.[18]

Jakob Huter strongly emphasized the importance of encouraging and strengthening members of the community who were suffering under the pressure of persecution and the temptation to recant. He admonished them to endure that suffering patiently and to wait upon God's intervention. The harvest was promised to those who endured. God led one into tribulations, but God also brought comfort. Already in the Old Testament, he wrote, God had encouraged Daniel with the words "Do not be afraid!" In one of his letters to Anabaptists imprisoned in Hohenwart, Huter quoted Jesus, writing: "I will never allow those who are mine to be torn from my hand, for the Father who gave you to me is stronger than all others." According

---

17   Fischer, "Jakob Huter," 48.
18   Ibid., 34.

to Huter, tribulation purified the believer. In a letter from 1534 he began with a hymn of praise to God who had made the Anabaptists worthy to suffer for the sake of his name.[19]

Be strong; trust in God; bear tribulations patiently—in light of the general situation this was good counsel, even though it was not so simple to actually put into practice. In a time of growing persecution, the constant threat of mass arrests at Anabaptist gatherings and the danger of being imprisoned and killed gave the following words an understandable and urgent meaning: we do not want to heed the "evil, godless, unrighteous, and damnable people," who "are unimaginably numerous," wrote Huter in a letter from 1535.

> For the person who is pious and upright before God, who lives and walks in truth, who stands firm and endures to the end; yes, the one who strives gallantly, who is unyielding in the face of all temptation, and remains true to the Lord and His people in all things—that person matters more to God and before God than 400,000 godless and apostate people. Yes, we want to stay focused on these people and follow them in the Lord.[20]

Every single believer has the task of committing themselves to prayer:

> That is my—indeed all of our—plea to you, for the Lord's sake, that you plead to God with utmost dedication and seriousness, day and night, without ceasing, for it is a necessity. We will also do the same for you, for we see and sense and know that God above hears your prayers in heaven.[21]

In his final letter, written from the Tyrol shortly before he was taken prisoner, Huter admonished the members of the community:

> You beloved and elect in the Lord, our body, soul, and possessions all belong to the Lord; yours do as well; you understand this completely. May you be comforted in your hearts. May God uphold us in his love and in the covenant of his peace forever. Amen.[22]

Thus, we hear Jakob Huter in his own words. The interrogation records of imprisoned Anabaptists in the Tyrol also convey a sense of Huter's

---

19  Ibid., 15f.
20  Ibid., 37.
21  Ibid., 34.
22  Ibid., 56.

powerful speech. According to Michael Ebner from Hörschwang, "His words are powerful—God speaks through him." Other Anabaptists also reported on their encounters with him. Before he came to know Jakob Huter, Valentin Luckhner of Taufers had come into a conversation with an Anabaptist named Mathes Schueknecht. Schueknecht asked him whether he had a New Testament, which Luckhner confirmed. He said that he read in it frequently and that he also believed what was in it. To this Schueknecht responded that it was not enough to merely believe what was in the New Testament; rather, one also needed to live according to the will of God and to be baptized as a believer.[23] Shortly thereafter, Jakob Huter and another Anabaptist, a cabinetmaker from Kufstein or Rattenberg, came to the house of Valentin Luckhner and requested food and drink. While they ate, the group entered into an open conversation. Huter asked Luckhner if he wanted to know divine truth. Luckhner responded with interest and they then entered into a very long conversation that concluded with a walk together in the meadow as Huter expounded on divine truth and baptism. As Luckhner himself reported, he was so moved by this that he knelt down and asked God to forgive him of his sins. Then Huter asked him if he believed in God, the Lord Jesus Christ, and the holy Christian church. Valentin Luckhner replied, "Yes." Huter then told him, "Now your sins are forgiven before God." He must now "renounce his flesh and blood, wife and children" and leave them. Clearly, Luckhner's family wanted nothing to do with Anabaptist beliefs. At that point, Huter took some water and baptized him "in the name of the Father, the Son and the Holy Spirit." As a member of the Anabaptist congregation, Luckhner openly acknowledged that he regularly attended worship services—at least as often as circumstances allowed—which mostly took place in the woods.

A central theme in Huter's sermons was that his listeners should acknowledge their own sins. Helena, daughter of Florian from Enneberg, testified in her interrogation that she knew that God was merciful and would forgive her of her sins. Once she had acknowledged her sins, she then followed the commandments of God. Many Anabaptists reported in their interrogations that Huter had warned them against participating in the Catholic Mass. Hans Peduller, who had been baptized by Huter in a wood close to Sterzing, reported to the authorities on his encounter with the Anabaptist preacher. Huter had counselled him to be pious, to work honestly, to distance himself from all forms of unrighteousness, and not to attend any church. Michael Ebner also reported that Huter had forbidden him to go to church. To be sure, Jesus Christ had told his disciples that he would rebuild the temple, but he had meant by this "a clean heart." Helena, the daughter of Florian from Enneberg mentioned above, claimed

---

23   Mecenseffy, *Österreich*, 3. Teil, 166.

that the sacraments on the altar were "an abomination and stench before God." Others claimed that the images in churches were "pure idolatry." In addition, Huter reportedly said that they should not pray to or make any requests of the saints—they should call upon God alone. Niklas Velder, who had also been baptized by Huter, described the Catholic church's understanding of the Lord's Supper as a "heresy and sorcery"; the church was "a temple to prostitutes and a temple of idols," filled only with idols of silver and gold. Velder called infant baptism a "child's bath and the sorcerer's bath." In it the priests wanted to drive the devil out of the infant even though it was the child who was actually pure while the priest was "full of the devil."[24]

## Community Life in the Tyrol under Jakob Huter

Persecution in the Tyrol made orderly congregational life impossible. The Anabaptists could meet only in secret, often far from settled areas in mountain pastures, woods, or in isolated inns. Although everyone who provided the Anabaptists with food and lodging, or merely avoided attending church, could be prosecuted, people were always willing to open their doors to the Anabaptists. For example, the farmstead of Hans Obern in Hörschwang, above St. Lorenzen, was available to the Anabaptists for meetings—Jakob Huter came regularly to Hörschwang. The location of the farmstead was perfect in that it took some time to travel there, which meant that the Anabaptists were protected from discovery and attack by the government. During a meeting there in 1532, the Anabaptists were reportedly warned that within three days the authorities would be showing up in Hörschwang for a raid on the gathering. This gave them enough time to promptly bring their meeting to an end and to disappear.

The sources also frequently mention the "Pecklhaube" inn as a place where Anabaptists gathered and spent the night. The inn—run by an elderly man, Ulrich Pecklhaube—was situated either directly in, or very close to, the town of Klausen. There are reports of meetings in which as many as 70 people gathered in the barn of "Pecklhauben." In addition, the proprietor of the inn frequently provided food for the Anabaptists.[25] These gatherings, however, did not remain undiscovered for long, and the old man needed to give an account to the authorities for his hospitality to the Anabaptists. Pecklhaube defended himself by insisting that he was not aware of the religious convictions of his guests and was only pursuing his business interests. Following Pecklhaube's release he no longer made his rooms available for Anabaptist meetings. Anabaptists also gathered at

---

24  Ibid., 21f., 151, 154, 198.
25  Ibid., 169.

Kniepasser, a farmstead close to St. Lorenzen in the Puster valley. In 1533, according to the sources, the Anabaptists frequently found lodging in the basement of "the poor farmer Kniepasser." Melchior Kniepasser and his wife would also supply the Anabaptists with food—for example, cornmeal or flour porridge. The Kniepassers themselves, however, did not undergo Anabaptist baptism.[26]

In addition to these farmsteads and inns, the Anabaptists gathered in alpine meadows and forest clearings. Something of the structure of these meetings is suggested by a report from the Anabaptist Valentin Fell from Flaas. Fell went to the woods in Brenner where more than 90 people had assembled. Jakob Huter read and preached from the Gospels. He also instructed his listeners that the Catholic understanding of the Lord's Supper and Mass was merely a "devilish phantom." One should not believe it; nor should one attend church or pray to the saints, but trust in God alone. In addition, baptisms took place at the meeting, the group celebrated the Lord's Supper, and letters sent by fellow believers in Moravia to the congregation in the Tyrol were read aloud. Furthermore, a report from Christoph Schuehknecht of St. Georgen, now part of Bruneck, makes it clear that the Anabaptists in the Tyrol already had a common purse. If someone contributed something to the congregation it was passed along to the treasurer (*Säckelmeister*).[27] Among other things, the fund provided support for the poor members of the congregation who did not have the resources to emigrate to greater safety in Moravia (described further in the next section).

The meetings often lasted for days, so the logistical challenge of providing for the needs of the participants was not simple. In January 1534, government authorities learned of a gathering in Getzenberg, close to Kiens in the Puster valley. The location of Getzenberg alone suggests why it would have been an ideal location for Anabaptist meetings. It was in an isolated region, thinly populated, and situated above the Puster valley on the road to Brixen and Eisacktal.[28] The testimony of the Anabaptist Hans Peduller provides a glimpse into how such meetings were organized. Prior to the gathering, the leader would send the treasurer and several trusted brothers to the neighbouring farmers to negotiate for the delivery of food. The food was then transported to an agreed-upon location, where the farmers were paid. At that point, other brothers brought the food to the site of the secret meeting.[29] One day, three Anabaptists came to the home of Michael Waldner—who was not himself an Anabaptist but was

---
26   Ibid., 173, 175.
27   Ibid., 72, 175.
28   von Schlachta, Forster, and Merola, *Verbrannte Visionen*, 67–69.
29   Mecenseffy, *Österreich*, 3. Teil, 198.

nonetheless willing to help them purchase supplies. They brought an ox with them and asked Waldner's wife to bake bread from three barrels of flour, i.e., some 90 litres. The wife agreed to bake the bread, whereupon an Anabaptist woman arrived with the flour. The Anabaptists then took the bread to their meeting. At another meeting, the sources report that two oxen were driven along the Ritten—that is, a ridge above the Eisack valley—and a total of fifty loaves of bread were carried there as well. When they celebrated the Lord's Supper, the Anabaptists drank wine.[30] But this would have also needed to be transported to a hidden location. Thus it was not a simple matter to organize these meetings, especially given the crucial fact that all the preparations had to happen without arousing attention. Government authorities were always on the alert.

Jakob Huter also reported in his letters regarding the work in the Tyrol. On the one hand, he wrote of the successes. In 1535, for example, he wrote that God was "bringing people daily…to the holy, Christian community where they are being saved." On the other hand, Huter also shared some looming problems with his Moravian brothers and sisters in the faith. For example, he complained that there were too few workers: "We have so much to do and accomplish for the Lord; but we simply cannot do this all at once."[31] The more the community in the Tyrol grew, the more difficult the situation became. The government began to use every means possible to root out the community and its meetings. One of the most pressing challenges came from former community members who had been expelled and were now eager to betray details of the congregation to the authorities. Several of them went to the government in Innsbruck out of "pure arrogance" and "evil intentions," making the situation more and more volatile for the Hutterites. The authorities therefore knew, or could surmise with relative precision, where Huter was lodging and where he would be travelling. But it was not only defectors who revealed hiding places and travel plans. The Tyrolean government also planted spies among the Anabaptists who then infiltrated the congregations. Ever since the events in Münster, where Anabaptists had seized power and then defended themselves against the troops of the bishop, fears had been growing about a treasonous underground Anabaptist conspiracy.

## Emigration to Moravia

Clearly, the situation for the Anabaptists in the Tyrol was dangerous. Since an orderly, structured congregational life was inconceivable, emigration appeared to be the only way for Anabaptists to continue practicing

---

30  Ibid., 23, 169.
31  Fischer, "Jakob Huter," 40.

their faith. Between 1528 and 1533, some 400 to 600 people successfully made the journey from the Tyrol to Moravia.[32] The Anabaptist Ruprecht Huber recounted in his 1533 interrogation in Michelsburg that the leaders of the Anabaptists did not want to leave any congregational members behind in the Puster valley, since it was simply too dangerous for them. Therefore they sent small groups over the Brenner Pass in the direction of northern Tyrolean cities like Schwaz.[33] From there the refugees floated by rafts eastward on the Inn River. Just before Vienna, the Anabaptists switched to travelling overland, north to the Hutterite communities in Moravia.

Just how closely the authorities observed the travelling Anabaptists is suggested by a decree issued by the government in Innsbruck of March 1532, addressed to all the mayors and provincial judges between Hall and Kufstein. One could assume, the edict read, that many Tyrolean Anabaptists would be travelling to Moravia again this year. They would be moving eastward on the Inn River. Therefore, the authorities were "strictly ordered" to "be diligently alert and attentive for any Anabaptists, and especially the aforementioned Jakob Huter" on the "docks at Hall"—that is, the point of departure for the rafts—"and on all other paths and roads in your jurisdiction." At the docks, "no unknown person should be permitted to board a boat who does not have a trustworthy advocate or guarantee, or a plausible explanation for where they intend to go."[34]

Travel in the sixteenth century was dangerous not only for the Anabaptists; it was a wearisome undertaking for everyone, since the roads were anything but safe. Therefore it was customary for travellers to be armed in order to protect themselves against attacks. This meant that travelling unarmed was a clear step of faith. The Anabaptists tried to travel at night, away from main roads, which meant that they had to face some truly adverse challenges. From a report on road conditions in the Tyrol from 1524, we know that many roads were tiny, often littered with fallen rocks that needed to be cleared away. Some were completely overgrown with shrubs, and still others were so ruined by irrigation ditches that they were filled with water. The report described one road as follows: "This path has not been improved for many years; the cobblestones are completely gone, the ruts are deep and rocky, and in rainy weather wagons sink up to their axles."[35] Not only were road condition terrible, but signage was also minimal.

---

32  Packull, *Hutterer in Tirol*, 224.
33  Mecenseffy, *Österreich*, 3. Teil, 177.
34  Ibid., 37.
35  *Wege ins Ungewisse: Reisen in der Frühen Neuzeit 1500–1800*, ed. Holger Th. Gräf and Ralf Pröve (Frankfurt/Main: Fischer, 1997), 78, 85.

Those who went on foot needed to travel lightly. Generally, it was customary to travel with a backpack or a sack attached to the coat, which meant that the coat contained one's entire possessions while walking during the day and could also serve as a blanket for sleeping at night. Rain and cold regularly accompanied travellers. Walking for days on end meant that one's shoes were eventually so soaked and so tattered that they hung from the feet like rags. Clothing made of felt and wool was also quickly soaked. Yet in the face of all of these adversities, the sources report that people everywhere helped the Anabaptists and gave them lodging, even though in doing so they made themselves liable for arrest.

## The Community in Moravia

When Anabaptists arrived in Moravia they must have felt as if they had reached paradise. Here the political situation was completely different than in the Tyrol, promising them much more freedom. Community life could now be structured in an orderly way. The various territorial lords in Moravia were generally quite tolerant. They accepted the Anabaptist refugees and offered them land on which to settle. To be sure, they did all this not out of pure generosity but in pursuit of their own economic interests. Welcoming new subjects meant productive land and new sources of revenues and taxes. The Hutterites—who among all the Anabaptist groups had settled in Moravia the longest—proved to be ideal subjects since they were skilled in various handcrafts and helped to revive and expand the local economy on various estates.

At the same time, however, the emergence of the Hutterite community in Moravia was not without debates and divisions. Already in 1528, a group of Anabaptists led by Jakob Wiedemann, whom the Hutterite *Chronicle* describes as "one-eyed Jakob," had split from the rest of the Anabaptists in Nikolsburg. At issue were questions regarding nonresistance and government. In Nikolsburg, Balthasar Hubmaier had developed a very close relationship with the local government. He had successfully won over the lords of the town of Nikolsburg, the noble family of Liechtenstein, to Anabaptist ideas, which was possible only because Hubmaier was less radical than the others and willing to be more flexible on the principle of separation from the "world," especially in regard to the government and politics. The group led by Jakob Wiedemann wanted to maintain a stricter position on separation and nonresistance. It seems likely that they also already held some notions about introducing a more comprehensive practice of community-of-goods. As Wiedemann's group left Nikolsburg, the well-known scene unfolded along the road close to Austerlitz, regarded today as the foundational moment for Hutterian community-of-goods. The *Chronicle* describes what happened in the following way:

> They started on their way and encamped in a deserted village between Dannowitz and Muschau and stayed there for a day and a night. They took counsel together in the Lord because of their immediate need and distress and appointed servants for temporal affairs…. These men then spread out a cloak in front of the people, and each one laid his possessions on it with a willing heart—without being forced—so that the needy might be supported in accordance with the teaching of the prophets and apostles. Isa. 23:18; Acts 2:44–45; 4:34–35; 5:1–11.[36]

Led by Wiedemann, the group was received on the estate of the lords of Kaunitz in Austerlitz where they quickly formed a community that attracted additional members.

A year later, in 1529, Jakob Huter became acquainted with the community in Austerlitz. The Hutterite *Chronicle* reports that the Anabaptists in the Tyrol had heard that "at Austerlitz in the Margravate of Moravia, God had gathered a people in his name to live as one mind, heart, and soul, each caring faithfully for the other."[37] For this reason the congregation in the Tyrol sent Jakob Huter and Simon Schützinger to observe what was happening in Moravia. There they came to realize that their two groups were "of one heart and soul in serving and fearing God."[38] Thus, they united with the community in Austerlitz. Huter, however, returned to the Tyrol to continue preaching there.

Unfortunately, in 1531 a new division emerged within the community in Moravia. In part, the schisms resulted from serious problems uncovered by Wilhelm Reublin, an Anabaptist from Württemberg. At the same time, the schism could also be clearly traced to a quarrel over the nature of authority in the community. Under Jakob Wiedemann, several teachings and practices contrary to the principle of equality that members experienced as coercive and burdensome had crept into the community. If we are to believe a letter by Wilhelm Reublin, in which he offered his perspective on the matter, several specific grievances had emerged. The elders, for example, enjoyed a better standard of living than the "ordinary" community members—they had better food and drink and did not participate in the communal meals. In addition, they wore fancier clothes and lived in their own homes, while the rest of the community members lived in collect-

---

36 Wolkan, *Geschichtbuch*, 62; *Chronicle*, 80–81.
37 Wolkan, *Geschichtbuch*, 64; *Chronicle*, 84.
38 Wolkan, *Geschichtbuch*, 64; *Chronicle*, 84.

ive housing. The community members were to give all of their money to the community, whereas Jakob Wiedemann and the elders enjoyed private luxuries. When he and his confidants went to the local Jews who were active in money exchanges, wrote Reublin, they learned that the elders had already exchanged "a handful of ducats." Moreover, the leaders taught that salvation came through baptism, not faith. Children who had not been baptized were "damned" and "consigned to hell" by the elders. The leaders had done away with the Lord's Prayer. And there was more. Under Jakob Wiedemann's leadership, the elders compelled single women to marry "with much coercion and force, absent the command of God." In closing, Reublin further noted that small children were not given sufficient milk and had become extremely emaciated.[39]

Reublin did not keep his observations to himself. Indeed, he preached about them when the elders were absent. According to his own account he won over many listeners, which brought him into serious conflict with the elders. After several rounds of argument and debate, Reublin—along with Jörg Zaunring, who supported him—decided to leave the community. "So it was that on the 8th day of January, for the sake of the truth and in the confidence and grace of God, we left the false brethren in Austerlitz, shaking the dust from our shoes as we went."[40] They found refuge in Auspitz, on lands owned by Johanka von Boskowitz, the abbess of the convent in Brünner.

Both parties—the group under Jakob Wiedemann and the group under Wilhelm Reublin—sent a call for help to the Tyrol in an effort to secure support from Jakob Huter. Subsequently, in the spring of 1531 Huter, together with Simon Schützinger, travelled to Moravia in order to get a better sense of the situation. The *Chronicle* reports that he judged the group under Jakob Wiedemann in Austerlitz "to bear the most fault" for the conflict.[41] Then, the text continues, when Huter "pointed out their error, they didn't want to hear anything more from him." Thus, Huter and Schützinger decided to join the community in Auspitz and to confide in Jörg Zaunring. However, this did not restore peace to the community, since there were further inconsistencies regarding private property. Ultimately, Wilhelm Reublin was also banned after it was discovered that he secretly possessed 40 gulden. The *Chronicle* describes him as a "lying, untrustworthy, treacherous Ananias."[42] In addition, Jörg Zaunring also came under scrutiny, since his wife had had an affair with another man.

---

39   The letter from Reublin can be found in Carl Adolf Cornelius, *Die Geschichte des Münsterischen Aufruhrs*, vol. 2 (Leipzig: T.O. Weigel, 1860), 256–258.
40   Ibid., 258.
41   Wolkan, *Geschichtbuch*, 70; *Chronicle*, 91.
42   Wolkan, *Geschichtbuch*, 79; *Chronicle*, 104.

Huter and Schützinger now sought contact with two other Anabaptist preachers, Philipp Plener and Gabriel Ascherham, who had established communities close by. For a short time, the groups enjoyed warm fellowship. However, conflicts also soon emerged in this relationship, which led to a new division. This schism actually marks the first point at which the "Hutterites" emerged. At the centre of the conflict was a debate between Simon Schützinger, whom Huter had installed as elder, and Jakob Huter himself. Schützinger accused Huter of using his charismatic and rhetorical gifts to seize leadership of the group. Gabriel Ascherham and Philipp Plener joined with Schützinger, also accusing Huter of grasping for power and describing him as a "haughty and proud spirit." A leadership struggle ensued in which Huter emerged as the victor. Once again, problems with implementing community-of-goods had clearly accelerated the conflict. After a service of admonition and rebuke, Jakob Huter called on his listeners to reveal all of their private possessions. Schützinger was exposed as possessing a secret stash of linens and shirts along with a sum of money. Following this upheaval, the community decided to appoint Jakob Huter as elder, although not before devoting themselves first to a week of prayer. In his letters, Huter went into great detail about the conflicts with Gabriel Ascherham and Philipp Plener. He regarded his actions as justified, emphasizing that his thoughts and deeds had been directed to God in a spirit of peace and unity. He attempted to refute all accusations that he had been the cause of the schism in the community, "for God knows that I came here to promote peace and unity, not to destroy it."[43] In retrospect, it is impossible to determine exactly who was striving for more power in the conflict.

## Persecution in Moravia and Huter's Letter to the Governors (*Landeshauptmann*)

In the final year of his life, Jakob Huter experienced yet another decisive moment in the history of the Anabaptist community in Moravia—the onset of persecution, the likes of which would have been unthinkable during the early years in Moravia. In 1534–35, a group of Anabaptists in the north German city of Münster came into a violent conflict with the bishop of the city. The consequences of those events were felt by Anabaptists throughout the Holy Roman Empire. Since authorities everywhere feared that other Anabaptist groups could also become political rebels, seize weapons, and challenge traditional forms of order, they responded with intense persecution. Caught in the backlash, the Hutterites in Moravia were ordered to relinquish all of their property and to cease practicing

---

43   Fischer, "Jakob Huter," edition section, 8.

community-of-goods. The *Chronicle* reported on the pain this caused for community members who wandered around the country for a time seeking shelter and were sometimes forced to simply camp in meadows: "Now we are here in the wilderness, on a wild moor under the open sky."[44]

Jakob Huter vehemently defended the group against these actions and wrote a letter to the Moravian governor Johann Kuna von Kunstadt. Clearly, the tone of the letter did not help to calm the situation. Huter wrote in a rage, sparing no polemics. Along with his letter, he sent two representatives to the government with a somewhat contradictory message. On the one hand, Huter emphasized that his community did not pose any danger, did not wish to do evil to anyone, and was not planning any sort of armed revolt. But on the other hand, he described Ferdinand I as a "tyrant," language which not only closed the door to the possibility of any sort of mercy but also called into question the very legitimacy of Ferdinand's rule. In addition, Huter described Ferdinand as an "enemy of godly truth and justice" and even as a "prince of darkness." Huter elevated these attacks even more with an appeal to the Moravian nobility that they should reconsider their obedience to Ferdinand I. In some sense, he was indeed calling them to an insurrection. They should be aware, he wrote, that if they were to join the general wave of persecution against the Anabaptists they would be departing from the godly path. Clearly, Huter's letter to the Moravian governor was politically explosive.

By contrast, Huter portrayed his communities as protected by God and standing under his sovereignty. He and his fellow believers, Huter insisted, would accept persecution and expulsion with patience, since they regarded this as something laid upon them by God. Through it, God "made the community worthy" of "suffering for his name's sake." God was the "governor and defender" of the community; he would engage the battle on their behalf. And the community would look to God for its leadership. God alone, not the government, would tell them where they should emigrate, even though, Huter continued, being forced to find a new place to live would make things difficult for the Hutterites, for "wherever we move, robbers and tyrants seek to consume us, like sheep among the ravenous wolf or the ferocious lion."[45]

The message that Jakob Huter sent to the Moravian governor with his letters must have been interpreted by the authorities as an act of resistance, calling into question or explicitly rejecting every form of secular and spiritual hierarchy. As the *Chronicle* reported:

---

44 Wolkan, *Geschichtbuch*, 109; *Chronicle*, 135.
45 Wolkan, *Geschichtbuch*, 111f.; *Chronicle*, 137–141.

> After the governor received and read the letter from the community that had been sent to them by their couriers, he immediately sent his servants back with strict orders to arrest and imprison Jakob Huter.[46]

The community received word of this order and sent their elders to the Tyrol. There, however, Huter's life came to an end.

## The End in the Tyrol: The Imprisonment and Death of Jakob Huter

In effect, the letter to the governor was the warrant for Jakob Huter's death. The return trip to the Tyrol would be his last journey between Moravia and his homeland. Persecution had intensified in the Tyrol and the authorities there were intent in their search for Huter and the Anabaptists. In August 1534, Wölfl the goatherd was arrested in Meran, South Tyrol. It was the same Wölfl who had first told Huter of the Anabaptist faith in the home of Huter's cousin. Eleven other Anabaptist men and women were captured along with Wölfl; but then, interestingly enough, they were all soon released. The government in Innsbruck was astonished that the authorities in Meran set them free, writing that Wölfl was "one of the reasons," why Jakob Huter was baptized.[47] In April 1535 the government in Innsbruck warned all of its lower-level authorities that very soon "hordes" of Anabaptists would be returning from Moravia to the Tyrol, since the Moravian parliament (*Landtag*) had recently decided to pursue them. Local authorities should therefore "stay well informed" in order to capture these Anabaptists.[48] The net tightened. A local judge from Schöneck, whose jurisdiction included a portion of the Puster valley, was ordered to watch very closely the location where Jakob Huter was lodging. According to the sources, the judge of Schöneck was to round up the appropriate people—that is, scouts and spies—and send them to the Anabaptist communities. For the Anabaptists this now became a significant danger.

The song "I Lament and Grieve the Whole Day Long," which has been passed down in the *Lieder der Hutterischen Brüder*, recalls this painful chapter of Anabaptist persecution.[49] The song names Jörg Frue, "a child of the devil and a child of Judas:"

---

46 Wolkan, *Geschichtbuch*, 114; *Chronicle*, 141.
47 Mecenseffy, *Österreich*, 3. Teil, 262.
48 Ibid., 269.
49 The nine-stanza song, "*Ich reu und klag den gantzen Tag*," is found in *Die Lieder der Hutterischen Brüder*, ed. Hutterischen Brüdern in Canada, 4th ed. (Cayley, Alb.: Macmillan Colony, 1974), 68–69.

> With a deceitful intent,
> he said with beautiful words: "Oh my brother,
> excuse me for a moment, I want to go home
> and fetch my wife and child."
> The Christian shepherd said to him:
>
> "Are you of those with false hearts?
> God will not banter with you."
> "Oh no, oh no," he said while drinking,
> "the Lord preserve me from such a deed.
> Come home with me to my house."
> And indeed the innocent man followed him,
> as if running straight to Pilate.[50]

Jörg Frue was active as a spy already in June 1533. He had taken part in an Anabaptist gathering on the Getzenberg and betrayed the Anabaptists. Nevertheless, the bailiff who hastened there could only capture eight Anabaptists. Jakob Huter and Hans Amon, who were the main ones being pursued, had already fled. Now, in the fall of 1535, Jörg Frue was commissioned once again to infiltrate the Anabaptist movement. In one of his last letters before being taken prisoner, Huter himself reported that two other believers, Martin Nieder and Christoph Bühler, had been expelled from the community and had then gone to the authorities in order to disclose everything they knew about the Anabaptists. They were "horrible people, in league with the devil; dreadful, evil scoundrels."[51]

Jakob Huter spent his last months in the Puster valley, with Hörschwang at the centre of his activities. Many of the inhabitants there were either Anabaptists or so disillusioned with the Catholic church that they no longer attended services. Sympathetic to the Anabaptist cause, they were eager to offer their assistance. From Hörschwang, Mair reported that he had slept in an oxen stall so that the Anabaptists could sleep in his house. In a letter from 1535, Huter himself reported on the situation in the Tyrol. He described how he and those accompanying him—including, at the very least, his wife Katharina as well as Jeronimus Käls, who later became a schoolmaster in the Moravian community—had arrived in the Puster valley and in the Etsch region. There they had been "received and

---

50  Ibid., 69. The original German is as follows: "*Mit falschen Schein: O Brüder mein, / Sprach er mit schönen Worten. / Verzieht ein klein, so will ich heim, / Mein Weib und Kind auch holen. / Der christlich Hirt bald zu ihm red, / Bist du eins falschen Herzens, / Gott wird mit dir nicht scherzen. / O nein, o nein, sprach er mit Wein, / Da b'hüt mich Gott von solcher Tat, / Kommt mit mir heim zu Hause. / Doch ging davon der züchtig Mann, / Tät zu Pilato laufen.*"
51  Fischer, "Jakob Huter," 40.

greeted with joy and godly love." In the days that followed the Anabaptist preacher travelled tirelessly "in mountains and valleys," "stirred everyone who hungered and thirsted after the truth," and "proclaimed and preached from the truth of the gospel." Some of them accepted the message with joy and "gave themselves over to God. The almighty God and Father has already established a congregation here once again and the Lord is increasing his people every day and is bringing them to his holy church." There was much to do, he wrote. They actually needed to be everywhere at once: "There should be many more of us—servants and other brothers—who are eager and prepared to do the work of the Lord. For the field is ripe unto harvest and the workers are few."[52]

But the net was steadily tightening—in the Puster valley, Peter Troyer, a judge whose daughter and son-in-law had joined the Anabaptists, cast a watchful eye on the movements of Jakob Huter and those accompanying him. Troyer passed along crucial information to the authorities. Huter, his wife, and Jeronimus Käls left the Puster valley in October of 1535. Since Katharina Huter was expecting a child, Troyer informed authorities to keep an eye open everywhere for "a poor maid who was about to deliver a baby."[53] Huter sensed the pressure, as is evident in his final letters. He knew where the government authorities were attacking and capturing Anabaptists, so he decided to send Jeronimus Käls, who would become a leading figure among the Hutterites following Huter's death, to carry letters back to Moravia. Huter himself, along with his wife and a friend, Anna Stainer, left the Puster valley and arrived in Klausen on November 30. There, they found refuge with the widow of the former sacristan of Klausen, who had once belonged to the Anabaptists but later had recanted her faith. Nevertheless, she provided Huter and his companions with lodging, so they could warm themselves by a fire. As was their custom, they travelled at night in order to remain unnoticed. Thus, Huter's companions wanted to continue their journey sometime after midnight. But just before they left, the city judge of Klausen took them by surprise. Huter, his wife, and Anna Stainer were imprisoned in the stronghold of the bishop of Branzoll, above Klausen.

For the government, the capture of Jakob Huter was a "great success," which it could use to intensify its attacks on the Anabaptists. Now it had the biggest ringleader and preacher in custody. While the women remained behind in Klausen, the authorities transferred Jakob Huter to Innsbruck, where he was to be tried. He was interrogated and tortured. According to the Hutterite *Chronicle* he was placed in ice-cold water and then beaten. Afterward, brandy was poured into his wounds and then set

---
52  Ibid., 27.
53  Mecenseffy, *Österreich*, 3. Teil, 277.

ablaze. In order to crush him spiritually and emotionally before his execution, Huter was transported to the Catholic parish church—today the cathedral of St. Jakob. The *Chronicle* reads as follows: "Putting a hat with a tuft of feathers on his head, they led him into the house of their idols and in every way made a laughing stock of him."[54] At the end of February or the middle of March—unfortunately, the sources are not entirely clear on this point—Jakob Huter was taken to Innsbruck and publicly burned to death in the square in front of the Goldenes Dachl. The *Chronicle* honours him with the following words:

> It is from this Jakob Hutter that the church inherited the name Hutterite, or Hutterian Brethren. To this day the church is not ashamed of this name. He stood joyfully for the truth unto death and gave his life for it. This has been the fate of all Christ's apostles.[55]

---

54 Wolkan, *Geschichtbuch*, 118; *Chronicle*, 145.
55 Wolkan, *Geschichtbuch*, 119; *Chronicle*, 146.

**James M. Stayer** is emeritus professor at Queen's University, Kingston, Ontario. He is the author of *Anabaptists and the Sword* (1972 and 1976), *The German Peasants' War and Anabaptist Community of Goods* (1991), and *Martin Luther: German Saviour, Evangelical Theological Factions and the Interpretation of Luther, 1917–1933* (2000).

# The Moravian Hutterites and the Beginning of Anabaptist History Writing: Kaspar Braitmichel, the First Historian of Anabaptism

## JAMES M. STAYER

It is the broadly accepted consensus that Anabaptist history began in Zurich in January 1525, but the writing of Anabaptist history began in the late 1560s in Moravia when Kaspar Braitmichel began *The Chronicle of the Hutterian Brethren* (*Das große Geschichtbuch der Hutterischen Brüder*).[1] In fact, although the *Chronicle* is the sole source that describes the Zurich baptisms of 1525, there are convincing reasons to accept its account.[2]

The sources of Anabaptist history have become ever more extensive, enriched by three multi-volume publications of archival holdings: *Quellen zur Geschichte der [Wieder]Täufer* (1930–),[3] *Quellen zur Geschichte der Täufer in der Schweiz* (1952–),[4] and *Documenta Anabaptistica Neerlandica* (1975–).[5] Jarold K. Zeman relied on a multi-volume Czech topographical series to greatly expand the geographical knowledge of Anabaptist settlements in Moravia in *The Anabaptists and the Czech Brethren in Moravia, 1526–1628*.[6] More recently, the opening of the Czech archives since 1990 to scholars fluent in Czech as well as German—most prominently Martin Rothkegel—has expanded the knowledge of Anabaptism in Bohemia, Moravia,

---

1 *The Chronicle of the Hutterian Brethren*, vol. I (Rifton: Plough Publishing House, 1987), LXXIII–LXXV.
2 James M. Stayer, "Was There a Klettgau Letter of 1530?" *Mennonite Quarterly Review* 61 (1987), 75–76.
3 Eighteen volumes to 2011.
4 Four volumes to 2008.
5 Volumes 1–3, 5–8 published to date.
6 Jarold K. Zeman, *The Anabaptists and the Czech Brethren in Moravia: A Study of Origins and Contacts* (The Hague/Paris: Mouton, 1968); Jarold K. Zeman, *Historical Topography of Moravian Anabaptism* (Goshen: Mennonite Historical Society, 1967).

and Silesia.⁷ During the Cold War, East Bloc historians confined themselves to already known sources, using the hypothesis of an "early modern revolution in Germany" to enrich them with Marxist theory. Zeman's and Rothkegel's efforts have tended in a similar direction—to increase the awareness of non-Hutterite and anti-Hutterite Anabaptists in Moravia and adjacent territories under Habsburg rule. Nevertheless, the Hutterites were undeniably by far the largest Moravian Anabaptist group from the middle of the sixteenth century to the expulsion of non-Catholic groups from Moravia in 1622.

Modern Moravian Anabaptist history began with the discovery and collection of Hutterite manuscripts by Josef von Beck, a judicial official of the Habsburg monarchy, in the middle of the nineteenth century. The Hutterites had been exiled from Moravia to the Kingdom of Hungary (modern Slovakia) in 1622, and when the Slovakian Hutterites were finally suppressed entirely in the eighteenth century their manuscripts were confiscated and placed in libraries and archives. Beck avidly collected Hutterite manuscripts and in 1883 in Vienna published *The History Books of the Anabaptists in Austria-Hungary*.⁸ After his death, his manuscript collection was utilized by Professor Johann Loserth of Graz University. After Loserth, the Beck collection came to the Moravian State Archives.

The concentration of Moravian Anabaptist historical studies on confiscated Hutterite manuscripts put a spotlight on the Hutterite telling of the story through their successive chroniclers. One facet of the undertaking was the search for a missing "Great Chronicle" of the Hutterites, which Beck confessed himself unable to find. *The Chronicle of the Hutterian Brethren* was eventually discovered, together with the modern Hutterites, in Canada and the United States. Rudolf Wolkan, Professor of German Literature at the University of Vienna, had published *The Songs of the Anabaptists*,⁹ which included Anabaptist songs of Moravian origin. Beck, Loserth, and Wolkan assumed that Moravian Anabaptism had died out with the forced conversion of the Slovakian Hutterites in the eighteenth century. When Wolkan's book was read in 1908 by John Horsch, a pioneering Mennonite church historian in Indiana, the Austrian Hutterite scholars were put in contact with real Hutterites in North America. Horsch introduced Wolkan to Elias Walter, a Canadian Hutterite bishop who had the Hutterite "Great Chronicle" in his possession. Walter copied the huge

---

7   Hans Martin Rothkegel, "Anabaptism in Moravia and Silesia," in *A Companion to Anabaptism and Spiritualism, 1521–1700*, eds. John D. Roth and James M. Stayer, (Leiden, Boston: Brill, 2007), 163–215.
8   Josef von Beck, *Die Geschichts-Bücher der Wiedertäufer in Oesterreich-Ungarn*, in *Schriften der Wiener Akademie der Wissenschaften*, F.R.A. 2, 43 (Vienna, 1883).
9   Rudolf Wolkan, *Die Lieder der Wiedertäufer: Ein Beitrag zur Deutschen und niederländischen Literatur- und Kirchengeschichte* (Berlin: Behre, 1903).

codex and sent this to Vienna.¹⁰ Then Wolkan edited the chronicle, using variant readings from the Beck collection, and produced the *Geschicht-Buch der Hutterischen Brüder*,¹¹ a volume of around seven hundred pages. Meanwhile, Loserth had researched the story of Hutterite survival: how a group migrated to Transylvania, then to Ukraine, and finally fled Russian conscription in 1874 and settled in Canada and the United States.¹² Wolkan's *Geschicht-Buch* was produced in modernized German; in 1943 it was replaced by A.J.F. Zieglschmid's *Die älteste Chronik der Hutterischen Brüder*,¹³ which reproduced the early modern German original text. *The Chronicle of the Hutterian Brethren* (1987) was translated from the Wolkan and Zieglschmid editions.

In 1923 Wolkan convinced Robert Friedmann, an ethnically Jewish veteran of the Habsburg armies in World War I, to take up research on the Hutterite epistles.¹⁴ Friedmann became the most prolific scholar of the Hutterites of his generation. Imprisoned by the Nazis in 1939, he escaped through England to America through the good offices of Roland Bainton and Harold S. Bender and established himself in 1945 at the University of Michigan, Kalamazoo, where he worked closely with the "Bender school" of Anabaptist historiography at Goshen, Indiana. His successor, Leonard Gross, taught at Goshen College—his book, *The Golden Years of the Hutterites*,¹⁵ traces the unfolding of the Hutterite communities. The approach to the history of Moravian Anabaptism of the Beck-Loserth-Wolkan-Friedmann-Gross succession was a "Hutterite in-group history," not in the sense that it was written by Hutterites, but in the sense that it was written by persons fascinated by and sympathetic to the Hutterites, who told their story from Hutterite chronicles and codices, and from the Hutterite point of view.

By the 1960s, marked by Harold Bender's death in 1962, this kind of history writing was starting to appear less than adequate both to Mennonite and Baptist historians, and to post-confessional historians such as myself. Jarold Zeman was interested in Bohemian Brethren as well as

---

10   *Chronicle of the Hutterian Brethren*, XVII.
11   *Geschicht-Buch der Hutterischen Brüder*, ed. Rudolf Wolkan (Macleod and Vienna, 1923).
12   Johann Loserth, "Decline and Revival of the Hutterites," *Mennonite Quarterly Review* 4 (1930), 93–112.
13   A.J.F. Zieglschmid, ed., *Die älteste Chronik der Hutterischen Brüder: Ein Sprachdenkmal aus frühneuhochdeutsch Zeit*, (Ithaca, NY: Cayuga Press, 1943).
14   Robert Friedmann, "The Epistles of the Hutterian Brethren," *Mennonite Quarterly Review* 20 (1946), 147–177.
15   Leonard Gross, *The Golden Years of the Hutterites: The Witness and Thought of the Communal Moravian Anabaptists during the Walpot Era, 1565–1578* (Scottdale: Herald Press, 1980; rev. ed. Waterloo: Pandora Press, 1998), 23.

Anabaptists, but he admitted that, despite striking similarities of belief, the case of Moravia did not show important connections between the Bohemian Brethren, who can be classed as medieval sectarians, and the Anabaptists, who were Reformation radicals. The linguistic and ethnic barriers between the German-speaking Anabaptists in Moravia, preponderantly a community of religious refugees, and the mainly Czech-speaking Bohemian Brethren were too impermeable for the two groups to influence each other.[16] A secondary conclusion of Zeman's scholarship was that the Hutterite chronicles and epistles did not give an adequate representation of the non-Hutterite Anabaptists in Moravia.[17] This theme was repeated insistently and vigorously in the solid scholarship of Martin Rothkegel, following his ThD thesis of 2000 on Balthasar Hubmaier and the humanist Reformation in Nikolsburg.[18]

The most important questioning of the historical authority of the Hutterite *Chronicle* has come very recently, with the source studies of Matthias Rauert. Robert Friedmann outlined the beginning of the writing of the *Chronicle*, which was based on the memory of survivors and a library of the writings of major early Anabaptist leaders collected at the central headquarters of the Hutterite brotherhood after the middle of the sixteenth century. The first chronicler, Kaspar Braitmichel, began his work in the late 1560s and brought his account to 1542, but the "Great Chronicle" was above all the project of Hauptrecht Zapff, chief scribe of the brotherhood (1578–93). He took up the project of Braitmichel, abandoned in the early 1570s, and brought the account to 1591, that is, to his own time. Rauert argues, convincingly, that in its time the *Chronicle* was a private project of Zapff—"an experimental writing that fell short of an official Hutterite statement," permitted but not endorsed by the leadership. The Anabaptist teachers whose works were preserved in the leaders' archive were not always on the same doctrinal line as the Hutterite brotherhood—clear examples of this were Balthasar Hubmaier and Pilgram Marpeck. According to Rauert, the *Chronicle* became the authoritative account of the Hutterite past only after the Brethren were expelled from Moravia to Slovakia, in the time of presiding elder Andreas Ehrenpreis (1639–62). Thus the first crucial ten years of the brotherhood were remembered at a distance of thirty-five years, and that memory became totally authoritative only at a distance of 135 years.[19]

---

16  Zeman, *Anabaptists and Czech Brethren*, 310–313.
17  Ibid., 242–309, 313.
18  Hans Martin Rothkegel, "Die Nikolsburger Reformation, 1526–1535: Von Humanismus zum Sabbatarianismus," (ThD diss., Prague, 2000).
19  Matthias Rauert, "Ein schön lustig Büchlein," *Mennonite Quarterly Review* 83 (2009), 425–470.

The *Chronicle*'s introductory section on the Reformation singles out Martin Luther and Ulrich Zwingli as the first Reformers but states that they failed to reform the papal church: "To speak in a parable, they struck the jug from the pope's hand but kept the broken pieces in their own."[20] The division between Luther and Zwingli is more or less correctly ascribed to Luther's belief "that the body of the Lord Christ is in the bread of the Lord's Supper" and Zwingli's belief "that the Lord's Supper was a memorial of the salvation and grace of Christ,"[21] although Zwingli's teaching is surely flattened and oversimplified here. The anticlerical animus of the early Reformation is perceptively registered: "Eating meat, taking wives, and reviling popes, monks, and priests (who of course richly deserved it) was the extent of their service to God."[22] The marks of the falsity of the early Reformation, according to the *Chronicle*, are the willingness of its leaders to defend their teaching with the sword and the continuance of infant baptism: "The pope had just as little scriptural foundation for infant baptism as for purgatory, the mass, the worship of saints, letters of indulgence, and the like."[23]

The beginning of the genuine Anabaptist Reformation is described in the *Chronicle*'s entry for 1525: "It began in Switzerland, where God brought about an awakening."[24] Ulrich Zwingli, Conrad Grebel, and Felix Mantz "realized that infant baptism is unnecessary and, moreover, is not baptism at all."[25] Zwingli, however, refused to act on his knowledge because of personal cowardice (he "shrank from the cross") and concerns for public order. Then Georg Blaurock, visiting Zurich from Chur, made contact with Grebel and Mantz:

> In the fear of God they agreed that from God's Word one must first learn true faith, expressed in deeds of love, and on confession of this faith receive true Christian baptism as a covenant of a good conscience with God.

Later, at a meeting,

> fear came over them and struck their hearts.... After the prayer, Georg Blaurock stood up and asked Conrad Grebel in the name of God to baptize him with the true Christian baptism on his faith and recognition of the truth. With this request he knelt down, and Conrad baptized

---

20 *Chronicle of the Hutterian Brethren*, 41.
21 Ibid., 42.
22 Ibid.
23 Ibid., 43.
24 Ibid.
25 Ibid., 44.

him, since at that time there was no appointed servant of the Word. Then the others turned to Georg in their turn, asking him to baptize them, which he did.[26]

The identification of the date as January 21, 1525, came as an inference from the archival documentation of believers' baptisms in the nearby village of Zollikon in the last days of January 1525.[27] The omission of mention of Wilhelm Reublin, who had been under pressure from the Zurich Council to accept infant baptism together with Grebel and Mantz, was almost certainly due to Braitmichel's disapproval of the role Reublin played in the Anabaptist settlements in Austerlitz and Auspitz in Moravia in the early 1530s. The 1526 mandate of the Zurich government threatening drowning to recalcitrant Anabaptists and the actual drowning of Felix Mantz on January 5, 1527, are both mentioned in the 1525 entry.[28] Clearly there was an accurate general memory of the beginnings of Swiss Anabaptism when Braitmichel began to write the *Chronicle* in the 1560s, but this is far from a precise description of *wie es eigentlich gewesen*. Naturally, Hutterite in-group historians recognized from the start that the *Chronicle* was far from a complete history of early Anabaptism, but they took it to be essentially reliable. Other historians of Anabaptism, like the Mennonite H.W. Meihuizen, sometimes stumbled in trying to discover early, independent non-Hutterite sources (in Meihuizen's case, the imaginary "Klettgau letter of 1530") for the first Zurich baptisms of 1525.[29]

The *Chronicle*'s entry for 1526 focuses on the arrival of Anabaptism in Moravia with the call of Balthasar Hubmaier to the reforming church of Nikolsburg (now Mikulov) in the territories of the lords of Liechtenstein. This is accurate, and Hubmaier was introduced as an Anabaptist adherent in the 1525 entry, but there is no mention of his earlier introduction of Anabaptism in Waldshut, or its context in Christian humanism and the German Peasants' War. The 1526 entry is used to discuss Anabaptism in Nikolsburg from its onset in 1526 to its division in 1528 between a settled congregation patronized by the Liechtenstein family and a separatist group of refugees from Switzerland and south Germany, inspired by the early church's community-of-goods as described in Acts 2 and 4. This continuance of a theme from the year of its beginning to the time it plays

---

26  Ibid., 45.
27  Leonhard von Muralt and Walter Schmid, eds., *Quellen zur Geschichte der Täufer in der Schweiz*, vol. 1: Zürich (Zurich: Zwingli Verlag, 1952), 38–42; cf. Fritz Blanke, *Brothers in Christ* (Scottdale, PA: Herald Press, 1960).
28  *Chronicle of the Hutterian Brethren*, 46–47.
29  H.W. Meihuizen, "De Bronnen voor een Geschiedenis van de eerste doperse Doopstoediening," *Doopsgezinde Bijdragen*, 1 (1975), 54–61; vs. Heinold Fast, "Wie doopte Konrad Grebel," *Doopsgezinde Bijdragen*, 4 (1978), 22–31.

itself out several years later is typical of Braitmichel's presentation of early Anabaptism. In other words, he uses his year headings rather loosely.

The *Chronicle*'s story of the Anabaptists in Nikolsburg extends from 1526 to Hubmaier's execution in Vienna in March 1528.[30] It is distorting primarily in its treatment of Hans Hut, the major Anabaptist missionary in south and central Germany and Austria. Hut had been a follower of Thomas Müntzer, and present at the battle of Frankenhausen. Baptized by Hans Denck in May 1526, he developed an apocalyptic message that attached significance to Müntzer's career and predicted the end of the world for Pentecost 1528, three and one-half years after Müntzer's death.[31] Braitmichel either did not know about or did not want to discuss Hut's failed apocalyptic message, which seemed to have accelerated the flight of south German-Austrian Anabaptists down the Danube to Moravia. Hut and Hubmaier did clash in Nikolsburg in May 1527, but the later Hutterite objection to "using the sword" and "paying war taxes" misrepresents the nature of their disagreement. At an earlier stage in Anabaptist historiography, the *Chronicle*'s entry for 1526 was preferred to Hut's recorded interrogations following his arrest in Augsburg in September 1527.[32] Hut died in prison in Augsburg in December 1527, but the *Chronicle* records his death among martyrs listed for 1529.[33] Conversely, the *Chronicle* records the martyrdom of Georg Blaurock in the South Tyrol under the year 1527, and some pages further under the correct year, 1529.[34] The martyr account of Michael Sattler appears correctly under the year 1527,[35] but without the Seven Articles of Schleitheim, which mirrored Hutterite practice. In Braitmichel's accounts prior to 1528 there is an imprecise mastery of Anabaptist history—including many accounts of the death of martyrs who were credited with authoring songs still used by the brotherhood, often together with descriptions of the unpleasant deaths of the persecutors.

It is only when Braitmichel repeats in greater detail the account of the division of the *Schwertler* and *Stäbler* in Nikolsburg and the exodus of the latter to Austerlitz in March 1528, this time listing it correctly in 1528 (not 1526), that the *Chronicle* begins to have true worth as a histor-

---

30  *Chronicle of the Hutterian Brethren*, 45, 47–51, esp. 47–49.
31  On Hans Hut, cf. Gottfried Seebaß, *Müntzers Erbe: Werk, Leben, und Theologie des Hans Hut* (Gütersloh: Gütersloher Verlag, 2002).
32  Herbert Klassen, "The Life and Teachings of Hans Hut," *Mennonite Quarterly Review* 33 (1959), 171–205, 267–304; vs. James M. Stayer, "Hans Hut's Doctrine of the Sword: An Attempted Solution," *Mennonite Quarterly Review* 39 (1965), 181–191.
33  *Chronicle of the Hutterian Brethren*, 60–61.
34  Ibid., 53, 82.
35  Ibid., 51–53.

ical source, although continuing to be a very partisan history.[36] Despite the valuable presentation of the first Zurich baptisms of 1525, it is not a usable account of such important early Anabaptist leaders as Balthasar Hubmaier and Hans Hut. For instance, although it correctly dates the deaths of Leonhard Schiemer and Hans Schlaffer to 1528,[37] it does not identify them as important representatives of Hans Hut's Anabaptist mission campaign. But when it explores the mutual relations of the followers of Gabriel Ascherham, Silesian Anabaptists settled at Rossitz, those of Philip Plener, west German Anabaptists settled at Auspitz, and the group under Jakob Wiedemann, who had emigrated from Nikolsburg to Austerlitz, its narrative greatly increases in historical worth.[38] Werner O. Packull recognized this in his excellent monograph, *Hutterite Beginnings: Communitarian Experiments during the Reformation*.[39]

According to the *Chronicle*, a community led by Gabriel Ascherham settled at Rossitz in 1528, after which a group led by Philip Plener "from Swabia" joined them. There were differences in practice between the "Gabrielites" and "Philippites," which led to the Philippites establishing their own community 25 kilometres away at Auspitz. There was no schism between the two groups, which maintained affiliation. From the later Hutterite viewpoint expressed in the *Chronicle*, "they still claimed to be brothers, but their hearts were disunited;"[40] and, in fact, the history of the Gabrielites and Philippites diverged after the major persecution of Moravian Anabaptists in 1535–36.

More detailed is the *Chronicle*'s account of the schism in the Nikolsburg Anabaptist congregation during the winter of 1527–28. Balthasar Hubmaier was surrendered to the Habsburg government in Vienna by his Liechtenstein overlords in Nikolsburg, as the *Chronicle* correctly reported.[41] This likely occurred in the summer of 1527, and it was probably due to Hubmaier's prior alliance with Peasants' War armies defending Anabaptist Waldshut against the Austrian government in 1525,[42] but it did not lead to the disappearance of the Anabaptist congregation that Hubmaier had established at Nikolsburg. Leonhard and Hans von Liechtenstein had accepted baptism from Hubmaier, as had the pastor of the Nikolsburg

---

36 Ibid., 79 ff.
37 Ibid., 55–58.
38 Ibid., 79–82.
39 Werner O. Packull, *Hutterite Beginnings: Communitarian Experiments during the Reformation* (Baltimore/London: Johns Hopkins University Press, 1995), chs. 4, 5: 77–132.
40 *Chronicle of the Hutterian Brethren*, 79–80.
41 Ibid., 47–49.
42 Torsten Bergsten, *Balthasar Hubmaier: Seine Stellung zu Reformation und Täufertum, 1521–1528* (Kassel: J.G. Oncken, 1961), 476–481.

church, Hans Spitelmaier. The *Chronicle* reports that the Liechtensteins defended their territory against the threat of a general persecution of Anabaptists directed from Vienna: "Then Lord Leonhard and Lord Hans von Liechtenstein warned the [Austrian] provost not to interfere within their boundaries or they would present him with a few bullets."[43] The fact that usually the aristocratic estates of Moravia resisted the Habsburgs' pressure for Catholic uniformity in the name of the multidenominational reality created by the Hussite Reformation of the fifteenth century was a major key to the survival of the several Anabaptist groups in Moravia until 1622 and the beginning of the Thirty Years' War.

The settled Anabaptists in Nikolsburg who lived under Liechtenstein protection were termed "the people of the sword"—*Schwertler*. Opposed to them were Anabaptist refugees from south and central Germany and Austria, led by Jakob Wiedemann from Memmingen, "the people of the staff"—*Stäbler*. They declared that the Liechtensteins' protection of Anabaptist Nikolsburg was contrary to their principles and they held strongly to the early Anabaptist veneration of the first-century Jerusalem church's "community-of-goods," as described in Acts 2 and 4. So the Wiedemann group undertook an act of separation—in a sense, they recapitulated the separation of the Zurich Anabaptists from Zwingli's church: "They met from time to time in different houses, received the pilgrims, guests, and strangers from other countries, and began living in community." When the Anabaptist pastor Hans Spitelmaier complained to his protector Lord Leonhard von Liechtenstein about the separatist group led by Jakob Wiedemann, Lord Leonhard ordered the Wiedemann group to attend his church or leave the territory. The separatists were tolerated through the winter of 1527–28, but in March 1528 Lord Leonhard, who is portrayed throughout the *Chronicle* as good natured, declining to confiscate their possessions, escorted Wiedemann and 200 of his followers ("not counting children") out of his property:

> [The leaders] then spread out a cloak in front of the people, and each one laid his possessions on it with a willing heart—without being forced—so that the needy might be supported in accordance with the teaching of the prophets and apostles. Isa. 23:18; Acts 2:44–45; 4:34–35; 5:1–11.

The group relocated to the territory of the lords of Austerlitz.[44]

The Austerlitz congregation sent missionaries to persecuted Anabaptists, particularly in Tyrol. In the entry for 1529, Jakob Hutter and Simon

---

43 *Chronicle of the Hutterian Brethren*, 51.
44 Ibid., 50–51, 80–82.

Schützinger, Anabaptist leaders from Tyrol, are described as visiting Austerlitz and affiliating with the community there.[45] Eighty or nintey Anabaptists from Krumau in southern Bohemia, including the future Hutterite leaders Hans Amon and Leonhard Lanzenstiel, moved to Austerlitz in that year.[46] Also in the 1529 entry, it is noted that "a man named Wilhelm Reublin came to Austerlitz, claiming to be a teacher or servant, but as nothing was known about him, he was not permitted to teach."[47] Reublin, in fact, had played an early role in the Swiss Reformation in Basel and Zurich, was closely associated with Grebel and Mantz in the beginnings of Zurich Anabaptism, and was instrumental in Hubmaier's joining the Anabaptist movement.[48] He tried to insert himself into the leadership of the Austerlitz community "early in 1530" and was resisted by Jakob Wiedemann, who retained the loyalty of the majority of the Austerlitz community. However, Reublin succeeded in drawing to his side a number of leaders at Austerlitz, most prominently Georg Zaunring, who insisted that Wiedemann should give Reublin a fair hearing, instead of simply standing on his authority. There is evidence that the rejection of war taxes, later a characteristic part of the Hutterite program, came from Reublin. One of his complaints against Wiedemann's leadership of the Austerlitz brotherhood was that they claimed to be peaceful but paid war taxes.[49] The dominant group at Austerlitz excommunicated the dissidents, without allowing them to recover the possessions they had surrendered to the community. So about 150 people set out with Reublin and Zaunring to Auspitz in 1531. The beginnings in Auspitz were quite difficult; they "had to suffer great need and hunger, for they were quite ignorant of the country, and the work in the vineyards." In their first year the Auspitz group, according to the *Chronicle*, were thoroughly exploited by a vineyard owner before they "purchased a house near the horse market by agreement with the nuns at Brünn, who owned the land and lent them money."[50]

---

45 Ibid., 83–86.
46 Ibid., 85.
47 Ibid., 86.
48 James M. Stayer, "Reublin and Brötli: The Revolutionary Beginnings of Swiss Anabaptism," in *The Origins and Characteristics of Anabaptism/Les débuts et les charactéristiques de l'anabaptisme*, ed. Marc Lienhard (The Hague: Martinus Nijhoff, 1977), 83–102; James M. Stayer, "Wilhelm Reublin: A Picaresque Journey Through Early Anabaptism," in *Profiles of Radical Reformers: Biographical Sketches from Thomas Müntzer to Paracelsus*, ed. Hans-Jürgen Goertz (Scottdale/Kitchener: Herald Press, 1982), 107–117; Peter Bührer, "Wilhelm Reublin: Radikaler Prediger und Täufer," *Mennonitische Geschichtsblätter* 65 (2008), 181–232; C. Arnold Snyder, ed., *Later Writings of the Swiss Anabaptists, 1529–1592* (Kitchener: Pandora Press, 2017), 27–40.
49 Wilhelm Reublin, "Letter to Pilgram Marpeck (1531)," trans. J.C. Wenger, *Mennonite Quarterly Review* 23 (1949), 67–75; *Later Writings of the Swiss Anabaptists*, 48–56.
50 *Chronicle of the Hutterian Brethren*, 87–90.

Jakob Hutter and Simon Schützinger were called from Tyrol to visit Austerlitz and Auspitz and to adjudicate the 1531 schism. Their conclusion was that Wiedemann and his followers were the "most guilty."

> In the first place they had acted unjustly in expelling the innocent; second, they had allowed freedom of the flesh, resulting in a return to private property; third, there had been marriages with unbelievers....[51]

After this, the Austerlitz Brethren more or less disappear from the *Chronicle*, although as recent scholarship shows they continued to be a significant part of Moravian Anabaptism.[52] Entries for the late 1530s mention persons converted to the Hutterian Brethren from "the lapsed group at Austerlitz." Seemingly the Austerlitz Brethren were no more Christians in Braitmichel's eyes than Roman Catholic persecutors. Just what the accusation of "a return to private property" meant is very obscure. Imitation of the early church in Jerusalem as described in Acts 2 and 4 was a widespread early Anabaptist ideal—certainly it included "support for the needy," but there was not at that time the complete communism of production and consumption achieved by the later Hutterites.[53] So a standard accusation of one group against another was that their version of Christian communism, in effect, was really a "return to private property."

The *Chronicle*'s 1531 entry includes the excommunication of Wilhelm Reublin, the moving spirit of the Austerlitz-Auspitz schism:

> Soon after, Reublin became extremely ill. Without the knowledge of the elders and the church and regardless of the great hunger among the people, he had hidden twenty-five gulden that he had brought with him from his home. In his illness he entrusted this money to a married sister named Katherina Loy, who immediately reported it.[54]

Hutter and Schützinger were asked to assess the matter and they immediately excommunicated Reublin (supposedly he acknowledged that the sentence was just). Is this account credible? Reublin lived to be eighty, long after the Anabaptist episode in his life was over. He was one of the few early Anabaptist leaders to escape an early death, either as a martyr

---

51 Ibid., 91.
52 Martin Rothkegel, "Pilgram Marpeck and the 'Fellows of the Covenant'," *Mennonite Quarterly Review* 85 (2009), 425–470. Arnold Snyder, however, observes that the major persecution of 1535 seriously weakened the Austerlitz Brethren, and possibly diminished the authority of Moravia over German missionaries like Marpeck.
53 James M. Stayer, *The German Peasants' War and Anabaptist Community of Goods* (Kingston/Montreal: McGill-Queen's University Press, 1991), 95–122, 200–208.
54 *Chronicle of the Hutterian Brethren*, 91.

or a fugitive. His remarkable talent for self-preservation makes it entirely credible that he would have secreted private wealth from the confiscations of the Austerlitz brotherhood under Jakob Wiedemann.

However, the person-by-person elimination of all Jakob Hutter's later competitors for leadership of the Auspitz community is more remarkable. First of all, it came to light that Georg Zaunring, who had joined Reublin in the 1531 exodus from Austerlitz to Auspitz, was himself impure. His wife had committed adultery with another member of the community; although Zaunring separated from her when her sin was discovered, he forgave her much too quickly and easily: "The whole church agreed unanimously that members of Christ should not be members of a harlot and therefore Zaunring and his wife should be excluded and separated from the church."[55] This left the Auspitz congregation without a leader, so Hutter and Schützinger were again summoned from the Tyrol to set things right. The solution was that Schützinger was to lead the Auspitz congregation, while Hutter was to return to embattled Tyrolean Anabaptism, directing the flight of many Tyrolean Anabaptists to Moravia. Further, a union was forged with the Gabrielites at Rossitz and the Philippites at Auspitz: "From now on the three groups were no longer to act separately in difficult matters but to seek each other's counsel as befits a united people."[56]

The union of 1531 continued until, under the pressure of intense persecution in Tyrol, Hutter decided to come to Auspitz, "arriving on August 11, 1533. The elders and the whole church welcomed him with great joy […]."[57] In the *Chronicle*'s detailed account, Hutter aspired merely to a co-leadership with Schützinger, but Ascherham and Plener insisted upon Schützinger maintaining complete authority at Auspitz. Ascherham is represented as telling Schützinger,

> I command you, Simon, to continue your service as shepherd to this people. If you were to lose courage for your service and allow it to be weakened because Jakob is more gifted and a better speaker than you, God would punish you.[58]

Then, Jakob Hutter got an inspiration about how to resolve the problem; the *Chronicle* remarks that "God had given Jakob the gift of discernment." The rooms of all the elders were searched, and it was discovered that Simon Schützinger had forty gulden hidden under his roof:

---

55  Ibid., 92–93.
56  Ibid., 93.
57  Ibid., 98.
58  Ibid., 101.

Jakob and the other servants were appalled. They could hardly believe that he would knowingly have done such a thing: he taught full surrender and community to others and yet did not hold to it himself.[59]

Schützinger was immediately excommunicated. The rub turned out to be that Gabriel Ascherham and Philip Plener would not concur with what had transpired. A struggle consuming much of October and November 1533 resulted in mutual excommunications between the Auspitz congregation, now fully under the control of Jakob Hutter, on one side, and the Gabrielites and Philippites, on the other.

From the side of the Gabrielites and Philippites, Jakob Hutter's personal charisma was the issue. Visiting Hutter's congregation on October 26, Philip Plener phrased the accusation against Jakob Hutter thus: "I have always said you are an idol and the people worship you. That is the plain truth."[60] The *Chronicle* ends its description of this fateful juncture with a long letter by Jakob Hutter to his followers in Tyrol, reporting on what had occurred.[61] The letter is full of the eloquence of a religious leader who, like many in subsequent centuries, had learned from the Bible to write in the tones and cadences of a New Testament apostle. This could not have occurred before the German Reformation made biblical eloquence so accessible and impressive. In subsequent years the Hutterian Brethren far outstripped their Moravian Anabaptist competitors. How much this was the personal achievement of Jakob Hutter is something of a conundrum.

Under 1534 the *Chronicle* registers a distant, but essentially accurate, awareness of the Anabaptist rule of Münster in Westphalia, concentrating on the leadership of Jan van Leyden:

> This Jan set up a government according to Jewish custom and a new religion, saying, for instance that a man could take as many wives as he wished. Then he made himself king in royal splendour and in his folly believed that he would rule the whole world and possess the throne of his father David until the heavenly Father would claim the kingdom from him.[62]

This echoed the numerous pamphlets about Anabaptist Münster, and whether its government aspired to literal world domination remains in

---

59  Ibid., 103–104.
60  Ibid., 106.
61  Ibid., 110–126.
62  Ibid., 133.

dispute, even among contemporary scholars.[63] The *Chronicle* acknowledged that the baptism of adult believers was taught in Münster but recognized no kinship with the Münster Anabaptists. It argued that the Münster episode caused the great persecution of Moravian Anabaptists in 1535–36. A contributing factor was the Hutterite declaration that because of her "idolatry," they would no longer work in the vineyards of the abbess of Brünn, their landlord at Auspitz. Expelled from the abbess's property, the Hutterites camped in open fields in Liechtenstein land.[64] Hutter wrote an open letter to the governor of Moravia, denouncing him and his overlord, King Ferdinand of Austria, for their persecution of God's peaceful flock.[65] Whatever else, Hutter showed himself totally incapable of tactical deference. When the governor responded to Hutter's defiance by ordering his arrest, Hutter hid himself, turned over leadership of the Moravian brotherhood to Hans Amon, and set out to join his followers in Tyrol.[66] He was arrested in November 1535 in the Adige region of Tyrol, taken to Innsbruck, horribly tortured, and burned at the stake in February 1536. In Moravia the Hutterites divided into small groups of eight or ten persons, with whom Amon and his assistants kept in touch as best they could: "The people wandered about the land in misery and suffering for almost a whole year."[67]

The Philippites at Auspitz were also scattered in a manner similar to the Hutterites. The *Chronicle* comments disparagingly on their return to west Germany, where they were unable to practice community in the Moravian manner: "[They] felt no desire to embrace the more perfect way, choosing private property and their own gain rather than patient surrender in Christian community."[68] Werner Packull in *Hutterite Beginnings* observes that "no evidence exists that Philip [Plener] advocated a unique or different form of Anabaptism generically at variance with Swiss Anabaptism.[69]" The Philippites were more or less Swiss Brethren when they came to Moravia, and they were absorbed into the Swiss Brethren after they returned to their homeland. But the Philippites did leave one important mark on Anabaptist history. The *Chronicle* notes that a large group of sixty Philippites were apprehended and imprisoned at Passau.[70] They are the source of the first Anabaptist hymnbook published in 1564. These hymns

---

63  Karl-Heinz Kirchhoff, "Das Phänomen des Täuferreichs zu Münster 1534/35," in *Der Raum Westfalen*, vol. 6/1, ed. Franz Petri (Münster: Aschendorff, 1989), 399–401.
64  *Chronicle of the Hutterian Brethren*, 134–135.
65  Ibid., 137–141.
66  Ibid., 142.
67  Ibid.
68  Ibid., 176–177.
69  Packull, *Hutterite Beginnings*, 86.
70  *Chronicle of the Hutterian Brethren*, 136.

were used both by Swiss Brethren and Hutterites. When first published, the hymns were attributed to "Swiss Brethren"—Packull shows that they came from the Philippites. Curiously, two of the original hymns praised community-of-goods; they were deleted from the *Ausbund*, the official Swiss Brethren hymnal, in its later editions.[71]

In the summer of 1537, Peter Riedemann, a Moravian Anabaptist who had been imprisoned in Nuremberg for four years, was released from prison. His first associates were Philippites, but he is described as determined to investigate the various inter-group schisms that had occurred since 1533. His decision to join the Hutterites appears to have been significantly influenced by the decision of the Austerlitz Brethren, Philippites, and Gabrielites to return to private property in response to the fierce persecutions of 1535–36.[72] Münster Anabaptism had flaunted its own version of community-of-goods. Early Anabaptists generally idealized the communalism of the primitive church as described in Acts 2 and 4—obviously this did not work out practically in the Nikolsburg church, which continued the medieval parish system under Balthasar Hubmaier and Hans Spitelmaier. But the Münster crisis led several Anabaptist leaders to regard excessive focus on the early church in Jerusalem as a mistake, and to reinterpret the New Testament narrative as compatible with private property. This change can be observed, for instance, in the writings of Pilgram Marpeck, as Werner Packull has noted.[73] The Hutterites vigorously continued their earlier commitment to community-of-goods; leaders like Riedemann drew some groups of Austerlitz Brethren and Philippites to the Hutterites in the aftermath of the 1535–36 dispersion of Moravian Anabaptists.

Peter Riedemann also mentions contact with Anabaptists, whom he refers to as "Swiss Brethren," when he was travelling on a Hutterite mission in 1539.[74] The *Chronicle* makes an earlier reference to "Swiss Brethren in Switzerland" in 1536 and the vain efforts of Hutterite missionaries "to stimulate them to a more perfect life."[75] Riedemann's comment refers to "Swiss Brethren" in Swabia, again with criticism.[76] Harold S. Bender was in his day fully aware that the term "Swiss Brethren" came into use only in the late 1530s, but he concluded that such Anabaptists had continued the original Anabaptism begun by Conrad Grebel and Georg Blaurock in

---

71  Packull, *Hutterite Beginnings*, 89.
72  *Chronicle of the Hutterian Brethren*, 163–168.
73  Packull, *Hutterite Beginnings*, 138; Stayer, *Peasants' War and Community of Goods*, 156–157.
74  *Chronicle of the Hutterian Brethren*, 183.
75  Ibid., 152.
76  Ibid., 183.

Zurich in January 1525, hence he titled his biography of Conrad Grebel *The Founder of the Swiss Brethren Sometimes Called Anabaptists* (1950). It seems clear that "Swiss Brethren" Anabaptists were not confined to Switzerland, and doubtful that they had a special founding moment distinct from the Zurich baptisms of January 1525.[77]

In entries for 1539 and 1540 the *Chronicle* describes a Habsburg raid on a Hutterite community at Steinebrunn, resulting in the imprisonment of 150 in Falkenstein Castle. When the Anabaptists resisted efforts to win them to Catholicism, it was decided to separate the men from the women and to sentence the men to be galley slaves in the fleet of Andrea Doria fighting the Turks. The men were subjected to a long march to Trieste where the fleet was waiting for them.

> On the twelfth night in Trieste they all got free of their bonds. They walked out of the prison, and God showed them a place where within an hour they could all let themselves down from the city wall with ropes. The ropes that had bound them and by which they had been led into the prison now served for their escape.

Most of the prisoners made their way back to the Hutterites in Moravia. Only twelve were apprehended in the pursuit.[78] Kaspar Braitmichel wrote a celebratory song about the event.[79] Escapes from prison were also part of the story of early Swiss Anabaptism, and there were New Testament precedents. Nevertheless, a fractious group of Hutterites questioned whether imprisoned Christians were not obliged to obey higher authority and stay in prison[80]—a sort of echo of the Jacob Wiedemann group taking exception to the Liechtensteins protecting their Nikolsburg Anabaptists from the Austrian provost.

Peter Riedemann was a Hutterite missionary to the Hessian Anabaptists, in the course of which he was imprisoned by Margrave Philipp of Hesse, a ruler notably unwilling to execute Anabaptists for their unwillingness to accept the official Reformation. Riedemann was held in a very mild confinement and engaged in doctrinal discussions with Hessian Protestant theologians, a situation which provided him with the occasion to work out a detailed articulation of Hutterite doctrine.[81] In the course

---

77 James M. Stayer, "Die 'Schweizer Brüder'—Auf der Suche einer neuen Definition: Selbstkritik und Dialog in der Täuferforschung. Im Gedenken an Heinold Fast," *Mennonitische Geschichtsblätter* 73 (2016), 7–18.
78 *Chronicle of the Hutterian Brethren*, 187–196, esp. 195.
79 Ibid., 196n2.
80 Ibid., 198–199.
81 Werner O. Packull, *Peter Riedemann: Shaper of the Hutterite Tradition* (Kitchener: Pandora Press, 2007).

of this imprisonment he expressed himself on a subject which helped to define the character of Hutterite community-of-goods. Against Hutterite dissidents he strongly endorsed the "double honours" accorded to the leadership, against the accusation that "they eat by themselves and of the best. They teach you community-of-goods but do not keep it themselves."[82] Riedemann replied by citing St. Paul's defense of living from the Gospel, instead of supporting himself from his tent-making craft. This contributed to reinforcing the authority of the Hutterite servants of the Word and servants of temporal needs. With the possible exception of the Swiss Brethren, most Anabaptist groups developed a strong principle of authority.

The antagonism between the Hutterites and the Austerlitz Brethren, which continued from the 1531 schism, was particularly strong. Pilgram Marpeck, who has won great attention in twentieth-century Anabaptist scholarship,[83] chose to remain affiliated with Austerlitz rather than to connect himself with Reublin and Schützinger in Auspitz. He nursed ambitions to overcome the division. In 1541 he and Cornelius Veh, an elder of the Austerlitz Brethren, made approaches to the Hutterites. The treatment of Marpeck in the *Chronicle* is particularly dismissive:

> He claimed he had come to the country to gather and unite all groups that had split up over matters of faith, but he straightaway proved the opposite. His very presence seemed to cause disturbance and confusion, and his slanderous talk confirmed this. When the brothers and sisters met to seek comfort and strength in the Lord's Word, this slanderer wanted to join them in prayer. The brothers and sisters did not permit this, because of his great lack of understanding […].[84]

In the winter of 1541–42, the plague killed many people in Moravia, including Jakob Hutter's successor, Hans Amon, who died in February 1542. Leonard Lanzenstiel was chosen to succeed him.[85] A bit later Peter Riedemann was released from his Hessian prison: "All the elders of the church gathered and decided unanimously that the brothers Leonhard Lanzenstiel and Peter Riedemann should together care for the church, which they did with great dedication."[86]

---

82 *Chronicle of the Hutterian Brethren*, 199–209, esp. 202.
83 Most recently, Walter Klaassen and William Klassen, *Marpeck: A Life of Dissent and Conformity* (Waterloo/Scottdale: Herald Press, 2008); *Studies in Anabaptist and Mennonite History*, 44.
84 *Chronicle of the Hutterian Brethren*, 210.
85 Ibid., 213–214.
86 Ibid., 216.

Braitmichel concluded his account with a table of martyrs and a general tribute to the martyrs of the church, occasionally mixed with accounts of God's exemplary punishment of their persecutors.[87]

> But now, although I would gladly have continued the work, I am unable to continue it because of physical weakness and a problem with my eyes. I brought the story only to the year 1542, when the church was entrusted to brother Leonhard Lanzenstiel. I still hope that through this beginning God will move others to carry on this work with even greater diligence, as completely as possible.[88]

Kaspar Braitmichel, with his particular commitments and his cloudy memories of the first years, is the first historian of Anabaptism.

---

87  Ibid., 217–225.
88  Ibid., LXXIV.

**Bruce Wiebe** is an independent researcher from Winkler, Manitoba. His primary research interests are the Mennonite West Reserve in Manitoba, the Reinlaender Mennoniten Gemeinde and their *Waisenamt*, Mennonite emigration to Mexico, and the establishment of Hutterite communities in Manitoba.

# "Despairing in Canada?"
# The Land Transactions of
# Hutterite Immigration to Manitoba

## BRUCE WIEBE[*]

When comparing the affluent Manitoba Hutterite communities of today with their immigration story, we are struck by sharp contrasts of hardship and despair occasioned by sometimes overwhelming financial obligations due to their land purchases. This essay examines the details of the Schmiedeleut Hutterites' immigration from South Dakota to Manitoba, but is not intended as a comprehensive history. Rather, this essay attempts to address the information gap in published works concerning the land purchases. The knowledge of these events has by now disappeared from the collective memory of the Hutterite community. Reconstructing the Manitoba land transactions tells a significant part of the immigration story, including from whom the lands were purchased, at what cost, and how the purchases were financed. Details about the South Dakota community sales that enabled the Manitoba purchases are another significant part of this story, as is information about earlier Hutterite settlement in Manitoba.[1]

---

[*] The author is grateful to Crystal Spring, Acadia, and Silverwinds Hutterite communities for the financial contributions to assist with the cost of document copies; to John Hofer, Patrick Murphy, and Tim Waldner for access to original documents as noted in footnotes and to Ian Kleinsasser and Tony Waldner for copies, scans, or transcriptions of significant primary documents without which this research would have been incomplete. Also, for their advice, feedback, and reading of the manuscript.

[1] Additional primary documents and Hutterite financial ledgers may still exist and become available to further clarify or revise certain transactions described here. The initial immigration period is the focus of this paper and, with few exceptions, later land transactions are not included.

Unless specifically stated on certificates of title, all acreages, whether individual parcels or totals for multiple parcels, are to be considered as approximate since they cannot be precisely verified. The number of acres per quarter section may vary slight-

The Schmiedeleut Hutterites of the early twentieth century faced significant hardship. Although many of the facts are no longer commonly known, even among Hutterites, the vestiges of history provide ample resources to help us understand and reconstruct the progression of events. For example, their distress is evident in a song written or recopied by Kathrina J. Waldner of Rosedale, Manitoba.

> …We came from the United States
> where it was more advantageous.
> Who knows how this will turn out!
> Despairing in Canada!
>
> Despairing in Canada,
> in dear Manitoba;
> We already owe half a million dollars.
> Is that not over the limit?
>
> To this we have sunk—
> is it not lamentable?
> The old depart this place
> and the young remain to pay.[2]

---

ly, but 160 is used as the average and unknown railway allowances are not deducted. Additionally, calculations of irregular parcels were sometimes approximate and therefore total acreages may vary from actual. The number of acres contained within any legal descriptions were, where possible, obtained from the Municipal Assessment and Collector Rolls, but these were also inconsistent. For brevity, smaller acreage exclusions from certain parcels are not included in the summarized legal descriptions, and where possible, property legal descriptions were combined. Unless specified, document dates are as of signing and not registration, which can vary considerably. Deeds refer to Old System registrations and transfers refer to registrations under the Real Property Act (RPA). Mortgages registered under the RPA were destroyed by the Property Registry and some details have been reconstructed, as possible. Balances owed on some assumed mortgages are undocumented, therefore informed estimates were occasionally necessary. Assumed mortgages discharged almost immediately after the property transfer were considered to have been included in the land payment calculations. Further transfers of certificates of title between trustees within communities and between different communities as well as title consolidations may have occurred beyond those documented here. Other than the Municipal Tax Rolls, and the Sharpe and Roseisle community details in the Morden Land Titles Office, all other Manitoba land transaction data was transcribed from microfilm in the Portage la Prairie and Winnipeg Land Titles Offices. In the event of a transcription discrepancy, refer to the relevant documents on said microfilms or abstracts. Municipal Assessment and Collector Rolls are not always clear as to actual ownership or tenancy or even residency. Tax rolls also consulted but not specifically identified were those of the Rural Municipalities of Cartier, Portage la Prairie, St. François Xavier, and Macdonald. All legal descriptions are west of the Principal Meridian except for those in the RM of Franklin and eastern portion of RM of Rhineland, which are specified as east. Cents were omitted for sums listed, but no rounding was done.

2  This song was discovered among the papers of Paul Waldner (Rosedale, MB) and

These poignant lyrics reveal the financial strain of immigration, but numerous references only become clear after knowing the full context. From the events described in this essay, it will be evident that in a true expression of community, the Schmiedeleut enabled the move for all Hutterite communities by intentionally choosing to immigrate to Canada as one group. Echoing the "greatest commandment" of both Matthew 22 and Mark 12, their inter-community mutual aid commitment was well summarized by Joseph Kleinsasser of Milltown, South Dakota, in 1919 when asked about their response should another community meet with disaster. He replied: "It is our duty and our practice to help them out as much as possible as if we were in the same condition ourselves."[3]

The first Hutterites to visit the new Canadian province of Manitoba were Paul Tschetter and Lorenz Tschetter, who accompanied the 1873 Mennonite delegation from Russia (present-day Ukraine) seeking settlement opportunities in North America.[4] Between 1874 and 1879, the Hutterite community immigrated to the southern part of Dakota Territory. Four branches can be identified there: the communal-living Schmiedeleut, Dariusleut, and Lehrerleut, as well as the non-communal Prairieleut. It was members of this latter group who made the first attempt at a permanent settlement in Manitoba.

---

    transcribed by Tony Waldner (Forest River, ND). Transcription in the author's collection, freely translated. The original, in its entirety, is as follows: *[Verloren in Kanada:] Ein schönes Lied zu betrachten. Geschrieben von Kathrina J. Waldner, Rosedale Colony, Elie, MB. (1.) Wir wollen euch jetzt vorsingen, / Wir sind so sehr bekümmert / Über unserm Zustand in diesem Land. / Was wird die Zeit noch bringen? (2.) Kamen von Vereinigten Staaten, / Dort ist alles gut geraten. / Wo kommt es doch hin; wer gibt's uns im Sinn? / Verloren in Kanada! (3.) Verloren in Kanada, / Im lieben Manitoba. / Wir schulden ja schon ein halb Million. / Ist das nicht über die Massen? (4.) So weit sind wir gefallen, / Ist das nicht zu beklagen? / Die Alten gehn fort, hinterlassen den Ort / Dem Jungen zu bezahlen. (5.) Dem Armen zu bezahlen, / Wie ist ihr Gut verfallen! / Sie erben nicht mehr als die Taschen ganz leer. / Wie werden sie es bezahlen? (6.) Das nimmt noch viele Jahren. / Wer kann so viel ersparen, / Zu zahlen die Schuld, wer hat die Geduld? / Der Mut ist schier verfallen. (7.) Es ist ja zu verzagen; / Das Land kann's nicht ertragen, / Den schrecklichen Lohn über ein halb Million. / Wer hat dran ein Gefallen?*

3    Circuit Court of the State of South Dakota, Ninth Judicial Circuit, Beadle County, E.P. Flowers and H.G. Spratt, Plaintiffs v. Frederick Waldner, Maria Waldner, R.O. Richards, Trustee and Attorney in Fact for Frederick Waldner and Maria Waldner; Hutterische Bruder-Gemeinde, a corporation, et al., Defendants. October 27–28, 1919, Joseph Kleinsasser testimony, partial trial transcript, 179. Courtesy of Ian Kleinsasser.

4    A.J.F. Zieglschmid, *Das Klein Geschichtsbuch der Hutterischen Brueder* (Philadelphia: Carl Schurz Memorial Foundation, 1947), 569–606. For a biography of delegate Paul Tschetter, see Rod Janzen, *Paul Tschetter: The Story of a Hutterite Immigrant Leader, Pioneer, and Pastor* (Eugene: Pickwick Publications, 2009).

As early as July 1890, it was reported that Joseph Wallman had moved to Manitoba,[5] but it was in 1891 that the Prairieleut began a documented presence on the Mennonite West Reserve. That is where the families of Paul Wallman, Jacob Waldner, and Andreas Wallman were living, immediately north of the American border at the village of Neuhorst, where Andreas was employed as the herdsman.[6] This village was the residence of Isaac Miller, former *Obervorsteher* (administrator) of the West Reserve and, significantly, himself of Hutterite lineage through his father, Andreas Miller, who was born in 1798 in the Hutterite Bruderhof at Vishenka. Other Mennonites of Hutterite ancestry residing in the village were Jacob Thiessen (whose maternal Knels grandparents had also left the Radichev Bruderhof) and Jacob Knelsen, of the same Knels lineage but whose mother was a Wipf.[7]

The tax rolls for the Rural Municipality (RM) of Rhineland indicate that in 1892, Jacob Waldner relocated to Edenburg, just east of Gretna, where Reverend David Waldner, David Waldner Jr., Andreas Kleinsasser, Heinrich Walter, and Hans Wipf now also resided. Although not yet landowners, in 1893 Rev. David Waldner was recorded on Section 3, Township 1, Range 1 WPM, his son David Waldner Jr. on 11-1-1W, Andreas Wallman at Gretna on 6-1-1W, and Andreas Kleinsasser on 21-1-1W. By the following year, 1894, further changes had been made: Andreas Wallman was recorded at Gretna village, Andreas Kleinsasser was now living on NW 34-1-2W, David Waldner Jr. had relocated to SW 35-2-2W, and Jacob Waldner was living on the adjacent SE 35-2-2W. Both of the latter were on land owned by the Massey Harris Company of Winnipeg.

By 1895, minster David Waldner was living at Schoenhorst and being assessed taxes on NW 18-1-1E, Andreas Wallman on SE 12-1-1E, Samuel Wipf on SW 22-1-1E, Paul Kleinsasser east of Plum Coulee on

---

5   Letter dated July 27, 1890 from Peter Janzen, Bon Homme, SD. *Mennonitische Rundschau*, August 6, 1890, 1.
6   RM of Rhineland 1891 Assessment Roll, digitized in 2015 by Bruce Wiebe at the Archives of Manitoba. See also Census of Canada, 1891, Library and Archives Canada (hereafter cited as LAC), last modified February 21, 2019, https://www.bac-lac.gc.ca/eng/census/1891/Pages/about-census.aspx.
7   Communication between South Dakota Hutterites and their Manitoba relatives was ongoing as evidenced by a letter from Andreas Miller in Freeman, SD, to his unnamed cousin in Manitoba—presumably Isaac Miller according to references in the letter (Andreas Miller to unnamed cousin, May 28, 1892; copy at Mennonite Heritage Archives, Winnipeg, Johan W. Thiessen collection, vol. 1600; location of original in Mexico is unknown). Andreas had just returned home from a visit to Manitoba and reported delivering greetings to various individuals. William Miller of Burwalde, MB, recorded that his father's Waldner cousin from South Dakota visited them in 1894 ("The Mueller Family Register," William Miller files, in author's collection).

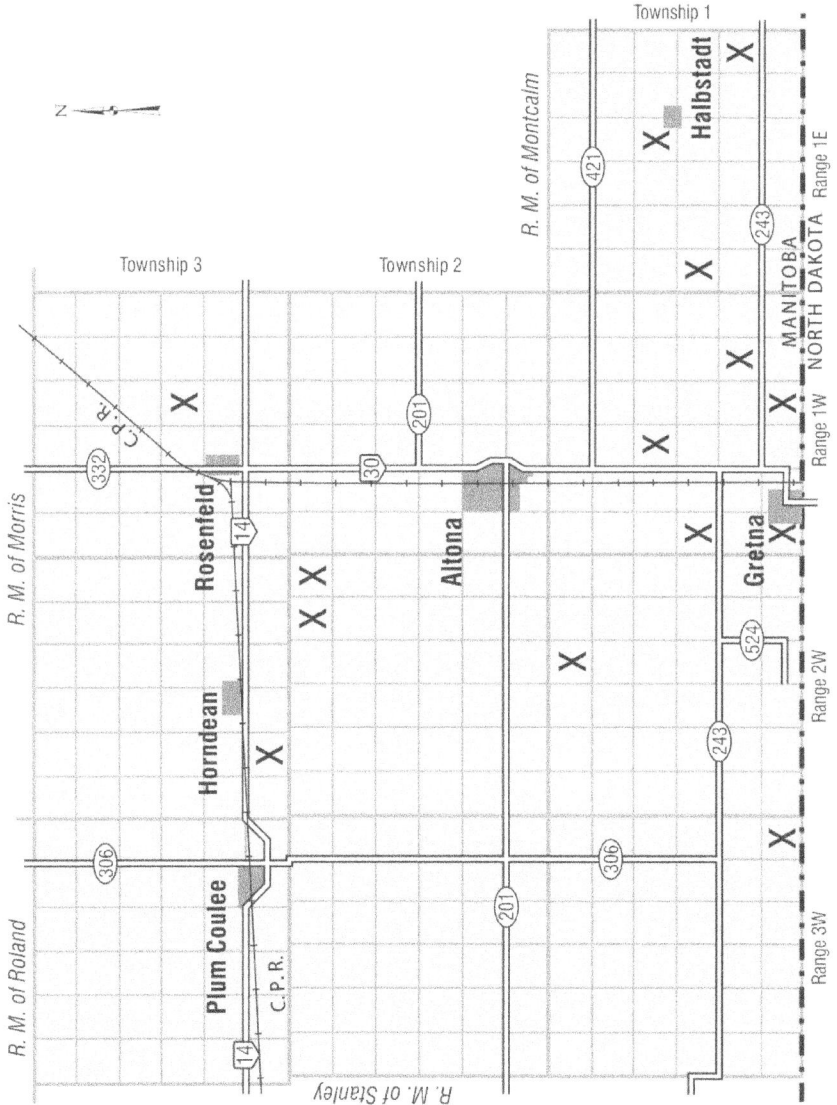

**Map 1.** Prairieleut settlement in the RM of Rhineland. Sections marked with an X are known to have portions of land on which Prairieleut were recorded as having lived, were assessed for, or paid taxes on at some point during the years between 1891 and 1902. (Map drawn by Weldon Hiebert)

SE 5-3-2W, and Heinrich Walter on Erdman Penner's property, SW 36-2-2W.[8] In 1895 Paul Tschetter was also at Plum Coulee,[9] but in 1896 he made enquiries as to whether NW 15-3-1W was available for entry. If it was available, he intended to make entry and by paying $3 per acre and residing on the property at least six months annually for the next three years, thereby acquire a patent. In the same year, Paul Kleinsasser enquired about making reduced payments for SE 15-3-1W,[10] while Joseph Waldner, residing in Gruenthal village near Gretna, borrowed $200 from the Mennonite West Reserve administration.[11]

The exact number and names of the Prairieleut families living on the West Reserve and precisely when they left is unknown. Approximately a dozen can be identified; their initial places of residence were temporary. The impermanence is attributable to them mostly being tenants, although some were earlier recorded by the municipality as landowners. Additionally, they were widely dispersed. How minister David Waldner served them spiritually is not evident, but his presence would have contributed towards a sense of community despite the distances. Waldner had been a minister in the non-communal Hutterite community at Hutterdorf in Russia, which had immigrated to America in 1874 and settled at Wolf Creek in Dakota Territory.[12] Seventeen years later he arrived in Manitoba.

Examples of this impermanence are numerous. For example, by 1897 the Heinrich Walter and Paul Kleinsasser families were no longer identified as being on their West Reserve properties. Andreas Wallman and Andreas Kleinsasser no longer appeared on theirs in 1898,[13] although Kleinsasser was still in the area in 1902.[14] In July 1898, minister David Waldner paid Johann Klassen $300 for a quitclaim deed to SW 15-3-1W, which included a partially built house and 20 acres broken, on which another $380 appeared owing to the Department of the Interior. Waldner was still required to meet a residency requirement before he obtained a patent in December 1901, at which time he was cultivating 100 acres and

---

8   RM of Rhineland Assessment and Collector Rolls.
9   June 25, 1895 Petition, RM of Rhineland Correspondence files, Altona and District Heritage Research Centre Inc.
10  Department of the Interior, Homestead Application File for SE 15-3-1W. Likely in error, it is also referred to as the north east quarter in one document.
11  This $200 plus accrued interest will have been repaid in 1899, since it no longer appears thereafter. (*Anschreibebuch des Bezirksamt zu Reinland, der Schlussrechnung vom 6. Juli 1875 bis 11. Januar 1878* [Ledger of the District Office of Reinland, final report for July 6, 1875 to January 11, 1878], 134, 136, and 138. Current location of original unknown, copy in author's possession.)
12  *Das Klein Geschichtsbuch*, 460.
13  RM of Rhineland Assessment and Collector Rolls.
14  Letter from Jacob D. Wurz, *Mennonitische Rundschau*, March 26, 1902.

had completed a 16' × 24' house with an 8' × 24' lean-to.[15] It appears that he resold as soon as possible. In 1900, Jacob Waldner's name did not appear on his property, but he remained in the area till at least 1902, when David Waldner Jr. also vacated his property.[16] The presence of Joseph Wallman and Joshua Wollman on the eastern portion of the West Reserve was noted in 1901,[17] and Samuel Wipf appeared as late as 1903. In addition, the Hutterite family surnames Hofer, Wurz or Wurtz, and Tschetter appeared on the West Reserve through marriages recorded there: Andreas Hofer and Maria Kleinsasser in 1900; Jacob Wurtz and Anna Kleinsasser in 1896; J.M. Janzen and Maria Tschetter in 1900; and David J. Janzen and Katharina Tschetter in 1901.[18]

Coinciding with their disappearance from the West Reserve was the entry of Prairieleut families east in the Rural Municipality of Franklin, across the Red River. For the year 1898, the municipal tax rolls recorded the following:

- Jacob Wurtz on NW 27-1-3E
- Michael Wurtz on SW 27-1-3E
- Andrew J. Kleinsasser on SE 33-1-3E
- Andrew Hofer on SW 34-1-3E
- Anna Kleinsasser on NW 34-1-3E

Recorded the following year, 1899, were these individuals:

- Paul Wallman on SE 25-1-3E[19]
- Andrew Wallman on SW 25-1-3E
- another Jacob Wurtz on NE 28-1-3E
- Paul Tschetter on N ½ 33-1-3E
- Paul J. and David Gross on S ½ 35-1-3E
- Jacob Hofer on SE 4-2-3E
- Anna Kleinsasser had added NE 34-1-3E, and Jacob Wurtz and Michael Wurtz were shown together on NW 22-1-3E
- further to the east, Heinrich Walter on SE 2-1-5E, and Jacob Walter on SE 16-1-5E[20]

---

15   Department of the Interior Homestead Application File for SW 15-3-1W.
16   Letter from Jacob D. Wurz, *Mennonitische Rundschau*, March 26, 1902.
17   Census of Canada, 1901, LAC, last modified February 21, 2019, https://www.bac-lac.gc.ca/eng/census/1901/Pages/about-census.aspx.
18   Data available via the Province of Manitoba Vital Statistics website: http://vitalstats.gov.mb.ca/Query.php.
19   Paul Wallman obtained a homestead patent for SE 25-1-3 East on April 13, 1904.
20   Heinrich and Jacob Walter are as yet unidentified as Hutterites.

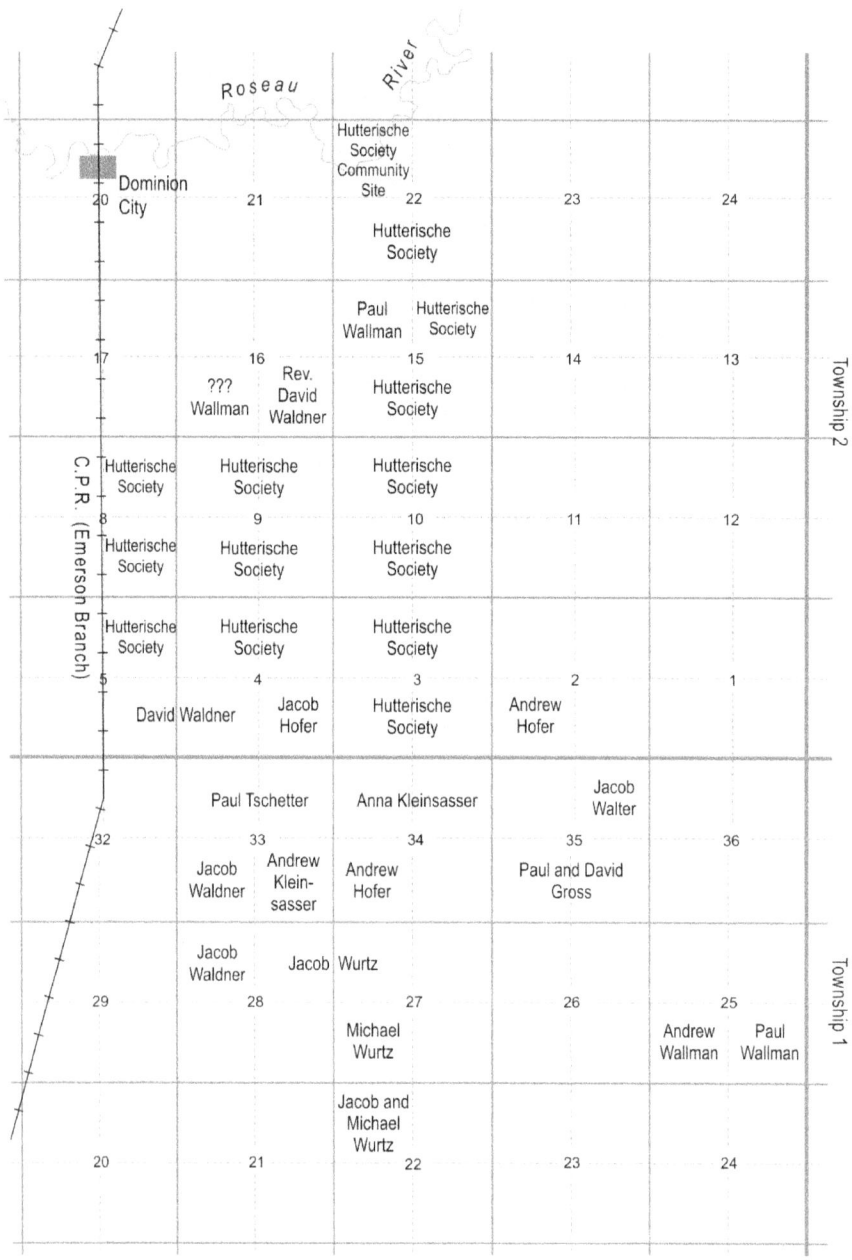

**Map 2.** Hutterische Society and Prairieleut property tax records in the RM of Franklin. Taxes on these lands were assessed and/or collected from either owners or tenants at some point between the years 1898 and 1905. (Map drawn by Weldon Hiebert)

Noteworthy is the contiguity of these lands, excepting the nearby 25-1-3E and the two parcels in 1-5E.[21]

Events of 1898 far beyond the borders of Manitoba are crucial to this narrative as well. A confrontation between the United States and Spain over Cuba's struggle for independence became inevitable on April 20, 1898, after President McKinley was authorized to use military force to aid the Cubans. On April 21, Spain severed diplomatic relations and the United States began a blockade of Cuba. Three days later, on April 24, Spain declared war on the United States, but on the previous day already, the Hutterische Society of Jamesville in Yankton County, South Dakota, reacted by sending a letter to the Department of the Interior in Ottawa, requesting information about lands in the Canadian Northwest.[22] They intended to send three delegates to North Dakota and wished to inspect Canada as well. The letter was first delivered to W.H. Rogers, the Canadian government immigration agent at Watertown, South Dakota, and the response from the Canadian authorities was rapid and favourable. By May 20, three delegates had already arrived in Winnipeg and were sent on to Rosthern, Saskatchewan, with expenses covered by the commissioner of immigration in Winnipeg.[23] The rationale of the Hutterische Society in considering Canada was now obvious, as the commissioner requested that the Department of the Interior locate and provide copies of whatever 1873 Order in Council or Act of Parliament was passed at the time concerning Mennonites, and specifically their military service exemption.[24] On June 20, Elias Walter,[25] who had been one of the three delegates, advised that provided they received the exemption from military service, they were resolved to make a settlement attempt in Canada.[26] On August 4, a second delegation left for the District of Saskatchewan.[27] It was composed

---

21  RM of Franklin Assessment and Collector Roll Microfilms, RM Office, Dominion City, MB.
22  Hutterische Society to the Department of the Interior, April 23, 1898, translation (LAC, Immigration Branch, Record Group [hereafter cited as RG] 76, vol. 173, file 58764, part 1).
23  W.F. McCreary to James A. Smart, May 20, 1898 (LAC: RG 76, vol. 173, file 58764, part 1).
24  Ibid.
25  There were two Dariusleut ministers by the name of Elias Walter: Elias Walter Sr., an uncle to the other, was ordained minister in 1891 and *Ältester* in 1903. He resided in South Dakota until 1918. Elias Walter Jr., the nephew, was ordained minister at Dominion City, MB, where he resided from 1899–1905. Other than by residence, it is sometimes unclear which of the two is being referenced.
26  Elias Walter to [W.F. McCreary, Commissioner of Immigration], June 20, 1898 (LAC: RG 76, vol. 173, file 58764, part 1.)
27  The District of Saskatchewan was a regional administrative district of Canada's North-West Territories. It was formed in 1882, later enlarged, and then ultimately abolished with the creation of the provinces of Saskatchewan and Alberta in 1905.

of John Wurz and Elias Walter of Jamesville, Darius Walter of Menno, John Kleinsasser of Rockport, and Peter Hofer of Elmspring, SD.[28] Before returning home, they advised Canadian officials that the choice between two locations—either Crooked Lake or the country between Rosthern and Hague—would be left to their community.[29] Before moving, they required the Canadian government to issue an agreement in writing, specifically granting them, the "*Hutterische Gemeinde*" "or any member of same," the privileges previously granted to Mennonites.[30]

The subsequent cessation of hostilities between Spain and the United States on August 12, 1898, and the Treaty of Paris signing on December 10, 1898, do not appear to have sufficiently allayed Hutterite concerns about American conscription. However, despite their earlier enthusiasm for the District of Saskatchewan, when immigration did occur the following year it was to the RM of Franklin in Manitoba.[31] Nor was it the immediate relocation of the entire community desired and anticipated by the Canadian authorities.

On May 17, 1899, ten Dariusleut settler families totalling fifty-two persons arrived at Dominion City with six railway cars of freight, including ten horses and thirty-seven milk cows. They had already purchased some $20,000 worth of land east and south of Dominion City which included Roseau River access.[32] Remarkably, their newly acquired lands were contiguous to those of the previous year's Prairieleut settlers. This could not have been coincidental, and the choice of the RM of Franklin by the Dariusleut is likely attributable to ongoing contacts with the already established Prairieleut in Manitoba. These Hutterische Society community lands, all in Township 2, Range 3 East, consisted of Section 3, N ½ 4, E ½ 8, W ½ 9; Section 10, S ½ and NE 15, NW 22. The Roseau River meandered through NW 22, and this is where the community buildings were constructed, which in 1900 included a steam-powered mill.[33] The settlers subsequently added the adjacent properties NE 5, E ½ 9, S ½ 22, and may also have had an interest in S ½ 27.

---

28  In my assessment, based on the individuals' location, the first three were Dariusleut while the latter two were from the Lehrerleut branch.

29  Hutterische Society Delegates Report, undated translation (LAC: RG 76, vol. 173, file 58764, part 1).

30  Quotation marks as in original. Charles Arthur Jones, German interpreter/officer to Commissioner of Immigration in Winnipeg, undated (LAC: RG 76, vol. 173, file 58764, part 1).

31  For further information on the Dariusleut at Dominion City, see Jerald Hiebert, "The Hutterite Story of a Pure Church: A Study of the Dariusleut Alberta Hutterites, 1918–2000" (MA thesis, Regent College, 2001), 47–52.

32  W.F. McCreary to James A. Smart, June 28, 1899, (LAC: RG 76, vol. 173, file 58764, part 1); *Dominion City Weekly Echo*, May 18, 1899; *Der Nordwesten*, May 25, 1899.

33  *Dominion City Weekly Echo*, December 13, 1900 and July 25, 1901.

The municipal tax rolls show the Prairieleut also expanding in subsequent years:

- In T2R4E: Andrew Wallman (N ½ 9)
- In T1R3E: Jacob Waldner (NW 28 and SW 33), Jacob Walter (NE 35)
- In T2R3E: Paul Wallman (NW 15), Andrew Hofer (SW 2), and David Waldner (SW 4 and SE 5); an unidentified Wallman as tenant on SW 16-2-3; and Reverend David Waldner on SE 16.[34] Reverend Waldner together with his married son, John, had arrived about 1902 from the West Reserve.

The precise number and name of all Prairieleut families living in the RM of Franklin is unknown and their exact status regarding land ownership has not been researched.

The contiguous settlements of both the communal Dariusleut of the Hutterische Society and the non-communal—but obviously community-minded—Prairieleut were, however, of brief duration. The original ten Dariusleut families had been joined in 1900 by several more families from South Dakota, but several also left thereafter.[35] By May 1905, the Hutterische Society's future in Manitoba had been decided: they would sell and return to South Dakota.[36] Other than delayed seeding due to poor drainage in springtime, they were not dissatisfied with conditions here, but rather, disappointed that the anticipated mass movement by the brethren to join them did not materialize.[37] By December they were gone, having disposed of their entire real property to the Deutsch-Kanadische Landgesellschaft.[38] Most of the Prairieleut appear to have similarly moved on, many of them to Saskatchewan, with some names disappearing from the tax rolls as early as 1904.[39]

---

34   RM of Franklin Assessment and Collector Roll.
35   *Dominion City Weekly Echo*, May 3, 1900; *Dominion City Church Book 1898*, courtesy of Tony Waldner. The RM of Franklin 1902 Property Assessment records 19 married males, 28 unmarried males, 19 married females, and 24 unmarried females living on NW 22-2-3 East.
36   Commissioner of Immigration, Winnipeg, to W.D. Scott, Superintendent of Immigration, Ottawa, May 15, 1905 (LAC, RG 76, vol. 173, file 58764, part 1).
37   Ibid.; W.J. White to W. Scott, June 14, 1905; *Winnipeg Free Press*, October 28, 1905, 5; untitled handwritten description courtesy of Tony Waldner: "*Es wollten sich aber die Brueder zu dieses neuen ansiedlung nicht schicken, besonders weil es so weit von der Gemeinde war und trachteten deshalb immerzu wie sie moechten zurueck kommen* [The brothers, however, couldn't resign themselves to this new settlement, especially because it was so far away from the community and therefore constantly tried to find a reason to return]."
38   *Der Nordwesten*, October 26, 1905; *The Winnipeg Tribune*, November 3, 1905, 1; *Dominion City Weekly Echo*, November 2, 1905.
39   Prairieleut from South Dakota had already settled between Saskatoon and Langham,

Whether he brokered a larger deal or merely sold several of his own parcels to the incoming Hutterites, the role of Emerson real estate agent Michael Scott in this early settlement attempt is unclear. He had reportedly sold 8,000 acres locally before August 1 in 1899 alone and sold many thousands more in subsequent years.[40] Whether or not he had a more formal involvement, his familiarity with the Hutterite community[41] stood him and them in good stead twenty years hence during the later immigration to Canada.

Although the Dariusleut settlers had arrived prior to receiving the 1898 requested written guarantees, on June 24, 1899, Elias Walter in South Dakota writing to German Interpreter/Officer Charles Jones reminded W.F. McCreary, the Winnipeg commissioner of immigration, that his promises had still not been acted upon by Parliament and that if they were, then he, Walter, hoped the rest of the brethren would immigrate as well.[42] Subsequently, on August 12, 1899, an Order in Council was issued exempting those members of the Hutterische Society permanently settled in Canada from military service.[43] Apparently not content with this, on September 5, 1899, Christian Waldner of Yankton, South Dakota, and Elias Walter of Dominion City, Manitoba, on behalf of "all the brethren of the Hutterische Community that are still in South Dakota" sent a petition through the commissioner of immigration requesting an Act of Parliament granting military service exemption (already dealt with in PC1676), religious freedom and private schools, freedom from taking oaths or holding office, and freedom to live in community and to own property communally.[44] Deputy Minister of the Interior James A. Smart responded to Commissioner McCreary at Winnipeg that the Order in Council had addressed the first issue, that freedom of religion prevailed

---

many as homesteaders. Subsequent Canadian census records confirm the presence of some families from Manitoba in that same general area while others initially appear to be living near Yorkton or Humboldt.

40   *Winnipeg Free Press*, August 1, 1899, 4.
41   Scott was also an adjacent landowner, acquiring a half interest in SW ¼ 36-1-3 East and was assessed for, or paid taxes on, numerous other parcels as well.
42   Hutterische Society to W.F. McCreary and C.A. Jones, 24 June 1899 (LAC, RG 76, vol. 173, file 58764, part 1).
43   Privy Council (hereafter PC) 1676, "Extract from a Report of the Committee of the Honourable the Privy Council, approved by his Excellency on the 12th [of] August, 1899" (LAC, RG 76, vol. 173, file 58764, part 1).
44   Hutterische Society to the Government of the Dominion of Canada, 5 September 1899, translated (LAC, RG 76, vol. 173, file 58764, part 1). Undated copy of the request in German, "*Eine demuethige Bitte an die Regierung von Canada* [A Humble Request to the Government of Canada]," courtesy of Tony Waldner. The request is on behalf of "*wir, und alle die Brueder des Hutterischen Gemeinwesens, welche noch in Süd Dakota sind* [we, and all the brethren of the Hutterian community which are still in South Dakota]."

throughout the country, that they could have their own schools provided a proper education was provided, and that the other requests were covered by the existing laws of the country.[45] This was forwarded to Elias Walter at Dominion City, who referred to them as the promised privileges.[46] These documents would also hold great significance twenty years later.

## The 1918 Immigration

The mere possibility of conscription during the brief 1898 Spanish American war paled in comparison to the actual experiences of the South Dakota Hutterite community during World War I. By October 1917, a group at Redfield referred to as "Mennonites" was negotiating for about 15,000 acres of land in Western Canada and on their behalf inquiries about admission were made to the Canadian government agent M.J. Johnstone at Watertown.[47] Johnstone followed this up with a visit to the community near Letcher and was informed that nearly four hundred wished to move and would require 15,000 to 18,000 acres of land. Their destination was either Saskatchewan or Alberta, with British Columbia also being a possibility, although they had already been approached regarding sugar beet farming at Raymond, Alberta.[48] In late January 1918, three representatives of the South Dakota Hutterite communities met with Commissioner of Immigration J.B. Walker in Winnipeg to discuss the movement of their communities to Canada. They were David Hofer (Lehrerleut) of Alexandria, Elias Walter (Dariusleut) of Frankfort, and Joseph Kleinsasser (Schmiedeleut) of Milltown. They were accompanied by none other than Michael Scott, who was still a real estate agent but now located in Winnipeg.[49] Again, Saskatchewan and Alberta were mentioned as destinations and military service exemption and other issues were discussed.[50] On January 31, 1918, they met with Manitoba Minister of Agriculture and Immigration and Member of the Legislature for Rhineland Valentine

---

45  James A. Smart to W.F. McCreary, October 27, 1899 (LAC, RG 76, vol. 173, file 58764, part 1).
46  Letter from Elias Walter, *Mennonitische Rundschau*, December 20, 1899. Includes both the James A. Smart letter and PC1676 translated into German.
47  M.J. Johnstone to W.J. White, Inspector of United States Agencies, October 15, 1917 (LAC, RG 76, vol. 173, file 58764, part 1). It should be noted that the Canadian government, through its American-based land agents, was extensively advertising in local American newspapers the availability of free 160-acre homesteads and lands for purchase at low prices in western Canada. This information, as well as Johnstone's name and location, would have been common knowledge.
48  M.J. Johnstone to W.J. White, October 23, 1917 (LAC, RG 76, vol. 173, file 58764, part 1).
49  J.B. Walker to W.D. Scott, January 30, 1918 (LAC, RG 76, vol. 173, file 58764, part 1).
50  Ibid.

Winkler[51] to enlist his support. Winkler immediately wrote to Minister of the Interior Arthur Meighen at Ottawa that "I am of the opinion they are very much the same class of people as our Mennonites in Manitoba, who have made first class settlers here."[52]

On February 4, 1918, the three Hutterites and Michael Scott met with Deputy Minister of the Interior W.W. Cory, in Ottawa.[53] They referred to their earlier residence from 1899–1905 at Dominion City and their desire to now return to Canada and settle in one of the western provinces. They requested that they be exempted from military service of any kind, combatant or non-combatant, and that in this respect they be extended all the privileges granted to the Mennonites already living there, and that they be allowed to follow their own community life.[54] Three days later, Cory responded favourably by telegraph to the representatives and Scott,[55] who were now in Chicago on their way home,[56] and followed this up with a letter to Scott in Winnipeg.[57] In March, Michael Scott visited the communities in South Dakota.[58] Thereafter, another delegation scheduled an extended April trip through western Canada, and at the request of Michael Scott,[59] the acting deputy minister provided documents relating to the exemption of Mennonites from military service.[60]

Later that month, Johnstone, the Canadian government agent at Watertown, visited the community at Letcher again and, now referring to them as the "Hutterische Brethren," reported that fifteen Communities intended to move and that along with their machinery and other assets, they would bring over one million dollars in cash.[61] He noted that one

---

51  The city of Winkler is named after Valentine Winkler.
52  Valentine Winkler to Arthur Meighen, January 31, 1918 (LAC, RG 76, vol. 173, file 58764, part 1).
53  Michael Scott to W.W. Cory, February 5, 1918 (LAC, RG 76, vol. 173, file 58764, part 1).
54  Ibid.
55  Telegram by W.W. Cory to M. Scott, February 7, 1918 (LAC, RG 76, vol. 173, file 58764, part 1).
56  M. Scott to Elias Walter, February 7, 1918, courtesy of Ian Kleinsasser.
57  W.W. Cory to M. Scott, February 7, 1918 (LAC, RG 76, vol. 173, file 58764, part 1 and Part 3).
58  Michael Scott to Joseph Kleinsasser, April 3, 1918, courtesy of Ian Kleinsasser.
59  After this initial involvement, there is as yet no evidence that Michael Scott was involved in the Manitoba land purchases by the Schmiedeleut. However, he was involved in Alberta as per *The Edmonton Bulletin* of March 19, 1919, 11, which cites Paul Wipf of Raymond, AB: "Mr. Wipf said all their land deals were arranged by Michael Scott of Winnipeg."
60  Michael Smith to Deputy Minister of the Interior, telegram, April 2, 1918 (LAC, RG 76, vol. 173, file 58764, part 1); Acting Deputy Minister to M. Scott, April 3, 1918 (LAC, RG 76, vol. 173, file 58764, part 1); Michael Scott to W.W. Cory, April 9, 1918 (LAC, RG 76, vol. 173, file 58764, part 2).
61  Johnstone to White, May 2, 1918 and May 8, 1918 (LAC, RG 76, vol. 173, file 58764, part 2).

community had already sold their land for $140,000 and intended to move within weeks to Saskatchewan or Alberta, while another group had just left for Canada to purchase land.[62] By now the Hutterites appeared satisfied as to their exemption status in Canada, but still questioned whether their young men might not still be subject to the United States draft law, to which Superintendent of Immigration W.D. Scott responded that this latter point was unclear, but he reassured them that they were not subject to military service in Canada under the Canadian Military Service Act.[63]

The number and composition of the various land-seeking delegations and their purchases, as well as the efforts to satisfactorily establish the requested military service exemptions, belongs to a more comprehensive history of Hutterite immigration to Canada. For this essay, suffice it to say that the Dariusleut and Lehrerleut both opted for Alberta. The Schmiedeleut, who had six established communities in South Dakota, selected ministers Michael Waldner of Bon Homme and Paul Gross of Rosedale, in addition to Paul Wollman, the steward from Huron, to travel to Canada as well.[64]

On April 19, 1918, Waldner, Gross, and possibly Wollman left for Edmonton via Winnipeg, taking with them five draft-age young men for whom they intended to find employment.[65] During May they travelled within Alberta, examining the many properties offered to them.[66] They were joined by another nine Hutterites who had travelled west through Winnipeg on May 15,[67] and by May 18, there were eleven South Dakota representatives in Alberta.[68] Their final visit was to the Peace River District and from there, Waldner, Gross, and Paul Wollman, together with Minnesota real estate broker Alvin Solberg, left for the Kindersley area and Saskatoon in Saskatchewan.[69] On May 31 Michael Waldner and possibly the other two arrived back in South Dakota.[70]

---

62  Ibid.
63  W. Scott to Johnstone, May 18, 1918 (LAC, RG 76, vol. 173, file 58764, part 2).
64  Ian Kleinsasser, email to author, March 30, 2016.
65  Michael Waldner, "*In kurzen, der erste Bericht von Michael Waldner* [In Brief, the First Report from Michael Waldner]." The "Michael Waldner Report" is a six-page transcript courtesy of Ian Kleinsasser. Although the young men accompanied Waldner and Gross to Alberta, subsequent documents indicate that they were eventually left in Saskatoon. Wollman is not mentioned in the provided transcript.
66  Ibid.
67  M. Scott to Joseph Kleinsasser, May 15, 1918, courtesy of Ian Kleinsasser.
68  This number likely includes members of all three *Leut*.
69  M. Scott to Joseph Kleinsasser, May 23, 1918. The "Michael Waldner Report" records only waiting for the train to Saskatoon where they will attend to the young men ["*nach die jungen Brüder sehen*"].
70  "Michael Waldner Report." Gross and Wollman may also have returned at this time, but are not specifically named.

Prior to their July 1905 South Dakota incorporation as the Hutterische Bruder-Gemeinde, the Schmiedeleut had elected trustees from each of the communities. Recorded as serving in those capacities for 1918 were: Bon Homme (Michael Waldner and Joseph Waldner); Milltown (Joseph Kleinsasser, Michael Maendel, and David Hofer); Huron (Joseph Waldner and Michael Waldner); Rosedale (Paul Gross, Zacharias Hofer, and Jacob Hofer); Maxwell (Samuel Hofer and Joseph Wipf); and James Valley (David Hofer).[71] Of these, Paul Gross was president, Michael Waldner was vice president, and Joseph Kleinsasser was secretary.[72]

Now, at a meeting on June 5, 1918, it was decided that one brother from each of the communities would travel to Canada to purchase land.[73] These brethren left on June 8, travelling first through Winnipeg and then on to meet the draft-age young men whom they had left at Saskatoon.[74] Accompanied again by broker Alvin Solberg, and now also by A.H. Davis, the Canadian Northern Railway general agent at St. Paul, Minnesota, they first inspected lands in Saskatchewan but, finding nothing suitable, returned to Winnipeg.[75] Back in Manitoba, the six were positively impressed by three properties (6,000, 3,040, and 9,600 acres) which were gumbo soil but still suitable for growing wheat, because the clods left after ploughing would disintegrate when dry. By June 26, they were inclined to purchase one of the properties and secure an option on the others. Solberg suggested offsetting the Manitoba purchase with one of the Dakota community properties.[76]

The establishment of a new communal home in Manitoba by the Schmiedeleut would require the acquisition of sufficient contiguous lands to support their population, and these had now been identified in the western portion of the RM of Cartier and the eastern portion of the RM

---

71 "*Verhandlung gehalten in Bon Homme Co.* [Proceedings held at Bon Homme Co.]," 1918, courtesy of Ian Kleinsasser.
72 Ibid.
73 "Michael Waldner Report." The six brothers were not named in the report, and Huron actually had two while Maxwell had none. This may have occurred since minister Joseph Wipf of Maxwell had recently died.
74 Minister Joseph Waldner to Bon Homme Community, June 11, 1918, transcript courtesy of Ian Kleinsasser. Although documents only mention the young men having been left at Saskatoon, it is possible that they stayed with the Prairieleut located between Saskatoon and Langham.
75 Ibid. The Davis referred to is identified in a later item in the *Winnipeg Free Press*, July 22, 1918, 5.
76 Joseph Waldner to Bon Homme Community, June 26, 1918, transcript courtesy of Ian Kleinsasser. Waldner noted that because the clods left after ploughing disintegrated when dry, the gumbo soil in Manitoba was unlike that in Buffalo County, SD: "*Der Grund ist Gumbo auf alle drei Plätze* [The soil is gumbo at all three locations]." He also wrote that he intended to bring Solberg to South Dakota to view their property.

The farmyard purchased by the Hutterites from Joseph Hackney in 1918. Photo by L.B. Foote, 1916. [Source: Benard Farm 1916, L.B. Foote fonds, P7392/1, Foote.9, Archives of Manitoba.]

Clockwise from top left: Aimé Bénard, Alvin Solberg, Fred D. McCartney, and Joseph M. Hackney.

of Portage la Prairie.[77] Although the initial Hutterite purchase occurred in 1918, it was the preceding transactions that enabled their acquisition of significantly large acreages. Speculators and intermediaries initially involved were two Americans and a Canadian: Joseph Malcolm Hackney[78]

---

77  Sufficient contiguous lands does not indicate that it was one parcel, but rather that there were parcels of contiguous lands in close proximity sufficient for several communities.

78  Joseph Hackney was the antithesis of a Hutterite communalist. He was born in Watonwan County, MN, to a Scottish father and a Canadian mother who had emigrated from Edwardsburg, ON, to Minnesota in the early 1860s. The Hackney family was involved in farming, agricultural implement manufacturing, and as investors, land speculators, and financiers. In 1900, Joseph Hackney and his brother Leslie, together with others, incorporated the Law Manufacturing Company which specialized in agricultural implement manufacturing. In 1909 it was renamed the Hackney Manufacturing Company, with Joseph as secretary-treasurer of the corporation. In 1911 it began production of the Hackney Auto-Plow which, although it had three underslung 14" shares, was bidirectional and functioned as a regular tractor of that era. The only one still running is a 1912 model located at the Dale and Martha Hawk Museum near Wolford, ND.

Hackney studied at Hamline University at St. Paul and the Faculty of Law at the University of Minnesota, eventually being elected to the Minnesota State Senate as a Republican, where he served from 1907 to 1915. He had been a shareholder in and secretary of the Hackney-Boynton Land Company, which in 1901 purchased all of the Northern Pacific Railway Company lands west of the Missouri River in North

from St. Paul, Alvin Solberg[79] from Minneapolis, and Manitoban Aimé Bénard.[80]

As early as 1914, a business, implied as being the Hackney Investment Company, which was located in the Hackney Building in St. Paul, was

---

Dakota, and then offered for sale these holdings, which exceeded one million acres. In 1904, he and his brothers, Leslie and William, incorporated the Hackney Land Company. He personally owned a model dairy farm, Arden Farms Inc., and also did business as the Hackney Investment Company. (The RM of Portage La Prairie 1917 Assessment Roll records this name; Hackney also used it in advertising his mortgage backed bonds in the United States.)

79   Little is known about Alvin Solberg. He was born in Fillmore County, MN, to Norwegian immigrant parents. He lived in Canada from 1910 to 1913, first giving his address as Calgary, then Edmonton, and was involved in the real estate business (Minnesota marriage license from March 18, 1913, and a U.S. passport application from September 3, 1920). By 1917, Solberg was a real estate broker with an office in the Plymouth Building in Minneapolis. Through his travels in Manitoba and Saskatchewan, Solberg likely also became acquainted with Mennonites, and after the events here described he became involved with their emigration to Latin America. From October through December 1920 he accompanied their Hague, SK, land-seeking delegation to Paraguay (U.S. passport application from September 3, 1920, and passenger manifest of the SS Martha Washington arriving New York, December 22, 1920, from Buenos Aires). In 1921 he accompanied a different delegation on a trip to Mexico where, on August 11, he rode on horseback over the Hacienda Bustillos lands, which were purchased the following month by the Old Colony Mennonites from Manitoba (see delegate Bernhard Toews' memoir, typewritten 1982 translation by W.J. Kehler). A Herbert, SK real estate broker, John F.D. Wiebe, also accompanied them, and an August 6 agreement existed between Wiebe and Solberg that the latter would receive a commission of twenty cents an acre for Mexican land sold to Mennonites with his assistance. Claiming that 300,000 acres were subsequently sold and the commission never paid, Solberg sued Wiebe for $60,000 in August 1922 and was awarded a default judgment (Mennonite Heritage Centre Archives, Winnipeg, vol. 4395 6, State of Minnesota Complaint No. 201484; *El Paso Herald*, August 30, 1922, 2; *Minneapolis Morning Tribune*, August 4, 1922). Prior to this suit but after returning from his 1921 Mexico trip with the delegates, while in Winnipeg, Solberg wrote to Morden lawyer John Black enquiring about a six-month option on the approximately 100,000 acres which Black had advertised for sale in Manitoba (Mennonite Heritage Centre Archives, A. Solberg to John Black, October 22, 1921). These were the lands which would be vacated by the Old Colony Mennonites emigrating to Mexico. The prospective buyers were not identified.

80   Aimé Bénard was born at Henryville, QC, where he also received his normal school education. After moving to Manitoba in 1893, he engaged in farming in the RM of Cartier, amassing thousands of acres of farmland and a large herd of cattle. At various times he also gave his occupation as hotel keeper and as a financial agent. He was politically active and served as a Conservative Member of the Manitoba Legislature from 1907–1917. Around 1915 or 1916 he was chosen and served briefly as interim party leader. In 1917 he was appointed to the Canadian Senate by Prime Minister Robert Borden, where he served until his death in 1938. Prior to his 1917 sale, Bénard acquired approximately 7,000 acres of land but also continued with further dealings thereafter (see *Winnipeg Free Press Trade Expansion Supplement*, March 16, 1918, 7; *Winnipeg Tribune*, December 26, 1922; *Winnipeg Evening Tribune*, January 10, 1938, 1–5).

advertising to buy good farms in Western Canada, and by 1915, Minneapolis broker Alvin Solberg was attempting to exchange cultivated South Dakota lands for unimproved lands in western Canada.[81] The following year, Solberg negotiated the purchase of Aimé Bénard's farm in the RM of Cartier by Joseph M. Hackney from St. Paul.[82] On November 27, 1916, Hackney and Solberg were in Winnipeg together, presumably looking over these properties.[83] By December 13, Hackney, now accompanied by Carlos M. Boynton of St. Paul, his former partner in the Hackney-Boynton Land Company, was back in Winnipeg.[84] There, on the following day, he signed a $50,000 mortgage in favour of Marie Bénard, wife of Aimé Bénard, on the south half and the north-west quarter of 11-11-4W, and the west half of Section 11, Township 10, Range 3. On February 10, 1917, Aimé Bénard deeded these lands to Joseph Hackney, but it was only on November 3, 1917, that patent from the Crown for W½-11-10-3 was finally issued in the name of Aimé Bénard. Already on October 14, 1917, Hackney had signed an application to bring this property under the operation of the Real Property Act, but that month was subsequently changed to November. These transactions might not have seemed unusual at the time, but Hackney mortgaged property that he did not yet own, and Bénard deeded property that he did not yet have patent for. This was the beginning. Many signatures on these transactions were witnessed by Winnipeg lawyer Alexander Adams, who had begun his practice of law with the firm of Tupper, McTavish and Tupper in 1916, and who continued to act on behalf of Hackney in subsequent transactions.[85]

Although he appeared to have taken possession in December 1916, during the month of February 1917, Joseph Hackney finalized the purchase of Aimé Bénard's large farm west of Winnipeg, which included some properties owned by Aimé's wife, Marie. Hackney paid the Bénards $111,602 for the 7,835 more-or-less acres. (It was also variously reported that he paid $376,000 for the farm, which included all the equipment and a couple of hundred head of cattle, or $250,000 for the farm and equipment.)[86] Of course, his actual cash requirement was reduced by the $50,000 he owed on the mortgage to Marie. In addition, that year Hackney also purchased 1,675 acres at a cost of $28,422 from other individuals,

---

81 *Winnipeg Tribune*, March 30, 1914, 12; *Winnipeg Free Press*, May 10, 1915, 15. The Hackney Investment Company is recorded at this address in the 1917 RM of Portage la Prairie Tax Lists.
82 *Winnipeg Free Press*, August 8, 1919, 5. Aimé Bénard stated that Alvin Solberg arranged Hackney's 1916 purchase from him.
83 *Winnipeg Free Press*, Nov 27, 1916, 4.
84 *Winnipeg Free Press*, Dec 13, 1916, 4.
85 See Appendix 3 for more on Adams.
86 *Winnipeg Free Press*, Feb 13, 1917, 8; July 13, 1918, 5.

for a total of 9,510 acres more or less. In actual fact, his documented cost for the total acreage was $140,024, or an average $14.72 per acre, including whatever buildings were located thereon.

In the United States, Hackney had been a shareholder in the Hackney-Boynton Land Company and, after 1904, its apparent successor, the Hackney Land Company; he also appeared to do business as the Hackney Investment Company.[87] However, his Canadian real estate purchases were registered in his own name, where he initially gave his occupation as "Capitalist" and later as "Farmer."[88] As a well-connected major investor, he had access to more innovative sources of funds should that be to his benefit. On September 1, 1917, he issued a $230,000 "First Mortgage 6% Gold Bond" through the Associated Mortgage Investors of Rochester, New York, and Calgary, Alberta.[89] The bond certificate maturity dates were $5,000 annually on January 1, 1919 through 1926 inclusive, and the remaining $190,000 on January 1, 1927.[90] Six percent annual interest was due by semi-annual interest coupons payable each January and July. The issue was denominated in United States currency. As security, Joseph Hackney mortgaged 11,268 acres of his own land (including the former Bénard farm, plus 958 acres at Sanford, Manitoba, and 800 acres in Saskatchewan) to the National Trust Company Limited as trustees for the bond issue under concurrent mortgages 30768, 90316, 386788, and AK2319.[91]

---

87  The RM of Portage la Prairie recorded the name Hackney Investment Company in its property assessment rolls.
88  "Capitalist" appears on the Saskatchewan certificates of title and "Farmer" in Manitoba.
89  This thirty-four-page document, inclusive of the mortgage, is sufficiently abstruse that the full extent of the Associated Mortgage Investors' involvement remains unclear. Its name appears only three times within the text but significantly is referred to as "the Company." The mortgagee, National Trust, was obligated to call a meeting of bondholders if so requested by Associated Mortgage Investors, which also had the responsibility to appoint a different mortgagee should National Trust "desire to be relieved." Associated Mortgage Investors was incorporated in New York State and in Canada licensed only in Alberta; that is likely the reason that the National Trust Company Limited became the trustee in Manitoba and Saskatchewan. Whether individual bonds were actually sold to investors by Associated Mortgage Investors cannot now be determined. Such bonds could optionally be registered with the mortgagee and, failing production of such a registration book, that information is unavailable. In a December 5, 1917 letter to the district registrar of the Portage Land Titles Office in reference to some of Hackney's lands, Alexander Adams does not provide any further clarity when he writes "the National Trust Co. Ltd., the trustees for the bond issue which was recently put upon this property."
90  This is the aggregate payable annually on the total bond issue which was to be sold as multiple $1,000, $500, or $100 individual bonds.
91  Portage Land Titles Office RPA and Old System mortgage, Winnipeg Land Titles Office RPA mortgage, and Moose Jaw, Saskatchewan, Land Registration District mortgage, hereafter referred to as the National Trust mortgage.

This nominal $1 mortgage was registered in Winnipeg, September 26, 1917, at 12:35 p.m. At 12:37 p.m. a second mortgage (30769) of $5,000 obtained by Hackney from Kingman Robins, the secretary-treasurer of Associated Mortgage Investors, was registered as well, but it affected only 320 acres (W ½ 5-11-3).

Added to Hackney's already documented $140,024 in land purchases were a known $24,000 for his farm at Sanford and an apparent $18,610 for the Saskatchewan property, for a total of $182,634.[92] However, through the bond issue he was able to borrow $230,000, which was significantly more than his cost. This was possible because the total 11,268 acres was appraised by E.B. Mount, the Calgary supervisor of the Associated Mortgage Investors, at $545,825 in his report of July 30, 1917.[93] How February 1917 selling prices could increase by 240 percent to equal the July valuations[94] is open to interpretation, but it suggests a less than arms-length relationship between Joseph Hackney and Kingman Robins, who had apparently loaned him the $5,000 personally.[95] (An obvious example of this over-appraisal would be the 276 acres south of the railway on W ½ 9-11-3, which Hackney swore in March 1917 had a value of $3,840, and which the Associated Mortgage Investors appraised at $16,599 in July!) Obviously, Hackney needed no personal cash inputs for his real estate acquisitions and an existing assumable mortgage would be a desirable resale feature.

As already mentioned, the Schmiedeleut representatives were favourably impressed by three different properties west of Winnipeg. One of these included the former Bénard farm, now owned by Joseph Hackney. Another was the less developed farm of Dakotan Fred Delos McCartney, president of the First National Bank at Oakes, North Dakota, and secretary-treasurer and partner in the Marshall McCartney Company. Although the current landowners were not named, the Hutterites reported

---

92  Hackney's 1915 Saskatchewan acquisitions included $7,360 paid for 320 acres in 1-26-5 and a value given as $11,250 for the 480 acres in 28-26-5 which were part of a land swap.
93  There are some deficiencies in that White's appraisal of the individual land parcels is incomplete, incorrectly multiplied, and does not appear to precisely equal his total appraised value.
94  Deducting the Saskatchewan lands and Sanford farm appraisal amounts from the total results in a $476,612 appraisal for the remaining Manitoba lands purchased by Hackney.
95  Kingman Nott Robins was also vice-president of the Farm Mortgage Bankers Association of America and author of *The Farm Mortgage Handbook* (Garden City: Doubleday, Page & Company, 1916). This $5,000 mortgage is perplexing in that Hackney would have had no need to privately borrow such a minor sum. Another interpretation could be that no such loan ever existed and that this was merely a kickback to be paid to Robins, not by Hackney, but by any subsequent purchaser of the property.

that Hackney's 9,600-acre property, of which 4,000 acres was under cultivation, had excellent facilities for dairying, as well as barns for horses and other animals, and was well equipped with machinery. The inclusive price for the farm with standing crop and equipment, but excluding the cattle, would be $52 per acre. McCartney's property was not as well developed and would accordingly be less expensive. The now unidentifiable third parcel, available at $45 per acre, consisted of 6,000 acres, of which 3,000 acres were under cultivation.[96] The Hutterite representatives were aware that Hackney had been a senator, and they intended to pay him a visit on their way home.[97]

## The Land Purchases[98]

### Purchase 1[99]

Precisely how the deal with Hackney was struck is unknown. The Hutterites' apparent agent, Alvin Solberg, who had negotiated Hackney's large purchase from Aimé Bénard in 1916 and who had accompanied the Hutterite land-seeking delegations of both May and June 1918, may indeed have done so with the objective of reselling Hackney's property to them.[100] From Winnipeg, Solberg was likely in close communication with Hackney before the visit from the representatives, if such a visit to St. Paul did indeed take place. What is known is that on June 29, 1918, the Hutterites, via a memorandum of agreement,[101] agreed to purchase certain

---

96 These 6,000 acres were liked best by the representatives and it is possible that the majority or portions thereof were also among those purchased from or through the individuals hereafter identified.

97 Joseph Waldner to Bon Homme Community, June 26, 1918, transcript courtesy of Ian Kleinsasser.

98 Purchases here refer to completed purchases and/or agreements to purchase. To distinguish between them, these "holding committee" purchases and agreements to purchase are numbered 1 through 40, and the later trustee acquisitions/purchases are lettered A through M.

99 Transfer 32066, summarized as follows: In Township 10-3: W ½ 11, NW 12, S ½ SW 13, N ½ NW 16, SW and N ½ NE 21, SE 28, NE and E ½ NW 32, NW and W ½ NE 33. In Township 10-4: NE and N ½ SE 13, SE and S ½ NE 24. In Township 11-3: W ½ 4, Section 5, NE 7, Section 8, W ½ 9 South of RR, NW and W ½ NE 16, W ½ and N ½ NE 17, Section 18 except S ½ SW, Section 19, Section 20 except E ½ NE, E ½ and SW 30. In Township 11-4: Section 1, S ½ and NW 11, S ½ and NW 12, W ½ and NE and N ½ SE 13. In Township 12-3: W ½ 1. See Appendix 6: Transfer of Land, Joseph M. Hackney to David Hofer Sr., et al.

100 In his June 26 letter, Joseph Waldner referred to Solberg as, "*unser Agent, der Solberg* [our agent, Solberg]." In an April 26, 1920 Department of Immigration memorandum, after meeting with Alexander Adams and Jacob Hofer of Rosedale, F.C. Blair wrote that Solberg negotiated the sale of all lands purchased by "the congregation" (LAC, RG 76, vol. 174, file 58764, part 6).

101 Declaration of Trust, February 21, 1919. Copy courtesy of Tony Waldner.

of Hackney's lands and made an immediate $15,000 payment to him.[102] After the representatives returned home to South Dakota, meetings were held in early July. At that time, it was decided that minister Joseph Waldner of Huron Community would move to Manitoba with the young men already registered for the draft but not yet called up for service.[103] It was also decided to purchase the herd of heifers on the Hackney farm and that the young men already in Saskatchewan should also relocate there to look after the property.[104]

On July 11, the sale was reported in the *Oakville Standard* and two days later in the *Winnipeg Free Press*. The actual transfer of land was signed on August 2, 1918, at Winnipeg by Joseph Hackney and registered on August 24. For half a million dollars the Brethren purchased 9,240 acres more or less, plus certain personal property. Alexander Adams again witnessed certain signatures.

Alvin Solberg's suggestion to offset the Manitoba purchase with one of the South Dakota properties was also acted upon. An August 7 Hutterische Bruder-Gemeinde resolution[105] authorized the sale of Huron[106] to Joseph Hackney for the sum of $146,200.[107] On August 14 the Hutterites made a further payment of $35,000 to Hackney,[108] but their purchase remained subject to the balances still owing by Hackney on the mortgages to National Trust, to Marie Bénard, and to Kingman Robins. Although the bond obligation secured by the National Trust mortgage was for $230,000, the deal with Hackney appears to have been that the purchasers would assume $197,453 thereof.[109] This would have been calculated by deter-

102 *Milltown Colony, SD, Income & Expense Ledger 1911*, 267. Copy courtesy of Tony Waldner.
103 "*Prediger Versammlung wegen ausziehen nach Kanada, Juli 3, 1918* [Ministers' meeting regarding emigration to Canada, July 3, 1918]" and "*Kirchen Versammlung wegen nach Kanada ziehen* [Church meeting regarding moving to Canada]," July 6, 1918. Transcripts courtesy of Ian Kleinsasser.
104 Ibid.
105 *Beadle County Register of Deeds*, book 202, 472.
106 The original Huron site in South Dakota is now the location of Riverside Community.
107 The exact dates are unknown but Hackney, together with Solberg, visited the South Dakota communities and, in addition to purchasing Huron, also considered purchasing James Valley. These details are revealed in the transcript of David Hofer's testimony at an October 27–28, 1919 South Dakota court case (Circuit Court of the State of South Dakota, Ninth Judicial Circuit, Beadle County, E.P. Flowers and H.G. Spratt, Plaintiffs, v. Frederick Waldner, Maria Waldner, R.O. Richards, Trustee and Attorney in Fact for Frederick Waldner and Maria Waldner; Hutterische Bruder-Gemeinde, a corporation, et al., Defendants, October 27–28, 1919, 26. Courtesy of Ian Kleinsasser).
108 *Milltown Colony, SD, Income & Expense Ledger 1911*, 267.
109 Mortgage balance courtesy of John Hofer. The existence of an agreement stipulat-

mining what percentage the appraised value of the lands they purchased represented of the total appraisal and then multiplying that by the mortgage principal. Hackney's earlier $50,000 mortgage (89411) from Marie Bénard, which had been refinanced for $53,281 (concurrent mortgages 30799 and 90324) was now reported to have a balance of $35,520.[110] The $5,000 mortgage from Kingman Robins was still unpaid. Accordingly, to complete the $500,000 property purchase the Hutterites, after deducting the Huron sale and the previous two payments, would presumably have required another $65,827 in cash,[111] and then remained indebted to National Trust and Marie Bénard for the balances owing on those mortgages, after the Kingman Robins mortgage was subsequently repaid and discharged by October 24.

Of the $500,000 purchase price, $422,901 was declared by the Hutterite purchasers as being the total value of the properties. They may have deemed the additional $77,099 to be the allowance for farm machinery, cattle, and the standing crop. Hackney's land costs for the 9,510 acres had been only $140,024, but his outlay for equipment and current year crop inputs is unknown. At the time of sale, he withheld 270 acres and still demanded $500,000.[112] His gain on equipment, crop, and also the livestock is indeterminable, but his astounding 210% profit on the land alone in just one and a half years—at the expense of a community seeking only to live in peace—was unconscionable.[113]

The six men in whose names this and all other land purchases made prior to March 1921 were registered constituted a "holding committee" for the real estate of the communities. This appears to be how lawyer Alexander Adams later described them[114] in a meeting with James Calder, the

---

ing the amount to be paid is referred to in a February 21, 1927 letter from lawyer C.J. Macleod to Joseph Hackney. Such an agreement should have included not only the purchase price, but also details of encumbering assumed mortgage amounts to be deducted. Letter courtesy of Ian Kleinsasser.

110 Mortgage balance is noted on a homemade map which included information about land purchases. This map is on display at James Valley Community, Elie, MB. Courtesy of John Hofer.

111 This sum could also have been reduced by any currency exchange on the Huron sale.

112 Hackney's profit was so astounding that someone with access to the transfer document at the time, for the purpose of comparison, noted on the statement of value their calculation of what the valuations would have been when Hackney purchased them.

113 Deducting Hackney's $3,700 cost of the properties not sold to the Hutterites from the $140,024 reduces his cost to $136,324.

114 Superintendent of Immigration to W.W. Cory, March 26, 1919, citing the minister's meeting that morning with Alexander Adams (LAC, RG 76, vol. 173, file 58764, part 3). They functioned as "the Trustees for the Hutterian Brethren of the Province of Manitoba and who are the owners as Trustees, of the real and personal property of the said Hutterian Brethren of the Province of Manitoba" according to a draft

Minister of Immigration and Colonization, but their actual role had yet to be defined. Their names, as recorded on the documents, were David Hofer the Elder, Paul Wallman, Zacharias Hofer, David Hofer the Younger, Joseph Michel Waldner, and Joseph Waldner. Collectively, on behalf of all Schmiedeleut, they purchased and took title to all lands, entered into agreements to purchase, registered caveats, and assumed liabilities through the purchase of mortgaged properties, or themselves mortgaged them to others. In a true expression of community, the Schmiedeleut enabled the move for all by intentionally choosing to immigrate to Canada as one.

The signatures of two of the named "holding committee" members differ somewhat from those recorded on the documents: Paul Wallman signed as Paul Wollman and Joseph Michel Waldner signed as Joseph Michael Waldner. The identities of the six individuals who had been entrusted with this responsibility would appear to be as follows:[115]

1. David Hofer Sr., born July 20, 1853, married to Sarah Hofer, was from Milltown Community, South Dakota. He immigrated in 1918 to Milltown Community, Manitoba, and later moved to Blumengart, Manitoba, where he served as Steward.[116]

2. Paul Wollman, born March 1, 1856, married to Katharina Kleinsasser, was from Huron, South Dakota. He immigrated in 1918 to Huron, Manitoba, and later moved to Sharpe/Thorndale, Manitoba.[117]

3. David Hofer Jr., born March 21, 1877, married to Rachel Stahl, was a son of the above David Hofer Sr. He was a minister who immigrated in 1918 from James Valley, South Dakota, to James Valley, Manitoba.[118]

4. Zacharias Hofer, born August 25, 1866, married to Susanna Gross, was a minister from Rosedale, South Dakota. He immigrated in

---

bond (LAC, RG 76, vol. 173, file 58764, part 3). The term "holding committee" will henceforth be used in this paper to differentiate these trustees from the 1921 and later individual community trustees.

115 The process of identifying the delegates was complicated because of the number of individuals with the same or a very similar name within the Hutterite communities. Identification sources included *The Schmiedeleut Family Record*, 2nd ed., compiled by David Gross (High Bluff: Sommerfeld Printshop, 1997); the 1915 South Dakota State Census; 1921 Canadian Census; John Hofer, "The Hutterian Brethren," in *Treasures of Time: The Rural Municipality of Cartier, 1914–1984* (Elie: RM of Cartier, 1985); Solomon Stahl, *The History of Bon Homme Colony, Manitoba* (Fordville: Forest River Colony, 2001); *Das Klein Geschichtsbuch*; and significant information compiled by and courtesy of Ian Kleinsasser and Tony Waldner.

116 *Schmiedeleut Family Record*, 200.08.

117 Ibid., 200.37.

118 Ibid., 112-2.

1918 to Rosedale, Manitoba, and later moved to Elm River, Manitoba.[119]

5. Joseph Michael Waldner, born September 12, 1883, married to Katharina Waldner, was a minister from Bon Homme, South Dakota. He immigrated in 1918 to Bon Homme, Manitoba, and his widow later moved to Plainview, Manitoba.[120]

6. Joseph Waldner, born March 27, 1879, married to Maria Waldner, was a minister from Huron, South Dakota, who immigrated in 1918 to Huron, Manitoba, and later moved to Poplar Point, Manitoba. In 1947, he was elected as Schmiedeleut *Ältester*.[121]

The initial local, public response to the sale was perhaps best articulated by the *Oakville Standard* on July 11, 1918, when it first broke the news of the Hutterite purchase:

> The Aimé Bénard farm, by which it is best known, though owned the last couple of years by Senator [H]ackney, of Minnesota, and managed by the popular Mr. Crooks, has again changed hands, if rumours are correct. The new owners are a colony of Minnenites [sic] from the U.S.A. who will take possession shortly. They number somewhere between fifteen hundred and two thousand souls, including men, women and children, and needless to say, the big farm comprising somewhere around ten thousand acres, will be a hive of industry when they arrive and commence making homes for themselves. We understand the farm will continue to be run as a whole, the Memenites [sic] working on a community or co-operative plan, pooling their expenses and labour and all sharing alike in the profits. They run their own places of business, which means a hamlet will spring up in connection with the place, all of which will be part and parcel of the farm. Their coming, therefore, will make little difference to the rest of the community, as they live to themselves, do their own business, worship in their own way, fight, quarrel and make up again like other people, get born in the old fashioned way, get married and in due time die as usual. It will be a new experience for this part of Manitoba, one that will be watched with a good deal of interest, but if it works anywhere should be a big success here.

---

119 Ibid., 58-2.
120 Ibid., 173-1.
121 Ibid., 178-3.

During July and particularly in August of 1918, a considerable number of Hutterites arrived to harvest the standing crop that had been included with their purchase of the Hackney farm.[122] However, the entry of these German-speaking pacifists—while the country was still at war in Europe—and their acquisition of lands that some considered should be made available for returning soldiers also caused an almost immediate backlash.[123] The *Oakville Standard* of September 5, 1918, opined:

> Objection is developing in more than one quarter to the influx of Mennonites into Canada from the United States, as instanced in the recent purchase and occupation of the Bénard farm by these people. It is said they are here because President Wilson recently asked all residents who wished to remain to take the oath of allegiance and assume the full duties of citizens. The duty of a citizen of the U.S., among other things, is to fight for it, and as the Mennonites are averse to fighting they came to Canada. It is suggested [that] they came here under special arrangement with the Government, and if so it is time such arrangements cease. This colony is said to be wealthy, but even wealth shouldn't entitle a class of people of any kind to secure and set themselves down in one of the garden spots of the west unless they are prepared to defend their property in common with other citizens when the necessity arises. It is evident they do not intend to confine themselves to the Bénard farm, as other farms adjacent are being acquired at fancy prices. These objections will have the result of showing whether they come here with any special privileges, and if that is the case it will be one more act the Union government will have to answer for when the gentle art of criticism once more becomes good form.

Despite this backlash, the Schmiedeleut, through the six brethren of the "holding committee," continued with their purchases and the six South Dakota communities were re-established in Manitoba: Milltown, Huron, Bon Homme, James Valley, Rosedale, and Maxwell. This was followed shortly thereafter by two more: Iberville in 1919, beside Rosedale, and

---

122 *Oakville Standard*, August 29, 1918. Alexander Adams to Percy Reid, March 10, 1919 (LAC, RG 76, vol. 173, file 58764, part 3). Permits were issued to seventy-nine persons. M.J. Johnstone to W.J. White, July 18, 1918 (LAC, RG 76, vol. 173, file 58764, part 2).

123 *Oakville Standard*, September 5, 1918. National newspapers carried significantly more hostile reports.

Barickman in 1920, near Maxwell. It should be noted that some vendors to the communities of these properties were long-time owners, while others had themselves purchased only recently, but still prior to 1918 when the immigration of Hutterites began. Some vendors were farmers and others were non-resident landowners. After the immigration commenced and Hutterite land acquisition began, real estate agents and other opportunists bought with the intention of quick profit on resale.

By now, Joseph Hackney's lawyer, Alexander Adams, appears to have transitioned into acting for the Hutterites and continued to do so in their subsequent purchases.

## Purchases 2, 3, 4, and 5

Without a written agreement for sale, the "holding committee" on August 22, 1918, agreed to purchase Section 36-10-4 from Louis Boyer for $28,800,[124] but it was reported only that they had bought a total of three unidentified quarter sections of land from him at $45 per acre. Although Boyer was being assessed for some of the property taxes, he was not the registered owner of this section. As a tenant, he might have been entitled to payment for the standing crop, but his undertaking to sell to the Hutterites suggests that he was an opportunist.[125] Accordingly, the land purchases 2, 3, 4, and 5 were made directly from the actual landowners, but Boyer will have been paid the $13,200 price difference to equal $28,800, as specified in the verbal agreement.[126]

### Purchase 2[127]

On August 31, from Elie farmer Alexander McKinnon—240 acres for $4,800, subject to the balance still owing by McKinnon on his $3,500 mortgage 22243 from the Scottish Ontario and Manitoba Land Company Limited.

### Purchase 3[128]

On August 31, from John Grant and Alexander McKinnon as executors of the David McKinnon Estate—160 acres for $3,200, subject to the

---

124 Recorded in a Declaration of Trust, February 21, 1919.
125 *Oakville Standard*, September 5, 1918; RM of Portage la Prairie Tax Records.
126 "Balance of purchase price to Boyer," information courtesy of John Hofer.
127 Transfer 32160: "The North West Quarter and the West Half of the North East Quarter both of Section Thirty-six (36) in Township Ten (10) and Range Four (4) West of the Principal Meridian in Manitoba."
128 Transfer 32161: "The South East Quarter of Section Thirty-six (36) in Township Ten (10) and Range Four (4) West of the Principal Meridian in Manitoba."

balance still owing on the John Grant et al. $3,500 mortgage 27860 from the Law Union and Rock Insurance Company.

**Purchase 4**[129]

On August 31, from Portage la Prairie farmer John Grant—160 acres for $5,600, subject to the balance still owing by Grant on his $2,700 mortgage 77895 from the Law Union and Rock Insurance Company.

**Purchase 5**[130]

On September 14, from Winnipeg manager William Skinner—80 acres for $2,000.

## Purchase 6[131]

On September 13, the six members of the "holding committee" entered into a $33,800 purchase agreement with Elie farmer August Larson, for 480 acres plus unspecified personal property.[132] Larson would retain title to his real property until the purchasers had paid for it under the terms of a payment schedule.[133] It is not evident whether any initial cash payment was involved in this transaction, but the final payment of $16,000 was due by November 1923. To protect themselves the committee registered Caveat 15987 against the property. (See Acquisition D below.)

## Purchases 7[134] and 8[135]

On September 13, the "holding committee," via a memorandum of agreement, agreed to purchase 1,920 acres of the Fred McCartney property for $73,000.[136] McCartney signed the necessary transfer and deed at

---

129 Deed 93107: "The South West Quarter of Section Thirty-six (36) in Township Ten (10) and Range Four (4) West of the Principal Meridian in Manitoba."
130 Transfer 32159: "The East Half of the North East Quarter of Section Thirty-six (36) in Township Ten (10) and Range Four (4) West of the Principal Meridian in Manitoba."
131 SE 14-10-3, S ½ NE 14-10-3, SW 14-10-3, S ½ NW 14-10-3.
132 The RM of Cartier taxation records list Larson as a resident farmer with an address at Elie. James Valley in its financial records list him at St. Paul, MN, in 1922.
133 Agreement details courtesy of John Hofer.
134 Transfer 32291: "The North Half of the North East Quarter of Section Fourteen (14); the East Half and the East Half of the North West Quarter of Section Twenty three (23); all of Section Twenty four (24); the South East Quarter and the West Half of Section Twenty five (25) all in Township Ten (10) and Range Three (3) West of the Principal Meridian in Manitoba."
135 Deed 93360: "In the Province of Manitoba being composed of the South Half of Section Twenty-six (26) in Township Ten (10) and Range Three (3) West of the Principal Meridian."
136 Declaration of Trust, February 21, 1919.

Oakes in North Dakota on October 7, 1918. The statement of value on the transfer was signed by David Hofer Jr. in Winnipeg only on November 1. Certain personal property described in a November 1, 1918 bill of sale was also included in the purchase.[137] McCartney extended financing of $41,000 via two concurrent mortgages (93361 and 32292) on the 1,920 acres.

Terms of repayment were $30,000 due December 13, 1918, and the remaining $11,000 due September 13, 1919, with 6% annual interest being charged. Although the signatures of all six purchasers were affixed, the mortgages were signed on October 12, 1918, at Milltown, South Dakota, by David Hofer Sr., Zacharias Hofer, and David Hofer Jr. (as witnessed by Joseph Kleinsasser), and on November 1, 1918, at Winnipeg by Paul Wallman, Joseph Michel Waldner, and Joseph Waldner (as witnessed by Alexander Adams). As noted having signed the statement of valuation, David Hofer Jr. was now also back in Winnipeg on the latter date. Both mortgages were discharged on May 26, 1919.

It was clear that Adams was becoming increasingly involved with the Hutterites in that their mortgage payments to McCartney were specified to be made at the office of the Tupper law firm, where Adams practised. It would appear that a $32,000 cash payment was made by the Hutterites ($73,000 purchase less $41,000 mortgage) but it may initially have been less, since their purchase was subject to a pre-existing $32,000 mortgage obtained from the Economic Trust Company by a previous owner who pre-dated McCartney. In any case, whatever balance remained on this latter mortgage would have been cleared prior to its release three months later. McCartney had paid $47,000 for 2,400 acres of the total 3,040 acres which he acquired in April 1917, but his obligations are unknown for the remaining 640 acres which had been deeded to him for $1. Disregarding those 640 acres, he profited substantially on this sale and still retained ownership of 1,120 acres.[138]

---

137  Ibid.
138  Although the Marshall McCartney Company was not registered in the province, and all Manitoba documentation unambiguously shows Fred McCartney as the registered owner, it was reported by the *Oakes Times* from Oakes, ND, on March 14, 1918, and August 29, 1918, that the property belonged to the Marshall McCartney Company of which Fred was the secretary-treasurer. His brother, Henry Clay McCartney, was vice-president of the company and a co-founder of the Toro Manufacturing Company, as reported in the *Oakes Times* of December 9 and 30, 1920, and the *Wall Street Journal*. https://quotes.wsj.com/TTC/company-people, accessed April 15, 2019.
The Marshall McCartney Company appears to have acquired these properties as part of a larger exchange, namely their irrigated lands in Washington for "4,000 [?] acres of choice lands in the Red and Saskatchewan Valleys near Winnipeg, Canada" (*Oakes Times*, December 30, 1920). Documents filed with the Manitoba Land Titles

## Purchases 9[139] and 10[140]

On August 21, the "holding committee," via a memorandum of agreement, agreed to purchase from St. Eustache area farmer Ferdinand Lafleche a total of 1,610 acres[141] for $80,500, which included some personal property.[142] The purchase was finalized on October 23 when Lafleche signed the two transfers for a total of $79,992. There were no mortgages on the property and the Hutterite purchasers would have paid this sum. Lafleche was the brother-in-law of Aimé Bénard (who had just been appointed to the Canadian Senate), and on November 2, only days after his sale, Lafleche, accompanied by Bénard, purchased $100,000 worth of Victory Bonds.[143]

## Purchases 13, 15, 16, 18, 19, and 22

Via an August 21, 1918 memorandum of agreement, the "holding committee" agreed to purchase certain lands from Aimé Bénard for the sum of $156,500.[144] None of these lands were yet owned by Bénard himself,

---

Office indisputably show McCartney paid $47,000 for 2,400 acres, while the other 640 acres were recorded for only $1. To further cloud the issue as to McCartney's profit, the *Winnipeg Evening Tribune* of March 28, 1917, inexplicably reports that James O. Smith of St. Norbert sold his 3,040 acre farm to the Marshall McCartney Company for $121,600.

139 Transfer 32295: "The East Half of Section Twenty-five (25) and the South Half and North East Quarter both of Section Thirty-six (36) all in Township Eleven (11) and Range Three (3) West of the Principal Meridian in Manitoba."

140 Transfer 399876: "The West Half of the North West Quarter of Section Thirty (30); the West Half of Section Thirty one (31); and the Fractional North East Quarter of said Section Thirty one (31); the South East Quarter of said Section Thirty one (31); all in the Eleventh Township and Second Range West of the Principal Meridian; Also all that portion of Fractional Section Six (6) in the Twelfth Township and Second Range West of the Principal Meridian in said Province contained within the following limits namely: Commencing at the South West corner of said Fractional Section, thence Northerly along the Western limit thereof Ten hundred and fifty feet, thence South Eighty three degrees and Forty minutes East Eight hundred and Seventy feet; thence North Sixty three degrees and ten minutes East Five hundred feet, thence North Seventy five degrees East Five hundred and twenty feet, thence South Seventy three degrees and Thirty five minutes East Eight hundred and seventy five feet, thence South Sixty five degrees and fifty minutes East Thirteen hundred and sixty one feet more or less to the Eastern limit of said Fractional Section, thence Southerly along said Eastern limit Five hundred and sixty eight feet more or less to the Southern limit of said Fractional Section, thence Westerly along said Southern limit Forty two hundred and fifty seven feet more or less to the point of commencement."

141 *Oakville Standard*, September 5, 1918, states 1,610 acres, which clarifies the fractional parcels on the actual transfers.

142 Declaration of Trust, February 21, 1919.

143 *Winnipeg Tribune*, November 2, 1918, 2; *Winnipeg Free Press*, November 4, 1918, 7.

144 Declaration of Trust, February 21, 1919.

although his wife, Marie, was the registered owner of some of the river lots since 1917. Bénard will have noted the windfall his 1917 purchaser, Joseph Hackney, had made on the 1918 resale to the Hutterites, and the senator himself now began a series of real estate flips. Including Marie's property, over the next nine months, he sold 2,227 acres more or less to the "holding committee" for a total of $111,566. Aimé Bénard's profit on these flips amounted to $24,876. However, he never did acquire all of the properties included in the August 21 memorandum of agreement, and those remaining lands were transferred to the "holding committee" directly by their owners, for a total of $34,840. The total cost of all the lands transferred amounted to $146,406, but it is assumed that Bénard received the additional $10,094 from the Hutterites to match the $156,500 specified in their August 21 agreement with him.

### Purchase 13[145]

From Aimé Bénard on November 29, 1918, for $12,025. Bénard had paid only $6,000 for this property, which he acquired on August 13, 1918, from Robert Gillete of Minneapolis.

### Purchase 15[146]

From Aimé Bénard on December 3, 1918, for $14,792. Aimé Bénard had signed this transfer prior to his receiving title from Member of Parliament and Minister of the Interior for Canada Arthur Meighen, from whom he then purchased it for $8,922. These transactions later became so controversial that it may have contributed to Meighen's 1921 electoral defeat.[147]

### Purchase 16[148]

From Aimé's wife, Marie Bénard, on December 27, 1918, for $33,963. Marie Bénard had been the registered owner of these lots since 1917.

---

145 Transfer 400939: "The North West Quarter of Section Sixteen in the Eleventh Township and Second Range West of the Principal Meridian in Manitoba and all that portion of the fractional North East Quarter of said Section Sixteen which lies to the West of a line drawn east of, parallel with, and perpendicularly distant Twenty Chains and Forty five Links from the Western limit of the said North East Quarter."

146 Transfer 33284: "Parcel No. 1: Parish Lots Five (5) and Six (6) in the Parish of Baie St. Paul in Manitoba. Parcel No. 2: The most Easterly Twenty (20) acres of Parish Lot Seven (7) of the Parish of Baie St. Paul in Manitoba, said Twenty (20) acres being a strip of land whose Western limit is parallel to the Eastern limit of said Lot Seven (7)."

147 See Bruce Wiebe, "A Politically Risky Land Sale," *Preservings* 32 (2012), 35–38.

148 Transfer 401585: "The most Westerly Two (2) Chains in width of River Lot One hundred and three (103); all of River Lots One hundred and four (104) One hundred and five (105) and One hundred and six (106) and all those portions of River

## Purchase 18[149]

From Aimé Bénard on April 14, 1919, for $11,550. Bénard had paid the Beatty Estate $6,930 for this parcel on March 19, 1919.

## Purchase 19[150]

From Aimé Bénard on April 19, 1919, for $17,736. On February 24, 1919, Bénard purchased this property for $12,335 from the Right Honourable Margaret Charlotte, Baroness Strathcona and Mount Royal, of Mount Royal in the Province of Quebec and of Glencoe in the County of Argyle, of the City of London, in England.

## Purchase 22[151]

From Aimé Bénard on May 27, 1919, for $21,500. On April 7, 1919, Bénard purchased River Lots 102 and 103 (except the westerly three chains of 103) from the estate of deceased Canadian Senator George Albertus Cox for $12,900, and in August he purchased outer Lot 102 from the Robert Jaffray estate for $5,640. Bénard's signed transfer to the Hutterite purchasers predated his actual acquisition of this latter property.

### Purchases 11, 12, and 14

Although included in the August 21, 1918 agreement to purchase from Aimé Bénard, these properties were actually transferred to the "holding committee" directly by their owners.

---

Lots One hundred and seven (107) and One hundred and eight (108) according to the Dominion Government Survey of the Parish of St. François Xavier in Manitoba lying to the South of the Main Highway according to a Plan of same filed in the Winnipeg Land Titles Office as No. 552."

149 Transfer 412962: "Fractional Section Twenty-one (21) in the Eleventh Township and Second Range West of the Principal Meridian in Manitoba containing Two hundred and thirty-one Acres more or less."

150 Transfer 33096: "Lot Two (2) and the most Westerly Six (6) Chains in perpendicular width of Parish Lot One (1) both of the Parish of Baie St. Paul in Manitoba."

151 Transfer 415844: "Parcel No. 1: River Lots One hundred and two (102) and One hundred and three (103) excepting out of said Lot One hundred and three (103) the most westerly two Chains in width thereof according to the Dominion Government Survey of the Parish of St. François Xavier in Manitoba. Excepting thereout the main highway according to a Plan filed in the Winnipeg Land Titles Office as No. 552. Parcel No. 2: Lot One hundred and two (102) according to the Dominion Government Survey of the Outer Two Miles of the Parish of St. François Xavier in Manitoba."

## Purchase 11[152]

On November 22, 1918, a purchase of 330 acres was made from Portland, Oregon banker Carl Hendrickson, for $8,250.

## Purchases 12[153] and 14[154]

Two purchases were made on November 29, 1918, from Elie farmer and former Kansan Albert Hammerquist: 90 acres for $4,400 and 446 acres for $22,190.

∼

It was at this juncture during the land purchases that the nature of the "holding committee" was defined and trusteeship of the landholdings was formalized. On February 21, 1919, David Hofer Sr., Paul Wallman, Zacharias Hofer, David Hofer Jr., Joseph Waldner, and Joseph Michel Waldner all signed a declaration of trust:

> AND WHEREAS the whole consideration or sum of money paid by us for the purchase of the said lands and personal property was the money of Hutterian Brethren and the said purchases were made by us as Trustees for and on behalf of the said Hutterian Brethren and we do hereby admit and declare:
>
> NOW THESE PRESENT WITNESS that in consideration of the premises, WE HEREBY ACKNOWLEDGE AND DECLARE THAT WE, our heirs, executors, administrators, and assigns do and shall respectively stand seized of the said lands and personal property with all the appurtenances conveyed to us IN TRUST for the said Hutterian Brethren, their successors and assigns forever, and we or our heirs, executors, administrators or assigns will convey, lease, sell, or dispose of the same in such manner as the said Hutterian Brethren shall direct and we

---

152 Transfer 32462: "Lots Three and Four according to the Dominion Government Survey of the Parish of Baie St. Paul in Manitoba."
153 Deed RPA 9375: "All of Parish Lot One (1) of the Parish of Baie St. Paul excepting thereout and therefrom the most Westerly Six (6) Chains in Width thereof."
154 Transfer 401143: "Parcel No. 1: All those Portions of Lots One hundred and seven (107) and One hundred and eight (108) according to the Dominion Government Survey of the Parish of St. François Xavier in Manitoba which lie between the main highway as said highway is shown on a Plan filed in the Winnipeg Land Titles Office as No. 552 and the Assiniboine River. Parcel No. 2: River Lots One hundred and nine (109) One hundred and ten (110) One hundred and eleven (111) and One hundred and twelve (112) according to the Dominion Government Survey of the Parish of St. François Xavier in Manitoba."

further admit and declare that all our right, title and interest in any of the said property is held as joint tenants and not as tenants in common, and we hereby further admit and declare that the above mentioned lands are held in trust for the following societies of the said Hutterian Brethren....[155]

The individual communities were then listed: Milltown Society, Bon Homme Society, Huron Society, Maxwell Society, Rosedale Society, and James Valley Society. These were followed by the legal descriptions of the properties already purchased and held in trust.[156] Individual declarations of trust were henceforth prepared when subsequent purchases were made. Alexander Adams and the Tupper Law Firm[157] prepared all such documents. Adams appears to have been most diligent on behalf of the Hutterites in that caveats in the name of Joseph Waldner were registered as needed on the certificates of title of those owners whose properties were to be purchased. By doing so, these lands were better secured until actual transfers were signed and registered.

∼

**Purchase 17**[158]

A March 13, 1919 purchase of 160 acres (less 1) for $8,000 from Murdoch McKinnon was also in the form of an agreement for sale where $100 was paid immediately as a deposit; $1,900 was due upon execution of the documents; $1,800 was to pay McKinnon's mortgage (79612) balance to the Law Union & Rock Insurance Company; and $1,400 was due on both March 13, 1920 and 1921, with the remaining balance due March 13, 1922. Included with the property (NW 25-10-4) were a binder, drill, harrow, truck, sleigh, jumper [?], mower, hay rake, grind stone, two ploughs (gang and walking), two wagons, seven horses, three head of cattle, an old harness, two sets of harnesses with collars, thirty-nine chickens, and twenty bushels of potatoes. The Hutterite purchasers again registered Caveat 16399 against the real property, to which they only received title in 1926 after the death of Murdoch McKinnon. (See Acquisition B below.)

---

155 Declaration of Trust, February 21, 1919.
156 Ibid.
157 I do not always specify the law firm's name due to name changes with the addition of new partners. At this point it was Tupper, McTavish, Foley, and Tupper.
158 RPA 9300: "The North West Quarter of Section Twenty-five (25) in Township Ten (10) and Range Four (4) West of the Principal Meridian in Manitoba, excepting thereout all that portion thereof consisting of the most Northerly Three (3) Chains and Sixteen (16) Links in depth of the most Westerly Three (3) Chains and Sixteen (16) Links in width of the said Quarter Section."

### Purchase 20[159]

From Chippewa County, Minnesota farmers Emmet Olson and Charles Olson, 240 acres for $10,000 on April 21, 1919.

### Purchase 21[160]

From St. Eustache farmer Ferdinand Moreau, 240 acres for $9,000 on April 23, 1919. The memorandum of agreement to purchase this property had been signed February 20, 1919.[161]

### Purchase 23[162]

From Voltaire, North Dakota farmer Albert Anderson, 240 acres for $11,400 on September 22, 1919.

### Purchases 24[163] and 25[164]

On October 8, 1919, from Winnipeg real estate agent/farmer James Wolfe, 240 acres for $11,064. Wolfe had just purchased 120 of these acres in July from Elie farmers David Roy and Joseph Roy for $850, and in September the remaining 120 acres from them for $2,000. Both his purchases were encumbered by an unspecified outstanding judgment. Whether the judgment required further capital input by Wolfe is unknown, but no doubt he was left with a substantial profit on his real estate flip.

---

159 Transfer 407296: "The North East Quarter and the East Half of the North West Quarter of Section Thirty (30) in Township Eleven (11) and Range Two (2) West of the Principal Meridian."
160 Transfer 406460: "The North West Quarter of Section Nineteen (19) and the West Half of the South West Quarter of Section Thirty (30) all in Township Eleven (11) and Range Two (2) West of the Principal Meridian."
161 Declaration of Trust, February 21, 1919.
162 Transfer 33777: "The North West Quarter and the North Half of the South West Quarter of Section Twenty-five (25) in Township Eleven (11) and Range Three (3) West of the Principal Meridian in Manitoba."
163 Transfer 418199: "In the Province of Manitoba and being composed of Legal Subdivisions One (1) Two (2) and Eight (8) of Section Twenty (20) in Township Eleven (11) in Range Two (2) West of the Principal Meridian in said Province excepting thereout all those portions thereof taken for the purpose of a Public Drain as the same is shown coloured pink on the Plan filed in the Winnipeg Land Titles Office as No. 1308."
164 Transfer 418200: "In the Province of Manitoba and being composed of Legal Subdivisions Three (3) Six (6) and Seven (7) of Section Twenty (20) in Township Eleven (11) in Range Two (2) West of the Principal Meridian in said Province excepting thereout all those portions thereof taken for the purpose of a Public Drain as the same is shown coloured pink on the Plan filed in the Winnipeg Land Titles Office as No. 1308."

## Purchases 26[165] and 27[166]

On October 10, 1919, transfers were signed by Winnipeg grain merchants Francis Kloepfer and Francis Klema, transferring clear title to Baie St. Paul Lots 12, 13, and 16 to the Brethren for $1. Lots 12 and 13 were valued at $11,280, and Lot 16 at $6,540, but no explanation is provided as to actual compensation. Since Kloepfer and Klema were in the grain business, it might be possible that payment equivalent to the land valuations was made by grain deliveries to them.

## Purchase 28[167]

Also on October 10, 1919, from Elie farmer Pierre Desilet, 237 acres for $9,492.

## Purchases 29[168] and 30[169]

Two purchases were made on October 13, 1919, from Portage la Prairie real estate brokers Charles Burley and Joseph Metcalfe, a total of 719 acres for $29,000.[170]

---

165 Transfer 33995: "Being Parish Lot Sixteen of the Parish of Baie St. Paul in Manitoba excepting thereout all special reservations as reserved in the Grant from the Crown."
166 Transfer 33996: "Being Parish Lots Twelve and Thirteen both of the Parish of Baie St. Paul in Manitoba excepting thereout all special reservations as reserved in the Grant from the Crown."
167 Transfer 33997: "In the Province of Manitoba and being composed of Lot Fourteen (14) Baie St. Paul in the Province of Manitoba containing Two Hundred and thirty-seven and thirty-one hundredths acres more or less."
168 Transfer 34003: "Situated in the said Province of Manitoba and being 1: The West Four (4) Chains of Lot Seven (7) and the East Six (6) Chains of Lot Eight (8) of the Parish of Baie St. Paul according to the Dominion Government Survey thereof. 2: The East Half of Lot Seven (7) and the West Half of Lot Eight (8) of the Parish of Baie St. Paul excepting thereout the most Easterly Twenty (20) Acres of the East Half of Lot Seven (7) being a strip of land of uniform width lying parallel with, West of, and immediately adjoining the Westerly boundary of Lot Six (6) of the said Parish described in Certificate of Title 15433 of the Portage la Prairie Land Titles Office."
169 Transfer 415463: "1: The Fractional North West Quarter of Section Thirty-two (32) and the South West Quarter and Fractional North West Quarter of Section Twenty-nine (29) in Township Eleven (11) and Range Two (2) West of the First Principal Meridian. 2: The Fractional South West Quarter of Section Thirty-two (32) in Township Eleven (11) Range Two (2) West of the First Principal Meridian."
170 The purchases, although registered in the Winnipeg and Portage Land Titles Offices respectively, were both recorded as being for $29,000. The Winnipeg Statement of Valuation was unavailable, but the Portage valuation was $14,812, thus indicating that $29,000 would have been the purchase price for both.

## Purchase 31[171]

From the Scottish Ontario and Manitoba Land Company, 204 acres for $4,000 on October 30, 1919. Grain merchants Francis Kloepfer and Francis Klema were being assessed taxes on these two lots, but were not the registered owners.

## Purchases 32[172] and 33[173]

Two purchases were made on November 26, 1919, from Pigeon Lake farmer George Crepeau, a total of 240 acres for $11,400, subject to Crepeau's $5,000 mortgage (399980) owing to Ferdinand Lafleche. This mortgage was refinanced on May 27, 1920, when the six Hutterites remortgaged (428857) the property for the same amount to William J. Tupper, a partner in the Tupper law firm and a son to Canadian Father of Confederation Sir Charles Tupper.

## Purchases 34[174] and 35[175]

There were two purchases from the Eastern Loan & Investment Company Ltd: 164 acres on December 3 for $8,000 and 335 acres on December 4 for $8,000. The vice-president of this company was John A. Flanders[176] of Winnipeg, but more interesting was that in May 1919, Michael Reilly of Fond du Lac, Wisconsin, had assigned to Aimé Bénard an articles of agreement document concerning an earlier 1910 sale of these same prop-

---

171 Transfer 33998: "Lots Seventeen and Eighteen of the Parish of Baie St. Paul in Manitoba."
172 Transfer 417964: "The South East Quarter of Section Nineteen (19) in the Eleventh Township and Second Range West of the Principal Meridian in Manitoba."
173 Transfer 417965: "The West Half of the South West Quarter of Section Twenty (20) in the Eleventh Township and Second Range West of the Principal Meridian in Manitoba excepting thereout that portion taken for a Public Drain as shown coloured pink on a Plan filed in the Winnipeg Land Titles Office as No. 1308."
174 Deed RPA 29274: "The fractional South East Quarter and the fractional North East Quarter of Section Twenty-nine (29) in Township Eleven (11) in Range Two (2) West of the Principal Meridian in the Province of Manitoba."
175 Transfer 34401: "In the Province of Manitoba and being Lots Nine (9) and Ten (10) according to the Dominion Government Survey of Baie St. Paul excepting out of said Lot Nine (9) that portion described as follows: Commencing at a point on the Easterly boundary of said Lot distant Northerly thereon fourteen-hundred and eighty three and six one hundredths (1483.06) feet from the South East corner of the said Lot thence Northerly along the said Easterly boundary three hundred and forty and seventeen one hundredths (340.17) feet thence westerly at right angles to the said easterly boundary two hundred and eighty six and two one hundredths (286.02) feet thence southerly parallel to the said Easterly Limit two hundred and fifty five feet, thence Easterly in a straight line to the point of commencement excepting of said exceptions Firstly the most Easterly thirty three feet in width thereof, secondly the most Southerly thirty three feet in depth thereof."
176 Cf. John Flanders, in Purchase 40.

erties, which had subsequently been reassigned to others in 1913 and then to Reilly himself in 1914. Bénard's actual financial interest, if any, in the properties at the time of their sale to the Hutterites is as yet unexplained.[177]

Lots 9 and 10 were subject to a $4,500 mortgage (20301) by Henry Anderson et al., owed to Dominion of Canada Investment and Debenture Company. On February 10, 1921, the "holding committee" obtained a $4,500 mortgage (37361) from the Excelsior Life Insurance Company which appears to have paid off the above Mortgage 20301.

## Purchase 36[178]

From Winnipeg horse dealer Edward Watchorn, 444 acres for $13,365 on December 11, 1919. These lots were subject to a $4,500 mortgage (18455) by C.M. Anderson owed to the North of Scotland Canada Mortgage Company.

## Purchase 37[179]

On December 15, 1919, the Brethren registered Caveat 16807 on Portage la Prairie merchant Thomas Millar's 240 acres. An agreement for sale would have been signed and the property thereby secured until its later transfer for $6,000. (See Acquisition A below.)

## Purchase 38[180]

From Porter, Minnesota merchant Christian Berg and the Samuel Berg heirs, 240 acres for $7,200 on May 18, 1920. An agreement for this purchase was entered into as early as May 1919,[181] but the estate formalities appear to have delayed the transaction.

## Purchase 39[182]

From Winnipeg farmer Amandus Nentwig, 374 acres[183] for $10,472 on September 29, 1920. For this transfer, Alexander Adams even signed

---

177 See footnote 203 regarding Bénard's possible involvement.
178 Transfer 34400: "Parish Lots Eleven (11) and Fifteen (15) of the Parish of Baie St. Paul in Manitoba."
179 SW 24-10-4, S ½ NW 24-10-4.
180 Transfer 432880: "The South East Quarter and the East Half of the South West Quarter of Section Thirty (30) in the Eleventh Township and Second Range West of the Principal Meridian in Manitoba."
181 Declaration of Trust, May 14, 1919, courtesy of Tony Waldner.
182 Transfer 36420: "The most Westerly Three (3) Chains and Sixty one (61) Links in width and the most Easterly Six (6) Chains in width, both of Parish Lot Nineteen (19) and the most Easterly Fourteen (14) Chains and Thirty nine (39) Links in width of Parish Lot Twenty (20) all of the Parish of Baie St. Paul, in the Province of Manitoba."
183 Manitoba Probate Court file 1144; the RM of Cartier collection rolls record 187

the valuation statement as agent for the Hutterite transferees. This was the property of the deceased Theodor Hundeby of Los Angeles, California, and a transfer from his widow and executrix, Randi Hundeby, to Nentwig preceded this purchase.

**Purchase 40**[184]

On October 8, 1920, the "holding committee" purchased 2,773 acres more or less from Winnipeg real estate broker John A. Flanders for

---

acres for the Lot 19 portion of this purchase, but some assessment rolls record only 157.

184  Transfer 437240: "In the Province of Manitoba and being composed of:
Parcel No. 1: River Lots Seventy three (73) Seventy four (74) Seventy five (75) Eighty (80) Eighty two (82) Eighty three (83) Eighty four (84) Eighty five (85) Eighty six (86) and Lots Seventy four (74) to Eighty (80) both inclusive and Eighty two (82) to Eighty six (86) both inclusive in the Outer Two Miles according to the Dominion Government Survey of the Parish of St. François Xavier excepting out of said River Lot Seventy three (73) that portion thereof taken for the purpose of a public drain as same is shown coloured pink on Plan filed in the Winnipeg Land Titles Office as No. 1380: and excepting out of all River Lots the main highway according to Plan of same filed in the said Land Titles Office as No. 552 and excepting out of said Lot Seventy four (74) in the Outer Two Miles that portion which lies South of a line drawn parallel with and One hundred (100) feet perpendicularly distant Northerly from the centre line of the Grand Trunk Pacific Railway as said centre line is shown on a Plan of said Right of Way filed in the said Office as No. 1304 and subject to Plan of Road filed as No. 666.
Parcel No. 2: River Lots Seventy-eight (78) and Seventy-nine (79) according to the Dominion Government Survey of the Parish of St. François Xavier containing One hundred and thirty-five and eighty-seven one hundredths (135.87) acres more or less. Lot Seventy-six (76) in the Inner Two Miles according to the Dominion Government Survey of the Parish of St. François Xavier excepting thereout the Public Highway as shown on a Plan of same filed in the Winnipeg Land Titles Office as No. 552. River Lot Seventy-seven (77) according to Dominion Government Survey of the Parish of St. François Xavier containing Ninety-six and nine tenths (96.9) acres more or less excepting that portion taken for a Public Highway as shown on a Plan filed in the Winnipeg Land Titles Office as No. 552. Excepting also that portion taken for a public drain as described in Certificate of Title 126648.
Parcel No. 3: The North half of the North West Quarter of Section Twenty five (25) and Legal Subdivisions Two (2) Three (3) Six (6) and Seven (7) of Section Thirty six (36) in Township Ten (10) and Range Two (2) West of the Principal Meridian excepting thereout those portions taken for the Right-of-Way of the Portage Extension of the Northern Pacific and Manitoba Railway according to Plan of same filed in the Winnipeg Land Titles Office as No. 366 and excepting out of said Legal Subdivisions Six (6) and Seven (7) all those portions thereof which lie between two lines drawn parallel with and each said line being Seventy five (75) feet perpendicularly distant on opposite sides from the centre line of the Grand Trunk Pacific Railway as said centre line is shown on a Plan of Right-of-Way filed in the said office as No. 1304 and also excepting out of said Legal Subdivision Seven (7) all that portion thereof taken for the purpose of a Public Drain as same is shown coloured pink on a Plan filed in said Office as No. 1380."

$137,004—although they had, however, registered Caveats 101141 and 101142 on these properties as early as May 27. The Mortgage Investors Agency had been a long-term owner of certain of these St. François Xavier lots, which it sold to Winnipeg merchant John Barickman for $83,397 on November 20, 1918. On March 13, 1919, Barickman transferred these same lots to Barickman, Barnum, Shaw Limited for $70,000: River Lots 73 through 75; 80 through 86; and Outer Lots 74 through 80; 82 through 86; plus N ½ NW 25-10-2 and Legal Subdivisions 2, 3, 6, and 7 of 36-10-2. On June 20, 1920, the latter company transferred them to Winnipeg Real Estate Broker John Flanders for $39,221, although they were valued at $105,000. The price variations in these transfers are unexplained.

On April 22, 1920, Flanders had acquired River Lots 76 through 79 in St. François Xavier from Isadore Zastre for $30,000. These lots, combined with the earlier parcels, were the properties that Flanders resold to the Hutterites for $137,004 subject to four existing mortgages: John Barickman owed to the Great-West Life Assurance Company (403973 for $30,000) and to the Mortgage Investors Agency (403974 for $36,017); John Flanders owed to Barickman Barnum Shaw (Mortgage 429695 for $5,000) and to Isadore Zastre (Mortgage 426267 for $20,000). The John Flanders mortgage owed to Barickman Barnum Shaw was discharged November 11, 1920. Had the full amounts still been outstanding on these mortgages, the cash required by the purchasers would have been $45,983. On this latter transfer, Alexander Adams again signed the valuation as agent of the transferees.

∼

The majority of the foregoing land acquisitions (Purchases 1 through 40) were made by the "holding committee" in 1918 and 1919, and all were made prior to March 24, 1921. During this period, however, the controversy over these land sales—incited by those persons and organizations opposed to the immigration of a pacifist community such as the Hutterites—had become intolerable for the government. Yielding to public pressure, the Canadian government first cancelled the military service exemption for those members of the "Brethren of the Hutterische Society"[185] who had yet to enter Canada as immigrants.[186] Then, commencing May 2, 1919,

---

185  The Order in Council (PC1676) of August 12, 1899, granted military service exemption to the "Brethren of the Hutterische Society" settling permanently in Canada. Alexander Adams took for granted that this designation included the Schmiedeleut, and advised the Minister of Immigration and Colonization that they preferred to use the term 'Hutterian,' rather than 'Hutterische' in Manitoba. Alexander Adams to J.A. Calder, 18 October 1918 (LAC: RG 76, vol. 173, file 58764, part 2).

186  PC768, April 8, 1919, which cancelled the Order in Council (PC1676) of August 12, 1899, rescinded military service exemptions for those who entered Canada as immigrants on or after April 10, 1919 (LAC: RG 76, vol. 173, file 58764, part 3). In

by an Order in Council, the government prohibited entirely further entry of Hutterites, Mennonites, and Doukhobors as immigrants.[187] Despite the entry prohibition, the land purchases in Manitoba continued, and the Order in Council was only rescinded on June 2, 1922.[188] During those three years, the Hutterites not yet in Canada were forced to remain in South Dakota,[189] where all but Bon Homme and those Milltown Community lands east of the James River had been sold.[190]

Since 1906, the Hutterische Bruder-Gemeinde as a corporation had been the registered owner of all South Dakota Schmiedeleut community lands. Accordingly, this corporation made all sales under the signatures of its corporate officers and corporate seal application.[191] In addition to any prior *Zeugbruder Rat* (council meeting) and *Prediger Versammlung* (ministers' meeting) decisions, at a meeting on August 7, 1918, the members of the Hutterische Bruder-Gemeinde authorized the corporation to sell the South Dakota real estate held by the corporation for a price of not less than $45/acre.[192] On August 2, 1918, the corporation had already agreed to sell Rosedale's 3,840 acres for $200,000 to F.L. Simmons and C. Mullenburg of Brookings, South Dakota. The amount of $25,000 was payable on that date, with another $25,000 on September 1, 1918, and the balance of $150,000 on October 1, 1918. However, on October 1, a warranty deed conveyed these properties to the purchasers for $188,000.[193]

---

a similar manner, PC2622 of October 25, 1918, had already rescinded such exemptions for Mennonites and Doukhobors but did not mention Hutterites (LAC: RG 76, vol. 173, file 58764, part 2).

187 PC923 (LAC: RG 76, vol. 173, file 58764, part 3). Subsequent to an amendment to the Immigration Act, on June 9, 1919, a new Order in Council (PC1204) essentially reaffirmed this entry prohibition (LAC: RG 76, vol. 174, file 58764, part 4).

188 PC1181 rescinded the entry prohibition for Hutterites and Mennonites (LAC: RG 76, vol. 174, file 58764, part 8).

189 Some families and individuals were, however, allowed temporary entry.

190 Refers only to Schmiedeleut and their known community lands. The Dariusleut appear to have been incorporated as "Hutterische Society" and the Lehrerleut as "Hutterische Gemeinde," as reported in the Scotland, SD, *Citizen Republican*, September 19, 1918.

191 These are the known transactions as registered in the various county courts. Mortgages or other encumbrances on these properties, if any, existing prior to sale date have not been researched. Dates and amounts of payments actually received from land sales were unavailable. A *lis pendens* filed on the South Dakota lands and disposition thereof, as well as involvement of the South Dakota Council of Defense and a reported requirement to invest 2.5 percent of the sale proceeds in Liberty Loan Bonds and donate 0.5 percent to the Red Cross have not been researched.

192 This is noted on several deeds of sale registered in South Dakota, including *Hutchinson County Book Q*, 631.

193 *Hanson County Register of Deeds, Book EM*, 618–619; *Book 43*, 383; *Das Klein Geschichtsbuch*, 489–490, provides details about this reduced sum.

Concurrent with their large Manitoba purchase from Joseph Hackney of St. Paul, Minnesota, the Hutterische Bruder-Gemeinde had sold Huron's 3,360 acres for $146,200 to him on August 8, 1918. Similar to what he did in Manitoba, Hackney financed a portion of the purchase price by issuing an $85,000 bond secured by a trust deed of the acreage to the Minnesota Loan and Trust Company.[194] In February 1919, Hackney resold this property for $214,200, thus realizing a $68,000 profit in less than a year.[195] On September 28, 1918, the corporation sold James Valley's 1,920 acres to E.P. Flowers and H.G. Spratt of Huron for $96,000, subject to two preexisting mortgages totalling $20,000.[196] Maxwell's property was sold by the corporation for $209,616 to Humphrey Statter of Sioux City, Iowa, on December 31, 1918.[197]

Initially, the corporation sold only the Milltown properties west of the James River: portions of Sections 3 and 4-99-59 to William Rardin for $11,200 on October 1, 1918; the East ½ 5-99-59 to George Moter of Parker for $23,200 on November 13, 1918; a portion of 34-100-59 to Frank Wright of Hutchinson County for $14,000 on July 1, 1919; the NW ¼ of the NE ¼ 3-99-59, excepting the town site of Milltown, to Andreas Goehring of Freeman for $3,244 on July 1, 1919; the South ½ of the SE ¼ of the SW ¼ and the South ½ of Lot 10, both in Section 2-99-59, to John G. Winter for $4,424 on July 1, 1919; and portions of Sections 2 and

---

194 An advertisement for these bonds, placed by the Minnesota Loan and Trust Company as trustee, appeared in the *Minneapolis Morning Tribune* of November 27, 1918, where the security was described: "These Bonds are secured by a first mortgage on 3,360 acres in Beadle County, South Dakota, excellently located as to market, being within 10 miles of Huron, a good town on the Chicago & Northwestern and Great Northern Railways. 1,516 acres are in cultivation, 1,115 additional acres cultivable, and the balance is better adapted to pasture and meadow. It is operated under the personal supervision of Mr. Hackney as a stock and grain-raising proposition; is improved with good buildings and is well stocked. It was formerly a Mennonite Colony and the character of the soil, condition of the property and standard of farming is in keeping with the reputation that these people had for selecting and owning good land. The property has been personally examined by two representatives from our Company and the valuations given represent their appraisal. Our business relations with Mr. Hackney have extended over a period of several years and we are pleased to recommend these bonds for investment, both because of the real estate and Personal security." The valuation then listed was: land $184,800, improvements $20,000, for a total of $204,800. This was the same property which Hackney had purchased for $146,200 only three months earlier.
195 *Beadle County Register of Deeds, Book 198*, 511–512; *Book 202*, 472; *Book 207*, 28; *Mortgage Book 183*, 572–577.
196 Ibid., *Book 198*, 525; *Book 208*, 521. *James Valley Untitled Ledger*, 181, records the two mortgages as $13,600 and $6,400 respectively. Courtesy of Patrick Murphy.
197 *Hutchinson County Register of Deeds, Book Q*, 556.

3-99-59 to Wesley Taylor of Parkston for $27,000 on July 21, 1919. This latter sale to Taylor had been authorized September 4, 1918.[198]

Land sales income statistics during 1918 alone, as recorded by the communities themselves, were: Maxwell, $76,000; Rosedale, $113,732; Milltown, $33,790; Huron, $138,579; and James Valley, $52,060; for a total of $414,161. Recorded as paid for land and on promissory notes that same year were: Bon Homme, $51,467; Maxwell, $81,000; Rosedale, $150,000; Milltown, $72,760; Huron, $173,522; and James Valley, $88,955; for a total of $617,704.[199] Although some South Dakota community assets had been sold at auction prior to emigrating,[200] most of their farm machinery, livestock, and household goods were brought to Manitoba by rail,[201] plus much had been included in the purchase of the Hackney farm. By March 1920, it was reported that the Hutterites had purchased 22,000 acres of land on which they had already made payments of $850,000.[202] Much had also been expended on the construction of family living quarters and on barns. The above actually documented[203] Manitoba land purchases, agreements to purchase, and/or declared value of purchases and caveats total $1,183,309 for 24,370 acres more or less.[204]

198 Ibid., 465, 488, 662, 625–631; *Book AL*, 588, 575; *Book M7*, 316–318. The May 1919 Order in Council barring further Hutterite entry to Canada will have caused Milltown to suspend further South Dakota sales.
199 Annual financial statistics courtesy of Ian Kleinsasser. Dates on which payments were received from the individual South Dakota land sales and the amounts are not recorded, nor are the dates and amounts of the individual payments made for the Manitoba purchases.
200 *Scotland Citizen Republican*, November 28, 1918. Maxwell scheduled an auction sale for December 16, 1918.
201 *Winnipeg Free Press*, April 11, 1919, refers to two railcar loads of livestock and effects in quarantine at the border. *Milltown Colony Ledger 1920*, 79, records 1922 freight expenses for rail cars of farm machinery and livestock to Canada. *Winnipeg Free Press*, April 25, 1947, 13, recalls that in 1918, Milltown, Bon Homme, and Huron "arrived with their 90 carloads of horses, cattle, machinery, and household goods." Eighteen rail cars were required by Milltown, SD, alone for the move to Blumengart in 1922–23. G.A. Cook to W.J. White, February 26, 1923 (LAC, RG 76, vol. 175, file 58764, part 9).
202 Arnold George to Department of Immigration and Colonization, memorandum, March 30, 1920 (LAC: RG 76, vol. 174, file 58764, part 6).
203 Acquisitions here numbered 1 through 40, as documented in Manitoba Land Titles Offices.
204 In the absence of further documentation, such as agreements to purchase, it has not been possible to determine whether other third parties facilitated acquisition of a larger parcel from multiple owners. It appears that prior to 1921, the Hutterites preferred to deal with large landowners or speculators and opportunists such as Hackney, McCartney, Lafleche, Flanders, Bénard, and Boyer. Purchases here numbered 23 through 36 appear unusual in that respect. However, some of these smaller individual purchases were from people like James Wolfe and Burley and Metcalfe, who were already involved in real estate, or grain merchants Kloepfer and Klema, all of whom were unlikely to cooperate with some third party enriching

Up to this point, the various Manitoba community parameters were indistinguishable within the land transactions, but on March 24, 1921, this changed. The "holding committee" transferred the until-now commonly held properties to the eight individual communities, where new certificates of title were registered in the names of three trustees for each community.[205] Henceforth, any new land acquisitions were made by those particular trustees for each individual community.

No documents regarding the individual communities' involvement in negotiating their respective purchases[206] have yet been made available,

---

themselves when they could have more profit. But the purchases from the Scottish Ontario & Manitoba Land Company and from Amandus Nentwig were made for a significantly lower per acre price than the others, and those from the Eastern Loan & Investment Company, Edward Watchorn, and Christian and Samuel Berg were somewhat below the average. Together these would be the most likely acquisitions to have had involvement by an opportunist. Such involvement would have increased the total cost to the Hutterite purchasers despite the third party never having held title. Although John Flanders was vice president of the Eastern Loan & Investment Company, it is the May 1919 Articles of Agreement assigned to Aimé Bénard which predated that company's sale to the Hutterites—plus his known dealings with George Crepeau—that suggest Bénard may have put together a larger acreage and was financially compensated for so doing. Alternatively or additionally, Kloepfer and Klema, beyond their own three Baie St. Paul lots, which were valued significantly higher than the average, also had some unidentified interest in the two lots belonging to the Scottish Ontario & Manitoba Land Company, and may have been involved in the latter transaction as well. The purchase from the Bergs had been negotiated about the time when adjacent purchases for higher sums were made from Lafleche, Olson, and Moreau, and the Hundeby lot purchase may have been delayed due to estate issues, all of which could suggest third-party involvement.

205 For a general summary of the lands transferred to the individual communities, as well as the known mortgages thereon, see Table 1 for "holding committee" transfers to the trustees.
206 Although the lands held in trust by the "holding committee" for each individual community were described in the various earlier declarations of trust and beginning in 1919 were so named in the RM of Cartier Collector Rolls, only after March 24, 1921, did the individual community parameters become evident after the property titles were transferred to their trustees: Milltown, Huron, and Bon Homme divided up Purchase 1 from Hackney. Bon Homme, in addition, also purchased 2, 3, 4, 5, 17, and 37. James Valley purchases were 6, 7, and 8. Maxwell purchased 11, 12, 13, 14, 15, 16, 18, 19, and 22. Rosedale's purchases were 9, 10, 20, 21, 23, 32, 33, 38, and 39. Rosedale and Iberville divided up purchases 24, 25, and 30. Iberville's other purchases were 26, 27, 28, 29, 31, 34, 35, and 36. Barickman's purchase was 40. Of these, only a very brief second-hand account is known to exist for Rosedale. In an April 26, 1920 Department of Immigration memorandum, after meeting with Alexander Adams and Jacob Hofer of Rosedale, F.C. Blair wrote: "Six men representing the seven congregations came to Canada on a tour of inspection and agreed to the purchase of certain lands. Mr. Hofer came across, as nearly as he remembers, late in August 1918 being committed by the report and action of the first six. He made a payment on a piece of land at Elie the area being about 3300 acres.... The purchase of land was to some extent negotiated through Senator Bénard. Part of the 3300 acres was

but the documentation that can be accessed suggests that prior to making any decisions the Schmiedeleut conferred in their *Zeugbruder Rat* regarding each community's purchases in Manitoba, as well as the sales of their respective South Dakota lands, including per-acre prices for both transactions.[207] However, from the wordings of the declarations of trust prepared for each land purchase, it is obvious that the monies for those purchases were considered Hutterian Brethren pooled, but not communal, funds. Unlikely to have been an actual bank account, this presumed pool could be considered to have been the sum generated through the combined sales of the South Dakota properties and other community resources from which the "holding committee" made all Manitoba land purchases on behalf of the individual communities. Some of these purchased Manitoba lands were already mortgaged, and it would be logical that the pooled fund took advantage of this existing longer-term financing in order to maintain the working capital of all the communities.[208] Initially these were the Milltown, Bon Homme, and Huron lands, which were heavily mortgaged to National Trust. Other lands, particularly those of Rosedale, Iberville, and Maxwell, were purchased largely without mortgage financing and had, with few exceptions, clear Certificates of Title. It would appear probable that expenditures for each community's purchases were proportional to their equity in the presumed fund, and that individual communities may have directly made the land payments specific to their respective purchases.[209]

---

    owned by Senator Bénard's brother-in-law Lafleche" (LAC: RG 76, vol. 174, file 58764, part 6). The documented land purchases are obvious proof that it was a much more complex process than Blair described. He does, however, confirm that the prior action of the six representatives tasked with purchasing land committed Hofer to so doing.

207  As an example of their unity, the July 3 and 6, 1918 meetings authorized James Valley to sell its South Dakota lands for $60/acre and purchase 3,040 acres in Manitoba for $45–50/acre. "*Prediger Versammlung wegen ausziehen nach Kanada, Juli 3, 1918* [Ministers' meeting regarding emigration to Canada, July 3, 1918]" and "*Kirchen Versammlung wegen nach Kanada ziehen* [Church meeting regarding moving to Canada]," July 6, 1918.

208  For example, if Huron had merely swapped its South Dakota lands for some of Joseph Hackney's Manitoba lands, then the National Trust mortgage thereon could have been immediately repaid and proportionally discharged. By pooling their resources and sharing existing financing, those funds initially remained available for further land purchases or as working capital rather than retiring mortgage principal. In addition, although Rosedale purchased none of the Joseph Hackney lands mortgaged to National Trust, nevertheless, in April 1925, it paid $300 to Milltown, "*für ein theil von Hackney Interessen* [as a payment toward the Hackney interest]," which could suggest that they initially also participated in the pooled financing and benefited from the continuance of the mortgage. *Milltown SD, Income and Expense Ledger 1920*, 162. Courtesy of Tony Waldner.

209  Joseph Kleinsasser of Milltown, SD, was secretary-treasurer of the South Dakota Hutterische Bruder-Gemeinde and, when recording the initial June 1918 cheques

## MILLTOWN

Registered on all these lands at time of purchase by the "holding committee" was the Hackney mortgage owed to National Trust (#30768/#90316) plus the Hackney mortgage owed to Kingman Robins (#30769) which encumbered only W ½ 5-11-3. Mortgage #30769 was discharged October 24, 1918. All lands conveyed by this 1921 transfer to the Milltown trustees remained encumbered by Hackney mortgage #30768/#90316.

Transfer #37759 – Milltown: John Hofer, David Hofer Sr., Jacob Hofer.
Valued at $117,493.
N ½ NW 16, SW and N ½ NE 21, SE 28, NE and E ½ NW 32, NW and W ½ NE 33, all in 10-3.
W ½ 4, Section 5, NE 7, Section 8, W ½ 9 South of RR, SW 17, N ½ S ½ and S ½ SE 18 except Easterly 1,729' of said N ½ SE 18, all in 11-3.

Transfer #37731 – Milltown: John Hofer, David Hofer Sr., David Hofer.
Valued at $900.
Easterly 1,729 feet of N ½ SE 18-11-3.

## BON HOMME

Murdoch McKinnon agreement for sale of the NW 25-10-4 was assigned on June 23, 1921, and is not included in this transfer. The Thomas Millar property, SW and S ½ NW 24-10-4, on which caveat #8120 was registered is not included.

Registered on these lands or portions thereof at time of purchase by the "holding committee" were the Hackney mortgage owed to National Trust (#30768/#90316) and Hackney owed to Marie Bénard (#30799/#90324), Alexander McKinnon owed to Scottish Ontario (#22243), and John Grant (#27860 and #77895) owed to Law Union and Rock. Subsequently, mortgages #30799 and #90324 were discharged December 17, 1919, mortgage #22243 on December 29, 1919, and mortgage #27860 on May 27, 1919. As per agreement with McKinnon, they were also responsible for his mortgage #79612 owed to Law Union and Rock. Certain lands conveyed to the Bon Homme trustees by this 1921 transfer were still encumbered by Hackney mortgage #30768/#90316, and Grant mortgage #77895. Mortgage #79612 still encumbered the McKinnon property.

Transfer #38118 – Bon Homme: Joseph Michael Waldner, Jacob Waldner, Jacob Wurz.
Valued at $156,314.
W ½ 11, NW 12, S ½ SW 13, all in 10-3. NE and N ½ SE 13, SE and S ½ NE 24, Section 36, all in 10-4. Section 1, S ½ and NW 11, S ½ and NW 12, N ½ and SW and N ½ SE 13, all in 11-4.

## HURON

Registered on these lands at time of purchase by the "holding committee" was the Hackney mortgage owed to National Trust (#30768/#90316). Partial discharges of this mortgage were registered during 1919 and 1920 as payments were made for their release. However, those lands yet encumbered and conveyed by this 1921 transfer to the Huron trustees remained encumbered by said mortgage.

Transfer #38119 – Huron: Joseph Waldner, Michael Waldner, John Waldner.
Valued at $115,656.
NW and W ½ NE 16, NW and N ½ NE 17, N ½ 18, Section 19, W ½ and SE and W ½ NE 20, E ½ and SW 30, all in 11-3. W ½ 1-12-3.

## JAMES VALLEY

Purchase agreement from Larson of the S ½ and S ½ N ½ 14-10-3 was assigned on June 23, 1921, and is not included in this transfer.

Purchases were enabled by David Hofer, et al. (i.e., holding committee) mortgages (#93361 and #32292) from vendor Fred McCartney, both of which were subsequently discharged on May 26, 1919. Lands were conveyed by this 1921 transfer to the James Valley trustees free of encumbrances. There remained the outstanding balance on the purchase agreement from Larson.

Transfer #37758 – James Valley: David Hofer Jr, Peter Hofer, David Hofer.
Valued at $73,600.
N ½ NE 14, E ½ and E ½ NW 23, Section 24, W ½ and SE 25, S ½ 26, all in 10-3.

**Table 1.** March 24, 1921 "holding committee" transfers to the trustees, including a general summary of the lands transferred.

## MAXWELL

"Holding committee" purchases were made without mortgage financing and were transferred unencumbered to the Maxwell trustees in 1921.

Transfer #37733 – Maxwell: Joseph Hofer, John Hofer Sr., John Hofer Jr.
Valued at $44,778.
Lots 1, 2, 3, 4, 5, 6, and Easterly 20 acres of Lot 7, all in Baie St. Paul.
Transfer #446562 – Maxwell: Joseph Hofer, John Hofer Sr., John Hofer Jr.
Valued at $101,228.
River Lots 102 through 112 both inclusive and Outer Lot 102, all in St. Francois Xavier. NW and Westerly 20 chains and 45 links of NE 16, Frac 21, all in 11-2.

## ROSEDALE

At time of purchase of parcels SE 19 and W ½ SW 20-11-2, the "holding committee" assumed the mortgage balance owed by George Crepeau (#399980) to Ferdinand Lafleche, which was then refinanced by the David Hofer Sr. et al. (the "holding committee") May 27, 1920, mortgage (#428857) from William Tupper. This latter mortgage still encumbered said lands at time of this 1921 transfer to the Rosedale trustees and was subsequently refinanced by Hofer, Maendel, and Maendel for $5,000 on December 23, 1925, by a new mortgage (#534409) in favour of William Tupper.

Transfer #37732 – Rosedale: Zacharias Hofer, Joseph Maendel, John Maendel.
Valued at $61,872.
E ½ and NW and N ½ SW 25, S ½ and NE 36, all in 11-3. Westerly 3 Chains 61 Links and Easterly 6 Chains Lot 19, Easterly 14 Chains 39 Links Lot 20, all in Baie St. Paul.
Transfer #447599 – Rosedale: Zacharias Hofer, Joseph Maendel, John Maendel
Valued at $88,082.
NW and SE 19, SW 20, SW 29, Section 30, W ½ and SE and Frac NE 31, all in 11-2. Frac 6-12-2.

## IBERVILLE

Purchases were made by the "holding committee" free of mortgages other than C.M. Anderson owed to North of Scotland (#18455) affecting Lots 11 and 15, and Henry Anderson to Dominion of Canada Investment and Debenture Co. Ltd. (#20301) affecting Lots 9 and 10. Mortgage #18455 was discharged December 31, 1920. Mortgage #20301 was refinanced February 10, 1921, by the David Hofer, et al. (holding committee) Mortgage #37361 from Excelsior Life. Although both of these latter mortgages encumbered Lots 9 and 10 at time of this March 1921 transfer to the Iberville trustees, mortgage (#20301) appears to have been immediately discharged on April 22.

Transfer #37678 ½ - Iberville: Paul Gross, Jacob Hofer, John Hofer
Valued at $74,879.
Parish Lots 7 through 18 both inclusive except Easterly 20 acres of Lot 7, all in Baie St. Paul.
Transfer #447370 – Iberville: Paul Gross, Jacob Hofer, John Hofer
Valued at $28,204.
Legal Subdivisions 1, 2, 7, 8 of Sec 20, Frac E ½ and Frac NW 29, Frac SW and Frac Legal Subdivision 12 of Sec 32, all in 11-2.

## BARICKMAN

At time of purchase the "holding committee" assumed the balances of John Barickman's March 1, 1919 mortgage #403973 owed to Great West Life and #403974 to Mortgage Investors Agency and John Flanders's June 8, 1920 mortgage #429695 owed to Barickman, Barnum, Shaw, and April 26, 1920 mortgage #426267 owed to Isadore Zastre. Mortgage #429695 was discharged November 1920, but the other three mortgages still encumbered the lands at the time of this 1921 transfer to the Barickman trustees.

Transfer #446065 – Barickman: Samuel Hofer, Jacob Wipf, Peter Hofer
Valued at $137,004.
River Lots 73 through 80 and 82 through 86, Outer Lots 74 through 80 and 82 through 86 all in St. Francois Xavier. N ½ NW 25 and Legal Subdivisions 2, 3, 6, 7 of Section 36, all in 10-2.

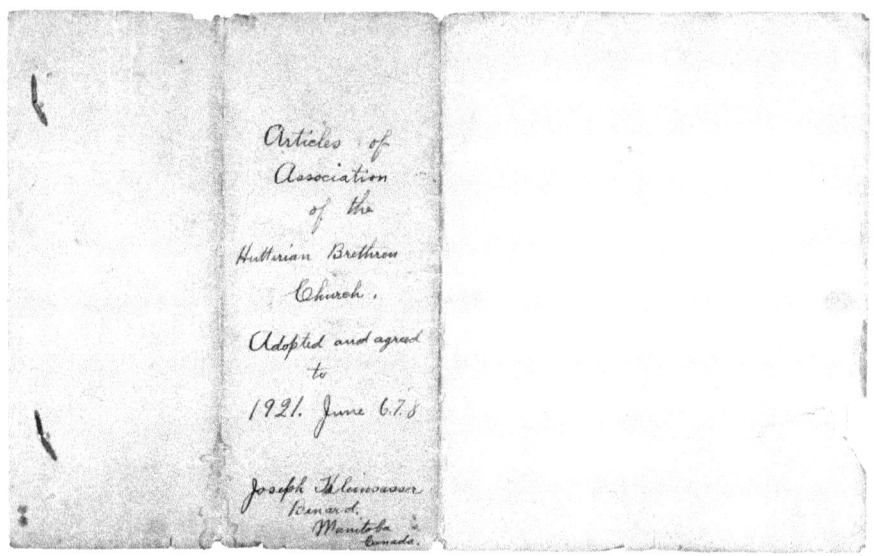

Cover of Joseph Kleinsasser's copy of the 1921 Articles of Association of the Hutterian Brethren Church. [Source: Courtesy of Tony Waldner.]

Subsequent to the March transfer of lands by the "holding committee" to the community trustees, the Manitoba Schmiedeleut in June 1921 adopted the Articles of Association of the Hutterian Brethren Church.[210] Specified among the forty-one articles were the following:

- "That the Officers of the Association shall consist of a President, a Vice-President, a Secretary, and a Treasurer, and twenty-five (25) Managers."

- "That the Minister, Business Manager and Farm Manager, (or where there are two Ministers the second one shall be chosen instead of the Farm Manager), of each Colony shall be appointed by each Colony to act as Trustees for the purpose of holding title to all of its real and personal property, and such trustees shall hold title as joint tenants, and shall execute a declaration of trust in favour of the Colony."

---

payable to Hackney, a new series was begun: the $15,000 cheque was B-1 and the $35,000 cheque was B-2. These payments could have been specific to Milltown's purchase but were more likely made on behalf of Bon Homme and Huron as well. Cheque B-28 was for Huron abstracts from Beadle County. It is not always certain whether Kleinsasser was recording Milltown or also certain Hutterische Bruder-Gemeinde expenses. *Milltown Colony, SD, Income & Expense Ledger 1911*, 267, 269. Courtesy of Tony Waldner.

210 Articles of Association of the Hutterian Brethren Church, adopted June 6–8, 1921, signed by Joseph Kleinsasser, Benard, Manitoba, Canada. Courtesy of Tony Waldner.

- "That the President, Vice-President, Secretary, and the Treasurer shall be eligible for election as both Managers and Trustees, and a Manager shall be eligible for election as a Trustee."
- "That the affairs, powers, privileges, business, and property of said Association shall be managed, administered, exercised, transacted, conducted and controlled by the Board of twenty-five (25) Managers...."

The following individuals were initially named as managers:
- Barickman: Samuel Hofer, Jacob Wipf, Peter Hofer
- Maxwell: Joseph Hofer, John Hofer Jr., John Hofer Sr.
- Iberville: Paul Gross, Jacob Hofer, John R. Hofer
- Rosedale: Zacharias Hofer, Joseph Maendel, John Maendel
- Huron: Joseph Waldner, Michael Waldner, John Waldner
- Milltown: John D. Hofer, David Hofer, Jacob Hofer
- Bon Homme: Joseph M. Waldner, Jacob Waldner, Jacob Wurz
- James Valley: David Hofer, Peter Hofer, David D. Hofer

These individuals were the named community trustees to whom the "holding committee" had already transferred the certificates of title in March. The Articles of Association also allowed for Communities to appoint two persons to do the banking for the community, including borrowing money "on the credit of such Colony, or if the consent of the Board of Managers has first been obtained upon the credit of the whole Association." The board of managers, with prior consent of the majority of the association members, could also mortgage the real property and were "authorized to instruct the Trustees of each Colony to sign, execute and deliver" such forms of securities as required.

By this point in time, portions of the National Trust mortgage had already begun to be repaid and discharges obtained for certain parcels of Huron land. Bon Homme had paid off the McKinnon and one John Grant mortgage and James Valley had repaid its mortgage due to Fred McCartney. Now, despite the separation of the community lands but consistent with the Articles of Association, in December 1921 a $250,000 mortgage from Great-West Life was collectively obtained[211] (concurrent Mortgage 39124 by J. Hofer et al., for lands in the Portage Land Titles Office District, and 460738 by Joseph Hofer et al., Paul Gross et al., and

---

211 Although the 1921 mortgages were already registered against the properties of the various communities, on January 3, 1922, Great-West Life registered Caveats 108183 (Winnipeg Land Titles Office) and 18465 (Portage Land Titles Office) on all of the same properties and thereby confirmed their shared responsibility.

Zacharias Hofer et al., for lands in the Winnipeg Land Titles Office District). Rosedale, Maxwell, and Iberville[212] mortgaged essentially all of their lands; Huron remortgaged its lands that were already unencumbered; Bon Homme remortgaged the N ½ and SE 36-10-4; and James Valley remortgaged the former McCartney property. Milltown and Barickman lands were not involved. However, the collective mortgage obligation was variably distributed between all eight communities.[213]

Although not the subject of this research, each community also had non-mortgage indebtedness such as private promissory notes and bank loans. Also consistent with the Articles of Association was the collective approach to some of these obligations, as evidenced by a resolution in a 1923 letter of guarantee for $75,000 given to the Molson Bank by the Hutterian Brethren Church:

> That the Association give to the Molsons Bank a Letter of Guarantee upon the form supplied by the Bank for the sum of Seventy-Five Thousand Dollars ($75,000.00), such guarantee to cover all of the indebtedness of each and all of the Colonies of the Association to the Molsons Bank; and that this Resolution be the consent of the majority of the Members of the Association to the Board of Managers for the signing and delivering of the said Letter of Guarantee to the said Bank.[214]

At the time of the 1925 Molson Bank merger with the Bank of Montreal, all communities were still indebted to the Molson Bank.[215]

## Trustee Acquisitions

After March 24, 1921, the individual communities, through their trustees, finalized the acquisition of certain properties and made further land purchases, as described below.

---

212 Iberville's Lots 9 and 10 in Baie St. Paul were not included, since they were already mortgaged to Excelsior Life.
213 *Untitled Milltown Colony Ledger*, 20–21. In a March 31, 1925 statement given to the Bank of Montreal, the communities reported their December 31, 1924 Great-West Life mortgage obligations: Barickman: $35,100 and $9,900, Blumengart: $28,00, Bon Homme: $32,400, Huron: $37,589, Iberville: $26,100, James Valley: $15,895, Maxwell: $51,624, Milltown: $9,160, and Rosedale: $32,800.
214 "In the matter of a Letter of Guarantee given by Hutterian Brethren Church to The Molsons Bank...," Resolution, May 22, 1923. Courtesy of Tony Waldner.
215 *Untitled Milltown Colony Ledger*, 20–21. Courtesy of Tony Waldner.

## Acquisition A

On December 15, 1919, the "holding committee" had registered Caveat 16807 on 240 acres,[216] and after the other land transfers to the communities, Caveat 8120 was registered August 6, 1921, on this same property by the Bon Homme trustees, Joseph Michael Waldner, Jacob Waldner, and Jacob Wurz. On August 24, 1922, they finalized the purchase from Portage la Prairie merchant Thomas Millar for $6,000 clear of encumbrances.[217] (See Purchase 37.)

## Acquisition B

The March 13, 1919 Murdoch McKinnon agreement for sale was assigned by the "holding committee" on June 23, 1921, to the Bon Homme trustees for $1, subject to Mortgage 79612. On June 23, 1921, the latter registered Caveat 18119, but actual transfer of the property by his executor, John Henry Chasely, to the trustees only took place on June 10, 1926, after the death of Murdoch McKinnon.[218] Mortgage 79612 was discharged in conjunction with this transfer. (See Purchase 17.)

## Acquisition C

On January 10, 1923, the Bon Homme trustees purchased the remaining one acre of NW 25-10-4 from Isabella Birse for $100.[219]

## Acquisition D

The September 13, 1918 purchase agreement (S ½ and S ½ N ½ 14-10-3) with August Larson was assigned on June 23, 1921, by the "holding committee" to the James Valley trustees David Hofer Jr., Peter Hofer, and David Hofer. They again registered Caveat 18121 against the property. Extensions of the repayment terms were agreed to by Larson (who had by

---

216  SW and S ½ NW 24-10-4.
217  Transfer 40480: "The South West Quarter and the South Half of the North West Quarter of Section Twenty-Four in Township Ten and Range Four West of the Principal Meridian in Manitoba."
218  Transfer 45548: "In the Province of Manitoba and being the North West Quarter of Section Twenty-Five in Township Ten and Range Four, West of the Principal Meridian. Excepting thereout the most Westerly Three chains and Sixteen links in perpendicular width of the most Northerly Three chains and Sixteen links in perpendicular depth thereof and also excepting all special reservations as reserved in the Grant from the Crown."
219  Deed 106626: "All that portion of the North West Quarter of Section Twenty-five (25) in Township Ten (10) and Range Four (4) West of the Principal Meridian in Manitoba, the said portion consisting of the most Northerly Three Chains and Sixteen Links (3.16) in depth of the most Westerly Three Chains and Sixteen links (3.16) in width of said Quarter Section."

now, in 1932, relocated to California) five more times: in January 1924, November 1926, November 1932, August 1934, and again in April 1935.[220] The actual transfer of the property only took place on January 17, 1950.[221] (See Purchase 6.)

## Acquisition E

On July 2, 1921, the James Valley trustees purchased 240 acres (SE and E ½ SW 15-10-3) from St. Eustache farmer Avila Lavoie, for $6,240, subject to his $4,500 mortgage 33106 from Lavina Chenier et al. Lavoie also took back a $755 mortgage (38315) as partial payment from the trustees.[222]

## Acquisition F

On April 24, 1929, the James Valley trustees registered Caveat 22902 on the N ½ 26-10-3. This 320-acre property had been owned by Fred McCartney in 1918 but was not purchased by the "holding committee" at that time. In April 1923, McCartney deeded this parcel, as well as all his other Manitoba lands, to his brother, Henry Clay McCartney, for a nominal $1.[223] In 1927, Alvin Solberg[224] of Minneapolis was involved in Henry McCartney's sale of these 320 acres, which subsequently changed hands several times until acquired in December 1928 by Aimé Bénard's son, Leon. On January 19, 1935, it was purchased by James Valley for $8,000 from Leon Bénard by the three trustees who mortgaged (53668) it for $2,178 to the Toronto General Trusts Corporation.[225]

---

220 Agreements, November 24, 1932 and April 6, 1935, courtesy of John Hofer.
221 Transfer 71732: "In the Province of Manitoba and being the South Half and the South Half of the North Half of Section Fourteen (14) in Township Ten (10) in Range Three (3) West of the Principal Meridian in said Province."
222 Transfer 38314: "The South East Quarter and the East Half of the South West Quarter both of Section Fifteen (15) in Township Ten (10) and Range Three (3) West of the principal Meridian in Manitoba excepting thereout all that portion thereof taken for Drainage purposes as the same is shown on a Plan thereof registered in the Portage la Prairie Land Titles Office as No. 337."
223 For additional details, see Appendix 5, "The Untold Story: Milltown, South Dakota, to Blumengart, Manitoba."
224 Although the 1927 sale was not to Hutterites, Alvin Solberg's contacts with and work for the Hutterite community may be more extensive and may have continued much later. During July and August 1932, Rosedale paid him an unexplained total of $355 "on his account." *Rosedale Income and Expense Ledger*, 112, 114, 116, 120, 122, 124, and 128. Courtesy of Tony Waldner.
225 Transfer 53667: "The North Half of Section Twenty six (26) in Township Ten (10) and Range Three (3) West of the Principal Meridian in Manitoba."

## Acquisition G

In August 1921, Paul Gross, Jacob Hofer, and John Hofer, on behalf of Iberville had registered Caveat 18122 on S ½ NW 36-11-3, and on January 28, 1922, they purchased these 80 acres from La Corporation Archiépiscopale Catholique Romaine de Saint-Boniface for $2,000, free of encumbrances.[226]

## Acquisition H

In August 1921, the Iberville trustees had also registered Caveat 106599 on NE 19 and N ½ 20-11-2, which were owned by farmers John Handeen and Frank Handeen from Montevideo, Minnesota. An agreement to purchase over a period of time will have been signed and the payments will have been made.[227] Since trustee Paul Gross had died earlier in the year, on November 23, 1929, these 480 acres were transferred to Jacob Hofer and John Hofer for $17,280, free of encumbrances.[228]

## Acquisition I

An already convoluted series of transactions continued to unfold when, on August 20, 1919, Aimé Bénard agreed to purchase the E ½ and E ½ W ½ 17-11-2 from Mary Kelly (wife of grain merchant Andrew Kelly) and real estate agent James Wolfe of Winnipeg, for the sum of $21,600. Bénard's agreement was, however, subject to a lease of the property held by George Crepeau, and therefore the latter became a signatory to the document as well. Bénard would be charged 6% interest and was to pay $7,500 principal on November 1, 1919, and $1,000 annually on November 1, 1920 through 1922, with the remainder due in full on November 1, 1923. On September 6, 1921, Bénard and cosignatory Crepeau agreed to resell the property to Paul Gross, Jacob Hofer, and John Hofer of Iberville for $1 cash and the balance of $21,599 at 8% interest, to be repaid by annually delivering one-half the crop therefrom to the elevator in the name of the

---

226 Transfer 39614: "The South Half of the North West Quarter of Section Thirty-six in Township Eleven and Range Three West of the Principal Meridian in Manitoba containing Eighty Acres more or less."

227 It was recorded in March 1925 that the Handeens were still owed $12,280, of which $5,100 was by Iberville and $7,180 by Rosedale. *Untitled Milltown Ledger*, 20–21.

228 Transfer 614720: "In the Province of Manitoba and being composed of: The North East Quarter of Section Nineteen (19) and the North Half of Section Twenty (20) in Township Eleven (11) and Range Two (2) West of the first Meridian according to a Plan of same filed in the Winnipeg Land Titles Office as No. 2628 excepting out of the said North East Quarter of Section Nineteen and the West Half of the North West Quarter of said Section Twenty all that portion taken for the purposes of a Public Drain as shown coloured pink on a Plan of same filed in the Winnipeg Land Titles Office as No. 1308."

vendors.[229] Bénard stood to gain 2% interest on the principal without any cash outlay, since the Hutterites would essentially be making his payments to Kelly and Wolfe. The wording of the agreement reflected this understanding, and provision was also made for the extension of the repayment period beyond 1923.

Bénard and Crepeau did not have outright actual ownership or title to any of this property, and on February 24, 1922, the Iberville trustees (P. Gross et al.) registered a caveat[230] on the NE and E ½ NW portion of the section, which had a certificate of title. On May 14, 1925, Bénard and Crepeau acknowledged receipt of the $21,600, and gave to the trustees a quitclaim deed[231] for the unpatented SE and E ½ SW 17-11-2, although this was not filed at Land Titles at the time. James Wolfe appears not to have had any apparent claim to the property, since this SE and E ½ SW 17-11-2 was deeded by the Thomas Robertson Estate to Mary Kelly alone on November 19, 1925, for $3,600. On December 4, 1925, she deeded it to Anderson Fanset for $4,348, who re-deeded it to the Iberville trustees for $9,000 on December 23, 1926.[232]

Similarly, Mary Kelly had herself only acquired the NE and E ½ NW 17-11-2 from James Griffin for $6,480 on July 20, 1920, and then transferred it to Anderson Fanset for $4,348 on December 4, 1925. This was the title on which the P. Gross et al. caveat had been registered, as well as Caveat 104837 filed by Aimé Bénard in March 1921. On December 22, 1926, Anderson Fanset transferred the property to Iberville trustees Paul Gross, Jacob Hofer, and John Hofer for $9,000.[233]

These Iberville purchases appear to have been financed through the Aimé Bénard Agreement for Sale (171176), as evidenced by Caveat 108621 and the till now unregistered quitclaim deed which was subsequently filed at Land Titles on April 1, 1927.[234] Bénard's actual profit is obscured due to the deeds and title transfers for varying sums.

---

229 Agreement for Sale 171176.
230 Caveat 108621.
231 RPA 34375.
232 Deed 187803: "In the Province of Manitoba being composed of the South East Quarter and the East Half of the South West Quarter of Section Seventeen (17) in Township Eleven (11) and Range Two (2) West of the Principal Meridian in said Province."
233 Transfer 557194: "In the Province of Manitoba and being composed of the North East Quarter and the East Half of the North West Quarter of Section Seventeen (17) in township Eleven (11) and Range Two (2) West of the Principal Meridian in said Province."
234 In March 1925, Iberville recorded a debt of $19,800 to Aimé Bénard, but their total indebtedness appears that amount less in March 1927. *Untitled Milltown Ledger*, 20–21, 26–27.

## Acquisition J

In 1922, John Hofer, David Hofer Sr., and Jacob Hofer, on behalf of Milltown, purchased the southern Manitoba Mennonite village of Blumengart, whose inhabitants were emigrating to Mexico. They acquired 3,600 acres including the village buildings,[235] which became a Hutterite community that retained the name Blumengart. Milltown's South Dakota lands east of the James River (2,174 acres) had remained unsold during the duration of the Order in Council that had prevented a minority of its members from emigrating to Canada.

Since funds needed to purchase from the Mennonites were still invested in those unsold South Dakota lands, a plan was devised whereby Winnipeg lawyer Ernest Fletcher would broker a deal. The Hutterische Bruder-Gemeinde would convey Milltown's 2,174 acres in South Dakota to Fletcher in exchange for Fletcher transferring to the Hofers clear title to the Blumengart, Manitoba, lands. A July 12, 1922 resolution authorized the South Dakota sale to Fletcher, and the conveyance to him was signed October 10, 1922. But without a buyer for the South Dakota lands and payment now due to the Mennonites for the Blumengart lands, Fletcher mortgaged the South Dakota lands for $60,000 to the Connecticut General Life Insurance Company and applied the funds towards the Blumengart purchase. He then financed the remainder of the purchase price via a mortgage of $31,141 in favour of the Blumengart villagers on the lands which they had already transferred to him. He then re-transferred said lands, now encumbered by the $31,141 mortgage, to John Hofer, David Hofer Sr., and Jacob Hofer.[236]

---

235 The church building in Blumengart belonged to the Reinlaender Mennoniten Gemeinde and was purchased by Hutterites from them separately, price unknown, but a cheque of $495 was received by them in April 1923.

236 Transfer 37969: "The South half of Section Twenty-eight (28) South-West quarter of Section Twenty-seven (27) South half of Section Twenty (20) All of Section Twenty-one (21) North half and South West quarter of Section Twenty-two (22) All of Section Fifteen (15) All of Section Sixteen (16) The North East quarter of Section Seventeen (17) The East half of the East half and the East half of the West half of the North West quarter of Section Seventeen (17) and the North half and the North half of the South half of the South West quarter of Section Seventeen (17) all in Township Two and Range Three West of the Principal Meridian in Manitoba [excepting out of the North West quarter of Section Fifteen all Mines and Minerals and the Right to work the same as reserved in the original Grant from the Crown and excepting out of the South West quarter of Section 27 the most Easterly forty (40) yards in width of the most Westerly two hundred and seventy (270) yards in width of the most Northerly eighty (80) yards in depth thereof]." The Land Titles Office destroyed the originals and the microfilm is unclear; the latter portion has been reconstructed using additional sources.

Undated *Altona Echo* photo, "Hutterian Colony, Blumengart," looking north in the North West corner of NW 15-2-3W. A row of former Mennonite village homes to the left and the former Mennonite Church, used as a kitchen here, to the right. [Source: Altona and District Heritage Research Centre, Altona, MB. Courtesy of Dave Harms.]

To further protect their interests, Fletcher gave to the Hofers his personal promissory note of $31,141, due March 31, 1923, and a mortgage for the same amount registered on the South Dakota lands now recorded in his name. To pay an unidentified commission he had also mortgaged those same lands for $3,000 to Northrup & Edmison of Sioux Falls. On March 5, 1923, Fletcher deeded those 2,174 acres to Oakes, North Dakota banker Fred D. McCartney, as payment for which McCartney agreed to pay all three mortgages: $60,000 due in full in 1932 plus annual interest payments; $3,000 repayable over ten years plus annual interest; and the $31,141 to the Hofers which was due in full within weeks, on March 31, 1923. In addition, McCartney was to transfer 320 acres in Ward County, North Dakota, to Fletcher. McCartney defaulted on the March 31 payment and foreclosure action was immediately initiated under the Fletcher mortgage in the Circuit Court of Hutchinson County, South Dakota. Ernest Fletcher, his wife Lenore, and Fred McCartney were named in case 2398, which resulted in a sheriff's sale of the 2,174 acres on December 1, 1923, at which the Hofers bid $33,434. A sheriff's certificate of sale was issued to them which, on November 14, 1924, they were able to assign to the Minneapolis Trust Company in exchange for a payment to themselves of $32,500.[237] This sum was sufficient to cover the $31,141 which had been owing at the time on the Fletcher mortgage of the Blumengart lands (but which the Hofers had already on May 31, 1923, repaid to the villagers with proceeds from a $33,000 mortgage obtained by them from Great-West Life.) The documentation clearly indicates that Ernest Fletcher was working in cooperation with the Milltown Hutterites in both Manitoba

---

237 *Hutchinson County Register of Deeds*, Book AN, 111–114, 142–143, 149, 303, 323–324; Book 77, 285, 287, 289; Book 76, 212; Book M7, 634; Book 52, 277–278; Book M8, 125. First Judicial Circuit Court for Hutchinson County, Case No. 2318.

and South Dakota and that as their attorney, Alexander Adams was involved as well. Although the Hutterites had recovered the amounts due to them, there were numerous subsequent transactions involving the South Dakota lands and the Fletcher mortgages thereon and further involvement of Fred McCartney through his partnership in the Marshall McCartney Company.[238]

## Acquisition K

On October 6, 1924, Joseph Waldner, Michael Waldner, and John Waldner, on behalf of Huron, arranged a lease with option-to-purchase for 2,660 acres south of Manitou, Manitoba (lease 107168). Since 1912, this property had been owned by Canadian Senator William Sharpe,[239] who in 1920 deeded it to Heinrich M. Klassen of Herbert, Saskatchewan. In March 1923, Klassen in turn deeded it to Thomas J. Clark, who then mortgaged it to Sharpe for $40,000. At the height of the 1919 agitation against Hutterite immigration and immediately prior to the May 2 Order in Council that barred further entry, Senator Sharpe had been accused of selling his farm to the Hutterites, something he strongly denied.[240] Now in October 1924 the farm, heavily indebted to Sharpe, was leased by Clark to the Hutterites with option to purchase. On September 17, 1925, Clark deeded the farm back to Sharpe for $1 and the Senator became the *de facto* landlord/seller to the Hutterites. The community established here was named Thorndale, but it was also referred to as Sharpe. The lease was for five years and required annual payments of $6,000, or it could be converted to a purchase for $82,500 to $90,000, depending in which year of the lease this occurred. A cash payment of $10,000 would then need to be made, and $6,000 annual payments thereafter with interest at 6%. The 2,660 acres were composed of Township 2-9: Section 34, W ½ 35, N ½ and N ½ of S ½ of Legal Subdivisions 15 and 16 of Sec 35, and Township 3-9: Section 2, SW 3, E ½ 3, SW 10, S ½ 11, SE of SE 10. The buildings, which included a very large brick house, were located on SE 2-3-9. Thorndale was not viable[241] and the community relocated south of Roseisle, Manitoba, where in 1929, David Glanzer, John Waldner, and Joseph Waldner as trustees purchased a total of 1,920 acres in Township 6 Range 7 for $49,920, which they mortgaged to the Prudential Insurance Company for $31,300. Purchased were NE 8 from William Lowery for $11,520; SE 8 and all of Section 5, also from William Lowery, for $19,200; N ½ 6 from Alexander Kerr for $8,000; N ½ SE 6 from William Bagnall for $2,400;

---

238  This is a brief synopsis. For further significant details, see Appendix 5.
239  Sharpe was appointed to the Senate in 1916.
240  *Winnipeg Free Press*, April 21, 1919, 5 and April 14, 1919, 3.
241  This happened despite the community having increased their cultivated acreage to 3,040 by January 1, 1928. *Untitled Milltown Ledger*, 46.

S ½ SE 6 from Earl McPhail for $2,400; SW 6 from the Soldier Settlement Board of Canada for $4,400; and W ½ 8 from the Hudson's Bay Company for $2,000. In addition, they were assessed property taxes on W ½ 9-6-7, which they may have rented. This was initially also referred to as Thorndale, but subsequently became Roseisle.[242]

## Acquisition L

On March 26, 1926, Joseph Hofer, John Hofer Sr., and John Hofer Jr., on behalf of Maxwell, purchased 25 acres (Fractional NE 16-11-2) from Anna Harvey of Winnipeg for $900, free of encumbrances.[243]

## Acquisition M

On December 15, 1924, Sir James Aikins,[244] Lieutenant Governor of Manitoba, on behalf of Rosedale, enquired of the Department of the Interior as to the availability of the westerly 3 chains and 61 links of Lot 20 in Baie St. Paul, which was presently not being cultivated.[245] Rosedale already owned the balance of this lot, and they were subsequently able to purchase from the department these 48.65 acres for $20 per acre, with the total $973 payable in four equal annual instalments plus 6% interest. On July 30, 1927, patent to the property was issued in the names of Zacharias Hofer, Joseph Maendel, and John Maendel.[246]

---

242 "Notice of application for incorporation of Thorndale Hutterian Mutual Corporation," *Winnipeg Free Press*, February 23, 1931, 14. "An Act to Incorporate the Roseisle Hutterian Mutual Corporation," *Statutes of Manitoba* 1931, Legislative Library.
243 Transfer 539329: "In the Province of Manitoba and being all that portion of the Fractional North East Quarter of Section Sixteen (16) in the Eleventh (11th) township and Second (2nd) Range West of the Principal Meridian in Manitoba which lies to the East of a Line drawn parallel to and Twenty (20) Chains and Forty-five (45) Links perpendicularly distant Easterly from the Western limit of the said Quarter Section; Containing Twenty-five and Sixty seven one-hundredths (25.67) Acres more or less."
244 Alexander Adams to W.W. Cory, May 2, 1925 (Archives of Manitoba, GR 2671, Parish Land Files, M1009, Parish of Baie St. Paul-Lots 1 to 25). Sir James was a land neighbour of the Hutterian Brethren.
245 Sir James Aikins to W.W. Cory, December 15, 1924 (Archives of Manitoba, GR 2671, Parish Land Files, M1009, Parish of Baie St. Paul-Lots 1 to 25.) Sir James writes, "I know something about the Rosedale Colony of Hutterites and am convinced that they are good farmers and by their cultivation would improve this part of the lot...."
246 The patent was registered in the Land Titles Office on April 8, 1932, as 116104. Application under the RPA was made the same day with instruction to issue a certificate of title in the name of the Rosedale Hutterian Mutual Corporation. However, the title was only issued in 1934 and, according to the wording of the patent, it was in the name of the three trustees. This particular parcel was therefore not included in the 1931 incorporation document.

There were only minor changes in ownership subsequent to the foregoing land acquisitions (A through M). As a result of the 1919 Order in Council barring entry, many members had remained at the unsold Bon Homme Community in South Dakota, and perhaps for this reason, in September 1922 Bon Homme in Manitoba sold 240 acres for $4,800 to Napoleon Girard. The transfer was signed by Joseph M. Waldner, Jacob Waldner, and Jacob Wurz, in whose names the Certificate of Title had been registered after March 24, 1921.[247]

It should also be noted that their purchased properties were not necessarily the only lands cultivated by the Hutterites. For example, as recorded by James Valley, in addition to the lands purchased from Fred McCartney, in 1919 they rented land from him on a one-third share basis. His share of the 4,700-bushel wheat yield that year was 1,566 bushels. In 1925, McCartney's share was 736 bushels. Other lands share-cropped that same year were those of the Emmert Foundation Land Company, to which 1,000 bushels were due, and to Anton Bischoff, 380 bushels. The Union Rock Land Company was owed 475 bushels of barley.[248] In 1927 Maxwell Community paid Aimé Bénard $242 as his share of oats, G. Leslie $171 as his share of barley, and $140 was paid to Bénard and Crepeau for pasture rent.[249] Other communities may have similarly rented as well.

As already mentioned, the Schmiedeleut Hutterites had purchased only 9,240 acres of the total 11,268 acres which Joseph Hackney had mortgaged to National Trust as security for his $230,000 bond issue. Hackney's astounding profit on their quick resale makes his subsequent dealings even more objectionable. Although, as recorded, $197,453 was the agreed upon Hutterite portion of the mortgage, the reality was that they, and any other purchaser of Hackney's lands, remained responsible for the whole unless released by National Trust. The terms of the National Trust mortgage required principal to be repaid proportional to the appraised value of any security to be released. Already prior to his Manitoba sale to the Hutterites Hackney had resold his mortgaged 800 acres in Loreburn Municipality, Saskatchewan, in January 1918 to Arthur Hitchcock and James Thomson of Moose Jaw.[250] These lands initially remained encumbered by that mortgage, but in December 1921 a partial discharge thereof was registered which affected only the W ½ 1-26-5. Hitchcock and Thomson would have been required to pay $3,591 for the release of this parcel, which they resold

---

247 Transfer 40481: "NW 12-10-3, S ½ SW 13-10-3."
248 *"Ausgaben* [Expenses]," *James Valley Untitled Ledger*, 1925, 87, 92–93. Courtesy of Patrick Murphy.
249 *Maxwell Ledger (1922–72)*, 76–77, 80. Courtesy of Ian Kleinsasser.
250 W ½ 1-26-5, E ½ 28-26-5, SW 28-26-5, W 3rd Meridian.

a year later.[251] They subsequently retained title to those lands in 28-26-5 W 3rd which remained encumbered by the mortgage.

Manitoba lands not purchased by the Hutterites included 80 non-contiguous acres (E ½ NE 28-11-3), which Hackney sold in 1921 to Wilfred Moreau for $2,400. Although they had been included in the mortgage, it has not been ascertained whether any payment on principal was made when they were released in March by National Trust. Baie St. Paul Lots 130 and 131, totalling 190 acres, were north of the Assiniboine River and further west. The property taxes were billed to Angus Smith, who resided on the property, and not to the owner, Joseph Hackney, in St. Paul. The non-payment of those taxes resulted in the transmission of the two lots to the Municipality of St. François Xavier, which nullified Hackney's National Trust mortgage thereon. The municipality then transferred the lots to Adjutor Picard in 1925. No payment was made on the mortgage principal.

Twelve miles to the south was the 958-acre Sanford Farm, which had been purchased for $24,000 in April 1917 by Joseph Hackney's wife, Jennie Hackney.[252] In August that same year, she transferred the farm to Joseph and he mortgaged it to National Trust, together with his other properties. Two months later, on October 13, he signed a transfer of the property back to Jenny, but this was not registered until March 1920, when it was to be resold. Thereby, Jenny became the seller of the farm that same month to Adolph Fast, from whom she took back a mortgage of $34,812 in favour of herself. This was subsequently transferred by her as mortgagee to Kydippe Russel;[253] this may have coincided with a request by Joseph Hackney that the National Trust release its mortgage on the Sanford Farm.[254] The farm had been appraised at $47,909, and accordingly should only have been released by them for a payment of $20,187. However, in June 1924, at the request of Joseph Hackney, National Trust approved the release for the much lesser sum of $9,200. Adolph Fast had defaulted on his mortgage payments to Russel, and by a final order of foreclosure on September 12, 1924, the property was transmitted to Kydippe Russel, but now totally free of the National Trust mortgage. How much the Hackneys gained financially on the Sanford Farm transactions is unknown.

---

251 The per-acre value of the 320 acres was $26.63, totalling $8,522, which was divided by the total Associated Mortgage Investors valuation of $545,825 and then multiplied by the mortgage principal of $230,000, which yields $3,591.
252 E ½ NE 34-7-1, NW 35-7-1, N ½ NE 2-8-1, W ½ 2-8-1, S ½ 3-8-1.
253 Kydippe Russell was the wife of Edward Russell, a Winnipeg builder. Her maiden name was Roupas.
254 Joseph Kleinsasser to C.J. Macleod, undated response. Courtesy of Ian Kleinsasser. This information appears in pencil, undated and unsigned, on the reverse of an April 11, 1927 letter from Macleod to Kleinsasser. The handwriting appears to match Kleinsasser's.

Besides the Hackney lands purchased by the "holding committee," the above two Manitoba properties, totalling 1,148 acres, were also collateral for the mortgage; as noted, they should only have been released by the National Trust subsequent to a proportional payment. Such failure to do so by Hackney meant that when making their mortgage payments, the Hutterites were making payments for lands they had not purchased. As they prepared to repay their portion of the remaining mortgage balance due January 1, 1927, the Hutterites were aware that Joseph Hackney had not fulfilled his obligations. Already in February 1925, they had sent their lawyer, Alexander Adams, to St. Paul to "investigate Hackney," and Adams' recommendation, which he communicated to them more than once, was to sue Hackney.[255]

In Saskatchewan, Arthur Hitchcock and James Thomson, despite paying National Trust $5,386 to clear their remaining unsold lands in 28-26-5 west of the third meridian, were in the same situation as the Hutterites, since none of the mortgaged lands could be cleared without payment of the whole. There remained an additional $13,369[256] to be paid on principal in order to obtain a discharge of the National Trust mortgage on all of their lands.

The Hutterites stated that they had overpaid, because of the Baie St. Paul lots and the Sanford Farm, an amount they calculated to be $18,029.[257] This was composed of $10,988 principal on the Sanford Farm and $2,381 on Lots 130 and 131, plus interest, premiums, bank fees, lawyers' expenses, etc. This sum was reduced to $17,368 after Hitchcock and Thomson paid an additional $661 as their proportional share of this overpayment. The National Trust mortgage was finally discharged in Manitoba on January 5, 1927, and in Saskatchewan on January 6.

For this unjust additional payment of $17,368, the Hutterites held Joseph Hackney responsible. As well, his lawyer, Alexander Adams (Hackney's former lawyer, but now theirs), the Tupper law firm, and the current owner of the Sanford Farm were also considered liable.[258] Unwilling to commence legal action and with their requests for compensation from Hackney unmet (they would have accepted a promissory note from him),[259]

---

255 Ibid., and "Hutterian Brethren Expense Records on Lots 130 and 131 and Sanford Farm from July 1, 1923 to January 5, 1927." Courtesy of Ian Kleinsasser.
256 This was composed of $2,381 owing for Lots 130 and 131, and $10,988 still owing for the Sanford Farm after Hackney's reduced $9,200 payment.
257 "Hutterian Brethren Expenses on Lots 130 and 131...." Calculation records on Hutterische Bruder-Gemeinde stationery with the South Dakota address crossed off and Benard, MB, substituted.
258 Hudson, Ormond, Spice & Symington to Joseph Kleinsasser, January 27, 1927. Courtesy of Ian Kleinsasser. *Untitled Milltown Colony Ledger*, 76, refers to them having had to pay because of Adams' negligence and fraud.
259 Hudson, Ormond, Spice & Symington to Joseph Hackney, February 21, 1927.

the Hutterites settled for a $6,769 mortgage from Kydippe Russel.[260] It appears that Russel either did not wish to risk a lawsuit or else recognized that she had gained financially through the injustice of Hackney's manipulations. She agreed to $5,861 plus interest accrued since June 1924, for a total of $6,769. This mortgage, payable to Joseph Waldner and Joseph Glanzer,[261] was registered March 17, 1927, and on April 8 they transferred it to Great-West Life. The net sum[262] thereby recovered was divided up, with Milltown receiving $3,171, Bon Homme $2,995, and Huron $208. All these events led to a parting of the ways between certain Hutterite communities and Alexander Adams of the Tupper law firm.[263] Joseph Hackney, however, went on with other land deals that subsequently saw him acting as an agent for Canadian Doukhobors who were considering emigration to Mexico.[264]

Just prior to the National Trust mortgage having been paid out, Bon Homme had, in December 1926, transferred roughly 480 acres of their mortgage-encumbered lands to Huron for a nominal $1.[265] The precise

---

Courtesy of Ian Kleinsasser. In this letter it is acknowledged that "the Hutterites do not wish to press you unduly for payment at the present time as they understand that you are not as well off financially as you were a few years ago." Such a contention of adversity by Hackney appears disingenuous since, in the *Minneapolis Morning Tribune* of July 23, 1922, he had claimed combined net assets of $1,350,000 for himself and Arden Farms. The reality of Hackney's Manitoba transactions refutes a statement in a May 6, 1920 *Minneapolis Morning Tribune* ad for his personal bonds: "MORAL RISK. Mr Hackney is an exceptionally desirable moral risk. He is one of Minnesota's best known and most successful breeders of pure-bred Holstein cattle. He has also made an enviable success as farmer and business man and has acquired an estate well over one million dollars. He has been twice State Senator, each time serving the people of Minnesota most capably. The ability he has shown in business, in farming, and in the legislature explains the wonderful success of Arden Farms."

260 Hudson, Ormond, Spice & Symington to Joseph Hackney, February 21, 1927; Hudson, Ormond, Spice & Symington to Joseph Kleinsasser, February 26, 1927. Both courtesy of Ian Kleinsasser.
261 Joseph Waldner is recorded as mortgagee on the Land Titles Office registration, but both he and Joseph Glanzer are so named in a letter from C.J. Macleod to Joseph Kleinsasser, February 26, 1927. Courtesy of Ian Kleinsasser.
262 Although the mortgage principal was $6,769, they recorded receiving $6,374 from Great-West Life. *Untitled Milltown Colony Ledger*, 40.
263 C.J. Macleod to Joseph Kleinsasser, March 29, 1927. Courtesy of Ian Kleinsasser. Rosedale and Iberville communities instructed Alexander Adams to retain their documents on file when at least Milltown's documents, and likely Bon Homme's and Huron's, had been transferred to the firm of Hudson, Ormond, Spice & Symington.
264 When that emigration failed to materialize, Hackney claimed that they still owed him a dollar per acre commission. He sued for $750,000 in a Yorkton, Saskatchewan, court but lost the case. *The Winnipeg Tribune*, November 21, 1932; March 7, 1938; March 9, 1938. *The Montreal Gazette*, June 28, 1938, 1.
265 Transfer 46121: "The N ½ and N ½ of S ½ 13-11-4 less portion of W ½ lying north of RR."

principal balance that had remained to be paid on January 1, 1927, by the Hutterites on the mortgage is unknown,[266] but it was collectively refinanced by a December 30, 1926 mortgage of $165,000 from Great-West Life (Mortgage 46143)[267] made by John Hofer et al. Remortgaged were the same Milltown, Bon Homme, and certain Huron properties previously still mortgaged to National Trust.

Consistent with the 1921 Articles of Association, the individual communities—by signatures of all community members—had designated proxies to attend a meeting and vote for a resolution authorizing a "Loan for $165,000 to be made by the Hutterian Brethren Church in the Province of Manitoba with the Great-West Life Assurance Company, of Winnipeg."[268] Despite security for this loan being a mortgage registered exclusively on lands belonging to the three communities, and they being the apparent beneficiaries, a collective responsibility for repayment is obvious.[269] The interrelationship between Milltown and Blumengart communities was evidenced the following year when Blumengart took over $40,900 of Milltown's Great-West Life mortgage obligation via an internal ledger entry.[270]

Barickman also refinanced a portion of its debt at this time. On January 20, 1927, a Samuel Hofer et al. mortgage of $45,000 from Great-West Life[271] discharged the John Barickman mortgages owed to Great-West Life and to Mortgage Investors Agency. The original $20,000 John Flanders mortgage, owed to Isadore Zastre on St. François Xavier River Lots 76 through 79, was not included in the refinancing and accordingly remained in effect.

The worldwide Great Depression of the early 1930s affected Canada and the Hutterite communities as well. Wheat prices reached new lows and land values dropped; this affected the Hutterites' debt-servicing ability and eroded the equity in their land. However, internal population growth

---

266 Reported as having been owed December 31, 1924, on the National Trust mortgage was $78,759 by Milltown, $66,875 by Bon Homme, and only $6,000 by Huron. *Untitled Milltown Ledger*, 20–21.
267 Although it appears to have been much greater, the balance now remaining on the National Trust mortgage could have been $128,461, provided that payments for known releases had been $61,539, and provided that the specified $40,000 principal payment composed of $5,000 annually had been made.
268 The available James Valley, Milltown, and Huron proxies. Courtesy of Tony Waldner.
269 A shared commitment is indicated by the wording "Hutterian Brethren Church," and the fact that, as a non-beneficiary whose lands were not involved, James Valley still approved the making of the mortgage.
270 *Untitled Milltown Ledger*, 43, 47, 76. There was a corresponding reduction in Milltown's recorded Great-West Life obligation between 1927 and 1928.
271 Mortgage 554704.

continued, and the need to establish new communities remained an issue that would shortly need to be addressed.[272]

In April 1931, the ten existing Hutterite communities—Barickman, Blumengart, Bon Homme, Huron, Iberville, James Valley, Maxwell, Milltown, Rosedale, and Roseisle—incorporated.[273] Individual memorandums of agreement dated February 27, 1931, signed by all members of each community, acknowledged the impending incorporation and that all real and personal property then held in trust for that particular community would become the property of the newly incorporated entities. Attached was another memorandum of agreement with the same date, which stated that "all of the aforesaid colonies are jointly and severally indebted to certain persons, firms, and corporations," and that upon dissolution of the former association these debts would need to be "apportioned." Attached to this was a list of the lands owned by the various communities.[274]

In subsequent years, transfers from their former trustees produced new certificates of title issued in their respective names, each as a "Hutterian Mutual Corporation." Ernest Fletcher's law firm documented the incorporations.[275] The later apportioning of the collective community debt, then resulted in certain communities being considered creditors or debtors of the others. Perhaps as part of this process, Bon Homme signed a transfer of 320 acres to James Valley for $1 in 1931, but this was only registered in March 1934.[276] In January 1932, Bon Homme, South Dakota, forwarded US$21,500 (C$26,095), of which $20,505 was used to variably reduce the individual community obligations on the collective Great-West mortgages.[277] That same month all ten corporations, by signatures of presidents and secretaries and applications of corporate seals, signed a $45,290 "On Demand 7% Bank of Montreal Promissory Note."[278] In April 1932, nine corporations also countersigned a $38,536 promissory note at 7%, which sum Roseisle owed to Peter Anderson[279] of the North West Commission

---

272 See Table 2: January 1, 1930, statistics recorded in *Untitled Milltown Ledger*, 58.
273 *Statutes of Manitoba 1931*, Manitoba Legislative Library. Bon Homme is spelled "Bonhomme" in this document.
274 "Milltown Colony of Hutterian Brethren Memorandum of Agreement" and "Memorandum of Agreement," February 27, 1931; also for Maxwell. Courtesy of Tony Waldner.
275 *Manitoba Free Press*, February 23, 1931, 14.
276 Transfer 52791: "W ½ 11-10-3."
277 *Untitled Milltown Ledger*, 72 and 90. Sums recorded as paid on behalf of the individual communities on the mortgages were as follows: Milltown, $2,529; Bon Homme, $4,171; Barickman, $3,731; Rosedale, $433; Iberville, $1,125; Huron, $3,641; Maxwell, $2,220; Blumengart, $1,939; and James Valley, $712. However, the cheque to Great-West Life was recorded as only $20,034.
278 Ibid., 73.
279 Ibid.

| POPULATION | Barickman | Bon Homme | Blumengart | Iberville | James Valley | Huron | Maxwell | Milltown | Rosedale | Thorndale |
|---|---|---|---|---|---|---|---|---|---|---|
| Adults over 60 | 2 | 3 | 2 | 4 | 5 | 5 | 8 | 3 | 6 | 2 |
| Males 15–60 | 35 | 32 | 25 | 23 | 25 | 30 | 30 | 16 | 32 | 13 |
| Females 15–60 | 31 | 32 | 27 | 22 | 23 | 32 | 38 | 23 | 32 | 20 |
| Children in School | 33 | 35 | 30 | 25 | 22 | 39 | 58 | 47 | 47 | 35 |
| Children in Kindergarten | 10 | 13 | 11 | 8 | 15 including under 2.5 | 12 | 17 | 16 | 15 | 10 |
| Children under 2.5 | 10 | 15 | 10 | 10 |  | 20 | 14 | 10 | 13 | 14 |
| Total Population | 121 | 130 | 105 | 102 | 90 | 138 | 165 | 110 | 145 | 94 |
| ACREAGE | | | | | | | | | | |
| Seeded acres 1929 (owned and rented) | 1860 | 1970 | 2000 | 2300 | 2025 | 2146 | | 2030 | 2615 | 1500 |
| Fallow acres 1929 (owned and rented) | 1000 | 460 | 740 | 980 | 600 | 936 | | 380 | 950 | |
| Total Acres | 2850 | 2430 | 2740 | 3280 | 2625 | 3082 | 3395 | 2500 | 3565 | 1500 |
| SUMMARY | | | | | | | | | | |
| Acres cultivated/Male 15–60 | 81 | 76 | 109 | 142 | 105 | 102 | 113 | 156 | 111 | 115 |

**Table 2.** January 1, 1930, statistics recorded in *Untitled Milltown Ledger*, 58.

Company.[280] Further similar transactions involving mutual guarantees may have taken place as well. Calculations for the separation of the various community mortgage amounts and the resulting actual inter-community creditor/debtor status occurred in October 1934.[281]

Responsibility for the 1921 Great-West Life $250,000 mortgages (39124 and 460738) was still being shared, with varying balances owing: Milltown, $9,679; Bon Homme, $31,828; Huron, $49,611; Iberville, $26,236; Barickman, $17,985; Rosedale, $8,598; Maxwell, $54,925; and James Valley, $17,598. Responsibility for the 1926 Great-West Life $165,000 mortgage (46143) was shared by several: Milltown, $50,174; Bon Homme, $66,841; Huron, $32,730; and Blumengart, $49,652.[282] In addition, Blumengart owed $9,000 on their 1923 Great-West Life mortgage (38637), which in 1931 the latter mortgagee had transferred to Jacob Friesen of Reinfeld.[283] Barickman reportedly now owed $53,629[284] on the 1927 Great-West Life $45,000 mortgage (554704).

During June and July of 1935, the foregoing mortgages were discharged and replaced by individual community corporation mortgages from Great-West Life at 6% interest. These were Maxwell (54013 and 676874) for $59,915, Rosedale (53993) for $53,437, Iberville (54012) for $51,183, Huron (53962) for $62,075, James Valley (54003) for $29,396, Milltown (53963) for $57,756, Bon Homme (53964) for $64,234, Blumengart (51828) for $65,629, and Barickman (676607) for $34,842.[285] However, although separation of the mortgage debt was now complete,

---

280 The North West Commission Company was incorporated in 1919 by grain merchants Peter Anderson, Hannes Lindal, and Henry Rosenblatt, and lawyer Walter Lindal. Peter Anderson was the company president and in 1924 became the principal shareholder (North West Commission Company Limited, Companies Office, corporation documents, Archives of Manitoba, 267n, CCA 0059, GR 6427 Q 24643). The Hutterite communities marketed some of their grain through the company and purchased coal, oil, flour, feed, and other supplies from them. Some of those purchases were on credit, but of more significance were the outright loans obtained by communities from the company or from Peter Anderson personally.
281 See Table 3: The inter-community creditor/debtor debt apportioning after separation of the mortgages, as recorded on inserted papers in *Untitled Milltown Ledger*, 84. Courtesy of Tim Waldner.
282 The 1934 balances recorded as owing on the Great-West Life mortgages appear rather high when compared to the original amounts. Accrued interest or certain other outstanding loans' balances may have been included in these numbers, as recorded in the *Untitled Milltown Ledger*, 84.
283 Jacob Friesen was the great-grandfather of the author of this paper. Friesen also extended personal loans to both James Valley and Blumengart communities.
284 *Untitled Milltown Ledger*, 84. This sum may have also included the Zastre mortgage balance.
285 Coinciding with repayment of the $250,000 mortgage, the collective responsibility for it ended in July 1935 when Caveats 108183 (Winnipeg Land Titles Office) and 18465 (Portage Land Titles Office) were discharged by Great-West Life.

October 1934 inter-community creditor/debtor debt apportioning after separation of the mortgages:

|  | Rosedale | Iberville | James Valley | Blumengart | Maxwell | Total |
|---|---|---|---|---|---|---|
| Milltown owes... | $1,006 | $560 | $265 | $156 | $111 | $2,098 |
| Huron owes... | $9,713 | $5,405 | $2,556 | $1,511 | $1,081 | $20,266 |
| Bon Homme owes... | $16,495 | $9,177 | $4,340 | $2,567 | $1,836 | $34,415 |
| Barickman owes... | $17,624 | $9,805 | $4,637 | $2,742 | $1,963 | $36,771 |
| Total | $44,838 | $24,947 | $11,798 | $6,976 | $4,991 | $93,550 |

December 2, 1936, recalculation to enable Milltown to owe only James Valley:

|  | Rosedale | Iberville | James Valley | Blumengart | Maxwell | Total |
|---|---|---|---|---|---|---|
| Milltown owes... | $0.00 | $0.00 | $2,098 | $0.00 | $0.00 | $2,098 |
| Huron owes... | $9,915 | $5,517 | $2,189 | $1,542 | $1,103 | $20,266 |
| Bon Homme owes... | $16,897 | $9,401 | $3,607 | $2,630 | $1,880 | $34,415 |
| Barickman owes... | $18,026 | $10,029 | $3,903 | $2,804 | $2,008 | $36,771 |
| Total | $44,838 | $24,947 | $11,797 | $6,976 | $4,991 | $93,550 |

**Table 3.** Inserted papers in *Untitled Milltown Ledger*, 84. Courtesy of Tim Waldner.

Great-West Life still required a "guarantee" that each community would reimburse them $2,500 in the event that any other community became bankrupt. This guarantee would no longer be required of the others once a community had reduced its own mortgage balance to $25,000, except for Barickman and James Valley, whose balances would first need to be reduced to $15,000.[286]

Also of interest is that Isadore Zastre[287] had died in November 1931, and the John Flanders mortgage owed to him—which had been assumed by the Hutterite purchasers—had, in December of 1931, been refinanced by a $16,000 mortgage (644548) by Barickman in favour of Zastre's executors. This was again refinanced by Barickman in January 1934 with Mortgage 664242 in favour of those same executors, Alexander Lafreniere and John Joseph Zastre. The mortgage principal appears to have been $10,400.

Because of the existing collective responsibility for certain community bank loans, non-mortgage debt redistribution also took place in October 1934. An example of this was the $45,290 Bank of Montreal loan;[288] it was specified as being owed by Huron at $21,090, Barickman $19,200, and Roseisle $5,000. This sum was now redistributed, with Huron retaining $11,690 of the debt, Barickman $3,000, and Roseisle $600, while the other communities each assumed $4,200, except for Gracevale at $600. In addition, the bank required a guarantee of $500 per community in the event of any other community's bankruptcy.[289]

Although post-incorporation-founded communities are not the subject of this research, two such Schmiedeleut communities did not survive:

1. Gracevale, also known as Teulon after the nearby town,[290] was established in 1932 by Barickman near Teulon, Manitoba, on Section 23-16-2 East and the adjacent East ½ of 22-16-2E, a total of 960 acres.[291] Titles to these properties were registered in the name of the Harris Abattoir Company (subsequent to a merger, after

---

286 *Untitled Milltown Ledger*, 84.
287 His name is recorded as Isidore Zace in Gail Morin's Métis genealogy at the Provincial Archives of Manitoba. Morin, *Metis Families, vol. 11, Sutherland-Zace* (Createspace, 2016), 317–325.
288 *Untitled Milltown Ledger*, 85. The actual loan balance was reduced to this sum after the bank cancelled approximately $5,000 thereof. Item 6, common to each 1931 incorporation document, specified that each community corporation "shall assume and be liable for all present indebtedness of the said Hutterian Brethren Church to the Bank of Montreal."
289 Ibid. See Table 4.
290 Tony Waldner advises that Gracevale was also referred to as New Barickman or Barickman Farm.
291 RM of Rockwood Assessment Rolls, Stonewall, MB. *They Came for the Future* (Teulon: Teulon and District History Book Committee, 1983), 437.

|  | Rosedale | Iberville | James Valley | Blumengart | Maxwell | Milltown | Bon Homme | Total |
|---|---|---|---|---|---|---|---|---|
| Huron owes… | $1,342 | $1,342 | $1,342 | $1,342 | $1,342 | $1,342 | $1,342 | $9,394 |
| Barrickman owes… | $2,228 | $2,228 | $2,228 | $2,228 | $2,228 | $2,228 | $2,228 | $15,596 |
| Roseisle owes… | $630 | $630 | $630 | $630 | $630 | $630 | $630 | $4,410 |

**Table 4.** The inter-community creditor/debtor debt apportioning after separation of the Bank of Montreal loan, October 1934. *Untitled Milltown Ledger*, 85.

1927 known as Canada Packers) or James Harris, James Stanley McLean, and Robert James Speers. Gracevale never owned the land and the community was liquidated by receivers W.S. Newton & Company in 1936. An auction sale, held at the farm on March 21 that year, disposed of the livestock and machinery.[292]

2. Sundale was established by Maxwell in 1932 on the large Andrew Anderson property in Alberta known as Fogelvick Farm.[293] A comprehensive agreement dated April 8, 1932, between Anderson as vendor and Joseph J. Hofer, Joseph Wipf, and John Hofer Sr. as purchasers detailed the land, buildings, farm machinery, farm inventories, and livestock purchased. Upon payment over time of $51,200, the Hutterites would acquire the farm assets, including 2,560 acres.[294] Noteworthy is that only $1 was paid to Anderson at the time of execution of the documents, and that specified annual payment amounts were based upon the dollar value of the wheat crop grown on lands that had been summer-fallowed the previous year. No doubt such arrangements were based upon the prevailing adverse financial and climatic conditions during the Great Depression. However, the reputation of Hutterites in general was a factor in Anderson's decision: "The vendor has entered into this agreement with the purchasers because of his belief in the skill and ability of the purchasers and of the Hutterian Brethren as farmers.... It is understood and agreed that the said Brethren will personally farm the said land."[295] Also signed on April 8, 1932, was a lease with option to purchase for additional lands owned by Anderson.[296] The combined agreement and lease totals were for 4,345 acres more or less. Despite Anderson's confidence in them, however, the Hutterite "skill and ability" was no match for the drought known as the Dirty Thirties,[297] and no payments on principal could be made. By mutual agreement in January 1935, the

---

292 *Stonewall Argus*, March 25, 1936; *Teulon Times*, March 25, 1936; *Winnipeg Free Press*, March 14, 1936, 2.

293 The farm was usually identified as being at Alsask, SK, since that was the Anderson family's postal address. The lands, however, were actually across the border in Alberta. According to the terms of the agreement, the Hutterite purchasers were not permitted to use the name "Fogelvick."

294 "In Township 29 Range 1 West of the 4th Meridian, all of Sections 21, 26, 27 plus E ½ of Sec 28 and North ½ of Sec 22."

295 "Agreement Sale of Land," April 8, 1932. The Anderson/Sundale documents can be found in the Glenbow Archives, Calgary, AB (file M-802-48, Magnusson, Anderson Family fonds, Series 2: Fogelvik Farms, 1911–1962).

296 "In Township 29 Range 1 West of 4th Meridian, Sec 3, SW 10, East ½ 36, Fractional West ½ 34. In Twp 30 Rg 1 W 4th, East ½ Sec 1, Fractional North ½ Sec 3."

297 Peter Tschetter, *Hutterite Life* (Trafford Publishing, 2013), 2. After the initial bumper crop of wheat, the rains stopped, and it remained the only one harvested.

sale agreement and lease were cancelled and a new lease for one year was entered into,[298] whereby Sundale would pay Anderson one-third share of the 1935 crop.[299] Thereafter Sundale ceased to exist.[300]

Unfortunately, Roseisle was also not financially viable, and its assets were liquidated by an October 1938 "winding-up order" made by the court and the real property was transferred to the Prudential Insurance Company. After its incorporation, the community had, in 1933, obtained a second mortgage of $36,600 from the Prudential Insurance Company, and by 1939 had no equity left in the land beyond the $39,299 still owing on the mortgage. The April 1932 Peter Anderson debt of $38,536 had, by October 1936, increased to $46,730, at which time it had also been redistributed. After Anderson forgave $3,730, all ten communities assumed responsibility for repayment of an equal portion of the remainder. Interest of 6% on each community's subsequent $4,300 debt was to be reduced to 5% if such community marketed its grain through the North West Commission Company.[301]

From all the known separation and redistribution data, it is obvious that despite individual community incorporation, the 1934 debt apportionment was not thereafter equivalent to total separation, in that a collective responsibility—albeit limited to a specific sum in certain cases—still existed, and the communities continued to provide aid to each other commensurate with their ability. How the inter-community creditor/debtor obligations were resolved over time has not been researched.

The Isadore Zastre mortgage obligation, which the "holding committee" had assumed with their 1920 purchase of St. François Xavier River Lots 76 through 79 from John Flanders, and then its subsequent remortgaging to the Zastre estate executors, became an issue for Barickman years later. Events suggest that during the Depression, Barickman Hutterian Mutual Corporation encountered financial difficulty and consequently two individuals on behalf of community members applied for protection under the Farmers' Creditors Arrangement Act of 1934.[302] Such protec-

---

298 The documents were prepared for January 1935 but signed on April 9.
299 Lease dated January 1935 and signed April 9, 1935 (Glenbow Archives, Calgary, AB: file M-802-48, Magnusson, Anderson Family fonds, Series 2: Fogelvik Farms, 1911–1962).
300 For additional details see Appendix 4: "The Establishment of Sundale, Alberta."
301 *Untitled Milltown Ledger*, 86. Includes details of debt to Peter Anderson, other mutual guarantees, and further reductions for prompt repayments. The per-community $4,300 remained an obligation which Roseisle Community was to repay to the other communities as possible.
302 *Winnipeg Tribune*, August 16, 1939, 1. Barickman was heavily indebted under a first mortgage, a vendor's agreement, and a chattel mortgage.

tion would have allowed Barickman to restructure its debt to a manageable level while continuing its farming operation. The community was initially successful in being allowed to make such an application, but the revelation that Barickman Colony was incorporated caused the executors of the Isadore Zastre estate to appeal to the Manitoba Court of Appeal, contending that Barickman was not a "farmer" as defined in the act. The court allowed the appeal, the result of which, in the event of payment default, could have meant foreclosure on the Zastre mortgage or action by any other creditor.[303] Barickman then appealed the Manitoba Court's judgment to the Supreme Court of Canada. Present were Justices Duff, Rinfret, Cannon, Kerwin, and Hudson. Barickman was incorporated, and among many points considered by the Justices was the wording of the preamble in the incorporation document:

> WHEREAS a religious community of farmers exists in this province under the name of Barickman Colony of Hutterian Brethren, who have associated themselves together for the purpose of promoting and engaging in the Christian religion, Christian worship and religious education and teachings according to their religious belief, and of having, holding, using, possessing and enjoying all things in common, and who are desirous that the said religious community may be incorporated.

The objects of the corporation were also noted:

- to promote, engage in and carry on the Christian religion, Christian worship and religious education and teachings, and to worship God according to the religious belief of the members of the corporation;
- to engage in, and carry on farming, stock-raising, milling, and all branches of these industries; and to manufacture and deal with the products and by-products of these industries.

The appeal was allowed in 1939, with only Justice Cannon dissenting. Barickman was considered a "farmer within the meaning of that word as used in the Farmers' Creditors Arrangement Act, 1934" and could seek protection under said act.[304] The mortgage owed to the Zastre heirs was finally discharged on July 30, 1948.

---

303 This had implications for all the communities since each of them had obligations under the known mutual guarantees required by creditors Great-West Life, Bank of Montreal, and Peter Anderson.
304 Barickman Hutterian Mutual Corporation v. Nault (Judgments of the Supreme Court of Canada), http://scc-csc.lexum.com/scc-csc/scc-csc/en/item/8536/index.do.

In the post-World War I period, the initial anti-immigrant rhetoric directed at the Hutterites rapidly changed. Already on February 7, 1922, prior to the June rescinding of the Order in Council barring entry, the Municipal Council of the RM of Cartier passed a resolution in which it referred to the Hutterites as "first class farmers" of which more were needed, and that the existing law should be changed to allow more to immigrate.[305]

Conversely, arguments had also been made that the Hutterites had "secured land located in such a manner as to interfere with the development of large sections of this locality by desirable settlers,"[306] and "that the scheme of settlement showed a deliberate effort…to freeze Canadian settlers out of their land in that territory."[307] It was also claimed that the main reason for the Hutterites' entry into Manitoba was "to enable certain land speculators to get out from under with a good profit on their transaction," and that in this there was "evidence obtainable of the complicity of men high in the public life of Canada."[308] From the documented land transactions, it is clear that the availability of these large contiguous parcels was initially due to American speculators Hackney and McCartney, and subsequently to Manitoba opportunists Aimé Bénard, John Flanders, Burley and Metcalfe, and others.

∼

Although the prospects of success seemed bleak for Schmiedeleut Hutterites in the early twentieth century, through faith and perseverance they overcame the hardships and challenges associated with a mass migration. They replaced foreign speculators Joseph Hackney and Fred McCartney with a permanent Canadian presence, but paid a steep price. They recovered ownership from the Canadian opportunists and vested it in themselves as farmers who had good reason to preserve the land for future generations. As a communal society, they eliminated the need for the land to change ownership with each succeeding generation. Their Christian communal ethic countered greed, deception, cronyism, misunderstanding, and animosity. One measure of their success is evident on a modern property ownership map, where the first nine communities to be established remain to this day. They overcame the despair expressed in Kathrina Waldner's song; Hutterites are no longer "despairing in Canada." ∼

---

305 RM of Cartier, meeting minutes, February 7, 1922.
306 *Winnipeg Free Press*, April 9, 1919, 9.
307 Ibid., April 21, 1919, 1.
308 Ibid., April 16, 1919, 1.

## APPENDIX 1
## Mennonites in Manitoba with Hutterite Roots

The following are Mennonites with known Hutterite ancestry who had emigrated prior to 1880 from Russia and were living on the West Reserve when the Prairieleut first arrived in Manitoba:

- **Isaac Miller** of Neuhorst, Manitoba; his brother, **Johann Miller** of Rosengart; and their sister, **Katharina Peters** (née Miller) of Ebenfeld. Their father, Andreas Miller, was born in 1798 to Peter Miller and Susanna Stahl in the Hutterite community at Vishenka.

- **Wilhelm Miller** of Schoendorf; and his sisters **Katharina Fehr**, previously Penner (née Miller) of Blumstein, later Blumenort; and **Susanna Neufeld**, previously Giesbrecht and Wall (née Miller), of Grossweide. Their father, Mathias Miller, was born in 1801 at Vishenka to Peter Miller and Susanna Stahl. This is the maternal Miller family ancestry of the author.

- **Peter Thiessen** of Schoenwiese. His mother, Susanna Kuhr, was born in 1811 at Radichev to Joseph Kuhr and Barbara Pullman.

- **Jacob Thiessen** of Neuhorst. His mother, Judith Knelsen, born in 1824, was the daughter of Jacob Knels, born in 1796, and Katharina Kuhr, born in 1798, both at Vishenka.

- Half-sisters **Katharina Driedger** (née Eitzen) of Gruenthal, and **Maria Unrau** (née Pankratz) of Schoenfeld. Their mother was Barbara Knels, born in 1801 to Abram Knels and Judith Wallman at Vishenka.

- Siblings **Jacob Knelsen** of Shanzenfeld, and **Anna Funk** (née Knelsen) of Shanzenfeld. Their father, Joseph Knels, was born in 1804 at Radichev to Abram Knels and Judith Wallman.

- **Abraham Knelsen** of Shanzenfeld. His parents, Jacob Knels born in 1796, and Katharina Kuhr born in 1798, were both born at Vishenka. Abraham's wife was **Susanna Wipf**, whose parents were Johann Wipf born in 1792 in the Bruderhof, and Maria Schrag born in 1792, a Mennonite who joined the Hutterites.

# APPENDIX 2
## Hutterites on First Nations and Métis Lands

Standing in stark contrast to the unrestrained greed of speculators, such as Joseph Hackney, was the original ceding of land by First Nations and subsequent sales for low prices by Métis, which enabled the later Hutterite purchases. The Schmiedeleut Hutterite entry into Manitoba first occurred fifty-one years after Canadian Confederation, and forty-eight years after Manitoba became a province. As described in this essay, the lands they acquired were from those persons registered as owners at the time of purchase. However, although the Hutterites received certificates of title guaranteed by the province under the Real Property Act, their title, derived through the earlier ownership, possession, occupation, or habitation of those same lands, is more complex.

These lands were once part of the vast area of North America inhabited by First Nations peoples that the British Crown granted to the Hudson's Bay Company (HBC) in 1669, and that was later transferred by the HBC to the Dominion of Canada. Prior to 1870, the HBC had surveyed and granted deeds for rows of lots along the Assiniboine and Red Rivers;[1] and thereafter the Dominion Land Survey divided the surrounding lands into townships of thirty-six square miles each. Registry offices were established that recorded the subsequent entries on these lands, which were part of Treaty 1, concluded with the First Nations in 1871. Soon ownership of river lots was registered, in many cases to Métis people, as well as land allotments to Métis children in portions of townships reserved for such purpose.

---

1   "Treaties with Indigenous Peoples in Canada," *Canadian Encyclopedia*, last modified September 11, 2017, https://www.thecanadianencyclopedia.ca/en/article/aboriginal-treaties.

Therefore, all the lands purchased by the Hutterites in Townships 10, 11, and 12, as well as the river lots, were first Treaty lands ceded by the First Nations; the majority had subsequently been Métis land grants as well.[2] A few examples are as follows:

1. Lot 8 of the Parish of Baie St. Paul, which the "holding committee" acquired in 1919 and which is today part of Iberville. In 1868, Paul St. Denis claimed this lot and in March 1873 he deeded the east 6 chains thereof to John Taylor. In September 1874, St. Denis deeded the west 6 chains to François Arcand. All three men were Métis. John Taylor, born in 1834, was a school teacher living in the Parish of St. François Xavier, who was first elected as a member of the Manitoba Legislative Assembly in 1871 and later served as Minister of Agriculture. François Arcand, born in 1840, was also living in St. François Xavier in 1870, but later fought in the Northwest Resistance of 1885.

2. Lot 5 of the Parish of Baie St. Paul, now part of Maxwell, was deeded in March 1873 by Pierre McKay to François St. Germain.

3. In 1877, patent to Lot 76 of the parish of St. François Xavier was issued to Jean Baptiste Bercier, and Lot 77 was issued to Gonzalve/Gonzaque Zastre, the father of Isadore Zastre. Both lots, now owned by Barickman, were included in the Zastre mortgage. Barickman also owns N ½ NW 25-10-2 and L S 2,3,6,7 of 36-10-2, the Métis grant of Jean Baptiste Roy.

4. In 1883, patent to the westerly 3 chains and 61 links of Lot 19 and the easterly 8 chains and 39 links of Lot 20 of the Parish of Baie St. Paul was issued to Antoine Desjarlais. These lots are now owned by Rosedale. As well, part of Rosedale is located on SW 31-11-2, which was the 1881 Métis children's allotment of Pierre Alphi Lesperance, after whose decease it was granted to his sole heir, Jean Lesperance.

5. A portion of James Valley is located on SE 23-10-3 and N ½ NE 14-10-3, lands that were the 1880 Métis allotment of Marie Desjarlais, wife of Baptiste Desjarlais.

6. Huron is located on NE 30-11-3, the former 1880 allotment of Julie Martin, daughter of Laurent Martin.

7. Bon Homme lands include NW 36-10-4 and W ½ NE 36-10-4, the 1880 allotment of Melanie St. Germain, daughter of François St. Germain.

---

2  Blumengart and Roseisle community lands were also Treaty 1 land, but not Métis land grants.

8. Milltown is located on SW 17-11-3, the former 1880 allotment of William Houle, son of Louis Houle. Milltown lands also include SW 9-11-3 and S ½ NW 9-11-3, the 1880 allotment of Patrice Leveille, son of Gabriel Leveille.[3]

The Hutterite community of today is no longer unaware of what preceded their ancestors' arrival in Manitoba and the details of land purchases. It is hoped that their own historical experience with injustice will guide how they now choose to respond.

---

[3] Information obtained primarily from the Archives of Manitoba, Township Plans and Plats, NR 0212; and LAC, Department of the Interior, Register of Grants to Half-Breeds [sic], Parishes of Saint-François-Xavier and Baie Saint-Paul (RG 15, vol. 1565).

## APPENDIX 3
## Alexander Adams

The Hutterites' lawyer, Alexander Adams, was born on July 6, 1887, in Winnipeg, of Scottish Presbyterian parents. In July 1916, he married Marion Whyte—the same year he began his practice of law with the firm of Tupper, McTavish & Tupper. Despite his earlier legal work for Joseph Hackney, the documentation shows Adams to have been most diligent on behalf of the Hutterites in all their land purchases. The Sanford Farm deception was attributable to Joseph Hackney alone, since it was he who requested and obtained the National Trust mortgage release for a lesser sum than was due. Nowhere is there indication that Adams was even aware of what occurred. It is a fact that in 1925, the Hutterites sent him to St. Paul to "investigate" Hackney, and his recommendation was that Hackney should be sued. This would not have been the recommendation of a person whose own failings or culpability would be revealed by such action.

Although not discussed in this essay, his efforts to secure admission to Canada of those Hutterites still in South Dakota when the Order in Council barring their entry took effect in May 1919 were noteworthy. Alexander Adams warrants sympathetic treatment when all correspondence in the Department of Immigration files at the National Archives is reviewed. His dogged persistence in seeking admission of those left behind is evident in his March 1, 1921 telegram to F.C. Blair, Secretary of Immigration:

> I am quite satisfied in my own mind that your Department has been furnished with evidence quite sufficient to warrant the admission of the small remnant of these people, and it is certainly unnecessary for me to go over all of the points we have already gone over. The one thing that is necessary is immediate action. It is simply impos-

sible to allow the matter to drag indefinitely, and I must ask you to kindly let me have a reply by telegram, stating definitely whether or not these people will be admitted.[1]

He then concludes: "In any event, I have no intention of dropping the matter, but if it is necessary to change the procedure, then I must do so at once."[2] Adams was an assertive and articulate advocate on behalf of the Hutterites.

---

1   LAC, Immigration Branch, RG 76, vol. 174, file 58764, part 7.
2   Ibid.

# APPENDIX 4
## The Establishment of Sundale, Alberta

Events and transactions involving the founding of the Sundale, Alberta community, and other Hutterite issues concurrent with and subsequent to it, are also significant and require explanation. Lawyer Ernest Fletcher first became involved with Hutterites when he brokered the 1922 deal to acquire Blumengart. At the time, he was a partner in the Winnipeg firm of Monteith, Fletcher, and David, which also had offices in other communities, including Altona.

Working in the Altona office in the early to late 1920s was Gabriel Gilbert Serkau, a rather controversial figure, as it later appears.[1] Serkau was an 1891 immigrant from Poland[2] who in various documents also gave his place of birth as Germany,[3] the United States,[4] Manitoba,[5] or Wapella, Saskatchewan.[6] Serkau had run unsuccessfully in a 1920 Manitoba provincial election,[7] but was now employed in Fletcher's law office. In this cap-

---

1 Kirk Niergarth and J.L. Black, "Revisiting the Canadian-Soviet barter proposal of 1932–1933: The Soviet Perspective," *International Journal* 71, no. 3 (2016), 415. Although he appeared to practice law, Serkau had not articled as a lawyer.
2 Census of Canada, 1901, LAC, last modified February 21, 2019, https://www.bac-lac.gc.ca/eng/census/1901/Pages/about-census.aspx.
3 Census of Canada, 1911, LAC, last modified February 21, 2019, https://www.bac-lac.gc.ca/eng/census/1911/Pages/about-census.aspx.
4 Census of the Prairie Provinces, 1916, LAC, last modified February 21, 2019, https://www.bac-lac.gc.ca/eng/census/1916/Pages/about-census.aspx.
5 Census of Canada, 1921, LAC, last modified February 21, 2019, https://www.bac-lac.gc.ca/eng/census/1921/Pages/introduction.aspx; Census of the Prairie Provinces, 1926, LAC, last modified May 14, 2019, http://www.bac-lac.gc.ca/eng/census/1926/Pages/default.aspx.
6 "New York, New York Passenger and Crew Lists, 1909, 1925–1957," FamilySearch, last modified 14 June 2016, http://FamilySearch.org. Citing NARA microfilm publication T715 (Washington: National Archives and Records Administration, n.d.).
7 *Winnipeg Free Press*, July 21, 1920, 7.

acity he had some involvement in the Milltown purchase of Blumengart, in that his signature appeared as a Commissioner of Oaths on the villagers' 1922 property transfers to Ernest Fletcher. His signature as commissioner also appeared later in Winnipeg on the 1931 land transfer to Maxwell Hutterian Mutual Corporation indicating that, till this point at least, he might possibly still have had a connection with Fletcher's law practice.

That same year, Serkau was involved with Hutterite immigration from Wolf Creek, South Dakota, to Alberta, but this appears to have been his own initiative. Although Wolf Creek in Alberta had been established in May 1930, movement in January 1931 of the remaining residents from South Dakota was impeded by the Alberta government. After David Wipf from Wolf Creek, South Dakota, was refused entry, Jacob Hofer of Iberville in Manitoba personally visited the Winnipeg Immigration and Colonization office on his behalf.[8] Perhaps it was Hofer who referred Wipf to Serkau at this time, since on July 20, Wipf and Joshua Hofer were temporarily allowed entry at Windsor, Ontario,[9] from where they presumably proceeded to Ottawa to meet Serkau. Serkau (and likely Wipf and Hofer) met with Canadian immigration officials,[10] and thereafter Serkau proceeded to Edmonton to meet with provincial authorities. After an August 5 meeting at Rockport with the heads of seventeen Alberta communities, Serkau and a delegation of four of the community heads spent a week in Edmonton, where they were advised of "the conditions under which the Wolf Creek Colony would be admitted, and the wishes of the Government in connection with the colonies generally."[11]

After conferring with all of the community leaders, Serkau drafted a letter on August 15 to Alberta Premier J.E. Brownlee, in which he wrote that "I am authorized by them to make, on their behalf, the following statement." Included in the six points that followed were two that defy credibility because of their negative implications for the future of the Hutterite community in Alberta:

> [2.] No Hutterian Colony in Alberta shall either by purchase, lease or otherwise, increase its holdings of land or exercise any option now held for the purchase of land, and upon incorporation, the corporation shall not be entitled to increase its holdings of land as aforesaid:

---

8   Thomas Gelley to A.L. Jolliffe, April 29, 1931 (LAC, Immigration Branch, RG 76, vol. 359, file 425971).
9   Inspector, Department of Immigration, Windsor, Ontario, to J.S. Fraser, July 20, 1931 (LAC, RG 76, vol. 359, file 425971).
10  G.G. Serkau to A.L. Joliffe, July 23, 1931 (LAC, RG 76, vol. 359, file 425971); G.G. Serkau to W.A. Gordon, July 23, 1931 (LAC, RG 76, vol. 359, file 425971).
11  G.G. Serkau to George Hoadley, October 19, 1931 (LAC, RG 76, vol. 359, file 425971).

[3.] No Hutterian Colonies which are not now in existence in this Province shall be established in Alberta.[12]

Inconceivably, this letter was also signed August 25, 1931, by the respective communities as being approved by them.[13] Thereupon, the Alberta government withdrew its objection,[14] and the Department of Immigration allowed the Wolf Creek community entry. Soon thereafter some of the communities understandably repudiated their approval of the August 15th letter.[15]

Serkau had already contradictorily diminished the letter's intent by writing that it "did not constitute an agreement or undertaking" but that he was "strongly of the opinion that its provisions should be carried out to the letter by the Hutterites in Alberta."[16] He appeared to be appeasing both his Hutterite clients and the Alberta government,[17] but was soon to disregard the statement by his own actions.

Back in Manitoba, Serkau's involvement with the law firm now known as Fletcher and David, and before year-end 1932 solely as E.A. Fletcher & Company, is at this point unclear. That year, Maxwell established Sundale Community not far from Sibbald in Alberta and, contrary to Serkau's own opinion that the agreed-upon statement of August 25, 1931, should be adhered to, he was directly involved. The sale of Fogelvik Farm to the Schmiedeleut Hutterites was reported in the *Winnipeg Free Press* by G.G. Serkau, who had just returned from "completing arrangements for the

---

12   G.G. Serkau to J.E. Brownlee, August 15, 1931 (LAC, RG 76, vol. 359, file 425971).
13   Ibid.; G.G. Serkau to George Hoadley, October 19, 1931 (LAC, RG 76, vol. 359, file 425971). Serkau's letter from August 15 1931 is a transcript and lacks signatures, while the letter from October 19, 1931 is ambiguous as to whose signatures were actually affixed and when.
14   George Hoadley, Acting Premier, to Wesley A. Gordon, Minister of Immigration, August 26, 1931 (LAC, RG 76, vol. 359, file 425971).
15   G.G. Serkau to George Hoadley, October 19, 1931 (LAC, RG 76, vol. 359, file 425971); G. Mullen to M.W. Jones, January 20, 1932 (LAC, RG 76, vol. 359, file 425971).
16   G.G. Serkau to George Hoadley, October 19, 1931 (LAC, RG 76, vol. 359, file 425971).
17   The Alberta government took point 3 of the August 25, 1931 letter as a commitment that "No Hutterian Colonies which are not now in existence in this Province shall be established in Alberta." Commissioner to Honourable Mr. Gordon, February 12, 1932 (LAC, RG 76, vol. 359, file 425971); W.A. Gordon to George Hoadley, Alberta Minister of Agriculture, May 9, 1932 (LAC, RG 76, vol. 359, file 425971); Commissioner of Immigration to W.A. Gordon, March 5, 1934, (LAC, RG 76, vol. 359, file 425971). This memorandum states that "the Prime Minister telegraphed Jacob Wipf on March 1st, pointing out that the Hutterites had in 1931 given a pledge that no Hutterite Colonies which were not then in existence in Alberta should be established in that Province." Obviously, the federal government also accepted this as a commitment.

transfer."[18] Maxwell had paid him a total of $115 early that year,[19] but Serkau appears to have been more directly involved in this transaction in that he also expected to be paid a commission of $800 by the owner, Andrew Anderson. In November and again in December 1932, as well as in January 1933, Fletcher wrote Anderson on behalf of Serkau, demanding payment of said commission.[20] Whether it was ever paid is unknown, but Anderson had in April 1932 been warned about Serkau in a letter from Boissevain businessman George McDonald, who brought the latter's business dealings into question.[21] McDonald was referring to a situation in which Serkau collected fees and commissions for a land deal to Mennonites in the Whitewater, Manitoba area.[22]

It was also in 1932 that Serkau (while representing a syndicate of Winnipeg businessmen that included Peter Anderson of the North West Commission Company,[23] with whom the Hutterites already had a business relationship) began promoting a plan to barter Canadian cattle for Russian coal and oil.[24] Such a deal could have raised the price of cattle and the potential benefit to Hutterite communities must have been obvious to them. Perhaps to further this plan, Rosedale, and perhaps other communities as well, made a payment to Serkau that year, Rosedale noting their $100 payment as "G.G. Serkau for Montreal."[25] Despite significant Canadian support, the Russian cattle barter plan came to naught, despite Serkau, now referred to as a Montreal Trader, promoting it as late as 1936.[26] By 1939 he was promoting American cotton sales to Russia,[27] and in 1940 he was sentenced to two to three years in prison in Bridgeport, Connecticut, on an unrelated embezzlement conviction that was later stayed pending an appeal.[28] Documentation may yet become available to more clearly explain Serkau's relationship with the Hutterites. ∽

---

18   *Winnipeg Free Press*, April 11, 1932, 16.
19   *Maxwell Ledger*, 1922–1972, 50–51. The reason for the payments is not recorded.
20   Ernest Fletcher to Andrew Anderson, letter, November 22, 1932; telegram, December 24, 1932; letter, January 9, 1933 (Glenbow Archives, Calgary, AB, File M-802-48, Magnusson, Anderson Family fonds, series 2: Fogelvik Farms, 1911–1962).
21   Ibid. George McDonald to Andrew Anderson, April 14, 1932.
22   *Boissevain Recorder*, February 9, 1933, 1.
23   Niergarth and Black, "Revisiting the Canadian-Soviet Barter Proposal of 1932–1933," 415.
24   *Brandon Sun*, Jan 4, 1933; *Winnipeg Free Press*, December 31, 1932, 1; "'Hooves for Gallons:' The Canada-Russia Barter Deal of 1932–33," *Alberta History* 49, no. 2 (Spring 2001), 12–19.
25   *Rosedale Ledger 1932*, 143.
26   *Winnipeg Evening Tribune*, October 13, 1936, 11.
27   E.R. Perkins, ed., *Foreign Relations of the United States: Diplomatic Papers: The Soviet Union, 1933–1939* (Washington: Government Printing Office, 1952), 318.
28   *Schenectady Gazette*, Nov 14, 1940, 17; *Lethbridge Herald*, Nov 14, 1940.

## APPENDIX 5
## The Untold Story: Milltown, South Dakota, to Blumengart, Manitoba[1]

In 1918–19, the South Dakota Hutterische Bruder-Gemeinde had sold all the Milltown community lands west of the James River. A minority of the Milltown members remained in the community buildings on the east side of the river, the rest already residing at the new Milltown community in Manitoba. The May 1919 Order in Council that had barred further immigration of Hutterites to Canada was rescinded on June 2, 1922. The border was now open and the unsold South Dakota lands east of the James River needed to be converted to cash to enable further purchases in Manitoba to facilitate their resettlement.

While these South Dakota Hutterites were immigrating *to* Canada to preserve their faith and way of life, many Old Colony (*Reinländer*) Mennonites were looking to emigrate *from* Canada for the same reasons. They had already begun their search for land and guarantees of religious privileges in Latin America in 1919, but their exodus to Mexico only commenced in 1922. The initially planned large block sales of their Manitoba West Reserve lands did not materialize, but in anticipation of a sale, residents of the village of Blumengart began preparations for emigration.[2] The village had been founded in 1875 and originally comprised eighteen

---

1 Further information concerning Blumengart village and its Mennonite residents was previously published in my article, "The Move to Mexico: The Sale of Three West Reserve Villages," *Preservings* 30 (2010), 35–46. Subsequent research in 2016 at the Office of the Register of Deeds, Hutchinson County, SD, and the First Judicial Circuit Court for Hutchinson County (Case File 2398), as well as the office of the Register of Deeds, Ward County, ND, and the Manitoba Court of Kings Bench (Case 515/23), provided the additional details in the present narrative.
2 In March and April of 1922 the Morden law firm of McLeod, Black & McAuley was assisting them to obtain certificates of naturalization.

quarter sections of land in Township 2 Range 3 West: Sections 15, 16, 21, 22, and the south half of Section 28. By 1922, the original village lands were owned by fifteen individuals, some of whom also owned lands outside the village parameters. In addition, there were other village residents, some without land, and the actual number of farmsteads in the village exceeded fifteen.

The Order in Council barring entry had not yet been rescinded when Ernest Fletcher of the Winnipeg firm Monteith, Fletcher, & David—which also had offices in Altona, Steinbach, and a newly opened office in Winkler—became involved in both of these issues: the Hutterite need for land and the Mennonite need to sell. Records of contacts made and deals discussed between the two communities were unavailable at the time of this writing, but a plan was devised whereby Fletcher would broker a deal. Milltown would convey its remaining 2,174 acres in South Dakota to Fletcher in exchange for Fletcher transferring to the Hofers clear title to 3,600 acres of the Blumengart lands in Manitoba, including the village farmsteads. In early May, Fletcher began preparing applications to bring the individual villagers' properties under the Real Property Act, which would allow the issuance of certificates of title. On July 12, 1922, the "Hutterische Bruder-Gemeinde," as the registered owners of the South Dakota lands, passed a resolution to convey their 2,174 acres at Milltown, South Dakota, to Fletcher.

On August 1 and 2, 1922, Frank Bastin from the Winkler office of Monteith, Fletcher & David was in Blumengart obtaining signatures from fifteen villagers on transfers of their properties to Fletcher personally. In total, 3,920 acres of land, including the village farmsteads and buildings, were signed over to him for the combined sum of $84,306.[3] Lands included in these transfers but outside the original village parameters totalled 1,200 acres. The villagers' transfers were not immediately registered, and no money changed hands, but the signatures thereon enabled Fletcher to continue putting the deal together.

Acting on their July 12, 1922 resolution, on October 10, the Hutterische Bruder-Gemeinde executed a conveyance of 2,174 acres in South Dakota—those Milltown lands situated east of the James River—to Ernest Fletcher for the sum of $165,000. Those members already in Manitoba signed a $1 quitclaim deed on October 14. Those members still in South Dakota had signed such a quitclaim on October 11. Again, no money will

---

3   The purchase and sale totals as recorded on the various Manitoba and South Dakota documents cannot be reconciled and the numbers are irrelevant to the stated intent, which was the free-of-encumbrances even-up exchange of the remaining Milltown, SD lands for the Blumengart, MB village.

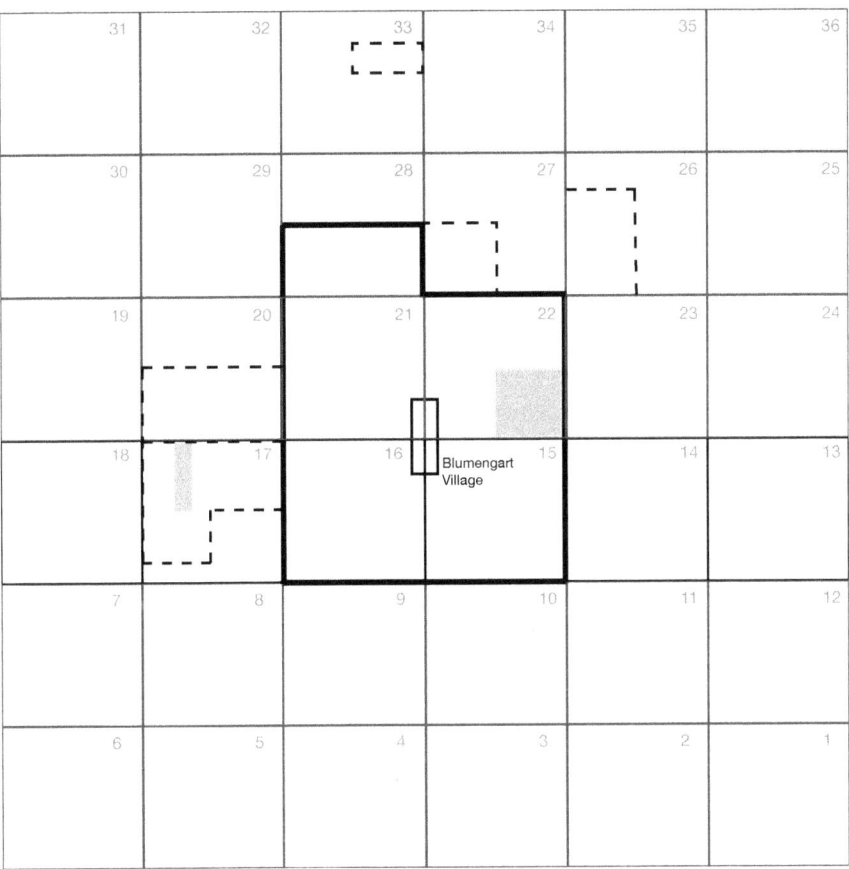

**Map 3.** A map of Township 2 Range 3 West showing the original Blumengart village land parameters in dark outline with the village proper in the centre. Other than the shaded parcels, all lands within the dark and dotted lines were purchased from the Mennonites by Ernest Fletcher. He initially transferred these same lands to the Hutterites, except the parcels in sections 26 and 33 and W ½ W ½ NW 17.

have changed hands, but Fletcher was now in a position to deal further with those lands.

Also on October 11, Fletcher and his wife, Lenore, mortgaged the 2,174 acres in South Dakota for $60,000 to the Connecticut General Life Insurance Company. This was registered as a first mortgage on the lands and although the principal was only payable in full on March 11, 1932, an annual payment of interest was still required. Fletcher used this sum as partial payment to the Blumengart villagers on their lands. Also that day, the Fletchers mortgaged the 2,174 acres for $3,000 to Northrup & Edmison of Sioux Falls, South Dakota. This was registered as a second mortgage on the lands and was repayable by ten equal annual payments. This sum was reported as for paying an unidentified commission.[4]

---

4    In his August 10, 1923 deposition, Ernest Fletcher referred to it as a "Commission Mortgage," but in his October 1, 1924 conveyance to the Minneapolis Trust Company, Fred McCartney referred to it as "a mortgage given for part of the interest

However, as he was subsequently unable to resell the South Dakota lands, Fletcher was unable to complete payment to the Blumengart villagers for their lands. After using the $60,000 from the Connecticut General mortgage as partial payment, he thus remained indebted to them for $31,141. As security he provided villagers Abraham I. Friesen, Jacob Harms, and Abram Rempel with a mortgage for this sum registered on 3,560 acres of the total 3,920 which the entire village had transferred to him. Payment in full was due March 31, 1923.

On October 31, 1922, Fletcher transferred to John Hofer, David Hofer Sr., and Jacob Hofer[5] these 3,560 acres,[6] which included the Blumengart village farmsteads, for the sum of $72,000. The remaining 360 non-contiguous acres of the total 3,920 on the signed transfers from the villagers to Fletcher were part of the 1,200 acres situated outside the original village parameters. Fletcher had now delivered title to the Hutterites, but not clear title as was agreed upon, since it remained subject to his $31,141 mortgage owing to Friesen, Harms, and Rempel, plus he still owed the Hutterites 40 acres to complete the total 3,600. As further collateral for the $31,141, on November 1, 1922, Fletcher gave to the Hofers his

---

of the above described mortgage," with the "above described mortgage" being the $60,000 mortgage.

5    The Hutterite purchasers of the Blumengart properties in whose names the certificates of title were issued were David Hofer Sr. and his two sons, Jacob and John. David was born in Russia in 1853 and immigrated to southern Dakota Territory in the United States in 1874. In 1918, he and these two sons, together with other families, emigrated from South Dakota to found Milltown, MB, at Benard Siding. (The 1921 Canadian Census lists these sons as Jacob and John and their families at Milltown, MB, although John's name is incorrectly recorded as Joseph. A seventy-four-year-old widower named David Hofer is also listed, who would appear to be David Hofer Sr., who was by then widowed, but only sixty-seven.) All three families subsequently moved to Blumengart. David Hofer Sr. and John Hofer remained there and are buried in the community cemetery. Jacob Hofer later moved to Crystal Spring Community.

6    Transfer 37969: "The South half of Section Twenty-eight (28) South-West quarter of Section Twenty-seven (27) South half of Section Twenty (20) All of Section Twenty-one (21) North half and South West quarter of Section Twenty-two (22) All of Section Fifteen (15) All of Section Sixteen (16) The North East quarter of Section Seventeen (17) The East half of the East half and the East half of the West half of the North West quarter of Section Seventeen (17) and the North half and the North half of the South half of the South West quarter of Section Seventeen (17) in Township Two and Range Three West of the Principal Meridian in Manitoba [excepting out of the North West quarter of Section Fifteen all Mines and Minerals and the Right to work the same as reserved in the original Grant from the Crown and excepting out of the South West quarter of Section 27 the most Easterly forty (40) yards in width of the most Westerly two hundred and seventy (270) yards in width of the most Northerly eighty (80) yards in depth thereof]." The Land Titles Office destroyed the originals and the microfilm is unclear; the latter portion has been reconstructed using additional sources.

personal promissory note for the same amount, plus he provided a mortgage for this sum on the 2,174 acres at Milltown, South Dakota, which was registered thereon as a third mortgage. Both the note and the mortgage were also made payable on March 31, 1923. In addition, he also provided them with a mortgage for this same sum on the 360 acres at Blumengart to which he still held title. Manitoba lawyer Alexander Adams was involved in drawing up many of these documents and seeing to their registration. In a deposition, he stated that Ernest Fletcher also gave to the Hofers a power of attorney whereby if Fletcher did not sell the South Dakota lands before March 31, 1923, then Fletcher authorized them to sell it for $90,000 and apply same towards repayment of the $60,000 first mortgage and their own claim of $31,141.

However, prior to that date, Fletcher found a buyer for the property in the person of Fred McCartney, a banker from Oakes, North Dakota. On February 24, 1923, an agreement for sale was signed whereby Fletcher would deed the 2,174 acres in South Dakota to Fred McCartney in exchange for McCartney repaying the three mortgages thereon as they became due: the Connecticut General $60,000 mortgage due in full in 1932, plus an annual payment of the interest; the Northrup & Edmison $3,000 mortgage, payable over ten years plus annual interest, which mortgage had on November 14, 1922, now been assigned to the Hutchinson County Bank; and the $31,141 due in full to the Hofers on March 31, 1923. In addition, McCartney was to convey 320 acres in Ward County, North Dakota, to Fletcher. On March 5, 1923, Ernest and Lenore Fletcher for $1 "and other good and valuable consideration" signed a deed of the 2,174 acres at Milltown, South Dakota, to Fred McCartney, but this document was to be held in trust by McCartney's agent at Winnipeg until McCartney had deposited the funds to pay $31,141 to the Hofers. Subsequently, McCartney claimed that he required the deed in order to raise the money, upon which Fletcher then waived this requirement, and the deed was registered on March 26 in Hutchinson County. Such confidence in Fred McCartney would not have appeared misplaced, since he was well known to the Hutterites after the 1918 purchase of his Manitoba lands for James Valley and their other land rental arrangements with him.

On March 6 and 7, 1923, Fred McCartney purchased 320 acres of land in Ward County, North Dakota. The acquisition of this would have allowed him to fulfill his obligations to Fletcher, but only days later, on March 10, he conveyed these same 320 acres to A.J. Rieger of Winnipeg.[7] Although this latter document was not immediately registered, this

---

7   In Ward County, ND: Lots three (3) and four (4) and the East half (E ½) of the Southwest quarter (SW ¼) of Section eighteen (18), and the Northeast quarter (NE

development could suggest that McCartney had no intention of fulfilling the terms of his agreement with Fletcher. More plausible, though, is that as part of his deal, Fletcher already had a buyer, Rieger, for the 320 acres, and to eliminate one transfer, the conveyance was made directly from McCartney to Rieger, but registration was delayed pending compliance with all conditions. However, McCartney then failed to make the March 31, 1923 payment of $31,141 that was due to the Hofers. This default meant that Fletcher's mortgage debt, owed to the Blumengart villagers on their Manitoba lands, remained unpaid, and thus the Hofers' title to the 3,560 acres could not be cleared as had been agreed upon. Since the South Dakota lands had been deeded to McCartney, the only recourse left to wrest ownership from him and enable a sale to a different buyer was through foreclosure, and this was apparently discussed between Alexander Adams, Ernest Fletcher, and the Hofers.

In early April 1923, action for mortgage foreclosure and sale of the 2,174 acres in South Dakota commenced in the Circuit Court of Hutchinson County, Case 2398, with John Hofer, David Hofer Sr., and Jacob Hofer as plaintiffs versus Ernest Fletcher, Lenore Fletcher, and Fred D. McCartney as defendants. On April 5 in Manitoba, in an attempt to protect his remaining assets after his payment default, McCartney deeded or transferred ownership of his remaining Manitoba properties, including the N ½ 26-10-3 (years later purchased by James Valley; see Acquisition F) to his brother, Henry Clay McCartney, for $1. On May 9, in Manitoba Court of Kings Bench Case 515/23, Ernest Fletcher filed a statement of claim on behalf of himself and other unnamed creditors versus Fred McCartney and Henry Clay McCartney, where he claimed that the transfer of his land by Fred to Henry was intended to defraud the creditors and therefore should be cancelled. A certificate of *lis pendens* (suit pending) issued by the Court was registered on May 11 in the Land Titles Office, which impeded further Manitoba land transactions by the McCartneys until the South Dakota controversy was dealt with. On June 28, Fred McCartney filed a statement of defence disputing the Fletcher claim in Manitoba Case 515/23.

To enable payment of the now overdue Fletcher mortgage ($31,141 plus interest) owed to the Blumengart villagers, on May 31, 1923, John Hofer, David Hofer Sr., and Jacob Hofer remortgaged the 3,560 acres at Blumengart to the Great-West Life Assurance Company for $33,000.[8]

¼) of Section Seven (7), all in Township One hundred and fifty-two (152) North, of Range eighty-six (86) West of the 5th P.M.

8   Of personal interest to the author is that whatever balance remained owing by John Hofer, David Hofer Sr., and Jacob Hofer on the $33,000 Great-West Life Assurance Company mortgage was subsequently transferred by Great-West Life to his

The mortgage due to Friesen, Harms, and Rempel was subsequently repaid and discharged on June 7.

On October 15, 1923, a trial took place at Olivet, South Dakota, concerning McCartney's payment default on the $31,141 Fletcher mortgage of the 2,174 acres, where final decree was issued ordering foreclosure and the sale thereof. Lawyer Coe Crawford from Huron, South Dakota, who had previously provided much valuable service to the Hutterites, acted on behalf of the Hofers, while the defendant, McCartney, was represented by his attorney. On December 1, 1923, a public auction of the 2,174 acres was held at the courthouse in Olivet. No bids were received other than that of $33,434 by the mortgagees, Hofer, Hofer, and Hofer, to whom the lands were then declared sold, and to whom a sheriff's certificate of sale was issued. As purchasers, they would be entitled to a deed of the property unless it was redeemed prior to the expiration of one year. The Hofers' deed would, however, still be subject to the $60,000 first and $3,000 second mortgages.

Just less than a year later, on October 1, 1924, Fred McCartney and his wife, Frances, granted, conveyed, and warranted the 2,174 acres to the Minneapolis Trust Company for $1 "and other good and valuable considerations." Whether the McCartneys had any actual interest in or claim to the lands is unlikely, and this would appear to have been a stipulation by Fletcher to eliminate any such claim.[9] On November 14, John Hofer, David Hofer Sr., and Jacob Hofer assigned the certificate of sale for the 2,174 acres to Minneapolis Trust in exchange for $32,500. The receipt of this sum by the Hofers essentially signified conclusion of the plan whereby they exchanged their lands east of the James River in South Dakota for the village of Blumengart in Manitoba.[10] That same day, November 14, in the Manitoba Court of Kings Bench, Ernest Fletcher filed a notice of discontinuance in Case 515/23, Fletcher v. McCartney, and on November 25 registered a certificate of discontinuance in the Land Titles Office. Fletcher discontinued the action without costs to either party, and the McCartneys were again free to deal with their Manitoba lands as they wished. On December 6, 1924, the sale of the 2,174 acres to Minneapolis Trust, subject to both $60,000 and $3,000 mortgages, was registered by the Hutchinson County sheriff. Also registered on January 25, 1925, was the until-now unregistered conveyance by McCartney to Rieger of the

---

    great-grandfather, Jacob Friesen, of Reinfeld, MB, as mortgagee on December 31, 1928.
9    See footnote 14.
10   The Hofers did not use the $32,500 proceeds to fully pay out their $33,000 Great-West Life mortgage, and it remained an encumbrance on their Manitoba lands.

320 acres in Ward County, North Dakota; it had been in abeyance after McCartney reneged on the Hofer mortgage payment.[11]

Although Milltown had now received sufficient funds from its South Dakota lands, equivalent to what Ernest Fletcher had left owing on the Blumengart property mortgage, Fletcher had earlier conveyed only 3,560 of the agreed-upon 3,600 acres to them. However, on June 29, 1923, Fletcher had, for $1, transferred to the Union Trust Company Limited, as trustee for John Hofer, David Hofer Sr., and Jacob Hofer, the 360 Blumengart acres not sold to the Hutterites but which were valued at $10,800. This land had still been subject to the $31,141 Fletcher mortgage owed to the Hofers. The following year, on April 15, 1924, the Union Trust had exchanged from these 360 acres the W ½ of W ½ of NW ¼ 17-2-3 for the W ½ of E ½ of the same quarter, which was owned by Cornelius Wall. This latter 40 acres was adjacent to the lands already owned by the Hofers and was then deeded directly to them by Wall. This had completed their 3,600-acre acquisition from Fletcher. Later that year, on November 22, Union Trust, for $1, transferred back to Ernest Fletcher the 320 acres that still remained of his original purchase from the Blumengart villagers. His mortgage owed to the Hofers on these acres was now also discharged. It appears that these lands were now considered personal assets by him, since he mortgaged and resold them in subsequent years. To this day, Ernest Fletcher's memory is preserved at Blumengart in that the parcel consisting of the west half of 26-2-3W is still referred to as "Fletcher."[12]

At Milltown, South Dakota, after November 14, 1924, the former community lands now owned by Minneapolis Trust continued to be encumbered by both mortgages: the Connecticut General $60,000 mortgage due in full in 1932, plus the annual payment of interest; and the Northrup & Edmison $3,000 mortgage payable over ten years, plus annual interest, which mortgage had on November 14, 1922, been assigned to the Hutchinson County Bank. On September 10, 1925, the *Hutchinson Herald* advertised the September 14 sale by auction of 2,174 acres: "The Milltown Colony Lands. Large number of buildings, water power flour mill with feed grinder. Grain elevator of 25,000 bushel capacity. Barns, sheds and houses. Alfalfa, hay and pasture land and several hundred acres of farm land." The paper's September 17 issue reported some sales that had been made. Subsequently, on February 1, 1926, the Hutchinson County Bank released 400 acres (primarily lands in 1 and 2-99-59) from the $3,000 mortgage for a payment of $500, and on February 19, Connecticut Gen-

---

11  There is no evidence available to suggest that this seemingly unrelated acreage was included in the February 1923 agreement other than as a financial incentive for Fletcher.
12  Personal interview with Blumengart resident.

eral released 418 acres (essentially those same parcels) from the $60,000 mortgage for a payment of $1 "and other valuable considerations" made by Andrew Kopprud of Hutchinson County.

On June 30, 1927, Minneapolis Trust conveyed the remaining approximately 1,756 acres (lands in 26, 34, 35, 36-100-59 and 31-100-58) to the Marshall McCartney Company of Oakes, North Dakota, for $1 "and other good and valuable consideration." Both Fred McCartney and Henry Clay McCartney were partners in the company, and it was Fred's 1923 payment default that had caused the foreclosure. The following year, on September 19, 1928, the Marshall McCartney Company conveyed essentially those same lands, now recorded as approximately 1,774 acres, to the Northwest Company of New York for $1 "and other valuable consideration."[13] Why they were still involved, or again became involved, and what benefits if any the McCartneys derived from these transactions is unknown.[14]

---

13  The Northwest Company, a corporation with an authorized capital of $5,000,000, was formed in 1925 by a number of banks with Henry Clay McCartney as president and Fred Delos McCartney an associate. Their stated, seemingly altruistic, plan was "bringing farmer relief to the Northwest" but only to owners of large acreages and not to individual farmers. They would do so by "acquiring deeds to such large holdings as may be available and then, instead of proceeding to ouster (the owners), arrange for carrying delinquent purchasers at a reasonable interest rate, to give them a chance to work out their own salvation without loss of what they already may have invested in their farms." *The New York Times*, September 24, 1925, 14.

14  There is as yet no clarification for this further involvement by the McCartneys but the Minneapolis Trust Company would appear to have held these lands for them on an interim basis since October 1924. Now as actual owners since June 1927, their Marshall McCartney Company could convey the property to another in which they had a stake, the Northwest Company, and the seemingly altruistic motives for the latter's incorporation fade. In none of these property conveyances, including subsequently to Judge F.J. Graham, is the actual financial compensation recorded. The Marshall McCartney Company was delinquent in the tax payments for 1928 and 1929 and also in arrears for the interest payment on the mortgage, both of which precipitated the Connecticut General foreclosure. However, Judge Graham subsequently still conveyed certain parcels to other individuals. What was unrecorded in Hutchinson County Court filings will remain shrouded.
    In Canada, the November 1927 sale by Henry C. McCartney of the majority of their remaining Manitoba properties only occurred shortly after the Marshall McCartney Company had reacquired the South Dakota properties from the Minneapolis Trust Company on June 30, 1927. As noted in Acquisition F, Alvin Solberg was involved in his capacity as a real estate broker with the November 22, 1927 sale of (a) the N ½ 26-10-3W, and (b) the SE ¼ 34, S ½ 35, S ½ of SW 36, all in Township 10 Range 3W, in Manitoba, and all to Minnesota State Treasurer Julius A Schmahl. Although the subsequent property transfers of these latter parcels have not been specifically researched, the N ½ 26-10-3W, after being deeded to Schmahl on November 22, 1927, was then re-deeded (together with unspecified other lands, probably those already listed) by Schmahl on December 27, 1927, to Edwin M. Parish (who had been the chief clerk to the Minnesota Secretary of State when Schmahl occupied that

On April 14, 1930, the land changed hands again when the Northwest Company conveyed them, still subject to both mortgages, to F.J. Graham of Ellendale[15] for $1 "and other good and valuable consideration." Only two months later, on June 21, a public auction of the 1,756 acres was held at the courthouse in Olivet, where no bids were received other than a total bid of $52,475 by the mortgagee, Connecticut General. The lands were then declared sold to them and a sheriff's certificate of sale was given. Although the $60,000 principal on the mortgage from Connecticut General was only due in March 1932, the annual payment of interest had not been made, nor had the property taxes been paid; therefore Connecticut General foreclosed. The principal outstanding at foreclosure had already been reduced to $49,000 by payments for partial releases, but interest of $3,353 was also due. Recorded as purchasers in the sheriff's certificate of sale, after one year Connecticut General was entitled to a deed of the property, but during that year five further entries were recorded.[16] Thereafter, on June 23, 1931, a sheriff's deed conveyed to Connecticut General such lands as had not yet been redeemed (lands in 26, N ½ 36, 34, 35-100-59 which still appeared subject to the $3,000 mortgage). Six years later, on July 7, 1937, the Hutchinson County Bank released those lands in 2-99-59 from the $3,000 mortgage.

There is no obvious date as to when all obligations were fully met and the original 1922 mortgages of Ernest Fletcher for $60,000 and $3,000 were fully discharged from all former Milltown community lands in South Dakota. However, on February 7, 1947, by a special warranty deed Con-

---

position). Parish thereupon re-deeded it January 20, 1928, to Mortimer A. Smith et al. (Smith was a grain merchant with Paterson Grain Company), who a year later, on December 15, 1928, deeded it to Leon Bénard (see Acquistion F). Three consecutive deeds of the same property within the space of two months involving three Americans seems unusual, but whether or not the timing of these transactions was merely coincidental is not as yet apparent.

15  F.J. Graham was a North Dakota Judge. *The Evening Star*, Washington, DC, August 7, 1928, 1.

16  August 27, 1930: The Hutchinson County Bank, for a payment of $200, released 160 acres from the $3,000 mortgage which Northrup & Edmison assigned to them. (Lands in 31-100-58); September 20, 1930: F.J. Graham and Ina Graham, for $1 "and other good and valuable consideration," conveyed 640 acres to J.F. Hoeck of Huron. (36-100-59, still subject to both mortgages or the foreclosure sale by Connecticut Life); December 4, 1930: F.J. Graham and Ina Graham, for $1, conveyed approximately 920 acres to S.C. Lassegard of Alexandria. (Primarily lands in 34, 35, 26 – 100-59, still subject to both of the mortgages or the foreclosure sale by Connecticut General); May 21, 1931: Notice of payment of taxes. Connecticut General paid certain outstanding property taxes, which sum was to be added to the total amount required should the property be redeemed from the mortgage sale. (Paid for lands in 26, 36, 34, 35 – 100-59); June 20, 1931: J.F. Hoeck paid $1,152 for the overdue interest and taxes on 160 acres and the exemption from foreclosure on same was extended to one year (S ½ of 36-100-59).

necticut General conveyed to F.S. Dilger of Yankton County primarily those lands in 26, 34, 35-100-59 for $1 "and other valuable consideration." Since Connecticut General had acquired these lands through foreclosure of the Fletcher mortgage, the proceeds of which had originally been used by Fletcher as payment for the Blumengart properties, perhaps this transaction could be considered the conclusion of the South Dakota story. In Manitoba, the Hutterites' acquisition of the 18 quarter sections of land originally comprising the former Mennonite village of Blumengart continued in 1938, when the Hutterite community entered into a $4,000 agreement with John H. Unger for the SE ¼ 22-2-3.[17] They agreed to pay him an immediate $1,000 and half of each crop plus 5% interest annually thereafter until fully repaid. The deed was only registered in 1942 to fully complete the transition from a Mennonite village to a Hutterite community.

---

[17] This parcel was situated within the original village parameters but sold to Unger before Ernest Fletcher became involved.

## APPENDIX 6
## Transfer of Land: Joseph M. Hackney to David Hofer Sr., et al.

The following images are of the original $500,000 Schmiedeleut land purchase in Manitoba. This transfer of land, dated August 2, 1918, and registered on August 24 in the Portage la Prairie Land Titles Office as no. 32066, provides the legal description of each parcel of land sold by Joseph M. Hackney to the "holding committee."

**Manitoba** } I, Sydney Lawler of the City of Winnipeg in the Province of Manitoba, Law Clerk make oath and say:

**To Wit:**
1. That I was present and did see Joseph Malcolm Hackney the within-named transferor execute the within transfer.
2. That it was executed at the City of Winnipeg aforesaid
3. That I know the said Joseph Malcolm Hackney and that he is in my belief of the full age of twenty-one years.
4. That I am a subscribing witness to the said instrument.

**Sworn** before me at the City of Winnipeg in the Province of Manitoba this second day of August A.D. 1918

*Sydney Lawler*
*Alexander Adams*
A Commissioner in B.R. &c.

**Manitoba** } I, Joseph Malcolm Hackney of the City of St. Paul, in the State of Minnesota One of the United States of America, Farmer make oath and say:

**To Wit:**
That I am the within-named transferor and that I am of the full age of twenty-one years.
That I am the registered owner of the lands hereby transferred.

**Sworn** before me at the City of Winnipeg in the Province of Manitoba this Second day of August A.D. 1918

*J M Hackney*
*Alexander Adams*
A Commissioner in B.R. &c.

---

Dated 2nd August 1918

Joseph M Hackney
to
David Hofer et al

**Transfer of Lands**

No. 32066

RECEIVED AUG 24 1918 LAND TITLES OFFICE

Tupper McTavish Tupper & Tupper
Winnipeg
Manitoba

---

**Memorial of Instrument**

| Name of Instrument | Time of its Production for Registration | Name of the Parties thereto | No. of Instrument |
|---|---|---|---|
| Transfer | 24th Aug 1918 at 10:01 am | Joseph M Hackney to David Hofer Sr. et al | 32066 |

I Certify that the within Instrument was presented for registration at time above mentioned, and that the same has been registered in the Land Titles Office as ____, and that a Memorial thereof has been entered in the Register Book on Certificate of Title Nos. 26651, 27133, 27114, 27183, 27419, 27114, 27146, 27145, 27154, 27454, 27584, 27585, and 27119

District Registrar

I Certify that at the time this Instrument was presented for registration no registrations appeared in the Caveat Book which would affect this land other than Nos. 26 Above, 27133, 27134, 27187, 27183, 27146, 27147, 27454, 27148, ...

Certificate Issued No. 28521, 28539

Manitoba
The Real Property Act
## Memorandum of Transfer

I, Joseph Malcolm Hackney of the City of St Paul in the State of Minnesota One of the United States of America Farmer being registered owner of an estate in fee simple in possession subject however to such encumbrances liens and interests as are notified by memorandum under-written (or endorsed hereon) in all those certain pieces or parcels of land known and described as follows:—

In the province of Manitoba and being composed of ~~The East Half of the North East Quarter of Section Twenty-eight (28) in Township Eleven (11) and Range Three (3) West of the principal Meridian~~

Parcel No. 1 The West Half of Section Eleven (11) in Township Ten (10) and Range Three (3) West of the principal Meridian Excepting out of the South West Quarter of said Section Eleven (11) all that portion thereof taken for a Public Drain as the same is shown on a plan thereof registered in the Portage la Prairie Land Titles office as N° 314 Excepting thereout all mines and minerals as reserved in the Grant from the Crown and subject to all taxes under the Manitoba Drainage Act

Parcel No. 2 The South half and the North West Quarter both of Section Eleven (11) in Township Eleven (11) and Range Four (4) West of the principal Meridian in Manitoba Excepting thereout all mines and minerals as reserved in the Grant from the Crown

Parcel No. 3 The South West Quarter of Section Eight (8) in Township Eleven (11) and Range Three (3) West of the principal Meridian

Parcel No. 4 The North Half and the South East Quarter of Section Eight (8) the South West Quarter of Section Nine (9) and all that part of the North West Quarter of Section Nine (9) which lies South of the Southern limit of the Right of Way of the Northern Pacific and Manitoba Railway as shown on a plan thereof registered in the Portage la Prairie Land Titles Office as N° 235 both in Township Eleven (11) and Range Three (3) West of the principal Meridian

Parcel No. 5 The South West Quarter, the South Half of the North West Quarter and the North Half of the North East Quarter all of

Witness
Sidney Lawler                                JM Hackney

Section Seventeen (17) and the South East Quarter of Section Twenty (20) all in Township Eleven (11), and Range Three (3) West of the principal Meridian in Manitoba excepting out of the South West Quarter of said Section Seventeen (17) that part thereof described as follows: Commencing at the intersection of the Western Limit thereof with the centre line of the Northern Pacific and Manitoba Railway as shewn on a plan thereof registered in the Portage La Prairie Land Titles Office as No. 235, thence Northerly along said Western limit one hundred and fifty eight and three-tenths (158 3/10) feet more or less to a point distant perpendicularly Northerly one hundred and fifty (150) feet from the said centre line, thence Easterly parallel to said centre line twelve hundred and seventy and one half (1270 1/2) feet, thence Southerly parallel to said Western limit to a point distant perpendicularly Southerly one hundred and fifty (150) feet from the said centre line, thence Westerly parallel to said centre line to the said Western limit thence Northerly along said Western limit to point of commencement.) Also excepting all that part of the South West Quarter of said Section Seventeen (17), lying East of the above described exception, and taken for the Right of Way of the said Railway as shewn on said plan No. 235 Also excepting those parts of the South West Quarter and the South half of the North West Quarter of said Section Seventeen (17) taken for Right of Way of the Grand Trunk Pacific Railway as shewn on a plan thereof registered in the said Land Titles Office as No. 346 Also excepting out of the South West Quarter of said Section Seventeen (17) the most Westerly twelve hundred and four (1204) feet in depth of the most Northerly Seventeen hundred and forty seven and one-tenth (1747 1/10) feet in width thereof—

Parcel No. 6 all 97884 The North Half of the North West Quarter of Section Seventeen (17) the East Half of Section Nineteen (19), the South West Quarter of Section Twenty (20) and the East Half of Section Thirty (30) all in Township Eleven (11) and Range Three (3) West of the principal Meridian

Parcel No. 7 all 97133 The North West Quarter and the West Half of the North East Quarter of Section Sixteen (16) in Township Eleven (11) and Range Three (3) West of the principal Meridian

Parcel No. 8 all 97482 The North West Quarter and the West Half of the North East Quarter of Section Twenty (20), in Township Eleven (11) and Range Three (3) West of the principal Meridian

**Parcel No. 9** The West Half of Section One (1) in Township Twelve (12) and
all 2 b 139  Range Three (3) West of the principal Meridian

**Parcel No. 10** The West Half of Section Four (4), all of Section Five (5) both in
all 22588  Township Eleven (11) and the North East Quarter and the East half
of the North West Quarter both of Section Thirty two (32) in
Township Ten (10), and the North West Quarter and the West
half of the North East Quarter both of Section Thirty three (33)
in Township Ten (10) all in Range Three (3) West of the
principal Meridian

**Parcel No. 11** Section One (1), the South half and the North West Quarter
all 22139  both of Section Twelve (12) and the West half, the North East
Quarter and the North Half of the South East Quarter all of Section
Thirteen (13) all in Township Eleven (11) and Range Three (3)
West of the principal Meridian; excepting out of the North West
Quarter of said Section Twelve (12) all that part thereof taken
for a public drain, as shewn on a plan thereof, registered in the
Portage la Prairie Land Titles Office as N° 335; also excepting
out of said Section Thirteen (13) all that part thereof taken for
the Right of Way of the Northern Pacific and Manitoba Railway
as shewn on a plan thereof registered in the said Land Titles Office
as N° 235 also excepting out of said Section Thirteen (13) all that
part thereof taken for the Right of Way of the Grand Trunk Pacific
Railway as shewn on a plan thereof registered in the said Land
Titles Office as N° 346; also excepting all that part of the
North West Quarter of said Section Thirteen (13) which lies North
of the Northerly limit of the Right of Way of the Grand Trunk
Pacific Railway aforesaid subject to all levees under the Manitoba
Drainage Act

**Parcel No. 12** The North East Quarter of Section Seven (7) and South half
all 22143  of the South East Quarter of Section Eighteen (18) both in
Township Eleven (11) and Range Three (3) West of the
principal Meridian; excepting thereout the most Northerly four
hundred and seventeen and four-tenths (417 4/10) feet in width
and the most Southerly two hundred and eight and seven tenths
(208 7/10) feet in width, both of the most Easterly two hundred and
eight and seven tenths (208 7/10) feet in depth and the most

Northerly two hundred and eight, and seven-tenths (208 7/10) feet in width of the most Westerly six hundred and twenty six and one tenth (626 1/10) feet in depth, all of Legal subdivision One (1) of said Section Eighteen (18).

**Parcel No 13** The South West Quarter of Section Thirty (30) and the North
all 27487 Half of the North West Quarter of Section Nineteen (19) in Township Eleven (11) and Range Three (3) West of the principal Meridian

**Parcel No 14** The South West Quarter and the South Half of the North West
all 27487 Quarter of Section Nineteen (19) in the Eleventh Township and Third Range West of the Principal Meridian, containing two hundred and forty one (241) acres more or less

**Parcel No 15** The North half of the South half and the North Half both of
all 27143 Section Eighteen (18) in Township Eleven (11) and Range Three (3) West of the principal Meridian excepting thereout all that part thereof taken for Right of Way of the Northern Pacific and Manitoba Railway as shown on a plan thereof registered in the Portage la Prairie Land Titles Office as No 236 also excepting thereout all that part thereof taken for Right of Way of the Grand Trunk Pacific Railway, as shown on a plan thereof registered in the Portage la Prairie Land Titles Office as No 316, also excepting thereout the most Easterly Seventeen hundred and twenty nine (1729) feet of the North Half of the South East Quarter of said section

**Parcel No 16** The North East Quarter and the North Half of the South East
all 27139 Quarter both of Section Thirteen (13), the South East Quarter and South Half of the North East Quarter both of Section Twenty-four (24) all in Township Ten (10) and Range Four (4) West of the Principal Meridian excepting out of the said North half of the South East Quarter of Section Thirteen (13) all that portion thereof taken for a Public Drain as the same is shown on a plan thereof registered in the Portage la Prairie Land Titles Office as No 337 Subject to all levies under the Manitoba Drainage Act

**Parcel No 17** The North West Quarter of Section Twelve (12) and the
all 27140 South Half of the South West Quarter of Section Thirteen (13)

both in Township Ten (10), and Range Three (3) West of the Principal Meridian subject to all levies under the Manitoba Drainage Act

Parcel No. 18 The South West Quarter of Section Twenty one (21) and the North Half of the North West Quarter of Section Sixteen (16) both in Township Ten (10), and Range Three (3) West of the Principal Meridian, subject to all levies under the Manitoba Drainage Act

Parcel No. 19 The South East Quarter of Section Twenty eight (28) and the North Half of the North East Quarter of Section Twenty one (21) in Township Ten (10) and Range Three (3) West of the Principal Meridian

Parcel No. 20 All that portion of the South West Quarter of Section Seventeen (17) in Township Eleven (11) and Range Three (3) West of the Principal Meridian described as follows:— Commencing at the North West corner of the said Quarter Section thence Easterly along the Northern limit thereof twelve hundred and four (1204) feet; thence Southerly parallel to the Western limit thereof seventeen hundred and forty seven and one tenth (1747 1/10) feet thence Westerly parallel to the said Northern limit to the said Western limit, thence Northerly along the said Western limit to the point of commencement; Excepting thereout the Right of Way of the Northern Pacific and Manitoba Railway as the same is shewn on a plan thereof registered in the Portage la Prairie Land Titles Office as No. 235 Excepting also the Right of Way of the Grand Trunk Pacific Railway as the same is shewn on a plan thereof registered in said Land Titles Office as No. 346 Excepting thereout also all that portion thereof conveyed to the Northern Pacific and Manitoba Railway Company for Station Grounds as described in registered instrument No. 18363 of the said Land Titles Office

Parcel No. 21 An undivided one-half (1/2) interest in all that piece or parcel of land known and described as follows:— The most Easterly Seventeen hundred and twenty nine (1729) feet of the North half of the South East Quarter of Section Eighteen (18) in Township Eleven (11) and Range Three (3)

West of the principal Meridian Excepting therout all that portion thereof which lies between two lines parallel to and distant perpendicularly One hundred and fifty (150) feet on opposite sides of the centre line of the Northern Pacific and Manitoba Railway as shown on a plan thereof registered in the Portage la Prairie Land Titles Office as N° 235 **do hereby** in consideration of the sum of *Five hundred thousand dollars* ($ *500,000*.⁰⁰) paid me by *David Hofer* the Elder, *Paul Wallman*, *Zacharius Hofer*, *David Hofer* the Younger, *Joseph Michel Waldner* and *Joseph Waldner* all of the Post Office of *Benard* in the Province of Manitoba *Farmers* the receipt of which sum I hereby acknowledge, **transfer** to the said *David Hofer* the Elder, *Paul Wallman*, *Zacharius Hofer*, *David Hofer* the Younger, *Joseph Michel Waldner* and *Joseph Waldner* all my estate and interest in the said pieces of land **In witness** whereof, I have hereunto subscribed my name this *Second* day of *August* A.D. *1918*.

*Signed* by said *Joseph Malcolm Hackney*
in presence of

Sydney Lamb

J M Hackney

Subject to Mortgages Numbers:—
30768; 90316; 90324; 30799 and 30769
And also subject to all levies under the Manitoba Drainage Act

Province of Manitoba } I, Joseph Waldner
to wit          of the West Shore of Bonard in the
                province of Manitoba, Farmer
                make oath and say:—

1. That I am one of the Transferees named in the annexed transfer
2. That the within described parcels, together with all buildings and other improvements thereon, are, in my opinion, of the value of Four hundred and twenty two thousand, nine hundred and one 90/100 dollars (@ $422901.90) and no more, made up as follows:—

|  | | |
|---|---|---|
| Parcel No 1 | $ 11,400.00 | 4,500 |
| Parcel No 2 | 21600.00 | 7,500 |
| Parcel No 3 | 7200.00 | 3,500 |
| Parcel No 4 | 34079.85 | 15540 |
| Parcel No 5 | 18830.70 | 6,240 |
| Parcel No 6 | 39600.00 | 12,900 |
| Parcel No 7 | 108.00.00 | 3,600 |
| Parcel No 8 | 108.00.00 | 3,600 |
| Parcel No 9 | 11400.00 | 4,600 |
| Parcel No 10 | 65105.10 | 21,300 |
| Parcel No 11 | 74767.95 | 24,100 |
| Parcel No 12 | 10840.95 | 3,400 |
| Parcel No 13 | 10852.20 | 5,000 |
| Parcel No 14 | 10936.80 | 5,422.50 |
| Parcel No 15 | 22067.10 | 6,400 |
| Parcel No 16 | 21616.65 | 7,000 |
| Parcel No 17 | 10800.00 | 3,500 |
| Parcel No 18 | 10800.00 | 3,500 |
| Parcel No 19 | 10800.00 | 3,600 |
| Parcel No 20 | 1704.60 | 852.50 |
| Parcel No 21 | 900.00 | 350 |
| | $422,901.90 | 147,905.00 |

Affirmed before me at the City of Winnipeg in the Province of Manitoba this 20th day of August A.D. 1918

Joseph Waldner

Alexander Adams
A Commissioner for BRO

**Leonard Gross** served as executive secretary of the Historical Committee of the Mennonite Church, editor of the *Mennonite Historical Bulletin*, and director of the Mennonite denominational archives and historical research program located at Goshen, Indiana, from 1979–1990. He has written, edited, or translated many works related to the Amish, Hutterites, and Mennonites. His monograph, *The Golden Years of the Hutterites: The Witness and Thought of the Communal Moravian Anabaptists during the Walpot Era, 1565–1578* (Scottdale: Herald Press, 1980), was a groundbreaking publication in historical scholarship on the Hutterites.

# *Community and Ethics*:
## Samuel Kleinsasser's Analysis and Interpretation of Schmiedeleut Faith and History

### LEONARD GROSS

Over the decades, numerous scholars have attempted to portray North American Hutterian faith and life, thought, and history, analytically and interpretively. Yet almost all such published attempts, whatever the language, have come from the outside—that is, until quite recently. The manifold bibliographies published at the end of many such publications on the Hutterites make the point; one need not list them here. But an early exception to this is Paul S. Gross's book, *The Hutterite Way: The Inside Story of the Life, Customs, Religion, and Traditions of the Hutterites*;[1] a more recent example is Linda Maendel's tome, *Hutterite Diaries: Wisdom from My Prairie Community*, wherein she writes: "When others write about us, things tend to get twisted, either intentionally or because the author couldn't grasp certain aspects of our communal life."[2] And by now, other genuinely Hutterite interpretive attempts could also be mentioned.

One such attempt, written a generation ago in 1998, that merits careful consideration as a worthy endeavour in interpreting present-day Hutterianism, is Samuel Kleinsasser's *Community and Ethics*.[3] What follows is

---

1 (Saskatoon: Freeman Publishing Company, 1965).
2 Linda Maendel, *Hutterite Diaries: Wisdom from my Prairie Community* (Kitchener: Herald Press, 2015), 13.
3 Samuel Kleinsasser (1927–2014) was a Schmiedeleut Group II minister from Concord Community, Stony Mountain, Manitoba. He is referred to four times in Rod Janzen and Max Stanton, *The Hutterites in North America* (Baltimore: The Johns Hopkins University Press, 2010). Kleinsasser wrote numerous articles, unpublished but circulating, including "Open letter to the Hutterian Church" (ca. 1992), and "Our Broken Relationship with the Society of Brothers," later published in *KIT Newsletter* 6, no. 7 (July 1994). See also Rod Janzen, "The Hutterites and the Bruderhof: The Relationship between an Old Order Religious Society and a Twentieth-Century Communal Group," *Mennonite Quarterly Review* 79 (October 2005), 505–44.

the background to how this book-length manuscript came into being, and a short analysis of the volume itself—followed by actual extended excerpts from the book itself, consisting of Kleinsasser's foreword, his Chapter 1, and the final three paragraphs of his volume.

I became acquainted with Samuel Kleinsasser in the 1980s and visited him numerous times. In looking over his library, I found volumes in English and German, spanning the whole spectrum of publications, among them highly scholarly works in theology, history, and ethics—including not only Beck, Loserth, and Wolkan, but also the two Niebuhrs. And it was obvious, in our discussions, that he had read them. We became friends, and during one visit around 1995 he showed me the first pages of a hand-written draft that he had been working on for quite some time, titled "Community and Ethics." I read through the first ten pages or so of the first chapter and showed deep interest, wondering if I could have a copy. He wondered if I could help him by editing and typing out the chapter, and I said I would do so.

This was the beginning of a three-year process: Kleinsasser would send me handwritten chapters, which I would edit and send back. He would then edit my version, the changes of which I would then also enter, the result of which was a final copy that was truly the genuine work of Samuel Kleinsasser. In the editing process, my goal was to maintain Samuel's substance and spirit. I wanted his thoughts to read well—something every author desires.

Samuel Kleinsasser's *Community and Ethics* may well be a first among Hutterites for the manner in which the author attempts to ferret out the primary motifs of the Hutterian Brethren. In fact, it aligns as a mirror image of Harold S. Bender's great essay, *The Anabaptist Vision*,[4] homing in on the same three pillars of sixteenth-century Anabaptism: discipleship (following Jesus), community (as the gathered Body of Christ), and love and nonresistance (intent on living out the forgiving and nonviolent love of Jesus)—themes which also crisscross the length and breadth of the Hutterian confession of faith: Peter Riedemann's *Confession of Our Religion, Teaching, and Faith*.[5]

---

4   Bender, Harold S., *The Anabaptist Vision* (Scottdale, Pennsylvania: Herald Press, 1944), still in print.

5   Of the many possible examples from Riedemann which underscore discipleship, community, and love/nonresistance, here are two passages from his Confession: "What [a person] does must be in keeping with the Lord's nature and character; then he will be conformed to his Master in word and life, and give those who follow an example of blessedness. Such a messenger was Paul, who said, 'Be imitators of me, as I am of Christ.' Everyone who wants to gather with Christ must be of his nature, mind, and spirit. Whoever does not have the Spirit of Christ is none of his. How could such a person gather with Christ?… First, we should gather with him as those

On discipleship, Kleinsasser writes in Chapter 2 (one of many examples):

> Let us now see what lies at the roots of Christ-like simplicity, keeping in mind that this is but one expression and function of humility, for *it is always Christ himself, and not so much our forebears, who presents for us a perfect model and example. It is from him that our forebears learned, following in his footsteps, and drawing power and life from him, even if it should cost them their life.* (emphasis added)

As for community, Kleinsasser writes in Chapter 1:

> We arrive at a bone of contention that has often been debated among some Christian churches, for many people state that one cannot find a direct legal demand in the Bible that followers of Christ are to live in community and pool all their resources. Maybe this cannot be found directly, but like higher ethics which are non-enforceable, it is there *indirectly*, which is another way of saying, nobody should seek to live in community because he *has* to, but because he *wants* to. Community is a test of love. (emphasis original)

As for love and nonresistance, Kleinsasser writes in Chapter 4 (one of many an example):

> Love for enemies can only make sense and be brought about when a follower of Christ realizes that a human enemy is spiritually blind, therefore ignorant of true causes, is being exploited and used by sinister plotting and evil forces, and is not only the victim of the evil in his nature. It then places the responsibility of standing in the gap, so to speak, and praying for an enemy, on the shoulders of the one who has received this light. Stephen prayed amidst hailing stones, 'Lord! Do not remember their sin against them!'

---

who have been sent by him. Second, we should do our utmost to keep those who are gathered, so that they do not again become scattered and torn apart by wolves." And "That is why Christ rebuked his disciples when they wanted to express their vengeance by calling fire to fall from heaven and consume those who would not receive them. He said, 'You do not know to what spirit you belong, for the Son of Man did not come to destroy people's souls, but to save them.' He means to say, 'What are you doing? That is not my purpose! If you want to be my disciples, you must not act in this way, for I have not been sent to practice vengeance.'" Peter Riedemann, *Peter Riedemann's Hutterite Confession of Faith*, trans. and ed. John J. Friesen (Waterloo: Herald Press, 1999; Walden: Plough Publishing, 2019), 184, 185, 218.

Another deep concern of Kleinsasser's was to keep Jesus central. He writes in his second chapter:

> Wherever Jesus is not central, even in community, only a rigid, socialistic system remains. The Hutterian Church to our dismay has lost much of this first love, hence God-reliance has waned and become stale. And so, proportionally many have lost zeal also for community living. Therefore to keep the system from falling apart, great emphasis was placed upon community living as being essential for saving and rescuing souls. Both in overstatement and by omission, community living was somehow directly connected with salvation of souls, and not seen only as an aid in this regard that it truly is. [...]
> Unless Jesus is constantly lifted up, with his power to save and restore magnified, and unless we proclaim him alone as the Way, the Truth and giver of spiritual Life that overcomes any and every human dilemma, we are heading for failure. All other attempts to advance within utopia without his leading the way are eventually doomed to failure. Human effort is simply too weak and handicapped by our fallen nature to handle severe crises on our own, and without his divine backing.

*Community and Ethics* is perhaps the sole in-depth and in-house theological, historical, and sociological interpretation of Schmiedeleut Hutterianism to have been written in the twentieth century. It represents the perspectives of one Hutterite who writes about the Hutterian past and present, warts and all—but optimistically so. And because of its depth and thoroughness, it needs to be taken seriously. Yet the perspectives of other Hutterite writers should also be forthcoming—those who come from Schmiedeleut Group I, and from the Dariusleut and Lehrerleut. With this in mind, I hope the reader of *Community and Ethics* will be able to separate Samuel Kleinsasser's vision from his analysis of group conflict, reacting to his interpretations and responding to his visionary ideas apart from his analysis of the encounters that led to the formation of two Schmiedeleut groups, the details of which may well be in contention.

In any case, a published volume that commemorates the century of Schmiedeleut life in Manitoba dare not bypass the profound thoughts of Samuel Kleinsasser, who spent years in preparing for and then writing what might well be his most significant life's work.[6]

---

6   Samuel Kleinsasser's *Community and Ethics* has been informally self-published for use in Hutterite communities. Copies are preserved in the Mennonite Historical Li-

In order to get a better feel for the whole of the Samuel Kleinsasser volume, this essay closes with excerpts from *Community and Ethics*, beginning with a condensed table of contents, followed by the foreword, Chapter 1 in its entirety, and finally, the last three paragraphs of the work.

∽

## [Excerpts from *Community and Ethics* by Samuel Kleinsasser]

### Table of Contents

**Foreword**

**Chapter 1:** The Golden Rule, Clue to Higher Ethics

**Chapter 2:** Spiritual Giants, Spiritual Dwarfs—The Past Twenty-Five Years

**Chapter 3:** The God of Love, and the god of Force

**Chapter 4:** The Power of Nonresistance

**Chapter 5:** Values Regained

### Foreword

Before the reader begins studying this book, I would like to bring to his or her attention a few brief personal comments. First of all, since this work is an analysis of our present-day Church and is not primarily historical in nature, I have tried to point my reader to the rock-bottom Christian principles and ethics upon which I attempt to base my argument. These principles represent the pillars and main support upon which our Church claims to be founded. Therefore, historical events are only periodically interspersed, in order to document the volume's broader purpose which centers on "Community and Ethics" in the here-and-now.

Secondly, there are several ways to approach the subject of ethics as applied to community. During the decades of the era of our founding fathers, and even much later, religious arguments that accepted the Word of God (our Bible) as their final authority were generally considered valid. In our present age, basing one's argument on the Bible has ceased to be a self-evident, valid axiom and basis for working at the myriad problems and

---

brary, Goshen College, Goshen, Indiana, and the Hutterian Brethren Book Centre Archive, MacGregor, Manitoba).

issues confronting society. In its stead, reason, logic, and dialectics have, to a great degree, taken the Bible's place.

Since my work is aimed mainly at the Hutterite mind, at those who as a Church still cling to the claim that God through the Bible should have the final word, I have thus tried to construct my argument along this line, based on Scripture, knowing that the Hutterite mind continues to favour this biblical approach and method in resolving disputes. At the same time, I have also tried to define my presentation so that others outside our society can grasp, and to some extent recognize and even identify with some of the ideals presented in this work. Therefore I have used terms and explanations with them in mind as well. But I also have squarely in mind the newer generations within our Church, many of whom, it appears, find it ever more difficult to identify with and grasp the older methods of explanation and thought patterns handed down to them from older generations.

As for myself, I do not claim that this work is solely my own idea and undertaking. I must pass on much of the credit to the society which has nourished and reared me. Hence, for the most part I am indebted to my fellow members, being but a reflection of the society which has produced me. But I must immediately add that the Gospel message of Jesus—so dear to the Hutterite mind—has led me beyond mere Hutterianism into a personal relationship with the Master Designer of Christianity.

In general, our Church as an institution does not cater to a personal commitment towards one's Creator, fearing defection into individuality. Yet this seeming contradiction and paradox is the very life-blood and core of Christianity.

It is true that worshippers, gathered together in church, tend to set each other on fire, and as a whole will generate a greater volume of spiritual light and warmth than can the individual alone. But too great an emphasis on this larger-scale phenomenon has a tendency to disregard and even take away from the equally essential need of each unique individual—whom God has created unequal—to establish and maintain a personal, one-of-a-kind relationship to one's Creator. Indeed, the Church as an institution cannot fathom the depth of a person's inner needs and total requirements, and hence, by the very nature of things, must forever stand outside and apart from this personal individual need which only the Holy Spirit can penetrate and enter into as His own private domain, empowering the individual with inner strength, wisdom, and knowledge.

To a large extent this work reflects an escape on my part from the mental chains and thought patterns that the institutional Church tries to implant in the individual, resulting in the freedom to express my personal opinion. At the very same time, however, by virtue of this aforementioned mysterious paradox, it brings me closer to, and into a oneness with the gathered community as a home base, yet not as a piece of community-owned property, but only as a lease. The sole owner of myself, therefore, is Jesus Christ who created me, and who finally purchased me, by the very nature of his death, as his very own. Not even my closest and dearest kin can come in between this personal one-of-a-kind relationship, mainly because earthly covenants are not permanent, but a covenant with God is everlasting….

Compiling this work has taken a lot of effort, but nonetheless, if only one precious soul finds his or her way to Jesus through this work, my effort is well rewarded.

– *Samuel Kleinsasser (July 15, 1998)*

## Chapter 1: The Golden Rule, Clue to Higher Ethics

In the past the Hutterian Church of North America represented a fairly stable and productive society. Stable, that is, in comparison to its immediate surroundings where value-changes are very rapid; where, in many areas, Bible standards are considered naive and outdated; and where values and ethics are given the roller-coaster treatment according to the dictates of new trends, tastes, and ever-changing fashions.

In spite of this change and rapidly decreasing moral vacuum within its immediate surroundings, the Hutterian Church enjoyed a strong, if not unique, identity that owed much of its stability to tolerating within its midst gradual change and adjustment on the secular side, and to a moderate Bible-oriented idealism on the moral, ethical, and spiritual side.

Struggle for survival gave cause for hard-labour ethics, which in turn curbed a too-excessive idealism and a super-spirituality. Long-lasting ties and a nearly continental-wide identity among member communities was due to a number of uncommon factors: community-of-goods, a similar code of apparel, common language, nonresistant teachings, identical church doctrines. Sermons and ritual practices presented in their mother tongue spoke to their heart as if it were a sacred language. Adhering to and devotion to a Reformation-era theology, with little change right into the present age, did much to separate them from other churches and strengthened their nonconformity.

Surrounded by a fast-changing sophisticated society, often misunderstood and picked on as an ethnic small-minority group, and sticking out like a sore thumb due to their peculiar life-style, they developed to some extent an inferiority complex, which was often wrongly interpreted as a chip on their shoulder.

Lacking sophistication, and being community centred, they sensed that they could not fit into modern society too well, for they had not yet learned the art of hiding their feelings, or of smiling when the heart was cold; therefore, for them, friendship to outsiders created a problem and became a threatening situation, because they had not built up a defense against it. For once they let somebody in, they thought this called for childlike trust and a total and unreserved friendship. Passive culturing had conditioned them to behave like that. They had their share of ups and downs, and internal and external struggles; but such challenges, so important for internal strength and growth, did not come in so thick and fast that they could not be handled.

But then, in came a new challenge for them, represented by the Society of Brothers, who by all appearances represented many ideals that the Hutterian Church was weakly striving and longing for. Some of these ideals the Hutterian Church, partly due to lukewarmness, partly due to adjustment and compromise, had neglected; and to some ideals its members paid lip-service only in part. Yet this also served to prolong, and in some cases even helped to upgrade community living on the positive side; but it also contributed to a gradual back-sliding on the negative side.

Let us take a closer look at several examples where adjustment by neglecting the ideal had actually enriched the community from an ethical viewpoint. According to the ideal's demand, if a family left a community, this family was not entitled to the house they lived in—or any community property for that matter—but by now it has become a common practice that such a family is permitted to take with them all the contents in that house.

This of course is a very notable discrepancy from the ideal's demand as presented in Acts 4:32, which we take quite literally, wherein it is stated that no one claimed that any of his possessions were his own. Or the baptismal vows where all belongings were voluntarily given up to the church. But when we take a closer look at this obvious discrepancy, we observe that even though it violates the Hutterian Constitution, it harmonizes with higher Christian principles—in other words, with an even higher ethic, *the Golden Rule* (do unto others as you wish to be treated yourself), which takes over. And so, mercy and compassion overrule legalities—for instance, as pointed out, by releasing a portion of property which according to the Church Constitution belongs to the Church, or at least to the individual community.

Let us look at another example. Discrepancy from the ideal is seen when a married person leaves the community. Even though each person vows individually to stay true to the Church, it is taken for granted that married partners and family belong together, and by no means are they asked to break up as a family—as is common within the Society, which holds firmly and rigidly to the ideal and to church vows.

Yet how do we know for sure that we are on the right track by practicing such negligence and lenience? Let us furnish ourselves with another example that will lend us more insights that legalities and the law do not always cover the entire need, and that, where legalities do not cover all or most needs, they proportionally cater to injustice.

We observe a somewhat similar problem wherein we note a clash between the ideals (the law) and higher ethics (the Golden Rule). In Israel, tithing was expected of all good Jews. But in many cases the desperately poor could hardly afford to tithe; it was very much like taking bread out of hungry mouths, and all too often this tithe found its way into the pockets of the already fabulously rich rulers and temple staff. Jesus called this robbing the widows and orphans and devouring their homes.

Now according to the Law of Moses, collecting tithes was perfectly legal and called for by the law to keep the religious system going, but at the same time part of this over-all tithe should have found its way back to the poor, not stopping till at least their basic needs were thus met, according to the Golden Rule. Higher ethics would then label the collecting of tithes—including other high-priced temple services practiced by the temple officials whereby they got rich at other people's expense—as *legalized robbery*.

And so we too must exercise caution, lest according to higher ethics (the Golden Rule) the legal measures that we try to obey and even enforce from time to time turn out also to be a form of pious-looking legalized robbery, which problem has confronted us many times lately.

With this in mind we are led to see in our case that this seeming discrepancy on our part from legalities—or better still, from the very Constitution that we all vouched to obey and honour—does not take away from community even though it appears to do so on the surface. Instead of impoverishing community it enriches it, because it harmonizes with so-called higher ethics. For in principle, Christian community, when lived right, is the outgrowth of love—even more so, the outgrowth of undeserving love. Community, like the Sabbath, exists not for the sake of community, *but for the sake of man*. Community is an extension of ourselves, an expression of our oneness, of our being our brother's keeper.

Now some of my readers might be prompted to ask: What does the term, "higher ethics," actually mean? Let us take to hand a very simple illustration, assuming that one of our communities was well to do and had stock-piled some savings. Down the road was a neighbour who too was in farming, but due to poor luck the bank had refused to loan him any more money to put the crop in. Now suppose this farmer would approach this community for him to borrow some money till fall in order to buy seed, fertilizer, and fuel for the spring seeding. And for security, this farmer would offer them a first mortgage on his tractor, of value equal to the loan. Come fall this farmer would have a complete crop failure and there was no way he could repay this loan.

What should the community do to get their money back? The law is on their side. With a signed note in hand they could legally drive the tractor away in the fall. Even the arm of the law could not stop them.

Now if the community would take away the neighbour's equipment, what they would be doing would be legally right, but morally and ethically wrong. It would be wrong because higher ethics—that is, the Golden Rule—would be broken by their action. Hence we who claim to be Christian must class such an act as breaking a higher law. But where do we find this law written? In the first place it is written in the New Testament by which laws we claim to live, and secondly in our hearts. But we must not mistake man's baser instinct as the voice of God through our conscience. In case of doubt we should always consult the Bible.

Higher ethics are usually not found in national law books; they are conspicuously absent in our Church Constitution in that it leans somewhat heavily on the rights of a majority, and grants the majority full power, but in real life the minority is also sometimes right. The written Church Constitution should not be underestimated; it is the best man can come up with.

Higher ethics, as just pointed out, are not found in law books; nevertheless, they are written in man's heart by their Creator. Since they cannot be found in the law books at the courthouse, no enforcing agency can enforce them; yet they will register and make themselves felt in man's heart when violated, as a very disturbing, uncomfortable, and guilty feeling, as if one had angered God, failed man, and betrayed one's better self.

We usually do not feel responsible beyond our close kin, but according to the teachings of Jesus, he held the rich man accountable for not feeling responsible toward poor Lazarus who lay at his door. And in the parable about the Good Samaritan, Jesus makes us responsible for total strangers who are in need of help.

The Apostle Paul (Rom. 2:15) declares that on Judgment Day God will judge all nations—even the people of all primitive and barbarian societies who had not heard about the Law of Moses or the Gospel of Jesus—by that inner light placed there by their Creator. It is an unwritten law that stands on its own merits and can easily be proven that it exists. Deny any person his or her rights to equal consideration and such will immediately feel mistreated. Society in every age has tried to subtract, add to, twist, and distort this inner code. In spite of all such efforts it still remains with us to this very day.

On Judgment Day none of us will be judged by how we lived up to the standards as presented by man-made laws, charters, or bills of rights, nor by the Hutterian Church Constitution, the rules and guidelines of which are frequently changed, added to, modified, and sometimes even reversed. Judgment will be based entirely on eternal, everlasting, concrete principles and higher ethical codes. They alone are the true fundamentals: constant, and never changing—and not man-made charters and bills of rights.

Let us elaborate a little further on ethical higher law and how it applies in daily living. The parable about the Good Samaritan is a prime example. The priest and Levite could legally bypass the wounded stranger by the roadside. They took refuge and were governed by the first law of nature: self-preservation and self-interest. To assure their survival, this first law of nature insisted that for survival and safety's sake they had better exercise caution and bypass this wounded stranger. Maybe those robbers were still hanging around. Or some ceremonial ritualism restricted them from touching strangers. Or they were on the way to an important summit meeting. We note that an escape always follows this order and sequence. Religion furnishes the cover-up.

Now the Good Samaritan too had that same first impulse, therefore could have claimed the same rights; but we read that compassion took over, and compelled him to go beyond the call of duty, beyond legal expectations, yes, to go beyond the call of first impulse and safety that always enquires: How can I get away with my whole skin? What's in this for me?—which, from a legal and survival viewpoint, is a very essential, sensible, and intelligent question. What the Good Samaritan was obeying was the principle of going the second mile, that extra mile not required by the law of nature, nor by the Law of Moses.

Jesus, who lived mainly by higher ethics, time and again clashed with the hard-core, cold-blooded legalists: the educated lawyers and scribes of that era. Such a clash was inevitable because Jesus who lived by a higher law constantly ended up outside the legally set boundaries. Hence the lawyers and scribes who made no distinctions, and had very little head knowledge of higher superior law, judged that Jesus had broken God's law and deserved to be put away. They were proud of their keen insights and hair-splitting knowledge of the Law of Moses. They thought they knew all there was to know. Self-righteousness stood in the way of a humble, teachable open mind that would lead them into seeing that there was yet much they did not know, and that they missed out on the blessings that follow hungering and thirsting after true righteousness.

Legally-set boundaries forbade and restrained the lawyers and scribes from entering the realm of higher law; by contrast, Jesus insisted that higher law (compassion and mercy) should overrule and override legalities. His whole life and even his voluntary death was governed by higher codes. If this were not so, he could and would have legally stayed in heaven. Compassion alone is what motivated him to come down to earth and lay down his life and die in our stead. And now he bids us: Go thou and do likewise.

Jesus himself states the following, concerning higher moral codes, and about his mission to bring light and understanding into the darkness of this world on this subject: I did not come to put away the law, but to fulfill it. In other words, to extend it, to clarify it, to bring to light and add to the law that missing dimension of human relationships, without which the law falls short of the demands and expectations of God.

Now the Law of Moses was just as true as the Gospel of Jesus. They both came from God. But the Law gave us only a shadow of good things to come; the real substance of the old and new Law was Christ himself. He gave it power, spirit and reality.

Jesus probably never made a more clarifying statement than when he said, I am the Light of the world. It is he who brought us enlightenment about God-pleasing relationships. We read of the first world, due to wickedness of heart, that they constantly refused to be led by God's Spirit. Man refused God's best offer, hence had to settle for God's second-best, a book of rules and regulations enforced by fallible rulers and kings.

Rules and laws are enforceable. A person can be forced to pay his bills. By ancient law, if a person could not pay his bills he could be sold as a slave like an animal, as payment for his legal debts. For the most part, this law was inflexible. A legally-signed document could not be broken. But higher ethics are non-enforceable laws. They represent inner laws and attitudes written in the hearts of men. All the forces and powers in the universe combined could never, ever, force a single drop of love out of a person.

According to 1 Corinthians 13, love can be imitated and copied at times, but to genuinely love one's fellow man is not under the jurisdiction of law; it cannot be legislated; it cannot be ordered into effect by law courts.

We often run into situations and conditions where the measures and the action that we take could be legally justified, but when compared to higher ethics or the Golden Rule they are cruel, inhuman, and un-Christlike.

Christian community cannot function or exist without rules and regulations, but the guidelines that should govern true community must mainly consist of higher laws, prompted by the Holy Spirit. Community rises and falls on this premise: the more higher ethics prevail, the higher the rating; when legalities in excess dominate, community declines; for legalities by the very nature of things limit a relationship by drawing *conditional lines*, hence hampering and blocking the second-mile principle. Christian community can only function properly within the framework and within that extra dimension consisting of higher ethics.

Again, let me repeat, because of the importance of this principle: Genuine community cannot exist for very long as a brotherly relationship without the aid of higher principles, without voluntarily going that second mile. Christian community is the result, the outcome, the outgrowth of putting higher ethics into practice. Genuine community is spontaneous; it cannot be brought into effect by imitating and simulating the saints of the first apostolic church in Jerusalem.

Here we arrive at a bone of contention that has often been debated among some Christian churches, for many people state that one cannot find a direct legal demand in the Bible that followers of Christ are to live in community and pool all their resources. Maybe this cannot be found directly, but like higher ethics which are non-enforceable, it is there *indirectly*, which is another way of saying nobody should seek to live in community because he *has* to, but because he *wants* to. Community is a test of love.

In John 3:16 we read, "For God so loved the world that he gave his only begotten son, that whosoever believes in him shall not perish but have everlasting life." According to this verse, if we believe in Christ, we have accepted salvation. This verse illustrates the love of God towards men. But the Bible does not stop here. As we dwell upon and ponder in our hearts God's love for all of us, we are changed more and more unto that upon which our hearts are fixed, and so good works will provide outward evidence of inward transformation. Good works are not the source of our merits, but an evidence of our faith. They put legs under our faith.

In 1 John 3:16 we are further instructed: "That is how we know what love is, Christ gave his life for us; *we too then ought to give our lives for our brother.*" This then is Christian growth, the outward evidence of our faith and love for Jesus.

Now, most of us have no problem with this first verse, John 3:16. We seem to agree that faith is the sole basis of salvation; we feel blessed and would be foolish not to embrace it for ourselves. But when we are called to go *beyond self*, this then becomes the test of our faith. Love towards our neighbour is evidence that our inward selfish nature has been truly transformed, and that we truly have a born-again experience. (Of course, there is much more to a genuine born-again experience.)

Any Christian in any setting and vocation who wholeheartedly seeks to serve Jesus through his fellow men meets this requirement. Nonetheless, it stands to reason that within the framework of a community setting, one is much better equipped to apply the Golden Rule in a practical, tangible way. All too often private ownership stands in the way of sharing our resources.

If we genuinely accept and appreciate God's unselfish love for us, we too become less selfish and more loving. We look for an expression, an outlet for our love; our fellow men in need furnish us with an outlet. If we keep this outlet closed, we have stopped and hindered God's flow of love towards us, and hence to others. Genuine love for God will always translate itself into love for fellow man as sure as day follows night.

The Apostle John brings this cycle (from God, to us, to our neighbour) to our attention *indirectly* when he writes: "For he cannot love God, whom he has not seen, if he does not love his brother, whom he has seen" (1 John 4:20). We can love our fellow man in a sentimental way, by words only, or in a more real and practical way, through action, through meeting a need.

Jesus tells us that the love we extend to our fellow man should be as unconditional as God's love, for God lets his sunshine fall on the good and bad alike. In Matthew 5:46 we read: "Why should God reward you if you love only those people that love you? Even the tax collectors do that; you must therefore be perfect just as your Father in heaven is perfect."

But without that inner motivation, through Christ and the Holy Spirit to guide and strengthen us, all attempts at fulfilling community will fail. Many attempts have been made at community living which have depended too heavily—or even entirely—on the innate natural goodness found in all men, which is not sufficient to carry us through long periods of severe droughts and acute crises.

This latter warning brings the following question to mind: If the Holy Spirit is responsible for—and adds holding power to—community living, does this imply that the Hutterian Church, which has existed for a considerable length of time, is held together by the Holy Spirit, more so than with non-community-seeking churches?

The Hutterian Church is a rare phenomenon. Much of what its members practice is conditioned by culture. That the Holy Spirit is active in their midst, constantly trying to lead them towards all truth, is of course understandable, for it is the Spirit's function to promote Christ wherever the name of Christ is mentioned and preached. That Hutterites at times have had rather long periods of dry spells and dry seasons is undeniable, especially where materialism and smug self-righteousness have crept in, for we know that a fully alive church is generally active in missionary work. Wherein do Hutterites lack?

But back to our former question: Is community living for Christians authorized in the Bible? Is it essential? One can answer this question with another, somewhat similar question: Is the Golden Rule demanded in the Bible? Is it essential? Jesus answers this question when he stated: Go thou and do likewise.

Now we all know that community living is a very high risk for higher gain, a higher cost for a higher reward and lifestyle. This high risk is the main reason why so few churches take the risk to invest totally in such a high-cost venture; they fear that if they fail the loss will be too great.

Besides, people find it twice as hard to put community living into practice in our age, because it is contrary to and runs against the grain of our Western civilization's highly competitive trends and conditioning. And so it has very little appeal, being a lifestyle that goes in nearly the opposite direction from that of popular trends and Western-style Christianity.

Lately, the truth of this *high loss* has been brought home to us *also*, very forcefully; many among us have nearly lost hope and faith in a continuation of community. This is mainly because we have become too dependent on secular and material benefits as our reward, instead of on spiritual benefits. For instance, we tend to forget that when we take care of the needy, we are serving Jesus. When we serve the needy and they do not show enough appreciation, or if they take advantage of us, we lose incentive.

But when we keep in mind what Jesus said, that in serving the needy we serve him; and when human beings, being who they are, often do not show enough appreciation, or as in Jesus' case as he was going about doing good the crowds still turned against him—in such a case, neither should we look to [humans] for appreciation (fine, if it is given). It is Jesus' appreciation that we should look forward to, when he will say: Well done, my faithful servant.

This type of motivation does not let us down as material benefits do, and as lack of appreciation by people does—the latter being a low, earthly reward; the former, a high, heavenly reward. In our case we have become too dependent on rules, regulations, and traditions to function well in community. But traditions are a very poor substitute for higher law. For one, traditions are in need of modification from time to time; higher ethics are never outdated.

Higher ethics are the very lifeblood of community living, the ground rules as presented by Jesus in his Sermon on the Mount. These are not legal demands that can be enforced; they are voluntary reflexes, triggering a response in us; they are spontaneous by-products aroused in us by God's love which we did not deserve, a love which was not forced on us. His love, if appreciated, arouses in us a counter-love which he lives and produces through us; it arises from him, hence is of no credit to us.

At best (being handicapped by our fallen human nature) we represent symbolically a dead, cold moon, which borrows light from the sun and reflects it down upon earth—or a light bulb which, in order to give light, has to be connected to the power station continuously. As Jesus said, a branch cannot bear fruit by itself; it has to be connected to the vine.

What helps keep us together in part is our cultural conditioning from the cradle up. Unlike the outside society, the we and us is much more dominating than the me and I, which becomes a great aid, and once established, as second nature. Due to force of habit it is not easily gotten rid of, if ever, as many ex-Hutterites can testify. Somewhat similar, as the saying goes, a sailor can be taken out of the sea, but the sea can never be taken out of the sailor. Also we must not lose sight of the major role that our German language in an English-speaking society plays. It separates us and protects us, in part, from faster assimilation.

And so, with non-community members who were reared in community, community will stay in their blood for the rest of their lives. This is not so much a gnawing conscience when given up, but a culturing and conditioning factor. For once a person has become highly institutionalized, where others make decisions for him, or where decisions are made together as a group, it is hard to de-program such a dependent person so that he does his own thinking. In his heart, such a person longs for the shelter of a brotherly institution. To some extent such a person is addicted and hooked on community.

The proper order in genuine Christianity makes a person accountable to God first and foremost, and only secondly, responsible to man-run organized institutions. This order takes care of the fear of man. For the more we fear God, so to speak, the less we will fear man. If men, or institutions, or systems, try to entice us to backslide and bow down to their wishes, fear of God will constrain us. This calls for a strong antithesis, and a strong individuality, due to feeling accountable first to God. But once transformed by his love, there will follow the feeling of responsibility towards men, yet never in conformity to the world.

Individuality in a community setting is not an antisocial drive, unless carried to excess. We each have different talents and gifts, and God expects us to develop these unique gifts. Each of us represents an organ with different functions in the body of Christ (his church) of which he is the head.

Let me summarize this chain of thoughts, and put them in proper order and sequence. Only as we love God supremely and totally is it possible to love our neighbour impartially and truly. For Paul in 2 Corinthians 8:5 reminds us: "They gave themselves first to the Lord, and then to us, in the keeping of God's will."

Community starts to fall apart when we, in a community setting, become too legalistic and insist more and more on our personal legal rights. People are sometimes forced into such a situation because a ruling, competitive spirit, instead of a serving spirit, has found its way into the system, and has stalemated self-giving, creating a threatening atmosphere where child-like trust and lamb-like innocence has been exploited, taken advantage of, and betrayed.

Or, some oversight could cause community to start crumbling, such as the example of the first Christian community at Jerusalem, where the Greeks complained that their widows were sometimes overlooked in the daily distribution. This problem had to be quickly remedied by the Apostles. Or, [it could be] a problem where the light shining upon these principles is missing, or where the crutch of human tradition has replaced Christian principles.

Once a too-legalistic attitude has entered our minds, followed by its practice, then, before we become aware of it, we begin more and more to feel entitled to a fair shake of the available goodies; and if we don't get what we consider our full share, we all too often hold back and refuse to comply, in a manner which sounds fair and square to our, by now, legalistic frame of mind.

And so, instead of going beyond the call of duty where the more gifted put in all their effort, do not hold back, do not feel entitled to special treatment, honour, role, or reward, due to their superior gifts over the less talented (the utilization of which is a must in a community setting)—rather than all this, risks are instead calculated, and service becomes conditional. This results in our becoming mere imitators of Christ; carrying each other's burden becomes a heavy load. At best it is a duty, instead of a privilege and delight, where one is aware that whatever each of us has done to the least of these, God's creatures, this will be reckoned and accounted unto us as if we had done it unto Him. This same God, who has done so infinitely much for us, even unto laying down his life for us, now bids us: Go thou and do likewise. What Jesus in effect is saying is: Love them, serve them for me in my stead.

Thus, in our case, a worldly fairness code and mentality, a legalistic atmosphere, has entered our midst. Now if this were our only lot, we could probably put up with it until we someday find our way back. But much that is worse has come our way. For once corruption and a fighting spirit has entered into a community setting where all resources have been pooled, the devastation and ruin is even worse than within an individualistic society where one can at least fall back upon some individual reserves.

## [Concluding paragraphs from the end of Chapter 5, "Values Regained."]

Throughout this work, time and again, I have mentioned the loss of values, and values that have been traded off and exchanged for something else. Now "value" means the prize, and the prominence and importance placed on a given thing. In this regard, the person who has learned the art of prayer is richer by far than a person with billions in the bank, but who shortchanges himself on prayer. Yet reliance on prayer is but one example of the many available virtues, saintly merits and high morals that make for true everlasting riches, wealth that does not rust, that no thief can steal. So let us dare to be different, for Christians indeed are to be different from non-Christians.

God took our church out of Russia just before all hell broke loose over there, and transplanted us like a vineyard into North American soil, a land where milk and honey flows in abundance. Here he expects us to grow and produce the Fruits of the Spirit. So let our lights so shine that others see The Light and glorify our Father in heaven. But this land is not the end of our journey. There is yet a journey ahead for each and every one of us. Life on earth is our schoolroom; our destination is heaven in the afterlife. To qualify and finally graduate, we have to sweat here on earth for the finals.

I can think of no more befitting words to close this work than to say with the Apostle Peter: "Let all men know … that salvation is to be found through (Jesus) alone: in all the world there is no one else whom God has given, who can save us." And with Paul: "I am not ashamed of the Gospel of Christ, for it is the power of God unto salvation to everyone that believeth…. For therein is revealed the righteousness that matters before God,… not having a righteousness of my own that comes from obeying the law, but that righteousness that comes from God and is by faith in

Jesus Christ." To him alone do I dedicate this work, and like millions of others who have accepted him as their Redeemer and Savior, I give him all praise, credit, honour, and glory! ∼

**Gerald J. Mast** is professor of communication at Bluffton University and editor of *Studies in Anabaptist and Mennonite History*. He is the author of *Separation and the Sword in Anabaptist Persuasion* (Cascadia, 2006), and *Go to Church, Change the World: Christian Community as Calling* (Herald, 2011). A member of First Mennonite Church, Bluffton, Ohio, he is married to Carrie Mast and is the father of Anna, Jacob, and Jorian.

# Navigating the Internet Question: Hutterite Leadership Practices and Schmiedeleut Smartphone Struggles

### GERALD J. MAST

The internet and its related technologies offer distinct attractions to Hutterite communities, successful as they have been throughout the twentieth century in adopting new farming and manufacturing technologies often shunned by other conservative Anabaptist groups.[1] The Hutterites have generally been eager to appropriate new technologies whose technical efficiencies complement the economic efficiencies of their communal lifestyle, so long as those technologies are focused on improved productivity rather than on new modes of entertainment or personal convenience. This is evidenced, for example, by their longstanding willingness to invest in large and well-equipped farm machinery, including, more recently, in GPS systems that enable precise and semi-automated planting of crops.[2]

---

1  Rod Janzen observes that "the traditional Hutterite approach to new technologies is to adopt them quickly, as long as they don't negatively influence Hutterite theology or culture," an approach that contrasts with the Amish and other old order groups that are far more reluctant to adopt new technologies. Rod Janzen and Max Stanton, *The Hutterites in North America* (Baltimore: Johns Hopkins University Press, 2010), 260. It's perhaps more accurate to say that Hutterites have drawn a distinction between entertainment technologies like television and radios that are regarded as unimportant to the community's economic success, on the one hand, and technologies that enhance economic efficiency of the community's enterprises. Radios are unnecessary and potentially harmful and so forbidden, whereas industrial farm equipment or robotic manufacturing technology is regarded as intrinsic to the economic vitality of the community and spiritually neutral. The challenge of the internet is that it combines entertainment and economic capacities in ways that don't easily fit former discernment paradigms.

2  These observations about Hutterite technology use and many that follow in this essay are drawn from my visit to several Schmiedeleut Hutterite communities in North Dakota and Manitoba during May 2014. Information gathered from these visits and the interviews I conducted during the visits is in my possession and is used by permission as part of an informed consent arrangement. Interviews from this

In communities that have developed manufacturing facilities, it is not unusual to see production lines equipped with robotic technology and computerized quality-control systems. In some cases, Hutterite communities have become not only the consumers of automated and computer-based equipment but also the producers and innovators of cutting-edge large-scale farming equipment, including top-of-the-line livestock feeders and remote-controlled irrigation systems. One community I visited during a research trip had purchased a 3D printer to facilitate the design of prototypes for its plastics molding company. Another community assembles a commercially available computer system for controlling sprinkler pivot points via smartphone, a system for which they also provide ongoing customer support.

At the same time, Hutterites have discovered that the distinctions between profitable technology and entertainment or convenience-oriented technology are increasingly more challenging to draw. A television is easier to categorize as an unnecessary or even harmful entertainment technology than is a smartphone, which can be used to control pivot points as well as to access Facebook.

The most conservative of the three main Hutterite groups, the Lehrerleut, have responded to the increasing convergence of business and entertainment digital platforms by eliminating even business- and accounting-related internet use on their communities in order to become completely internet free, consciously accepting the economic consequences.[3] Among the Dariusleut, internet usage varies from community to community, with the more conservative communities following the Lehrerleut model of becoming internet-free and the more assimilated communities accepting business and commercial uses of the internet, while seeking to restrict entertainment and non-commercial use.[4] The Schmiedeleut, generally seen as the most liberal of the Hutterite groups, include communities that have accepted modestly filtered internet access for not only business but also educational and household use as a matter of routine.[5]

---

     research trip will be identified in citations as either Schmiedeleut Group I interviews, May 2014, or Schmiedeleut Group II interviews, May 2014.

3    Janzen and Stanton, *The Hutterites in North America*, 265.

4    Ibid.

5    For example, a pamphlet published by Group I Schmiedeleut designed to introduce Hutterite practices and beliefs to the public includes a photograph of a Hutterite classroom equipped with computers, along with a caption stating that "technology is integral in our schools." *The Hutterian Brethren: Living in Christian Community* (St. Agathe, MB: Crystal Spring Colony, 2000), 15. During my visits to Group I Schmiedeleut communities I observed that computers in these classrooms were clearly internet accessible. Indeed, the high school classrooms at these Hutterite

Behind such choices about internet access, a lively conversation has been unfolding among the Hutterites about the costs, benefits, and unintended consequences of internet use, a conversation that in recent years has focused specifically on the potential and ubiquity of smartphones—which for most Hutterite communities who use them means the various iterations of Apple iPhones and iPads.

The conversation is shaped significantly by leadership decisions and pronouncements at both the conference and community levels, as well as by the way leadership actions are received, interpreted, and discussed by ministers during church and prayer services—but also by community members during informal conversations at daily coffee breaks and communal meals, as well as during many other occasions for discussion that are part of Hutterite community life. Such opportunities for daily conversation about community policies distinguish the Hutterites to some extent from other Anabaptist churches, such as the Amish or Mennonites, who do not live communally. Thus even though Hutterites follow a hierarchical and patriarchal model of authority, there is also a significant capacity for dissenting views or practices to develop momentum in resistance to decisions made by community or conference leaders.

Historically this has meant that there is typically some distance between many of the official community rules that have been established by Hutterite leaders and actual personal and community practices. For example, while there may be official rules against cameras or musical instruments, it is not unusual for such items to be tolerated so long as they are kept hidden from public view.[6] In principle, the Hutterites share all of their wealth and property in common; in practice, many participate in what is sometimes called the Hutterite "black market," where individuals may sell crafts or other items for personal profit in order to acquire spending money for gifts or possessions.[7] These are generally small-scale enterprises and are mostly tolerated by leaders who struggle to know how to effectively curb such activity other than preaching against it. At the same time, such enterprises can serve as a kind of safety valve for the individual ambitions that are generally suppressed for the sake of the common life.

This distinction between official rules and actual practices plays an important role in the contested arena of internet use. Those leaders who oppose routine or non-business uses of the internet struggle with how to enforce official rules against personal online activity that many Hutterites regard as unofficially negotiable in private. The complex relationships

---

    communities were linked together through a Hutterite-owned broadband network that made video-conferenced classes possible.

6    Janzen and Stanton, *The Hutterites in North America*, 231.

7    Ibid.

between conference-wide policies, community implementation of those policies, and individual Hutterite responses to such official decisions can best be understood through a closer examination of how internet-related conversations and practices have played out thus far in communities related to one or the other of the two Schmiedeleut groups.

## Hutterite Leadership Practices and the 1992 Schmiedeleut Division

The communalist Hutterites in North America have historically been organized into three different groups or *Leut*, rooted in distinctive founding stories associated with the renewal of communal living in nineteenth-century Russia. The Schmiedeleut originate with the leadership vision and community begun by the blacksmith (*Schmied*) Michael Waldner in 1857, who led a group of Hutterites from the Ukraine to Dakota Territory in 1873–74 to establish the Bon Homme Community. During the same year, another group of Hutterites, organized and led by elder Darius Walter and therefore known as the Dariusleut, migrated to what is now South Dakota to establish the Wolf Creek Community. The third *Leut* arrived in the Dakotas in 1877, led by ministers Jacob Wipf and Peter Hofer, and were known as the Lehrerleut because Jacob Wipf was a *Lehrer*—a teacher.[8] In 1918, fifteen Hutterite communities moved from the Dakotas across the border into Canada, with six Schmiedeleut communities choosing to settle in Manitoba. The Dariusleut and the Lehrerleut settled in Alberta.[9]

Among these groups, the Schmiedeleut have been considered the most open to cultural change and the Lehrerleut the most restrictive and conservative, with the Dariusleut incorporating greater diversity than either of the other two groups. At the same time, since 1992, the Schmiedeleut have been divided into two bodies that have essentially functioned as two different *Leut*—one more conservative and the other open to greater innovation.[10]

Hutterite leadership is organized hierarchically, both within the community structure and in the conference bodies that provide community accountability to the larger church. Within the community, a council of elders has authority to make significant decisions for the community. This council consists of the community's senior minister, the assistant minister, if there is one, the steward, the farm manager or work distributor, and two or three other trusted men, sometimes including the so-called German

---

8  Astrid von Schlachta, *From the Tyrol to North America: The Hutterite Story Through the Centuries* (Waterloo: Pandora Press, 2008), 167–68.
9  Ibid., 180.
10  Janzen and Stanton, *The Hutterites in North America*, 64–73.

teacher who is responsible for the religious instruction of children. These leaders are either elected to their positions or, in the case of the ministers, chosen through a combination of election and selection by lot. An executive committee consisting of the ministers and the managers convenes on a daily basis to handle routine community decisions. Additional community members are assigned to direct specific areas of work on the community, such as the care of various livestock operations, servicing vehicles and farm equipment, tending the gardens, and managing the cooking teams. These department heads are elected by vote of the male members of the community, who also constitute a body that may ratify or challenge decisions by the council of elders.[11]

Each community belongs to one of the larger church conferences—which are derived from the distinctive *Leut* that emerged in early North American Hutterite history. An executive committee that includes a senior elder and representative ministers drawn from various communities provides conference governance and is charged with enforcing the *Gemeindeordnungen* (ordinances or regulations) of their conference.[12] Historically, each of the conferences also elected three ministers to a board charged with representing all the Hutterite groups under the common constitution of the Hutterian church.[13] This constitution was adopted in 1950 in order to incorporate the broader Hutterian Brethren Church consisting of the communities in all three conferences and presided over by a nine-member board with representation from each of the conferences.[14]

The larger Hutterite conference system was tested in the 1980s during a crisis in authority that culminated in the 1992 Schmiedeleut division. Among the events leading to this division were a raft of inter-Hutterite lawsuits about matters that are still highly contested among the groups involved, which included practically all communities in the Schmiedeleut and, in a fairly peripheral way, the other two Hutterite conferences as well. Each of the two sides in the schism regards itself as the true continuation of the original Schmiedeleut Conference (and therefore in the right) and both sides have nicknames for the other faction that arise from the peculiar circumstances of the division. Following the lead of internal reconciliation attempts, namely that of the Hutterian Education Committee (a formal group that survived the schism longest, although it also eventually reorganized relatively peacefully into two groups along schism lines), scholars have taken to calling these two factions Group I and Group II.

---

11 Ibid., 206–08.
12 Ibid., 205.
13 Ibid.
14 Alvin Esau, *The Courts and the Colonies: The Litigation of Hutterian Church Disputes* (Vancouver: UBC Press), 2004.

For their part, those associated with Group I allude to the other faction as the "Gibbs," referring to the last name of a banker who at one point circulated a lengthy manuscript accusing a number of Group I leaders of various misdeeds. Group II, on the other hand, identifies Group I as the "Oilers"—referencing the mismanagement of oil-well investments by some of the Group I communities. It is worth noting that the use of the pejorative labels of "Gibbs" and "Oilers" is in decline among Schmiedeleut, particularly with renewed hopes in the possibility of reunification of the two groups following the appointment of Arnold Hofer as the new elder for Group I after the death of Jacob Kleinsasser.

A number of accounts of this division have appeared, the most comprehensive being Alvin Esau's book *The Courts and the Colonies*, which is written from a legal studies perspective and appears to favour the Group II viewpoint. Another informative, but less comprehensive, account by Jeff Longhofer—somewhat more sympathetic than Esau to Group I—focuses on the structural inconsistency in Hutterite polity between intra-community communalism on the one hand, and inter-community ambiguity between autonomy and cooperation on the other hand.[15] In my account of the division here, I will focus on only those aspects of the conflict that are relevant to the contrasting ways these different Schmiedeleut groups have approached the use of the internet.

The most important root of the division, from my perspective, is the controversial and complicated relationship between the Hutterites and the Bruderhof—a modern communalist movement begun by Eberhard Arnold in Weimar Germany. Arnold visited North American Hutterite communities in 1930 in order to establish a relationship between the Bruderhof and the Hutterites, a visit that culminated with Arnold being ordained as a Hutterite minister and representative missionary in Germany.[16]

The Bruderhof was forced out of Hitler's Germany and, after resettling first in England and for a longer stretch in Paraguay near the Mennonite colonies, the Bruderhof established several locations in New York and Pennsylvania.[17] The Bruderhof relationship with the Hutterites was tested early on by a conflict centred at the Forest River Community in North Dakota, leading to the breaking of ties between the two groups in 1955. This rupture lasted until 1974, when full fellowship was re-established

---

15   Jeff Longhofer, "All Things in Common? The Contingent Nature of Communalism Among the Hutterites," *Journal of Mennonite Studies* 11 (1993), 174–93.
16   Markus Baum, *Against the Wind: Eberhard Arnold and the Bruderhof* (Farmington: Plough Publishing House, 1998), 192–203.
17   Yaacov Oved, *The Witness of the Brothers: A History of the Bruderhof* (New Brunswick: Transaction Publishers, 1996), 93–205.

between the Bruderhof and the three Hutterite *Leut*.[18] Although the Bruderhof-Hutterite relationship would ultimately fail again, during nearly twenty years of working together there was a significant exchange of ideas, practices, and marriage partners between the Bruderhof and the Hutterites, especially the Schmiedeleut branch.[19] The Bruderhof adopted many of the historic clothing and grooming practices of the Hutterites as well and grafted themselves onto the larger and older founding narrative of the sixteenth century—the Anabaptist movement.[20] The Hutterites, especially the Schmiedeleut, were influenced by the more expressive piety and modern organizational practices of the Bruderhof.[21] For example, during the 1973 reunification of the Bruderhof with the Schmiedeleut, the grounds for affiliation emphasized spiritual unity more than agreement about "points" of "traditional rules."[22] That priority of spiritual unity over traditional rules has continued to be attractive for some Schmiedeleut leaders and communities.

Nevertheless, this exchange of gifts led to tension and conflict, not only between the Bruderhof and the Hutterites, but also within Hutterite communities, as they debated about how far to go in accepting Bruderhof innovations. Some Hutterites felt that the Bruderhof was a positive spiritual force that could renew the original missionary impulse of the historic Hutterite movement and strengthen their witness to the world.[23] Other Hutterites were anxious that the Bruderhof influence was undermining the separation from the world that was central to Hutterite life and faith, as well as a traditional Anabaptist teaching shared more broadly with communities such as the Amish and the Mennonites.[24] In North America, separation had become identified more closely with a practice of sectarian withdrawal—an outcome of centuries of conflict and persecution in Europe. Yet Anabaptist separation had not always meant withdrawal, and those who argued for more mission and outreach were not advocating assimilation.[25]

In any event, such cultural anxieties and theological differences led ultimately to a fracturing of ties between the Bruderhof and Hutterite

---

18   Ibid., 190–96; 245–50.
19   Janzen and Stanton, *The Hutterites in North America*, 289.
20   Oved, *Witness of the Brothers*, 289.
21   Yossi Katz and John Lehr, *Inside the Ark: The Hutterites in Canada and the United States* (Regina: CPRC Press, 2012), 181.
22   Merrill Mow, *Torches Rekindled: The Bruderhof's Struggle for Renewal* (Rifton: Plough Publishing House, 1991), 220.
23   Ibid.
24   Oved, *Witness of the Brothers*, 288–89.
25   For an account of Hutterite missionary activity in Europe that aligned with a more activist posture of separation, see Gerald Biesecker-Mast, *Separation and the Sword in Anabaptist Persuasion* (Telford: Cascadia Publishing House, 2006), 150–60.

communities that has never been repaired.[26] The Lehrerleut and Dariusleut broke fellowship with the Bruderhof in 1990, followed by Group II Schmiedeleut in 1992 and Group I Schmiedeleut in 1995.[27]

Accounts of the 1992 internal Schmiedeleut division typically feature the bitter courtroom battles over patent rights to a hog feeder design, as well as the long-term litigation of disputes over financial settlements associated with community conflicts resulting from the Schmiedeleut division.[28] Moreover, such accounts also usually give considerable attention to the extraordinary and controversial influence of the senior Schmiedeleut elder Jacob Kleinsasser, who until 1995 was a firm advocate for closer ties with the Bruderhof and who exhibited sympathy for the Bruderhof's social outreach and advocacy.[29] While such details are certainly an important part of the story, my own interest in Hutterite responses to digital technology leads me to give greater attention to theological and ideological differences between the two groups that ultimately emerged in the Schmiedeleut division: Group I, which was shaped to a greater extent by the expressive piety and organizational rationalism of the Bruderhof; and Group II, which adhered more strongly to traditional Hutterite spiritual practices and governance. Both groups understood themselves to be loyal to their sixteenth-century spiritual forbears. But Group II tended to emphasize to a greater extent the necessary obedience to the rule of Christ—expressed concretely in practices of submission and yielding. Group I, for its part, sought to recover the original missionary activism and spiritual solidarity of the early Hutterite communities. These two views are not mutually exclusive, and both groups incorporated some version of both of these distinctive Anabaptist commitments; however, each group emphasized one over the other in ways that invited conflict.

The most significant cultural differences between the groups relate to differing understandings of authority, including the status of *Ordnungen* made by church leaders, as well as the attitude toward the outside world that is increasingly available to Hutterites who enjoy internet access. On the one hand, both groups were influenced by the Bruderhof's emphasis on a centralized leadership hierarchy that tended to follow a modern managerial understanding of procedural authority. On the other hand, this influence was inflected in divergent ways among the two groups, with the divergence sometimes occurring between the groups and at other times within the groups. In terms of current community polity as articulated in organizational documents and practices, the Group II Schmiedeleut, along

---

26  Ibid., 288–97.
27  Janzen and Stanton, *The Hutterites in North America*, 68.
28  For example, Esau, *The Courts and the Colonies*.
29  See, for example, Katz and Lehr, *Inside the Ark*, 180–86.

with the Lehrerleut and Dariusleut Conferences, adhere to a more traditional view of leaders as shepherds and shapers of an often-contested consensus that is given expression in *Gemeindeordnungen*, or rulings by conference leaders about community practices that relate to the spiritual and social welfare of the community.[30] Group I Schmiedeleut express greater deference to ordained and elected leadership, more than to rules and *Ordnungen*, even while granting more apparent participation in decisions to both male and female members. Both groups value consensus but define it differently: for Group II, consensus entails a willingness to tacitly accept decisions and rules made by the leadership, even if not in full agreement with them; Group I prefers that decisions express a more inclusive and willing support by all in the community. Group II emphasizes readiness to yield—the traditional Anabaptist virtue of *Gelassenheit*.[31] Group I speaks more favourably about the role of conscience—spiritual discretion and conviction—in guiding moral choices.[32] At the same time, one might find Group I communities that are oriented by a more traditional Hutterite focus on rules or a Group II community that is oriented more by deference to a leadership vision.

This distinction in leadership and polity should not be overdrawn. Both Schmiedeleut groups retain a traditional Anabaptist commitment to the authority of the church community over personal choices and decisions, along with the responsibility of the church's ministers to enforce and implement decisions made by the Hutterite church, including decisions made by the respective Schmiedeleut Conferences.

The crisis in leadership authority among the Schmiedeleut precipitated by the 1992 schism serves to illustrate emerging polity differences within a shared communalist ethos. When the ministers now associated with Group II communities voted not to recognize the authority of Jacob Kleinsasser as their spiritual leader, they were in a sense declaring that they no longer regarded Kleinsasser as a leadership embodiment of their spiritual commitments. The response of Jacob Kleinsasser and his supporters—Group I—was to argue that the vote was not procedurally legitimate. In the conflict, Group II focused on leadership credibility (Jacob Kleinsasser can no longer be trusted); whereas Group I focused on process legitimacy (Jacob Kleinsasser was unfairly treated).

---

30  According to social ethicist Gerald Schlabach, "Leaders in traditional cultures represent their communities in their very person, because they only emerge as leaders by accumulating the community's wisdom and embodying its values over time." Gerald Schlabach, "The Case for Conference Authority, part 1: Patterns of Church Life," *The Mennonite* (September 15, 1998), 8–9.
31  Schmiedeleut Group II interviews, May 2014.
32  Schmiedeleut Group I interviews, May 2014.

Because the senior elder of the Schmiedeleut was historically also recognized as the senior elder on the board of managers representing all Hutterite *Leut* or conferences, the rejection of Kleinsasser's authority by Group II leaders also forced the Lehrerleut and the Dariusleut to take sides in the dispute. The Lehrerleut and Dariusleut ended up aligning with Group II to form the Hutterian church's board of directors—which in 1993 revised their 1950 Constitution. Among the revisions was a stipulation that the senior elder on the board of directors cannot also be a senior elder of one of the *Leut*, as Jacob Kleinsasser had been.

The polity decisions of the more traditional Hutterite *Leut*, including the Group II Schmiedeleut faction, appear to be designed to reduce the centralization of authority at the levels of conference and board of directors—as is illustrated by the 1993 constitutional revision that forbids an elder of one of the *Leut* to be the senior elder of the broader Hutterite church. By contrast, the modernizing Group I Schmiedeleut continue to adhere to the 1950 Constitution and insist that their senior elder is the rightful leader of all Hutterites. The Group I stance included a controversial ruling by their elders that forbade routine marriages of Group I members with Group II members, a ruling that has been lifted in a recent *Ordnung* letter.

My understanding of this difference in polity is that the traditional groups seek a polity that permits some diversity of conference and community practices—including support for the continuation of more traditional Hutterite customs and convictions. Many Group I Schmiedeleut, by contrast, seek a more expressive spiritual unity in their embrace of more advanced education, mission outreach, and other "modernizing" practices. This distinction between decentralized traditionalism and expressive unity can be illustrated in the practical management of church discipline in community culture.

As mentioned earlier, in many traditional Hutterite communities some limited stretching or even breaking of the *Ordnungen* is permitted so long as it is not done in public view, especially if it involves younger members. A story told by Rod Janzen and Max Stanton illustrates this distinction between official church rules and unofficial exceptions. When a Hutterite youth was heard playing a guitar by a minister who was his uncle, the minister came into his bedroom where the youth was playing the guitar and broke the guitar over his knee, making the statement: "I don't want to ever have to do this to you again." The youth, when asked by a visitor whether that was the end of his guitar-playing days, explained what his uncle meant: "He was not angry that I was playing a guitar. Everybody in the community knows that and I'm not the only one who does. It's just that I was playing loud enough for him to hear me when he was passing by. As the community minister, he had no other choice but to take action."³³

The Group II Schmiedeleut mostly continue to accept this traditional view of Hutterite *Ordnungen*: rules to be followed in public, even if not always in the basement. However, Group I Schmiedeleut tend to be critical of this traditional distinction between the living room and the basement, between outward obedience and private dissent, a distinction they believe undermines trust and a sense of fairness in the community. These different views about rules lead to quite different practices related to internet use between Schmiedeleut II and Schmiedeleut I communities.

## Contrasting Habits of Hutterite Internet Use

In 2002, the leadership of the Schmiedeleut Group II issued a letter containing *Ordnungen* related to the use of the internet. This statement is the first in a long series of letters and rules about the internet issued by the conference ministers, all of which express alarm about the use of the internet in Hutterite communities and urge against its use. The 2002 letter, for example, stated that all computers unauthorized by the community should be put away.³⁴ It also acknowledged that computers were increasingly being used for entertainment purposes, such as games and videos, and urged that computers "remain in barns and shops" and that any computers found in homes should "have all games removed."³⁵ With respect to the internet, the letter was unequivocal: "The internet should not be allowed and those who have it must remove it from houses, barns, shops, and schools." This rule describes the internet as an "alarming abhorrence" and "a great evil for God's people," displaying "impure, heathenish things" that "should not even be mentioned."³⁶ The 2004 conference report reiterates that the internet not be tolerated under any circumstances.

In 2006, the conference report recognized the overuse of cellphones as an emerging problem, although not requiring a rule. People should use common sense and good conscience to make wise choices about cellphone use. Phones should not be distributed to every household in a community but rather allocated as needed.³⁷ A separate rule forbade any use of "camera

---

33   Janzen and Stanton, *The Hutterites in North America*, 103.
34   *Ordnungen und Konferenz Briefen*, 2002, #7. For an English translation, see "Ordnances and Conference Letters of the Schmiedeleut, 1762–2009" in Katz and Lehr, *Inside the Ark: The Hutterites in Canada and the United States*, 375. This translation is a good reference guide to the "Ordnances and Conference Letters" but not always accurate in its translation. The direct quotations in this paper are checked against the original German text of the letters and altered where necessary for accuracy.
35   *Ordnungen und Konferenz Briefen*, 2002, #8; Katz and Lehr, *Inside the Ark,* 375.
36   Ibid., 381.
37   *Ordnungen und Konferenz Briefen*, 2006, #13; Katz and Lehr, *Inside the Ark*, 386.

phones."[38] The 2006 rule on the internet states clearly that "the internet is simply not allowed" while noting that "many have taken the liberty to install it." All the ministers and stewards "were questioned about this and those who took this liberty were required to apologize to the large assembly for their disobedience."

The 2006 letter then makes an appeal regarding the internet: "Dear brothers, it is a dishonour that we as leaders of the community consider it not to be important when something is forbidden, or that we directly oppose the rule and thus create conflict with the older ministers." Expressing concern for the young people, the letter characterizes the addictive nature of internet activity and poses the question: "Why don't we see it more negatively? Many people of the world do not permit this abomination in their homes to protect their children from such vulgarity. We should strive against it with much greater effort so that we are not also led into temptation." The letter also anticipates the argument that community business enterprises need to use the internet: "We shall not think that we need it to go about our business since there are communities with large businesses and manufacturing operations that do not have it." The distinction between the World Wide Web and e-mail is considered: " We can try all we want to filter it and lock it out and only allow e-mail. But anyone you talk with about this will tell you that before you even get to e-mail, the image of an exposed woman already appears." Nevertheless, "several stewards have been appointed to see whether it is possible to use only e-mail in communities with manufacturing operations."[39]

This 2006 conference report exhibits a number of responses to the internet that are quite common among conservative Anabaptist communities more generally. First, there is a lament that not everyone feels the sense of urgency to address the issue. Second, there is a central concern about the influence of the internet on the habits of young people. Third, there is recognition of the pressures that business enterprises experience to utilize the internet. Fourth, there is consideration of the difference between email and the World Wide Web more generally. And fifth, a committee of community managers with expertise in digital technology is charged with further research.

In 2008, there appears to be a kind of watershed in the thinking of Schmiedeleut Group II leaders regarding the internet. The 2008 letter says that during the conference's elders' meeting, "it was discussed at great length as to whether it is possible to conduct our business without the internet and it was acknowledged by everyone that it brings much vice and

---

38   *Ordnungen und Konferenz Briefen,* 2006, #14; Katz and Lehr, *Inside the Ark,* 386.
39   *Ordnungen und Konferenz Briefen,* 2006, #15; Katz and Lehr, *Inside the Ark,* 386.

great danger with it." A significant concession now appears in the letter: "But the communities with manufacturing claim that they cannot work without it. It was recognized by the great majority that it can be allowed in communities with manufacturing, but nowhere else, not by the ministers and stewards, not in schools and not in homes." The letter then goes on to propose a set of practices whereby exceptions to the rule against internet use can be considered and granted. The communities that feel they need to use the internet because of their involvement in manufacturing must apply to the executive committee of the conference. Only those communities who are granted permission may use the internet and these communities must keep strict track of who is given permission to use it in the community. Even in these communities, however, the internet is not to be used in schools or in the homes or offices of ministers and stewards. Moreover, anyone who uses the internet without permission is to be punished.[40]

The 2009 elders' letter tightens up and clarifies the 2008 rules and their application by strengthening the division between home and business use and opposing all use in Hutterite homes, "not even in the homes of ministers and stewards." Moreover, the letter states, "where it is found that the internet is being used for manufacturing without employing all means to block everything except e-mail, and someone commits a sin through it, this shall be punished with *Unfrieden*" (that is, those who are responsible will be proclaimed to be at odds with the community).[41]

This rule against any internet use, except for business needs that have been vetted by the conference elders and community leaders, continues to be the official rule for Schmiedeleut Group II communities. At the same time, five years later the unofficial practices of many communities stretched this rule considerably, as I discovered when I visited three Group II communities in 2014.

In the Group II communities I visited, it was clear that the official policy was that internet use was forbidden, apart from necessary use for community enterprises or, in some cases, for access to educational and publishing resources. In these communities, internet access is typically controlled by password-protected Wi-Fi access. Those with permission to use the internet are given the password while other uses of the internet are limited to a computer that is kept in a locked room in the shop.[42]

When I discussed this policy with a few young women of one of the communities, they agreed that the community forbade internet use for any purpose except approved business or instructional needs; however, they

---

40   *Ordnungen und Konferenz Briefen*, 2008, #2; Katz and Lehr, *Inside the Ark*, 393.
41   *Ordnungen und Konferenz Briefen*, 2009, #7; Katz and Lehr, *Inside the Ark*, 398.
42   Schmiedeleut Group II interviews, May 2014.

also admitted that they had Facebook and Pinterest accounts, just like most of the other youth in the community. In fact, they told me that the recipe for the salad included in the menu for the community's evening meal had been found on Pinterest. Clearly, the Wi-Fi password for the community was known beyond officially approved users.[43]

However, all such unofficial use of the internet is kept hidden from public view, a practice that is facilitated by the use of iPods and smartphones. In Schmiedeleut Group II communities, there seems to be little disruption of community life and routines thanks to this avoidance of public use. In this community the German teacher is also responsible for supervising the care of the community's large garden plot, usually by young women. He told me that he insists the young women leave their cellphones and iPods at home, so as not to interfere with work. "Texting should stay in the privacy of the home," he said.[44]

In one Group II community I visited, my conversation partner described a leadership conflict in the community between the junior minister and the business manager over the use of smartphones. The junior minister wants the community to get rid of them, but the business manager opposes such a policy, especially since the community has begun manufacturing digital management systems for farm equipment that rely on smartphones for functionality; for example, systems that control irrigation sprinklers via GPS. According to my source, most of the community's members agree with the business manager. Moreover, most of the members regard the smartphone and the internet as simply the latest items in a parade of technology innovations that were at first opposed by the Hutterites and then eventually accepted, at least unofficially, such as tape recorders and radios.[45]

In the view of some Group II community members I spoke with, the tension that exists between official prohibitions and unofficial toleration, as well as the contrasting positions that are often expressed among community leaders and members, are healthy conflicts in a close-knit and mutually dependent community such as the Hutterites maintain. For example, the German teacher mentioned earlier describes these conflict-accepting processes by comparing them with the Bruderhof's style of decision-making: "When the Bruderhof makes a decision, everyone needs to agree with the decision before they move forward. Here, when we make decisions, those who disagree go along with the decision for the sake of the group, but they aren't expected to express agreement."[46]

---

43  Ibid.
44  Ibid.
45  Ibid.
46  Ibid.

Hutterites who live in Schmiedeleut Group I communities tend to see things a bit differently, as I discovered when I visited two prosperous Group I communities. In both of these communities, manufacturing has played a significant role in the community's economic success and identity. I was hosted at one of these communities by a family in which the husband and father was a member of their company's management team, and the wife and mother was one of the community's schoolteachers and a graduate of Brandon University's Hutterite education program.

When I met with my host in his office at work, he was working at a station with two computer screens and frequently consulted his iPhone. In this Schmiedeleut I community, there is no prohibition of the internet and Wi-Fi access is readily available anywhere in the community. The only apparent restriction is what my host described as a modest filtering system that prevents anyone from accidentally stumbling into pornographic or indecent sites. The filtering system is furnished by the internet service provider used by the community—the Hutterian Broadband Network (HBNi)—a system designed and managed by Group I Hutterite technicians. HBNi was created especially to provide the online and video-conferencing capabilities that connect classrooms among Group I community schools, especially high school classes. The network is an impressive achievement that links Schmiedeleut communities and classrooms across the entire southern part of Manitoba. While the main purpose of HBNi has been to connect community classrooms through video-conferencing, it also provides a full range of internet-related services to member communities: phone service, filtered internet connectivity, website hosting, e-mail service, business-related video-conferencing, and so on.[47]

At the Schmiedeleut Group I communities I visited, all community members who wish to have a smartphone receive one, along with a data plan. Although some Schmiedeleut Group I communities block social media sites such as Facebook, the communities I visited had no such restrictions; in fact, the wife in my host family explained that social media is a primary way for her to stay connected to her friends and the broader Christian community. She reads Christian women bloggers such as Rachel Held Evans and Jen Hatmaker and considers Facebook to be a place where she is able to have substantive conversations.[48]

The small group of friends who showed up at my host family's house to discuss technology with me included one of the community's ministers, who shook his head when I asked him whether he thought there should be any restrictions or rules about internet use set by the community. "We

---

47    Information about HBNi can be found on the network's website, http://www.hbni.net.
48    Schmiedeleut Group I interviews, May 2014.

don't need any more rules," he said. "We have enough rules. Conscience should be our rule."[49]

Although the minister left after about an hour, the remaining group of young adult men and women laid out their hopes for the future of communities like theirs: more open and responsive to the world around them, less rule-governed and more collaborative in decision-making, more inclusive of women in positions of community authority, more embracing of education, and more committed to mission.[50] These views are clearly shaped by the vision of the Hutterite future articulated by Group I's senior elder Jacob Kleinsasser; they also reflect the influence of spiritual and theological visions from beyond Hutterite communities, including those discovered in the higher education experiences of an increasing number of Hutterites as well as through online sources that are now freely accessible.

This group of young adults acknowledged that the internet had brought some challenges and problems into their community. Some young ministers were sending people text messages of admonishment rather than visiting in person. "No, you can't use text messages to talk about problems and issues," someone pointed out. The internet had opened the door to addictive behaviours on the part of some community members, which needed to be addressed. My host noted that his children are quite attached to the iPad, but said he preferred that to television, which he thought of as a more passive medium, although he also acknowledged that some people used the internet just like a television, in a very passive, consumption-focused way.[51]

In any event, "problems such as these shouldn't be addressed by a few leaders making decrees that no one follows," as one young adult put it. These are problems that community members should work at solving together as sisters and brothers. And, he pointed out, there are many opportunities for open discussions of technology issues in routine community life, from the daily gathering of managers and workers before the work day begins—at least in Hutterite communities organized around manufacturing—to morning and afternoon coffee breaks, the three communal meals shared each day, and the late-night social gatherings of the kind I had the privilege of participating in. When an individual member exhibits problematic behaviour related to internet use, this should be viewed more as a pastoral challenge to be resolved with the help of personal intervention by the ministers and not as the basis for new rules for the whole community, from this Group I perspective.[52]

---

49  Ibid.
50  Ibid.
51  Ibid.
52  Ibid.

Not all Group I communities are as critical of conventional Hutterite practices of authority as the young adults I interviewed during my research. And many Group II individuals express the same concerns that have been emerging with great energy in Group I about traditional leadership practices and authority patterns.

## *Gemeindeordnungen* and Changing Leadership Communication

What is clear from the discussions about smartphones and digital networks and how to regulate them for church members is that among the Schmiedeleut, and perhaps especially among Group I, the traditional model of Hutterite leadership and authority is being questioned and, in some cases, reformed. This traditional model relies on the issuing of *Gemeindeordungen*, or church ordinances, that admonish church members to "live up to the requirements of life in a perfect community of goods" and that advance "the battle against *Eigennutz* (selfishness, greed, profit-motive)," as Robert Friedmann has described the tenor of Hutterite church ordinances.[53]

The use of *Gemeindeordnung* to govern Hutterite church communities and conference networks is shaped by the long-term influence of Andreas Ehrenpreis—an elder from the seventeenth century who sought to recover the original zeal and discipline of the Hutterite church. Ehrenpreis left behind a substantial body of letters, confessional statements, and tracts, including significant *Gemeindeordnungen* whose form and spirit continue to be reflected in the church letters and rules issued by Hutterite conference elders. The significant 1651 communal discipline associated with Ehrenpreis can serve as a touchstone for the persistent framing of Hutterite problems within a spiritual discourse organized by:

1. a grounding in communal discernment by elders;

2. an enumeration of threats (instances of *Eigennutz*) to the integrity of the community along with stating and restating rules that address such threats as well as consequences for breaking the rules; and

3. an exhortation to faithful Christian discipleship and virtue—recovering the original faith of the founders.[54]

The 1651 *Gemeindeordnungen*, for example, begins with a reminder of the biblical roots of communal discernment by elders. It appeals to the ac-

---

53   Robert Friedmann, *Hutterite Studies: Celebrating the Life and Work of an Anabaptist Scholar*, 2nd ed. (MacGregor: Hutterian Brethren Book Centre, 2010), 112.

54   John Hostetler, Leonard Gross, and Elizabeth Bender, *Selected Hutterian Documents in Translation* (MacGregor: Hutterian Brethren Book Centre, 2013), 97–11.

count of Jethro's advice to Moses in Exodus 18 to delegate discernment to trustworthy leaders, as well as to Solomon's wisdom that "in an abundance of counsellors there is safety" (Proverbs 11:14).[55] It then offers a long list of problems and failures in Hutterian communities: too much buying and selling among church members, overconsumption of wine, unfair access to communal resources by some, clinging to money and possessions, and other habits that undermine community-of-goods.[56] Finally, it concludes with a stirring vision of the church of God as Jerusalem—the "city where all band together, where all fare well, where all love one another as is testified in Scriptures."[57]

It appears that over the centuries, Hutterian *Gemeindeordnungen* have increasingly emphasized the enumeration of threats and corresponding rules as the main purpose of these texts. One way to understand the critique of traditional patterns of authority emerging in Group I is the desire to more strongly emphasize a discourse of appeal and exhortation than one of rules and threats. A recent *Ordnung* letter issued by Group I elders Arnold Hofer and Samuel Waldner reporting from the January 30, 2018 meeting of ministers and stewards reflects this shifting direction in spiritual communication among the leadership of Group I Hutterites.

It is significant that while this letter was at first sent exclusively to Group I ministers, because it was distributed not only as a print document but also as an e-mail attachment, it soon became available to Group I members apart from the public reading of the letter by the elders of each community—which had been the traditional method of conveying decisions and rules made by the conference leaders. In this way, the decision to use e-mail to send out the letter ended up bypassing the traditional channel of authority and communication by which the community's ministers mediate between the conference and the community.

This letter begins with greetings of blessing, acknowledges the traumas of the 1992 division, and expresses a desire to "extend an olive branch."[58] The rest of the letter is focused primarily on lifting restrictions on relationships with Group II communities, including restrictions on intermarriage and attendance at funerals and worship services. The letter concludes with a reference to Romans 15:7, encouraging members to "welcome one another just as Christ has welcomed you for the glory of God." While this letter certainly includes all of the elements found in traditional *Gemeindeordnungen*, it exhibits a significant shift in tone and focus: more rules

---

55  Ibid., 97.
56  Ibid., 98–109.
57  Ibid., 110–11.
58  "*An alle Gruppe I Schmiedeleut Hutterer-Gemeinde in Manitoba, Kanada; Minnesota, Nord and Süd Dakota, USA*," (March 8, 2018), 1.

are lifted than maintained, and the exhortation is more a future-oriented appeal for generosity and forgiveness than a past-recovering admonition to hold to the old foundations. It may be that this letter represents a significant shift in leadership communication patterns among Schmiedeleut Hutterite leaders, at least in Group I. If so, the emerging pattern appears to be drawing from the traditional form of *Gemeindeordnungen* while shifting the emphasis from threat-managing rules toward unity-seeking appeals. Whether this shift can lead toward reunification of the two Schmiedeleut groups remains to be seen.

It is clear, in any event, that experiments with more procedurally-focused decision-making are emerging among Schmiedeleut Group I, many of them focused around policies related to the internet and education. From the HBNi board of directors to an education committee that gives oversight to problems and issues in community schools to a committee charged with managing the archives of Group I, committee processes appear to be redistributing at least some authority from the conference elders to community members and leaders.

## Conclusion

This essay has highlighted two distinct, if somewhat overlapping, approaches by Schmiedeleut Hutterites to qualifying and managing their communities' use of the internet and related technologies such as networked computers and smartphones. These two approaches arise from a divergence among the Schmiedeleut in their understanding of church polity and decision-making.

Group II tends to follow the more traditional Hutterite approach that expects spiritual leaders to make and enforce strict rules for faith and life, including restrictions on entertainment technology (or use of the internet for entertainment purposes), with the informal expectation of some diversity of implementation among the different communities and even among different households or individuals in a community. This approach assumes a healthy and persistently negotiated tension between high-demand leadership expectations and the often less-than-perfect practices of yielding to those expectations by church and community members with varied personalities, roles, and experiences.

Reflecting this approach, Group II tactics for negotiating the internet have evolved toward official public avoidance of internet use, except for specific business and educational uses, while demonstrating a keen attentiveness to the way that human communities are shaped by mimetic peer behaviour. Group II seems aware that we pick up habits of digital consumption not just from the form of the technology but from peer influence. When someone gets out a smartphone and checks a Facebook account while eating in a social setting, this contributes to the social assumption that such an act is a valid and perhaps even desirable behaviour. Group II Schmiedeleut are essentially asking the question: "What kinds of social practices and interactions do we want to reinforce or discourage by what we do when others are around us?"—which in Hutterite communities is almost all the time, of course. By framing their internet negotiation this way, the Group II Schmiedeleut significantly reduce the amount of internet-related communication that takes place on their communities, while at the same time giving space for some unofficial liberty that arguably helps make the official rule easier to follow in principle, because it is less absolute in practice.

By contrast, Group I prefers its leaders to cultivate a more spiritually expressive and less rule-driven unity of faith and practice, with choices about such matters as internet use based on authentic commitment to the well-being of the person and the community. This approach assumes a pastoral and perhaps even therapeutic responsibility on the part of spiritual leaders when members develop bad habits or make poor choices.

Following this approach, many Group I Schmiedeleut display an embrace of internet communication that is qualified by a constant, open, and relatively non-anxious conversation about the costs and benefits of digital communication technology. One young man, an enthusiastic user of the internet who has his own web page and a Facebook account that he accesses with an Apple laptop and an iPhone, asked me in the spirit of this approach: "So how do you avoid overuse of this technology? How do you keep it from taking over your life?" This is, of course, the question that almost every twenty-first-century person plugged into the internet is now asking. Group I Hutterites have the advantage of a spiritually curious and socially supportive community to help answer this question well.

In their struggle to work around the internet, Schmiedeleut Hutterites provide two useful if somewhat paradoxically related insights: Group II practices suggest the value in reducing public use of digital devices—keep your smartphones hidden from view to avoid negative peer influence. Group I practices highlight the strength of an open and accountable use of digital devices—use your smartphones in good company to keep your conscience clear.

**Ian Kleinsasser** is an independent researcher based out of Crystal Spring Hutterite Community near St. Agathe, MB. He and his wife, Jolene, are parents of five lively children who are a constant reminder of why he pursues historical research. He holds a Bachelor of Arts and an Education after-degree from Brandon University. Ian has given numerous presentations at the annual conference for Hutterite German teachers and the International Conference for Hutterite Educators. Kleinsasser's research focuses primarily on the Hutterianism of the nineteenth and twentieth centuries.

# Voices of Conflict: A Perspective of the 1992 Schmiedeleut Church Schism

### IAN KLEINSASSER

More than thirty years have passed since the Schmiedeleut Conference of the Hutterian Brethren Church suffered a devastating schism. Many events of this history show our communities in a poor light. Some might be tempted to think that these stories are best swept into the dustbin of the past and forgotten. Such a sterilized history, however, would be not only false, but also harmful to the future of the Hutterian church.

In Deuteronomy 26, the children of Israel are reminded of the importance of passing on the collective stories of Israel, good and bad, to each new generation. History is about understanding the past to make sense of the present. Many of the forces driving the disunity and conflicts within the Hutterian Brethren Church today stem from what happened in the past. As we and our children seek to understand the complex historical factors that have shaped our story, we can gain the wisdom and resources necessary to move beyond conflict and pain, towards a story of redemption.

During the last decade of his life, I assisted my uncle *Ältester* or Elder Jacob Kleinsasser in historical and archive-related tasks.[1] On the many occasions when we discussed the 1992 schism, I was struck by his deep sense of pain at what had happened. Whenever the discussion turned to writing an account of what had happened, he became very cautious, often citing 1 Peter 3:9: "Do not repay evil with evil or insult." He would ask, "How can we tell our version of what happened without adding further hurt and pain to others? How can we avoid repaying evil with evil?" At other times, particularly in the half year before he died in 2017, Kleinsasser struggled with doubt because he felt that as an elder, it was his duty to record what had

---

1   Jacob Kleinsasser held the office of *Ältester* from 1978 to 2017.

happened. On one occasion as we were working together, he paused and quietly mused, "Will they understand what it was that we were trying to do?" This question stands at the centre of this essay, for it was his vision of renewal and what the church ought to be that shaped many of the events related to the schism. Indeed, Kleinsasser's legacy will always be weighed against the 1992 schism and the subsequent conflicts that developed from it. This legacy must be understood as one that not only shaped the present era in Hutterite history, but was itself shaped by a period of broader disruption and radical change in Hutterite society through factors such as education, industrialization, individualism, and acculturation.

Jacob Kleinsasser was filled with a passion for God's people, and he desired to see his church regain the splendour of the Hutterite "Golden Years" (1565–92). His openness and compassion, which reached beyond the borders of the Hutterite communities, awakened a small missional movement within the Group I Schmiedeleut. His vision for education has seen Hutterite men and women attending university to receive training as educators and nurses. In pursuing this vision, Kleinsasser did not always make the right decisions, say the right things, or follow best practices for communal decision-making, but that is the risk faced by any leader who chooses to go down the uncertain path in hopes of a better future.

In this essay, I first explore a wide array of factors that contributed to the 1992 schism of the Schmiedeleut Hutterite Conference. These include the historic dynamics of the Bruderhof-Hutterite relationship, tensions between American and Canadian Schmiedeleut communities around leadership structure, a growing divide between traditionalist and progressive-minded communities and leaders, financial challenges and mismanagement as Hutterite communities shifted their means of livelihood from farming to manufacturing, and conflicts between the Lehrerleut, Dariusleut, and Schmiedeleut conferences, as well as struggles within the Schmiedeleut Conference itself.

The resulting breakdown, which split the Schmiedeleut Conference into Groups I and II and ultimately affected the entire Hutterite Church, is described in the second part of this essay. In the final part, I discuss some of the consequences of the split, including the dispute over Vital Statistics records. This conflict ultimately led to a broad set of changes that in many ways rewrote the definition of what and who the Hutterite Church is. The essay concludes by exploring ways in which the two Schmiedeleut groups might work towards a process of reconciliation and healing.

# Background to the 1992 Schism

## Bruderhof Relationship

In 1920, a small intentional community took root in Hesse, Germany. The Bruderhof movement was founded by Eberhard Arnold, who believed that love and unity were fruits of a Christian life that would in turn lead all sincere seekers into a common life. In 1928, Arnold began a correspondence with Dariusleut *Ältester* Elias Walter from Stand Off, Alberta, in which Eberhard declared his determination to unite with the Hutterites. In May 1930, Arnold set out for North America, where he visited all the Hutterite communities and personally requested that the two groups unite. On December 9, 1930, Eberhard was incorporated into the Hutterian Brethren Church at Stand Off. Ten days later he was confirmed in the service of the Word, with the laying on of hands by the Lehrerleut and Dariusleut elders. However, following Eberhard's untimely death in 1935, rifts between the Hutterites and the Bruderhof began to develop.[2]

In 1954, when the Bruderhof founded Woodcrest in New York state, Hutterite carpenters were sent to help with the construction of the new community. However, tensions between the two groups increased until the relationship ruptured in 1955, when a large group of sixty-six Hutterites left Forest River near Grafton, North Dakota, to join Woodcrest.[3] The report of a 1955 meeting in James Valley, Manitoba, between members of the Bruderhof, *Ältester* Peter Hofer,[4] and a group of senior Hutterite ministers reveals the differences between the two groups.[5] Where the Hutterite ministers stressed compliance with Hutterite ordinances, the Bruderhof representatives argued that many of the Hutterite regulations were a hindrance to mission work and the free working of God's Spirit. The

---

2  For a thorough account of this, see Emmy Barth, *An Embassy Besieged: The Story of a Christian Community in Nazi Germany* (Eugene: Cascade Books; Rifton: Plough Publishing House, 2010).

3  A smaller group of forty-two led by the minister Andreas Hofer stayed with the Hutterite church. In many Hutterite sources, it is stated that the Bruderhof took over Forest River. This, according to Tony Waldner, resident historian at Forest River, is not entirely true. Many of the people living in Forest River were discontented with the Hutterite church and had invited the Bruderhof to come to Forest River. Even after the Bruderhof members left in 1955, the disagreements in Forest River continued until 1957 and resulted in divided families and communities, including in some Manitoba Schmiedeleut communities. Many Hutterites conflate these events into one conflict, yet they were not necessarily related. See Tony Waldner, *History of Forest River Community* (Fordville: Forest River Community, 1990), 16–25; *The Forest River Story, 1954–1957: Extracts from Letters Written by Heini and Annemarie Arnold and Emmy Arnold* (Farmington: Plough Publishing House, 1999).

4  *Ältester* from 1951–66.

5  Author unknown. Informal meeting notes made at a minister's conference in James Valley, August 1955, in author's collection.

Michael Waldner Bon Homme, SD (1876–1889).
No Elder from 1889–1934.
Joseph Kleinsasser Milltown, MB (1934–1947).
Joseph Waldner Huron, MB (1947–1951).
Peter Hofer James Valley/Miami, MB (1951–1967).
Joseph Kleinsasser Sunnyside, MB (1967–1978).
Jacob Kleinsasser Crystal Spring, MB (1978–2017).

**Table 1.** List of Schmiedeleut Elders up to 1992.

relationship was eventually severed, and a deep-seated distrust towards the Bruderhof took hold among certain Hutterite leaders and within many communities, particularly those hurt by the events in Forest River.

In 1973, when Bruderhof leader Heinrich "Heini" Arnold asked the Hutterite Church for forgiveness for its actions in Forest River in 1955, *Ältester* Joseph Kleinsasser took a different approach.[6] Whereas the 1955 meeting had revolved around points of contention with Hutterite customs and traditions, Kleinsasser intentionally avoided these issues in order to discourage dissension.[7] Arnold and other Bruderhof representatives were told that the Hutterites would not ask the Bruderhof to adopt the traditions and customs of the Hutterian church.[8] It was determined that it was enough if they lived according to the leading of Christ's Spirit.[9] *Ältester* Joseph Kleinsasser and his successor, Jacob Kleinsasser, openly supported the Hutterite relationship with the Bruderhof because they hoped that God would use the Bruderhof to strengthen the Hutterite people's awareness of their rich heritage and to help them see the superficiality that had crept into the church. However, as the renewed relationship with the Bruderhof developed, so did the unease with which some other Hutterite ministers viewed this union.[10]

---

6   Joseph Kleinsasser served as Schmiedeleut *Ältester* from 1967 to 1978.
7   Merrill Mow, *Torches Rekindled: The Bruderhof's Struggle for Renewal* (Rifton: Plough Publishing House, 1991), 220.
8   Some historians have argued that the Bruderhof was a progressive influence which sowed disunity among the largely traditional-minded Hutterites. I contend that, on the contrary, a progressive tendency already existed within some Hutterite communities. The relationship with the Bruderhof simply provided additional opportunities to express this tendency which, in the Schmiedeleut context, was empowered by the support of progressive-minded elders.
9   David Decker Jr., to "all concerned," May 17, 1993, in author's collection.
10  This openness should not be interpreted as a rejection of traditions and *Ordnungen* (ordinances) as such, but rather as a willingness to recognize that inherited traditions need ongoing and thoughtful modifications through a process of communal discernment and an openness to the guidance of the Holy Spirit. What both elders resisted was the attempt to see traditions and *Ordnungen* as articles of faith. When traditions

## American-Canadian Conflicts

By the 1960s, other strong tensions had begun to emerge between some American and Canadian Hutterites regarding church leadership structure. Oral histories and personal correspondence between *Ältester* Joseph Kleinsasser and key American Schmiedeleut leaders show that there was growing resentment among some American communities towards the church eldership, which was located in Canada. The lack of high-speed transportation and sparse availability of telephone technology meant that community leaders had to rely mainly on the postal service to communicate. In that era, all major issues or decisions were made by a majority vote of all the ministers or, in some cases, all voting members of each colony. This meant that when problems arose within the American communities, they were relayed in writing to the elder in Manitoba. If necessary, the elder would then write to all the Schmiedeleut communities, asking them to discuss and vote on the issue. The responses were tallied and returned to the elder, who then sent the answer back to the American Schmiedeleut communities. This created a significant delay in processing issues, and the American communities felt that their concerns were being inadequately addressed. The American ministers pushed elder Peter Hofer[11] from James Valley, Manitoba, to appoint an assistant from South Dakota to work with the elder.

The church eventually agreed, and in 1962 Peter Hofer selected Joseph Hofer[12] from Maxwell, South Dakota, as the first American assistant to the *Ältester*. However, by doing so, the church soon found itself in a power struggle. When Hofer fell ill and couldn't carry out his duties, a small group of American Schmiedeleut ministers decided to take matters into their own hands. Without consulting the Manitoba elder—the newly appointed Joseph Kleinsasser from Sunnyside, Manitoba—a group led by Joseph Wipf from Plainview, South Dakota, removed Joseph Hofer and elected Wipf as the American assistant elder.[13] When *Ältester* Joseph Kleinsasser heard about this, he and the Manitoba ministers requested that those responsible come to Manitoba for a hearing. Instead of complying, Wipf sent Joseph Waldner (Platt, South Dakota),[14] Jacob Waldner[15] (Bon Homme, South Dakota), and Michael Waldner (Pearl Creek, South Dakota). At the meeting, Joseph Kleinsasser asked where the real

---

become enshrined as articles of faith, they create an environment of inflexibility towards any meaningful change, which then becomes an obstacle to the spiritual welfare of the church.

11  Served as *Ältester* from 1951 to 1966.
12  Also known as *Singer Vetter* (1888–1977).
13  David Decker Jr., to "all concerned," May 17, 1993, in author's collection.
14  Also known as *Michela-Joe*.
15  Also known as *Michela-Jake*.

"culprits" were, and received the reply that Wipf had sent the three of them. Kleinsasser sent them back home with the instructions to tell Wipf he should personally report to the elder.

A few weeks later, Joseph Wipf came to Sunnyside, where the meeting was held. After discussing the issue at hand, Wipf as well as a few other South Dakota ministers were asked to leave the meeting while the remaining ministers debated how to deal with these transgressions. The Manitoba leadership and ministers decided to put the incident behind them, but first Wipf would be asked to make a public apology. In a show of good faith, *Ältester* Kleinsasser then appointed Joseph Wipf to be the new South Dakota assistant.[16] Years later, ministers who had been present at this meeting observed that Wipf never forgot this "humiliation" and in subsequent years actively worked to undermine the Manitoba eldership.[17]

During this time, and particularly during the eldership of Joseph Kleinsasser, further tensions began to develop between Hutterite leaders regarding contrasting visions of the Hutterite church. Some felt that by maintaining the traditions and ordinances of the forefathers, they were honouring their memory and sacrifice. "Do not remove the cornerstones" and "We need to hold fast to what we have" were their watchwords. Others, including *Ältester* Joseph Kleinsasser and his Manitoba assistant, Jacob Kleinsasser, felt that the church had largely failed to live up to the example of its forefathers who, among other exemplary initiatives, sent out missionaries in accordance with Jesus' teachings (Matthew 28:19).

These two conflicting visions came to a head in 1977, when *Ältester* Joseph Kleinsasser refused to call the annual conference of the Schmiedeleut. Joseph Wipf demanded to know why the *Ältester* had cancelled the yearly Conference. Joseph Kleinsasser replied,

> I believe that our heavenly Father has very little pleasure in such meetings where very little godly conversation takes place, but mostly temporal or practical matters are discussed or dealt with. In contrast, our Saviour's last command to his disciples (Matthew 28:19) is completely disregarded. "For my people have committed two evils:

---

16  Samuel Waldner (Decker Community), interview by Mark Waldner, 2017, transcript in author's collection.
17  The impact that American versus Canadian, or even progressive versus conservative, tensions had on the larger conflict needs further research and is outside the scope of this essay. Future research will also have to explore how this dynamic played out among the Dariusleut and Lehrerleut communities. Both these Conferences have communities located on either side of the international border and in both Conferences there has been noticeable tension between the American and Canadian communities. See Joe Wurtz and Danny Gross, *Washington Tagebuch, January 18–24, 2010* (self-published, 2010).

they have forsaken Me, the fountain of living waters, and hewed out cisterns for themselves, broken cisterns, that can hold no water" (Jeremiah 2:3).[18]

In 1978, the year he passed away, Joseph Kleinsasser addressed a church gathering in Sunnyside with a lamentation from Jeremiah 11:13: "For your gods have become as many as your towns, O Judah; and as many as the streets of Jerusalem." Kleinsasser then asked, "Is this also true among the Hutterite brotherhoods and communities?"[19]

> For one seeks righteousness with a collar on a jacket; if you do not have one or have a different one than I, then I will not recognize you as a Christian. The other says, if you have pants with a crooked zipper, or if you do not have the same kind of hat that I have, you are going toward perdition and mock your salvation. Such imaginings abound as if our salvation were to be found in mere rags. Why don't such think instead about what the apostle Paul wrote to the Roman church (6:23): "For the wages of sin is death, but the gift of God is eternal life in Christ Jesus our Lord." Those who hold to these things, rob Jesus Christ of the honour that He alone deserves and try to honour themselves.[20]

These events make it clear that distinct fracture lines over matters such as maintaining traditional Hutterite practices versus seeking a renewal of the church were forming within the Schmiedeleut Conference well before 1992.

### A New *Ältester*

When Joseph Kleinsasser passed away, his serving assistant Jacob Kleinsasser from Crystal Spring, Manitoba, was elected as *Ältester*. Like his predecessor, Jacob Kleinsasser worked to improve the spiritual and financial situation of the church. The study of history demonstrates that any time changes are introduced into a society, they invariably cause anxiety, concern, and even hostility. As such, Jacob Kleinsasser's eldership was fraught with controversy. Some have portrayed him as the polarizing figure who caused the Hutterite church to split into two factions, while in reality, the Schmiedeleut had already begun to splinter well before his eldership. Once Kleinsasser was elected, his personality and assertive leadership style forced some underlying issues out into the open. Many Schmiedeleut did

---

18  Joseph Kleinsasser to Joseph Wipf, September 26, 1977, in author's collection.
19  Joseph Kleinsasser, "Lament for the Hutterite People," 1978, in author's collection.
20  Ibid.

not approve of his leadership style or vision, fundamentally disagreed with his proposed changes, and began to resist.[21]

Because *Ältester* Jacob Kleinsasser shared the late Joseph Kleinsasser's vision for the future, he worked to realize the reforms his predecessor had initiated. However, the new elder had inherited a church mired in spiritual distress and plagued by financial troubles. In this context, he advocated for improved baptismal instruction to cultivate spiritual development instead of relying on the accepted *schena Elter*[22] criterion for those requesting baptism. He emphasized prudence, chastity, and temperance within courtship to address loose dating practices and promiscuity among Hutterite youth. Describing the state of the church at this time, David Decker from Starland, Minnesota, wrote,

> The greatest evil creeping into the colonies, and the sickness of all humanity from the beginning of history was sexual impurity. The elder in 1974 and later our present elder Jacob Kleinsasser inherited a sick church community … [The elder] immediately went to the task of cleaning up the mess, without cleansing we were headed for destruction. Illegitimate births were quadrupling, and no end was in sight. Many meetings were called to stop the fire [that was burning] out of control.[23]

Knowing the devastating consequences of alcoholism experienced in many communities, the new elder pushed for limiting alcohol at weddings. He challenged the popular practice of *Eigennutz*—earning money for personal use—among the Schmiedeleut.[24] At the time, many community stewards had a reputation of being severe and stingy, refusing to supply essential items for their people and forcing them to earn money privately. In the long run, this practice promoted a culture of selfishness and individual-

---

21  Studying the Schmiedeleut conference reports from the 1970s and '80s clearly demonstrates this point. What also clearly emerges is the growing tension between the traditionalist communities and leaders and those who favoured a more progressive approach. For instance, the traditionalist leaders began to demand stronger enforcement of rules and practices, particularly dress codes. During Joseph Kleinsasser's eldership (1967–1978), much of this pressure came from the South Dakota leadership. For further reading on this see Samuel Kleinsasser, "Values Regained," in *Community and Ethics* (unpublished manuscript, 2010).

22  *Schena Elter* (meaning "fitting age" or "old enough") is a phrase commonly used to communicate the attitude that age is a sufficient indicator of a person's preparedness for baptism or marriage.

23  David Decker Jr., to "all concerned," May 17, 1993, in author's collection.

24  Another harmful practice that Jacob Kleinsasser tried to stop was that of feed companies giving Hutterites tips, bribes, or alcohol to encourage them to stay with their company or to get them to promote their products. The elders understood that these "gifts" were received at the expense of the communities' well-being.

ism that was detrimental to the community. Kleinsasser often stressed the example of Acts 2:45: "And [they] distributed ... to all, as any had a need." These are only a few of the issues *Ältester* Jacob Kleinsasser addressed; his calls for reform, however, were rejected and criticized by a very vocal minority among Hutterite ministers, stewards, and members.

## Financial Context

Many of the accusations that came to be levelled against *Ältester* Jacob Kleinsasser involved financial projects that unfolded in a particular economic context. Following the move from South Dakota to Manitoba in 1918, some Schmiedeleut communities had struggled financially because of huge mortgages and loans incurred from buying land at high prices. By the 1950s, however, the Hutterites were benefiting from an upswing in the world economy, a period of prosperity that lasted until the early 1970s. During this time, many Hutterite communities began to spend more money than they could afford.[25]

Things changed in the 1980s and '90s, when the Schmiedeleut Conference faced significant financial difficulties. In the early 1980s, a recession hit North America, causing the Hutterites to experience high inflation and interest rates. In 1981, the average inflation rate was over 12%, and the Bank of Canada's interest rate climbed to 21%. The Hutterite communities most affected by the recession were those that needed to finance the purchase of more land to establish daughter communities.[26] The elder and other ministers met with many bankers, stockbrokers, fund managers, and financial advisors in an attempt to find answers to these challenges.[27] In some situations, financial advisors hired by communities betrayed them by saying they would charge lower interest rates, and then took advan-

---

25   This increased focus on earning money had an extremely detrimental impact on Hutterite education. Children were pulled from school as soon as possible so that they could begin to earn money. Brothers who were deemed of little worth in the workforce were appointed as "German" school teachers. This led to a sharp drop in the level of education offered to Hutterite children.
     At the same time, unhealthy competition began to develop between wealthier and poorer communities as the poorer communities tried to match the living standards of their wealthier counterparts. This led communities to build unnecessarily large housing units, purchase the best vehicles and trucks, etc. See also John [Hans] Decker, "Overview of Hutterite History," [ca. 1980s], in author's collection.
26   Group II historian Tony Waldner acknowledges Jacob Kleinsasser's concern regarding high interest rates, but points out that it was precisely these crippling interest rates that made many Schmiedeleut stewards and leaders protest what they deemed as "imposed taxes." Waldner acknowledges that Kleinsasser discussed the ventures at various meetings but that "many recall being intimidated to obey." Personal interview, November 5, 2018.
27   Michael F.C. Radcliffe to Jacob Kleinsasser, September 22, 1992, in author's collection.

tage of them. In one case, acts of fraud and financial mistakes brought two South Dakota communities, Rosedale and Millbrook, to the verge of bankruptcy. The financial advisors who deceived these two communities, Harold E. Cornell and Alfred L. DeLeo, were prosecuted and ended up going to jail.[28] As financial details regarding the Rosedale/Millbrook and Crystal Spring fraud issue emerged, allegations were made that *Ältester* Kleinsasser had compromised the church fund through the Crystal Spring power-of-attorney agreement, then used church funds to pay off Crystal Spring's debt.[29]

## Donald I. Gibb and the Rosedale/Millbrook Fraud

One individual who played a considerable role in misleading and deceiving many Hutterites was a former farmer, financial advisor, and banker named Donald Gibb.[30] Gibb was born near Rosebank, Manitoba, where his family had owned a large farm that went into bankruptcy in 1980. Because of his farming roots, Gibb was well acquainted with Hutterites. When he ran for political office in Manitoba, several members of the Miami and Darlingford area communities purchased memberships in the Manitoba Conservative Party in order to vote for him at the nomination meeting.

In 1981, Gibb joined the First National Bank of Chicago (First Chicago) and began to make connections with Hutterite communities in the United States. He established a lending company which serviced approximately forty Hutterite communities in the Dakotas. When Gibb

---

28   Cornell and DeLeo first advertised their plan for making low-interest funds available to Hutterites in 1982. Two communities, Crystal Spring and Rosedale/Millbrook, signed the necessary legal documents, which included assigning powers of attorney to the DeLeo-Cornell Group. Crystal Spring withdrew its power-of-attorney agreement due to concerns with the wording. Rosedale/Millbrook did not recall their power of attorney, which enabled DeLeo-Cornell to commit numerous fraudulent transactions that neither Rosedale/Millbrook nor Crystal Spring were aware of or authorized.

29   It has been established that none of the communal church funds contributed by other communities went to pay any of the losses suffered by Crystal Spring. Daniel Hofer, his brother Paul Hofer, and their lawyer, Donald Douglas, spent an entire day during the Lakeside pretrial examinations poring over all the financial reports and papers held by David Norris and were unable to point to any funds which had been misapplied by Jacob Kleinsasser. Michael F.C. Radcliffe to Jacob Kleinsasser, September 9, 1992, in author's collection.

30   The derogatory name "Gibb" refers to those Schmiedeleut who accepted Donald Gibb's assertions against *Ältester* Jacob Kleinsasser; later the name Schmiedeleut Group II was formalized. The name "Oiler" was used to label those who sided with the elder in reference to the oil-well servicing rigs purchased by the DeLeo-Cornell Group using powers of attorney granted by Rosedale/Millbrook; later known as Schmiedeleut Group I.

left First Chicago, however, the communities were ordered by the bank to close their accounts. From First Chicago, Donald Gibb moved on to Rabobank Netherlands in New York, where he again looked after the Hutterite portfolio. In 1988, Rabobank and Donald Gibb[31] parted ways after the Rosedale and Millbrook loan fraud came to light. The exact role played by Donald Gibb and other South Dakota players in this whole affair still needs further research.[32] What is known is that after leaving Rabobank, Gibb wrote an accusatory letter and released a collection of documents known colloquially as "The Gibb Book," which contained unfounded allegations against Jacob Kleinsasser. Kleinsasser, Jeff Cristall (an accountant with the accounting firm Meyers Norris Penny),[33] Michael Radcliff (who served as a lead counsel in the lawsuits),[34] and James S. Youngblood (an attorney hired by Welk Resources Ltd.[35] to investigate related affairs)[36] repeatedly stated that many of Gibb's assertions were presented out of context and deliberately misleading.[37]

Even before these events, the elders had looked for ways to help the financially struggling communities. These projects included H.B. Credit, H.B. Trust, H.B. Mutual Insurance, and H.B. Medical, all of which were initiated with the full support of Schmiedeleut ministers in Manitoba and the United States. These companies were all run by a Hutterite board of directors, but managed by non-Hutterites. All monies handled by the

---

31  Jeff Cristall to "whom it may concern," July 16, 1992, in author's collection.
32  David Martin and James Inglis to "whom it may concern [Jeffrey Sveen and Donald Gibb]," February 5, 1993, in author's collection.
33  Jeff Cristall to "whom it may concern," July 16, 1992.
34  Michael F.C. Radcliffe to Jacob Kleinsasser, September 22, 1992, in author's collection.
35  Welk Resources Ltd. was established as a limited partnership to clean up some of the financial messes that ensued because of the DeLeo-Cornell Group's activities, either by shrugging off any commitments not too firmly tied down, or assuming responsibility for the investments DeLeo-Cornell had made and selling them for what they could get. However, many of the decisions made by the various people involved in the DeLeo-Cornell cleanup were not always prudent. Some of the early decisions were made under pressure, and based on insufficient information or reports that had been deliberately presented with missing information. In general, the practice of permitting Welk managers the authority to make decisions on their own did not work out well for the Hutterites in the long run. Despite these setbacks, Welk did accomplish the goal of reducing the overall damages. Welk Resources Ltd. was closed on May 5, 1986.
36  James Stuart Youngblood to Federal Bureau of Investigation, February 18, 1985, in author's collection.
37  According to Tony Waldner, a Group II minister and historian, the Rosedale/Millbrook issue is one area in which the Group II communities have a distinctly different narrative than Group I communities. I acknowledge this concern and am hopeful that a group consisting of historians from both sides will one day be able to work together to more fully understand these competing narratives.

various organizations were monitored by provincial and federal insurance regulatory bodies and by the accounting firm Meyers Norris Penny. It is important to note that every company, organization, and joint venture, as well as the methods for collecting the appropriate fees, was always approved by a majority vote of Hutterite ministers and stewards. During the Lakeside trial (discussed below), Mr. Justice Patrick Ferg stated that "nothing was or is amiss with any of the subsidiary corporations of the Hutterian brotherhood, or their financial affairs. [...] The fund is audited annually; nothing is amiss, every cent is accounted for."[38] Despite the fact that these ventures initially had the full support of the church, they triggered a further rift between *Ältester* Kleinsasser and the South Dakota assistant elder, Joseph Wipf, who began to criticize the church projects in private and thereby influenced those around him.[39]

## More American Dissension

By the early 1990s, the American Schmiedeleut communities, along with some Canadian ones, began to withdraw from these projects without the consent of the rest of the Manitoba communities. They demanded a share of the equity of H.B. Mutual Insurance Corporation, even though the company had not been dissolved. This demand was contrary to the laws governing such companies.[40] American communities accused the Manitoba communities of collecting taxes from Manitoba Schmiedeleut communities without providing the larger church with account of how the funds were used.[41] This was patently untrue. Any Schmiedeleut minister had the full right and authority to view the records, the only restriction being they could not view confidential information belonging to individual communities. In addition, monthly financial statements were sent to all the directors in the United States and Canada.[42]

Two incidents which occurred in late 1991 help illustrate some of the tensions that brought the conflict between the Manitoba and South Dakota communities to a boiling point. The first incident concerns two North Dakota Schmiedeleut communities, Willowbank and Fairview, that

---

38 Lakeside v. Daniel Hofer et al. (Court of Queen's Bench of Manitoba, October 31, 1989), 23–24.
39 David Decker Jr., to "all concerned," May 17, 1993, in author's collection.
40 See Article 352(3) of the Manitoba Insurance Act.
41 The South Dakota communities' demand failed to consider the acts of goodwill, such as when the Manitoba communities gave up $300,000 of their dividends to help the U.S. communities pay their medical insurance costs.
42 Directors for Manitoba were Jacob Kleinsasser (Crystal Spring), Michael Waldner (Milltown), Jacob Hofer (Valley View), David Waldner (Milltown), and David M. Miller; for South Dakota, Joseph Wipf (Plainview), David Decker (Starland), and John "Hans" Decker (Wolf Creek).

filed fraudulent claims with the H.B. Mutual Insurance Company. These communities had received free services from Mercy Hospital and then filed papers with H.B. Insurance to reclaim money that was never spent. When this was discovered, the two communities attempted to deny any wrongdoing. Further, two of the senior South Dakota elders, Joseph Wipf (Plainview) and Jacob Wipf (Spring Creek), attempted to defend these two communities, claiming they had done nothing wrong. It was only after the Manitoba ministers pointed out that they had committed fraud, which, if not corrected immediately, would lead to criminal charges, that the perpetrators grudgingly admitted their dishonesty.[43]

The second 1991 incident involved Joseph Wipf accusing *Ältester* Jacob Kleinsasser of stealing money from a church fund. This was a special fund which had been established to help Hillcrest, South Dakota, which would have had to declare bankruptcy if the church had not intervened. At a December 12, 1991, meeting, Wipf accused Kleinsasser of stealing $600,000. The elder was shocked and deeply hurt by this accusation, as neither he nor anyone present at the meeting knew what Wipf was talking about. The elder ordered an investigation into this charge. What was discovered was that not a cent was unaccounted for and that Wipf himself signed all the transactions enabling the withdrawal of funds from the account.[44] Because Wipf had falsely and publicly accused the elder, he was asked to make a public apology.[45] This was the same Joseph Wipf who had been asked to apologize to the Manitoba elders in 1978 for his leadership role in a faction that tried to establish an independent eldership in South Dakota.

As tensions mounted around the various conflicts described above, it became increasingly clear that the Schmiedeleut Conference was heading towards a serious crisis, revolving in part around the financial institutions established by the Schmiedeleut church, the Hutterite-Bruderhof relationship, and accusations of mismanagement of church funds by *Ältester* Kleinsasser.

## Lakeside Community Difficulties

The mounting tensions between the various Hutterite conferences and congregations were aggravated by conflicts at Lakeside community, Manitoba, that had begun in the mid-1970s.[46] Like many of the other

---

43  Jacob Kleinsasser, "*Versammlung wegen Samuel Waldner, New Port* [Meeting to Address Various Disturbing Events]," December 12, 1991, in author's collection.

44  First Bank Aberdeen, "Deposits & Cheques/Withdrawals/Transfers," 1987–1991, in author's collection. Courtesy of David Martin.

45  Jacob Kleinsasser, "*Bei Starlite Gemeinde wegen Pembrook SD Beschuldigungen* [Meeting at Starlite Regarding Accusations made at Pembrook, SD]," December 12, 1991, in author's collection.

46  Full details of the Lakeside litigation against Daniel Hofer between 1986 and 1991

struggles described here, the problems in Lakeside had roots that went back to before Jacob Kleinsasser's eldership. In the 1970s, Lakeside was facing financial and spiritual ruin, owing to disunity and conflict between various factions within the community. Financially, the community was in trouble in part because it had very few enterprises that were generating a cash flow. The bigger problem, however, was that many of the Lakeside members were working for personal gain rather than for the community. Several people even had private bank accounts. The church, first under *Ältester* Joseph Kleinsasser and later under Jacob Kleinsasser, sought to stop the infighting so that Lakeside could become financially solvent again.

During this time, Lakeside management consisted of minister Joseph Hofer, steward Daniel Hofer Sr., and farm manager Joseph Hofer. These managers were so uncooperative and hostile towards each other that the church had to appoint three overseers from other Manitoba communities to help manage Lakeside: Michael Wollman (Springhill), Jacob Hofer (James Valley), and steward David Waldner (Milltown).[47] Before and after the appointment of the overseers, conflicts at Lakeside were at times so violent that the police had to be involved. In one altercation, Daniel Hofer took a community vehicle, presumably without permission, and went for a drive. Minister Samuel Kleinsasser from Sturgeon Creek and a group of others gave chase. When Kleinsasser got too close, Hofer reversed his truck and smashed into Kleinsasser's pickup. Some of the parties involved brought charges against each other, thus involving lawyers and the police. At a church meeting, it was decided that all involved in the pickup incident should apologize at a Sunday morning church service.[48] Four other members of Lakeside were put under church discipline (*Unfrieden*).

## Patent Dispute

During this period, Daniel Hofer Sr. held a number of different positions in the Lakeside community, first as steward and later as German school teacher. However, because he repeatedly refused to cooperate with the church-appointed overseers, he was removed from these positions. By 1984, Hofer was working in the Lakeside blacksmith shop, where he

---

are beyond the scope of what can be adequately covered in this essay. Only the most relevant factors that connect this conflict to the larger conflict are described here.
47  Already in July 1982, Lakeside's overseers and leadership met with elder Jakob Kleinsasser to resolve internal issues. In particular, Lakeside leadership was uncooperative with church-appointed overseers to the point that the church considered abandoning Lakeside to its fate. This strained relationships between the overseers and Lakeside leadership undoubtedly contributed to the later conflict. See "Rejecting Lakeside Overseers," July 4, 1982, in author's collection.
48  "*Lakeside Gemeinde Versammlung* [Lakeside Community Meeting]," June 30, 1978, in author's collection.

manufactured a variety of steel products, including a hog feeder. Initially, Hofer worked on a hog feeder for which he hoped to acquire a patent. By 1986, his feeder had evolved into a wet and dry feeder design that was very similar to a feeder already patented and marketed by the Crystal Spring community. Hofer later claimed that Crystal Spring had stolen his design and wrote letters to the patent office, demanding they cancel Crystal Spring's patent, as he felt he was the rightful patent holder. The patent office, however, declined Hofer's request.[49] Daniel Hofer may have believed that he had invented the wet/dry feeder system but his invention, though similar to the Crystal Spring feeder, had significant functionality problems. One of the Lakeside overseers told him that if he wanted to see a well-made feeder, he should go to James Valley and look at the Crystal Spring feeder there. Hofer then sent one of his helpers, Samuel Hofer, to James Valley to purchase two Crystal Spring feeders.[50] Hofer then proceeded to manufacture an exact copy of the Crystal Spring feeder.

By 1986, Hofer had been notified numerous times by C. & J. Jones that he could not manufacture the Crystal Spring feeder.[51] Hofer stated that Crystal Spring did not legally own the patent, but that he did. When Brian Miller, owner and president of C. & J. Jones, asked for proof, Hofer could not produce the required evidence to back up his claim. When he continued to manufacture the Crystal Spring feeder, C. & J. Jones instructed their solicitors to demand damages from Lakeside for patent infringement.[52] This caused much concern for the Lakeside management, who then arranged a meeting with Brian Miller and the patent agent, Adrian Battison, on January 12, 1987. Together they reviewed all the documentation, diagrams, and correspondence, and were convinced that the feeder Daniel Hofer was making infringed on the Crystal Spring patent.

---

49  A 1988 study carried out by the Sim, Hughes, Dimock law firm, specialists in intellectual property and commercial litigation, stated that "from the correspondence between Mr. Hofer and his patent agent which we have reviewed and also from an examination of his prototype feeder, we are of the opinion that Mr. Hofer cannot make a proper claim to ownership of the Kleinsasser invention and does not have a proper basis for alleging that the Kleinsasser patent is invalid as a result of any inventive act by Mr. Hofer." Mirek A. Waraksa to Michael Radcliffe, February 2, 1988, in author's collection.
50  Michael F.C. Radcliffe to Alvin Esau, August 8, 2001, in author's collection; Michael F.C. Radcliffe to Jacob Kleinsasser, September 22, 1992, in author's collection.
51  Crystal Spring filed a patent application on June 10, 1985, and subsequently sold their Canadian patent to C. & J. Jones (a Manitoba-based hog equipment dealership) on April 25, 1986, for $15,000, and later their U.S. patent to Gro Master, Inc., because they did not want to deal with possible patent infringement litigation, which they knew would be forthcoming if anybody started manufacturing their feeder. Jonathan Kleinsasser, interview by author, 2018.
52  Lakeside v. Daniel Hofer et al. (Court of Queen's Bench of Manitoba, October 31, 1989).

The Lakeside overseers, therefore, agreed to pay C. & J. Jones $10,000 to settle the lawsuit. On January 21, 1987, the Lakeside overseers informed their brotherhood about the settlement with C. & J. Jones, which they felt they had to make to keep Lakeside out of the courts. Daniel Hofer voiced his displeasure at the $10,000 settlement, which he felt was unfair,[53] and walked out of the brotherhood meeting.[54]

Shortly after this, Hofer convinced the Bank of Montreal to stop Lakeside's payment of the $10,000 settlement. The Lakeside overseers immediately called a series of meetings, first with the members of Lakeside, and then with *Ältester* Kleinsasser.[55] The elder counselled that all those who signed the stop-payment document should be placed under church discipline. In a separate, specially convened meeting, Hofer was informed that he was under church discipline for initiating the stop order on the payment to C. & J. Jones and for not listening to the overseers. Hofer refused to accept the discipline and stated that he appealed to a higher court. The Lakeside brotherhood, under the leadership of church-appointed overseers, decided that because of his continual refusal to accept church discipline, Daniel Hofer Sr. should be excommunicated from the community. This likely only served to heighten Hofer's frustration that he was not being heard or understood, and he again refused to accept church discipline.

In a further demonstration of frustration, Hofer locked the Lakeside management out of the hog barn on February 6, 1987, preventing them from marketing hogs. Throughout February, Hofer took Lakeside hogs to market without authority from community leadership and interfered

---

53 In his judgement, Justice Ferg made the following observation: "In fairness to Daniel Hofer Sr., one must conclude that probably in his own mind he believed he had invented the wet and dry feeder, and was entitled to patent it, but from all the evidence on file, the documents, descriptions, and diagrams, the evidence is clear that the invention of the wet and dry feeder was probably that of the members of Crystal Spring Colony who had, at least, patented it long before Hofer Sr., conceived his idea" (ibid., 15).

54 In the Hutterite context, walking out of a brotherhood meeting in anger may put a member in *Unfrieden*, a formal state of disunity with the brotherhood. A member who does so is usually granted an opportunity to apologize for their actions, and only if they refuse to accept the offer are they put into *Unfrieden*.

55 Later, Group II leaders questioned *Ältester* Kleinsasser's involvement in the Lakeside issue, considering the patent dispute involved his community of Crystal Spring, and suggested that he should have recused himself from the situation. However, Hutterite church practice has always been that when a community runs into spiritual or financial difficulties, the elder and his assistants appoint overseers to assist the ailing community. In this situation, the elder and his assistants were always involved only to the extent that they serve as advisors if the overseers need extra council. This was the practice in Lakeside, and the argument could be made that it was Daniel Hofer's filing of a counterclaim against the church which pulled the elder personally into the dispute.

with the payment to the community. During this time, he also continued to manufacture the patented feeder, thus exposing Lakeside to the risk of further action from the patent holder.[56]

On February 16, because Hofer kept deliberately violating the community's rules and rejecting the church-appointed overseers, the church ordered its legal counsel, Baker, Zivot, and Company, to serve Daniel Hofer Sr., Daniel Hofer Jr., and David Hofer with an eviction order. Hofer Sr. immediately wrote back to legal counsel Michael Radcliffe, rejecting the excommunication and eviction, claiming that if the church had wanted him excommunicated, he would have been notified in person. Hofer concluded his letter by stating, "We will be challenging patent no. 7202840 in a federal court, as advised. We claim it's our invention. Then we'll have the church meeting."[57]

As the seriousness of the eviction order settled in, however, it triggered a heartfelt plea from Daniel Hofer, Sr. and deepened his resolve to keep fighting. In a follow-up letter written on the evening of the same day to legal counsel for the church, Michael Radcliffe, Hofer expresses his and others' deep angst about the church's expulsion order.[58] This letter is heart-wrenching, as it demonstrates how the innocent are often dragged into other people's conflicts. It also highlights the deeper ramifications of the church's legal actions against its members. In this letter, Daniel Hofer states: "Some of the men you've addressed these [expulsion] letters to have pregnant wives. They/we received these letters 20 minutes ago. […] David just reported to me the women (pregnant approx. 7 to 8 months) are crying over the contents of your poison letter."[59]

Hofer wrote another letter on February 25, "To our ex-officers (Lakeside Col. Ltd.) Mike W., Jacob H., Josh H.,"[60] notifying the church overseers that he, Daniel Hofer Sr., and Daniel Hofer Jr., "have opened a partnership bank account to carry on business for Lakeside Col. Ltd."

---

56  In a letter dated February 16, 1987, Daniel Hofer threatened that he would challenge the patent in a federal court to force the requested church meeting.
57  Daniel Hofer Sr., to Mr. [Michael F.C.] Radcliffe, February 16, 1987, in author's collection.
58  Daniel Hofer Sr., to "I'm not going to call you dear Mr. Radcliffe now." [Michael F.C. Radcliffe], February 16, 1987, in author's collection.
59  If any lessons are to be learned from this, it is hoped that all Hutterite conferences would explore ways in which to deal with voluntarily or involuntarily excommunicated members. What is the church's responsibility towards people who leave the Hutterite faith? Past practice was that people leaving the church did so of their own accord and did not receive any form of compensation. This is still largely practiced, but in recent years, Group I communities have begun to informally support people leaving communities in various ways.
60  Daniel Hofer Sr., to "our ex-officers, Mike W[ollman, Springhill], Jacob H[ofer, Starlite], Josh H[ofer, Lakeside]," February 25, 1987, in author's collection.

They demanded that the "ex-officers" of Lakeside hand over "the sum of approximate four or five thousand dollars." Again, this request was backed up by a threat to take the "necessary [legal] action by us to resolve this payable problem."[61]

After this, the conflict escalated, with Hofer refusing to obey the eviction order. He acquired a lawyer, Donald Douglas, and filed a counterclaim against the church on May 27, 1987.[62] This, in turn, led to a series of court battles that went all the way to the Canadian Supreme Court and took an additional four to five years to resolve. A full survey of these litigations is well outside the scope of this essay, but I will attempt to touch on some of the key points of the conflict that played a significant role in the disunity that led to the 1992 schism.[63]

## Daniel Hofer Sr. and the Schmiedeleut Elder

Daniel Hofer, increasingly isolated and chastised, launched a letter-writing campaign against *Ältester* Jacob Kleinsasser.[64] In letters addressed

---

61  Ibid.
62  By filing a counterclaim against the church's eviction order, Daniel Hofer Sr. initiated the Lakeside v. Daniel Hofer et al. court cases. Because, however, Daniel Hofer filed the counterclaim, Lakeside, the church, and *Ältester* Jacob Kleinsasser automatically became the plaintiffs. This became the basis of the accusation against Kleinsasser by the other Hutterite *Leut* and Jacob Wipf that he was "going to worldly courts" to settle church matters.
    To highlight the duplicitous nature of this accusation, it is helpful to consider an example where this practice is later declared acceptable. On May 19, 1994, the Dariusleut, Schmiedeleut Group II, and Lehrerleut met in Rosetown, SK, to discuss church matters. At this meeting, the Lehrerleut challenged the Group II American delegates to explain why they were plaintiffs in a court case. Minister Michael Tschetter explained they were automatically drawn into the case as plaintiffs because Group I members had appealed an eviction order. The Darius- and Lehrerleut stated that "…we could not object to [their action], that it was sinful […*welches wir ihnen nicht konnten widersprechen dass es Sünde sei*]." They did, however, encourage them to end the court cases as soon as possible. Joseph Waldner, *Beschreibung und Gründung der Lehrerleut Gemeinden, 1887 to 1998* [A Written Account of the Establishment of the Lehrerleut Communities] (Havre), 412.
63  The timing of the Lakeside v. Daniel Hofer et al. court cases overlapped with the time of the Schmiedeleut schism. The schism had solidified by the time the court case was resolved. By 1996, Daniel Hofer and others had established a new Hutterite community, Heartland, and became incorporated under the Schmiedeleut Group II constitution from 1993.
64  Daniel Hofer's letter-writing campaign was significant in that, even though it predated social media of today, it was highly successful in sowing doubt against *Ältester* Jacob Kleinsasser. In his "Reasons for Judgement Delivered," Justice Ferg wrote, "During all of the time, in that year, Daniel Hofer Sr., had been writing letters and sending epistles to all colonies, the bank, RCMP, and others, damning in the most vitriolic and malicious terms, Reverend Kleinsasser and the overseers, accusing them of fraud, deceit, conspiracy and theft, and made other equally serious accusations. It

to "All Hutterites of the World," he accused Kleinsasser of using his position as Elder to silence any opposition to Crystal Spring's claim to the hog feeder patent.⁶⁵ (The patent office and Justice Ferg would later reject Daniel Hofer's accusations.) On December 16, 1987, Hofer wrote a letter addressed to "All ministers of the Hutterian Church," stating that Lakeside was now effectively under his control: from now on, President Daniel Hofer Sr., and Secretary Daniel Hofer Jr., would be making all decisions at Lakeside. As for the rest of the brotherhood, those who did not support him were in effect excommunicated. He wrote:

> An unanimous decision was reached, that we (the Hutterian Brethren Church) baptized members of the Hutterian Brethren will no longer tolerate the actions and behaviour of Jacob Kleinsasser (head minister of the church) (at present) and any associates being in harmony with his actions regarding breaking church and colony rules set out in the New Testament (which is of our religion) and the corporation rules also the breaking of the articles of association. [...] All ministers guilty of above-stated offenses be prepared to return to the order of the church or colony. Also, all secretary-treasurers. (Anyone by keeping silent on issues when brought up is declared guilty) [sic].⁶⁶

The "unanimous decision" referred to in Daniel Hofer's letter addressed to "All Ministers of the Hutterite Church" lists seven accusations aimed at *Ältester* Jacob Kleinsasser and the church:

1. Breaking the community rules as set out in the Articles of Association;

2. Expelling members of the church without as much as a hearing;

3. Using the Lakeside issue as cover for his [Jacob Kleinsasser's] supposed financial losses to "New York gangsters;"

---

will be remembered all the overseers had done was devote hours and hours of their time, energies and wisdom to put Lakeside back on its feet, both spiritually and temporally. All they wanted, all the ministers wanted, was peace, but the defendants would have none of it. Words cannot really describe, although witnesses tried, how disturbing this whole matter was to the particular Hutterian brethren involved, and as well, to the whole Hutterian brotherhood" (Lakeside v. Daniel Hofer et al, October 31, 1989, 21–22). Although Daniel Hofer's accusations of conspiracy and fraud were soundly rejected by the courts, the damage caused within Hutterite communities could not be reversed.

65  Daniel Hofer Sr., to "All Hutterites of the World," January 14, 1991, in author's collection.
66  Daniel Hofer Sr., to "All the Ministers [of the] Hutt[erian] Church," December 16, 1986, in the author's collection.

4. Expelling Lakeside members (in good standing) merely because they opposed the payment of $10,000 to C & J Jones;
5. Breaking up families, thus causing divorce;
6. Abusing power by enforcing *Meidung* (church discipline); and
7. Forcing Hutterite communities to pay into the failing (Springhill) killing plant[67] (imposed by withholding the Lord's Supper).[68]

These and other points raised by Daniel Hofer in the above letter are instructive in not only highlighting Hofer's personal grievances against Jacob Kleinsasser, but very likely acted as a catalyst for the discontentment and disillusionment that were present in the many Hutterite communities. Through his circulation of letters addressed to "All Hutterites of the World," Hofer gave voice to this discontent and at the same time ignited the Hutterite rumour mills with wild speculation and falsehoods.

At the same time, Hofer's letters are filled with unsubstantiated accusations and even prophetic claims with which he tries to bolster his arguments.[69] Throughout the Lakeside v. Daniel Hofer et al. trials (1987–1991), the judges carefully examined all these accusations and concluded they were groundless.

In their Trial Decision report, Justices O'Sullivan and Huband rejected Daniel Hofer's assertions of fraud and conspiracy as reasons for his expulsion. Rather, Hofer's expulsion came about because of his stop-payment directive to the Bank of Montreal in 1987 and his subsequent refusal to accept church discipline for his actions.

Justice Huband, one of the Manitoba Appeals judges, wrote:

> Daniel Hofer Sr., was expelled from his church, for his total disobedience to the baptismal vows of his church, which he in fact had made on two separate occasions, when he was first baptized, and again in 1981, when all

---

67 Hofer alleged that Michael Wollman required substantial financial support to bolster the financially struggling Springhill Farms abattoir and that the *Ältester* was using his position to direct church monies to the project. In return, Wollman was to stop Hofer from manufacturing the hog feeders that were competing with Crystal Spring. In short, Hofer alleged that the elder was using Wollman (overseer) to get rid of him because he was exposing this corruption. In his judgment, Justice Ferg stated "there is no evidence before me of any such conspiracy, for any reason, and I reject any such suggestion" (Lakeside v. Daniel Hofer et al., 19).
68 Daniel Hofer Sr., to "All the Ministers [of the] Hutt[erian] Church," December 16, 1986.
69 For instance, in one letter Hofer claims that it was revealed to him by God in a dream that "Kleinsasser will not outlive the year of 1991," referencing Hananiah, the false prophet mentioned in Jeremiah 28:16–17. Daniel Hofer [Sr.,] to "All Hutterites in the World," January 14, 1991, in author's collection.

the then members of Lakeside applied for a remission of their suspensions, and renewed their vows before the whole congregation.[70]

Both Justices recognized that by refusing to accept the church's attempts to settle the dispute and turning to legal counsel instead, Daniel Hofer waived any possibility or opportunity of reaching an understanding and reconciliation.[71]

Daniel Hofer's second and fourth charges against *Ältester* Kleinsasser alleged that he (Hofer) and his supporters were expelled from membership without a proper hearing. The facts do not support this. After refusing to attend multiple community meetings in January of 1987, the Lakeside brotherhood agreed to place Daniel Hofer under church discipline. When he refused to accept church discipline, it was agreed to excommunicate him in January 1987. A meeting on February 10, 1987, with eighty-one ministers confirmed Daniel Hofer's excommunication, and he was asked to vacate Lakeside Colony.[72] At a March 11, 1987 meeting at Woodland, forty-one Hutterite ministers invited Daniel Hofer to appear before the group to present his arguments or reactions to the church's decision. He again declined to attend. On May 17, 1988, in Milltown,[73] 106 ministers voted on whether Daniel Hofer should be given a hearing;[74] eighty-three were in favour of extending him an invitation, and twenty-three were against extending the invitation.[75] Once again, Hofer refused to attend.

The day after this meeting, David Miller Sr., David Miller Jr., Barney Martin, and David Norris were all called to give an account of the church corporations, H.B. Insurance and H.B. Credit. In particular, they were asked to respond directly to allegations read out by Joseph Wipf at the previous day's meetings. After lengthy reports, it was "unanimously agreed" by all present[76] "that the accusations outlined and read out by the

---

70   Lakeside v. Daniel Hofer et al. (Court of Queen's Bench of Manitoba, October 31, 1989), 23.
71   Ibid., 25.
72   Michael F.C. Radcliffe, "Lakeside Colony v. Daniel Hofer Synopsis," April 20, 1988, in author's collection.
73   This meeting was not chaired by *Ältester* Jacob Kleinsasser, but by his assistants, Joseph Wipf (Plainview, SD) and Jacob Hofer (Woodlands, MB).
74   This vote was taken at the court's request. In actual fact, Daniel Hofer had already been excommunicated by the Lakeside Brotherhood. However, to ensure it was done properly according to natural justice, Daniel Hofer was given another opportunity to present his case to the gathering of Hutterite ministers.
75   Joseph Wipf and Jacob Hofer, "Meeting at Milltown about Daniel Hofer Concerning Handling of Funds (Day 1)," May 17, 1988, in author's collection.
76   Present at this meeting were the following U.S. Representatives: Joseph Wipf (Plainview), Sam Hofer (Big Stone), Jacob Wipf (Spring Creek), Mike Waldner (Millbrook), Zack Wollman (Fordham), Mike Tschetter (Elmspring), and Nathan

chairmen Rev. Joseph Wipf and Rev. Jacob Hofer were without foundation."[77] All present declared themselves entirely satisfied with the answers they received.

On August 3, 1989, the church held a special meeting to address concerns raised by some ministers about the court proceedings and whether it was permissible to go to court in light of scriptural teachings and the witness of Hutterite ancestors.[78] Ministers from both the United States and Canada raised concerns about the allegations brought against the elder and about the appropriateness of going to a secular court. *Ältester* Kleinsasser defended the decision to turn to the court for protection from Daniel Hofer by reminding the ministers that neither he nor his assistant, Joseph Wipf, had made this decision on their own but through the consent of the majority of the Schmiedeleut ministers. The elder reminded the ministers that all attempts to stop Hofer from taking over Lakeside through "police and other methods" had failed.[79] Furthermore, the decision to turn to the courts had been made through a process of church discussion and discernment, where it was made clear that there was no alternative but to turn to the legal system for protection. The church had initially sought an application of eviction, which Daniel Hofer refused to obey. Hofer then acquired a lawyer, Donald Douglas, and filed a counterclaim against the church on May 27, 1987, which triggered the Lakeside litigation.[80] The elder reminded those present that this decision was in line with Peter Riedemann, who wrote that it is permissible to turn to government for protection.[81] The elder also listed numerous examples from church history in which the church had asked the government or the courts for assistance.[82] The meeting concluded with ministers and stewards signing their

---

Decker (Pembrook). Canadian representatives included: Jacob Kleinsasser (Crystal Spring), Jacob Waldner (Blumengart), Samuel Waldner (Springfield), Michael Wollman (Springhill), Jacob Hofer (Starlite), Jacob Hofer (Valleyview), John Hofer (Riverbend), Michael Waldner (Rosedale), Jacob Gross (Iberville), Michael Waldner (Waldheim), Leonard Kleinsasser (Delta), David Waldner (Rosevalley), and Elias Maendel (Hidden Valley).

77 Joseph Wipf and Jacob Hofer, "Meeting at Milltown about Daniel Hofer Concerning Handling of Funds (Day 2)," May 18, 1988, in author's collection.

78 Jacob Kleinsasser, "*Versammelt und Gehandelt wegen verschiedenen Welt Gericht* [Meeting and Deliberations Regarding Various [Examples of Using] Worldly Courts]," August 3, 1989, in author's collection. This document contains the signatures of Schmiedeleut ministers and stewards supporting or opposing the Lakeside lawsuit

79 Jacob Kleinsasser, "*Eltester Jakob Kleinsasser bericht* [sic]. [Report by Elder Jacob Kleinsasser]," July 21, 1989, in author's collection.

80 Ibid.

81 Peter Riedemann, *Peter Riedemann's Hutterite Confession of Faith*, trans. and ed. John J. Friesen (Waterloo/Scottdale: Herald Press, 1999; Walden: Plough Publishing, 2019), 130–31.

82 The examples cited by the elder were: 1. The Apostle Paul appealed to Caesar

name in support of the Lakeside court litigation. A total of 165 ministers and stewards signed their name in favour of the lawsuit; six members were against litigating in court.[83]

## *Meidung* Conflict

Daniel Hofer's sixth point contended that the elder was abusing his power by enforcing *Meidung*, or church discipline. Allegations were made that Jacob Kleinsasser was using Woodcrest- or Bruderhof-style discipline in expelling members from the community.[84] This was not true. The practice of excommunicating members had been a part of Hutterite tradition from the earliest days and is still practised by all Hutterite groups.[85] Numerous examples are found in the church chronicles[86] and in Peter Riede-

---

(Acts 25:10); 2. Hutterite forebears turned to governments and local authorities for protection; 3. Migration from Transylvania to Russia was made under the military protection of General Romanzov; 4. In Russia they turned to the government when questions came up about religious freedom; 5. In the United States, Hutterites requested government protection and religious freedom from President Grant; 6. In South Dakota the communities sought court protection from *Mitch-Michl* who left the community and demanded a share; 7. In Bon Homme, SD, the community protected itself against Jakob Hofer; 8. During World War I, vandalism and thefts occurred when the sheriff and police withdrew their protection; 9. During the Interlake court case all the communities and the church were united in seeking court protection against the demands of the Hofer brothers; 10. Sunset, USA court case; 11. Bon Homme and the Jim Wainscoat court case; 12. Many other cases in which Hutterite communities turned to the police for protection and assistance. Jacob Kleinsasser, "*Conference Bericht* [sic] [Conference Report]," August 24–25, 1989, in author's collection.

83   The ministers and stewards who openly criticized the *Ältester* and accepted the false accusations were called on to make public apologies.

84   Daniel Hofer Sr. and other Hutterite ministers were opposed to the practice of sending unrepentant members away from the community so that they might find repentance. They alleged that *Ältester* Kleinsasser borrowed this idea from the Bruderhof communities. The reality was that the church was experiencing more frequent gross violations by members: individualism, theft, smuggling, sexual immorality, and instances of sexual abuse were becoming increasingly apparent. Old and young were taking advantage of "cheap grace" to wipe the slate clean before the Lord's Supper, but falling back into their previous lifestyles shortly thereafter, thus making a mockery of grace and forgiveness. The elders and other ministers attempted to put a stop to what many Hutterites recognized as serious violations against biblical principles and teachings.

85   In the Lakeside appeal, all three trial judges stated that, even though the church had the legal right to expel members without any share, they felt it was unethical. In my view, this is one area where all Hutterite groups might explore more ethical and effective alternatives. Unfortunately, opposition to this is often framed with religious language: "We can't give those who leave the church anything because the money belongs to the widows and orphans." This is tantamount to using scripture to avoid recognizing the image of God in the other (see Mk 7:11).

86   *The Chronicle of the Hutterian Brethren*, vol. 1 (Rifton: Plough Publishing House, 1987), 403 and 777.

mann's *Rechenschaft*,[87] showing how the church established various practices of disciplining erring members.[88] Daniel Hofer's complaint refers more specifically to an amendment to the church's disciplinary procedure which allowed for more severe discipline for unrepentant members, and outlined how to deal with those who left the community and wanted visitation rights.[89] This issue was addressed at the June 2, 1980 church conference, but there appears to have been considerable dissension regarding this decision. On May 20, 1980, at a church meeting in Woodlands, Manitoba, the issue was raised again with thirty ministers. The assembly discussed and clarified the church's approach to dealing with members who had been under severe church discipline—*Ausschluss*, which normally annuls membership—and how they should be taken back into the brotherhood.[90] The ministers again ratified the June 2, 1980 decision to use the same procedure as when somebody joins the church who has already received baptism. This process, called *Einverleiben* or incorporation,[91] required the candidate to affirm several of the Hutterian baptism questions.[92] In this case, members who had been placed under *Ausschluss* would be asked to kneel before the congregation and reconfirm their membership vows.[93]

---

87  Riedemann, *Peter Riedemann's Hutterite Confession of Faith*, 152–53.
88  Historically there have been three processes: 1. *kleinen Unfrieden*; 2. *grossen Unfrieden*; and 3. *Ausschluss*. In the Schmiedeleut context, *grossen* and *kleinen Unfrieden* are the same, and denote a lesser level of discipline. Riedemann states: "If, however, one does not sin wilfully or maliciously but through weakness of the flesh, that person is disciplined without being completely separated from the church or excluded from fellowship" (ibid., 153). When a person is under the church ban (*Ausschluss*), they are separated from the church and "we have no fellowship with him and nothing to do with him" (ibid.).
89  The amendment states: "*Dies betreffe aber nur solche die unordentlich, lieblos, und unversöhnlich oder auch wo alle Straf und Warnung nichts mehr gilt, und mehrere Ursachen, soll darum in Gottes Furcht gehandelt werden.* [This applies only to those who are disorderly, loveless, and irreconcilable or where all discipline and warning are no longer effective, and [with] several reasons. This should therefore be done in the fear of God.]" Woodland Gemeinde [Meeting], April 29, 1980, article 3.
90  The older practice of prescribed or systematic discipline did not always lead to true repentance. The practice has therefore been called into question in cases involving sexual abuse of minors. In some Hutterite communities, the emphasis is still on placing the perpetrator under church discipline for a specific time period and then reinstating their membership and/or position. This practice has become increasingly problematic, especially when the perpetrator is a minister. In some instances, the minister is permanently removed from service, and there is an increased focus on seeking counselling for victims of sexual abuse.
91  The Schmiedeleut do not always require people who join the community from other faith traditions to be rebaptized. The process of *Einverleiben* or incorporation was first used in 1810. This issue remains an area of contention between the two Schmiedeleut groups.
92  This decision was confirmed four weeks later at another church meeting. Jacob Kleinsasser, "Woodland Gemeinde [Meeting]," May 20, 1980, in author's collection.
93  Ibid.

The application of *Meidung* can be understood as an attempt on the part of church leaders to address the increasing number of infractions happening on a wide scale within the Hutterite church against a growing resistance against the disciplinary processes established by the church.

**Springhill Farms**

Daniel Hofer's final point against *Ältester* Kleinsasser had to do with the building of the Springhill Farms abattoir.[94] This hog processing plant was a joint project started by the Schmiedeleut Hutterites in Manitoba around 1984–1985. At that time, the Manitoba government informed the Hutterite leaders that Canada Packers intended to close its plant in St. Boniface. As the Schmiedeleut communities in Manitoba produced approximately 33% of all hogs marketed in Manitoba, this news concerned them greatly. With the closure of Canada Packers, the Hutterite communities knew they would have to do something to protect their market for hogs or suffer the economic consequences.[95] Several church meetings were held where the issue was presented to all stewards and ministers. The Springhill community near Neepawa, Manitoba, proposed to build a processing plant. The project was to be financed by government grants and loans from H.B. Credit. However, Springhill would also need the support of the wider church to carry out this project. As all the Schmiedeleut communities stood to benefit from this abattoir, a church conference was convened in 1985 to discuss the project. The minutes of the meeting read, "All see it very necessary that a killing plant is needed very much, because there are too many pigs raised already, and we would run short of killing plants."[96] The gathered ministers and stewards voted unanimously to accept both the project and a levy of $2.00 per hog to help finance the project.[97] In October 1985, this decision was again ratified at a meeting in Milltown by all ministers and stewards of the Manitoba Schmiedeleut. All the communities were to sign a paper notifying the Manitoba Marketing Commission that the levy would be withdrawn from their accounts to finance the Springhill

---

94 The Springhill Farms hog abattoir is another issue too large to adequately cover in this essay. I limit my description of the issue to the connection to Lakeside litigation and how these two issues were catalysts for the greater conflict which erupted in 1992.
95 Lakeside v. Daniel Hofer et al., 24–25.
96 Jacob Kleinsasser, "Neepawa Killing Plant Decision at Milltown Colony," meeting minutes, [July 20, 1985].
97 The initial agreement was that the levy would be paid back after five years. The minutes state that it was "unanimously agreed to implement the hog levy, $2.00 upon each head that is sold, for one year[.] It shall be a contribution towards the use of the Neepawa killing plant" (ibid.). The original, somewhat arbitrary levy of $2.00/hog was later increased to $2.75; as the plant's finances stabilized, the amount was reduced to $1.75.

Farms abattoir. If everything worked out well, the levy would be repaid to communities in four to five years. However, if the current amount were not sufficient, the issue would be revisited in a year.[98] Because of the huge financial undertaking required for this project, the ministers and stewards were instructed to place the question of the levy and killing plant before each of their communities so that they could have the final vote. All votes were to be collected and sent to Edward Kleinsasser from Sunnyside, who would forward the results to *Ältester* Kleinsasser in Crystal Spring. Edward Kleinsasser later reported that 85% of the Schmiedeleut were in favour of the levy and killing plant. A few communities sent their votes directly to the elder at Crystal Spring. The combined tally amounted to over 90% of the votes in favour of building the abattoir and implementing the levy according to need.[99]

Even though a clear majority of Schmiedeleut communities supported the initial process, as the project broke ground, the implication of the huge financial commitment began to sink in.[100] Communities that had initially agreed to the project began to find ways to avoid paying the required levy even while benefiting from shipping hogs to the plant. What became obvious was that many people had either not been well informed about the scale of the project, or had simply not understood that large projects like the abattoir usually look quite different on paper than in reality. The initial debt load caused by building the plant seemed like an insurmountable expense to many Hutterites, who had little if any experience with such large financial projects. Also, to my knowledge, a joint project of this magnitude had never been undertaken by all the Hutterite communities. The Constitution of the Hutterian Brethren Church, under the Articles of Association section, stated that "No congregation or community of said Church shall be liable for the debts, liabilities, or any financial obligation whatsoever of any other congregation and/or community of said Church."[101] However, there existed significant concern and confusion over whether a

---

98  Jacob Kleinsasser, "*Versammlung Wegen Schlacht Haus bauen mit den Manitoba Gemeinden* [Meeting regarding building a slaughterhouse with Manitoba communities]," meeting minutes, July 30, 1985.

99  Jacob Kleinsasser, "Neepawa Killing Plant Decision at Milltown Colony," meeting minutes, [July 20, 1985]. Despite the fact that the minutes indicate 90% of church leaders supported the endeavour, the reality was that many did not. Many community leaders found loopholes to avoid paying the levy and undermined the work of those tasked with oversight of the project.

100 There was and remains disagreement around the nature of this "agreement." Both Group I and II leaders have raised concerns about how this decision was reached. Many felt that not enough information was presented or that those involved in making the decision on behalf of their community did not fully understand the project's scope.

101 *Constitution of the Hutterian Brethren Church and Rules as to Community of Church Property*, August 1, 1950, article 34.

joint project such as the abattoir would also entail joint liability should the project run into financial difficulty. This raises the question: did the growing concern over the abattoir project justify attempts made by some communities to withdraw from the project, even when the initial agreement between the communities was that all communities were to participate? In his 1991 ruling on the Lakeside litigation, Justice Ferg stated:

> Whether the plant is saved or not, the decision taken, with the knowledge available at the time, cannot be criticized, much less by Mr. Hofer Sr., who, as a single member of one colony, has really no say in the matter.[102]

Nevertheless, Daniel Hofer Sr. had a hugely negative effect on the Springhill Farms abattoir's future. Hofer's conspiracy claims levelled against Michael Wollman (from Springhill, and one of the appointed overseers for Lakeside), and *Ältester* Jacob Kleinsasser, coupled with his campaign of misinformation, caused widespread disillusionment in the project. Communities began to overtly or covertly withdraw their financial support.[103] Hofer's direct attack against the elder cast a long shadow of doubt against the church leadership, which played into the growing discontent manifesting itself in many corners of the church. Nothing, it seemed, could turn the tide of discontent and open malice against the elder. Church minutes show a beleaguered elder almost breaking under the increasing assault from all corners of the church. The elder's emphatic denial of all the allegations and his repeated attempts to explain the situation fell on deaf ears. Even Justice Ferg's findings that the accounts for the Springhill abattoir project were "properly kept and audited," that "nothing is amiss," and that "nothing could be further from the truth"[104] were completely ignored by those who had already passed judgment against their elder. Despite all claims of innocence or judicial acquittals, the die was cast, and the church was on an unstoppable course that would end in its division.

## The Hutterian Brethren Church Biennial Meeting

A final issue that played an important role in increasing tensions between the three Hutterite groups revolved around the biennial meetings. These meetings were established to manage the governing body of the federally incorporated Hutterian Brethren Church. From its inception in the 1950s, the biennial meeting maintained, at best, a tenuous peace between the Schmiedeleut, Dariusleut, and Lehrerleut.

---

102 Lakeside v. Daniel Hofer et al., 10.
103 Those communities who withdrew their support from the project increased the financial risk and burden of those who attempted to see the project through.
104 Lakeside v. Daniel Hofer et al., 22–24, in author's collection.

To understand the complexity of the relationship between the three *Leut*, a brief overview of some critical areas of conflict between the Schmiedeleut, Lehrerleut, and Dariusleut is required. When the Hutterites settled in Dakota Territory (1874–1877), attempts were made by all three groups to unite as one group. When Michael Waldner, also known as *Schmied-Michl*, was elected elder of all three groups, an attempt was made to establish an *allgemeine Kasse* (general church treasury). Attempts were also made to consolidate the landholdings of the individual communities into one central holding company. Most Hutterites voted against this measure and chose instead to leave land ownership with the individual communities. However, conflict soon developed between the elder and the Dariusleut management over land titles. When Wolf Creek was originally settled, it had apparently been founded in various individuals' names. When the Wolf Creek brotherhood and the elder insisted that land titles should be written over to the Wolf Creek community, the leadership refused to comply. They were put under church discipline, which they refused to accept. This conflict was later resolved through the mediation of the Lehrerleut.

Another issue stemmed from when the Lehrerleut immigrated to Dakota Territory in 1877. Before leaving Ukraine, the Lehrerleut sent the bulk of their money to the Dariusleut. When *Ältester* Michael Waldner heard about this, he asked that the money be handed over to the *allgemeine Kasse*, but the Dariusleut refused.

A final conflict ensued when *Ältester* Michael Waldner went back to Russia on a mission trip. Each of the groups gave him one thousand dollars, which was to be used to assist Hutterite settlers in Russia to immigrate to the Dakota Territory. In Russia, Michael Waldner received an additional thousand dollars from a millionaire of Hutterite descent named Andreas Wallmann.[105] When Waldner returned to America, he brought along a group of Hutterites who had promised him that if he paid for their passage, they would join one of the communities. However, once in America, some of the new immigrants opted for private ownership instead. Others stayed in the communities for a while, but never fully submitted themselves to the communal lifestyle and eventually left the brotherhood. The Darius- and Lehrerleut used this as grounds to break away from the united church, saying that Michael Waldner could no longer be their elder as he had wasted the money entrusted to him. After this, all three groups elected their respective elders.

In the 1950s, the Hutterites were experiencing outward pressure from private individuals, local governments, and the federal Canadian government, which pushed for stricter land and taxation restrictions to curb the

---

105 Wallmann was part owner of the Lepp and Wallmann Factory in Chortiza, Ukraine, which manufactured farm equipment.

expansion of the Hutterite communities. The Hutterian Brethren Church Corporation was created primarily to advocate and negotiate such issues with the federal government. At the time, the three groups agreed to hold biennial meetings to keep everybody informed regarding these efforts. In the following decades, however, many of these external conflicts were resolved, and as a result the latent issues that had been set aside while the Hutterite communities fended off external attacks began to re-emerge.

In the early 1970s, an incident involving an accountant from Alberta named Fred Stagg renewed longstanding tensions between the three *Leut*. Stagg had worked together with the Dariusleut to amend the Hutterite Constitution and the Articles of Association.[106] The Dariusleut tried to convince the Lehrerleut and the Schmiedeleut leadership to ratify the amendments.[107] The rationale behind the amendments was an attempt to avoid paying income taxes, but the federal government made it clear it would not accept these changes. The Dariusleut, with the help of Fred Stagg, launched a lawsuit against the federal government to force this issue through. Both the Lehrerleut and the Schmiedeleut refused to have anything to do with the amendments or the lawsuit,[108] and as a result were severely criticized by Dariusleut leadership.

These deep rifts between the three groups were never healed. By 1987, issues of contention between the different *Leut* begin appearing in the minutes.[109] These issues had to do with the relationship to the Bruderhof communities and, to a lesser degree, the Lakeside litigation. On April 13, 1987, Samuel Waldner from Raley, Alberta, wrote a letter attacking both the Bruderhof communities and *Ältester* Jacob Kleinsasser.[110] Two months later, a group of ten Schmiedeleut ministers travelled to Alberta to meet with the Darius- and Lehrerleut leaders to express their disappointment with Waldner's letter. While there, the Schmiedeleut delegates faced verbal abuse from the Darius- and Lehrerleut ministers, who insisted that they would no longer recognize the Bruderhof as Hutterites.[111] On October 7, 1987, a day before the biennial meeting in Milltown, Manitoba, a group of twenty-seven Darius- and Lehrerleut ministers arrived unexpect-

---

106 Fred A. Stagg to Jake Waldner, July 3, 1970, in author's collection.
107 The firm of Roy Baker, Zivot, Radcliffe, Murray, and Singnock, "The Hutterite Brethren Church [Fred Stagg Issue]," received by Mr. Ed Rasmussen, Director of Saskatchewan Farm Ownership Board, March 22, 1982, in author's collection.
108 "Minutes of a Meeting of the Hutterian Brethren Church of Canada," July 3, 1968, in author's collection.
109 "Minutes of a Meeting of the Hutterian Brethren Church Held at Milltown Colony," October 8, 1987, in author's collection.
110 Samuel C. Waldner to Michel Stahl, April 13, 1987, in author's collection.
111 "Schmiedeleut Delegate's Report of Trip to Alberta," July 5, 1987, in author's collection.

edly at Crystal Spring and confronted *Ältester* Kleinsasser. They again repeated their demand that the Bruderhof be removed from the Hutterite Brethren Conference. Kleinsasser refused, and serious disagreements ensued. Kleinsasser eventually postponed the discussion until the scheduled biennial meeting the following day.[112]

Two years later, at the 1989 biennial meeting in Alberta, the Schmiedeleut delegation faced further accusations. John Wurtz of Wilson Siding, Alberta, opened the meeting by reading the by-laws of the church and reminding attendees that "each group is on its own financially so things on courts and monies should not be brought up at this meeting and whoever has these problems are on their own [*sic*]." Nevertheless, the rest of the meeting was spent attacking the Schmiedeleut delegates over precisely these points. When the discussion became too heated, Wurtz closed the meeting.[113]

The disagreements expressed at the biennial meetings came to a head on December 11, 1990, when the Dariusleut and the Lehrerleut sent a letter in which they listed their reasons for no longer recognizing the Bruderhof as members of the Hutterian Brethren Church. The Schmiedeleut responded that they would not attend the biennial conferences until the Dariusleut and Lehrerleut retracted their statement about the Bruderhof, and until they apologized for the allegations and accusations levelled against *Ältester* Kleinsasser at the 1989 biennial meeting.[114] This was still the state of the relationship between the Schmiedeleut, Dariusleut, and Lehrerleut in 1992.

## The 1992 Schism

As the first part of this essay has shown, there were many conflicts simmering within Hutterite communities prior to the 1992 schism, ranging from historic tensions between the three *Leut*, to financial and manufacturing disputes, to dissatisfaction over changing methods of church discipline. *Ältester* Kleinsasser became a focal point for much of this dissatisfaction and a target of accusations from not only individuals like Daniel Hofer but also other ministers. The following sections attempt to lay out the details of what happened in 1992, which resulted in the split of the Schmiedeleut Hutterites into Group I and Group II.

---

112 Jacob Kleinsasser, summary of conversation, October 7, 1987, in author's collection. I could not locate the official minutes of the 1987 biennial meeting; by all accounts, it was a turbulent meeting.
113 "Hutterian Brethren Church Meeting Held at Lakeside Colony, Cranford, Alberta, Canada," August 16, 1989, in author's collection.
114 Roy Baker and Jacob Kleinsasser to John Wipf, June 18, 1991, in author's collection.

## November Starlite Meetings

On November 5, 6, and 7, 1992, all the Schmiedeleut ministers met at Starlite, Manitoba, to address the accusations brought against *Ältester* Jacob Kleinsasser. Joseph Wipf, Kleinsasser's assistant, acted as spokesman for the dissenting ministers and read out multiple accusations, claiming he had proof for every charge but producing none. Kleinsasser and other ministers disputed the allegations and tried to explain the complexity of each situation, to no avail: Wipf and his supporters rejected Kleinsasser's explanations and instead made accusations that had emerged from the Lakeside litigation and from Donald Gibb, the financial advisor who had been involved in the Rosedale/Millbrook loan fraud of the 1980s. The meeting at Starlite concluded with the request that all those who stood with Joseph Wipf's letter of accusation against the elder sign their name. All forty-nine signatures on the document were ministers from South Dakota.[115] *Ältester* Kleinsasser closed the meeting by asking the ministers to go home and carefully reconsider their accusations against him. For his part, the elder rejected the allegations as false,[116] and indicated another meeting would be scheduled to further discuss the situation.

In the meantime, news of the November meeting tore through Hutterite communities. While some were deeply dismayed over what had transpired, others rejoiced and spread additional rumours, thus fanning the flames of the conflict.

On December 1, 1992, Joseph Wipf and five other ministers[117] from American communities held a secret meeting with Lehrerleut and Dariusleut leaders at Springwater community in Montana, without the elder's knowledge or consent.[118] At this meeting, Lehrerleut and Dariusleut elders counselled and encouraged the American ministers to reject Jacob Kleinsasser's eldership.[119] They accepted as true the accusations brought against him by Donald Gibb, the American Schmiedeleut ministers, and

---

115 "Signatures Opposing Jacob Kleinsasser's Eldership," November 5, 1992, typescript, in author's collection.
116 Jacob Kleinsasser to "All brothers [i.e., Schmiedeleut minister]," November 23, 1993, in author's collection.
117 The five ministers were Jacob Wipf (Spring Creek, SD), Michael Tschetter (New Elm Spring, SD), Johannes Wipf (Maxwell, SD), Samuel Glanzer (Greenwood, SD) and Daniel Wipf (Willowbank, ND).
118 Jacob Kleinsasser to Joe Wipf, August 26, 1992, in author's collection.
119 This interference by the Darius- and Lehrerleut Conference was in direct violation of the 1950s Constitution, which states in paragraph 23: "The Conference Board shall exercise control over the Church dogma and Church discipline within their respective Conference, and shall have charge of all matters pertaining to Hutterian Brethren generally within their respective Conferences, and shall have power to take such action as they deem meet in respect to matters affecting or pertaining to the Hutterian Brethren *within their respective conferences*" [emphases added].

Daniel Hofer. Passing judgment without consulting the accused runs contrary to basic Christian principles of honesty and integrity (Matthew 7:5) that are a part of Hutterite practice.

Considering that many of the allegations levelled against Kleinsasser centred on financial loss or mismanagement, it is instructive to consider similar losses among the Dariusleut and Lehrerleut and the responses by the other *Leut*. For instance, in 1964, Hutterite communities in Alberta and Washington State lost $2.2 million in what became known as the Wheatland scam.[120] In the 1970s, the Dariusleut communities in Alberta were defrauded of approximately $3 million when they issued full power of attorney to Fred Stagg, the accountant hired to help fight their lawsuit against the federal government regarding income tax.[121] In 1987, some Darius- and Lehrerleut communities lost approximately $30 million when the Principal Group,[122] a savings company with which they had deposited millions of dollars, went bankrupt.[123] In all these situations, the Schmiedeleut did not interfere or demand an explanation. They accepted that mistakes could easily be made in the world of big business, and they trusted that the Alberta leadership had acted in good faith and in the best interests of their communities.

On December 6, emboldened by the support he had received from the Darius- and Lehrerleut Conferences, Joseph Wipf called another secret meeting at Plainview in Huron, South Dakota.[124] The question on the table was whether the ministers of the American communities should attend the December 9 meeting in Starlite, which had been scheduled by *Ältester* Kleinsasser as a follow-up to the November meetings, or whether they should demand that he appear before them in South Dakota. Apparently, the majority felt that they should attend the meeting.

## December Starlite Meeting

The American delegation arrived in Starlite on December 9, 1992, bringing a copy of the letter given to them by the Lehrerleut and Dariu-

---

120 Peter Menzies, "No one knows what Ken Oxborrow did with millions," *Yakima Herald-Republic* 82, no. 47 (1984).
121 Paul S. Gross to Joshua Hofer, August 1, 1980, in author's collection.
122 Paul S. Gross to Jacob Kleinsasser, September 22, 1887, in author's collection. By 1987, most of this money was recovered with the help of Meyers Norris Penny, who joined other investors in filing a class-action lawsuit against the Principal Group founders and partners. See "Principal Group Debacle Settled," *The Globe and Mail*, April 11, 2018, accessed August 23, 2019, https://www.theglobeandmail.com/report-on-business/principal-group-debacle-settled/article25704010/.
123 This is by no means an exhaustive list and does not include more recent losses, i.e., money hedging and contract scandals, insurance fraud, the South Dakota turkey scandal, and bitcoin investment losses, etc.
124 Anonymous to Joseph Wipf, [1993], in author's collection.

sleut,[125] as well as a letter consisting of grievances against the elder.[126] This letter was based on the accusations brought against the elder by Joseph Wipf and certain South Dakota communities. Some of these points had already been raised by Wipf at a meeting in Plainview a few months earlier, on August 8;[127] by December the accusations had increased to twelve.[128]

The December 9 meeting opened with Joseph Wipf objecting to the presence of a Bruderhof minister at the meeting.[129] Wipf argued that this affair did not concern the Bruderhof, and that their minister, Glenn Swinger, should leave. *Ältester* Kleinsasser maintained that Swinger had as much right to be at the Schmiedeleut meeting as any other minister. Next, Wipf asked that the elder step aside and not participate in "the hearing," likely meaning that the elder not chair the meeting. The elder refused to approve the motion, and so it was dropped. Kleinsasser proceeded to chair the meeting, as was the practice.

*Ältester* Kleinsasser opened the meeting by stating the reason for the gathering. He mentioned that at the November meeting everyone had been asked to reconsider what they had done and to consider the dangerous consequences of false testimony and unfounded accusations. Those who wished to change their minds had been invited to write a personal letter to the elder stating as much. However, no letters had been received,

---

125 M.S. Stahl and Johannes P.S. Wipf to "whom it may concern," December 1, 1992, in author's collection.
126 Joseph Wipf to "*Liebe Brüder* [Dear Brothers, i.e., all Schmiedeleut ministers]," August 29, 1992, in author's collection.
127 Jacob Kleinsasser, "Meeting at Plainview Col[ony], S. Dakota," summary note, August 11, 1992, in author's collection.
128 The twelve points consisted of the following: 1. Rosedale/Millbrook situation needs to be re-examined and the debt placed upon Rosedale remitted. Michael Waldner must be disciplined again; 2. Allegations that Jacob Kleinsasser had signed a power-of-attorney agreement by which the whole church would have been pledged; 3. The collection of the Donald Gibb book should have been done with council of all ministers; 4. Communities being dragged to court, i.e., the patent issue; 5. Complaint that the U.S. communities were deprived of their 1990 dividend (H.B. Mutual Insurance); 6. Dissatisfaction regarding financial contributions or "imposed taxes" made by Manitoba communities (i.e., Springhill Farms, truck wash, etc.) and allegations that no proper account is given of the monies spent; 7. Complaint about the Oak Bluff situation and how the church handled it; 8. Complaint about the Rock Lake situation and how the church dealt with it; 9. Reuniting with the Dariusleut and Lehrerleut; 10. Opposition to the elder going on mission trips or spending so much time in Woodcrest; 11. Dissatisfaction with a letter written by Woodcrest on November, 28, 1992, in which they stated that Joseph Wipf and the 49 American ministers should be removed from the service of the Word; 12. Re-examination of Rosedale situation to make sure that the borrowed money is repaid (Sirach 29:2).
129 Glenn Swinger was visiting Manitoba and had been invited to participate in the meeting.

since Joseph Wipf had stated that "he felt it would be better to write one letter for all instead of each one for himself."[130]

Once again, Kleinsasser asserted that the twelve points raised at the November meeting "were unfounded, untrue, and erroneous and caused nothing but mistrust and confusion which in turn would give rise to dissension and rebellion."[131] Jacob Kleinsasser later recounted:

> This was no hearing or meeting according to Christ's teaching, which says, "Ask your brother whether or not he has said this." Instead, they [those opposing Kleinsasser] were unreasonable in their purpose and made ill-considered charges and evil accusations, mistreating the elder with their accusations and false statements in a way that not even a vagabond should be treated in a Christian or brotherly gathering. They did not believe a word and would not allow their misrepresentations to be corrected regardless of how Jacob Kleinsasser defended himself.[132]

Various ministers spoke out in support of the points in Joseph Wipf's letter. Dissenting ministers asked that the Millbrook/Rosedale financial situation be re-examined. Accusations of fraud and deception were brought against minister Michael Waldner (Millbrook) and against the elder. In response, *Ältester* Kleinsasser read the church minutes in which the Rosedale matter had been dealt with through the church's disciplinary process. Some felt that Millbrook community had not divided the debt equitably, and that Millbrook owed Rosedale money. The same minutes the elder referred to state that the reason both communities agreed to split the debt was that at the time of the investment, the two communities had not officially separated. Despite this, Joseph Wipf and Leonard Kleinsasser (Delta, Manitoba) kept insisting that the whole matter needed to be re-examined and those who were found guilty should be re-disciplined.[133]

---

130 Jacob Kleinsasser, "Meeting at Starlite Colony, December 9–10, 1992," translation of meeting minutes, in author's collection.
131 Ibid.
132 Ibid.
133 In 1986, at a church gathering in Rosedale, SD, the situation leading up to the financial disaster was explained to everyone present. The DeLeo-Cornell Group had fraudulently made investments which neither Rosedale nor Millbrook were aware of. When the deception was uncovered, the two communities needed a loan so they could pay off the creditors. Michael Waldner borrowed the necessary funds from Rabobank in New York. In the end, they were still $3.2 million in debt, which was then divided between Millbrook and Rosedale ($1.5 million each). However, correspondence between Donald Gibb and Barney Martin indicates that Rabobank was not willing to allow Millbrook to assume responsibility for Rosedale's debt because, as a relatively new community, Millbrook did not have the asset base to justify, or the ability to repay, indebtedness of $3.2 million. (Donald Gibb to Barney Mar-

Joseph Hofer (Cypress, Manitoba), Jacob Gross (Mayfair, Manitoba), John Hofer (James Valley, Manitoba) and others brought up the Springhill Farms abattoir and insisted that *Ältester* Kleinsasser and Michael Wollman (Springhill) were involved in a conspiracy. Some maintained that the abattoir had been built without a majority vote.[134] Another issue raised was

tin, October 28, 1985, in author's collection.) The church accountant, Jeff Cristall, attempted to find a way to rectify this situation. At the Rosedale meeting, they suggested that Crystal Spring, as a financially strong community, could offset the Millbrook/Rosedale debt by absorbing $750,000. This debt was later further divided between Crystal Spring and Concord (MB) communities. *Ältester* Jacob Kleinsasser, as representative for Crystal Spring, agreed to this suggestion but stated that he wished to make it absolutely clear that Crystal Spring had no more obligation to take on this debt than any other Schmiedeleut community. The only reason Crystal Spring took on this debt was to stop the bank from foreclosing on Rosedale.

In 1988, the church convened another meeting in South Dakota to deal with the Millbrook and Rosedale financial issue. Rosedale refused to make payments on its share of the debt, insisting that the entire debt belonged to Millbrook because Michael Waldner, their minister, was the person primarily responsible for it. As a result of their refusal to pay interest on their debt and as a result of overall poor management, Rosedale had accumulated another $500,000 debt for a total of $2.4 million. At this meeting, the Rosedale management and members attacked Jacob Kleinsasser and Michael Waldner. In 1986, at a meeting in Crystal Spring, Rosedale and Millbrook leadership had acknowledged that both communities were liable for the debt; they now stated that Millbrook and Crystal Spring were liable for the debt. This greatly upset the elder as the accusations were completely unfounded. In his preamble to the October 26, 1988, minutes, the elder wrote, "Firstly, I feel that this accusation is completely out of line. As long as this accusation stands, especially against the elder, no council in this matter will be of any help for Rosedale. I find myself completely unsettled and unprepared to come up with any plan or council because, as it appears, there are many ministers who are not in agreement with the decision reached in Crystal Spring regarding the splitting of the debt. They want to impose a debt on Crystal Spring without just cause. […] Despite this, the situation cannot be altered. The reality is that Rosedale has to assume its debt and if they refuse to do so, they will have to declare bankruptcy [*versinken*]." (Jacob Kleinsasser, summary notes of Rosedale Meetings, 1986–88, in author's collection.) Because of the disastrous state of Rosedale's financial situation, the ministers decided that Rosedale would be placed under the management of Millbrook leadership.

In the 1990s the Rabobank was no longer willing to finance the Rosedale debt. The debt was therefore refinanced and reduced from $1,600,000 to $1,100,000. Fourteen Manitoba communities signed a letter of credit ($100,000 each), which resulted in a reduction of approximately $640,000. This manoeuvre also allowed the Rabobank debt to be transferred to H.B. Credit. (Unsigned letter to *"Alle Brüder* [All brothers]," annual conference report, August 20, 1990.) The fourteen Manitoba communities that signed a letter of credit for Rosedale's debt were Crystal Spring, Glenway, Rosedale, Milltown, Newhaven, Riverbend, James Valley, Oakridge, Baker, Greenwald, Miami, Oak Bluff, Sommerfeld, and Sunnyside.

134 This is partially true. The Springhill Farms abattoir was originally built by Springhill community, not the church. When it ran into financial difficulty, Michael Wollman, Springhill's minister and founder of the abattoir, approached the church and asked if it could buy the plant. If the church had not bought the plant, it would have been sold to other prospective buyers. Also, as stated earlier, many felt that they received

whether it was right to threaten to withhold participation in the Lord's Supper from communities that stopped supporting the abattoir. The elder explained that disobedience and disunity were two common reasons for withholding the Lord's Supper. Those communities that refused to comply with the majority decision that all communities were to participate in the project were being disobedient and were causing disunity, thus jeopardizing the project.[135]

As the accusations at the Starlite meeting piled up, more Schmiedeleut ministers stood and declared themselves in agreement with the twelve points in Joseph Wipf's letter. Jacob Kleinsasser kept denying the accusations, stating that the letter read by Joseph Wipf was unacceptable with "no proof or foundation to justify such an uprising and rebellion."[136]

Next, Jacob Wipf (Spring Creek, South Dakota) and Joseph Wipf introduced a letter written by the Lehrerleut and Dariusleut, dated December 1, 1992. This letter was not accepted to be read out at the present meeting because it was signed by the Dariusleut and the Lehrerleut elders, who had no authority to interfere in a Schmiedeleut meeting or affair.

Jacob Wipf and Joseph Wipf brought out a letter dated December 9, 1992, and signed by Joseph Wipf. Initially, Kleinsasser refused to accept this letter,[137] but Jacob Wipf threatened to make the letter public if it were not read, and send the elder a copy via registered post. Kleinsasser reluctantly consented to the letter being read out at the meeting, which Joseph Wipf did. The letter was a summary of accusations against the elder:

> Dear brothers,
>
> This is to inform all ministers and all our colonies of the growing decline of true community.
>
> May the almighty God and Lord grant that this ministers' meeting brings a blessing, and that it does not take place out of habit or to pass the time, but that we may seek ways

---

    insufficient information or did not fully understand the scope of the commitment as presented by the elder.

135  The fact that there was a clear discrepancy between the "majority" decisions and the reality that many ministers and stewards did not fully support the decisions raises serious questions about the processes by which these decisions were reached. As a church, we need to review and reflect deeply on the discernment processes and practices that shape collective decisions.

136  Jacob Kleinsasser, "Meeting at Starlite Colony, December 9–10, 1992."

137  According to ministers standing next to the elder when Joseph Wipf handed him this letter, Jacob Kleinsasser quickly scanned it and attempted to convince Wipf to take it back. He said, "You don't realize what you are doing with this letter. You are not only going to tear apart the church, but communities and families."

and means to heal the damage in Israel and to stop the ruin instead of increasing it.

Things already look sad and discouraging because the elder Jacob Kleinsasser and his helpers are no longer a brightly shining light and strong salt of the earth, which we are called to be as followers of Christ.

This was made sufficiently clear to us all at our meeting on November 5–7, 1992, at the Starlite Colony in Manitoba.

Things have come to pass such that sin is no longer sin. Instead, the greatest effort was made to dismiss it through cunning and loose talk. More time and effort were spent and is still being spent to continue covering it up instead of admitting the truth and putting an end to the disgraceful affairs, like that of Rosedale Colony, SD, whose property and money was taken away by deceit and cunning. Those who are guilty of borrowing money for Rosedale in a deceitful way should pay it back with interest, so that they may find forgiveness in this life for their sin and evil and will not have to appear before God with the burden of this sin.

As also the feeder patent clearly shows, and the burden of the enormous sum of money levied on the Manitoba colonies without specific reasons what the money is being used for. There we demand and request that a clear account be given of all money without delay.

The same goes for all the other points of August 21, 1992, and November 19, 1992, such as the impertinent actions of Woodcrest, especially their meeting of November 27, 1992, at 1:00 p.m. when all baptized members were present (2,000 souls) as reported in their letter of November 28, 1992, where they condemned all 49 U.S. ministers as well as all those who agreed with them in their absence (by proxy), without a hearing. Who gave Woodcrest the power and the right to pass judgment on Schmiedeleut, Lehrerleut, and Dariusleut or to consider them as deserving punishment, while they themselves are mere apprentices (novices)? It is nothing but their domineering spirit, power struggle, and impudence. One would like to ask: "Friend, how did you get in here" (Matt. 22:12)?

And the other insults that have been mentioned, which were made in a callous way: the longer it goes, the worse it gets, and no warning or admonishment helps. It is all in vain. It is stubbornness and lust for power, which we have brought up before, and our letters of warning clearly show how far we have strayed from the truth, and WHY?? [*sic*]

As also the letter of December 1, 1992, from our dear brothers the Lehrerleut and Dariusleut, makes clear and should serve greatly to encourage, admonish, and teach us, and we are fully satisfied and in agreement with it. We cannot thank God enough that help is still forthcoming and he still raises upright brothers and ministers to be untiring and fearless fighters for the truth.

Dear brothers: Therefore, we have recognized in the fear of God that Jacob Kleinsasser is not worthy to be acknowledged as a leader, elder, and minister of the Hutterian Church of the Schmiedeleut[138] with all these faults which have been discussed at length.

Also, we can no longer recognize his supporters and followers as brothers in the faith.

Your lowly and saddened helper,

Joseph Wipf[139]

At this point, *Ältester* Kleinsasser had no choice but to place the question before the meeting, asking those who still supported him to stand up so they could be counted. Some objected to this question, as they did not want the meeting to come to such a decision. There was considerable confusion,[140] but in the end, somebody indicated that approximately eighty

---

138 Group II leaders have repeatedly insisted that this statement was taken back on day two of these meetings. When the dissenting ministers met in Westroc, the Manitoba ministers apparently objected to the statement which declared that Jacob Kleinsasser was no longer an elder or minister. According to historian Tony Waldner, the Manitoba ministers insisted that Joseph Wipf strike that statement from his letter. This may well be, but Group I ministers insist that the statement, as read by Joseph Wipf on day one of the meeting, was never officially retracted.
139 Joseph Wipf to "Dear Brothers," December 9, 1992, in author's collection.
140 According to eyewitness accounts, this is an understatement; the room was in pandemonium. During reported votes, ministers often couldn't decide whether to stand or sit. Some stood up but saw some of their friends or relatives sitting, so they also sat down. The reverse was also true. Some ministers reportedly left the room as they did not want to make such a momentous decision. The official minutes are equally

people stood up. Michael Tschetter (1933–2013) from New Elm, South Dakota, mentioned a majority, but Kleinsasser replied, "This affair does not go by the majority." Kleinsasser stated that he could not accept Joseph Wipf's letter because it was full of untruths and false accusations.[141] At this, Wipf got up and said, "Whoever stands for the truth should be in Westroc tomorrow at 1:30 p.m.[142] We will have our own meeting."[143] The elder responded: "All of you who stand with the church and elder shall be here tomorrow at 1:00 p.m."[144] This was unanimously accepted by everybody present.[145]

The following day, December 10, when the elder and his supporters met in Starlite, all the ministers who had aligned themselves with Joseph Wipf the previous day came to the meeting uninvited. Kleinsasser asked, "What do you want here? We parted yesterday [and you stated] that you will have your meeting in Westroc. You have separated yourself from us, and that is the way it will stay." To this Joseph Wipf replied, "If God can change his mind, we can too."[146]

The December 10 meeting continued in much the same way as the previous day's meeting. Arguments erupted between various ministers on the floor, so that no clear progress could be made. The elder asked for order and read out a lengthy statement he had prepared after the previous day's meeting, excerpts of which are shown here:

> Now, dear brothers, the contents [of the last page of Joseph Wipf's twelve-point letter] ends with what has been

---

confusing. The elder claimed that in the days following "the vote," he received calls from a number of ministers who wished to retract their decision.
141 Jacob Kleinsasser, "Meeting at Starlite Colony, December 9–10, 1992."
142 At a meeting between the two Schmiedeleut groups in 1996, Leonard Kleinsasser pointed out that many Canadian Schmiedeleut ministers had not agreed with Joseph Wipf regarding having their own meeting in Westroc. This supports the assertion that the American ministers were the driving force behind the division. What seems equally clear from reading early Group II documents is that some Manitoba ministers had second thoughts about removing the elder and causing a schism. That is why the interference of the Dariusleut and Lehrerleut in encouraging and supporting the establishment of a new constitution is so unfortunate.
143 Jacob Kleinsasser, "Meeting at Starlite Colony, December 9–10, 1992."
144 Ibid.
145 At the close of the November and the December meetings, *Ältester* Kleinsasser tried to leave an opening for the ministers to reconsider. Twice he asked the ministers to return home, and after careful consideration, write him a letter expressing their opinion and position. Both times Joseph Wipf interfered with the elder's attempt at reconciliation by stating that he would write a letter representing everyone. This action of Joseph Wipf likely silenced many Canadian Group II leaders who might have had second thoughts about the direction things were going if they had been given the opportunity to put their thoughts into writing.
146 Memorandum by Jacob Kleinsasser, "Motion for the Closing of the Meeting at Starlite," December 9, 1992, in author's collection.

intended all along, but unfortunately is regrettable: that it has come so far among us and that there are so many who are guilty of this sin, although they say: "We cannot remain silent anymore about the sin." Regardless of whether there is cause or proof for any of these points, they still try to find accusations. They use all their strength and energy to prove what they have said against the elder, [accusing him of] "fraud and cunning, lying and avarice, power struggles that are waged without the fear of God and without further thought, dragging other colonies before a worldly court, just for the sake of money." [...]

Moreover, now it is said in the latest letter that Jacob Kleinsasser can no longer be elder and preacher and that all his followers and supporters are no longer their brothers in the faith. It is appalling to pronounce such a judgment without a hearing, without reason and proof of all those points, and without giving credence to any of Jacob Kleinsasser's explanations.

Just as in the very beginning of the meeting, the elder was assumed to be untruthful, for which reason the elder, with all his supporters, was not to sit in judgment. All of this had been prepared ahead of time, and the meeting began with this intention.

It was said, sin is no longer sin, referring to other points. However, the dreadful sin of slander and defamation, of spreading falsehoods all the way to the [far] west, is not taken seriously. Or taking part in a meeting in Montana with the Lehrerleut and Dariusleut, with a letter full of accusations, and to pass judgment at a distance of a thousand miles in the elder's absence.

Moreover, the way things look, that time has come. The church is being destroyed and torn apart so that one will have to say: Is there no balm in Israel to heal the damage?[147]

When the elder had finished reading this statement, Joseph Wipf stood up and requested that Jacob Kleinsasser call a general meeting in South Dakota in January 1993 with all Schmiedeleut communities. Many, however, expressed opposition to this motion. Some of the elder's sup-

---

147 Jacob Kleinsasser, "Meeting at Starlite Colony, December 9–10, 1992.

porters pointed out that since Wipf had rejected Kleinsasser as elder the previous day, how could he ask him to call such a meeting? First, they would have to revoke their statements and re-accept the elder. Second, the false statements and the open rebellion against the elder would have to be made right before any further meetings. Despite this, Wipf's supporters kept requesting a meeting in South Dakota. The account mentioned previously states that "[a] great commotion and loud dispute ensued."[148] Things got out of hand."[149] At this point, David Decker (1922–2009) of Starland Community, Minnesota, stood up and reiterated,

> [T]his rebellion and sin cannot be set aside without serious repentance, and no meeting can be held before this has happened. For it is a great sin thus to rise up like rebels. Moreover, the elder would accept nothing less.[150]

Other Schmiedeleut ministers who supported the elder concurred with Decker's statement.

When it became apparent that no further progress could be made, *Ältester* Kleinsasser asked the dissenting brothers to return home and consider the situation they had put themselves into and to refrain from preaching the word of God. Joseph Wipf, however, interjected, saying, "Everyone go home and preach the Word of God."[151]

To end the meeting, Kleinsasser said, "All that are with the church shall stay and sign their name, so we know where you are from. The rest shall go home and think about what you have done."[152] Kleinsasser's request was not a formal motion asking members to vote for or against him. Eyewitnesses recall that there was a lot of confusion at the conclusion of the meeting, and many in attendance were, understandably, conflicted and could not decide whether to sign their support of the elder or not. In the confusion that ensued, it was impossible to collect a clear record of signatures. For his part, the elder always maintained that he had never called for a vote[153] but was merely trying to clarify which members were not in agreement with Joseph Wipf's letter. The official minutes of the meeting show that there were 159 ministers present: ninety signed for the church and in support of the elder and seventy-eight signed as dissidents.[154]

---

148 Ministers present at the meeting reported the elder was physically attacked; ministers surrounded him, shouting, and even shoved him. Eventually, minister Jacob Hofer from Starlite forced his way into the crowd and escorted the elder from the room.
149 Jacob Kleinsasser, "Meeting at Starlite Colony, December 9–10, 1992."
150 Ibid.
151 Ibid.
152 Ibid.
153 As stated earlier, such a vote was impossible for multiple reasons.
154 The so-called vote that concluded the December 1992 meeting in Starlight was and

## A Parting of Ways

Later, leaders of the group that broke away would claim that *Ältester* Jacob Kleinsasser had lost a non-confidence vote. A close examination of Hutterian leadership structure and election process, as well as what transpired at the meeting and the legal wrangling which followed, suggests that no vote took place, or could take place, for two reasons.

First, the mechanism for voting an elder out of office does not normally exist within the Schmiedeleut leadership structure, nor for a minister or a steward. In Schmiedeleut practice, an elected person can only be promoted, not demoted. For instance, a steward can be elected or voted out of his position only if he is appointed as minister. The exception to this rule is if that member commits a clear, provable violation or sin. For instance, in 1621, Rudolf Hirzel had the eldership taken from him, and in the 1730s, Jörgl Frank was also removed from service. However, the context makes it clear that these individuals were removed for violations to which they admitted. In Jacob Kleinsasser's situation, the elder denied all the allegations brought against him, and to date none have been proven.[155] This prompts the question of whether the ministers overreached their authority in trying to remove an elder. Considering the process that the Schmiedeleut use in electing an elder, one might suggest that if it were permissible to remove an elder by vote, such a vote should only be taken by those people who voted him into the position in the first place.[156] Such a process would require the thoughtful and meaningful discernment of the entire body of Schmiedeleut baptized members.

---

    remains a heavily contested issue. Both groups claim that the numbers fell in their favour. The numbers, however, are not entirely clear. As reported earlier, some ministers reportedly changed their mind several times during the meeting, others were reported by the elder to have later revoked their signature, while others walked out of the meeting during the turmoil and only returned toward the end of the gathering. What complicates matters even further is that two sets of signatures exist: one for the November meetings, and one for the December meetings.

    The eight loose-leaf sheets with all the Schmiedeleut signatures were added as an appendix to the meeting minutes and are in the Jacob Kleinssaser Collection at Crystal Spring (MB). As indicated above, great caution is needed when interpreting these numbers because of the general confusion and turmoil that ensued during the proceedings. Some ministers initially sided with the elder, but when they returned to their home communities, a majority of their members informed them they no longer had a community to lead. This caused some to switch sides, as they felt it was their duty to remain with their congregation.

155  As stated earlier, these allegations were repeatedly dismissed during the many court cases. Allegations that the elder had bribed the judges border on the ridiculous.

156  Prior to the 1992 schism, all three Hutterite groups had an *Ältester* as the head of their conference, though each conference used a different selection process. In Schmiedeleut practice, the elder is elected by majority vote of *all baptized male members* of the conference.

The second reason for discounting the claim of a non-confidence vote is that when the dissenting ministers left the December 9 meeting with the intention of calling their own meeting, they separated themselves from the church. Any "vote" they may claim to have "won" after that is pointless, because they could hardly have a vote in a church they had voluntarily left. The 1993 Reaffirmation Constitution, which claims to hinge on this vote, has no authority in the Schmiedeleut Conference. This document was established by the Lehrerleut, the Dariusleut, and the dissenting group of Schmiedeleut. However, the Dariusleut and Lehrerleut Conferences cannot, by virtue of the 1950s Constitution, interfere with the affairs of the Schmiedeleut without their consent,[157] nor did the communities that supported Jacob Kleinsasser as elder sign the new 1993 Constitution. The Hutterian Brethren Church Federal Corporation has traditionally only been used to lobby the federal government in Ottawa and not as a vehicle exercising any real authority over the temporal or spiritual affairs of the communities in Canada.[158] As such, each of the three *Leut* function as autonomous entities so far as the Hutterian Brethren Church is concerned. Because this organizational structure is more congregational than episcopal,[159] the Federal Corporation has no authority as far as the individual communities are concerned.[160]

Because the Group I Schmiedeleut—those who continued to support *Ältester* Kleinsasser—refused to sign the Reaffirmation Constitution, allegations have been made that they are no longer part of the Hutterian church, as they refused to reconfirm[161] and have thus broken ranks with the established Hutterite church and started their own church. The Group II leadership—those who rejected Kleinsasser's eldership—claimed that they were the ones who remained with the Hutterian Brethren Church which includes the Lehrerleut and Dariusleut. However, the division caused a legal problem for the Group II Hutterites. Because of legal barriers that exist between the American and Canadian system, only the Canadian communities were signatories to the 1950s Constitution. In a legal sense, the American communities were thus never members of the constituted Canadian Federal Corporation. So even though the American Hutterites were technically part of the Schmiedeleut Conference, they were not part of it in a legal sense (they had retained their own constitution, which is different from the Canadian Hutterite Constitution). In essence, under the

---

157 *Constitution of the Hutterian Brethren Church*, August 1, 1950, Article 23.
158 Michael F.C. Radcliffe to Jacob Kleinsasser, June 25, 1993, in author's collection.
159 In a congregational structure, each congregation independently governs itself, whereas an episcopal structure is governed by bishops.
160 Michael F.C. Radcliffe to Jacob Kleinsasser, May 20, 1993, in author's collection.
161 John M. Wipf, Joseph P. Hofer, Peter A. Kleinsasser, M.S. Stahl, Joseph Wipf, and John Stahl to Hutterian Brethren Church, May 20, 1993, in author's collection.

leadership of Joseph Wipf, the Group II Hutterites formed a new group which left or disassociated itself from the original grouping of the Hutterian Brethren according to the meaning and expression of the Hutterite documentation itself.

## After the Schism

The tragic result of the December 9–10 meetings was that the Schmiedeleut Conference split into two parts, known as Schmiedeleut Group I and Group II. The ramifications of this split took some years to unfold and crystallize. Though it is agreed that the schism officially took place in December 1992, it took several months for the distinct sides to emerge. Some of the further disagreements that followed came about as a result of both groups wrestling with the practical consequences of the split. Because the Group II ministers and communities had rejected the eldership of Jacob Kleinsasser while Group I continued to recognize him as their leader, two distinct congregations of Schmiedeleut now existed in Manitoba, both claiming to be the genuine Hutterian Brethren Church. The existence of two competing groups had legal ramifications.

**Vital Statistics Conflict**

Sometime in March or April 1993, Jacob Kleinsasser was asked to update the list of registered officiants with the Manitoba Vital Statistics Agency. Because of the division of the Schmiedeleut Conference, Kleinsasser decided that he could no longer vouch for or confirm ministers as clergy who were no longer in harmony with him and who so openly rejected any attempts he made at trying to explain the situation, and so he asked Vital Statistics to remove their names from the list of recognized Schmiedeleut officiants under his authority.[162] Vital Statistics compiled

---

162 What may have triggered this event was a meeting that took place at Delta, MB, on February 22 and 23, 1993. Present were 110 dissident Schmiedeleut, ten Lehrerleut, and nine Dariusleut ministers. The purpose of the meeting was to listen to a report by Donald Gibb and Jeff Svenn (attorney for the U.S. Schmiedeleut communities) about the financial affairs in which Jacob Kleinsasser had supposedly been personally involved. At this meeting, the dissident group accepted as true the outlandish, twisted narrative woven by Gibb and Svenn, thereby rejecting the explanations given by Jacob Kleinsasser. When some of the dissident ministers suggested another attempt should be made to talk with the elder, the Lehrerleut objected. One of them chronicling a report of the meeting wrote, "*Wir waren zum Theil* [sic] *auch furchtsam, daß sie einen Vertrag mit Jakob Kleinsasser wollten machen um den Riß aufzuhalten, der ihnen schwer auf die Hertzen liegt, und ihren Gemeinden drohet. Sie aber hielten an und drangen hart darauf.* [Some of us were also afraid they might want to reach an agreement with Jacob Kleinsasser in order to prevent the split, which is heavy on their hearts and threatens their communities. Nevertheless, they pressed on hard.]" The report goes on to say it was the Lehrerleut who insisted that Elder

a list of dissident ministers, and Kleinsasser indicated that the dissident minsters would have to establish their own signing authority for their group. The Group II leaders were understandably upset at being removed from the registry, which they saw as a deletion. How were they to perform and solemnize marriages if they were essentially deleted[163] from the list of qualified clergy?[164] An emergency meeting with the Lehrerleut and Dariusleut was held on April 23, 1993, in Rosetown, Saskatchewan. It was decided that the six managers of the Hutterian Brethren Church would travel to Winnipeg and retrieve the semi-annual minute book from the office of their then-lawyer, Michael Radcliffe, who represented Group I. Radcliffe was surprised by this request and asked for a few of hours to consider the request. When the group returned the following day, Radcliffe gave them the requested book, but warned them that they were making a grave mistake that would cause a division. The group thanked him for his service and left. On April 25, the six managers, lawyer Sid Wolchuck, and minister Leonard Kleinsasser (Delta, MB) met with Marlene Zyluk from Vital Statistics. They tried to convince Zyluk that they represented the true Hutterite Church and that Vital Statistics should reject Jacob Kleinsasser's claim to have sole signing authority. They argued that the six managers, *as the true leaders* of the Hutterian Brethren Church, should be allowed to authorize the Group II Schmiedeleut ministers, and requested that Vital Statistics recognize Leonard Kleinsasser and Jacob Waldner (Blumengart, MB) "as qualified ecclesiastical authorities within the confines of the

---

Jacob Kleinsasser should be placed under exclusion. Report of meeting at Delta, MB, February 23, 1993, signed by Isaac Wurz, John M. Wipf, Peter A. Kleinsasser, Joseph P. Wipf, Michael P. Entz, John K. Wipf, Paul P. Wipf, David P. Kleinsasser, Jakob P. Wipf, and Joseph P. Hofer, in author's collection.

This meeting was followed by a letter from John Wipf, President of the Hutterian Brethren Church, which stated that "everyone should know that Reverend Jacob Kleinsasser is no longer an Elder of the Church and has no right or authority to speak for the Hutterian Brethren Church. I wish to make it clear in this letter that no one is to take any Instructions [*sic*] from Reverend Jacob Kleinsasser because he has no authority to speak for or on behalf of the Hutterian Brethren Church and the Schmiedeleut Congregation." John Wipf to "All Members of the Hutterian Brethren Schmiedeleut Congregations," April 8, 1993, in author's collection.

163 Jacob Kleinsasser and his supporters insisted that they had not, at least intentionally, deleted the Group II ministers from the Vital Statistics record. As a matter of fact, Group I never objected to Group II calling themselves Schmiedeleut or Hutterian Brethren and made it clear to Vital Statistics that they would not object as long as it was clear that Group II represented a different, breakaway group of Schmiedeleut. As such, they needed to set up their own classification and registry for their minsters. Group II leaders, however, saw this manoeuvre as a deliberate "deletion," viewing themselves as the rightful Schmiedeleut Hutterites.

164 In actual fact, no marriages were ever stopped. They could still perform marriages, but would have difficulties registering the marriage with Vital Statistics until a registration number and signing authority for their group was established.

Schmieden-Leut [*sic*] Conference of the Hutterian Brethren Church who would advise the director who the qualified clergy could be."[165] Understandably, this caused considerable confusion for Vital Statistics, which was placed in the awkward position of deciding which of the two groups represented the real Schmiedeleut Conference. Initially, Vital Statistics tried to mediate the situation and suggested that both groups could share the role of governing authority or seek arbitration. Group I leadership rejected this offer, feeling it would effectively undermine the authority of *Ältester* Kleinsasser.[166] The basis for Group I leadership's rejection of this offer was the fact that the Group II leadership did not recognize Kleinsasser as an elder or minister and they refused to recognize him or his members as Hutterites.[167]

One of the objections raised by the Group I legal counsel was that authorizing Group II ministers would "implicitly give equal standing to the renegades in their claim to be the authentic Hutterian Brethren Church, rather than refusing to recognize them or, at least, recognizing them as a new, break-away, group."[168] This became the central point in a new round of conflicts; namely, which group was the original group and which group should be designated a "new" or "breakaway group." Group I leadership claimed that the Group II leadership had created a breakaway group when they voluntarily walked out of the December 1992 meeting at Starlite and when they rejected the leadership of Jacob Kleinsasser. For their part, Group II leadership needed to come up with a way of either countering or bypassing Group I's claim.

### We are the "Real" Hutterites!

On June 9, 1993, a meeting was called in Calgary at which twenty-six leaders from all three *Leut* were present, in addition to three lawyers: Jeff Sween (representing American communities), Sid Wolchock (representing

---

165  Michael Radcliffe to Jacob Kleinsasser, May 20, 1993, in author's collection.
166  Gregory B. Bordan to David Hill, January 7, 1994, in author's collection. Central to this phase of the conflict was Group II leadership's absolute rejection of Kleinsasser's standings as either an elder or a minister.
167  Both groups may not have fully comprehended what Vital Statistic meant with "[sharing] the role of governing authority." On November 22, 1994, Joan E. Alty wrote to Group II counsel Sidney Wolchock, and informed him: "…as you may be aware, there is no requirement on a group practicing a religious undertaking to incorporate or file a name notation. As well, under The Religious Societies Lands Act there are no name prohibition sections, so the Director would have no authority to refuse to incorporate under that Act on the basis of the name." Joan E. Alty to Wolchuck and Company, November 22, 1994, in author's collection.
Group II counsel knew this fact as early as August of 1993. Myron Pawlowsky to Sidney Wolchock, August 2, 1993, in author's collection.
168  Gregory B. Bordan to David Hill, January 7, 1994, in author's collection.

Manitoba communities), and Philip K. Matkin (representing Alberta communities). No Group I leaders were present, nor had any notice been sent to them regarding the meeting. Earlier, on the basis of Kleinsasser's refusal to attend the 1991 biennial meeting, the Darius- and Lehrerleut removed him as a manager and appointed new managers from Group II.[169] Attendees at this meeting decided that to bypass Jacob Kleinsasser's claims, they would reaffirm the 1950s Constitution.[170] The Hutterian Brethren Board of Managers then sent a letter to all Hutterite communities in Canada and the United States, stating that the Board "deemed it necessary to require a Reaffirmation of Membership in the Hutterite Brethren Church."[171] Michael Radcliffe, counsel for Group I, responded by pointing out that what the Board of Managers was attempting to do was unprecedented and possibly illegal. In a letter to Phil Matkin, Radcliffe pointed out that

> [t]he Hutterian Brethren Church Federal Corporation, of which Mr. [John] Wipf is a President, has been traditionally used, until this date, to be a lobbying focus when approaching the Federal Government in Ottawa and has not been a vehicle exercising any real authority over the temporal or spiritual affairs of the Colonies in Canada. I would caution the Colonies in Manitoba not to sign the documentation.[172]

---

169 Article 10 of the 1950 Constitution allows for the expulsion or removal of a manager. Group I, however, viewed the appointment of new Schmiedeleut members by the Darius- and Lehrerleut as a violation of Article 23, which states that "The Conference Board shall exercise control over the Church dogma and Church discipline *within their respective Conference* [emphasis mine]." *Constitution of the Hutterian Brethren Church*, August 1, 1950.

170 At the June 9 meeting, it was specifically mentioned that they were not changing the 1950s Constitution. An unpublished manuscript states they would "*erneuern, aber nicht ändern, wegen der Zeit in der wir kommen sein mit Jacob Kleinsasser, Manitoba und seinen Anhang. Sie wollen die Hutterische Kirche bleiben und wir sagen: sie sein abgetreten. Drum können sie diesen Namen nicht brauchen, entweder sie tun buss und ändern ihren Sinn* [renew, but not alter, because of the time in which we have come to with Jacob Kleinsasser, Manitoba, and his followers. They want to remain the Hutterian Church, and we say they have abdicated. Therefore, they cannot use this name, unless they repent and change their ways]." Joseph Waldner, *Beschreibung und Gründung der Lehrerleut Gemeinden* [Written account of the establishment of the Lehrerleut Communities], 1887 to 1998 (Havre, Montana), 394. Despite the above assertion, this was not merely a reconfirmation of the 1950s constitution, but changed it in significant ways.

171 John M. Wipf, Joseph P. Hofer, Peter A. Kleinsasser, M.S. Stahl, J. Wipf, and John Stahl to "All Members of the Hutterian Brethren Church," June 9, 1993, in author's collection.

172 Michael F.C. Radcliffe to Jacob Kleinsasser, June 25, 1993, in author's collection.

Nevertheless, most of the Lehrerleut, Dariusleut, and dissident Schmiedeleut chose to reorganize under what became known as the 1993 Constitution.[173] Those Schmiedeleut who stayed loyal to Jacob Kleinsasser refused to and retained the 1950s Constitution.[174]

## Naming Dispute

What had begun as an argument regarding signing authority to register officiants with Vital Statistics thus turned into a much larger dispute about who the "real" Hutterites were. By drafting a revised constitution and asking all the Hutterite communities in Canada and the United States to accept it, Group II leadership hoped to establish that Jacob Kleinsasser and his supporters were no longer part of the Hutterian Brethren Church. The legal counsel for Group I recognized the seriousness of this manoeuvre and warned all Hutterite communities against signing the new constitution. He pointed out that

> [the new constitution] effects a number of important changes to the original constitution, notably concentrating power in the hands of a Board of Managers which is given the power to make decisions binding on the Conferences. Under the original Constitution, decisions of the Board of Managers are only binding if ratified by each of the Conferences.[175]

The Group II leadership responded by sending out notices demanding that Group I stop using the name Hutterian Brethren Church.[176]

In 1994, the conflict over the name began to escalate out of control as attempts were made to garner the support of the provincial Conservative Party under Gary Filmon. Michael Radcliffe, as counsel for Group I,

---

173  Those who signed the 1993 Constitution on June 29 were all the Lehrerleut; all the Dariusleut in Alberta; only six Dariusleut communities in Montana; all the Dariusleut communities in Saskatchewan except one, Belle Plain. Interestingly, none of the Washington communities signed the new constitution.

174  The first biennial meeting after the church division took place on July 21, 1993. Group I objected to this meeting taking place and requested permission to attend. No Schmiedeleut managers had been appointed yet, though the Schmiedeleut did not have any managers up to this point [this fact alone should raise serious concerns about the validity of the amended Constitution]. Philip K. Matkin, the counsel for the Alberta Conferences, replied, "Reverend John M. Wipf has requested that I advise you that you would not be welcome at the meeting." Philip K. Matkin to Michael Radcliffe, July 19, 1993, Re: Hutterite Brethren Church, in author's collection.

175  Gregory B. Bordan to David Hill, January 7, 1994, in author's collection.

176  Mike Hofer and Leonard Kleinsasser to Michael Wollmann, Sam Kleinsasser, Jacob Waldner, Jacob Hofer, and Sam Hofer, February 8, 1995, in author's collection.

outlined the problem for James Ernst, the government's Minister of Consumer and Corporate Affairs. Ernst had appointed Michael Radcliffe to

> gather information by telephone from the Directors/Registrars of vital statistics of the various provinces, particularly those with legislation similar to Manitoba's Marriage Act. The purpose of this information is to guide the Minister of Corporate and Consumer Affairs Jim Ernst in resolving the issue of who is entitled to register clergy of the Hutterian Brethren church to solemnize marriages under the Act.[177]

Further correspondence demonstrates the involvement of cabinet minister Bonnie Mitchelson and Izzy Frost of the Department of the Attorney General. After reviewing the arguments of both sides, Ernst concluded that

> the issues you have raised are by their very nature complex and cannot, in my view, be determined through an exchange of correspondence. I am advised by my legal advisors that these issues must be investigated by a court of competent jurisdiction in terms of evidence, and arguments as to facts and law in light of the Constitution of the Hutterian Brethren Church. Indeed, you have made reference to the Wollman and Hoffer [sic] decision delivered March 21, 1994 in the Court of Queen's Bench of Manitoba which contains a finding of fact "that the Senior Elder Jacob Kleinsasser put himself out of office on December 10, 1992 by challenging the Assembly by asking for a vote of confidence and losing it, and in effect consenting to his removal or disposition." The Court further goes on to state that from "a review of the proceedings leading to the adoption of a new Constitution, I must conclude that the Constitution was validly passed at the Bi-Annual [sic] Meeting of July 21, 1993." I have quoted the above passages from the decision in support of the obvious conclusion that the issues which you have raised are by their very nature subject to controversy and must ultimately be resolved either by consensus between the parties or in a Court of Law.[178]

---

177 Michael Radcliffe to James Arthur Ernst, May 5, 1994, in author's collection.
178 James Arthur Ernst to Michael F.C. Radcliffe, December 13, 1994, in author's collection.

Ernst stated that because of the controversial nature of the claims put forward by both groups, the department would continue "to hold the view that the Department's original position, namely, designating Reverend Jacob Kleinsasser, Reverend Jacob Waldner, and Reverend Leonard Kleinsasser as the three governing authorities within the Hutterian Brethren Church remains appropriate."[179]

Recognizing Ernst's observation that this issue could only be resolved by consensus between the two groups or in a court of law, Group I leadership prepared for what they saw as inevitable litigation by hiring the Montreal law firm Ogilvy Renault. The firm was asked to examine the legal claims of both groups and to come up with a legal opinion on the possible outcome, should the conflict end up in the courts. In their initial study, Ogilvy Renault found that Group II had violated the amendment process outlined in the 1950 Constitution, which states:

> These Articles of Association may be repealed or amended, or new Articles may be adopted from time to time at any annual, general or special meeting of the Board of Managers or any other meeting of the member Conferences called for that purpose by the Board of Managers.[180]

Ogilvy Renault took the position that the 1993 Constitution was never adopted at a duly constituted meeting as required by the original 1950 Constitution. They were prepared to argue that

> [t]he failure to respect the amendment procedures mandated by the Original Constitution, in our view, is fatal to the validity of the New Constitution as an amendment or restatement of the Original Constitution. This conclusion is unaffected by the number of colonies which may have subscribed to the New Constitution. The law does not, in our view, permit the legal rights and the property interests of members of Church, as these are created by the Original Constitution, to be changed, or in some cases removed entirely, without respecting the procedures set forth in the Original Constitution and courts have shown their willingness to enforce the respect of mandatory pro-

---

179 Ibid.
180 *Constitution of the Hutterian Brethren Church*, August 1, 1950, article 49. It is worth noting that the Schmiedeleut had no legal representation during the amendment period or the creation of the 1993 constitution. The existing Schmiedeleut managers were barred from the process because of the conflict, and only after the new constitution was ratified was Group II able to elect managers. A question to ponder is whether this was a violation of the amendment process as outlined in the 1950 constitution.

> visions of the constitution of an association and to sanction the use of illegal procedures. […][181]

> In our view, if the New Constitution has any legal validity, it can only be as a constitution separate from the Original Constitution. In other words, those colonies subscribing to the New Constitution have chosen, by so doing, to cease respecting the Original Constitution and to form, instead, a new association governed by the New Constitution.[182]

This legal opinion proved to be overly optimistic. In his judgment delivered on March 21, 1994, Mr. Justice DeGraves found that the December 10, 1992 vote in Starlite was valid and that *Ältester* Jacob Kleinsasser had been voted out of office. The legal counsel and the leadership of Group I realized the DeGraves' conclusions might prove harmful to the strategies they had set out for themselves. For example, the idea of launching a legal challenge against the new constitution would have to be examined or shelved indefinitely, as DeGraves' findings could be interpreted to favour Group II.

At the same time, Simon V. Potter from Ogilvy Renault pointed out that although Mr. Justice DeGraves' findings were heavy in consequence, they could be challenged. For instance, the legal counsel found it odd that the judge allowed himself unnecessary findings, particularly in light of his caution to himself in the ruling to avoid ecclesiastical matters if at all possible. If a legal challenge were mounted, they would ask the court to clearly state that the judge's *obiter dicta* (expressions of opinion) are just that, not essential to the decision or establishing precedent.[183] In his book *The Courts and the Colonies*, Alvin Esau recognized that "DeGraves J. drew conclusions that *might be interpreted* as giving legitimacy to the claim of Group II leaders that they were the true Hutterian Brethren Church [emphasis added]."[184] Esau goes on to point out:

> These findings of DeGraves J. that the elder had been removed and that the affirmed conference was the legitimate offspring of the original Schmiedeleut did not amount to a definitive ruling that the Group One Kleinsasser wing was no longer entitled to the assets of any colonies or the

---

181 The cases Ogilvy Renault cited as legal precedence are omitted.
182 Ogilvy Renault to "The Hutterian Brethren Church," January 24, 1994, in author's collection.
183 Simon V. Potter to Jacob Kleinsasser, March 22, 1994, in author's collection.
184 Alvin J. Esau, *The Courts and the Colonies: The Litigation of Hutterite Church Disputes* (Vancouver: UBC Press, 2014), 237.

conference, which were held in trust for the church. However, the findings could point in that direction, and certainly at minimum contradict the claims made by Group One that it was the only group with the rightful claim to be in the Hutterian Brethren Church and hold church assets. The conclusion of Mr. DeGraves could be valuable to the Group Two leaders in negotiations with Group One and in resisting the litigation brought against them by Group One,[185] despite the statement by DeGraves J. that his findings were *only to apply to these proceedings* [emphases added].[186]

---

[185] This is a misleading statement because it implies Group II communities were passive victims. The same can be said for the articles and manuscript written by minister Samuel Kleinsasser, who glosses over misdemeanours and acts of vandalism and violence. The reality is that Group II communities also expelled and removed Group I supporters from a number of communities, i.e., Huron, Rocklake, Cypress, James Valley, Kamsley, and a number of American communities such as Pointset and Tschetter among others. Both parties involved in this dispute have much to repent.

[186] Alvin J. Esau, *The Courts and the Colonies: The Litigation of Hutterite Church Disputes* (Vancouver: UBC Press, 2014), 237. Esau's book has, unfortunately, become the standard on Schmiedeleut conflicts. Even though Esau raises important issues and criticisms, his account is decidedly lopsided. His book either ignores or is ignorant of the long history of conflict involving Lakeside, Daniel Hofer Sr., and Hutterite leaders and elders prior to the infamous Lakeside case. Esau accepts the accusations levelled against Jacob Kleinsasser without looking at many of the primary documents which would have undoubtedly provided an important corrective. Michael Radcliffe, legal counsel for Group I, contacted Mr. Esau and submitted a review of the manuscript he sent to Josh Hofer of Lakeside, in which he pointed out numerous deficiencies in the manuscript. One of the most significant shortcomings in *The Courts and the Colonies* is that it presents an unbalanced view of the actual historical factors that contributed to the conflict. On at least two occasions, Radcliffe invited Esau to interview members from the "Group One camp who were involved with many of the events" and to interview Jacob Kleinsasser. This offer was never accepted. When members of Group I tried to contact Esau to raise objections to his one-sided account of the Lakeside conflict, he also declined the contact. Michael F.C. Radcliffe to Alvin Esau, September 8, 2001, in author's collection.
Another problematic aspect of *The Courts and the Colonies* is Esau's reliance on Donald Gibb's document, which he cites as a primary authority. As Radcliffe pointed out in his review, "For the most part, Don Gibb had no personal firsthand knowledge of the facts that he makes reference to. In many cases Don Gibb relied upon suspicions, gossip in the Hutterite community which was totally unsubstantiated by facts, prejudice, and I would even say on a 'without prejudice' basis, that his remarks in many cases are defamatory. I would therefore note that unreserved reliance on Don Gibb as a source of information, apart from being very biased, could be problematic from a truth standpoint. I do believe that Don Gibb may have collaborated with a number of Hutterites who were detractors of Jacob Kleinsasser and hence have an adversarial perspective." Michael F.C. Radcliffe to Alvin Esau, August 8, 2001, in author's collection.

By November 1994, it seemed that Mr. Justice DeGraves' findings would be put to the test in the Precision Feeds v. Rock Lake lawsuit. A quotation from the affidavit of Arthur Russel Holmes, senior vice-president of Deloitte and Touche, demonstrates how the issue of who had the legal right to call themselves Hutterites was a central part of these conflicts.[187] Holmes found that

> [b]oth Groups may legitimately lay claim to being the rightful inheritors of the trust which is the basis for the existence of the Colony, subject only to the determination by the Court of the issue of whether the continuing allegiance by the members of Group One to the leadership of Reverend Jacob Kleinsasser and their refusal to recognize the re-affirmation of membership of the Colony in the Church and the new constitution thereof is sufficient to disentitle them from the benefits of church membership.[188]

Should the courts find that Group II's claim is superior to Group I's, Holmes noted, the implications would be serious:

> If failure to reaffirm membership in the Hutterian Brethren Church and adopt the new constitution means a loss of membership in the Church, and if only members of the Church are entitled to the use and enjoyment of colony assets, then entire colonies, or substantial portions of the membership thereof, may be disentitled and may have to turn over control of their colonies to either the Church itself or to members in good standing thereof, without the right to retain any assets whatsoever for their own use.[189]

## First Steps toward Resolution

As demonstrated by these legal discussions, the state of affairs within the Schmiedeleut Conference was only growing more chaotic. By the end of 1994, there were at least five litigations before the courts in Manitoba and several others in the American courts. On April 5, 1995, Group II leadership drafted a letter, signed by committee members Jacob Waldner (Blumengart, Manitoba) and Jacob Wipf (Spring Creek, South Dakota), which called for Jacob Kleinsasser to "resign and lay down his position

---

187 Deloitte & Touche had been appointed as the receiver and manager of Rock Lake.
188 Affirmation of Arthur Russel Holmes, File No. CI 93-01-75639 3-4, Court of Queen's Bench of Manitoba, November 14, 1994.
189 Ibid.

as Elder of the Hutterian Brethren Church. Then both parties can come together and hopefully can make a peaceful settlement."[190]

At this point, both sides of the dispute were upset at the direction in which matters were going. A peaceful settlement seemed impossible while individual communities were still being torn apart, families forced out of their communities, and close to a dozen lawsuits pitting one Schmiedeleut group against the other were still before the courts. Even the Dariusleut and Lehrerleut Conferences were becoming increasingly uncomfortable with the direction they saw the two Schmiedeleut groups heading. At a meeting in Rosetown, Saskatchewan, they counselled the Group II leadership to do whatever they could to put an end to this church battle.[191]

Eventually, renewed efforts at finding a peaceful solution brought about a landmark agreement in May 1995. The written statement begins, "Whereas the Hutterite Colonies by their representatives from Group One and Group Two have agreed to the resolution of a number of issues and wish to record their agreement in writing."[192] The issues addressed by this agreement were the disagreements around the Springhill Farms abattoir, H.B. Credit, H.B. Farm, H.B. Mutual, and Pembina Poultry. Most importantly, Group I and Group II representatives agreed that in the communities where problems currently existed, there would be a *pro rata* division of the assets of the communities. In regards to the pending litigations, the agreement stated:

> The parties hereto agree that upon execution of this agreement, both parties will do all acts necessary to end all of the current court action including without limiting the generality of the forgoing, Rock Lake vs. Precision Feeds, Joseph Hofer vs. Paul Wollmann et al., Joe Wollmann vs. Dave Wollmann et al, and Maendel vs. Maendel at Oak Bluff, and the litigation at Huron Colony currently with the Royal Bank vs. Huron Colony et al. (subject to the decision of the Royal Bank of Canada).[193]

The May 1995 agreement brought about an important but fragile peace. What this demonstrated was that there were parties on all sides who

---

190 Jakob Waldner and Jacob Wipf to Mike [Michael] Wollman (Spring Hill, MB), April 6, 1995, in author's collection.
191 Joseph Waldner, *Beschreibung und Gründung der Lehrerleut Gemeinden, 1887 to 1998* [A Written Account of the Establishment of the Lehrerleut Communities] (Havre), 412.
192 Michael Wollman, Sam Waldner, Jake Hofer, Michael Hofer, Levi Gross, John Hofer, and Leonard Kleinsasser, "Agreement between Manitoba Schmiedeleut Group One and Two," May 2, 1995, in author's collection.
193 Ibid.

wanted to resolve the conflict peacefully, but that relationships between the individuals brokering the peace deal and between the two Schmiedeleut groups were so severely damaged that the agreement had a tenuous foundation at best. Despite this, the May 1995 agreement achieved its primary objects. The Group II communities agreed to release any holds they had on the church's financial institutions, and, for the most part, the contested Schmiedeleut communities were divided on a *pro rata* basis, thus avoiding costly litigation. However, in some of the contested communities, the animosity and distrust were so deep-rooted that the agreement broke. In three Manitoba communities, Oakbluff/Prairie Blossom, Cypress/Millshof, and Sprucewood/Fairway, major disagreements erupted about the value of the assets which were to be divided. In the end, both groups bitterly accused each other of violating and breaking the agreement, and the proverbial trenches were dug deeper as both sides refused to compromise their position to reach a consensus.

By the end of 1996, there were clearly two Schmiedeleut Conferences in Manitoba. Under the May 1995 agreement, both groups had agreed to recognize and accept that there existed two Schmiedeleut Conferences in Canada and the United States, identified in the agreement as "Group One, known as the Hutterian Brethren Church 1950 Constitution, Group Two, known as the Hutterian Brethren Church 1993 Constitution."[194] Both groups had been granted signing authority by Vital Statistics Manitoba and could add or delete names of ministers as they wished. However, by 1999–2000, the issue of which group had the legal right to call themselves the real Hutterian Brethren Church once again raised the possibility of litigation. In August of 1999, Group I legal counsel was served notice by Industry Canada that "they had received letters from S.R. Wolchock asking the Director to require your corporation to change its corporate name."[195] Group I legal counsel Paul D. Edwards responded with a report outlining the previous history of this conflict and how both groups had agreed, in principle and practice, that they no longer objected to the other group using the name "Schmiedeleut Conference" or "Hutterian Brethren Church."[196] What had happened within the Schmiedeleut Conferences to stir up this contentious issue yet again?

The genesis of this problem was a conflict over a longstanding publication project. Prior to 1995, the Bruderhof and the Group I Schmiedeleut had been working together to publish *The Chronicle of the Hutterian Breth-*

---

194 "Agreement between Manitoba Schmiedeleut Group One and Two," May 2, 1995, in author's collection.
195 Narayanan Iyer to Neil J. Duboff, August 18, 1999, in author's collection.
196 Paul D. Edwards to Narayanan Iyer, August 9, 1999, in author's collection.

*ren*, vol. 2.[197] In 1995, however, the Bruderhof and Group I Schmiedeleut parted ways. In 1997, Jacob Kleinsasser contacted the Bruderhof's Plough Publishing House and enquired about their plans for making the chronicle available in Canada.[198] Joseph Keiderling, then working in corporate affairs for the Bruderhof, responded by stating that

> Plough Publishing House of the Bruderhof Foundation holds the copyright to the translation, and since we have invested thousands of dollars in the translation and the research required to publish the English version of Vol. II, we would need to consider carefully any agreement whereby we grant publication rights to another organization.[199]

Kleinsasser strongly disagreed with the Bruderhof's claim, reminding them that the project had been a joint effort and the only reason the Bruderhof held the copyright was because the Schmiedeleut had granted it to them for publication purposes. As co-editor and advisor, Kleinsasser had in his possession a digital copy of the final draft of the *Chronicle*, vol. 2. He approached Friesens Printing in Altona, Manitoba, and made inquiries about printing the book. The Bruderhof communities were deeply hurt by this manoeuvre, as they had invested much time and considerable resources in this project.[200]

Bruderhof leadership objected to the publication of the Chronicle, and reminded Kleinsasser that they held the copyright. Legal counsel for Group I Schmiedeleut had anticipated this objection, however, and had taken out the Canadian copyright for the title *The Chronicle of the Hutterian Brethren*, vol. 2. They had also filed to register the trademark names "Schmiedeleut Conference of the Hutterian Brethren Church Inc." in 1996.[201] According to oral accounts, Bruderhof leader Johann Christoph Arnold had contacted Jacob Kleinsasser directly and indicated that they

---

197 Volume 1 was published in 1989.
198 Jacob Kleinsasser to Derek Wardle and Christoph Arnold, January 24, 1997, in author's collection.
199 Joseph Keiderling to Jacob Kleinsasser, February 11, 1997, in author's collection.
200 After meeting with Bruderhof representatives in 2018, I feel a recognition of the tremendous amount of personnel and financial resources the Bruderhof communities invested in this project on behalf of the Hutterite Brethren Church is in order. The publication of *The Chronicle of the Hutterian Brethren*, vol. 2, by Group I was an unfortunate byproduct of the conflict between Group I and the Bruderhof, and it is my hope that this could be resolved in the near future.
201 The Schmiedeleut I had applied for trademark in June 1996 shortly after the break with the Bruderhof communities. However, in their application, they specifically disclaimed the right to the exclusive use of the Conference of the Hutterian Brethren Church except for trademark purposes.

were no longer pursuing any claim for copyright of the *Chronicle*, vol. 2.[202] However, unknown to Jacob Kleinsasser, Group II and Bruderhof representatives had convened a meeting to discuss Schmiedeleut Group II's interest in publishing the *Chronicle*, vol. 1 and 2, in Canada. They agreed on a deal in which Group II would purchase Hutterite materials the Bruderhof no longer needed in exchange for the right to publish both chronicles. Only after the deal had been finalized and the books purchased did the Group II representatives learn about the copyright held by Schmiedeleut Group I. This revelation irritated and hurt Group II representatives and leadership as they felt a sense of betrayal. This, then, was the catalyst that reignited the naming conflict.

In his August 16, 1999 letter to Narayanan Iyer, Examiner for Industry Canada, Group I's legal counsel, Paul Edwards, wrote,

> It should be noted that the Corporation secured its name through a public process under the Corporations Act, as well as under the Trade-mark Act and has carried on business for in excess of 3 years. The 1993 Constitution group has delayed in raising any concern clearly is a factor to be considered by the Directorate in assessing the credibility of the complaint.[203]

In his response, Iyer stated that the issue would be handed over to a "committee within the Branch to either require a name change or dismiss the allegation of confusion; either party would have recourse to the federal court by way of appeal."[204] By March 1, 2000, Industry Canada had made its determination and served Group I's legal counsel with its decision:

> Based on our study of the representations made by both parties and in the light of the regulations respecting corporate names, it has been decided to order a change of corporate names. In our view, Schmied-leut [*sic*] Conference of the Hutterian Brethren Church Inc. was granted a name which was likely to cause confusion with the corporate name, The Hutterian Brethren Church. The two corporations appear to be related when they are not. If the corporation has not changed its corporate name within 60 days of receipt of this letter, the Director will be obligated to revoke that name and assign to it another name.[205]

---

202 David B. Kovnats to Robert B.G. Horowitz, July 28, 1998, in author's collection.
203 Paul D. Edwards to Narayanan Iyer, August 16, 1999, in author's collection.
204 Memorandum by Paul Edwards, September 30, 1999, in author's collection.
205 Robert Weist to Paul D. Edwards, March 1, 2000, in author's collection.

This was a severe blow to Group I, which now faced one of two choices: appealing to the federal court, or attempting to negotiate another agreement with Group II that would allow both groups to retain the name Hutterian Brethren Church. When faced with the stark reality of litigation of this proportion, both Schmiedeleut groups realized they did not want this issue decided by the court system. Groups I and II held a series of meetings which proved critical to the peaceful settlement of the naming conflict. On March 10, 2000, Samuel Waldner (Decker, Manitoba) met with Jacob Gross (Mayfair, Manitoba) to discuss the pending lawsuit. Waldner, as a representative for Group I, stated that should Group II push forward with attempts to stop Group I from using the name The Hutterian Brethren, Group I would have no choice but to appeal the decision at the federal level, and this could lead to another court case. Gross indicated that he knew very little about the naming conflict but that he would bring it up at a Group II church meeting scheduled for March 15. Additionally, he declared his willingness to try and stop the pending litigation. With this Waldner concurred, saying, "It is high time to stop putting up walls and time to start building bridges instead. It is time that we start acting like the Christians that we claim to be."[206] That same day, Samuel Waldner had a phone conversation with Michael Hofer (Sommerfeld, Manitoba) and told him about his conversation with Jacob Gross. Hofer agreed that the naming conflict needed to stop; he said, however, he would first like to discuss the situation with Jerry Lupkowski from the accounting firm Meyers Norris Penny.

On March 14, another meeting took place in Fargo, North Dakota, between John Waldner (Spring Prairie, Minnesota)[207] and representatives from Group I. Waldner expressed his concern that he did not know enough about what attorney Sidney Wolchock was doing on behalf of Group II members from Canada. The Group I representatives explained the current situation and pointed out that should it come down to a court case, all Hutterites, including the Dariusleut and Lehrerleut, would be pulled into the litigation. From these meetings, it became clear that everybody wanted to put an end to this conflict before it came before the judicial system. By March 30, 2000, a rough draft agreement between the two groups was on the table.[208] Aside from a few minor details, by April

---

206 Samuel Waldner, "Compilation of Minutes of Group I and II Uniting Talks," March 3, 2000, in author's collection.

207 Others present at this meeting were Samuel Waldner (Decker, MB), Mike Waldner (Millbrook, SD), Mike Waldner (Rosedale, MB), and George Waldner (Hutterville, SD).

208 The four people from the Schmiedeleut Conferences present at this meeting who deserve recognition and acclaim for this landmark agreement were Samuel Waldner (Decker, MB), Leonard Waldner (Wingham, MB), Mike Hofer (Sommerfeld, MB), Leonard Kleinsasser (Delta, MB).

30, 2000, Schmiedeleut Groups I and II had ratified and signed a Letter of Understanding in which they agreed to settle all outstanding disputes between them in a peaceful manner, without recourse to the legal system.[209] The Letter of Understanding openly expressed the wish of both sides to leave behind the conflicts which had torn the Schmiedeleut Conference apart and which were once again threatening to cause heartache and sorrow. The letter reads in full:

> The Hutterian Brethren Church consists of 3 conferences: Dariusleut, Lehrerleut, Schmiedeleut.
>
> The Schmiedeleut Conference consists of 2 groups.
>
> Both groups of the Schmiedeleut Conference are in agreement that the Schmiedeleut Conference will live under the umbrella of the Hutterian Brethren Church.
>
> Neither group wishes to pursue either group in the courts; they both wish to continue on as Hutterian Brethren and desire to live harmoniously with each other within the Hutterian Brethren Church.
>
> This understanding replaces all prior statements and is made as a result of a desire by the 2 groups of the Schmiedeleut Conference of the Hutterian Brethren Church to put to rest their disputes regarding their names and status.
>
> Signed, [Michael Hofer (Group II), Samuel Waldner (Group I), Leonard Kleinsasser (Group II), Mike Waldner (Group I)]

After the signing of the Letter of Understanding, meetings were held with the intention of finding a way towards full reconciliation. The general sense one gets from reading the minutes of those meetings was that both sides longed to find a way to fix what had happened at the Starlite meeting in 1992 but could not affect any further, meaningful progress. In subsequent years, additional, unsuccessful attempts have been made at reconciliation. As we continue to seek ways to heal the painful and tragic schism, we need to remind ourselves of Christ's benediction, "Blessed are the peacemakers, for they will be called children of God" (Matthew 5:9).

## Conclusion

This essay is by no means an exhaustive examination of the factors that led to the 1992 schism in the Schmiedeleut Conference. Neither should

---
209 "Letter of Understanding," April 10, 2000, in author's collection.

it be considered the final word about what happened and why.[210] Like most conflicts, this one has deep roots in the past. As pointed out earlier, underlying problems were exacerbated by false accusations and strong tensions between Schmiedeleut groups in Manitoba and South Dakota. At the same time, numerous changes were taking place within Hutterite communities concerning education, mission, and new financial projects, with an increasing trend towards manufacturing, and a gradual acculturation to the national identities of the host countries. Elder Jacob Kleinsasser promoted some of these changes; many of the changes, however, were merely a manifestation of the time, something neither Kleinsasser nor any other minister could control. It is easy to look back and imagine how we could or would have acted differently. Hindsight is, after all, 20/20.

## Forgiveness and Reconciliation

I hope this account will prompt necessary conversations to move us towards forgiveness and reconciliation.[211] There are many Schmiedeleut Hutterites on both sides of this division who are actively seeking paths toward forgiveness and reconciliation. For genuine reconciliation to occur, both sides must commit to carefully and honestly consider the historical factors that led to the 1992 schism. This work will need to be undertaken with sensitivity so as not to deepen old wounds and inflame grievances, which could only serve to further entrench enmity and embitter people on both sides of the conflict.[212] Recent conference-wide changes made by the Schmiedeleut Group I surrounding *Meidung* and regulations dealing with intermarriage between the various Hutterite groups will, it is hoped, lead towards establishing positive relationships, which in turn will help

---

210 History is not written in a vacuum; I acknowledge my personal bias. My greatest hope is that this essay may serve as a catalyst for scholars in both groups to enter into dialogue so that we can faithfully wrestle in a meaningful and constructive way in our mutual search for truth.

211 Truthfulness and forgiveness, as outlined in Matthew 6:14 and Mark 11:25, are a prerequisite to reconciliation. In these passages, Jesus clearly warns us that God will not forgive our sins if we do not forgive those who sin against us. As Christians we are not allowed to hold a grudge or be angry with our brothers. If they hurt us, we must forgive them; withholding forgiveness directly affects our relationship with God. Forgiveness does not, however, automatically bring about reconciliation. Reconciliation is focused on restoring broken relationships. Where trust is deeply broken, as it was and is in this case, reconciliation is and will be a long and difficult journey.

212 I realized that in writing this essay, I may be doing just that. In particular, I am sensitive about the sections dealing with the Lakeside v. Daniel Hofer et al. conflict. I am deeply empathetic towards those caught in this conflict, especially women, children, and extended family. It is my personal view that a church should never use either the police nor the courts to evict members, but rather find ways to seek resolution, restoration, or financial restitution for those who wish to leave the church community.

create the environments in which reconciliation flourish.²¹³ Our journey of reconciliation, however, will take the goodwill of all Hutterites—Lehrerleut, Dariusleut, and both Schmiedeleut groups—working together to seek God's guidance. May God grant that we honestly commit to understanding the causes of conflict and how they drive us further and further from reconciliation.

There are three elements to conflict between groups: first, the "certitude that our group is morally superior;" second, "a refusal or incapacity to see or admit to any possible errors or faults in our group;" third, "a refusal to believe that any other group possesses truth or can contribute anything of value."²¹⁴ As long as the four Hutterite groups cling to their respective narratives with attitudes of moral and ethical superiority, condescension, or Pharisaic injustice and self-righteousness, any attempt at reconciliation will be futile.

What are some practical steps that can be taken by the parties involved in this situation that may contribute to the creation of an environment in which reconciliation can happen? As in any conflict, both sides must identify and acknowledge the factors that led to the schism and also identify the ongoing issues in the divided church. As we begin this journey of healing, we all need to cloak ourselves with the humility of Christ so that we can confess our collective sins of disunity, strife, and pride, which have torn deeply into the fabric of our existence as a people of God. Any attempt to ignore what happened or to ignore the differences in culture and practices which exist among the various groups, especially at the leadership level, would be merely committing our church to another, possibly much worse schism down the road.

Too often conflict becomes destructive when we try to avoid it, or because we do not know how to face it well. Instead of seeing conflict as entirely negative, we need to make a conscious move towards acknowledging that conflict is a normal part of our life in the church (Romans 14:1–8, 10–12, 17–19; 15:1–7). As Christians, we are called to accept one another and not judge and condemn each other over issues of dress or adherence to particular ordinances. We should make every effort to do what leads to peace and mutual edification. To move this conflict in a positive direction, we must find ways to infuse our lives and our conversations with hope. We must affirm that God is present with us when we seek to work through our conflicts openly and honestly. When all parties seek to become more

---

213 Arnold Hofer and Samuel Waldner to "All Hutterite Communities of Schmiedeleut Group I in Manitoba, Canada, Minnesota, North and South Dakota, USA," annual conference report, March 22, 2019, in author's collection.
214 Jean Vanier, *Becoming Human* (Mahwah: Paulist Press, 1998), 47.

faithful to Jesus by practicing Christ-like love towards one another, we will be able to see conflict as an opportunity to grow.

In Matthew 18:15–22, Jesus describes the process of addressing conflict and restoring relationships in the church. Jesus' words "If your brother [or sister] sins against you" and "If your brother [or sister] refuse to listen" assume that there will be conflict within the church or community. These passages speak to our present situation, in which brothers and sisters sinned against each other and then refused to listen or even speak to each other. What followed were divided families, congregations, and church. As we wrestle with the painful questions of our schism, the apostle Paul reminds us that we need to "speak the truth in love," and in so doing we will "grow to become in every respect the mature body of him who is the head, that is Christ" (Ephesians 4:15–16).

Reconciliation will not happen on its own but must be pursued with sincerity and earnest prayer for one another. The apostle James encourages us to "confess [our] sins to one another, and pray for one another, that [we] may be healed," for "the prayer of a righteous man has great power in its effects" (James 5:16). Here the apostle emphasizes the importance of prayer, which leads to a mutually satisfactory solution. Such a prayer can only be effectual when we no longer pray for our justification or for the other to change, but instead pray to find a common way through consensus. Opening ourselves to the possibility of finding a common solution can empower us to look beyond our conflicts and see the intrinsic value and beauty in those opposite us. When we choose to focus on hope and faith, we are accepting God's call to "choose life so that [we] and [our] descendants may live" (Deuteronomy 30:19).

Our responsibility is to align our lives and speech with life and away from death and despair. In this light, one of the great sins of our conflict was unbridled slander, which spread darkness and death within our church. In his book *Smart Compassion*, Wesley Furlong points out that "slander is etymologically tied to the word devil. To slander another is to give our voice to the devil—the accuser—and speak untruth which includes anything that's not oriented towards life."[215] In our journey towards reconciliation, let us choose faith, hope, and love, which will lead us to life.

In an old letter, *Ältester* Michael Waldner (*Schmied-Michl*) recounts a dream:

> One of our sisters had a vision; she saw three wells, one belonged to us, one to the Dariusleut, and one to Jake

---

215 J. Wesley Furlong, *Smart Compassion: How to Stop Doing Outreach and Start Making Change* (Harrisonburg: Herald Press, 2017), 74.

Wipf [Lehrerleut]. Moreover, when water was drawn from one well, it ran together from all three. I rejoice in it, and it makes me hope for a true uniting. May God the Almighty allow me to experience this joy![216]

*Schmied-Michl*'s dream of uniting did not happen, but perhaps this vision can remind us that Christ should be the single source from which we all draw our strength. When dealing with conflict, we need to clothe ourselves with Christ's courage and humility so that we can acknowledge the guilt of the past and seek to live lives of faithful discipleship, love, and forgiveness in our communities. When we do this, we can begin to become the salt of the earth, the light of the world, the city on a hill.[217] Such healing can only take place in the proper *kairos*.[218] ∽

---

216 Michael Waldner to Bonhomme Community, 23 February 1885, in author's collection.
217 Matthew 5.
218 *Kairos* refers to an appointed time in the purpose of God. In Romans 13:11–12 the word *kairon* is used by the apostle in a call to action, conversion, and transformation—a change of life. "And do this, knowing the time [*kairon*], that now it is high time to awake out of sleep; for now, our salvation is nearer than when we first believed. The night is far spent, the day is at hand. Therefore, let us cast off the works of darkness, and let us put on the armour of light."

**Simon M. Evans** was adjunct professor of geography at the University of Calgary, where he earned his doctorate in 1976. He visited a Hutterite community within a few days of arriving in Canada, and his retirement after twenty-five years at Memorial University of Newfoundland enabled him to focus and intensify his research. He visited communities from the Peace Country of Alberta to the old community sites along the James River in South Dakota, and has published a score of articles on various aspects of Hutterite culture from diffusion to demography. A collection of his work was posthumously published by University of Nebraska Press in 2021: *A Geography of the Hutterites in North America*. Simon Evans died in 2019.

**Peter Peller** is the director of the Spatial and Numeric Data Services group at the University of Calgary Library. He assists university researchers and students with accessing and customizing the geospatial data they need and with using GIS software to visualize and analyze that data. He has co-authored four articles with Simon Evans on Hutterite culture.

# Beating the Squeeze:
# Adaptive Strategies on Hutterite Communities

## SIMON EVANS and PETER PELLER

Hutterites attempt to mirror the life of the early Christian church by "holding all things common."[1] Theirs is an all-encompassing faith; God's name is hallowed by their lives lived in full community-of-goods. Work in the field or in the kitchen is esteemed as worship just as much as time spent in their church services.

Unlike many other ethnic groups that have settled in the Canadian Prairies and northern Great Plains, Hutterites have resisted assimilation and maintained their dialect and culture since arriving in North America in 1874. The community is the essential unit of Hutterite culture. It consists of a farm village occupied by some fifteen to twenty families in which all members have prescribed roles and contributions to make, whether it is a ten-year-old girl babysitting younger siblings or a bearded *Wirt* (business manager or steward) wrestling with next year's cropping plan. It is within the borders of this community that Hutterites strive to live in harmony with one another. They meet for meals three times a day and for church in the evening. Young and old move from home to home to visit, borrow items, or exchange the news of the day. Children regard all adults as extended family and address them as *Vetter* and *Basl*,[2] and the adults keep an eye on all the youngsters as if they were their own. In order to preserve this intimate sense of community, when a community becomes too large it is divided into two and a new daughter community is established. This complex process of community division, often referred to as "hiving" or "fission," has become formalized over the decades. Years before a commun-

---

1   Acts 2:44; and Victor Peters, *All Things Common: The Hutterite Way of Life* (New York: Harper Torch Books, 1965). For a thorough introduction to all aspects of Hutterite life, see Rod Janzen and Max Stanton, *The Hutterites in North America* (Baltimore: Johns Hopkins University Press, 2010).
2   Literally uncle and aunt; also widely used generally as terms of respect for elderly individuals or people in positions of authority.

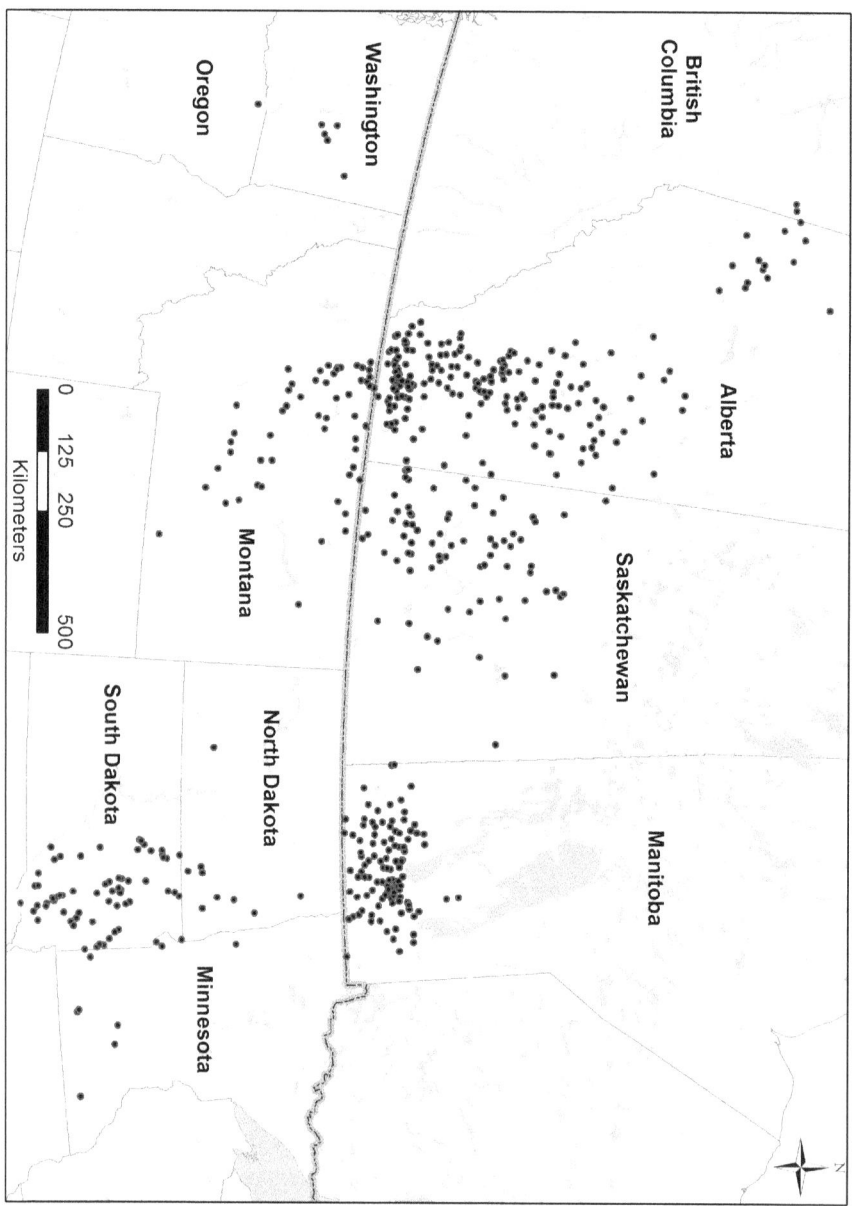

**Map 1.** North American Hutterite Communities, 2015. [Drawn from locations in Hutterite Directory and Global Anabaptist Mennonite Encyclopedia Online (GAMEO).]

ity has reached a threshold size of 120 to 150 people, planning will have begun to acquire a new location. As a strategy, community division has served the Hutterites well; indeed, one might argue that it is an important reason for the group's longevity.

Communal Hutterites are divided into four clan groups, or *Leut*. One of the communal groups that undertook the hazardous journey from the Ukraine to the Dakota frontier was led by Michael Waldner, who was a blacksmith. They became known as "the smith's people" or Schmiedeleut. Another group followed Darius Walter and were soon referred to as the Dariusleut, while a third party was loyal to Jacob Wipf, a teacher, and were christened the Lehrerleut.[3] At first, relations with non-communal Hutterites, the Prairieleut, who had moved from Russia with them, were close and intermarriage was common.[4] By 1914, however, boundaries between the three communal groups and their neighbours had become less porous. When the Hutterites were forced to leave South Dakota in 1918, an important geographic division took place. The Schmiedeleut moved just across the Canadian border into Manitoba, while the Dariusleut and the Lehrerleut moved to Alberta.[5] During the 1990s, a split took place among the Schmiedeleut. Hutterites now recognize two groups, Schmiedeleut I (the more progressive group) and Schmiedeleut II (the more traditional group).[6]

There were some 520 Hutterite communities in 2015, distributed across five States and four Provinces. Communities are found from the foothills of the Rocky Mountains in Alberta and Montana to the margins of the Canadian Shield in Manitoba. They range from the Peace River country and the parkland belt of the northern prairies, southward across the international border to the Missouri River. There is also a small but growing outlier in the rolling Palouse country of Washington and Oregon (see Map 1).[7]

The success of the Hutterites in maintaining their cultural identity, their remarkable growth in numbers, and their territorial diffusion has been sustained by their ability to make a good living from agriculture.

---

3   Janzen and Stanton, "Four Hutterite Branches," in *Hutterites in North America*, 54–75.
4   Rod Janzen, *The Prairie People: Forgotten Anabaptists* (Hanover: University Press of New England, 1999).
5   Simon M. Evans and Peter Peller, "The Hutterites come to Alberta," *Alberta History* 63, No. 4 (Autumn 2015), 11–19.
6   For a sympathetic account of this division, see Janzen and Stanton, *Hutterites in North America*, 62–73.
7   Simon M. Evans and Peter Peller, "Mapping an Ethnic Isolate: The Diffusion of Hutterite Colonies across the Prairies and Northern Great Plains," *Great Plains Quarterly* 38, No. 4 (Fall 2018), 357–386.

Working the land has allowed them to locate their communities discretely in the countryside and to maintain their distance from the host society. The Hutterites see themselves as an ark afloat and tossed about on the sea of the sinful world. They seek to control and limit their contacts with non-Hutterites as much as possible. The scale and diversity of their agricultural operations have protected them from the worst vagaries of environmental and economic cycles. Philosophically, too, agriculture has demanded the wholehearted commitment of the community while providing meaningful jobs for men, women, and older children. Victor Peters, who knew the Brethren so well, went so far as to say "The Hutterite dedication to farm life is motivated by a conviction that for them this way of life is the most pleasing to God."[8]

During the last twenty years, the dominant all-pervasive role of agriculture among Hutterites has been challenged by mechanization and globalization. Clearly, mechanization of field operations has a long history on the communities, but the scale and sophistication of new equipment is unprecedented and has further decreased the need for field hands. At the same time, machines have replaced workers in the livestock barns, whether it is with an egg sorting and packing system, automated milking, or processes for slaughtering and meatpacking. Globalization has increased competition, lengthened the supply chain, and reduced returns to primary producers. As production costs have risen and returns have stagnated, farmers everywhere have been squeezed by declining profit margins.

The Hutterites have responded to this evolving economic environment in a number of ways. Some communities have fine-tuned their cropping patterns to exploit new cash crops; others have explored ways of adding value to their products by cutting out the middleman or by processing products in the community. An alternative strategy has been to slash energy costs by adopting innovative systems based on renewable resources. Finally, the past few decades have seen a significant growth in the number of non-farm enterprises on the communities. Led by the Schmiedeleut in Manitoba and South Dakota, more and more communities have started to use their metalworking facilities and carpenters' shops to provide goods and services for regional markets. This is by no means a new departure. Many communities have worked on neighbours' farm machinery during the winter or undertaken some custom carpentry on an ad hoc basis. However, it is entirely new to find a community like Baker, Manitoba, which has leased most of its land and has concentrated on producing ventilation systems and heat exchangers for a North American market.

---

8  Victor Peters, *All Things Common: The Hutterian Way of Life* (New York: Harper Torch Books, 1965), 107.

The aim of this essay is to examine and describe these responses to twentieth-century economic realities, and to evaluate the prevalence of non-farm activities on the communities. This will put us in a position to answer the broader question: What are the implications of these developments for the "Hutterite way"? Is this the first perilous step on a slippery slope towards assimilation and the integration of the sect into the host society? Or is it merely a logical extension of a long-existent practice—another example of what Eaton called "controlled acculturation" all those years ago?[9]

After a brief explanation of our methodology, we will examine the pressures for change and the motives for adopting new strategies, and the links to Hutterite history will be established. Then we will discuss three initiatives: adding value to agricultural products; slashing costs by exploring new technologies; and adopting light-manufacturing, using existing infrastructure to create jobs. Finally, we will weigh some objections to adopting new ways and summarize our findings in order to reach some tentative conclusions concerning change and the future of the Hutterites.

## Methodology

To determine the extent of non-farming activity taking place on North American Hutterite communities, information was collected by searching through the internet, business directories, and newspaper databases. In addition, some Hutterites and non-Hutterite business and academic experts were consulted regarding their perspectives on Hutterite non-farming activities.[10] This environmental scan netted 117 communities that were engaged in non-farming activity. The communities involved were subdivided by *Leut* (see Table 1) and their activities were classified into the categories (Table 2). Some communities were involved in multiple non-farming enterprises, and that is why the total number of non-farming activities in Table 2 is greater than the 117 communities. Although this was neither a random nor systematic survey, the sheer number of communities found participating in these kinds of activities validates the notion that this practice is fairly widespread; in fact, the numbers don't reflect many of the smaller non-farming operations that may have been missed

9    Joseph W. Eaton, "Controlled Acculturation: A Survival Technique of the Hutterites," *American Sociological Review* 17, no. 3 (1952), 331–340.
10  In alphabetical order: Sascha Hausman, Freie University, Berlin; Rod Jansen, Fresno Pacific University, CA; Joanita Kant, University of South Dakota; Ron Kroeker, Farmshift, Winnipeg, MB; Johnathan Maendel, Baker Community, MB; Tom Mandel, Brant Community, AB; Duane Schrag, Heritage Hall Archives, Freeman, SD; Lisa and Ben Stahl, Estuary Community, AB; Duane Stoltzfus, Goshen College, IN; Jacob Waldner, Decker Community, MB; Glenn Webber, Parks Canada, Calgary, AB; Paul Wipf, Viking Community, AB.

through this process. This survey was then followed up with field work entailing visits to fifteen communities in Alberta, Saskatchewan, Manitoba, and South Dakota that were selected because of their mix of enterprises. It should be pointed out that this focused field work is in addition to over forty years of visits to more than one hundred communities.

## The Nature of "the Squeeze"

For over a century, their success as farmers has enabled the Hutterites to accumulate capital to establish new communities when they become necessary. As Paul Wipf explains:

> The whole plan of [community] life is to take care of the next generation. It is no different from your parents helping you through university, [...] but we do it to a greater extent.[11]

Saving for a daughter community is a constant and pressing obligation; indeed, if Hutterite culture is to survive, provision must be made for the next generation. However, it is becoming more and more difficult to generate monetary surpluses from agriculture. We are witnessing a paradigm shift among community leaders from reliance on agriculture to an economic plan that is more diversified and includes a variety of light manufacturing ventures. Already, almost half of the Schmiedeleut communities have adopted some non-farm enterprises. Dariusleut communities are not far behind, and the momentum of change is quickening. This profound shift in orientation is being driven by three factors that are affecting communities from South Dakota, through the Peace River country of Alberta, to Washington and Oregon states. The first is the inexorable rise in the costs of establishing a new community. The second is the declining profit margins in agriculture. Hutterites, like most North American farmers, are being squeezed between rising costs of production and stable or declining returns. The third factor occupying the minds of Hutterite leaders is how to find meaningful year-round jobs for their young people.

### The Costs of Establishing a Daughter Community

Much has been written about Hutterite community division and the establishment of daughter communities. The role of this process in maintaining the culture by limiting the size of communities has been discussed, as has the manner in which splitting multiplies the number of managerial jobs. Elsewhere, the fact that fission, or branching, provides an opportunity to release social tensions and to dissipate bad feelings between sub-groups

---

11   Paul Wipf, steward of Viking, AB, quoted in Lisa Guenther, "A New Venture," *Country Guide*, April 9, 2015.

| Leut | Communities | Number Engaged in Non-Farming Activities | Percent Engaged in Non-Farming Activities |
|---|---|---|---|
| Dariusleut | 162 | 46 | 28% |
| Lehrerleut | 141 | 13 | 9% |
| Schmiedeleut | 63 | 25 | 40% |
| Schmiedeleut | 122 | 33 | 27% |
| Schmiedeleut Unclassified | 2 | 0 | 0% |
| | 490 total | 117 total | 24% |

Table 1. Observed Prevalence of Non-Farming Activities by Hutterite *Leut*.

| Non-Farming Activity | Dariusleut | Lehrerleut | Schmiedeleut | All *Leut* |
|---|---|---|---|---|
| Agriculture | 7 | 5 | 4 | 16 |
| Manufacturing | 29 | 7 | 50 | 86 |
| Construction | 5 | | 3 | 8 |
| Automotive | 3 | | 3 | 6 |
| Resource Extraction | 2 | 1 | | 3 |
| Energy | 2 | 3 | | 5 |
| Miscellaneous | 4 | 1 | 6 | 11 |
| Total Non-Farming Activities | 52 | 17 | 66 | 135 |

Table 2. Non-Farming Activities by Category and *Leut*.

has been noted.[12] However, surprisingly little detail has been forthcoming about the costs involved in this vital undertaking. One has to agree with Schlabach's comment: "Surprisingly few authors have investigated the influences of market forces on individual group behaviour."[13]

The work of John Bennett is an exception. Based on his fieldwork during the 1950s and 1960s, he estimated that the total cost of establishing a daughter community was about $315,000. His case study was located in an area of marginal land in southwestern Saskatchewan. The land purchase—11,000 acres at $17 an acre—accounted for $200,000 of the total.[14] A brief but penetrating economic description of the Hutterites in Montana states that community land purchases for new communities in the early 1960s averaged around $400,000 but had doubled to $800,000 per community by 1969. The authors estimated the value of a typical community at one million dollars.[15] In Alberta, the report by a special government committee of the assembly on communal property had access to the tax returns of almost all the existing communities. However, the authors had little to say about the costs of establishing a new community, but merely quoted a researcher who estimated that a community would have to save some $59,000 per annum if it were to be ready to establish a new community after seventeen years.[16] John Ryan, to whom we owe a debt for his detailed analysis of the costs and returns of Manitoba communities, has nothing to say about the establishment of new communities.[17]

Recent books on Hutterites continue to emphasize the important role of community division in Hutterite culture but do not go beyond generalities. Janzen and Stanton state:

> Communities start saving money for expansion that is the establishment of daughter communities, as soon as their

---

12 For an overview, see Janzen and Stanton, *The Hutterites in North America*, 235–240; John A. Hostetler, *Hutterite Society* (Baltimore: Johns Hopkins University Press, 1974), 185–190; and for a case study, see Victor Peters, "The Process of Colony Division among the Hutterites: A Case Study," *International Review of Modern Sociology* 6, No. 1 (1976), 57–64.
13 Theron F. Schlabach, "The Historiography of Mennonites and Amish in America: Reflections on the Past and Future," *Mennonite Quarterly Review* 81, No. 1 (2007), 49–75.
14 John W. Bennett, *Hutterian Brethren: The Agricultural Economy and Social Organization of a Communal People* (Stanford: Stanford University Press, 1967), 69, 185–187.
15 Hans D. Radtke, "The Hutterites in Montana: An Economic Description," *Montana Agricultural Experiment Station Bulletin* 641 (Bozeman: Montana State University, 1971).
16 Select Committee of the Assembly, *Report on Communal Property, 1972* (Edmonton: Queen's Printer, 1972).
17 John Ryan, *The Agricultural Economy of Manitoba Hutterite Colonies* (Toronto: McClelland and Stewart, 1977).

debts are paid off or the population exceeds one hundred. [...] Hutterites are always saving money and looking for available land.[18]

In a similar vein, Katz and Lehr stress that a community

> must accumulate large capital resources to establish a daughter [community]. To achieve this they must maximize income from work and minimize living expenses.[19]

In neither book are figures for land acquisition and construction costs of infrastructure mentioned. This essay suggests that the race to generate capital savings to fund a new daughter community may be more and more difficult to win. The incentive to explore new revenue streams is growing.

In the absence of precise data, we are forced to rely on partial and anecdotal information about the costs involved in establishing a new community. These scraps of information—inadequate as they are—hint at the way in which such costs have inflated to reach startling new heights. In Canada, the need to acquire quotas for the production of milk, eggs, and poultry adds significantly to these costs. A dairy herd has been the sheet anchor of the economy of many communities because it provides cash returns throughout the year. But to establish a new dairy herd of 100 cows would cost about $4 million for the quota alone. Again, quota costs for laying hens amount to some $400 per bird. A modest barn with 13,000 layers would mean an outlay of $5.2 million. These are daunting figures indeed, especially when added to the rising costs of land and buildings. It is little wonder that Hutterite leaders are exploring new ways of making a living, which they hope will offer better and more regular returns on investment.[20]

Sascha Hausmann spent several months living on a community in southern Alberta during 2017. He had ample opportunity to hear discussions about "hiving" and stories about various communities that had recently split. He reported that Hutterites generally felt that it would require at least $50 million to establish a daughter community.[21] This figure corresponds to my own findings. When I visited a community in southeastern Alberta, which was well into the process of community division, the parent

---

18   Janzen and Stanton, *Hutterites in North America*, 236.
19   Yossi Katz and John Lehr, *Inside the Ark: The Hutterites in Canada and the United States* (Regina: Canadian Plains Research Center, 2012), 103.
20   Hutterite colonies in the US do not have to purchase quotas; however, their returns from milk, eggs, and poultry are much lower than the price-supported ceilings mandated in Canada.
21   Sascha Samuel Hausmann, "Working at the Hutterites: Motivation in a Communitarian Group" (MA thesis, Freie Universität, Berlin, 2017), 16.

community had purchased a huge ranch of 15,000 acres at $3,000 an acre.[22] The land had cost $45 million, so the necessary quotas and construction costs would push the total figure well above $60 million.[23] This big prosperous community faces the prospect of being deeply in debt for more than twenty years. This makes it vulnerable to increasing interest rates. It is not surprising that community leaders listen to political debates on the future of supply management with deep interest. Some communities have transferred their dairy quota to their daughter community and have closed their own dairy.[24] A land purchase by an Alberta community in northern Saskatchewan seems to have been rather less expensive. The purchase, near Tisdale, included 7,900 acres with some farm equipment and grain storage facilities, and the cost was reported to be $26.5 million.[25] On the basis of the fragmentary evidence, we must agree with Gordon Tait, who has spent thirty years working with the Hutterites, when he remarked: "Today they [Hutterite leaders] are making million dollar decisions that ten years ago were only $100,000 decisions."[26]

## Declining Profit Margins in Agriculture

In Canada, farm income was forecast to decline modestly in 2016 and 2017, mostly as a result of lower livestock prices resulting from increased meat production in the United States. Total operating expenses were expected to increase somewhat in 2017.[27] South of the border, analysts were less sanguine. In an article entitled "The Great Margin Squeeze," the authors remark that projected profit margins in agriculture are much tighter than they have been for some time: "The expected level of losses for 2015 are unprecedented over the period 1991–2015."[28]

They go on to explain that the prevalence of fixed costs in agriculture, land, equipment, and labour, make the industry slow to adjust to changing output conditions.

---

22  All first-person references refer to Simon Evans.
23  On-site visit, July 2016.
24  MacMillan Community, AB, interview, July 2016.
25  "Alberta Hutterite colony pays $26.5M for Saskatchewan farm," *Calgary Herald*, September 30, 2016, B2.
26  Tait was the director of Hutterite services with MNP, a financial consulting company that has acted as advisor to 95% of the Hutterites in western Canada for over fifty years. "Business Lessons from the Colonies," agadvance.com, September 22, 2014.
27  Agriculture and Agri-Food Canada, "Canadian Agricultural Outlook, 2017," 1.
28  Brent Gloy, Michael Boehlje, and David A. Widmar, "The Great Margin Squeeze: Strategies for Managing Through the Cycle" (Purdue Agriculture, January 2015), https://ag.purdue.edu/commercialag/home/wp-content/uploads/2015/01/201501_GloryBoehljeWidmar_GreatMarginSqueeze.pdf.

In the light of these general trends, Hutterite farm managers view the future with some apprehension. They feel that, over the next few years, their objectives will be focused on increasing efficiency rather than on growth of acreage, and they predict a decline in the importance of livestock.[29] The concentration of large hog operations in parts of Manitoba has raised concerns about the disposal of effluent and its possible effects on surface and ground water. In 2008, further expansion in the Red River Valley and Interlake regions was forbidden.[30] Later, this measure was extended to cover the whole province. This effectively stopped any plans for expansion and cast a chill over the hog industry in Manitoba. In March 2017, the new Conservative government removed the restrictions, but attempts to streamline planning applications have been only partially successful.[31] Profit margins on hogs are slim, and the costs of expanding infrastructure to meet an ever-more-stringent regulatory environment have risen sharply. As one Hutterite farm manager remarked, "Most of our income used to come from hogs, but that's a thing of the past. Not much is going to be invested in that anymore."

One of his peers went on:

> We actually went out of beef because it just didn't turn out. In my opinion […] with all the legislation that's out there on food safety and this stuff, I can't see us expanding. I think eventually they are going to kill us […] with pigs[.] We've been in pigs all our lives, since we've been here, but I can't see us surviving with pigs.[32]

These pessimistic forecasts suggest that demand for hogs and prices have been steadily declining. Such is not the case.[33] Although the price index shows considerable volatility from year to year, the trend has been stable or slightly upward. The point is that margins have been eroded by increased input costs. Some communities have been able to sidestep these strictures by establishing long-term relationships with agribusiness. Brant Community, for example, produces custom hogs for the Japanese market through its contract with Maple Leaf Foods in Lethbridge. Across the border in Montana, communities have links to veterinarians in Minne-

---

29  Blacksheep Strategy, "Farm Shift: Insight from Canada's Leading Farmers," 2009, 14.
30  Katz and Lehr, *Inside the Ark*, 104.
31  In Ontario, Alberta, and Saskatchewan, planning approval can be obtained in two to four months, while in Manitoba it takes more than a year. *Western Producer*, December 7, 2017.
32  Blacksheep Strategy, "Farm Shift," 41.
33  Statistics Canada, "Farm Product Price Index (FPPI), monthly weights," table 32-10-0100-01, https://www150.statcan.gc.ca/t1/tbl1/en/tv.action?pid=3210010001.

sota and slaughterhouses in California, as well as to markets in Japan and China.[34] But not all communities have been as successful.

**Providing Work for all Community Members**

On a Hutterite community, working in the fields or stock barns is much more than merely "a job." Work is worship for these communal people, and wholehearted commitment to labour for the community is as important to their spiritual welfare as is attendance at the evening service.[35] "To the Hutterite, work itself is a purposeful ingredient of life, and idleness is almost sinful."[36] Thus, a primary responsibility for community leaders is to ensure that there is regular meaningful work for all of their flock. As larger and more efficient machines have replaced labourers in the fields and the hog and egg barns, this duty has become more and more difficult to fulfill. In particular, the declining emphasis on livestock reduces the need for a team of dairy workers to carry out milking twice a day, and for others to feed hogs and clean their barns. These full-time and responsible jobs may be lost. Perhaps work in manufacturing will provide an alternative. During the late 1970s and 1980s, there was much discussion among Hutterite leaders and researchers about surplus labour and underemployment.[37] Ministers voiced concerns that "the devil found work for idle hands." Sam Hofer describes one such situation vividly:

> From the mid 1970s to the early 1980s we had more men on the field than were needed. For a few years far too many of our summer days were spent on the fields, picking rocks. We sat around a lot playing cards and listening to the radio. Incentives or feelings of accomplishment among our young people were dangerously low. […] In a period of about nine years, Baildon Colony lost fifteen young men to the outside world.[38]

In these circumstances, the creation of year-round jobs in non-farm occupations must seem an appealing prospect, both to managers and to young Hutterites. The task of community leaders to keep their community

---

34   Simon Evans, "Hutterite Agriculture in Alberta: The Contribution of an Ethnic Isolate," *Agricultural History* 93 no. 4 (January 2019), 656–681; "Montana Hutterites key to region's hog industry, *Grand Forks Herald*, November 26, 2013; and Joanita Kant, *Gentle People: A Case Study of Rockport Colony Hutterites* (Brookings, SD: Prairie View Press, 2011), 7.
35   Janzen and Stanton, *The Hutterites in North America*, 197.
36   Peters, *All Things Common*, 106.
37   Summarized by Karl A. Peter, *Dynamics of Hutterite Society* (Edmonton: University of Alberta Press, 1987), 160ff.
38   Samuel Hofer, *The Hutterites: Lives and Images of a Communal People* (Saskatoon: Hofer Printers, 1998), 128. Only two of the men returned to the community.

meaningfully occupied is complicated by the seasonal nature of the demand for labour. As one farm manager explained:

> I would have to say it's a problem to keep everybody employed on the farm […] there's a couple of times of year when you need everybody and then when it rains or something, all of a sudden you've got a bunch of people unemployed. And it's a big problem and I am always out there looking for opportunities where we can maybe do something seasonally during the winter.[39]

However, not all communities will have a pool of under-employed labour looking for meaningful and exciting jobs. A newly established daughter community of sixty souls might have fifteen to twenty adult males. Of these, the senior men would be responsible for various agricultural endeavours, one would be the field boss, others departmental heads and tradespeople. This would leave fewer than ten young men to provide muscle for the community—to drive tractors, clean the barns, and respond to the myriad of daily requests for help from the managers. Some communities are experiencing labour shortages. One minister said that he could use five or six men immediately. He even asked me about the Temporary Foreign Worker Program.[40] Jake Hofer, steward of Airport Community in Manitoba, remarked: "We are just as shorthanded as the other guys—now we have three outside guys working on the community. Help is hard to find for everyone."[41] Thirty years of declining birthrates coupled with defections among the fifteen-to-twenty-five age group mean that some communities have had to close one or more enterprises because of labour shortages. Serious underemployment will only occur during the later stages of a community's population cycle when the community has reached 120 people or more.

The cycle of the gradual growth of a community over decades, followed by its split and the establishment of a daughter community, has another less-obvious impact on the availability of skilled labour for starting a non-farm enterprise. For several years prior to community division, the skilled craftsmen on the community will be fully occupied building the new community. Even after the daughter community has finally separated and become a distinct functioning entity, the tradespeople at the parent community will be faced with an equally herculean task. The older buildings will require a makeover so that they conform to the elevated standards

---

39   Blacksheep Strategy, "Farm Shift," 43; Joanita Kant, *Hutterites of South Dakota: The Schmiedeleut* (Coral Springs: Llumina Press, 2006), 21.
40   On-site visit, Codesa Community, AB, July 13, 2013. For general context see Evans, "Hutterite Agriculture in Alberta."
41   "Business lessons from the colonies," Agadvance.com, September 22, 2014.

of the daughter community. This refurbishment of the parent community may take several years.[42] Thus, it would be a serious oversimplification to view the adoption of non-farm businesses as a means of finding jobs for underemployed Hutterites. Some communities are labour deficient, while on others key personnel are fully occupied. New enterprises will likely involve the reassignment of community members from one job to another. Already, on some communities during the winter months, men will spend the morning in the barns, and the afternoons in the various workshops.[43]

## The Historical Context of Non-farm Activities on Hutterite Communities

Hutterite leaders will often make the point that the adoption of non-farm activities on the communities is far from being an innovative departure; it is in fact a return to Hutterite tradition and to their cultural roots. They point out that during the "Golden Age" in southern Moravia in the late sixteenth and early seventeenth centuries, the economic success of the Bruderhofs was based on their craft skills.[44] They were also leaders in education and medicine.

Two hundred years later, during their sojourn in the Ukraine, Hutterite communities concentrated on agricultural production and learned progressive techniques from their Mennonite neighbours. But their craft skills continued to thrive. In the 1860s, they were producing pottery, clocks, cabinets, and fine linen. Some Hutterite leaders expressed concern as some of these industries flourished, lest the participants become too worldly.[45]

Not surprisingly, the Hutterites brought these skills with them when they established their first communities along the James River in Dakota Territory in 1874. Their building skills are still demonstrated by the survival of many original buildings, especially at Bon Homme Community in South Dakota. The new arrivals soon established mills to grind their own and their neighbours' corn. By 1897, there were five water-powered flour mills, and the colonists were engaged in spinning, weaving, carpentry, shoe-making, tanning, blacksmithing, and bookbinding.[46] A visitor in 1912 remarked on the modernity of their operations. Gasoline engines powered cream separators and butter churns, water flowed to houses and barns from artesian wells, and a large tractor was used for ploughing, although horse

---

42  See Simon Evans and Peter Peller, "Hutterite Colonies and the Cultural landscape: An Inventory of Selected Site Characteristics," *The Journal of Amish and Plain Anabaptist Studies* 4, 1 (Spring 2016), 51–81.
43  Hausmann, "Working at the Hutterites," 55.
44  Hostetler, *Hutterite Society*, 42. Hostetler lists more than thirty different crafts.
45  Janzen and Stanton, *The Hutterites in North America*, 29.
46  Hostetler, *Hutterite Society*, 125.

teams were in evidence everywhere. One community already had a dynamo for electric lights and other communities were following suit.[47]

No account of the emergence of non-farm activities on the communities during the twentieth century would be complete without a discussion of the role of Jacob Kleinsasser of Crystal Springs Community in Manitoba. A charismatic and visionary leader, Kleinsasser became *Ältester* (Bishop) in 1978 and has had an indelible impact on the Schmiedeleut for the past forty years.[48] Kleinsasser immersed himself in the writings of the Hutterite leaders of the sixteenth century and in the history of the sect in Europe. He became concerned that contemporary Hutterites might become complacent without the stimulus of outside hostility. In his view, worship had become moribund, and change was needed to reinvigorate spiritual life and to regain some of the passion and intensity of their ancestors. To this end, he encouraged Hutterite youth to embrace education. He envisioned a day when all Schmiedeleut children would complete high school and many would attend university. He was also committed to outreach and the mission field.

Kleinsasser renewed the connection between the Hutterites and the Bruderhof. This group was founded by Eberhard Arnold in the 1920s and had enjoyed a close relationship with the Hutterites during the 1930s and 1940s. Kleinsasser visited the Woodcrest Bruderhof at Rifton, New York, the movement's headquarters. He was impressed with the joy and spontaneous enthusiasm of their worship. He introduced musical instruments and praise songs to some Schmiedeleut communities.[49]

The Bruderhof drew its recruits from urban centers and from all walks of life. They sustained their communities through light industries and craft production. An astute Hutterite observer, writing in 1994, remarked:

> The bishop [Kleinsasser] saw the difficulties in acquiring sufficient land, dairying and egg quotas, and so on. Thinking ahead, he was looking to the eastern communities as

---

47  Paul K. Conkin, *Two Paths to Utopia* (Lincoln: University of Nebraska Press, 1964), 52–55.

48  Kleinsasser died in August 2017. His obituaries hint at his controversial leadership style. To some he was, "energetic, creative and visionary," and should be recognized as one of the greatest Hutterite leaders. *Winnipeg Free Press*, August 9, 2017. To others his death "marked the end of the most internally divisive era in our 500 years of existence." Mary Ann Kirkby, "New Bishop for Schmiedeleut 1 Hutterites: Renewed Hope for Reconciliation," Polka Dot Press, September 12, 2017, https://www.polkadotpress.ca/single-post/2017/09/12/new-bishop-for-schmiedeleut-1hutterites; see also *Mennonite World Review*, September 5, 2017.

49  For an account of the interaction between the Hutterites and the Bruderhof, and Kleinsasser's role, see Brian Preston, "Jacob's Ladder," *Saturday Night*, April 1992.

models for non-agricultural communal life that the Hutterites might someday need to adopt.⁵⁰

Thus, Kleinsasser was prescient and foresaw pressures on the status quo that would become difficult to ignore twenty years later. During a visit to Crystal Spring Community in the early 1980s, I remember seeing a huge machine for drying and making pellets from alfalfa; a machine shop devoted to turning out equipment for pig barns; and a classroom full of computers.

Unfortunately, his activism and his determination to push a reform agenda led to a widespread perception that he was an authoritarian leader, although he was not acting alone; many senior ministers supported these efforts and contributed to the movement. Under his leadership the threat of excommunication was used to daunt opposition; this is not unprecedented in Anabaptist history where the ban was commonly used to "non-violently" deal with conflict. Kleinsasser also took part in civil court actions as a last resort against those who resisted; these decisions being made collectively by the council of senior ministers. Thus, Kleinsasser was largely responsible for the division of the Schmiedeleut into two groups: Schmiedeleut I (his followers and the more reform-minded), and Schmiedeleut II (the majority of the more traditional communities).⁵¹ His successor, *Ältester* Arnold Hofer of Acadia Community, has a difficult task ahead of him. However, it is clear that some of the trends foreseen by "Jake *Vetter*" have come to pass in the new millennium.

All farmers are by necessity wonderfully skilled at fixing things and making delinquent machinery work. The Hutterites have an advantage; because of their relatively large labour force, they can specialize. Young men with particular attributes become full-time carpenters, welders, mechanics, electricians, or plumbers. They employ their talents in maintaining the complex systems at their home community and in building a daughter community from the ground up. High school graduates or school leavers of fifteen or sixteen years old are apprenticed to these established tradespeople. Thus there is a pool of skilled labour, brought up in a rural and agricultural milieu but available to develop non-agricultural enterprises.

---

50   Samuel Hofer, *The Hutterites*, 133. John Ryan, an economic geographer at the University of Winnipeg, and a close acquaintance of Kleinsasser, expressed the same idea: "Jake [Kleinsasser] is ahead of his time. He says 'In order to survive, we will have to change. In the past, Hutterites were craftsmen, not farmers. Just because we were farmers for the past hundred years or so doesn't mean we'll always be farmers.'" Preston, "Jacob's Ladder," 80.
51   Janzen and Stanton, *Hutterites in North America*, 62–73.

## New Initiatives in Non-farm Activities

### Adding Value to Agricultural Production

Most Hutterite communities continue to devote most of their efforts to agriculture. Therefore, one response to lower returns and shrinking margins is to look for ways to add value to their products and to reduce their dependence on the middleman by establishing co-operative marketing strategies.

Feed mills are ubiquitous on Hutterite communities. Most communities dry and mill some of their grain to feed their livestock. This has a long history. The group brought its skill and expertise as millers with them from the Ukraine. An early visitor to the communities along the James River explained that they were "distinguished by their stone buildings, by their herds of geese and flocks of pigeons and by their ice houses and tall flour mills."[52] In the frontier environment of Dakota Territory during the 1890s and the early twentieth century, grain mills on Hutterite communities provided an important service for the wider community. When the Hutterites were forced to relocate to Alberta, a flour mill was built on Rosebud Community, which served the three communities along the Rosebud River and attracted customers from miles around.[53]

One community in southern Alberta has a particularly long and successful history in producing food products for people rather than feed for livestock. Soon after arriving in its new location south of Magrath, Alberta, Rockport Community started using a traditional recipe to produce a pancake mix. Ninety years later, Coyote Pancake Mix is still flourishing. Don Bodnarchuk, president of NuStart Marketing, which handles the promotion and marketing of the product, explained:

> The community continues to grow their own wheat and it is something that really adds to the longevity of the product. They find it important to manufacture this mix at their community for their large following that has grown wider and stronger over the years.[54]

Bodnarchuk said that the regionally based product was now sold across Canada, and that the traditional processes are still used although they encompass technological advances and contemporary food safety standards.

---

52  Conkin, *Two Paths to Utopia*, 55.
53  Rockyford and District History Book Society, *Where We Crossed the Creek and Settled: Rockyford* (Calgary: Alcraft Printing, 1982), 67; and Evans and Peller, "The Hutterites Come to Alberta," 11–19.
54  Demi Knight, "Magrath Area's Rockport Hutterite Colony still flipping over pancakes after 90 years," *Prairie Post West*, April 13, 2018.

In contrast to the venerable processing facility at Rockport is a new soybean crushing plant under construction at Granum Community.[55] Soybean meal is the most popular protein supplement for livestock, especially for poultry and hogs. While soybean acreages in Manitoba and southeast Saskatchewan have been growing rapidly, cooler night temperatures and a shorter growing season inhibit similar growth in Alberta, where the community is located.[56] Almost all the soybean meal used by provincial farmers is imported from mills in Minnesota, to the tune of 55 to 60 million a year. Granum imports soybeans from Manitoba and plans to distribute processed meal to other communities and farmers in southwestern Alberta. The community is an "early adopter" in this field and its long-term investment may become increasingly profitable as shorter-season varieties are developed.[57]

A major project that illustrates both the power of cooperation between communities and the potential benefits of investment in processing facilities is Dakota Turkey Growers of Huron, South Dakota. It is worth recounting the story of how this successful venture started. During the early 2000s, Hutterite turkey growers in South Dakota were becoming frustrated with the prices they were being offered by processors. It seemed that all their efforts and investments to streamline their production were still not yielding a living for their families.[58] The communities had already worked together with their legal advisors to organize co-operative purchase of soybean feed, and this initiative had proved highly successful. Now the Hutterite leaders wanted to explore the possibility of building their own processing facility. Neither they nor their advisors underestimated the difficulties facing them. No major turkey processing plant had been built in the United States since the 1980s. The prospect of raising some $40 million seemed daunting.

In fact, the vague concept was translated into a concrete project remarkably fast. Within a few days after the initial meeting, the state governor had been informed, and he embraced the idea of helping family farms and creating jobs.[59] He went so far as to purchase an abandoned

---

55  On-site visit, Granum Community, AB, August 1, 2018.
56  Ron Gietz, "The Potential for Soybeans in Alberta," *Alberta Agriculture and Forestry*, August 2014.
57  Ron Gietz, personal communication, August 13, 2018.
58  The communities raise about 80% of the 6.2 million turkeys grown in the state. Kathy Cobb, "Color them Plain but Successful: Growing Hutterite Colonies Find Successful—and Sizable—Niches in District Economy," *Fedgazette*, January 6, 2006, 1–5.
59  We are extremely grateful to Jeff Sveen, a lawyer with the firm of Siegel, Barnett and Schulz, of Aberdeen, SD, who has worked with the colonies for 25 years. Having gained the permission of his clients, he met with us to tell us the story of Dakota Turkey Growers, May 17, 2018.

factory and offer it as a possible site for a processing facility. With political support and more than forty communities committed, Dakota Turkey Growers was established in 2003. Initially, the Hutterite communities provided $12 million, while the state came up with $9.2 million and some loan guarantees. Over the next three years, under the guidance of an experienced CEO, an ultra-modern processing facility was built. The initial labour force of 300 has now grown to 1,000, split into two shifts. The plant handles 40,000 birds a day and processes 200 million pounds of product a year. The company sells a variety of packaged meat products throughout the United States; its chefs and dietitians are constantly monitoring the marketplace and looking for new niches to fill. Currently, Dakota Turkey Growers plans to expand into the "ready-to-eat" market.

Initially, it was difficult to recruit and retain a labour force from the region. With cooperation from the town of Huron, South Dakota, the company worked to attract new immigrants. After one Karen family from Myanmar moved to Huron, other families soon followed.[60] Today there are 600 Karen immigrants in the town. People from South America have also been drawn by the prospect of jobs. They make up some 16% of the labour force. The town has helped the new arrivals with housing arrangements, and the schools have hired specialists in English as a second language to teach the children of immigrants, who now make up nearly half the student body. The cooperation between the company and the town to provide for the needs of newcomers has yielded positive results. The turnover of workers has declined to 15 to 20 percent, much lower than elsewhere in the meat packing industry.

Overall, this has been a very positive investment on the part of participating communities. Not only do they have a say in the prices paid them for their turkeys, but also they share in the profits of Dakota Provisions.[61]

Many communities are investing in slaughtering facilities and are preparing livestock products for niche markets. When we visited South Peace Community, British Columbia, in 2011, we were shown the recently completed meat processing facility. It had been designed and built by the community and represented a large capital outlay. As we considered the relative isolation of the community, we could not help wondering if it would attract enough custom to ensure viability. We need not have worried; a recent visitor reported that the facility was working five days a week and employs three or four men full time. There is more work than they can handle. The facility processes buffalo as well as beef and pork, and

---

60  This paragraph is based on a news report, *PBS News*, July 2, 2016.
61  One steward reminded me that Hutterite communities are also exposed to the risks faced by food processing companies—however diligent they are—of an outbreak of E. coli or salmonella.

is especially busy during the hunting season. A German neighbour has taught the community much about making sausages and salami.[62] Viking Community, Alberta, is investing in deboning equipment to maintain and expand sales of chicken to Chinese restaurants in Edmonton.[63] Paul Wipf, the steward, asks:

> Why ship poultry to Lilydale when we can process the birds on the farm? What makes Hutterite chickens better than the usual grocery-store birds? It's the freshness. […] People seem to trust the Hutterites and the way they do a good job of raising their food.[64]

The same trend is apparent at Iron Creek Community in Alberta where workers slaughter their pigs, and cut and wrap pork for specialized markets.[65]

A co-operative venture among Hutterite communities around Great Falls, Montana, is transforming egg production there. In 2006, thirty communities came together to form Montana Eggs Limited Liability Company. Working with the well-established distribution company Wilcox Family Farms, this new co-operative planned and built an egg sorting plant. The $6.6 million facility employs twenty people and ships 280 million eggs annually, and has a full-time inspector from the U.S. Department of Agriculture. In a recent development, the company has obtained a contract to supply eggs to Costco stores in Montana and eastern Washington. With this assured market and streamlined processing facilities, communities are investing heavily in new free-range chicken barns and expanding their flocks significantly.[66]

## Slashing Costs: Exploring New Technologies

One of the largest expenses faced by Hutterite communities is the cost of heating and cooling residences and barns. Poultry and hogs require carefully monitored constant temperatures to flourish. Humans are somewhat more tolerant of summer heat and winter cold, but residential heating costs are by no means inconsequential. Individual communities have been exploring ways to reduce energy costs for decades. In this quest they have two major advantages: they can experiment and invest for the long term without being answerable to impatient shareholders, and each

---

62 On-site visit, Granum Community, AB, August 1, 2018. Leonard Hofer's daughter lives at South Peace, and he had recently returned from a four-day visit there.
63 On-site visit, Viking Community, AB, June 28, 2018.
64 Guenther, "A New Venture."
65 On-site visit, Iron Creek Community, AB, June 28, 2018.
66 "$6.6 million sorting plant coming to Great Falls," *Great Falls Tribune*, September 2, 2016. The adoption of cage free nesting systems was part of the deal with Costco.

community enjoys some economies of scale when compared to a family farm. Enough energy is required to sustain a community of one hundred or more, as well as the demands of extensive livestock infrastructure.[67]

Political, economic, and technological developments have combined to create a very favourable environment for the expansion of renewable energy resources in western Canada. Hutterites have been quick to "jump on the green band wagon", as Jeff Collins put it.[68] The province of Alberta's Climate Leadership Plan, 2016, aimed at reducing greenhouse gas emissions by phasing out coal-fired energy generation and promoting renewable energy.[69] Currently, 18.9% of Canada's primary energy comes from renewables. Solar voltaic and wind energy are the fastest growing sources of electricity in Canada. In June 2016, the CBC reported that over the next decade up to $50 billion would be invested in renewable energy in Alberta and Saskatchewan.[70]

Technological developments coupled with the momentum generated by increasingly rapid uptake have meant a 64% decrease in utility-scale solar photovoltaic costs from 2008–14. The climate of western Canada means that solar systems installed here produce approximately 50 to 60 percent more energy than similar systems installed in Germany, which has the highest installed solar capacity in the world. Likewise, the costs of land-based wind energy projects have decreased by 41%. There is a sense of excitement in the field as research and experimentation continue on methods of storing electrical power and transmitting it more economically. Those involved in the field believe that the development of renewable energy in western Canada has reached a critical mass and that the momentum generated will withstand political changes. At the end of 2016, Alberta Electric System Operator listed eighty-five proposed and operating projects over one megawatt; of these, thirty-three were solar and fifty-two were wind based.[71]

Hutterite communities will play a significant role in promoting the growth of renewable energy on farms and in rural areas. In some cases, this will be through direct investment, in others by providing land for

---

67  Jeff Collins, *Hutterite Harvest: Green Energy on the Colonies* (Cache Project Production, Storyhive) YouTube video, October 12, 2017, https://youtu.be/aezPlSM6qEc?si=WvHvHQP_oiaLDMvl.
68  Ibid.
69  For a summary, see Vern Solbak, "Renewable Energy Strategies or Communities in Alberta," October 12, 2016, https://www.alberta.ca/system/files/custom_downloaded_images/tr-solar-energy-for-alberta-final.pdf.
70  Sandra Moore, "Southeast Alberta energy diversification report: Our Region, Our Jobs, Our Communities," Economic Development Alliance of Southeast Alberta: Medicine Hat, 2017.
71  Ibid., project list.

wind farms or extensive arrays of solar panels. Some communities have developed revolutionary new boilers that halve heating costs, while still others have plumbed the earth's surface to exploit geothermal energy. These varied strategies will be discussed under four subheadings: wind power, solar energy, improved boilers, and geothermal heating.

*Wind Power*

Pincher Creek Community in Alberta was among the first to host a wind farm in the eminently suitable area near the Crowsnest Pass. The first turbines started turning in 2000 and today there are sixty on the 8,500-acre community. They provide both electricity and cash flow to the community year round, as the steward Mike Gross remarks: "At the time of the year when there's no crop—in winter time—these windmills, they pay very, very, good."[72] Across the border in Montana, Springwater Community shares a somewhat similar windy location in the Judith Gap between the Little Belt and the Big Snowy Mountains. Opened in 2006, the wind farm of ninety turbines has been a boon to the county and a second source of income to the community, which collects a substantial rent while still using the land around the turbines. As one commentator put it, "The landscape tells the picture with wind turbines sprouting out of wheat fields and sheep grazing right up to the doorstep."[73] Not far away at Martinsdale Community, the relationship between the renewable energy company Two Dot Wind and the community is even closer, a perfect marriage of Hutterite mechanical expertise and the company's far-reaching contacts.[74] Community blacksmiths, welders, and electricians refurbish used turbines, and this reduces the costs of installation by two-thirds. The nearby shop at Forty Mile Community shares the work. The power generated is sold to Montana Power.

In British Columbia, on the margins of the boreal forest close to Dawson Creek, two wind farms, each containing seven turbines, have been established on South Peace Community. The company involved—Renewable Energy Systems Canada—was lured to invest by BC Power's Standing Offer Program, which enables small power projects to feed into the grid.[75] Farther south, Sunshine Community received approval to con-

---

72  Geoff Morgan, "The Power of Change," *Alberta Venture*, October 1, 2010.
73  "Wind Power is Blowing up Local Economies," *Prairie Populist*, August 1, 2018, http://prairiepopulist.org/judith-gap-wind-farm/.
74  *Billings Gazette*, July 9, 2005. The wind farm was recently sold to NorthWestern Energy for $18.5 million.
75  Jonny Wakefield, "Wind Farms on Hutterite Land Approved," *Dawson Creek Mirror*, August 12, 2016, https://www.dawsoncreekmirror.ca/regional-news/prrd/wind-farms-on-hutterite-land-approved-1.2322018.

struct four 600-kilowatt turbines, generating 2.4 megawatts, in March 2014. The community bought its turbines from Tacke Windtechnik, and they provide enough power for all the community's needs. Surplus power flows through the Fortis distribution network. Similarly, OK Community in Alberta purchased two used turbines from a Danish company, Bonus Energy, that generate 300 kilowatts. Prairie Home Community has a similar project underway while Pine Meadows is expecting to benefit from the growth of Next Era Energy Canada, which has fifty-one turbines already operating as part of its Ghost Pine Wind Energy Centre in Kneehill County.[76] These examples hint at the excitement and momentum developing in this field, but the pace of development means that many other projects have not been mentioned.

*Solar Energy*

The 7,600 solar modules at Green Acres Community, near Bassano, Alberta, generate two megawatts of electricity and make Green Acres one of western Canada's largest solar farms.[77] The community leaders embarked on the $4.6-million project with the objective of providing a long-term solution to the soaring costs of power. They stress that harvesting the power of the sun is consistent with their philosophy of striving to be self-sufficient. Their "solar harvest" is just another crop, albeit one that continues to amaze Jake Hofer, the community electrician responsible for much of the installation work. He remarked:

> It still blows me away to this day […] you look at the system day after day, and there's nothing moving […] no moving parts and yet it creates all this energy.[78]

Indeed, one of the reasons Green Acres decided to pursue a solar project rather than a wind power installation was the lower maintenance costs. Hofer boasts that after four years of operation, his main maintenance headache is weed control! Community labour inputs during the installation reduced costs from $2.80 per watt to $2.40. One megawatt of power is used in the community's plastics recycling plant, while the other serves the residences and barns. The original business plan, based on 2015 electricity

---

76  Alberta Utilities Commission (AUC), Decision 2014-074, March 27, 2014, Sunshine Colony; AUC Decision 2010-365, December 8, 2010, OK Colony; AUC Decision 2011-173, April 26, 2011, Prairie Home Colony; and *Virden Empire Advance*, June 30, 2018.
77  *Green Energy Futures*, November 16, 2015; and *New Energy Economy*, April 17, 2018.
78  Green Energy Futures, "124. Green Acres Solar Farm - The largest in Western Canada." YouTube video, 2:33. November 16, 2015. https://www.youtube.com/watch?v=ZDW2Yg0SOB0.

prices, projected a fifteen-year payback on their investment, but decreasing prices have extended this period.[79]

The solar installation at Brant Community, Alberta, is much smaller, but it may play a significant role as a model of what can be achieved using the power of the sun.[80] The "net-zero" chicken barn generates as much power as it uses. The project is a partnership between the community, Egg Farmers of Alberta (EFA), and Alberta Agriculture. It was supported by a $250,000 grant from the Albert government's Growing Forward 2 plan.[81] Tom Mandel, the community steward, explained that the community was planning to build a new chicken barn anyway, to replace the existing cage system with a free-range barn. The community was persuaded by EFA researchers to look carefully at a solar heating option. The potential savings made sense, and it was clear that a Brant "net-zero" barn, through its partners, might be a model for other chicken farmers and livestock producers. At the opening, an expert on sustainability praised the barn:

> This project really is the first of its kind in Canada [and] is trialing new technologies that could potentially define the new normal for energy efficiency and reducing climate impacts for animal husbandry.[82]

A hidden cost to the community was a certain loss of autonomy. While the barn was under construction by community tradespeople, every input and output was measured and documented by outsiders. The 100 solar panels on the barn roof produce 25.5 kilowatts of electricity, while heat exchange pumps, LED lighting, and extreme insulation techniques all contribute to efficiency. The careful instrumentation of every step in the process has produced data that will be invaluable to those who follow after. Closed-circuit television cameras help monitor the well-being of the birds and provide opportunities for the public to view the barn. Much of the electronic equipment installed came from the Netherlands, and Darrel Mandel, the community chicken boss, said he was in frequent contact with the Dutch firm. The boilers came from Germany.[83] At the barn opening,

---

79  When the project came online, the price of electricity was 14–15¢ per KW hour. Today it is only 2–3¢. Personal communication, David Vonesch, Skyfire Energy, September 14, 2017.

80  Community visits, July 6, 2016; and October 25, 2017. A video of the Brant barn was shown at the Annual Meeting of the Egg Farmers of Canada, Westin Inn, Calgary, July 13, 2018.

81  Barb Glen, "Barn Aims to make the energy it uses," *Western Producer*, August 18, 2016.

82  Kyle Bakx, "Net-Zero Egg Barn with Solar Energy Opens in Alberta," CBC News, July 27, 2016, https://www.cbc.ca/news/business/brant-colony-net-zero-solar-egg-farms-alberta-1.3695571.

83  On-site visit, October 25, 2017.

Alberta Minister of Agriculture Cheil Carlier commented that, "the colony here has taken a leap of faith."[84] It is to be hoped that other producers may follow their lead.

Turin Community, Alberta, was a real pioneer in 2006 when it built a solar-thermal system. Philip Waldner looks after the system that has met the community's needs for heat for more than a decade with very little maintenance. He emphasizes again what a good fit "harvesting the sun" is for the Hutterites: "It is just another crop and plays a role in reducing greenhouse gases."[85]

Granum Community is playing a more passive role in another solar energy project. It is providing land for a $210 million, 880 solar-module farm to be located northeast of Claresholm, Alberta.[86] The project manager in Alberta is Daniel Andres of Perimeter Solar, but a key partner is Obton A/S, a Danish firm and one of the largest solar farm operators in Europe. Andres explained:

> We got interested because the cost of solar has come down so quickly in the last eight years. It has come down about tenfold, making solar costs competitive with other sources of power generation.[87]

The site selected is in a saline basin and is marginal agricultural land. This reduces "species at risk" issues that would occur if native prairie land were involved. It is also adjacent to a transmission line.[88] From the community's point of view, the project is a win-win situation. Granum Community is paid rent for the land—which exceeds the returns from agricultural use—while at the same time continuing to graze sheep under the solar panels. The project began operations in October 2021.

*Improved Boilers*

For several decades, Decker Community was well known throughout western Canada as the maker and distributor of Decker Brand Boilers.[89] Their integrated system produced savings of more than 70% in heating bills for greenhouses, manufacturing plants, livestock facilities, and machine shops. Designed for multi-fuels, coal, biomass, biofuels, wood pellets,

---

84 Egg Farmers of Alberta, "Brant Colony Net-0 Grand Opening," July 28, 2016, https://eggs.ab.ca/about-us/news/brant-colony-celebrates-grand-opening-of-net-zero-layer-barn/#:~:text=July%2028%2C%202016%20(Calgary%2C,first%20net%2Dzero%20layer%20barn.
85 Jeff Collins, *Hutterite Harvest*.
86 On-site visit, Granum Community, AB, August 1, 2018.
87 "Solar farm proposed for east of Claresholm," *Claresholm Local Press*, August 9, 2017.
88 Personal communication, Daniel Andres, August 14, 2018.
89 On-site visit, Decker Community, MB, May 9, 2018

natural gas, and fuel oil, most of their boilers in fact used coal. However, the Decker boiler was among the cleanest burning boilers in the industry, and mandatory emission testing ensured that government standards were exceeded. Quality materials and careful engineering meant that the heating system required little maintenance and provided years of trouble-free service.

How did a rather isolated Hutterite community on the parkland margins of Manitoba become the production centre for a much-sought-after boiler with distribution across western Canada, into the United States, and even to Europe? As is so often the case, the "story of the boilers" began with the needs of the community.[90] Soon after the community formally separated from its parent community, Brightstone, in 1981, the costs of heating its barns and shops with propane "went through the roof." The community found an alternative heating source, the All Canadian Boiler built by Lawrence Redke. It worked well and reduced heating costs substantially. Decker bought a second boiler and became a dealer for the system. Through the early 1990s, Hutterite engineers worked to integrate and streamline each step in the process from fuel hopper to ash auger and multi-clone dust collector. The biggest innovation was to move from an open to a closed system. This increased efficiency greatly and allowed the use of rust inhibitors that greatly extended the life of the boiler. The downside of this major step was that it meant government regulation and a flood of red tape. However, sales continued to grow, as did the reputation of the Decker boiler. Both employment in the metalworking shop and income from the enterprise provided a good balance to the ongoing agricultural activities at the community.[91] Pincher Creek Community, faced with natural gas bills of $8,000 a month for their new pig barn, bought a Decker boiler in 1999 and slashed their costs to $1,200 a month.[92]

Unfortunately, sales of the boiler have fallen off in the past decade, and when we visited during the spring of 2018, the demonstration boiler system was gathering dust at the back of the shop. Community leaders were weighing whether it was worth the costs and the time spent to keep their certifications current. Two external changes undermined the competitive edge that the community product had enjoyed. First, fracking had opened new natural gas fields and reduced the price of gas to a point where it could compete with the economies achieved by coal-fired boilers. Second,

---

90   The following paragraphs draw heavily on an email from Decker Community steward, Jacob Waldner, June 6, 2018.
91   CBC reported that sales amounted to $2 million, more than half of the annual turnover of the community. "Hutterite Colony Diversifies beyond Farming," CBC News, January 23, 2012, https://www.cbc.ca/news/canada/manitoba/hutterite-colony-diversifies-beyond-farming-1.1261806.
92   Geoff Morgan, "The Power of Change."

governments introduced carbon taxes and moved to ban the use of coal. While the boilers can use a variety of biomass fuels as alternatives, these are in short supply and therefore expensive.

Iron Creek, Alberta, is a small community that has grown slowly since it was established in 1979. Today, it is home to eighty Hutterites but has proved to be a dynamic centre of innovation. Faced with high heating and water costs, and nagging problems with effluent disposal from its pig barns, the community worked with PDF Biofuels to install a furnace that used methane gas from hog manure to generate electricity.[93] A University of Alberta study in 2007 reported that the community was saving $146,000 in electricity and $203,000 in heating costs.[94] The plant was generating enough power to sell a surplus back to the grid. Perhaps the greatest achievement of the scheme was to reduce odour and water use, and to eliminate the costs of injecting manure.[95] Unfortunately, this imaginative and potentially lucrative solution to a major problem plaguing many communities—effluent disposal—hit some snags, and the furnace was mothballed after three years of operation. The furnace was installed when the price of natural gas was rising and the cost of electricity was soaring. Since that time the price of electricity has decreased and has been deregulated. The community also had to truck water to the site to maintain the anaerobic digestion process. Grant Meikle, the CEO of Open Energy, says that the technology is still intact and could be reactivated if and when prices change.[96]

The hub of innovation using biomass furnaces has moved to Manitoba, where there is more suitable material available, from wood chips to cattails.[97] In 2018, Vermillion near Sanford, Manitoba, faced a decision. The coal-fired furnace that the community used to heat its chicken barn was being phased out by the government. A new natural gas system could be installed for $450,000, but thereafter the running costs would top $100,000 a year. Alternatively, a biomass furnace would cost more to install ($600,000), but the annual energy costs would be much less. The

---

93  The original digestion technology came from Luxembourg. Europe is twenty years ahead of North America in this area because of its high costs of energy and government subsidies.
94  "More from Manure," *Green Matters* 27 (Spring 2006), 2.
95  Tony Kryzanowski, "Manure biogas developer ready for round two as green power trend grows," *Manure Manager*, July 10, 2008, https://www.manuremanager.com/manure-biogas-developer-ready-for-round-two-as-green-power-trend-grows-1598/.
96  The installation of very efficient European furnaces is a low-risk option for tackling heating costs. During a recent visit to Granum Community, the steward said that he was negotiating with a German firm for a new furnace system which would halve their costs.
97  Bill Redekop, "Hutterite Colonies greening up their act: Biomass generators provide cheap, sustainable fuel," *Winnipeg Free Press*, March 28, 2018.

community chose the innovative alternative, and the costs for the first two years of operation have been between $15,000 and $20,000 a year. "It's already paid for itself," said community steward Shawn Gross. The community buys woodchips from South-East Pallet and Wood Products of Blumenort, Manitoba. A side benefit is that the wood is not left to rot and produce methane gas. Sturgeon Creek Welding, a Hutterite manufacturing business on the Sturgeon Creek Community outside Headingley, makes the biomass generators. Triple Green Energy, which promotes and sells the system, reports that twenty of the generators have been sold in Manitoba, mostly to other communities. Six more communities have furnaces on order.[98]

*Geothermal Heating*

Millbrook Community, South Dakota, could claim to be the "poster child" of communities that have embraced non-farm enterprises. The fact that a relatively isolated agricultural ethnic community could develop a highly sophisticated geothermal heating system with sales across North America has attracted considerable attention.[99] Not long after the split from parent community Rosedale in 1983, Millbrook leaders started to look for activities that would provide year-round jobs for their people and additional income to supplement returns from their mixed farming operations. They concluded that a geothermal system would provide big savings in heating costs while at the same time leaving a benign ecological footprint.[100]

A geothermal heating and cooling system exploits the difference in temperature between the constant temperatures found at some depth beneath the earth's surface and the variable temperatures at the surface.[101] The key component in such a system is the pump, which circulates liquids deep underground and maximizes the heat differential on the surface. Hutterite engineers developed and patented the Hydron Model Ground Source Heat Pump. It worked so well that demand for the pump increased rapidly. In 1995, Energy Dynamics Incorporated was founded to act as the exclusive distributor of the pump, which was manufactured in expanded facilities close to the community. Continuing success and growth meant that more and more non-Hutterites were hired, and Millbrook's primary function as a faith community was jeopardized. In 2007, the business was

98  Interestingly enough, the residences at Vermillion are heated with a geothermal system.
99  Janzen and Stanton, *Hutterites in North America*, 215; Cobb, "Color them plain but successful;" and Kant, *Hutterites of South Dakota*, 21.
100 On-site visit, Millbrook Community, SD, May 16, 2018.
101 For explanation and helpful diagrams of geothermal systems, see the website of Enertech Manufacturing, https://enertechusa.com/.

sold to Enertech Manufacturing, which has again remodelled and expanded the plant at Mitchell, South Dakota.

The advantageous sale of the geothermal enterprise has underwritten the establishment of two daughter communities: Spruce Lane at Blanchard, North Dakota, and Meadow View at Bridgewater, South Dakota.[102] The parent community has been reduced in numbers to only fifty souls. The story of Millbrook Community over the past thirty years is one of extraordinary innovation and entrepreneurship. One could argue that the success of the heat pump exposed the community to "worldly influences." If this was indeed the case, it is clear that the present much-reduced community is firmly reestablishing its Hutterite roots, and its invention has provided a unique heating option for many other communities.

When White Lake in Alberta built its daughter community, Jumbo Valley, it decided to install geothermal heating and cooling systems in all the residences.[103] Leaders felt that "harvesting heat from the ground" was in line with their philosophy and their tradition of innovation. It was an expensive undertaking, although Hutterite electricians did most of the work. It will take a generation to pay off the installation costs and to reap the benefits of negligible running costs. When I visited Eli Hofer in his spacious new home on a hot day in August, the house was deliciously cool. Eli said that he never needed to adjust the temperature.[104] The parent community, White Lake, has used the principle of geothermal heating to develop and patent an innovative stock watering system. It consists of a thick rubber tube of insulation that can be sunk eight feet into the ground. This protects the water pipes, allowing the slightly warmer ground water to prevent the surface water from freezing. Its major advantage is that it does not require an external energy source and it is easily maintained. The community has agents in Montana, Manitoba, Pennsylvania, and Arizona; a trailer load of units had just been shipped the morning I visited.[105]

**Light Manufacturing Enterprises**

The most overt response by Hutterites to changes in the economic milieu has been their willingness to use existing infrastructure and the skills of their people to develop a variety of light industrial enterprises. These will be grouped for discussion under a variety of subheadings, from "Metalworking" to "Miscellaneous."

---

102 "New Hutterite Colony planned near Hillsboro," *Rapid City Journal*, December 18, 2011.
103 Jeff Collins, *Hutterite Harvest*.
104 On-site visit, Jumbo Lake, AB, August 1, 2018.
105 On-site visit, White Lake, AB, August 1, 2018.

*Metalworking*

Holden Community, Alberta, is the original home of Versa Frame Inc., a metal fabrication company with some fifteen participating sites across western Canada, several of them on Hutterite communities.[106] The company makes metal siding and roofing. Once again, the community's venture into manufacturing grew out of its own needs. It was buying a lot of construction materials from an Edmonton producer that had cramped facilities and had trouble meeting Holden's needs.[107] The community had space and skilled labour available, so the brothers who owned the business and the community leaders reached a deal. A large barn on the community, which had been used for seed potatoes, now houses three rolling mills and associated presses. Rolls of steel in thirty-four colours are imported from South Korea via Vancouver. The mill employs five men full time. Most of the output moves to a warehouse and sales centre in Nisku, just south of Edmonton, but when we visited, two contractors were loading finished products at the factory door. Most of the sales and contacts with customers are handled by non-Hutterites, allowing the community to concentrate on production.

Just across the road in the community looms another large building with its own reception centre and sales room, Holden Colony Portable Buildings. This facility uses the building materials produced on the community to turn out a variety of portable buildings: storage sheds, garages, and summer cottages are typical. These buildings can be tailored to the customers' requirements, and delivery and set up are included in the price. Attractive show homes are displayed at the community and the company website is comprehensive and easy to use.

Valley View Community, Alberta, planned to make manufacturing a central part of its daughter community from its inception. It started turning out sidewalls, roof cladding, and structures for the oil industry at the site of the new May City Community in 2006, long before formal community division. The new plant was recognized by Versa Frame—the parent company—for having the most aggressive first quarter sales in 2007, and output grew by 10% in 2012.[108] Across the border in central Montana, Golden Valley Community has launched a million-dollar facility—Valley

---

106  These include: Pibroch, Hillview, Rockport, and Box Elder in Alberta; Leask, Springwater, and Arm River in Saskatchewan; and Sommerfeld and Decker in Manitoba.
107  On-site visit, Holden Community, AB, June 27, 2018.
108  "Valley View Hutterites launch ambitious plans for new colony," *Mountain View Gazette*, May 7, 2013. Several other communities have built manufacturing facilities at daughter community sites prior to building residences or agricultural facilities. Examples are Millbrook, SD, and daughter community Spruce Lane, ND, and Fairview, ND, and daughter community Wheatland, ND.

Steel LLC—to produce custom steel trim, siding, and roofing for both commercial and residential customers.[109] Goldridge Industries, owned and run by Turin Community in Alberta, has a successful history reaching back to 1994. It produces a wide range of products for the cattle feedlot industry and for the oil and gas industry. "We manufacture anything that has to do with moving water in the oil patch, from pumps to road crossings and more—pretty much anything you need for pumping water," explained the steward.[110]

Baker Community, Manitoba, has been successful in creating a manufacturing industry that has expanded to fill a niche in North American agricultural support infrastructure. Under the company name Better Air, it manufactures and sells complete ventilation systems for animal barns and for facilities that store vegetable products like potatoes and apples.[111] Hogs, dairy cattle, and poultry produce humid air contaminated with $CO^2$, methane, and solid dust particles from food. A negative ventilation system extracts the foul air and draws in clean air, which can be controlled for temperature and humidity according to daily and seasonal changes in the external environment. A key component in the Better Air system is a heat exchanger, which uses the hot stale air to partially warm clean incoming air. This item and several robotic machines used in production were invented and built on the community. Alongside complete ventilation systems, the facility produces a variety of plastic and PVC products, from chimneys and fan hoods to feed carts and auger hoppers.

The factory provides year-round work for the majority of adult males on the community. In addition, five non-Hutterites are employed to handle sales and promotion, while some other young men from the neighbourhood work on the production line. Retired seniors from the community help with packing small items, and women provide additional hands when there is a deadline to meet. Better Air's sales area reaches westward deep into Saskatchewan and Alberta, and to a more limited extent, eastward into Ontario. The company has penetrated the U.S. market and has supplied customers in Texas. The steward remarked that the size of the U.S. market made it a rather daunting prospect; suddenly, instead of thinking in terms of producing hundreds of items, they were faced with the prospect

---

109   Rob Rogers, "After centuries of farming, Hutterite colony expands into building construction," *Billings Gazette*, October 15, 2017.
110   Robert Hoshowsky, "Alberta-Based Manufacturing Expertise," *Business In Focus* (May 2017), https://www.businessinfocusmagazine.com/2017/05/alberta-based-manufacturing-expertise/.
111   On-site visit, Baker Community, MB, May 11, 2018. This was a most interesting visit. Jonathan Maendel explained the unique origins of the community, and its commitment to education and outreach in Haiti and Nigeria. See also the company website: www.betterair.ca.

of thousands. The community plans to control growth and to continue to emphasize quality.

Most of Baker Community's land is leased to Mennonite neighbours. The community steward explained that the rental returns usually exceeded those they could expect from agriculture. Nevertheless, though the hog barns are empty, the community had just invested $250,000 to seed several hundred acres of corn and was planting a big garden. A miniature barn houses goats, chickens, hogs, horses, and rabbits, so that community children do not lose their farm heritage and can play a major role in looking after the livestock.[112]

For thirty years, Whiteshell Community in Manitoba prospered and grew, supported by diversified agriculture that saw the majority of its crops of soybeans, canola, and wheat fed to hogs, chickens, and dairy cows.[113] In the late 1990s, the community sold its dairy herd and expanded its hog operation. A decade later, Whiteshell was experiencing "irregular cash flow and surplus labour." Or, as the steward put it more forcefully: "Hog prices tanked and we had some bad years. Moreover, environmental regulations prevented us draining some of our heavy land." A communal decision was made to establish Whiteshell Chairs, a manufacturing business that would provide chairs and tables for the hospitality industry. While production started in the old dairy building, the company now has a modern production facility complete with a showroom. Sales have gone well, with contracts to supply Days Inn Hotels, and sales in the North West Territories and Mexico. Building on its initial successes, the company has widened its product line to include picnic tables, fire pits, and bike racks. All products are powder coated at the plant for quality and durability. In 2013, the company purchased Homestile Roofing to further diversify the output of its metalworking shop. Seven or eight Hutterite men are employed full time in the plant, while four or five women handle the upholstering work. Today, the problem is finding extra hands to do the work rather than having an underemployed labour force. In the steward's view, this is a much more healthy state of affairs.

In spite of this successful diversification, farming and livestock remain the main source of income for the community. It has 5,000 acres sown to soybeans, canola, and wheat, a 1,200-sow operation, and 10,000 laying hens. The steward's task is to manage his labour force to keep both factory and farm running smoothly, and perhaps more importantly, to keep his brothers and sisters supplied with varied and meaningful work.

---

112 Janzen and Stanton, *The Hutterites in North America*, 216.
113 The community was established from Iberville in 1962. The following paragraphs are based on a community visit, May 12, 2018; and "Whiteshell Colony Farms," in *Whitemouth River Valley: Visitor and Community Guide*, 2017–2019.

Metalworking—using a community's existing shop and the skills of Hutterite workers—is widespread among the communities. To briefly mention a few more examples: one thinks of Millerdale, South Dakota, and White Lake, Alberta, which produce all kinds of doors and windows; of Starland, Minnesota, which makes steel tools, metal parts, and accessories for manufacturing companies in the Twin Cities; and Riverside Community, South Dakota, with its shop producing stainless steel equipment.[114] The list could be extended.

*Woodworking*

The narrative of the development of woodworking at Springfield Community, Manitoba, is rather typical.[115] During the 1990s, the community started using its carpentry shop to make custom bedroom furniture for neighbours and other communities. One customer then asked for kitchen cabinets, and the gradual shift from "hobby shop" to sleek, highly automated production facility began. Today, the 70,000-square-foot factory produces 100 to 150 cabinets a day and is among the leading suppliers in Manitoba. It boasts $50 million worth of woodworking, finishing, and painting equipment from Germany and the United States. Twenty Hutterite men are employed, and the labour force is augmented with an equal number of non-Hutterites. This is a community in which there have been more girls born than boys, and women play a key role in the office while also being involved in the final sanding and polishing of the products.

The dramatic growth of this enterprise owes much to the drive and vision of the CEO, Pauly Kleinsasser. He explained, "As a young punk of sixteen, I travelled to New York State to the Bruderhof. There, I worked in the carpenters' shop and loved it. I promised that I would have my own shop one day."[116] Pauly has travelled frequently and widely to evaluate and purchase state-of-the-art machinery and materials. His enthusiastic promotion of Springfield Woodworking is matched by his overt expression of his commitment to his faith and the Hutterite way of life.[117] The community has a showroom in Winnipeg for its products, and its sales area reaches eastward to the cottage country around Lake of the Woods.

---

114 Cobb, "Color Them Plain but Successful;" Kant, *Hutterites of South Dakota*.
115 On-site visit, Springfield Community, MB, May 12, 2018.
116 During the 1970s the Schmiedeleut re-established relations with the Bruderhof, a twentieth-century religious movement. Exchanges of personnel took place in both directions. For an account of this, see Janzen and Stanton, *Hutterites in North America*, 62–73.
117 Pauly Kleinsasser regularly attends European trade fairs, and has visited the historic Hutterite sites in Austria and Moravia. He has also travelled to Asia five times in search of countertop materials.

The woodworking business balances the community's farming activities. It crops 6,000 acres of soybeans, canola, barley, and wheat, and feed hogs and chickens. Young community members are rotated between different jobs so that they gain experience in the fields and garden, with the livestock, and in the factory.

Two communities in the Peace River country of Alberta make use of local timber to produce wood products. Birch Hills Community makes attractive, if rather massive, beds and furniture using wood ravaged by the pine beetle.[118] Cleardale Community turns out a variety of sizes of sheds and storage facilities on an assembly line. This enterprise is a major contributor to the income of this young and rather isolated community. When we visited, the German teacher was preparing to travel to the U.S. Midwest to look at automated precision saw equipment, with a view to further investment.[119]

*Construction*

Many of the Hutterite-run enterprises already mentioned sell products to contractors and the building trades. Some communities have gone further and offer "one-stop" supplies to their customers. Hutterite-owned companies have staked out a growing foothold in the supply of construction materials to Manitoba builders. This area of manufacturing is a natural fit for communities because they build their own homes and agricultural infrastructure. Their shops already have some of the metal- and woodworking equipment they need, and community members have skills and experience. It is not surprising that their market share has been growing during the past two decades.[120] In Manitoba, two big companies lead the way: Domtek, owned by the Newdale Community, and Can-American Corrugating Corporation, run by its neighbour, the CanAm Community. Other communities produce siding or roofing materials as part of their product line but sell more locally.

Newdale Community is totally committed to manufacturing.[121] Almost all its land is leased to neighbours and the community relies on its company—Domtek Building Products—for its livelihood. The company has grown steadily over the past twenty-five years. Ten community members work in the plant full time, while five or six non-Hutterites look af-

---

118  On-site visit, Birch Hills Community, AB, July 16, 2013.
119  On-site visit, Cleardale Community, AB, July 19, 2013. Other examples of woodworking enterprises are Fab-a-Tek at White Rock Community, SD; Mayfield Truss at Mayfield Community, SD; and Douse Woodworking at Lakeside Community, MB.
120  *CBC News*, "Unfair competition," November 10, 2010.
121  On-site visit, Newdale Community, MB, May 10, 2018; and www.domtek.ca.

ter the state-of-the-art office on the community and the sales room in Winnipeg. Domtek products include steel panels for the walls or roofs of agricultural, residential, and commercial buildings. Selling points include features developed on the community, like special panel overlap and hidden fasteners, and a five-step painting system that allows it to offer a forty-year warranty with confidence. For interiors, it produces PVC interlocking liner panels, which compete well with more traditional systems like painted drywall. Domtek's sales area is centred in Winnipeg, but reaches into Saskatchewan and Alberta.

Near-neighbour CanAm Community, located at Margaret, Manitoba, is another important producer of building materials. Founded in 1999, Can-American Corrugating Corporation has grown into one of the largest dealers for metal roofing, laminated poles, and rebar in western Canada. Its use of state-of-the-art manufacturing equipment and high-quality materials have earned it a solid reputation. The company emphasizes customer service and ongoing technical support. CanAm's huge facility employs twenty-five community members and seven non-Hutterites. The community has retained 2,600 acres of land and grows dairy-grade alfalfa as a cash crop.[122]

Brentwood Community at Faulkton, South Dakota, has developed an extremely successful custom home-building business that fits well into community life.[123] When the community leaders were looking for an enterprise to balance their agricultural output and contribute to their bottom line, the shortage of housing in North Dakota, caused by the shale oil boom, was constantly in the news. This sparked the idea of building homes, though ironically none of the completed products have been sold in the oil-rich region.

ProComm Builders was established in 2010, and five show homes were constructed. However, sales proved elusive.[124] In 2012, the company developed the idea that the prospective buyer should "call all the shots," from the size and plan of the home to the kitchen cabinets, the colours, and the carpets. Since then, ProComm has sold seventy homes, each one unique, and has a comfortable waiting list of orders. One of the company's selling points is that it takes much of the mystery and intimidation out of building a new home. The customer can make all the choices, with the help of an experienced designer, before construction starts. But it is the quality

---

122 On-site visit, CanAm Community, MB, May 10, 2018; and personal communication, William Waldner, June 4, 2018.
123 On-site visit, Brentwood Community, SD, May 16, 2018.
124 *Outdoor Forum*, June 29, 2013.

of the materials and the workmanship that command the admiration of buyers.[125]

The homes are constructed in a 33,000-square-foot production centre where three homes can be built at a time. When we visited, two men were completing the base of a new house, while a second home was framed and roofed, and work was being done on interior drywall. One could appreciate the advantages of working in a controlled environment rather than on a wet and windy building site. The homes are extremely energy efficient. ProComm offers houses of 1,300 to 2,600 square feet, with a maximum footprint of 35 × 85 feet. The huge production facility includes state-of-the-art extractor fans for dust, and changing rooms, lockers, and showers for the work crew. It takes about fourteen weeks to complete a home, and customers are encouraged to visit while building is in progress. Outside, there were two more houses, one completed and awaiting delivery, the other nearing completion. The carpets were laid, the painting completed, and two Hutterite tradespeople were installing kitchen equipment. Seven men are employed full time while four or five more help out when their other responsibilities allow. A team of women clean and polish a completed home before delivery. As many as nine local suppliers are involved; they provide floor materials, bathroom accessories, cabinetry, kitchenware, countertops, electrical fittings, and carpets.

Typical customers include retiring farmers who are moving to small towns, first-time home-buyers, and those looking for a lakeside cottage as a second home. Most deliveries are made within a radius of fifty miles, but deliveries can be completed up to 100 miles. In the past, ProComm had sales centres in Faulkton and Aberdeen, but now its sales staff prefer to draw potential customers to the site. Word of mouth and an excellent website entice new customers.

*Plastics*

A number of communities have established successful businesses based on plastics. A pioneer in this field was Green Acres Community, Alberta. Its company, Crowfoot Plastics, performs an invaluable service by providing a place for farmers to recycle their plastic waste. Giant grain bags like huge white sausages are a common sight on Alberta farms. They are used to protect fodder crops from the weather. The disposal of large quantities of this plastic material posed a problem. Some chose to burn it, others to bury it; neither is a good option. Now farmers can simply roll their bags and take them to the Crowfoot Plastics plant, where they receive some

---

125 "ProComm Builders," May 8, 2017, http://procommbuilders.com. [Editor's note: This website now indicates that ProComm Builders has become a cabinet-making company called Kiwi Cabinets & Closets.]

compensation, which at least pays for their gas. The Hofer brothers run the company and report:

> Our company is five years old and we recycle approximately five million pounds of plastic a year: high-density polyethylene plastic and gas pipe, and low-density polyethylene grain bags.[126]

In the plant, which runs on solar power, materials are shredded, washed, dried, ground up, melted at 200°C, and extruded as plastic beads. This output makes up a vital part of the raw materials used at Crawling Valley Plastics, located nearby on Clearview Community. Crawling Valley Plastics produces plastic bags both for garbage and for the food and service industries. The availability of relatively low-cost recycled plastic makes the business viable. Five full-time operators run the extrusion machines and the presses, which are housed in the old dairy barn.[127] The computers in the state-of-the-art office run spreadsheets, which track the progress of every order. When the community started the company, it employed an outside agent to handle sales and distribution. Today, it has a well-established base of 300 customers and handles all sales from the community. Its location close to the Trans Canada Highway provides easy access for tractor-trailers that can move the products to Calgary and Edmonton.[128] Here, as is so often the case, Hutterite engineers have fine tuned the machines they bought to reduce waste, while steward John Hofer uses his years of experience working to optimize the diet of his hogs, tinker with raw material inputs, and ensure the right weight and strength of the bags his plant produces.

Clearview's daughter community, Ridgeland Community, operates Seiu Lake Plastics and has a more diverse product line. The company produces "bubble" packing products and plastic foam products. In Manitoba, Maple Grove Community runs Maple Grove Plastics, which produces air and radiator filters, patented under the name Screen-O-Matic, and hot water heating pads for farrowing crates. It also uses plastic tubing in its custom-built boat docks.[129]

After the setback with their biomass boiler, Iron Creek soon found another interesting manufacturing venture to explore. They produce Fox

---

126 Linda Maendel, "Who Will Help Recycle This Bag?," *Hutterian Brethren Blog* (May 31, 2012), http://www.hutterites.org/news/who-recycle-bag/.
127 On-site visit, Clearview Community, AB, July 21, 2018. John Hofer, the steward, explained that the dairy barn was old fashioned and due to be replaced, but to make it economical, they would have to increase the size of their milking herd. This was deemed impossible because of the costs of milk quotas.
128 A rather similar plastics business at OK Community, south of Raymond, AB, failed after two or three years because of high transport costs.
129 Maple Grove Plastics, http://maplegroveplastics.com.

Blocks for the Airlite Plastics Company of Omaha, Nebraska. These Lego-like plastic blocks clip together to form walls, and the hollow core of each block is stiffened with rebar and filled with concrete. This provides a tough wall with some five inches of insulation and both interior and exterior surfaces that are ready to cover with stucco or paint. The raw material consists of bags of plastic granules, which look like salt, imported from South Korea. Heated and extruded through a number of machines, the plastic is formed into blocks into which steel spreaders are fitted.

The plant provides jobs for four or five Hutterites, sometimes more when the machines are run for twenty-four hours to catch up with back orders. When we visited, the huge barn was stacked to the rooftop with relatively light and easily shipped bundles of prefabricated walls. At present, much of the output moves to Vancouver and southern British Columbia. The parent company, Airlite Plastics, has three other Canadian production centers: at Starbuck, Manitoba, Cap-Pelé, New Brunswick, and Montreal. The company handles management and sales, and the community's responsibilities are confined to manufacturing.

We had a chance to see Fox Blocks being used to construct new residences on the community. All the forty-year-old houses were being replaced. Stucco was being applied to the Fox Block walls on the outside of one house while the interior was completely finished and occupied. Windows with triple glazing and doors had been imported from Germany.[130]

Oak Bluff Community, Manitoba, like other Manitoba communities, was forced to look for a new enterprise when its hog business collapsed about a decade ago. It cast around for a green business opportunity. As steward Jack Maendel explained:

> There are too many [communities] in woodworking and metalworking already. We don't want to be copycats. We wanted something unique, and it is hard to find anything unique anymore.[131]

They came up with EcoPoxy, which uses bio-ingredients to make an odorless epoxy glue. Its advantages are that it uses renewable materials rather than an oil base, and can be more easily and safely used by DIY customers and professionals alike. At present, the product is made with linseed and cashew oil, but the company is experimenting with soybeans, which will cut costs significantly. The company has landed a government grant for

---

[130] Eastend Community, SK, handles imports of these top-of-the-line articles and distributes them to other communities. The door has six locks rather than just the customary one near the handle.

[131] Bill Redekop, "Hutterite colony carving out epoxy niche," *Winnipeg Free Press*, March 7, 2018.

$167,000 to enable it to develop its own laboratory facilities. There are fifteen employees, including five non-Hutterite chemists, salespeople, and accountants.

*Sand and Gravel*

Many communities in Alberta and Saskatchewan make use of the outwash sands and gravels that were deposited by the glaciers into open quarries to provide materials for use in constructing their communities and maintaining their roads. In some cases, they have invested in crushing and washing infrastructure. These communities sell sand and gravel to neighbours, contractors, and municipalities. Examples are: Cayley, Riverbend, and White Lake, all communities in Alberta. Peace View, British Columbia, is a special case. A small quarry on its newly acquired property turned out to have a valuable deposit of pea-sized gravel that hardly needed any treatment. The community has exploited this resource over the past decade and has ongoing contracts with the BC Roads Department. Further to the east, in Alberta, but still in the Peace River Country, Birch Meadows Community has a cement truck and carries out custom work for both private and municipal customers.

Several communities in central Alberta and Saskatchewan have exploited deposits of clay and sand to make pre-cast concrete walls. For example, Spring Ridge, near Wainwright, Alberta, began manufacturing walls for use in construction projects on the community in 2000.[132] In 2006, the community incorporated the enterprise as Twin Valley Precast, and began to sell to customers. In 2015, the plant was upgraded and expanded. It now has two bays, each with a 20-ton crane, and can handle large projects such as wall panels and oil pump bases. The Workers' Compensation Board has evaluated the operation to be quite separate from the farm operations, and has determined that the community should insure those Hutterites working in the plant.[133]

## Miscellaneous Enterprises

In the preceding paragraphs, we have attempted to outline many of the principal strategies used by the Hutterites to "beat the squeeze" and improve their returns. However, there are a multitude of individual in-

---

132 Jeremy Simes, "Alberta Hutterite Colony Ordered to Pay WCB Dues for Workers in Concrete Plant," *The Western Producer*, November 14, 2017, https://www.producer.com/daily/alberta-hutterite-colony-ordered-to-pay-wcb-dues-for-workers-in-concrete-plant/.

133 Claire Theobald, "Alberta Hutterite Colony Ordered to Pay WCB Dues for Workers in Concrete Business," *Edmonton Journal*, November 14, 2017, https://edmontonjournal.com/news/local-news/alberta-hutterite-colony-ordered-to-pay-wcb-dues-for-workers-in-concrete-business.

itiatives that fall outside our generalized categories. A few examples will hint at the breadth of these eclectic enterprises. Millerdale Community, South Dakota, has a flourishing business producing promotional items for companies, and teams of women rotate from kitchen and garden duties to work in the shop. When we visited, three young Hutterite women were minding a bank of eight automated sewing machines that were turning out baseball caps with embroidered company logos.[134] It takes hours to digitize each new pattern for the machines to copy. An older Hutterite in a wheelchair managed a laser-engraving machine that turned out knives and pens engraved with company names. They even customize three sizes of clocks for retirement gifts. At Lajord Community, Saskatchewan, steward Darius Hofer was having trouble finding a suitable weigh scale for the community's trucks. The community decided to build its own, but before it was installed, a neighbouring community bought it.[135] Since that time the community has kept building and selling the scales, keeping a stock on hand to meet the demand. Recent sales were to Hines Creek Community in the Peace River Country and to a community in Montana. Barrickman, Manitoba, exploits its proximity to the Trans Canada Highway to run a salvage business. Community members recover wrecked semi-trailers and sell their contents, whether it be women's clothing or chocolate bars. Then they either fix the rig or break it up for scrap and parts. Birch Hills, at Wanham, Alberta, does the same kind of work, although it also handles damaged grain bins and obsolete agricultural machinery.[136] Miami, Manitoba, runs a redolent but profitable tanning business. Community members process bison hides, moose and deer hides, as well as cattle, and make gloves, bridles, and leather goods. Finally, Ayers Ranch, in Montana, runs a popular meat shop that processes wild game during the hunting season, while Clear Lake, Alberta, promotes its "Traditional Hutterite Meats" online, boasting that its members have been producing meats since 1547.[137]

## Second Thoughts: Objections to Change

The leadership in some communities remains dubious about the wisdom of adopting light industrial enterprises. They fear that this change from the seasonal rhythms of agriculture, and the varied tasks which it implies, may be detrimental to the "Hutterite way."[138] These leaders envision their people harnessed to machines, their days arbitrarily divided

---

134 On-site visit, Millerdale Community, SD, May 16, 2018.
135 On-site visit, Lajord Community, SK, May 8, 2018.
136 On-site visit, Birch Hills Community, AB, July 17, 2013.
137 A date towards the end of the Hutterites' "Golden Period" in Moravia. Janzen and Stanton, *Hutterites in North America*, 20–22.
138 Hausmann, *Working at the Hutterites*, 56; and Janzen and Stanton, *Hutterites in North America*, 216.

into eight-hour shifts, and their ability to interact with their brothers and sisters inhibited by their specialized tasks and the safety equipment that they are forced to wear. They suggest that there could be resentment between those working in the warm dry conditions in the shop, and those facing the elements on the farm. They worry, too, that businesses dealing with customers and suppliers will increase the interaction between community members and the outside world, and they point to the fact that several communities have hired outside workers, thus bringing the outside world right into the community. Professor Kant described this problem graphically; she asked us to envision a young Hutterite working alongside a young man from the local town who is boasting about the truck he is saving for with his wages, or the stock-car races he is going to attend.[139]

We raised these points with the leaders of communities that had adopted light-manufacturing enterprises. They reported that their family men welcomed the regular hours in the shop, which allowed them more time at home. They argued that work in the plant and the coffee breaks in the rest area actually brought workers closer together.[140] They pointed out that shop managers are not "time management experts," and some of the leisurely tempo of work in the fields is carried over to work on the production line. The work must get done, but they are relaxed about timing; what does not get done today will get done tomorrow. Finally, they pointed out that not all young people are suited to farm life. One young Hutterite told us in no uncertain terms that he hated animals; one hopes he was fascinated by machines and computers. We asked Pauly Kleinsasser at Springfield Community, Manitoba, which employs twenty non-Hutterites, whether employing outsiders posed a threat to young Hutterites and their beliefs.[141] He replied that it all depended on how you bring up your young people. If they are firmly rooted and grounded in their faith, there is little danger of worldly influences.

In our—admittedly limited—experience, we found that light-manufacturing activities were regarded as just another set of possible jobs, adding diversity and interest to those offered on the farm. There was a lot of flexibility; men and women would spend a morning in the garden or the livestock barns and the afternoon in the shop. One steward explained that they were running behind on a contract for doors and windows, but that they would soon catch up when seeding was finished and extra hands

---

139  Interview with Professor Juanita Kant, South Dakota State University, Brookings, May 15, 2018.
140  Interview with Jonathan Maendel, Baker Community, MB, October 31, 2016.
141  On-site visit, Springfield Community, MB, May 12, 2018. Kleinsasser's thoughts were echoed by Wayne Waldner, Millbrook Community, SD, which has a number of non-Hutterites working in its feed mill. On-site visit, Millbrook Community, SD, May 16, 2018.

became available. Only a handful of communities rely entirely on manufacturing.

The growing number of communities engaged in various non-farm activities may result in competition with non-Hutterite companies. This is particularly true in the building supply industry. Construction companies in Manitoba asked the government to step in and end what they believed was an unfair advantage given to Hutterite competitors. Gino Koko, general sales manager of Vicwest, a company that manufactures metal building supplies, said:

> Every year they gain a bit more market share and they gain a bigger customer base. When the playing field is different and there's advantages that are outside something we could do, that's when we don't like the competition.[142]

But Jonathan Wollman of Newdale Community, the home of Domtek Building Supplies, ridiculed the idea that Hutterites do not have to pay wages:

> We have to pay the workers, not in the form of money, we pay them with a well-furnished house and three, four, or five meals a day. They [non-Hutterite companies] should take their employees, build them a house, furnish it, feed them, and totally look after them. They'd be surprised.[143]

Similar objections were voiced when Hutterville, South Dakota, sought a zoning change for its daughter community Sunrise, so that it could develop a blacksmith shop and garage for truck repairs.[144] Millbrook, South Dakota, also provoked a hostile response when it proposed a manufacturing plant for its daughter community Spruce Lane, North Dakota.[145]

There are dangers inherent in the adoption of non-farm activities, an important one being that manufacturing enterprises enjoy shorter product runs than is customary in farming. There is a constant need to reinvent

---

142 CBC News, "Hutterite Competition Worries Man. Firms," CBC/Radio Canada. November 8, 2010, https://www.cbc.ca/news/canada/manitoba/hutterite-competition-worries-man-firms-1.885702.
143 Ibid.
144 "JSR" wrote, "Giving exemption is a slap in the face to other businesses who are already in commercial classification. At this new shop no labour will be hired, no wages will be paid." JSR, July 8, 2015, comment on Cory Allen Heidelberger, "New Spink County Hutterite Colony may end Hutterville Conflict," *Dakota Free Press*, July 8, 2015, https://dakotafreepress.com/2015/07/08/new-spink-county-hutterite-colony-may-end-hutterville-conflict/.
145 "New Hutterite Colony Planned near Hillsboro," *Rapid City Journal*, December 19, 2011, https://rapidcityjournal.com/news/new-hutterite-colony-planned-near-hillsboro/article_5581dc70-29bb-11e1-ae9b-001871e3ce6c.html.

oneself, to innovate and to pursue new market niches, and to react to regulatory changes with respect to the environment or health and safety standards. But Hutterite businesses have established an enviable reputation for the quality of their workmanship and the reliability of their products. They display integrity and a commitment to excellence. Outside firms can establish contracts with the communities knowing that they are not going anywhere, and they can build trust, which gives Hutterite communities the stability they crave.

## Conclusion

To what extent have Hutterite communities adopted new enterprises to improve their bottom line and to accumulate capital? The concepts and language of diffusion theory are helpful in framing an answer to this question.[146] There are wide differences between the clan groups. The Schmiedeleut were "early adopters" and have pursued non-farm activities most vigorously. They started manufacturing enterprises during the 1980s, and with each success, more communities have 'come on board'. With 67% of Schmiedeleut communities reporting non-farm enterprises, they are classified as being in the "late majority" stage of diffusion. Their early adoption of new strategies owes much to the dynamic leadership of Jacob Kleinsasser, who acted as a "change agent," and to the *Leut*'s intense interaction over several decades with the Bruderhof in New York State, a group whose primary source of income comes from light manufacturing. More recently, escalating land prices have encouraged Schmiedeleut communities to look for alternatives to farming; when planning a daughter community they will purchase only enough land to ensure privacy and invest in manufacturing enterprises. These businesses will benefit from the expertise, skills, and contacts already fostered at the parent community.

Almost one third of Dariusleut communities have taken up some non-farm activities, placing them in the "early majority" category. There are pockets of innovation in central Alberta, like the communities around Holden, Iron Creek, and Viking, and also in the Peace River country. As far as we could see, few Dariusleut communities in the core area south of Lethbridge were transitioning to new manufacturing endeavours, and it is here that further change may be anticipated.

The Lehrerleut are still in the "early adopter" stage of diffusion, with less than 10% of communities involved with non-farm activities. This *Leut* is the most conservative of the clan groups and has the strongest inter-community organization, which may inhibit individual communities

---

146 Everett Rogers, *Diffusion of Innovations*, 5th ed. (New York: Simon and Schuster, 2003); for the geography of diffusion, see Lawrence A. Brown, *Diffusion Processes and Location* (Philadelphia: Regional Science Research Institute, 1968).

from innovating. Moreover, the Lehrerleut tend to have large, well-established farms, where the emphasis is upon grain production rather than livestock. So far, the communities in this group have reinvested in agriculture rather than manufacturing. It seems likely that some may follow the lead of Brant Community and look to slash energy costs by adopting new technology, while other Lehrerleut communities may look for ways to add value to their farm products.

The differences between clan groups are mirrored by those differences within each *Leut*. The communities blessed with vigorous entrepreneurial leadership and a willingness to take risks demonstrate innovation in not one but in several fields. For the sake of organizational clarity, various categories of non-farm enterprises have been discussed separately in this essay. In fact, some communities are pursuing a range of strategies. They may be investing in innovative energy solutions, while adding value to their agricultural products by processing and careful attention to marketing, and also pursuing one or more manufacturing activities. When I spent a morning with a community steward, I was impressed with the number of active files on his desk. These included reports on a new automated dairy barn, a soybean crushing plant, a solar energy project, and a plan to extend the community's gravel pit. At another community, I was shown the shop and manufacturing enterprise that had brought me to the community, and then the steward took me on a tour. We saw the new "drive-through" sheep barn, which had greatly increased returns by cutting down on losses during lambing. Then the steward explained that the community had doubled its acreage of potatoes because it had secured one of the first contracts with a new processing plant in Lethbridge. Success in one area spills over into others.

In complete contrast, there are communities in each of the clan groups where leadership does not have the drive or vision to pursue new paths.[147] They are risk averse and insist that what has been done in the past will continue to sustain them in the future. These are old communities, where it has been at least forty years since they split. Their population is aging, they are losing young people to the outside world, and the young men who remain find it hard to attract wives. Their housing stock is old and even their agricultural infrastructure is obsolescent. If one accepts the premise that the continuing health of Hutterite culture depends on finding the means to establish daughter communities when they are needed, then the

---

147 The following remarks should not be taken as an indictment of all communities which have not yet adopted non-farm activities. As explained earlier, some young communities will be employing all their capital to build up their farm, and all their tradespeople will be fully occupied.

dangers of not employing new strategies to generate capital far outweigh the risks inherent in innovation.

At the start of this project, we expected to be investigating a shift in emphasis from agriculture to light manufacturing industry that was 'revolutionary' in nature, involving precipitate change and resulting in tumult. How wrong we were. There has indeed been a steady expansion of non-farm enterprises on the communities, but it started decades ago and has proceeded at a measured pace. Innovation has been accommodated within the fabric of existing communities. Buildings once used for agriculture are now used for light engineering. Skills honed in community shops and used to build daughter communities and renovate older headquarters are now deployed in enterprises that help the community pay its way and accumulate capital. Only a handful of communities rely solely on manufacturing. In most cases, new ventures employ four or five Hutterite workers and earn some 10% of the community turnover. Agriculture remains an economic sheet anchor and a source of seed capital for new endeavours. What we observed was incremental change in response to a changing economic environment—a situation very close to that defined by Joseph Eaton as "controlled acculturation," and a process that will strengthen rather than threaten the continuity of the "Hutterite way."[148]

---

[148] Eaton defined controlled acculturation as "the process by which one culture accepts a practice from another culture, but integrates the new practice into its own existing value system." Eaton, "Controlled Acculturation," 338.

**Cheryl Rockman-Greenberg** (MD, CM, FRCPC, FCCMG) works at the Children's Hospital Research Institute of Manitoba and the Departments of Pediatrics and Child Health, and Biochemistry and Medical Genetics at the University of Manitoba. Dr. Rockman-Greenberg was inducted into the Canadian Medical Hall of Fame in 2018 and into the Order of Canada in 2019.

**A. Micheil Innes** (MD, FRCPC) works at the Departments of Pediatrics and Medical Genetics at the University of Calgary.

**J. Michael Charette** (PhD) works in the Department of Chemistry at Brandon University and at the Children's Hospital Research Institute of Manitoba.

# Genetic Research with the Hutterites: Its Importance and Projections for the Future

## CHERYL ROCKMAN-GREENBERG, A. MICHEIL INNES, and J. MICHAEL CHARETTE[1]

It is a privilege to contribute an essay in honour of the one-hundred-year anniversary of the arrival of the Hutterian Brethren on the Canadian prairies. As geneticists and university researchers, we are pleased to share some of the advances we have seen in understanding the cause of certain genetic conditions among Hutterites. One of our responsibilities as researchers is to ask questions for which there are limited answers, or no answers at all. As we discover better ways to answer these questions, we create new knowledge, which is our further responsibility to share.

The past thirty years have witnessed a rapid increase in the identification of the genetic basis for many genetic disorders, some of which have only been reported in people of Hutterite descent. With these gene discoveries has come the drive to better understand how errors in these genes cause disease. Gene identification now allows for the development of genetic tests that can be offered to individuals who wish to learn their genetic status for certain conditions and, possibly most importantly, permits the development of new strategies to treat genetic conditions that were previously both poorly understood and not treatable.

Gene discoveries have been possible not only because of the remarkable advances in technology and science but also because of the incredible

---

[1] The authors wish to thank the many colleagues with whom we have worked, especially Dr. Barbara Triggs-Raine, Dr. Klaus Wrogemann, Dr. Beth Spriggs, Dr. Teresa Zelinski, Gail Coghlan, Dr. Patrick Frosk, Dr. Joy Armistead, Dr. Jillian Parboosingh, Dr. Ryan Lamont, Dr. Francois Bernier, Caitlin Goedhart, Dr. Carole Ober, Dr. Ken Morgan, Dr. Mary Kujiwara, and Dr. Kym Boycott. We express our sincere appreciation to all the families who have shared their experiences and contributed so much to the advances in this research. This article is dedicated to the memory of Selma Maendel (1961–2014).

Selma Maendel (1961–2014) was instrumental in assisting researchers establish positive relationships with the Hutterite community.

support we have received from the Hutterite communities throughout the prairies. We are immensely grateful to all our Hutterite colleagues, true partners in our research endeavours; working in partnership with Hutterian families has allowed our work to flourish. In particular, we are indebted to Selma Maendel from Fairholme Community, a spokesperson for many Manitoba Hutterites who unfortunately passed away several years ago. Selma was the driving force behind forging and solidifying the partnership between Hutterite families and researchers. She was a champion for empowerment through knowledge, and for actively participating in even the most controversial of topics as a way to achieve understanding. Beginning in 1990, Selma, together with David Gross (Sommerfeld Community), helped organize many town hall meetings in Manitoba Hutterite communities, where we were able to share our research goals, progress, and challenges.

Even before Selma became such an important liaison between researchers and the Hutterite communities, many families had contributed blood samples for genetic studies conducted at different universities in the 1960s, '70s, and '80s. Their participation greatly furthered our understanding of human blood groups, especially the Rh factor, and many people became regular blood donors as a result—this can probably be considered the point where large family studies began.

Selma once shared a story from one of her favourite movies, *Ben-Hur*. The main character, Judah Ben-Hur, has returned home to find his former steward awaiting his return. The steward, who has lost both legs, has befriended a man with no tongue. The steward assures Ben-Hur that the two of them manage very well: the steward does the talking, and the friend, who is big and strong, can easily carry the diminutive steward wherever he needs to go. "Together," he tells Ben-Hur, "we make a considerable man!"

We are reminded of this line when we consider the realized strength and potential for the future as Hutterites and researchers continue to work together to improve the lives of Hutterian children and their families. In the remainder of this essay, we will first give a brief overview of the science of genetics and recent advances in genomic sequencing, then focus on genetic research among Hutterite communities and describe the progress that has been made in understanding a particular single gene disorder, Bowen-Conradi Syndrome.

## A Genetics Primer: It all Begins with a Recipe

The term "genetics" is now part of our everyday vocabulary. Whether we are talking about a gene for a common trait such as eye colour or height, or a gene associated with a disease, a gene is essentially a series of instructions that the cell reads and interprets. Much like a recipe with instructions that a cook follows in making a dish, genes are instructions read by a cell in making proteins. In turn, proteins are what make up most of the cell, allowing it to grow and do its designated jobs in the human body. Genes are made up of DNA, the double helix (two strands wound around each other) depicted so often in popular science. However, while words in the English language are made up of letters chosen from the twenty-six letters of the alphabet, there are only four letters that make up a gene. These, representing the four different molecules in DNA, are designated by the letters A, T, G, and C in the DNA alphabet. There are a total of three billion A, T, G, and C letters in every cell in our body. All genes are made up of these four letters, and the difference between genes lies in the number of letters and the order in which these letters appear. It is now believed that each cell in our body has approximately 25,000 distinct genes that code for proteins and that these genes are mostly located in the part of the cell known as the "nucleus"—the command centre. What makes a liver cell a liver cell and brain cell a brain cell is in many ways determined by which of the 25,000 genes are "turned on" and actively coded for protein, and which genes are "turned off."

## The Cookbook of Life

The past twenty years have seen an incredible revolution in genetics because of discoveries in a related discipline, namely that of genomics. By analogy, if a gene is the recipe for a protein, a genome is the cookbook, a collection of all the recipes—from appetizers to desserts—needed to make and maintain a cell. This new field of genomics, not even thirty years old, aims to catalogue the order of all the As, Ts, Gs, and Cs in a genome (the collection of all the DNA in a cell). The information allows for the identification of all the recipes, or genes in a genome. A problem that immediately arises is the enormous size of a genome. The human genome contains approximately 3,234,830,000 (over three billion) As, Ts, Gs, and Cs. To return to our analogy, all these letters would fill about 3,000 large books with around 25,000 different recipes.[2] Except it would be a 3,000-volume

---

2   This analogy is modified from Terence A. Brown, *Genomes*, 2nd ed. (New York: Wiley, 2002).

cookbook of recipes written in no particular order—appetizers mixed in with desserts—and without a table of contents.

## The Miracle of Technology

The first sequencing (determining the order of the As, Ts, Gs, and Cs) of the human genome remains one of the largest and most expensive scientific studies to date. Beginning in 1990, a team of over 1,000 scientists from the United States, the United Kingdom, France, Germany, Japan, and China worked for thirteen years to sequence the first human genome. On April 14, 2003, after spending around US$2.7 billion, the sequencing of the human genome was considered complete—the order of all the letters was determined. However, using our analogy of the 3,000-volume cookbook, the manual creation of a table of contents for the genes in the human genome (identifying where all the recipes are) remains incomplete some fifteen years later. In the meantime, the scientific community has seen a huge explosion of technical advances that have significantly reduced the time and resources needed to sequence the genome of one individual. Currently, genome sequencing can be done by one researcher over an afternoon and at a cost of less than $1,000. This dramatic improvement in feasibility has resulted in a number of research labs and hospitals embracing genome sequencing as a routine diagnostic strategy, transforming previously impossible research into standard studies.

The increasingly routine sequencing of the human genome has ushered in a new era of medicine. Genomic medicine can now make use of a patient's genomic information in the initial diagnosis of disease and then in selecting the most appropriate treatment. This is also known as "precision medicine," tailoring a specific treatment for a condition to the particular type of genetic problem associated with the disease in question. Specific changes (often called mutations) in the order of the As, Gs, Cs, and Ts in the genome have the effect of typos in the instruction manual of the cell and can cause disease—much as a recipe that calls for baking soda instead of baking powder will not turn out as well. In DNA, the effect of these misprints can range from the susceptibility to developing certain disorders to cancers and genetic diseases.

It is important to note that most changes in the order of the As, Gs, Cs, and Ts do not cause disease and are instead associated with normal human variations in height, hair and eye colour, and other differences—in the same way that swapping apples for peaches will result in an equally delicious pie. Therefore, genomic medicine is now confronted with an avalanche of data and the enormous task of comparing all three billion letters of one person's genome to that of another's, trying to distinguish between changes in the DNA letters that are part of normal human variation and those that are associated with disease. This important work can only be done through the collaboration of research scientists, physicians, and families who are willing to give DNA samples for genomic sequencing and can provide detailed, multi-generation family histories. This is where the Hutterite community offers a particular advantage and has already contributed greatly to our understanding of the genes that are involved in disease.

## Single Gene Disorders among Hutterites

Genetic disorders can result from an abnormality in the number or structure of chromosomes, the large units of heredity on which our genes are located, from an abnormality in a single gene, or from a combination of numerous genetic variants interacting with environmental factors. The discussion that follows focuses on research advances in our understanding of single gene disorders, specifically autosomal recessive conditions.

There are over 7,000 single gene disorders described in the general population, and only in about half of these diseases has the causative gene been identified.[3] Humans have two copies of every gene in their body: one copy from their mother and the other from their father. One type of single gene disorder is an autosomal recessive disorder, which can happen if both copies of a particular gene have a misprint. When an autosomal recessive disorder is diagnosed in an individual (whether Hutterite or non-Hutterite), both parents usually prove to be "carriers" of one copy of the genetic misprint. Individuals who carry a single copy of a misprint in a gene typically do not have any signs or symptoms of the disorder in question, as one normal gene copy is usually sufficient to prevent disease—it is only when an individual inherits a copy of the genetic misprint from each parent that they may develop an autosomal recessive disorder.

The Hutterite population has made a disproportionately large contribution to the identification of many autosomal recessive disorders and their causative genes. At least thirty-six single gene disorders have been described in individuals of Hutterite descent.[4] Multiple new single gene diseases and disease-causing variants continue to be reported. However, there are still Hutterite patients who remain undiagnosed, in spite of modern gene technology.

---

3  Ibid.
4  Caitlin Goedhart, "Further Delineation of the Genetic Architecture of Rare Genetic Disease in the Hutterite Population to Better Inform Patient Care," University of Calgary, 2018.

The carrier frequency for many of the autosomal recessive disorders seen in Hutterites is often between one in five to one in ten individuals. This is higher than the carrier frequency for most autosomal recessive conditions in the general population. The explanation for this relates to the fact that the approximately 45,000 Hutterites of today living on colonies on the prairies in Canada and the United States are the descendants of a much smaller number of individuals who came from Europe to North America in the late 1800s.[5] Population bottlenecks (when the population shrinks to a small number of individuals), coupled with reproductive isolation and population expansion, have resulted in the distinct group of genetic disorders that are over-represented and, in some cases, unique to the Hutterites. Both demographic and genetic studies indicate that shortly after the founding of the Hutterites, individuals from South Tyrol in Austria, Germany, and Switzerland settled to form a thriving population in Moravia. After being banished in the early seventeenth century to Transylvania, Hutterite numbers dwindled to a low of only sixty-seven individuals—the genetic bottleneck. In 1770, persecution forced them to Ukraine, where they were granted religious freedom and amnesty from military service. However, in 1874, this amnesty was revoked, causing 1,265 Hutterites to emigrate to the United States. During World War I, Hutterites moved to the Canadian prairie provinces of Manitoba, Alberta, and Saskatchewan to avoid the mandatory military draft that is contrary to Hutterite pacifist beliefs. Since that time, the Hutterites have been one of the most rapidly growing populations in the world, with over 450 communities across central and western Canada and the United States as of 2019: 107 communities in Manitoba, sixty in Saskatchewan, 168 in Alberta, two in British Columbia, fifty-four in South Dakota, seven in North Dakota, nine in Minnesota, fifty in Montana, and five in Washington State.[6]

Just like the rest of the population, where everyone carries three to four silent genetic misprints, Hutterite founders also carried misprints in different autosomal recessive genes. With successive generations, it is not unexpected that both husband and wife could emerge as carriers for recessive misprints in the same gene and that autosomal recessive conditions would appear in their offspring. It should be noted that Hutterites, as well as individuals in the general population, are often carriers for more than one recessive misprint. This is only of clinical significance if both the husband and wife are carriers of a misprint in the same gene. In that case, there is a one in four chance in every pregnancy that a child will inherit two copies of the misprint, one from each parent, and thus be affected with the condition in question.

---

5   Hutterian Brethren website, http://www.hutterites.org/.
6   Ibid.

## Bowen-Conradi Syndrome

Bowen-Conradi Syndrome (BCS) is an example of a single gene disorder that is possibly unique to the Hutterite community. The condition, which has not been confirmed in the general population, is an autosomal recessive disorder that occurs when a child is born with two copies of a misprint in the gene known as the EMG1 gene. Parents who are the carriers of one copy of this EMG1 misprint have no signs or symptoms of BCS, as one normal EMG1 gene copy is sufficient for normal functioning of the cell. Children who have inherited a copy of the EMG1 misprint from each parent, however, are born very small and do not grow and develop like children without BCS. In addition to remaining small, they have difficulty eating and swallowing and experience severe developmental problems. They usually have distinctive facial appearances (prominent nasal root, small jaw) and often have curved fingers and feet in the shape of the rockers of a rocking chair. Sadly, children with BCS typically only live for a few days to a few years, with the average life expectancy of thirteen months. At the present time, there is no known medical treatment or drug available specifically to treat BCS.

BCS was first described in the medical literature in 1976 as a distinct genetic condition in Hutterite children by two physicians at the University of Alberta, Dr. Peter Bowen (a specialist in internal medicine and genetics) and Dr. Gerhard Conradi (a pediatrician).[7] A subsequent paper was published in 1979 by Dr. Alasdair Hunter and colleagues,[8] describing in more detail the features of BCS and the evidence that it is an autosomal recessive disorder affecting males and females equally. It is believed that the genetic misprint that causes BCS likely was present in the Hutterite population in the 1500s, centuries before the first emigration to North America. It was not until 2009, thirty years after Dr. Hunter's research was published, that the research team of Dr. Barbara Triggs-Raine (University of Manitoba Department of Biochemistry and Medical Genetics, and the Children's Hospital Research Institute of Manitoba) identified the EMG1 gene responsible for BCS.[9] Fortunately, the function of EMG1 had been

---

7   P. Bowen and G.J. Conradi, "Syndrome of Skeletal and Genitourinary Anomalies with Unusual Facies and Failure to Thrive in Hutterite Sibs," *Birth Defects Original Article Series* 12, no. 6 (1976), 101–108.
8   A.G. Hunter, S.J. Woerner, L.D. Montalvo-Hicks, S.B. Fowlow, R.H. Haslam, P.J. Metcalf, et al., "The Bowen-Conradi Syndrome—A Highly Lethal Autosomal Recessive Syndrome of Microcephaly, Micrognathia, Low Birth Weight, and Joint Deformities," *American Journal of Medical Genetics* 3, no. 3 (1979), 269–279.
9   J. Armistead, S. Khatkar, B. Meyer, B.L. Mark, N. Patel, G. Coghlan, et al., "Mutation of a Gene Essential for Ribosome Biogenesis, EMG1, Causes Bowen-Conradi Syndrome," *American Journal of Human Genetics* 84, no. 6 (June 2009), 728–739.

### Arrhythmogenic Cardiomyopathy (*DSC2*)

This serious cardiac disorder causes failure of contraction of the muscle of both the right and left chambers (ventricles) of the heart, abnormal electrical activity and rhythm disturbances, as well as aneurysms of the heart muscle of the left ventricle, and can lead to sudden death in young adults.

### Beaulieu-Boycott-Innes syndrome (*THOC6*)

In this condition affected individuals show variable degrees of intellectual disability with a small head size associated with characteristic facial features including a high forehead, deep-set eyes, a relatively long nose, and dental problems. There may or may not be congenital heart and kidney problems.

### Bardet-Biedl syndrome (*BBS2*)

This is one form of Bardet–Biedl syndrome which can have the following: obesity, decreased vision due to retinitis pigmentosa (abnormal pigment deposits in the retina), extra fingers, abnormal pubertal development, and kidney disease. Learning problems may also be present.

### Bowen-Conradi syndrome (*EMG1*)

The features of this disorder are usually readily apparent at birth. The baby is often underweight compared to a full-term baby, has stiff joints, and has distinct "rocker bottom feet." These babies often do not grow well, gain weight very slowly, and have severe developmental delay. There is no known effective treatment as yet.

### Carnitine Palmitoyltransferase 1 deficiency (*CPT1A*)

This is a "metabolic" disorder that results from decreased activity of an enzyme called CPT1A. CPT1A is a key enzyme that allows fatty acids to be metabolized to meet the energy needs of cells and to keep blood sugar level normal. Individuals who have CPT1A deficiency are prone to low blood sugar and other metabolic problems, especially during times of illness. All newborns are screened for this disorder and there is effective treatment.

### Cerebellar atrophy, short stature or CASS (*SLC39A8*)

This condition affects children who have an undeveloped cerebellum (part of the brain which helps control coordination), short stature, and manganese deficiency.

### Combined pituitary hormone deficiency (*PROP1*)

In this condition several hormones that are produced by the pituitary gland in the brain are lacking. An abnormality in the PROP1 gene leads to low levels of thyroid hormone and cortisol as well as hormones important for normal puberty. The first signs of this condition can be slow growth and short stature.

### Congenital hyperinsulinism (*ABCC8*)

In this condition babies have very high levels of insulin circulating in their blood and this results in a very low blood sugar, which can cause seizures. The high levels of insulin are produced by an abnormal collection of insulin-producing cells in the pancreas. There is effective treatment.

**Table 1.** Select autosomal disorders seen in Hutterite individuals. The responsible gene is in italics in brackets after the name of the disorder

Table 1 continued

### Cranioectodermal dysplasia (*DPH1*)

This condition is characterized by bony abnormalities, including early fusion of skull bones, narrow rib cage, short limbs and fingers, and skin abnormalities. Some affected individuals can develop progressive kidney problems and problems with vision have also been described.

### Cystic Fibrosis (*CFTR*)

This condition causes lung and digestive problems due to abnormally thick mucous produced by sweat glands in the lungs and pancreas. Treatment advances have greatly improved the outcome of both children and adults with cystic fibrosis. It is also more commonly seen in people who are of northern European ancestry.

### Dilated cardiomyopathy with ataxia syndrome or DCMA (*DNAJC19*)

This condition affects children and causes variable degrees of developmental problems, an unsteady gait, and poor coordination. It can be associated with heart problems, specifically a weakened, enlarged heart muscle and an irregular heartbeat.

### Hypophosphatasia (*ALPL*)

This condition is a disorder of bone mineralization where calcium and phosphorus do not deposit normally in bones. It has only been reported once in a Hutterite baby.

### Joubert syndrome (*TMEM237*)

This disorder is associated with an underdeveloped cerebellum and an abnormally formed brain stem with a characteristic finding on brain MRI called the "molar tooth sign." Affected children show low body tone, slow motor development, poor control of muscle function, abnormal breathing patterns, and a variable degree of intellectual disability.

### Leigh disease (*NDUFS4*)

This severe neurological disorder of energy metabolism presents in early childhood with loss of motor and cognitive skills, is associated with seizures, and leads to severe disability and often early loss of life.

### Limb girdle muscular dystrophy 2H (*TRIM32*)

This is a type of muscular dystrophy, meaning there is slow loss of muscle strength, especially involving the muscles around the hips and shoulders. This results in difficulty walking, problems going up and down stairs or getting up from a seated position in a chair, as well as difficulty lifting objects above the head. This condition usually begins to manifest in adolescence or early adulthood and is generally very slowly progressive, but is also highly variable from one affected person to another. There is no known treatment to prevent the muscle weakness in this form of muscular dystrophy.

### Limb girdle muscular dystrophy 2I (*FKRP*)

This form of muscular dystrophy is similar to limb girdle muscular dystrophy 2H, but in limb girdle muscular dystrophy 2I, the heart muscle can also be affected, leading to heart failure or a disturbance in the heart rhythm. These heart complications if they arise can be treated with medications and a pacemaker if necessary.

Table 1 continued

### Limb girdle muscular dystrophy 2S (*TRAPPC11*)

LGMD 2S is a form of limb girdle muscular dystrophy associated with muscle weakness, but some affected patients can also show excessive movements or unusual posturing of the limbs and developmental delay.

### Methylmalonic aciduria (*MUT*)

This is a metabolic disorder in which the body is unable to process certain amino acids and fatty acids properly. Affected infants develop vomiting, dehydration, poor feeding, poor weight gain and growth, as well as acidosis and liver failure. The form of methylmalonic aciduria seen in Hutterite infants is a very severe one and treatment is not generally effective in reversing the signs and symptoms.

### Nephronophthisis-juvenile (*NPHP1*) and (*KIAA1009*)

In this condition cystic kidneys leads to kidney failure in childhood or adolescence.

### Oculocutaneous albinism (*TYR*)

Individuals with this condition lack pigment in their skin, hair, and eyes causing their skin to be very fair and their hair to be almost white. The lack of pigment in the usually coloured part of the eye known as the iris and the light-sensitive tissue at the back of the eye known as the retina causes increased sensitivity to light, decreased visual acuity, and shaky movements of the eye known as nystagmus. The skin must be protected from the sun to reduce the risk of skin cancer.

### Non-syndromic sensorineural deafness, DFNB1 (*GJB2*)

The form of deafness is sensorineural in nature, i.e., nerve deafness, and is present from birth. Non-syndromic means there are no other associated features.

### Non-syndromic mental retardation (*TECR*)

This is a hereditary form of intellectual disability with no other associated features such as congenital malformations or known biochemical abnormalities.

### Restrictive dermopathy (*ZMPSTE24*)

This is a very severe disorder where affected babies are born with very tense and translucent skin, severe joint contractures, and underdeveloped lungs. Affected babies are not able to live very long.

### Segawa syndrome (*TH*)

This is a neurological condition that presents as a progressive movement disorder with abnormal posturing and stiffness of the arms and legs. The condition can be very debilitating but very effective treatment specifically with the drug dopamine is available, which dramatically reverses the neurological problems. Treatment with dopamine is needed lifelong.

### Sitosterolemia (*ABCG8*)

This rare condition is associated with excessive absorption and decreased excretion of plant sterols ("phyto"sterols) leading to high cholesterol and early development of atherosclerosis.

### Succinylcholine sensitivity (*BCHE*)

In this condition there is deficiency of the enzyme that metabolizes the drug succinylcholine, a drug often used by anesthetists who are giving a general anesthetic prior to surgery. Anesthetists usually avoid using succinylcholine when administering a general anesthetic to Hutterite individuals.

Table 1 continued

---

**Thyroid dyshormonogenesis (SLC5A5)**

One of the many causes of an underactive thyroid gland is this genetic disorder, which is characterized by a lack of iodide transport in the thyroid gland to make mature thyroid hormone. This condition is identified at birth on newborn screening and when treatment is started very early in life it is completely treatable.

**Usher syndrome Type 1B, (MYO7A)**

There are 2 forms of Usher syndrome seen in Hutterite people, Usher syndrome type 1B and Usher Syndrome type 1F. Both have a combination of hearing loss present from birth and visual impairment caused by abnormal development of the retina, with symptoms of night blindness, tunnel vision, and progressive visual loss.

**Usher syndrome Type 1F (PCDH15)**

Similar to Usher syndrome Type 1B, see above.

**VLDLR with cerebellar hypoplasia (VLDLR)**

In this condition there is early onset of an unsteady gait, poor balance, mild tremor, slurred speech, and developmental delay. There is also an underdeveloped cerebellum.

---

described a few years earlier in 2001[10] as a protein involved in the assembly of ribosomes, molecular machines found in all cells that translate genetic information into proteins. Thus, the discovery that a specific misprint in the EMG1 gene caused BCS established the root cause of the disease as problems in the assembly of the ribosome.

The Hutterite community was very instrumental in the research effort to track down and identify the disease-causing BCS gene. This success was the direct result of the community's openness and willingness to participate by providing DNA samples through cheek swabs, blood samples, and further genealogical information.

Identifying the source of the problem is the first step in being able to propose new avenues for research, which we hope will ultimately lead to better treatments. Now, some ten years after the discovery of the relationship between the EMG1 gene and BCS, we still don't fully understand EMG1's role in the cell, though a number of possibilities are being pursued. One of the labs researching the role of the EMG1 protein and the cause of BCS is Dr. Michael Charette's laboratory at Brandon University.

Table 1 lists some of the single gene disorders and their responsible genes that have been described in Hutterite communities. For many of these disorders, definitive treatment is available; for others, no specific treatment has been identified yet, but genetic counselling and carrier test-

---

10  P.C.C. Liu and D.J. Thiele, "Novel Stress-Responsive Genes EMG1 and NOP14 Encode Conserved, Interacting Proteins Required for 40S Ribosome Biogenesis," *Molecular Biology of the Cell* 12, no. 11 (Nov. 2001), 3644–3657.

ing for individuals and families involved are available for many of these autosomal recessive conditions in genetic centres across the prairies and throughout Canada. Genetic counselling and genetic testing are always voluntary and a personal decision. Results of such testing are only shared with the individual requesting or offered testing and his or her care provider. As well, newborn screening, which is routine for all newborns in Canada, can detect some of the autosomal recessive conditions seen in Hutterite children. This allows treatment, if available, to be started before any symptoms of the condition in question become apparent and can sometimes be beneficial in slowing the progression of the disorder.

## The Future

Research on the Hutterite population of Manitoba is and continues to be successful because of the strong partnership established between members of the Hutterite community and local researchers and clinicians. The rapid development of new technologies, such as faster and more economical genome sequencing methods, will facilitate the identification of new genetic misprints along with better genetic screening and diagnostic methods. This will be coupled with our rapidly increasing understanding of the fundamental mechanisms of health and disease. The ultimate goal of researchers and clinicians is always to generate new knowledge at the service of society—be it by increasing our understanding, alleviating pain, providing better management options, or proposing new treatment options. When we walk together, knowledge is indeed empowering![11]

---

11  The website of the Canadian Association of Genetic Counsellors (https://www.cagc-accg.ca/) lists all the genetic centres across Canada and is an excellent resource on how to access more information about genes and genetic disorders.

**Jesse D. Hofer** is a high school teacher at Silverwinds Community, Sperling, Manitoba. He graduated from Canadian Mennonite University (2008) and serves as a member of the Hutterian Brethren Education Committee.

# Building Capacity for Communal Conversation: *Gemeindeordnungen*[1] and Discernment in the Hutterite World

## JESSE D. HOFER

On January 30, 2018, Schmiedeleut Group I pastors and stewards met at Acadia Community for the first conference since Arnold Hofer was elected *Ältester* (elder) on August 30, 2017.[2] The principal issue on the agenda was how to proceed with the conference's broken relationship with Schmiedeleut Group II.[3] In 1992, the Schmiedeleut Conference of the Hutterian Brethren suffered a painful schism that led to the creation of separate constitutions and church conferences.[4] In the years since 1992, much of Group I's ecclesial energies had been devoted to navigating the aftermath of the division. Of particular concern were the policies surrounding intermarriage and interaction between the two groups.

At the inaugural January conference, participants had the opportunity to speak about the issue for several hours in an open microphone format.

---

1 *Gemeindeordnungen* are communal orders or regulations designed to guide or instruct members of the church community. Synonyms include: orders, regulations, ordinances. In some ways, *Gemeindeordnungen* are similar to monastic orders, such as the Order of St. Benedict. Traditionally, *Gemeindeordnungen* are made and revised at an annual conference of ministers. In this essay, I will use *Ordnungen* as a shorthand for *Gemeindeordnungen*.
2 All male Schmiedeleut members vote to elect an elder. The ordained minister with the most votes becomes the new elder. A meeting is held, usually at the predecessor's community, to announce the new elder.
3 Arnold Hofer and Samuel Waldner to "*alle Gruppe 1-Schmiedenleut Hutterer-Gemeinden in Manitoba, Kanada; Minnesota, Nord und Süd Dakota, USA* [all Group I Schmiedeleut Hutterite Communities in Manitoba, Canada; Minnesota, North and South Dakota, USA]," January 15, 2018.
4 See Ian Kleinsasser, "Voices of Conflict: A Perspective of the 1992 Schmiedeleut Church Schism" in this publication for a more detailed account of the church division.

Following the sharing of personal reflections and the exchange of diverse viewpoints on how best to proceed on this issue, it was decided that the church[5] would initiate a policy of "cautious openness" toward Group II communities in an attempt to cultivate a healthier relationship between the two groups. In addition to opening the floor for participants to express their concerns, questions, and longings, *Ältester* Arnold Hofer emphasized the need for leaders to initiate and lead conversations with their respective congregations about this issue.

## A Call for Communal Discernment

Several days after the conference, Arnold Hofer reminded ministers about their responsibility to initiate discussions in their local communities about how the church division had been handled in their respective case:

> This brief letter is a reminder that I have requested that all ministers should address their communities in a spirit of openness about how our group has dealt with the division in the past twenty years. I want to encourage you and all our brothers and sisters to share what is on their hearts without fear of repercussion. Particularly I am concerned with how we as *Prediger* have had to draw hard lines; where this was done with unkind words toward our brothers and sisters—the sheep we are tending—let us lead the way and say, "*Es tut mir Leid*. [I am sorry.]"[6]

The fact that this reminder was sent out so soon after the conference highlights the significance of this point for the church's leaders.

The instruction that leaders communicate with their congregations about issues addressed at a church conference is not new. Elder Arnold Hofer's predecessor, Jacob Kleinsasser, who served as elder from 1978–2017, frequently urged his fellow "servants of the Word" to communicate church policies and decisions to their community members, although in many cases, his exhortations seem to have fallen on deaf ears. What is new in this church memorandum is that it makes it incumbent upon ministers to lead discussions in their respective communities about how they have dealt with the issue of the church division in general, and in particular, how they have treated members with respect to visiting rights for Group II relatives. The assumption is that some leaders have not dealt wisely or sensitively with this matter and they are expected to acknowledge this and change their ways. It is also noteworthy that actions which may have been

---

5 "Church" is used here for simplicity's sake to denote the Schmiedeleut Group I Conference of the Hutterian Brethren.
6 Arnold Hofer to [Schmiedeleut I] ministers, February 3, 2018.

seen as a sign of faithfulness earlier, namely taking a stand for the church, are now being called out as a problematic abuse of power. For close to twenty-five years, many ministers had acted as gatekeepers who enforced church policies around shunning in their respective communities, often without much community-level dialogue; now, their actions were being called into question by new church leadership. Clearly, these developments reflect an important shift in Schmiedeleut I church polity and deserve careful attention and reflection.

The February communication was followed about a month later by the official conference report, which reiterated the need for congregational-level dialogue and discernment with respect to the church division:

> Ministers are reminded of their important assignment clearly outlined in the letter dated the third of February 2018. It stated that each community must have its own discussion on how members stand in regard to the state of affairs with our church division and, where needed, repent for slander, lovelessness, and injustice. Ministers, in particular, have the task to listen with open hearts and gentleness because they have an important responsibility toward those who experienced pain and trauma due to the division. This openness will make the way to reconciliation and healing possible in cases where power and authority were unwisely wielded and abused.[7]

Building on the February document, the official report goes further by highlighting the need for renewal through effective leadership, communal dialogue, self-examination, confession, and repentance. Ministers are reminded that they have a special responsibility to listen to their members and acknowledge hurts and injustices, especially with respect to the handling of the policy of *Meidung* in connection with the church division. The emphasis on grassroots discussion is seen as fundamental for paving the way for reconciliation at the church level.

There is much to celebrate and affirm about these developments at the Group I Conference level. First, it is encouraging to see the tradition of *Gemeindeordnungen* in the form of a conference letter addressing the broader Hutterite church being revived, albeit in a modified form and tone. There is a noticeable shift away from specific rules governing behaviours to general exhortation and instruction that invites further reflection and discussion. While the church's tradition of guiding its members through annual *Gemeindeordnungen* at the conference level is not without its

---

[7] Arnold Hofer and Samuel Waldner to "all Hutterite communities of Schmiedeleut Group I...," Schmiedeleut Group I Conference Report, March 8, 2018.

problems, the absence of *Gemeindeordnungen* is arguably even more problematic. Second, the official conference report draws attention to the significant issue of how Hutterite *Prediger* understand and exercise leadership, an issue that has been plaguing the church for some time.[8] Leaders bear a special responsibility to regularly communicate church issues and policies to their congregations, as well as to initiate and facilitate discussion about issues of common concern. Unfortunately, some leaders used the period of uncertainty and instability following the 1992 schism to shore up their power, leaving many members indifferent and deeply disillusioned with their leaders and communal life. Finally, the emphasis on involving the wider church membership—the brothers and sisters who comprise the church, the body of Christ—in meaningful congregational-level discernment and conversation is an encouraging development.

Despite the hopeful tone and message of the 2018 conference report, some significant obstacles stand in the way of its implementation to any meaningful extent. It is difficult to imagine how the church's recent shift in policy can have the intended effect when many of its leaders lack the necessary skills or inclination to invite open conversation and wider participation within their congregations. In the rest of this essay, I will explore how an unhealthy or deficient culture of discussion and discernment within many communities will likely conflict with the recent policy of "cautious openness" in the Schmiedeleut Group I Conference with respect to how their communities wrestle with the church division. Part of the challenge confronting the church is a recent shift in the form and function of the *Ordnungen*, which have provided moral guidance since the beginning of the Hutterite movement; navigating this transition well is of utmost importance. Several biblical and theological reasons why conversation is vital for the life and witness of the church will be examined. Finally, a number of examples and practical suggestions for developing a stronger, healthier culture of discernment will be considered. It is my hope that this can become a starting point for rich discussions around these vital questions as we seek to be more faithful witnesses to the *Gemeinschaftsleben* (communal life) that God is calling us to.

## Evolution of *Gemeindeordnungen* among Hutterites

In 1527, Swiss Anabaptists met at the border town of Schleitheim to debate and discuss the common convictions they shared in the dynamic early years of the Anabaptist movement. The outcome of the conference was a document known as "Brotherly Union," or the "Schleitheim Confes-

---

8    Leonard Gross to "the Dariusleut, Lehrerleut and Schmiedeleut," May 19, 1993. See also Peter Riedemann's letter addressing the issue of "double honour" in early Hutterite congregations in *The Chronicle of the Hutterian Brethren*, 200–209.

sion," one of the earliest Anabaptist orders. Its purpose was to seek unity among a minority movement in danger of fragmentation and to provide practical guidance on how Anabaptist believers and communities ought to order or conduct themselves.

Early Hutterites followed this example of writing church ordinances to establish an orderly community life. One example is the Community Order of 1529, which outlines, among other things, how leaders should serve the needs of the people, how members should be disciplined, and how *Gütergemeinschaft* (community-of-goods) should be practiced.[9] Significantly, the seventh point in the Order deals with how to conduct healthy conversations as a community: "At community gatherings only one should speak and the rest listen and judge what is spoken, and not two or three standing at once. No one should curse or swear and pursue idle chatter so that the weak are spared."[10] From the beginning, Hutterites recognized the importance of effective communal conversation.

As the charismatic leadership of the Jakob Hutter era (1533–35) was gradually formalized and institutionalized, *Gemeindeordnungen* became more prominent. The earliest *Schulordnung* was produced in 1558 under Leonard Lanzenstiel and updated numerous times by Peter Walpot (1565–78) in 1568 and Hans Krӓl (1578–83) in 1578.[11] Its purpose was to instruct schoolmasters and schoolmothers on how to properly care for the children in a boarding school context. The *Kuchlordnung* regulated the roles in the communal kitchen and gave dietary guidelines for different groups of people. Krӓl described the late-sixteenth-century Hutterite mindset with respect to *Ordnungen* in this way: "There has to be order in all areas for the matters of life can be properly maintained and furthered only where order reigns—even more so in the house of God whose mas-

---

9 See Werner Packull, *Hutterite Beginnings*, 33–37. Although the Hutterite *Chronicle* dates it to 1529, Friedmann argues for an earlier date. In any case, it is significant that this Order (also known as the Church Discipline) and not the Schleitheim Confession was included in what eventually became *Das Große Geschichtsbuch*, the first volume of *The Chronicle of the Hutterian Brethren*. However, the Schleitheim Confession was included in at least one Hutterite codex. See Josef von Beck, *Die Geschichts-Bücher der Wiedertäufer in Oesterreich-Ungarn [Schriften der Wiener Akademie der Wissenschaften]*, F.R.A. 2, 43 (Vienna, 1883), 41–44.
10 *The Chronicle of the Hutterian Brethren*, vol. 1 (Rifton: Plough Publishing House, 1987), 78. The original found in *Das Große Geschichtsbuch* reads: "*Zum siebenten: In der Gemein Versammlung soll Einer reden, die andern zuhören und richten, was geredt wird, und nicht zwei oder drei zusammen stehn. Keiner soll fluchen oder schwören und daß kein unnütz Geschwätz getrieben werden, auf daß der Schwachen verschont werde*," 61.
11 The earliest *Schulordnung* was produced in 1558 under Leonard Lanzenstiel (1542–65). See Martin Rothkegel, "*Die älteste Schulordnung: Ein Ordnungszettel von 1558*," *Mennonitische Geschichtsblätter* 55 (1998), 85–105.

ter builder is the Lord himself. Where there is no order there is disorder. There God does not dwell, and the house soon collapses."[12]

Throughout the sixteenth and seventeenth centuries a number of new *Gemeindeordnungen* were produced. Some regulated the work departments, acting as a form of quality control, while others addressed spiritual concerns such as commitment to *Gütergemeinschaft* and non-violence. During his eldership when communities were ravaged by the Thirty Years War, Andreas Ehrenpreis (1639–1662) attempted to reverse the community's decline by writing, collecting, and enforcing a number of these orders.[13] Later Hutterites relied on these church orders to organize their communities and inform their decision-making process. For example, when communalism was revived in Transylvania in the early 1760s, the brothers and sisters "were led to establish and maintain true Christian order for their practical and spiritual life."[14] Among other documents, they looked to the old School Order for direction. Later, when the community in Russia was embroiled in a bitter dispute about the proper mode of prayer, they "searched carefully through our forefathers' writings" for guidance.[15] According to chronicler and elder Johannes Waldner, the purpose of recording the community's conflicts was "to warn against any of us presuming to introduce a new practice he has invented himself and thereby alter, disturb, and displace the old, well-proved order of the church."[16]

As elder, Johannes Waldner showed remarkable openness to other groups, especially the Moravian Brethren. He corresponded regularly with Johann Wiegand, the Moravian minister at Sarepta, and he clearly admired their devotion and piety.[17] Writing as the official Hutterite chronicler in about 1781, Waldner lamented the breakdown of the order of worship introduced by *Ältester* Hans Kleinsasser and the departure of Mathies Hofer.

> I do not mean to commend this neglect, nor am I glad for it. The gatherings for prayer and especially the reading at midday helped build up the young people's faith. As previously described, each read in turn and so each was involved, and it often led to a talk about the meaning of

---

12 *The Chronicle of the Hutterian Brethren*, vol. 2 (Ste. Agathe: Crystal Spring Colony, 1998), 761.
13 Wes Harrison, *Andreas Ehrenpreis and Hutterite Faith and Practice* (Kitchener: Pandora Press, 1997). See especially Chapters 3 and 4.
14 *The Chronicle of the Hutterian Brethren*, vol. 2, 393.
15 Ibid., 493.
16 Ibid., 495.
17 Astrid von Schlachta, *"Holding Fast to What is Good? Tradition and Renewal in Hutterite History,"* trans. Jesse Hofer (MacGregor: Hutterian Brethren Book Centre, 2020), 41–42.

a passage of Holy Scripture. At that time each one took pains to be able to read out the Scriptures fluently, and such a practice could still be used with a good conscience today. Now each young brother wants to have a good, well-bound Bible with big print, but many of them (always excepting the zealous) know little of what is inside. Paul taught in 1 Thessalonians 5:2, "Prove all things hold fast to what is good." It would have been possible to drop what was unnecessary and exaggerated and to keep what was good. But each can judge the matter as he sees fit.[18]

This passage clearly shows that Waldner was able to critically evaluate how the church's orders impacted the spiritual life of the church community, and he was confident that the community could have discerned a prudent way forward.

In the twentieth century, Hutterite church orders increasingly focused on the minutiae of dress code, home furnishing, and technology; overall, they sought to limit contact with the non-Hutterite world and cultivate an ascetic piety. In the second half of the twentieth century, both *Ältester* Joseph Kleinsasser (served 1967–1978) and *Ältester* Jacob Kleinsasser (served 1978–2017) resisted creating new *Gemeindeordnungen*. Instead, they favoured a policy of moral instruction and intrinsic motivation or conversion that is closer to the philosophy of chronicler Johannes Waldner (served 1794–1824), who observed, perhaps somewhat nostalgically, "Regulations for daily work were not present in the beginning nor were they necessary since each member in a right, simple, and child-like spirit, served God and the devout with all faithfulness and each gave freely of his entire ability."[19] A well-known proverb among Hutterites is that it takes more wisdom to write a new *Ordnung* than to observe it: "*Es get herter eh gueta Ordnung mochn, as wie ahna holtn* [It is more difficult to make a good ordinance than to maintain one]."

---

18  *The Chronicle of the Hutterian Brethren*, vol. 2, 504–505. The first three sentences of this passage appear in all caps, suggesting an emphasis by the author.

19  *The Chronicle of the Hutterian Brethren*, vol. 2, 761. This quotation contrasts with the one cited in footnote 16. Perhaps one reflects the outlook of a younger, more idealistic leader and the latter, the thought of a leader who has experienced considerable upheaval in his community. In this essay, I use Hans Kräl and Johannes Waldner as representatives of two ways of thinking about *Ordnungen* and as two possible ways forward for Hutterites today. The historical characters very likely would not correspond neatly to this dichotomy, since the historical reality is always much more complex than such a sharp dualism would allow. Indeed, one can see how in some ways, Waldner was very cautious and conservative, while in other respects he was open to new ideas and willing to try new things to inspire the community he led.

It could be said that the tension between Kräl's emphasis on external order via communal ordinances and Waldner's emphasis on the spiritual basis for an orderly communal life was one of the factors that contributed to the 1992 Schmiedeleut church schism. In general, Schmiedeleut Group II has emphasized the use of ordinances to regulate dress, technology, and home furnishings, while Group I has been more drawn to education and missions as the means of moral formation. For Group I, the upheaval and destabilization caused by the schism and a different understanding of the purpose and utility of *Gemeindeordnungen* resulted in less energy devoted to organizing annual conferences and drafting new *Ordnungen* and increasing attention to managing the boundaries between the two groups through policies surrounding intermarriage and boundary maintenance.[20] Since 1992, with the exception of policies dealing with interaction with Group II, Group I has produced virtually no ordinances that provide guidance in other important areas of church life such as leadership, material wealth, sexual ethics, education, and issues related to technology. This shift was widely welcomed by Group I members, many of whom were unhappy with what they perceived as legalism and over-regulation through top-down church legislation.

A lack of formal discussion and guidance on these pressing moral issues is not a development that ought to be welcomed by a Christian people. The new reality without regular church ordinances made room for individual congregations to make more decisions locally, which might have presented an opportunity to develop local discernment skills.[21] In reality, however, the change meant that each community was left to grapple with these challenges more or less on its own, which resulted in a growing level of disconnection or disunity between many communities.[22] The election of a new elder and the drafting of new conference letters under his leadership represents an opportunity to recognize the deficiency of an order-less church on one hand, while acknowledging the unhealthy, legal-

---

20   For example, Jacob Kleinsasser, "*Bericht von der Konferenz* [Conference Report]," July 30, 1997, in author's collection.
21   Unfortunately, in most communities this did not happen, which is not surprising, because in many communities both community leaders and brothers and sisters have been socialized to obediently follow their leaders without asking questions and without the benefit of open dialogue. As such, members are not schooled in the discipline of participating in essential communal conversations. Often, this is justified by references to the baptismal vow of obedience and the related posture of *Gelassenheit*. Instead, in many cases, leaders took the opportunity to become the main agent of decision-making, which helps to explain our leadership problem today.
22   Some communities formed informal alliances where leaders did things in similar ways; others were left alone until problems erupted. There are some benefits to this lack of conference pressure; local autonomy limits the coercive nature of broad church policies that may be the work of a vocal minority.

istic over-regulation which ruled in the church for much of the twentieth century on the other. This is the time to give congregations more room for local discernment and to equip and form leaders who are courageous and vulnerable enough to be servants of the Word, who facilitate congregational conversations while fostering unity within the broader church.[23]

However, it is one thing to revive the tradition of writing church orders to assist local congregations in their discipleship and faith formation, and quite another challenge to cultivate the conditions for holding healthy discussions in local congregations. Grassroots[24] participation in creating church and perhaps congregational orders is another approach worth exploring. This would require discussion within each congregation about its vision and priorities and would invite greater participation in the life of the church. When drafting new *Ordnungen* of a more general, hortatory nature, the conference might find a way to hear from a representative cross-section of members on a given policy using surveys and other tools. Addressing the culture of communal conversation will be crucial to the effectiveness of any new *Ordnungen* that are produced, especially if the content of the orders requires communal dialogue in the first place, as the January 2018 conference document does.

## Diagnosing the Issue

What are the signs that Hutterite communities are suffering from a culture deficient in dialogue as a means of discernment and decision-making at the congregational level? To my knowledge, no formal studies of this question have been made. There are, however, numerous relevant clues, one of which is the financial struggles experienced by many communities. A recent document outlining the implementation of an Economic Stewardship Council among Schmiedeleut Group I reports that as many as twenty-five communities (close to 50%!) are dealing with significant financial challenges.[25] To take an extreme example, in one newly founded community, members were unaware that the community had accumulated

---

23 Brené Brown, *Dare to Lead: Brave Work. Tough Conversations. Whole Hearts.* (New York: Random House, 2018). See especially Part I, "Rumbling with Vulnerability," which addresses a number of common myths associated with vulnerability, contrasts daring and armoured leadership, and explores the relevance of shame and empathy for leadership.
24 The fact that I'm distinguishing between "grassroots" and "leadership" levels in our communities suggests an existing, problematic divide or distance between many of our leaders and the people they are charged to lead. We would do well to recover our confidence in Jesus' promise that all believers are empowered to participate in discernment: "Where two or three are gathered in my name, I am there among them" (Matthew 18:20).
25 Hutterite Brethren Stewardship Council Mission Statement, August 2018, in author's collection. Schmiedeleut Group II has organized a similar advisory committee.

$8 million of debt over five years![26] The authors of the economic stewardship document recognize that one of the ways to address growing financial troubles in our communities is to facilitate closer communication, not only about the financial status of the community, but also about sustainable living standards.[27] In his report at the 2019 conference, council liaison Jack Waldner cites "on-going concerns such as a lack of accountability and transparency" as one of the main factors contributing to financial mismanagement. "Leaders need to encourage the thorough discussion of issues, plans, and ideas with members before making decisions. There must always be fair and due process which prevents nepotism."[28]

Furthermore, strong anecdotal evidence suggests that many leaders communicate very little of what gets discussed at conference-level meetings to their congregations, and that they are making more decisions about large purchases without consulting the brotherhood than was traditionally the case. At a meeting of Group I leaders in March of 2019, Elder Arnold Hofer told ministers, "In my analysis of the challenges our church is facing today, I have come to believe that a lack of good communication, disrespect, and the disunity that comes from this, is increasingly separating us."[29] If that is true, it is difficult to imagine the same leaders initiating discussions over complex and controversial issues.

There is another important reason why it is imperative that Hutterite communities develop a healthy culture of conversation. As we react to the rapidly changing economic and technological landscape, we find ourselves navigating another shift of seismic proportions in our communities—the changing face of education. Since the late 1990s and the advent of the Brandon University Hutterian Education Program (BUHEP), close to 100 teachers have graduated from universities in Brandon and Winnipeg and are teaching in their local communities. As a result, we have produced a generation of high school graduates who have been taught to think, question, and discuss issues at a level that is foreign and even intimidating to the older generations. The significance of this development for the culture and internal dynamics of Schmiedeleut Group I communities cannot be overstated. For the first time in their history, a significant number of individuals were sent to university in the hopes of taking back the responsibil-

---

26 Arnold Hofer and Samuel Waldner to "Brothers and Sisters in Jesus Christ [Schmiedeleut I membership]," June 18, 2018, in author's collection.
27 Hutterite Economic Stewardship Council Mission Statement, August 2018, in author's collection.
28 Arnold Hofer and Samuel Waldner to "all Hutterite communities of Schmiedeleut Group I in Manitoba, Canada; Minnesota, North and South Dakota, USA," "Schmiedeleut Group I Conference Report 2019," 5.
29 Arnold Hofer, "Concerning Leadership in our Communities." Speech notes for H.B. Mutual Shareholders' meeting, March 28, 2019, in author's collection.

ity of educating their own children.[30] What many community leaders did not anticipate, however, were the unavoidable tensions and growing pains that would result from new ideas and ways of thinking chafing against traditional beliefs and cultural norms, especially in a context where the necessary conditions for conversations were not adequately cultivated.[31]

Without a robust culture of conversation, these developments in the Hutterite education system hold great potential for misunderstanding, alienation, and disunity. Many older members do not consider that encountering new ideas at university for five years will (and should!) inevitably change anybody. What else is the point of attending an institution of higher learning? To learn is to be changed. The challenge for each community is to bring the wisdom of the community's tradition into dialogue with the best ideas learned by its members at university through ongoing, honest conversations. Clearly not everything learned at university will be beneficial to the community; members who attend university need help digesting, filtering, and metabolizing what they learn so they can help build up the community. Members who have had the luxury of studying history, literature, psychology, sociology, philosophy, theology, and other subjects, may have some helpful, albeit painful, critiques for their community and the wider church. As I have already noted, teachers or other members gifted in facilitating conversations can also play a role in leading communal discussions that will support this process.

At the same time, university-trained members will need to be sensitive to the fact that they have had the benefit of reading, learning, and interacting with diverse conversation partners over several years and have been changed in significant ways as a result. Other community members have not had the same experience and will naturally be at a very different place in their thinking. Regularly reflecting on one's intellectual development is one way to cultivate awareness and humility in this regard, because it is a reminder that absent the reading and learning we have been privileged to experience—to say nothing of the patience and generosity shown to us by

---

30  Shortly after emigrating to the United States of America, about a dozen Hutterites took a year of education in neighbouring colleges and taught in their respective colony schools. About half a dozen Hutterites received their teachers' training between 1970–1990. The numbers that graduated from 1999–2015 is simply unprecedented in Hutterite history.

31  Two unpublished papers that show some awareness of these challenges are Raymond Kleinsasser, "Hutterite Education: Growing Pains" (MA thesis, University of Manitoba, 2007) and Tim Waldner, "Hutterites and High School: Do they Match?" (2000). While the people who were pushing for higher education were willing to challenge the status quo and welcomed the changes it would bring, many others were less prepared for the adjustments.

our teachers and conversation partners—we would think and talk in ways similar to the people whose logic we may reject.[32]

These brief forays into the economic and educational realities Hutterites are navigating show why they would benefit from developing practices and cultures that encourage community-level conversations that promote transparency and help to bridge differences. Next, we turn to consider why conversation should matter to people of faith.

## Conversation in the Body of Christ

The words community and communication share the Latin root *communis*, which means "shared by all" or "to have in common." A healthy community exists when members have a shared sense of why they are living together. What purpose does our life together serve? What is the church's vocation, and how does it relate to our congregation's priorities? Is it primarily an economic purpose, or is there a larger spiritual vision of achieving wholeness through living out the gospel together and sharing that witness with the world? Conversation can help a community reflect on its vision and assess whether its current practices and priorities are congruent with its stated goals.

One of the most consistent metaphors for the gathered people of God in the New Testament is the human body.[33] This assembly of believers (Greek *ekklesia*) or "called out ones" is also referred to as the body of Christ.[34] Through the church, Christ is bodily present with the world (Matthew 25). In other words, the church is called to embody the ministry of Jesus, to be the healing presence of its Master through the power of the Spirit. As such, the heart of the church's mission is to be salt and light to the world. What does conversation have to do with the church's mission? Conversation has many practical benefits in the workplace, in family life, and in other social contexts. Its usefulness, however, may have been obscured to many Hutterites by ingrained attitudes and beliefs about leadership, conflict, and the Christian life in general. For example, if we have been taught that conflict should be avoided we will not value the kind of communication skills that are necessary to deal well with conflict. If we have been socialized to believe that our leaders bear the full burden of decision-making, we will be less likely to expect to be consulted about decisions. If we think that Christian discipleship is primarily about following the community's or the

---

32 A useful discussion of this is found in Alan Jacobs, *How to Think: A Survival Guide for a World at Odds* (New York: Penguin Random House, 2014), 123, 144–146.
33 See Eph 2:16 and 4:1–16; Col 3:15; 1 Cor 12:12–31; the famous meditation on love found in 1 Cor 13 appears within a discussion of the spiritual gifts of believers, "so that the church may be built up" (14:5).
34 Rom 12:5; 1 Cor 12:27; Eph 5:23; Col 1:18 and 1:24.

church's rules, we will not see the importance of ongoing and active reflection and participation in discernment in order to build up the community. To that end, I want to suggest three biblical and theological reasons why engaging in healthy communal conversation should be taken seriously. All three are deeply rooted in the church's vocation to be a witness and faithful presence to the world. The three features are not meant to be exhaustive. Rather, they are representative of the kind of witness the church should be as it lives out its vocation as the body of Christ.

**1. Conversation is Essential for Church Unity**

The body of Christ is called to pursue unity. In John 17, Jesus prayed that his disciples "may all be one," as Jesus and the Father are one "so that the world may believe that you have sent me" (v. 21). The church's unity is both a reflection of the intimate relationship between Father and Son and the Trinity as a whole; and it is an argument for the incarnation, making it possible for people to believe what might otherwise be inconceivable or fanciful. The church's unity is essential because when the church is united, it is more effective in being the hands and feet of Jesus, ministering to a hurting world and pointing people to the good news of his lordship.

There are various examples in church history of leaders and members meeting to talk through difficult issues. One of the earliest examples is described in Acts 15. A controversial issue that divided the early church was how to treat Gentile converts: should they be required to practice Jewish law, including circumcision and dietary customs, or should they be accepted simply on the basis of their faith in and allegiance to Jesus? The leaders resolved this thorny question by calling the first church council: they met at Jerusalem to debate the matter and eventually reached a decision that would pave the way for the expansion and flowering of the Christian faith.

As mentioned earlier, the early Anabaptists also convened a conference to work towards unity during the Reformation period. The Swiss and South German Anabaptists met at the Swiss border town of Schleitheim to discuss and work out seven articles that they agreed on. It is worth noting that the document they produced was entitled "Brotherly Union"—an attempt to work for unity in an age of chaos and fragmentation. In the introduction to "Brotherly Union," the author (probably Michael Sattler) declared,

> Joy, peace, and mercy from our Father, *through the reconciling* [vereinigung] *blood of Christ Jesus*, along with the gifts of the Spirit […] be with all who love God and the children of the light who are scattered about wherever God

has deigned to place them and wherever they are gathered in unity in the one God and Father of us all. Grace and peace of heart be with you all.[35]

Unity is not the same as uniformity or conformity; it does not mean that everybody is the same or that everyone agrees about everything. Rather, unity is about being united by the same Spirit to serve the same Lord through the rich and diverse collection of individual members that make up the body of Christ, otherwise known as the church. We can strive for unity by talking about our differences and by discussing our hopes and dreams for our community, instead of secretly gossiping about how we have been mistreated or how somebody made the wrong decision. In this way, we can contribute to the community's welfare and be appropriately disciplined and corrected by our fellow brothers and sisters.

There is a common misconception that all conflict is unhealthy, or even un-Christian. In fact, conflicts and disagreements are a natural part of human experience. A conflict is an opportunity to deal with an existing problem in an honest, healthy way. What matters is how the conflict is processed or dealt with. A conflict can be avoided, manipulated, angrily confronted, or talked about respectfully, in a spirit of generosity, patience, and forbearance, with the goal of getting to the bottom of the issue at hand. If the church's unity is to help the world believe that God has sent Jesus to save us (John 17), it will need to be motivated by the Spirit of unity expressed in the letter to the Ephesians:

> I therefore, the prisoner in the Lord, beg you to lead a life worthy of the calling to which you have been called, with all humility and gentleness, with patience, bearing with one another in love, making every effort to maintain the unity of the Spirit in the bond of peace. There is one body and one Spirit, just as you were called to one hope of your calling, one Lord, one faith, one baptism, one God and Father of all, who is above all and through all and in all (4:1–5).

Working for unity in the church has always been challenging. Today, unity is threatened by a polarized political climate and by individualism in the West. Now more than ever the world needs the witness of Christ's body gathering in humility to seek unity through gracious conversation.

---

35  Jesse Hofer and Kenny Wollmann, editors. *For God's Truth: A Hutterite History Reader* (MacGregor: Hutterian Brethren Book Centre, 2024), 90. Emphasis added. John Howard Yoder notes that "A most significant concept in the thought of Michael Sattler is that of *Vereinigung*."

## 2. Conversation is Essential for Reconciliation in the Church

Reconciliation is at the heart of the gospel and the church's vocation (Matthew 5:9; 2 Corinthians 5:16–21; Romans 5:1–11). "In Christ," Paul writes to the Corinthians, "God was reconciling the world to himself" (19). Those who are "in Christ" are a "new creation" called to serve in the ministry of reconciliation as "ambassadors for Christ." They share and embody the message that through Christ, God is reconciling the world to himself.

Problems with communication are a major contributing factor in most conflicts. Often, conflicts and misunderstandings erupt as a result of a failure to communicate honestly, clearly, and charitably. Sometimes conflicts happen when people do not listen patiently enough or do not watch their words carefully enough. When we learn to communicate in a timely and open manner, and when we learn the necessary skills to dialogue well, we become better equipped to prevent conflicts and better able to resolve them once they happen. This is especially important for Hutterites, who live in close proximity to their brothers and sisters and because of their commitment to Christian community.

The rule of Christ found in Matthew 18:15–20 recommends a redemptive process for resolving conflicts and is premised on the ability of brothers and sisters to talk frankly about difficult matters. This was a favourite text for early Anabaptists and remains foundational for how the church understands conflict resolution. The familiar promise of God's presence "where two or three are gathered in my name" assumes that believers will be people who meet in a variety of ways to address broken relationships and to discern what is essential for ongoing faithfulness. "Truly I tell you, whatever you bind on earth will be bound in heaven, and whatever you loose on earth will be loosed in heaven. Again truly I tell you, if two of you agree on earth about anything you ask, it will be done for you by my Father in heaven. For where two or three are gathered in my name, I am there among them" (vv. 18–20). This passage appears in a chapter devoted to teachings and parables about forgiveness and reconciliation, suggesting that God is present in a special way to those who meet to talk about issues that divide them.

## 3. Conversation is Essential for Discernment and Moral Formation in the Church and is Consistent with the Theology of Believer's Baptism

The early church theologian Tertullian once observed, "Christians are made, not born." Often we assume that most of the formation into the Christian life happens prior to baptism. In reality, discipleship is a lifelong process of growing into the fullness of Christ in the context of the believing community.

Believer's baptism assumes that when regenerated, believing men and women are incorporated into the body of Christ through baptism, and are therefore responsible for contributing to the body's welfare and wellbeing. Hutterite baptismal vows include a promise to give and receive admonition to keep the body honest, to help it grow in a healthy manner, and to ensure that its witness is effective. At the same time, young disciples need ongoing guidance and nourishment to grow into their faith and mature in their discipleship. Giving and receiving admonition is not simply an obligatory, spur-of-the-moment response to a misstep or sin, but an invitation to conversation in order to encourage or counsel a brother or sister in need of direction, ideally in the context of a cultivated relationship.

Baptism is also a commitment to share the struggles and glories of the body of Christ, particularly those of one's local congregation. Paul writes to the believers at Rome that God's Spirit reminds them of the glorious fact that they are children of God and joint heirs with Christ, "if in fact, we suffer with him so that we may also be glorified with him" (Romans 8:14–17). This pattern of cross and resurrection is, of course, patterned after the life of Jesus and is basic to Paul's understanding of the Christian life. Involving members in sharing the burden of making difficult decisions so they can take responsibility for the community's future is a way to help them mature as believers and participate in the work God is doing through the local congregation.

Hutterites are very familiar with the descriptions of the life of the early believers in Jerusalem found in the Acts of the Apostles. Acts 2:44–45 and 4:32–35 in particular are pivotal texts, because they describe how the early believers practiced community-of-goods in response to the outpouring of the Spirit of God. Another striking feature of the early Christian communities described in Acts is their commitment to be together in fellowship (German *Gemeinschaft*; Greek *koinonia*). This section in Acts begins with the description "When the day of Pentecost had come, they were all together in one place." Once the Spirit pulsed through the gathered believers, they were moved to change their lives in a radical way. Besides economic sharing, "they devoted themselves to the apostles' teaching and fellowship, to the breaking of bread and prayers" (2:42). "Day by day, as they spent much time together in the temple, they broke bread at home and ate their food with glad and generous hearts" (2:46). While *Gemeinschaft* is often associated primarily with economic sharing (*Güter-gemeinschaft*), its meaning refers to the dynamic togetherness and mutual support experienced by believers who share the same Spirit and worship the same Lord. The purpose of the fellowship among believers is no doubt multi-faceted, but surely one reason for it is to encourage growth and understanding among believers through edifying conversation.

To reiterate, learning to talk within the body of Christ is essential for the growth and maturity of its members, who are thereby knit together in love and equipped to better serve each other and the world through mission.

> But speaking the truth in love, we must grow up in every way into him who is the head, into Christ, from whom the whole body, joined and knit together by every ligament with which it is equipped, as each part is working properly, promotes the body's growth in building itself up in love (Ephesians 4: 15–16).

In the final section we will consider examples of several practices that hold potential for developing greater capacity for robust conversations in our communities.

## Practices for Nurturing Dialogue Skills and Encouraging Participation

One of the issues confronting Hutterite communities in recent years is how to develop guidelines around the wise use of technology, particularly smartphones and the internet. While some *Leut* groups have responded to this challenge through legislation (i.e., creating new *Ordnungen*), the Schmiedeleut Group I's approach has—intentionally or otherwise—left each community to develop its own policy.[36] In this section I will describe the process of discernment my home community of Silverwinds, Manitoba, went through as we wrestled with the challenges surrounding technology. Along the way I will reflect on what lessons this experience might offer for recovering a stronger culture of dialogue and discernment, both at the congregational and conference levels.

The internet, computers, and cellphones made their appearance in Silverwinds gradually and innocently enough. Their first sanctioned use was as business tools whose utility was difficult to argue against, since they were an economic benefit to the community—the traditional, though by no means foolproof, Hutterite litmus test for adopting new technologies. In the early 2000s, when flip phones were used primarily as communication devices for travellers, our community shared five cellphones. Around 2008, all baptized brothers received a personal cellphone, but only brothers in leadership positions in the various work departments subscribed to a data

---

36   One exception is the establishment of Hutterian Broadband Network initiative (HBNi), a church organization that provides filtered internet to many Hutterite communities.

plan. Internet access was available to adults mostly through desktop computers at the school computer lab, which was designed with transparency and mutual accountability in mind. Content was filtered and access shut off at 9:00 p.m. Youth received an internet account once they graduated and had demonstrated a certain level of maturity; students who wished to use the internet had to be signed in and monitored by teachers. There were some discussions among the teachers and parents in those early days about how best to manage the evolving ecosystem of online access, but very little dialogue was happening formally at the community level.

With the advent of the smartphone and Wi-Fi, the urgency for a wider communal conversation and clearer policies increased. Now, anybody with a digital device and a password could access the internet. Several other potential changes appeared on the horizon around 2016: smartphones for female members and blanket Wi-Fi across the community.[37] To help us wrestle with the bundle of difficult questions surrounding our use of technology, our *Rot*, or community council, appointed a committee to organize a series of meetings.[38] As older leaders, they recognized that they were not in the best position to lead a conversation around technology use, so they delegated the responsibility to younger members who were more familiar with the technical details and who were more capable of facilitating the discussion. This delegation of responsibility was crucial to the success of the process and required courage and vulnerability from our leaders. The process was built on a relationship of mutual trust and goodwill, which has to be cultivated on an ongoing basis. Of special note is that several members of the planning committee were teachers.

With respect to issues in the wider church, how can the church delegate responsibility to members who have the necessary gifts, so that they can deal with complex questions and issues more effectively, instead of assigning somebody a task because he is already in a leadership position?[39]

---

37  In general, gender roles in Hutterite culture are traditional and patriarchal: the men are active in managerial and bread-winning roles in the community's barns, shops, and fields, while the women assume responsibility in the domestic sphere. The earliest justification for personal cellphones as a business tool meant that access for women came about a decade later, when it was taken for granted that cellphones were also vital for communication purposes.

38  Our community used a similar approach when dealing with the challenges surrounding COVID-19 beginning in the spring of 2020. A committee was appointed to review provincial regulations and safety recommendations from the Hutterite Safety Council's COVID-19 Task Force, discuss and implement a plan for ensuring the community's compliance with these regulations, and to regularly communicate changes to our members.

39  Three examples where this is already happening are the Hutterian Broadband Network Inc. initiative, the H.B. Stewardship Council mentioned above, and the Hutterian Safety Council, an inter-*Leut* committee tasked with spearheading safety policy and programming.

How can trust and goodwill be effectively nurtured and nourished among our leaders and between leaders and the people they lead?

At our first community meeting we did two things: we reviewed the current situation and policies with respect to digital access in our community and gave participants (anybody fifteen years or older) a chance to raise questions and concerns around the use of technology. The committee planned several opportunities over the course of the meeting for participants to talk with each other in small groups in order to build trust in the process and in each other, to develop discussion skills, and to give everybody a chance to hear from their group members and voice their own thinking. This process was important, because people are not born with the ability to participate well in discussions or to exercise discernment. Communication skills are learned, and we learn best through guided practice. Too often we take for granted that people should be able to have quality discussions without ample time and opportunity to exercise or practice the necessary skills. How can we create time and space for discussions—both at the congregational and conference levels—in order to involve more people in decision-making and discernment around crucial issues so that the community can benefit from the diverse gifts among us and to wrestle together with how to be faithful Christians today? This challenge takes on a new urgency at a time when conversations are especially threatened by the highly attractive and addictive, but socially non-demanding, low-investment culture of digital communication.[40]

After having several opportunities to talk, small groups sorted their technology questions and concerns into categories such as "Effects of Technology on Child Development" and "Technology and Conscience Formation" and "Social Media Concerns." As a large group we brainstormed categories and narrowed them down to a manageable number. Questions of a technical nature were addressed first because they were the easiest to answer. Further research and investigation were needed to answer many of the questions, and participants were invited to volunteer to prepare presentations to help the community learn about the different aspects of technology use.

In a series of four follow-up meetings the presentations were shared, often by a team of two or more presenters, in an attempt to deepen the

---

40 For a sustained and insightful treatment of this topic, see Sherry Turkle, *Reclaiming Conversation: The Power of Talk in a Digital Age* (New York: Penguin Press, 2015). I think here of WhatsApp groups, particularly where Hutterite ministers are tempted to think they are having serious and meaningful conversations. While this medium can be effective for communicating trivial information such as the time and location of a meeting, it is far from ideal for conducting authentic conversations about real issues. In order to develop their ability as conversationalists, Hutterite leaders need a forum to regularly meet face-to-face to discuss relevant topics.

learning and potential discernment regarding technology. Preparing these presentations was an enriching experience in itself, as volunteers met to plan and discuss their learning and find a way to effectively share it with community members. By attending and responding to the different presentations, members practised and improved their communication skills and became more connected with people they had never had a deep conversation with before.[41] The outcome of these meetings was not a finely tuned policy regulating the use of digital devices, but a way to remind everybody that technology use has an enormous influence on our personal and social health, and that everybody has a responsibility to use it wisely. It is also worth mentioning that this process requires considerable patience and forbearance, and will be more difficult for people who are introverts by nature or may not particularly enjoy discussing a topic at length.

To return to the January 2018 Schmiedeleut Group I Conference meeting for a moment, there are several relevant points worth mentioning. Given the fact that dialogue skills are developed over time and depend on mutual trust between participants, spending a couple of hours discussing a complex, controversial policy that had held sway in the church for over twenty-five years is insufficient. A more patient, structured approach would honour the questions and concerns on both sides of the issue and would allow the time necessary to carefully study the Scriptures and the historical record in search of guidance and direction. Beginning this difficult conversation is certainly a courageous and necessary first step, but the conversation must continue beyond the preliminary stage if it is to bear the fruits of understanding and unity. Tasking groups of ministers to study particular issues and leading discernment on them is one way to encourage learning and engagement. Building capacity for discussion among the ministers is also a crucial first step before they can have the confidence to lead similar discussions in their local congregations. One way to do this might be to organize a reading group where ministers can meet regularly to read and discuss literature relevant to their ministry.

---

41 By way of background, it is important to say a bit more about our context in Silverwinds. From 2012–2014, interested adults—about 25 people from teenagers to young and middle-aged parents to seniors, both males and females—participated in a community book club led by the author. From 2015–2016, parents met on a weekly basis to view and discuss Dr. Gordon Neufeld's *The Power to Parent* series on child development and parenting. Most recently about a dozen members participated in a weekly Reading Circle during February and March 2020. I believe these experiences were formative in helping our members develop interest and engagement in a broader set of issues, as well as competency as thoughtful readers and conversationalists. Book clubs hold a lot of potential for stimulating thinking about important issues and for developing capacity for healthy conversation.

## Sharing Circles

Another practice that has the potential to elevate discussion and discernment in our communities is regular brotherhood or community-wide meetings. In most Hutterite communities, important day-to-day decisions are made by a council that consists of the minister(s), steward, farm manager, and in some cases, one or more witness brothers. The larger (male) brotherhood is consulted when large purchases and decisions are considered, church discipline is enforced, and important public announcements such as baptisms and marriages are communicated. Theoretically, members have the opportunity to ask questions and provide insights that aid the discerning process when matters are brought before the brotherhood. In practice, however, the culture of decision-making in many Hutterite communities does not invite much critique, discussion, and participation.[42]

Over the last several decades, many Manitoba Hutterite communities have transitioned from a predominantly agrarian economy to one where industry represents a significant source of income. Formerly members worked in relative isolation for most of the day in the various barns and shops on the *Hof*. Manufacturing has afforded the possibility of the majority of the workforce working in close proximity. Together with the obvious need for regular communication between workers and the leadership team in a factory setting, these circumstances gave rise to a meeting I will call a sharing circle.[43] The male members of the community gather regularly, typically once a week, to provide an update on the various work departments and to discuss issues that pertain to the larger community. Paul J. Wollmann has called it a "venting meeting" because it provides opportunities for members to express their concerns and grievances in a healthy manner. "Somebody who vents publicly can be helped," he observed. Overall, he thinks the sharing circle is an important forum "to iron out issues, allowing us to work peacefully in the workplace and in the larger community."[44] Further, he believes that the meeting space is a training ground that has improved Silverwinds' decision-making process by acting as a mechanism that keeps both the members and the leaders better in-

---

42  For the perspective of an outsider who joined a Hutterite community for several years see Robert Rhodes, *Nightwatch: An Inquiry Into Solitude: Alone on the Prairie with the Hutterites* (Intercourse: Good Books, 2009).
43  A growing number of communities have circle meetings in one form or another. Some meet on a weekly basis while others meet daily. There are, of course, many different ways to organize a meeting. The benefits of the circle format are that it emphasizes equality, which invites participants to lower their defences and be vulnerable. Seated in a circle, members can make eye contact and the audio is optimal, approximating the ideal of face-to-face conversation. The circle also symbolizes unity and inclusion.
44  Jesse Hofer, interview with Paul J. Wollmann, July 2010.

formed about the needs and challenges the community is facing and thus more responsive and accountable to each other.[45] Zacharias Hofer, the facilitator of Silverwinds' weekly meetings, sees them as crucial for building a culture of openness and trust in the community.[46]

In the sharing circle setting, members become aware of what is going on in the wider community and develop the essential communication skills of listening, asking good questions, responding clearly and respectfully to questions, contributing expertise, and being involved in decision-making, all of which are essential for effective participation in the life of the community. In the close to twenty years that Silverwinds has practised this type of meeting, I have noticed how underdeveloped basic discussion and communication skills were for many community members, and also how they have improved with practice. In many communities there is a serious lack of communication and participation between the leadership team and the wider membership. Even within the management council itself there can be serious communication problems, leading to unsound financial investments and unresolved conflict.[47] Sharing circles are also a way to bridge the education divide. Teachers and older students—whose work in the school can easily isolate them from the community's adult population—have the opportunity to learn about what is happening in the rest of the community. In turn, other members get a weekly update on what is happening in the school. Of course, the weekly conversations also allow the exchange of ideas on many other fronts.

For the full potential of sharing circles to be realized, they would have to be expanded in several directions. First, such meetings would need to move from their mostly workplace function to invite discernment on other moral issues affecting the community, such as how to minister effectively to our youth, how to engage positively with non-Hutterite neighbours, and how to reach out to serve the less fortunate in our world—concerns that are at the heart of the gospel and the church's mission. Second, the voices of both men and women should be invited and respected in such public forums. If we take the body metaphor for a healthy church com-

---

45  When members are not informed of the financial circumstances of their community, they cannot help to address the causes of the financial problems by spending less, being more frugal, lowering the standard of living, developing stronger work ethic, travelling less, etc.
46  Jesse Hofer, interview with Zacharias Hofer Sr., August 24, 2019.
47  Interview with a member of Silverwinds' community council, July 2010. Asked whether the lack of communication between management and the wider membership was a key factor responsible for widespread financial problems among Hutterites, he responded: "There is no question that that is the case. What I hear [about communities' financial circumstances] at the accountants' advisory meetings confirms this."

munity seriously, as the Scriptures and our sermons clearly teach, then we should be prepared to empower brothers and sisters—who took the same baptismal vows of faithfulness and accountability—as moral agents in the communal decision-making process.[48] The discernment process will vary between communities, given their unique needs and contexts. It will also require a robust, courageous faith and vulnerability as members grow at different rates in maturity and understanding and learn to accept differences. Finally, sharing circles require competent, sensitive leadership and facilitation to function in an effective and healthy manner.[49]

### Conversation and Daily Council Meetings (*Rot*)

Besides public meetings at the community level, there are many other opportunities to develop our capacity for conversation and connection in smaller settings. One such forum is the daily *Rot*, or council meeting, which is tasked with day-to-day planning, coordinating members' travel plans, and processing inquiries, complaints, and requests. The daily council meeting was first implemented in 1973 as a means to encourage closer collaboration between the secretary-treasurer, the farm manager, and the minister.[50]

A common understanding of what happens at these daily council meetings is that members ask for permission from the community council to travel somewhere or to follow a certain course of action. In that understanding, leaders wield ultimate, unquestioned authority, and members are discouraged from engaging in an open dialogue or offering any opposition to the decisions of their leaders. Understandably, individuals who hold this understanding often find it intimidating to approach the council. Further,

---

48    Hutterite teaching, "*Erste Pfingsten Rede* [First Pentecost Teaching]," 4. Demonstrating the participation of God the Father and God the Holy Spirit in the life of the community, the author invokes Paul's instructions to the Corinthians in 1 Cor 12:11, 28. In the former reference, the Holy Spirit is said to direct the diversity of gifts in the community, while the latter reference describes how God ordained an order of offices that serve the community: apostles, prophets, and teachers, as well as diverse gifts and forms that work together to build up the church community.

49    Significantly, Hutterites traditionally called their ministers "servants of the Word" (*Diener des Worts*) and their financial stewards "servants of material needs" (*Diener der Notdurft* or *Haushalter*). This Christian servanthood terminology has to a large extent been replaced by worldly business terms such as "boss" or "management," reflecting a troubling trend of acculturation. The shift in language may also be related to our legal structure, where typically the minister is the president of the corporation, the steward the vice-president, and so on. Words are not neutral or arbitrary; changes in the language we use to describe our world are usually accompanied by changes in our thinking about the things we are describing, and finally, about how we live.

50    *Ordnungen und Conferens Brief* [sic] [Ordinances and Conference Reports] (n.p., n.d.), 70. See also Yossi Katz and John Lehr, *Inside the Ark: The Hutterites in Canada and the United States* (Regina: Canadian Plains Research Center, 2012), 297.

many council members have been socialized to understand their leadership role in this way, which makes it a difficult dynamic to address. One problematic consequence of this approach is that members commonly rely on their leaders to make difficult decisions for them instead of discerning on their own whether a certain course of action is beneficial for the whole community. In effect, it is a way for members to avoid the responsibility to be directly involved in their community's decision-making and in the process to develop their voice, their conscience, and their ability to discern.

An alternative and arguably healthier approach is to understand the leadership team as a body nominated by the members to represent the interests of the community and give advice[51] to members with the big picture in view. For example, if I share my travel plans with the council, car-pooling with others can be coordinated. With this approach I am not asking for permission to do something, but sharing my plan or request and inviting the community's leaders to help me fit my plans into the rhythm of the larger community. In other words, when we come to *Rot*, we are participating in a conversation among brothers and sisters about our plans and the community's larger needs and goals. Understood in this way, community leaders are wise, patient conversation partners and not authoritarian gatekeepers who say "yes" or "no" without giving any justification or engaging in any kind of brotherly discourse. This understanding respects the individual integrity and dignity of each member and is consistent with the meaning of believer's baptism: it assumes that all brothers and sisters in the community are responsible and accountable decision-makers who are being formed as disciples through their participation in the life of the community.

At Silverwinds the council's meeting space includes an empty chair, which invites members to sit down and engage in a longer conversation with the council members if necessary.[52] This simple accommodation sends a powerful signal: that dialogue is a strength, an essential feature of a flourishing community. It is a reminder that leaders are there to serve and listen to their people, and they can do this best when people have the space, invitation, and freedom to speak their minds.

## Conclusion

The Schmiedeleut church division of 1992 and the economic difficulties many communities face have brought to the surface a number of serious underlying conflicts and issues, including the underdeveloped cap-

---

51  The *Hutterisch* term, *Rot*, comes from the German *Rat*, which means "council," and can also mean "advice" or "counsel."
52  Jesse Hofer, interview with Silverwinds council member, Zacharias Hofer Sr., August 24, 2019.

acity for communication among leaders and within Hutterite communities. Unfortunately, the skills necessary for healing any conflict—patient, charitable listening and open, honest speaking—have been largely absent and will need to be cultivated to make progress in finding reconciliation and preventing similar schisms from happening in the future. Moreover, one of the marks of a healthy church is its ability to dialogue in order to foster unity, to work for reconciliation, and to exercise moral discernment. There are a number of serious issues and questions that all Christian congregations need to address through tough, vulnerable conversations if they want their communities to flourish. At the same time, communities need guidance and resources (possibly in the form of regular, albeit repurposed, *Gemeindeordnungen*) from the church conference level that can foster unity and encourage moral formation. It is encouraging that the current elder is speaking clearly to ministers about their responsibilities to lead their people in conversations, not least with respect to issues relating to the church division. At the same time, church leaders will need to be aware that leadership skills, especially the ability to facilitate a healthy discussion, are developed over time and will require much practice, patience, and perseverance.

# Hutterites in Manitoba: A Selected Bibliography

## COMPILED BY KENNY WOLLMANN

This bibliography includes recent sources on Hutterites, with an emphasis on Manitoba Hutterites. Publications beyond that are included if they are considered classics of enduring value in the field and/or published after 1980. Bibliographies with different emphases and earlier sources can be found in the "Bibliography" section below.

Making distinctions between historical and theological texts in the Hutterite tradition can be challenging because the history is thoroughly theological, and vice versa. For the sake of organization and simplicity, however, choices were made based on what I perceived to be the overarching theme. Additionally, some titles fit well into several categories; in most cases dual listings were resisted, except when the overlap might be unexpected or unusual.

This bibliography makes a first attempt at recording internal publications produced by Hutterites not published via traditional publishing channels.

### Primary Sources

Barth Maendel, Emmy, and Jonathan Seiling, trans. and ed. *Jakob Hutter: His Life and Letters*. Walden: Plough Publishing House, 2024.

Beck, Joseph, ed. *Die Geschichts-Bücher der Wiedertäufer in Oesterreich-Ungarn, betreffend deren Schicksale in der Schweiz, Salzburg, Ober- und Nieder-Oesterreich, Mähren, Tirol, Böhmen, Süd-Deutschland, Ungarn, Siebenbürgen und Süd-Russland in der Zeit von 1526 bis 1785* [The Chronicles of the Anabaptists in Austria-Hungary, concerning their fate in Switzerland, Salzburg, Upper and Lower Austria, Moravia, Tyrol, Bohemia, Southern Germany, Hungary, Transylvania and Southern Russia in the period from 1526 to 1785]. vol. 2, 43 of *Fon-*

*tes Rerum Austriacarum*. Vienna, 1883. Repr. Nieuwkoop: B. De Graff, 1967, and MacGregor: Hutterian Brethren Book Centre, 2018.

*The Chronicle of the Hutterian Brethren*, vol. 1. Rifton: Plough Publishing House, 1986. An English translation of *Das große Geschichtbuch der Hutteritesche Brüder*.

*The Chronicle of the Hutterian Brethren*, vol. 2. Ste. Agathe: Crystal Spring Colony, 1998. An English translation of *Das Kleine-Geschichtsbuch Der Hutterischen Brüder* with additional sources.

Decker, Hans, ed. *Anfang von den Hutterischen Schmieden Gemeinden* [Beginnings of the Hutterite Schmiedeleut Community-of-Goods]. Hawley: Spring Prairie Printing, 1986.

_____. *Der Geist gegen den Fleisch* [The Spirit Versus the Flesh]. Wolf Creek Gemeinde, 1986.

Ehrenpreis, Andreas. *Ein Sendbrief an alle diejenigen, so sich rühmen und bedünken lassen, dass sie ein abgesondertes Volk von der Welt sein wollen…* [An Epistle to all those who Profess and Consider Themselves to be a People Separated from the World, 1652]. Wilson: Hutterischen Brüdern, 1953; Cayley: Macmillan Colony, 1975; Falher: Twilight Hutterian Brethren, 1988.

_____. *La communauté fraternelle: La plus grande exigence de l'amour*. Translated by L'Église de maison. MacGregor: Hutterian Brethren Book Centre, 2007. A French edition of the Ehrenpreis *Sendbrief*, 1652.

_____. 완전한 사랑의 공동체 [Brotherly Community]. Translated by Young-Pyo Jun. Korea Anabaptist Press, 2009. A Korean edition of the Ehrenpreis *Sendbrief*, 1652.

Ehrenpreis, Andreas, and Claus Felbinger. *Brotherly Community: The Highest Command of Love*. Rifton: Plough Publishing House, 1978; Kitchener: Pandora Press, 2006. An English edition of Ehrenpreis *Sendbrief*, 1652.

Entz, Johann. *Biblische Geschichten Auslegung: Zusammengetragen im Jahre 1886–1887 […]*. Elm Creek: Wingham Gemeinde, 2020.

_____. *Biblische Geschichten Auslegung*, fourth edition. Bassano: Fairville Colony and New Dayton: New Rockport Colony, 2018. Kurrent script edition.

Felbinger, Claus. 클라우스 펠빙거의 신앙고백 [Claus Felbinger's Confession of 1560]. Korea Anabaptist Press, 2008.

Friedmann, Robert, ed. *Glaubenszeugnisse oberdeutscher Taufgesinnter*, vol. 2. Quellen zur Geschichte der Taufer 12. Gerd Mohn: Gütersloher Verlaghaus, 1967.

Friesen, Frank, trans., and Walter Klaassen, ed. *Sixteenth Century Anabaptism: Defences, Confessions, Refutations*. Waterloo: Conrad Grebel College, 1982.

Hauser, Joseph. *Der Christ und das Eigentum*. Edited by Alexander Bassner. Wien: Für die Gemeinde Christi, 2017.

Hiebert, Clarence, comp. and ed. *Brothers in Deed to Brothers in Need: A Scrapbook about Mennonite Immigrants from Russia 1870–1885*. Newton: Faith and Life Press, 1974.

Hofer, David. *Ein kurzer Bericht von unserer Reise nach Europa* [A Short Report on our Trip to Europe, 1937]. Johann Hofer, copyist. N.p., 1970.

Hofer, Jesse, and Kenny Wollmann, eds. *For God's Truth: A Hutterite History Reader*. MacGregor: Hutterian Brethren Book Centre, 2024.

Hofer, Joseph. *The Diaries of Joseph "Yos" Hofer*. Translated and edited by Arnold M. Hofer. Freeman: Hutterite Mennonite Centennial Committee, 2012.

Hostetler, John A. *Child Rearing Sources: The Hutterian Brethren*. Willow Grove, n.d.

Hostetler, John A., Leonard Gross, and Elizabeth Bender. *Selected Hutterian Documents in Translation, 1542–1654*. Philadelphia: Communal Studies Center at Temple University, 1975; MacGregor: Hutterian Brethren Book Centre, 2013.

*Die Hutterischen Episteln, 1527–1763*. 4 vols. Elie: James Valley Book Centre, 1986–1991.

Klassen, Walter, ed. *Anabaptism in Outline: Selected Primary Sources*. Walden, Plough Publishing House: 2019.

Kleinsasser, Jacob, et al., trans. and eds. *A Book of [Hutterite] Prefaces*, vol. 1. Ste. Agathe: Crystal Spring Colony, 1997. The contents of this book include the following *Vorreden*: Concerning the Blessing of the Word of God; Concerning the Comfort and Joy of the Faithful; Concerning Watchfulness and Temperance; Concerning the Correct Use of Grace; About Choosing to Suffer with God's People; Concerning Repentance and Conversion; Concerning how we Must Persevere to the End; Concerning Christian Virtues; Concerning the Flight of Jesus into Egypt; Concerning the Duty of Parents to their Children and the Duty of Children to their Parents; Concerning how the Church should Shine Forth; Concerning our Duty to Speak Up; Concerning the Fight against the Lusts of the Flesh; Concerning release and redemption through Christ; Concerning the Frailty of Mankind; Concerning the Fear of God; Concerning Discipleship of Christ and Self Denial; Concerning how we Must Follow and Obey Jesus; Concerning Preparation for Tribulation; How to Strive for Humility and Lowliness; Concerning the Cross and Tribulation; Concerning the Suffering and Trials of the Devout; Concerning True Faith and its Characteristics; Concerning the True Discipleship of Christ; About True Christian Life, a Plea for Power and Strength, and Exhortation to Zealous Prayer.

_____. [Hutterite] *Prefaces*, vol. 2. Ste. Agathe: Crystal Spring Colony, 1996. This collection of prefaces contains the following: Concerning our Vows and Covenant; Concerning the Seriousness of the Devout; Concerning Heavenly Wisdom and Grace; Concerning the Counsel of Parents; Concerning Admonition and Discipline; On Praising God and an Admonition to be Faithful; We Should Never Forget our Promise to God; We Should Hold Firm to our Beginning; Concerning Christian Virtue; About the Protection of the Devout; One Should not Fail to Teach and Admonish; About the Strengthening of our Faith; About the Fear of God; We are Always to Pray; How One Should Prove Oneself in Love; Concerning the Suffering of the Devout with Joy and Delight; A Preface for the Second Easter Day; A Reminder to be Diligent, Fair, and Just; Concerning Faithfulness to our Position; Concerning Our Whole Life and Conduct; Concerning Faithfulness to God and the Avoidance of Evil Speech; Concerning the Scriptures and the Bliss of Jesus; Concerning Sin and Salvation; Preface to the Teaching on Joy, Concerning the New Creation; God Wants to Save all Men.

_____. *Hutterite Teachings*, vol. 6. Ste. Agathe: Crystal Spring Colony, 2001. This volume contains translations of the following teachings: Preface 86 for the New Year; Second Preface for the New Year; Luke 2:21–32; Preface on the Wise Men; Preface 87 on the Three Kings; Matthew 2:1–12; Preface 9 on the Flight of Jesus into Egypt; Matthew 2:13–23; Preface on the Flight of Jesus into Egypt; Preface on When Jesus was Twelve Years Old; Luke 2:36–52; Luke 3:1–22.

_____. *Hutterite Teachings*, vol. 7. Ste. Agathe: Crystal Spring Colony, 2001; 2009. This volume contains translations of the following teachings: Luke 24:13–53 (preface and teaching); Luke 23:24–46 (preface and teaching); Matthew 28:1–15 (preface and teaching); Luke 24:13–

53; Preface for Ascension Day; Preface 79 for Ascension Day; Acts 1:1–11; Luke 24:50–53.

———. *Hutterite Teachings*, vol. 8. Ste. Agathe: Crystal Spring Colony, 2000; 2006. This volume contains translations of the following teachings: Matthew 4:1–11 (preface and teaching); Luke 4:14–27; Matthew 5:1–12; Matthew 5:13–48; Matthew 6:1–18; Matthew 6:19–23; Matthew 7:1–12; Matthew 7:13–23; Matthew 8:23–27.

———. *Teachings on the Gospel of Luke* [vol. 9]. Ste. Agathe: Crystal Spring Colony, 2002. This volume contains translations of the following teachings: Luke 13:23–30; 14:1–14; 15:1–32; 16:1–18; 16:19–31; 17:11–37; 19:1–10.

———. *Teachings on the Psalms* [vol. 3]. Ste. Agathe: Crystal Spring Colony, 1998. This volume contains translations of the following teachings: Psalm 15; Psalm 19; A Preface Concerning True Faith and Teaching; Psalm 22; Psalm 33; Psalm 127:1–5; A Thanksgiving Preface and Teaching; Psalm 133; Psalm 139; Dialogue Between Jesus and the Soul.

Loserth, Johann. *Anabaptism in Tyrol*. Translated by Hugo F. Brinkman, edited by Jonathan Seiling. St. Catherines: Gelassenheit Publications, 2022. A translation of *Der Anabaptismus in Tirol*, vols. 1-2.

Mecenseffy, Grete, ed. *Quellen zur Geschichte der Täufer: Österreich I. Teil* [Sources on the History of the Anabaptists: Austria, Part I.]. Vol. 11. Gütersloh: Mohn, 1964.

———. *Quellen zur Geschichte der Täufer: Österreich II. Teil* [Sources on the History of the Anabaptists: Austria, Part II.]. Vol. 13. Gütersloh: Mohn, 1972.

———. *Quellen zur Geschichte der Täufer: Österreich III. Teil* [Sources on the History of the Anabaptists: Austria, Part III.]. Vol. 14. Gütersloh: Mohn, 1983.

Oswald, Hans Georg. *Als die Brüder ins Land zogen: Claus Felbinger und sein Bekenntnis zur Vollkommenheit Christi, 1560*. Pfeffenhausen: Hallertauer Bienenhof, 2010.

Peter, Karl, Franziska Peter, and Paul S. Gross, eds. *Der Gemein Ordnung: Die Gemeindeordnung der Hutterischen Brüder im 16th und 17th Jahrhundert* [The Community Order: The Community Ordinances of the Hutterian Brethren in the 16th and 17th Centuries]. Rearden, 1980.

Ri[e]demann, Peter. *Rechenschaft unserer Religion, Lehr und Glaubens, von den Brüdern, so man die Hutterischen nennt, ausgangen durch Peter Ride-*

*man* [sic]. Ashton Keyes: Verlag der Hutterischen Brüder in U.S.A., Canada und England Cotswold-Bruderhof, 1938.

Riedemann, Peter. *Confession of Faith: Account of our Religion, Doctrine and Faith Given by Peter Rideman of the Brothers whom men call Hutterians.* Rifton: Plough Publishing, 1970.

_____. *Liebe brennt wie Feuer: Die Rechenschaft und Glaubensbekenntnis eines Täufers*. MacGregor: Hutterian Brethren Book Centre, 2010.

_____. *Love is like Fire: The Confession of an Anabaptist Prisoner*. Translated by Kathleen Hasenberg. Farmington: Plough Publishing House, 1993; Kitchener: Pandora Press, 2006; Walden: Plough Publishing House, 2016.

_____. "Peter Riedemann's Rechenschaft des Glaubens der Hutterischen Brüder." In *Mittheilungen aus dem Antiquariate von S. Calvary & Co. in Berlin*, vol. 1. Berlin: S. Calvary & Co., 1870, 254–417.

_____. *Rechenschaft unsrer Religion, Lehre und Glaubens*. Berne: Witness Print "Verlag der Huterischen Brüder Gemeine," 1902.

_____. *Rechenschaft unserer Religion, Lehr und Glaubens, von den Brüdern, so man die Hutterischen nennt, ausgangen 1565*. Ashton Keynes: Cotswold Bruderhof, 1938.

_____. *Peter Riedemann's Hutterite Confession of Faith*. Edited and translated by John J. Friesen. Scottdale: Herald Press, 1999; Walden: Plough Publishing House, 2019.

_____. 피터 리더만의 후터라이트 신앙고백서 / *Piteo Rideoman ui Huteoraiteu sinang gobaekseo*. Translated by Yeongpyo Jeon. Nonsan: Daejanggan Publisher, 2018.

Snyder, C. Arnold, ed. *Sources of South German/Austrian Anabaptism*. Translated by Walter Klassen, Frank Friesen, and Werner O. Packull. Kitchener: Pandora Press, 2001.

Waldner, Michel. *Ein Bericht von einer Reise nach Europa von Amerika von zwei Diener des Worts, David Hofer und Michael Waldner, im Jahr 1937* [An Account of a Journey to Europe from America by two Servants of the Word, David Hofer and Michael Waldner, in 1937]. Copied by Joseph Y. Kleinsasser. Hawley: Spring Prairie Printing, n.d.

Walpot, Peter. *Schuel* [sic] *Ordnung von Peter Walpot aus O[e]sterreich von 1568* [School Ordinance by Peter Walpot of Austria, 1568]. Edited by David Waldner, 1969.

Zapff, Hauprecht. *Johannes der Evangelist über alle Kapitel erklärt: Ein täuferischer Bibelkommentar von 1597*. Edited by Martin Rothkegel. MacGregor: Hutterian Brethren Book Centre, 2017.

## Historical Works

### I. Surveys or General Histories

Friedmann, Robert. *Hutterite Studies: Essays by Robert Friedmann, Collected and Published in Honor of His Seventieth Anniversary*. Edited by Harold Stauffer Bender. Goshen: Mennonite Historical Society, 1961.

_____. *Hutterite Studies: Celebrating the Life and Work of an Anabaptist Scholar*. MacGregor: Hutterian Brethren Book Centre, 2010. This publication is a reprint of the 1961 edition.

Gross, Paul S. *The Hutterite Way*. Saskatoon: Freeman Publishing Company, 1965.

Hofer, John S. 후터라이트 공동체의 역사 [The History of the Hutterites]. Korea Anabaptist Press, 2008.

Hofer, John S., and Mike M. Maendel. *Geschichte der Hutterischen Brüder in kurzen Zügen für den Gebrauch in der deutschen Schule* [History of the Hutterian Brethren in Brief for use in German Schools]. Elie: James Valley Book Centre, n.d.

Horsch, John. *The Hutterian Brethren 1528–1931: A Story of Martyrdom and Loyalty*. Goshen: The Mennonite Historical Society, 1931; Repr. Cayley: Macmillan Colony, 1985; Falher: Twilight Hutterian Brethren/Bassano: Fairville Hutterian Brethren, 1994.

Hostetler, John A. *Hutterite Life*. Scottdale: Herald Press, 1965.

_____. 후터라이트 사람들, 그 삶의 이야기 [Hutterite Life]. Korea Anabaptist Press, 2002.

_____. *Hutterite Society*. Baltimore: Johns Hopkins University Press, 1974.

Janzen, Rod, and Max Stanton. *The Hutterites in North America*. Baltimore: Johns Hopkins University Press, 2010.

Osborne, Troy. *Radicals and Reformers: A Survey of Global Anabaptist History*. Harrisonburg: Herald Press, 2024.

Stayer, James. *Essays*. [Kingston, 2015?].

Taylor, Dean. *Anabaptist History Class Notes and Handouts*. Amberson: Scroll Publishing Company, 2012; CreateSpace, 2016.

von Schlachta, Astrid. *Die Hutterer zwischen Tirol und Amerika: Eine Reise durch die Jahrhunderte*. Innsbruck: Universitätsverlag Wagner, 2006.

_____. *From the Tyrol to North America: The Hutterite Story through the Centuries*. Translated by Werner and Karin Packull. Kitchener: Pandora Press, 2008. Translated from the German *Die Hutterer zwischen Tirol und Amerika*.

———. *"Holding Fast to What is Good?" Tradition and Renewal in Hutterite History*. Translated by Jesse Hofer. MacGregor: Hutterian Brethren Book Centre, 2020.

———. *Täufer: Von der Reformation ins 21. Jahrhundert* [Anabaptists: From the Reformation to the 21st Century]. Tübingen: Narr Francke Attempto Verlag, 2020.

Waldner, Samuel A. *Hutterian Church Time Line, 1528–2012: From [Europe] to North America*. Rose Valley Colony, [2013].

## II. Europe

Bayerischen Nationalmuseum München. *Die Hutterischen Täufer: Geschichtlicher Hintergrund und handwerkliche Leistung* [Hutterite Anabaptists: Historical Background and Artisanal Achievements]. Weierhof: Mennonitische Forschunsstelle, 1985.

Bonikowske, Adam Michael. "Anabaptist Masculinity in Reformation Europe." MA thesis, University of Wisconsin-Milwaukee, 2013.

Brown, Andrew Dylan Klassen. "Peace in the End Times: Apocalyptic Expectation and Sixteenth Century Peace Theology." MA thesis, Canadian Mennonite University and Mennonite Brethren Biblical Seminary, Winnipeg, 2021.

Buchinger, Erich. *Die Geschichte der Kärntner Hutterischen Brüder in Siebenbürgen und in der Walachei (1755–1770), in Rußland und Amerika* [The History of the Carinthian Hutterian Brethren in Transylvania and Wallachia (1755–1770), in Russia and America]. Offprint from *Carinthia I (1982). Zeitschricht für geschichtliche Landeskunde von Kärnten* 172. Klagenfurt: Verlag des Geschichtsvereines für Kärnten, 1982.

———. *Die "Landler" in Siebenbürgen: Vorgeschichte, Durchführung und Ergebnis einer Zwangsumsiedlung in 18. Jahrhundert* [The "Ländler" in Transylvania: Prehistory, Implementation, and Result of a Forced Resettlement in the Eighteenth Century]. München: Büchreihe der Südostdeutschen Historischen Kommission, 1980.

Chudaska, Andrea. *Peter Riedemann: Konfessionsbildendes Täufertum im 16. Jahrhundert*. Gütersloher Verlaghaus, 2003.

Chung-Kim, Esther. "Hutterites in Moravia." In *Economics of Faith: Reforming Poor Relief in Early Modern Europe*. New York: Oxford University Press, 2023.

Clasen, Claus-Peter. *Anabaptism: A Social History, 1525–1618: Switzerland, Austria, Moravia, South and Central German*. Ithaca/London: Cornell University Press, 1972.

Darlage, Adam W. "An Anabaptist's Tale: Christoph Erhard and the Recantation of the Ex-Hutterite Hans Jedelshauser." In *Grenzen des Täufertums/Boundaries of Anabaptism: Beiträge der Konferenz in Göttingen*, August 23–27, 2006, edited by Adam Schubert, Astrid von Schlachta, and Michael Driedger, 126–44. Schriften des Vereins für Reformationsgeschichte 209. Gütersloher Verlaghaus, 2009.

———. "Double Honor: Elite Hutterite Women in the Sixteenth Century." *Church History* 79, no. 4 (2010): 753–82.

———. "The Feast of Corpus Christi in Mikulov, Moravia: Strategies of Roman Catholic Counter-Reform (1579–86)." *Catholic Historical Review* 96, no. 4 (2010): 651–77.

———. "'*Mit was für Gewissen kan man sie…* [With what kind of conscience can one…]?' Conscience and Toleration in Christoph Andreas Fischer's *Vier und funfftzig erhebliche Vrsachen* [Fifty-four Significant Reasons]." *Journal of Germanic Studies* 48, no. 3 (2012): 289–300.

———. "Priests under Pressure in Southern Moravia: History and Identity in Roman Catholic Polemics (1575–1615)." PhD thesis, University of Chicago, 2009.

———. "'*Qui tacet consentire videtur* [He who is silent is understood to consent]': Christoph Andreas Fischer's Polemical Exchange with the Hutterite 'King' Klaus Braidl (1603–04)." *Renaissance and Reformation* 32, no. 3 (2009): 29–50.

———. "'They are to be pitied and wept over, not envied': Hutterite Responses to Persecution in the Chronicle." *Mennonite Quarterly Review* 83, no. 3 (2009): 403–23.

Eichinger, Reinhold, ed. *Auf den Spuren der Täufer in Tirol und Vorarlberg* [In the Footsteps of the Anabaptists in the Tirol and Vorarlberg]. Rev. ed. Wien/Nürnberg: Verlag für Theologie und Religionswissenschaft, 2018.

———. *Die Hutterer und ihr Gemüsse: Wie durch religiöse Flüchtline die gesamte Landwirtschaft rund um Thaya und March entscheidend bereichert wurde / Von den Gemüsegärten der Reformationszeit bis in die Prärien Nordamerikas* [The Hutterites and their Vegetables: How Religious Refugees significantly enriched the entire Agricultural Sector around the Dyje and Morava Rivers / From the Vegetable Gardens of the Reformation Period to the Prairies of North America]. Wien: Hutterischer Geschichtsverein, 2019.

Eichinger, Reinhold, and Josef F. Enzenberger. *Täufermuseum Niedersulz: Museumsführer [Niedersulz Anabaptist Museum: Museum Guide]*. Nürnberg: Verlag für Theologie und Religionswissenschaft, 2009.

Forster, Ellinor, Ersula Stanek, and Astrid von Schlachta. *Frauenleben in Innsbruck: Ein historisches Stadt- und Reisebuch* [The Life of Women in Innsbruck: A Historical City and Travel Book]. Salzburg: Verlag Anton Pustet, 2003.

Gerlach, Horst. *Hutterites in West Prussia: A Bruderhof in Wengeln at Lake Drausen*. Translated by Shirley Tschetter. Sioux Falls: Pine Hill Press, 1999.

Gross, Leonard. *The Golden Years of the Hutterites: The Witness and Thought of the Communal Moravian Anabaptists during the Walpot Era, 1565–1578.* Scottdale: Herald Press, 1980; rev. ed., Kitchener: Pandora Press, 1998.

Hamman, G. *Peter Riedemann in Wolkersdorf: 1541 schrieb hier die große "Rechenschaft" der Täufer und ihres Glaubens* [Peter Riedemann in Wolkersdorf: The great "Account" of the Anabaptists and their faith was written here in 1541]. Bottendorf: Evangelische Lutheranische Pfarramt, 1975.

Hofer, Rodney J. *Hutterites in Romania: A Brief History and Guide.* Createspace, 2016.

Huebert Hecht, Linda A. *Women in Early Austrian Anabaptism: Their Days, Their Stories.* Kitchener: Pandora Press, 2009.

Kalinová, Alena, Brigitte Fassinder-Brückler, and Theodor Brückler. *Täufer-Hutterer-Habaner: Geschichte, Siedlung, Keramik in Südmähren, Westslowakei und Niederösterreich* [Anabaptists-Hutterites-Habans: History, Settlement, Ceramics in Southern Moravia, Western Slovakia and Lower Austria]. Horn/Wien: Verlag Berger, 2004.

Kaufmann, Thomas. *Die Täufer: Von den radikalen Reformatoren zu den Baptisten* [The Anabaptists: From the Radical Reformers to the Baptists]. München: C.H. Beck, 2019.

Kluger, Hartmut. "Das 'Dicke Buch' der Gemeinde Gottes: Zur literarischen Selbstdarstellung der Huterischen [*sic*] Täufergemeinschaft [The 'Big Book' of the Church of God: On the Literary Self-Representation of the Hutterite Anabaptist Community]." In *Literatur und Laienbildung im Spätmittelalter und in der Reformationszeit: Symposion Wolfenbüttel, 1981*. Wolfenbuttel, 1981, edited by L. Grenzmann and K. Stackmann. Stuttgart: J.B. Metzlersche Verlagsbuchhandlung, 1984: 152–172.

Kneeland, Alma, comp. *Stories from the Chronicle of the Hutterian Brethren.* Farmington: Plough Publishing House, 1992.

Krisztinkovich, Maria H. "Bonne Espérance, Labrador, and the Hutterites: Further Notes on a Sixteenth Century Migration Plan." *Lectures and Papers in Hungarian Studies* 41. Hungarian Studies Association of Canada, 2003.

*Landkarten zur Bibel und hutterischen Geschichten* [Maps of the Bible and Hutterite History]. Starbuck: Starlite Colony, 2006.

Meyer, Therese, and Kurt Karpf. *St. Peter und darüber hinaus: Zur Geschichte der Menschen und ihrer Höfe in St. Peter, Aich, Tangern, Amlach und Kleinsaß bei Spittal in Kärnten* [St. Peter and Beyond: The History of the People and their Farms in St. Peter, Aich, Tangern, Amlach, and Kleinsass near Spittal in Carinthia]. Vol. 3 of Beiträge zur Kulturgeschichte Oberkärntens. Spittal an der Drau: Stadtarchivs Spittal/Drau, 2006.

Packull, Werner O. *Die Hutterer in Tirol: Frühes Täufertum in der Schweiz, Tirol und Mähren* [Hutterites in the Tirol: Early Anabaptism in Switzerland, the Tirol, and Moravia]. Translated by Astrid von Schlachta. Innsbruck: Universitätsverlag Wagner, 2000. Translation of *Hutterite Beginnings*.

_____. *Hutterite Beginnings: Communitarian Experiments during the Reformation.* Baltimore: Johns Hopkins University Press, 1995.

_____. *Peter Riedemann: Shaper of the Hutterite Tradition.* Kitchener: Pandora Press, 2007.

_____. "Weite Wege von Mähren nach Hessen: Die Zweite Missionsreise Peter Riedemanns [Distant Journeys from Moravia to Hesse: The second Missionary Journey of Peter Riedemann]." In *Aussenseiter Zwischen Mittelalter und Neuzeit: Festschrift für Hans-Jürgen Goertz zum 60. Geburtstag*, edited by Norbert Fischer and Marion Kobelt-Groch. Leiden: Brill, 1997: 171–85.

Pajer, Jiří. "Newly Discovered Anabaptist Settlement at Čermákovice (Alinkov farmstead, municipality of Horní Kounice, Znojmo District)." *Acta Ethnographica Hungarica* 60, no. 2 (2015): 463–82.

_____. *Sídla Novokřtěnců Na Moravě* [The "New Christians" in Moravia]. Strážnice: Nakladatelství Etnos, 2021.

Rauert, Matthias H. "*Die 'Brüder-Schreiber' in Mähren* [The 'Brotherhood Scribes' in Moravia]." *Mennonitische Geschichtsblätter* 56 (1999): 103–138.

Riedemann, Peter. *Rechenschaft unserer Religion, Lehre und Glaubens, von den Brüder, die man die Huterischen nennt: für den Gebrauch an hutterischen Schulen und Sonntagsschulen in heutigem Deutsch bearbeitet und mit einer Einleitung über "Die Anfänge der Hutterer und Peter Riedemann"* [Account of our Religion, Doctrine and Faith, by the Brethren who are called Hutterites: edited in modern German for use in Hutterite schools and Sunday schools and with an introduction on "The Beginnings of the Hutterites and Peter Riedemann"]. Edited by Lothar G. Korff. Krefeld, 1999.

Robertshaw, Eileen, comp. *Over the Mountains: A Story Based on the Second Chronicle of the Hutterian Brethren and other Contemporary Records.* Plough Publishing House, 2012.

Rothkegel, Martin. "Learned in the School of David: Peter Riedemann's Paraphrases of the Gospels." In *Commoners and Community. Essays in Honour of Werner O. Packull*, edited by Arnold Snyder. Kitchener: Pandora Press, 2002: 233–55.

Schroeder, William. *Hutterite Migrations in Europe.* Winnipeg, 2001.

Scribner, Robert W. "Konkrete Utopian: Die Täufer und der vormoderne Kommunismus [Actual Utopias: Anabaptists and Pre-modern Communism]." In *Religion und Kultur in Deutschland 1400–1800*. Göttingen: Vandenhoeck und Ruprecht, 2002.

Snyder, C. Arnold, and Linda A. Huebert Hecht, eds. *Profiles of Anabaptist Women: Sixteenth-Century Reforming Pioneers.* Waterloo: Wilfrid Laurier University Press, 1996

von Schlachta, Astrid, Ellinor Forester, and Giovanni Merola. *Verbrannte Visionen? Erinnerungsorte der Täufer in Tirol* [Scorched Visions? Anabaptist Memorial Sites in Tyrol]. Innsbruck: Innsbruck University Press, 2007.

von Schlachta, Astrid. "Die Hutterer: Jacob Hutter aus St. Lorenzen mein Hutterischer Sommer aus der Geschichte Lernen." *Südtirol: In Wort und Bild.* 2, 66 (2022).

_____. "'Du sollst nicht töten!' Täuferische Wehrlosigkeit als Lebenshaltung in der Reformationszeit ['Thou shalt not kill!' Anabaptist defenselessness as a way of life in the Reformation era]." In *Reformation und Militär: Wege und Irrwege in fünf Jahrhunderten* [Reformation and the Military: Paths and Missteps over Five Centuries], edited by Angelika Dorfler-Dierken. Gottingen: Vandenhoeck & Ruprecht, 2019: 49-61.

_____. *Hutterische Konfession und Tradition (1578–1619): Etabliertes Leben zwischen Ordnung und Ambivalenz.* Mainz: Verlag Philipp von Zabern, 2003.

Taylor, Dean. *The Hutterite Mission Machine: The Marine Corps of the Early Anabaptists.* Foreword by Jake Gross. N.p., n.d.

Waltner, Emil J. *Banished for Faith*. Rev. ed. Jasper: End-Time Handmaidens, 1979.

Wild, Geoffrey Milner. "Comenius, Education and the Hutterite Anabaptists: An Investigation of the Possibility of Influence on the Educational Thought of Comenius by the Hutterite Anabaptists." MA thesis, University of Western Australia, 1977.

Winkelbauer, Thomas. "*Die Vertreibung der Hutterer aus Mähren 1622: Massenexodus oder Abzug der letzten Standhaften?* [The Expulsion of Hutterites from Moravia in 1622: Mass exodus or Deportation of the Remaining Faithful?]" *Mennonitische Geschichtsblätter* 61 (2004), 65–96.

Wiswedel, Wilhelm. *Bilder und Führergestalten aus dem Täufertum: Ein Beitrag zur Reformationsgeschichte des 16. Jahrhunderts* [Scenes and Leaders of Anabaptism: A Contribution to 16th-Century Reformation History], Bd. 3. Kassel: Oncken, 1952.

Wolkan, Rudolf. *Die Hutterer: Österreichische Wiedertäufer und Kommunisten in Amerika* [The Hutterites: Austrian Anabaptists and Communitarians in America]. Wien: Wiener Bibliphilen-Geselschaft, 1918.

Zeman, Jerold K. *The Anabaptists and the Czech Brethren in Moravia, 1526–1628: A Study of Origins and Contacts*. The Hague: Mouton, 1969.

_____. "Historical Topography of Moravian Anabaptism." *Mennonite Quarterly Review*, 40 (1966), 266–78 and 41 (1967), 40–78, 116–60.

## III. Russia and Ukraine

Donner, Heinrich. *The Migration of Hutterites to South Russia*. Copied by Jacob Wall. Conference of Mennonites in Canada, 1975.

Dyck, Harvey L., and John R. Staples, eds. *Transformation on the Southern Ukrainian Steppe: Letters and Papers of Johann Cornies, Volume I: 1812-1835*. Translated and edited by Ingrid I. Epp. Toronto: University of Toronto Press, 2015.

_____. *Transformation on the Southern Ukrainian Steppe: Letters and Papers of Johann Cornies, Volume II: 1836–1842*. Translated and edited by Ingrid I. Epp. Toronto: University of Toronto Press, 2020.

Giesinger, Adam. *From Catherine to Khrushchev: The Story of Russia's Germans*. Battleford: Marian Press, 1974.

Klaus, Alexander. *Unsere Kolonien: Studien und Materialien zur Geschichte und Statistik der ausländischen Kolonisation in Russland* [Our Colonies: Studies and Materials on the History and Statistics of Foreign Colonization in Russia]. Translated from the Russian by J. Töws. Odessa:

Verlag der Odessaer Zeitung, 1887; Hildesheim: Georg Olms Verlag, 2009.

Staples, John R. *Johann Cornies, the Mennonites, and Russian Colonialism in Southern Ukraine*. Toronto: University of Toronto Press, 2024.

**IV. North America**

Canaday, Dayton W., ed. *South Dakota Historical Collections* 37. Pierre: State Publishing Company, 1977.

Clark, Bertha W. *Die hutterischen Gemeinschaften* [The Hutterian Communities]. Fulda: Eberhard Arnold-Verlag, 1929.

———. "Turners of the Other Cheek," *Survey* 47 (December 31, 1921): 519–524.

Clément, Dominique, and Renée Vaugeois, eds. *Alberta's Human Rights Story: The Search for Equality and Justice*. [Edmonton]: John Humphrey Centre for Peace and Human Rights, [2012].

Fuller, Millard, and Diane Scott. *Love in the Mortar Joints: The Story of Habitat for Humanity*. Chicago: Association Press, 1980.

"Granola Chronicles: Culinary Tales from Tall Grass Bakery and Winnipeg's Wolseley Community." *Anthologie Monthly* 1 (January 2021).

*Grunthal History, 1874–1974*. Grunthal: Grunthal History Book Committee, 1974.

Gross, Clarence, comp. *Schmiedeleut Prediger Verzeichnis* [Directory of Schmiedeleut Ministers]. Rev. ed. [High Bluff]: Sommerfeld Colony, 2007.

Hofer, D[avid] M. *Die Hungersnot in Rußland und Unsere Reise um die Welt* [The Famine in Russia and our Travels Around the World]. Chicago: K.M.B. Publishing House, 1924.

*History of 1990–2020*. N.p., 2023.

Hofer, John. *The History of the Hutterites*. Rev. ed. Altona: D.W. Friesen & Sons, 1988.

Hofer, Johnny, ed. *Briefe von Michael Waldner, Bon Hom[m]e, South Dakota, USA. geschrieben an seinen Sohn, Paul Waldner, aus England, 1937* [Letters from Michael Waldner, Bon Homme, South Dakota, USA. written to his son, Paul Waldner, from England, 1937]. Miami: Miami Colony, 2001.

Hiebert, Jerald. "The Hutterite Story of a Pure Church." MA thesis: Regent College, Vancouver, 2001.

*Hutterite CO's in World War I*. Hawley: Spring Prairie Printing, 1997.

Janzen, Rod. *Paul Tschetter: The Story of a Hutterite Immigrant Leader, Pioneer, and Pastor*. Eugene: Pickwick Publications, 2009.

Janzen, Rod A. *Perceptions of the South Dakota Hutterites in the 1980s*. Freeman: Freeman Publishing Company, 1984.

Jones, Clifton H., ed. "'The Hutterisch People:' A View from the 1920s." *South Dakota History* 7, no. 1 (1976): 1–14.

Kleinsasser, Ian. *Blessings and Burdens: 100 Years of Hutterites in Manitoba*. MacGregor: Hutterian Brethren Book Centre, 2019.

Kohl, Seena B. "A Comparison: Hutterite Women and their Families." In *Working Together: Women and Family in Southwestern Saskatchewan*. Toronto: Holt, Reinhardt and Winston of Canada, 1976.

Maendel, Dora. "Hutterites in Alcatraz." In *Cultivating Peace: Courage, Conscience and Resistance to War*. Kitchener: MCC Ontario, 2006.

Mumelter, Gerhard. *Die Hutterer: Tiroler Täufergemeinden in Nordamerika* [The Hutterites: Tyrolean Anabaptist Communities in North America]. Innsbruck: Kaymon, 1986.

[Rhodes, Robert]. *The Hutterian Brethren: Christians in Community*. Gibbon: Starland Hutterian Brethren, 1997.

Riley, Marvin P., and Darryll R. Johnson. "South Dakota's Hutterite Colonies, 1874–1967." *Bulletin* 565 (January 1970). Brookings: Agricultural Experiment Station, South Dakota State University.

Riley, Marvin P., and James R. Stewart. "The Hutterites: South Dakota's Communal Farmers." *Bulletin* 530 (February 1966). Brookings: Agricultural Experiment Station, South Dakota State University.

Stoltzfus, Duane C.S. *Pacifists in Chains: The Persecution of Hutterites during the Great War*. Baltimore: Johns Hopkins University Press, 2013.

———. "Armed With Prayer in an Alcatraz Dungeon: The Wartime Experiences of Four Hutterite COs in Their Own Words." *Mennonite Quarterly Review* 85 (April 2011): 259–292.

von Schlachta, Astrid. "Das Politische in der 'apolitischen' Geschichte: Robert Friedmann zwischen täuferischen Ideen und religiösem Sozialismus—Eine Annäherung." In *Politische Philosophie versus Politische Theologie? Die Frage der Gewalt in Spannungsfeld von Politik und Religion*, edited by Wolfgang Palaver, Andreas Oberprantacher, and Dietmar Regensburger. Innsbruck: Innsbruck University Press, 2011: 305–24.

Werner, Hans. "'Something…we had not seen nor heard of': The 1873 Mennonite Delegation to Find Land in 'America'." *Preservings* 34 (2014): 11–20.

Wiebe, Bruce. "A Politically Risky Land Sale." *Preservings* 32 (2012): 35–38.

## Community Histories

Gross, Mike D., and Jacob S. Waldner. *A History of Pincher Creek, [Alberta] and the Story of a Conscientious Objector*. Ste. Agathe, Crystal Spring Colony, 2021.

Hiebert, Jerald. *The Hutterite Story of a Pure Church*. MA thesis: Regent College, Vancouver, 2001.

[Hofer, John.] *Treasures of Time: the Rural Municipality of Cartier, 1914–1984*. Elie: RM of Cartier, 1985.

[Hofer, Johnny]. *The History of James Valley Hutterite Colony, 1918–2018*. Elie: James Valley Book Centre, 2019.

Stahl, Solomon. *The History of Bon Homme Colony, Manitoba*. Fordville: Forest River Bookbindery, 2001.

Waldner, Tony. *History of Forest River Community*. Fordville: Forest River Community, 1990.

———. *Reviving Memories of Milltown, SD Hutterite Colony 1886–1923*. Fordville: Forest River Bookbindery, 2024.

Youmans, Vance Joseph. *The Plough and the Pen: Paul S. Gross and the Establishment of the Spokane Hutterian Brethren*. Boone: Parkway Publishers, 1995.

## Theological Writings

Biesecker-Mast, Gerald. *Separation and the Sword in Anabaptist Persuasion: Radical Confessional Rhetoric from Schleitheim to Dordrecht*. Telford: Cascadia Publishing House, 2006.

Chatfield, Graeme R. *Balthasar Hubmaier and the Clarity of Scripture: A Critical Reformation Issue*. Eugene: Pickwick Publications, 2013.

Finger, Thomas N. *A Contemporary Anabaptist Theology: Biblical, Historical, Constructive*. Downers Grove: Intervarsity Press, 2004.

Godwin, Colin. *Anabaptist Meditations: Thirty Days of Biblical Reflection from the Founders the Tradition*. Thunder Bay, Pandora Press: 2022.

———. *Baptizing, Gathering, and Sending: Anabaptist Mission in the Sixteenth-Century Context*. Kitchener: Pandora Press, 2012.

Gross, Paul S. *Hutterian Brethren: Life and Religion.* Pincher Creek, n.d.

Harrison, Wes. *Andreas Ehrenpreis and Hutterite Faith and Practice.* Kitchener: Pandora Press, 1997.

Hiebert, Jerald. *Hutterian Brethren Foundations and their Formation in the Sixteenth Century.* Raymond, 2009.

———. *The Essence of Hutterite Faith and Values.* Raymond, 2007.

Hofer, Jacob E. *Ein schönes Taufbüchlein: Zu brauchen wenn die Kinder mit Gott und allen Frommen einen Bund aufrichten wollen* [A Beautiful Baptism Booklet: to be used when [Young People] desire to establish a Covenant with God and all the Devout]. [Grand Prairie: Grandview Colony, 2020].

Hofer, Kathrina, comp. *Weide mein Lämmer: Eagle Creek Schul Versammlung für Eltern, Lehrer, Jünglinge und Jungfrauen, Januar 14–15, 2015* [Feed my Lambs: Eagle Creek School Meeting for Parents, Teachers, and Young People, January 14–15, 2015]. Scotford Colony, 2015.

Hofer, Peter. *The Hutterian Brethren and Their Beliefs.* Starbuck: Hutterian Brethren of Manitoba, 1955.

*The Hutterian Church Responds to Questions of Faith.* Elie: Hutterite Education Committee and James Valley Book Centre, 2000.

*Im Weinstock treu bleiben: Hilfsquelle für hutterische Täuflinge / Abiding in the Vine: Resources for Hutterian Baptismal Candidates.* MacGregor: Hutterian Brethren Book Centre, 2018.

Kleinsasser, Jacob. *Seeking Purity: A Talk to Young People.* Ste. Agathe: Crystal Spring Colony, 2002.

Kleinsasser, Samuel. *Community and Ethics.* Unpublished manuscript, 2010. Portions of this work are published in this volume.

Maendel, Dora, and Clara Wollmann, eds. *Johannes Kapeteins Entzückung: Eine Ermahnung* [Johannes Kapetein's Vision: An Admonition]. MacGregor: Hutterian Brethren Book Centre, 2006.

Saxby, Trevor J. *Pilgrims of a Common Life: Christian Community of Goods through the Centuries.* Scottdale: Herald Press, 1987.

von Schlachta, Astrid. "Jakob Huter aus St. Lorenzen und die Hutterer." *Südtirol in Wort und Bild* 54, no. 4, (2009): 15–19.

Waldner, Adam. *The Great Deception.* n.p., [2014].

Wurz, Joeseph [sic], George Tschetter, and David Tschetter. *Hear my Cries! Oh Lord.* Wanham: Shady Lane Colony, 2019.

## Sociology, Ethnography, Anthropology, Geography

Conkin, Paul K. *Two Paths to Utopia: The Hutterites and the Llano Colony.* Lincoln: University of Nebraska Press, 1964.

Deets, Lee Emerson. *The Hutterites: A Study in Social Cohesion.* Philadelphia: Porcupine Press, 1975.

Evans, Simon. "Alberta Hutterite Colonies: An Exploration of Past, Present and Future Settlement Patterns." *Communal Studies* 30, no. 2 (2010): 27–63.

_____. "Hutterite Agriculture in Alberta: The Contribution of an Ethnic Isolate." *Agricultural History* 93, no. 4 (2019): 656–681.

_____. "Hutterite Colonies and the Cultural Landscape: An Inventory of Selected Site Characteristics." *The Journal of Amish and Plain Anabaptist Studies* 4, 1 (2016): 51–81.

_____. "The Hutterites Come to Alberta." *Alberta History* 63, no. 4 (2015): 11–19.

_____. "Some factors shaping the expansion of Hutterite colonies in Alberta since the repeal of the Communal Property Act in 1973." *Canadian Ethnic Studies* 45, no. 1/2 (2013): 203–236.

Evans, Simon, and Peter Peller. "A Brief History of Hutterite Demography." *Great Plains Quarterly* 35, no. 1 (2015): 79–101.

_____. "Mapping an Ethnic Isolate: The Diffusion of Hutterite Colonies across the Prairies and northern Great Plains." *Great Plains Quarterly* 38, No. 4 (Fall 2018): 357–385.

Flint, David. *The Hutterites: A Study in Prejudice.* Toronto: Oxford University Press, 1975.

Groulx, Nicolas. "La littérature de jeunesse huttérite: Thèmes, perspectives et perceptions d'une pratique littéraire [Hutterite Children's Literature: Themes, Perspectives, and Perceptions of a Literary Practice]" MA thesis, Université de Montréal, 2023.

Hostetler, John A. "Communal Socialization among the Hutterites." In *Sociology Canada: Readings*, edited by Christopher Beattie and Stewart Crysdale. Toronto: Butterworths, 1974: 109–133.

_____. *Communitarian Societies.* New York: Holt, Rinehart and Winston, 1974.

_____. *Hutterite Life.* Scottdale: Herald Press, 1965.

_____. *Hutterite Society.* Baltimore: Johns Hopkins University Press, 1974.

Hostetler, John, and Gertrude Enders Huntington. "The Hutterites: Fieldwork in a North American Communal Society." In *Being an Anthropologist: Fieldwork in Eleven Cultures*, edited by George D. Spindler. Prospect Heights: Waveland Press, 1970: 194–219.

_____. *The Hutterites in North America*, 3rd ed. Orlando: Harcourt Brace College Publishers, 1996.

Huntington, Gertrude Enders. "Children of the Hutterites." *Natural History* 90, no. 2 (February 1981): 34-47.

Infield, Henrik F. *Cooperative Communities at Work*. New York: Dryden Press, 1945.

_____. *Utopia and Experiment: Essays in the Sociology of Cooperation*. Port Washington: Kennikat Press, 1955.

Janzen, Rod, and Max Stanton. *The Hutterites in North America*. Baltimore: Johns Hopkins University Press, 2010.

Kant, Joanita. *Gentle People: A Case Study of Rockport Colony Hutterites*. Brookings: Prairie View Press, 2013.

Kaplan, Bert, and Thomas F.A. Plaut. *Personality in a Communal Society: An Analysis of the Mental Health of the Hutterites*. Lawrence: University of Kansas Publications, 1956.

Katz, Yossi, and John Lehr. *Inside the Ark: The Hutterites in Canada and the United States*. Regina: Canadian Plains Research Centre Press, 2012; rev. ed., 2014.

Kephart, William M. "The Hutterites." In *Extraordinary Groups: The Sociology of Unconventional Life-Styles*. New York: St. Martin's Press, 1979; 2nd ed., 1982.

Kienzler, Hanna. *Gender and Communal Longevity among Hutterites: How Hutterite Women Establish, Maintain, and Change Colony Life*. Aachen: Shaker Verlag, 2005.

Kraybill, Donald B., and Carl Desportes Bowman. "The Hutterites." In *On the Backroad to Heaven: Old Order Hutterites, Mennonites, Amish, and Brethren*. Baltimore: Johns Hopkins University Press, 2001: 20–59.

Längin, Bernd G. *Die Hutterer: Gefangene der Vergangenheit, Pilger der Gegenwart, Propheten der Zukunft* [The Hutterites: Prisoners of the Past, Pilgrims of the Present, Prophets of the Future]. Hamburg/Zurich: Rasch und Röhring, 1986.

Luther, Helmut. *Aus der Zeit gefallen: Mein Besuch bei den Hutterern in Nordamerika* [Disconnected from Time: My Visit to the Hutterites in North America]. Bozen: Raetia, 2023.

Mackie, Marlene. "Ethnic Stereotypes and Prejudice: Alberta Indians, Hutterites and Ukrainians." *Canadian Ethnic Studies* 6, no. 1/2 (1974): 39–52.

_____. "Outsiders' Perception of the Hutterites." *Mennonite Quarterly Review* 51 (January 1976): 58–65.

Martin, Alexander J.F. "Hutterite Colonies and Canopy Cover: A Remotely Sensed Analysis of the Effects of Cultural-Religious Beliefs on the Treed Landscape." *Trees, Forests and People* 14 (December 2023).

Masuk, Lesley C. "Patriarchy, Technology, and the Lives of Hutterite Women: A Field Study." MA thesis, University of Saskatchewan, 1998.

Mathieu, Barbara Altman. "The Door as Cultural Symbol: A Contrast of Hutterian Community and Middle-Class Society." PhD diss., University of California Los Angeles, 1987.

Miller, Ann, and Peter Stephenson. "Jakob Hutter: An Interpretation of the Individual Man and His People." *Ethos* 8, no. 3 (1980): 229–252.

Peter, Karl. "The Communal Settlements of the Hutterites in America." *German Canadian Yearbook* 1 (1973): 145–148.

_____. "The Decline of Hutterite Population Growth." *Canadian Ethnic Studies* 12, no. 3 (1980): 97–110.

_____. *The Dynamics of Hutterite Society: An Analytical Approach*. Edmonton: University of Alberta Press, 1987.

_____. "The Instability of the Community of Goods in the Social History of the Hutterites." In *Western Canada Past and Present*, edited by A.W. Rasporivich. Calgary: McClelland & Stewart West, 1975: 99–119.

_____. "Problems in the Family, Community, and Culture of Hutterites." In *Canadian Families: Ethnic Variations*, edited by K. Ishwaran. Toronto: McGraw-Hill Ryerson, 1980: 221–236.

_____. "Rejoinder to 'The Decline of Hutterite Population Growth: Causes and Consequences.'" *Canadian Ethnic Studies* 12, no. 3 (1980): 118–123.

_____. "Religion, Community Relations, and Self-Identity among the Hutterites." In *The Canadian Family*, edited by K. Ishwaran. Toronto: Gage Publishing, 1983: 177–188.

Peters, Victor. *All things Common: The Hutterian Way of Life*. Minneapolis: University of Minnesota Press, 1965.

_____. *Die Hutterischen Brüder (1528–1992): Die Geschichtliche und Soziale Entwicklung einer Erfolgreichen Gütergemeinschaft* [The Hutterite Brethren (1528-1992): The Historical and Social Development of a Successful Communal Movement]. Translated by Jack Thiessen. Marburg: N.G. Elwert Verlag, 1992. A German translation of *All Things Common: The Hutterian Way of Life.*

Pickering, W.S.F. *The Hutterites: Christians Who Practise a Communal Way of Life.* London: Wardlock Educational, 1982.

Redekop, Calvin, Victor A. Krahn, and Samuel J. Steiner, eds. *Anabaptist/Mennonite Faith and Economics.* Lanham: University Press of America; Waterloo: Institute of Anabaptist and Mennonite Studies, 1994.

Ryan, John. *The Agricultural Economy of Manitoba Hutterite Colonies.* Toronto: McClelland and Stewart, 1977.

Shenker, Barry. *Intentional Communities: Ideology and Alienation in Communal Societies.* London: Routledge & Kegan Paul, 1986.

Stanton, Max E. "All Things Common: A Comparison of Israel, Hutterite, and Latter-day Saint Communalism." David O. McKay Lectures, February 12, 1992, Brigham Young University–Hawaii.

_____. "The Maintenance of the Hutterite Way: The Family and Childhood Life-Cycle in the Communal Context." *Family Science Review* 2, no. 4 (November, 1989): 373-388.

Stephenson, Peter H. "A Dying of the Old Man and a Putting on the New: The Cybernetics of Ritual Metanoia in the Life of the Hutterian Commune." MA thesis, University of Calgary, 1973.

_____. "'He died too quick!': The Process of Dying in a Hutterian Colony." *Omega* 14, no. 2 (1983–84): 127–134.

_____. "The Hutterian People: Ritual and Rebirth in the Evolution of Communal Life." MA thesis, Lanham: University Press of America, 1991.

_____. "Persecution and Response: The Hutterites and Communal Practices Associated with Peace Building." In *Religious Diversity Today: Experiencing Religion in the Contemporary World*, vol. 3: Religion Transforming Societies and Social Lives, edited by Jean-Guy Goulet. Praeger: Santa Barbara, 2016: 121–144.

Tschetter, Rueben. "Communication Technology and Hutterite Culture: A Theoretical Analysis of ICT Uses and Practices within the Hutterite Community." Hons. Thesis, University of Calgary, 2011; Saarbrücken: Lambert Academic Publishing, 2014.

Wurm, Shalom. *Das Leben in den historischen Kommunen* [Life in the Historic Communes]. Köln: Bund-Verlag, 1977.

## The Law and the State

Esau, Alvin J. *The Courts and the Colonies: The Litigation of Hutterite Church Disputes*. Vancouver: UBC Press, 2004.

Hamilton, Jonnette Watson. "Space for Religion: Regulation of Hutterite Expansion and the Superior Court of Alberta." In *The Alberta Supreme Court at 100: History and Authority*, edited by Jonathan Swainger. Edmonton: University of Alberta Press; Toronto: Osgoode Society for Canadian Legal History, 2007: 159–192.

Janzen, William. *Limits on Liberty: The Experience of Mennonite, Hutterite and Doukhobor Communities in Canada*. Toronto: University of Toronto Press, 1990.

Moore, Howard W. *Plowing my own Furrow*. Syracuse: Syracuse University Press, 1985.

Sharpe, Robert J., and Kent Roach. *Brian Dickson: A Judge's Journey*. Toronto: University of Toronto Press, 2003.

## Medical Studies[1]

Amish, Mennonite, and Hutterite Genetic Disorders Database. Biochemical Genetics Laboratory, London, ON, August 2006. http://www.biochemgenetics.ca/plainpeople/index.php.

Anderson, Rebecca L., Kathleen Murray, Jessica X. Chong, Rebecca Ouwenga, et al. "Disclosure of Genetic Research Results to Members of a Founder Population." *Journal of Genetic Counseling* 23, no. 6 (2014): 984–91.

Armistead, Joy, Sunita Khatkar, Britta Meyer, Brian L. Mark, Nehal Patel, et al. "Mutation of a Gene Essential for Ribosome Biogenesis, EMG1, Causes Bowen-Conradi Syndrome." *American Journal of Human Genetics* 84, no. 6 (2009): 728–39.

Barbara, Angela M., Mark Loeb, Lisa Dolovich, Kevin Brazil, and Margaret Russell. "Agreement Between Self-Report and Medical Records on Signs and Symptoms of Respiratory Illness." *Primary Care Respiratory Journal* 21, no. 2 (2012): 145–52.

Bowen, Peter. "Workshop on Genetic Disorders in the Hutterites, Edmonton, Canada, October 12–13, 1983." *American Journal of Medical Genetics* 22 (1985): 449–51.

---

1  This section was enriched by the expertise of Drs. Hans Pasterkamp, Cheryl Rockman-Greeberg, Micheil Innes, and Michel Charette.

Bowen, Peter, and G.J. Conradi, "Syndrome of Skeletal and Genitourinary Anomalies with Unusual Facies and Failure to Thrive in Hutterite Sibs." *Birth Defects Original Article Series* 12, no. 6 (1976): 101–8.

Boycott, Kym M., Jillian S. Parboosingh, Bernie N. Chodirker, R. Brian Lowry, et al. "Clinical Genetics and the Hutterite Population: A Review of Mendelian Disorders." *American Journal of Medical Genetics* 146A (2008): 1088–98.

Brunt, J.H., B. Reeder, P. Stephenson, E. Love, and Y. Chen. "A Comparison of Physical and Laboratory Measures between two Hutterite Leute and the Rural Saskatchewan Population." *Canadian Journal of Public Health* 85 (1994): 299–302.

Cacciatore, Joanne, and Rebecca Ong. "Through the Touch of God: Child Death and Spiritual Sustenance in a Hutterian Colony." *Omega: Journal of Death and Dying* 64, no. 3 (2011): 185–202.

Campbell, Catarina D., Jessica X. Chong, Maika Malig, Arthur Ko, Beth L. Dumont, et al. "Estimating the human mutation rate using autozygosity in a founder population." *Nature Genetics* 44, no. 11 (2012): 1277–81.

Chong, Jessica X., Rebecca Ouwenga, Rebecca L. Anderson, Darrel J. Waggoner, and Carole Ober. "A Population-Based Study of Autosomal-Recessive Disease-Causing Mutations in a Founder Population." *The American Journal of Human Genetics* 91 (2012): 1–13.

Clark, Peter Gordon. "Dynasty Formation in the Communal Society of the Hutterites." PhD diss., University of British Columbia, 1974.

Converse, Thomas A., Richard S. Buker Jr., and Richard V. Lee. "Hutterite Midwifery." *American Journal of Obstetrics and Gynecology* 116, no. 5 (1973): 719–25.

Cusanovich, Darren A., Minal Çalişkan, Christine Billstrand, Katelyn Michelini, Claudia Chavarria, et al. "Integrated Analyses of Gene Expression and Genetic Association Studies in a Founder Population." *Human Molecular Genetics* 25, no. 10 (2016): 2104–12.

Eaton, Joseph W., and A.J. Mayer. "Man's Capacity to Reproduce: The Demography of a Unique Population." Glencoe: Free Press; repr., *Human Biology* 26 (1954): 206–64.

Eaton, Joseph W., and Robert J. Weil. *Culture and Mental Disorders: A Comparative Study of the Hutterites and Other Populations*. Glencoe: Free Press, 1955.

———. "Some Epidemiological Findings in the Hutterite Mental Health Study." In *Interrelations Between the Social Environment and Psychiatric Disorders*. New York: Milbank Memorial Fund, 1953: 222–31.

Eaton, Joseph W., Robert J. Weil, and Bert Kaplan. "The Hutterite Mental Health Study." *Mennonite Quarterly Review* 25 (January 1951): 47–65.

Gushuliak, Elizabeth Theresa. "Value Orientations of Hutterian Women in Canada." MA Thesis, University of Alberta, 1990.

Hartzog, S.H. "Population Genetic Studies of a Human Isolate: The Hutterites of North America." PhD diss., University of Massachusetts, 1971.

Hostetler, John A., "History and Relevance of the Hutterite Population for Genetic Studies." *American Journal of Medical Genetics* 22 (1985): 453–62.

Howells, W.W. *Hutterite Age Differences in Body Measurements*. Cambridge: The Peabody Museum, 1970.

Hunter, Alasdair G.W., Sarah J. Woerner, Lucy D.C. Montalvo-Hicks, S. Beatrice Fowlow, Robert H.A. Haslam, et al. "The Bowen-Conradi Syndrome: A Highly Lethal Autosomal Recessive Syndrome of Microcephaly, Micrognathia, Low Birth Weight, and Joint Deformities." *American Journal of Medical Genetics* 3, no. 3 (1979): 269–79.

Huntington, Gertrude Enders, and John A. Hostetler. "A Note on Nursing Practices in an American Isolate with a High Birth Rate." *Population Studies* 19 (1966): 321–24.

Kim, Tae H., Margaret L. Russell, Kevin Fonseca, Fred Aoki, Gregory Horsman, et al. "Characteristics of Respiratory Viral Infections during Influenza Season in Canadian Hutterite Communities." *Influenza and Other Respiratory Viruses* 7, no. 6 (2013): 1088–92.

Laing, L.M. "Declining Fertility in a Religious Isolate: The Hutterite Population of Alberta, Canada, 1951–1971." *Human Biology* 52, no. 2 (1980): 289–310.

Lilley, Margaret, Susan Christian, Stacey Hume, Patrick Scott, Mark Montgomery, et al. "Newborn Screening for Cystic Fibrosis in Alberta: Two Years of Experience." *Paediatrics and Child Health* 15, no. 9 (2010): 590–94.

Loeb, Mark, Margaret L. Russell, Lorraine Moss, Kevin Fonseca, Julie Fox, et al. "Effect of Influenza Vaccination of Children on Infection Rates in Hutterite Communities: A Randomized Trial." *Journal of the American Medical Association* 303, no. 10 (2010): 943–50.

Loeb, Mark, Paramjit K. Singh, Julie Fox, Margaret L. Russell, Kanti Pabbaraju, et al. "Longitudinal Study of Influenza Molecular Viral Shedding in Hutterite Communities." *Journal of Infectious Diseases* 206, no. 7 (2012): 1078–84.

Morgan, Kenneth. "Mortality Changes in the Hutterite Brethren of Alberta and Saskatchewan, Canada." *Human Biology* 55 (1983): 89–99.

Morgan, Kenneth, and T. Mary Holmes. "Population Structure of a Religious Isolate: The Dariusleut Hutterites of Alberta." In *Current Developments in Anthropological Genetics: Ecology and Population Structure*, vol. 2, edited by Michael H. Crawford and James H. Mielke, 1980: 429–48.

Motika, Caroline A., Charalampos Papachristou, Mark Abney, Lucille A. Lester, and Carole Ober. "Rising Prevalence of Asthma is Sex-Specific in a US Farming Population." *Journal of Allergy and Clinical Immunology* 128, no. 4 (2011): 774–79.

Ober, Carole, Terry Hyslop, and Walter W. Hauck. "Inbreeding Effects on Fertility in Humans: Evidence for Reproductive Compensation." *American Journal for Human Genetics* 64 (1999): 225–31.

Ober, Carole, Anne I. Sperling, Erika von Mutius, and Donata Vercellid. "Immune Development and Environment: Lessons from Amish and Hutterite Children." *Current Opinion in Immunology* 48 (2017): 51–60.

Peter, Karl A. "The Decline of Hutterite Population Growth." *Canadian Ethnic Studies* 12 (1980): 97–123.

Pichler, Irene, Christian Fuchsberger, Christa Platzer, Minal Çalişkan, et al. "Drawing the History of the Hutterite Population on a Genetic Landscape: Inference from Y-chromosome and mtDNA Genotypes." *European Journal Human Genetics* 18, no. 4 (2010): 463–70.

Schroth, Robert, Pamel R. Dahl, Mohammad Haque, and Eleonore Kliewer. "Early Childhood Caries among Hutterite Preschool Children in Manitoba, Canada." *Rural and Remote Health* 10, no. 4 (2010): 1535.

Science, Michelle, Jonathon L. Maguire, Margaret L. Russell, Marek Smieja, et al. "Low Serum 25-Hydroxyvitamin D Level and Risk of Upper Respiratory Tract Infection in Children and Adolescents." *Clinical Infectious Diseases* 57, no. 3 (2013): 392–97.

Smith, Christine. "An Analysis of Hutterite Breastfeeding Patterns." MA Thesis, University of Montana, 2006.

Stein, Michelle M., Cara L. Hrusch, Justyna Gozdz, et al. "Innate Immunity and Asthma Risk in Amish and Hutterite Farm Children." *New England Journal of Medicine* 375, no. 5 (2016): 411–21.

Thompson, Emma E., Ying Sun, Dan Nicolae, and Carole Ober. "Shades of Gray: A Comparison of Linkage Disequilibrium Between Hutterites and Europeans." *Genetic Epidemiology* 34, no. 2 (2010): 133–39.

Triggs-Raine, Barbara, Tamara Dyck, Kym M. Boycott, A. Micheil Innes, Carole Ober, Jillian S. Parboosingh, Alexis Botkin, Cheryl R. Greenberg, and Elizabeth L. Spriggs. "Development of a Diagnostic DNA Chip to Screen for 30 Autosomal Recessive Disorders in the Hutterite Population." *Molecular Genetics Genomic Medicine* 4, no. 3 (2016): 312–21.

Weiler, Tracey, Cheryl R. Greenberg, Teresa Zelinski, Edward Nylen, Gail Coghlan, et al. "A Gene for Autosomal Recessive Limb-Girdle Muscular Dystrophy in Manitoba Hutterites Maps to Chromosome Region 9q31-33: Evidence for Another Limb-Girdle Muscular Dystrophy Locus." *American Journal of Medical Genetics* 63 (1998): 140–47.

Yao, Tsung-Chieh, Gaixin Du, Lide Han, Ying Sun, et al. "Genome-wide Association Study of Lung Function Phenotypes in a Founder Population." *Journal of Allergy and Clinical Immunology* 133, no. 1 (2014): 248–55.

Zelinski, Teresa, G. Coghlan, J. Mauthe, Barbara Triggs-Raine. "Molecular Basis of Succinylcholine Sensitivity in a Prairie Hutterite Kindred and Genetic Characterization of the Region Containing the BCHE Gene." *Molecular Genetics and Metabolism* 90 (2007): 210–16.

## Education

Armstrong, Helen D., Jacob Kleinsasser, and Ray Hoeppner. "Hutterian History and Brandon University's Hutterian Education Program (BUHEP): A University Responds to the Needs of the Community." In *Examining the Practice of School Administration in Canada*, edited by Helen D. Armstrong. Calgary: Detselig Enterprises, 2005: 349–72.

Hildebrand, Bodo. "Erziehung zur Gemeinschaft: Geschichte und Gegenwart des Erziehungswesen der Hutterer [Education for Community: The History and Present of the Hutterite Education System]." MA diss., Freie Universität Berlin, 1989; Pfaffenweiler: Centaurus Verlag, 1993.

Hostetler, John A. *Education and Marginality in the Communal Society of the Hutterites.* University Park: Pennsylvania State University, 1965.

———. "Total Socialization: Modern Hutterite Educational Practices." *Mennonite Quarterly Review* 44 (January 1970): 72–84.

Huenemann, Mark W. "Hutterite Education as a Threat to Survival." *South Dakota History* 7, no. 1 (1976): 15–27.

Kleinsasser, Raymond. "Hutterite Education: Growing Pains." MA thesis, University of Manitoba, n.d.

Mann, George Adolf. "Functional Autonomy among English School Teachers in the Hutterite Colonies of Southern Alberta: A Study of Social Control." PhD thesis, University of Colorado, 1974.

Paulson, Lloyd M. *The Distance Delivery of a High School Program to Hutterite Colonies*. Brandon: Brandon University Rural Development Institute, 1998.

"Public Schools among Hutterites." *The Western School Journal* 15, no. 8 (1920): 304–7.

Rodger, William Randall. "The Role of the Teacher-Principal on Hutterite Colony Schools in Saskatchewan." *Journal of Amish and Plain Anabaptist Studies* 4, no. 1 (2016): 82-97.

St. Jacques, Paul. "The Hutterites: A Survey of their History, their Beliefs, and their School Systems." MA thesis, University of Saskatchewan, 1987.

## Hymnology, Music, and Discography

Acadia Hutterite Choir. *Behold our God*. Acadia Community, 2018. CD.

———. *Voices of Victory*, n.d., CD.

*alleluia, Sing! Songs of Faith and Worship: Guitarbook*. Rev. ed. Petersfield: Netley Colony, 2013.

*alleluia, Sing! Songs of Faith and Worship: Christmas/Easter Book*. Petersfield: Netley Colony, 2013.

Basnar, Alexander. *Ein Lied aus längst vergang'ner Zeit: Die Lieder der Taufer*. Wien, 2013.

*Beliebte Lieder: Morgen- und Abendlieder*. MacGregor: Hutterian Brethren Book Centre, 2019.

Brednich, Rolf Wilhelm. "Beharrung und Wandel im Liedgut der hutterischen Brüder: Ein Beitrag zur empirischen Hymnologie." *Jahrbuch für Volksliedforschung* 26 (1981): 44–60.

Cascade Hutterian Youth Choir. *Home*. 2015. CD.

*Come to the Manger: Our Christmas Songbook*. Rifton: Plough Publishing House, 1978.

Decker *Diene. Beginne du all meine Tage*. Decker Community, 2013. CD.

Decker Hutterite Choir. *Hello, Little Baby*. 1995. Audio-cassette.

Duerksen, Rosella Reimer. "Anabaptist Hymnody of the Sixteenth Century." PhD thesis, Union Theological Seminary, New York City, 1956.

*Easter Songbook/Osterliederbuch*. Compiled and edited by the Hutterian Brethren also known as the Bruderhof. Ulster Park: Plough Publishing House, 1990.

*Evangelisches Gesangbuch* [Gospel Songbook]. Hawley: Spring Prairie Printing, 1984.

*Favorite Gospel Songs and Hymns*. Hawley: Spring Prairie Printing, 1988.

Franz, H. *Choralbuch zum Gebrauch in den Mennonitischen Schulen und Kirchen in Kanada* [Choral book for use in Mennonite Schools and Churches in Canada]. 13th Canadian ed. Altona: D.W. Friesens & Sons, 1978.

Fretz, Clarence Y. *Handbook to the Anabaptist Hymnal*. Hagerstown: Deutsche Buchhandlung, 1989.

*Gesangbuch der Mennoniten* [Mennonite Hymnal]. Wiesbaden: Haus der Musik, 2007. This hymnbook of the Paraguayan Mennonites contains a transcription and arrangement of the Hutterite oral tradition's "*Ich habe nun den Grund gefunden*" (332).

*Gesang Büchlein. Lieder für Schulen und häuslichen Gebrauch*, herausgegeben von den Hutterischen Brüder, 1919; 2nd ed., Macleod, 1930; 3rd ed., Herausgegeben von den Hutterischen Brüdern in Canada [*sic*], 1940; 4th ed., David Hofer [James Valley, MB], 1941; 7th ed., Cayley: [Macmillan Colony?], 1961; unnumbered [8th?] ed., Rosholt: White Rock Bruderhof, 1976; 9th ed., Cayley: MacMillan Colony, 1978; 11th ed., Elie: James Valley Colony, 1982; 12th ed., Elie: James Valley Colony, 1988; 1st rev. ed., MacGregor: H.B. Book Centre, 1995. Edited by Edna Jory, Pauline Maendel, and Gisela Sann. Published in Fraktur and Latin lettering; rev. ed., Hawley: Spring Prairie Printing, 1998; 2nd rev. ed., MacGregor: Hutterian Brethren Book Centre, 2017. Latin lettering only.

*Gesang-Büchlein: Gesammelt aus den Liedern der Hutterischen Brüder. Mit einem Anhang schöne Lieder, die bisher nur in Abschriften vorhanden waren, aber sehr wichtig sind*. Herausgegeben von den Hutterischen Brüdern in Amerika, 1917.

Hofer Family. *While the Ages Roll I'll Keep on Praising Him*. Silverwinds Community, MB, 2018. CD.

Hofer, G.M. *Kleine Schul Büchlein: Lieder, Gebetlein, Wünschlein, Regeln und Biblische Fragen und Sprüchen besonders für kleine Kinder zu Haus oder kleine Schul gebräuchlich*. Hodgeville Gemein[de], 2012.

Joldersma, Hermina, and Louis Grijp. *Elisabeth's Manly Courage: Testimonials and Songs of Martyred Anabaptist Women in the Low Countries*. Milwaukee: Marquette University Press, 2001.

Kleinsasser, Courtney. *Nearer, My God, to Thee*. B Inspired Gifts and Books, [2020]. CD.

Knight, Matthew Emersen. "'When my kids get to heaven, they're gonna know how to sing': Performing Salvation in Hutterite Choirs." MA diss., University of Alberta, 2011.

Koldau, Linda Maria. *Frauen—Musik—Kultur: Ein Handbuch zum deutschen Sprachgebiet der Frühen Neuzeit* [Women—Music—Culture: A Handbook of the German-Language Region in the Early Modern Era]. Köln: Böhlau Verlag, 2005.

Letkemann, Peter. "The German Hymnody of Prussian Mennonite's: A Tale of Two *Gesangbücher*." *Preservings* 18 (June 2001): 120–130.

———. "The Hymnody and Choral Music of Mennonites in Russia, 1789–1915." PhD diss., University of Toronto, 1985.

———. "Singing the New Song Together: MB–GC Relations in Music." Unpublished paper, November 1983.

*Lieder-Büchlein für Schul-kinder*. Newton Siding: Die Hutterischen Brüder, Sunnyside Colony, 1958.

*Die Lieder der Hutterischen Brüder*. Scottdale: Mennonite Publishing House, 1914.

Lieseberg, Ursula. *Die Lieder des Peter Riedemann: Studien zum Liedgut der Täufer im 16. Jahrhundert*. New York: Peter Lang, 1998.

———. "The Martyr Songs of the Hutterite Brethren." *Mennonite Quarterly Review* 67 (July 1993): 323–336.

———. *Studien zum Märtyrerlied der Täufer im 16. Jahrhundert*. Europäische Hochschulschriften/European University Studies 12. Frankfurt am Main: Peter Lang, 1991.

Maple Grove Hutterite Choir. *The Path That's True*. Lauder: Maple Grove Colony, 2011. CD.

Martens, Helen. "Hutterite Melodies from the Strassburg 'Psalter.'" *Mennonite Quarterly Review* 48 (April 1974): 201–214.

_____. *Hutterite Songs*. Kitchener: Pandora Press, 2002.

Netley Choir. *Christmas Has Only Begun*. [Petersfield: Netley Community], 2003. CD.

Oyer, John S. "A newly-discovered Hutterite codex at Copenhagen." *Mennonite Quarterly Review* 44 (January 1970): 122–125.

Rankin, Diana M. "Hutterite Music: Sixteenth Century Melodies in a Twentieth Century World." MA thesis, Mancato State College, 1972.

Rosedale *Diene. Speak, Oh Lord*. Elie: Rosedale Community. CD.

Silverwinds Hutterite Choir. *The Joy of Christmas*. 2014. CD.

_____. *His Flag is still Flying*. MacGregor: Hutterian Brethren Book Centre, 2018. CD.

_____. *We Stand Amazed*. MacGregor: Hutterian Brethren Book Centre, 2007. CD.

*Sing unto the Lord: Spiritual Songs in English and German*. Hawley: Spring Prairie Printing, 2005.

*Songs of Light: The Bruderhof Songbook*. Compiled and edited by the Hutterian Society of Brothers. Music editor, Marlys Swinger. Rifton: Plough Publishing House, 1977.

*Sonnenlieder: Lieder für Naturfreunde, Menschheitsfriede und Gottesgemeinschaft*, vol. 1. Sannerz/Leipzig: Eberhard Arnold Verlag, 1924.

*Sonnenlieder: Lieder der Lebensgemeinde, wie sie aus Anregen des Geistes verfaßt und hervorgebracht und so auch zu singen seien*. Fulda/Leipzig: Eberhard Arnold Verlag, 1933.

Springhill Choir. *Let us Serve Him!* Neepawa, 2003. CD.

_____. *Secure*. Neepawa, 2010. CD.

Stoesz, Donald. *Canadian Prairie Mennonite Ministers' Use of Scripture: 1874–1977*. Victoria: FriesenPress, 2018.

Tschetter, George K. *Kleine Schul Buch*. [Wanham]: Birch Hills Colony, 2002.

Waldner, James. *Lead us on, Lord*. [Elm Creek: Wingham Community]. 2001, Audio-cassette and CD.

Waldner, Michael. *History in Song*. Ste. Agathe: Crystal Spring Colony, 2001.

Waldner, Tony. *"Wo bleiben meine Sinnen:" A Free-Verse English Translation*. Forest River Community, 2012.

Windy Bay Choir. *Let us Run*. [2013]. CD.

Wipf, Butch G. *Hutterian Songs: A Selection of Christian Songs Suitable for all Occasions*, vol. 1. Decker: Decker Hutterian Colony, 2013.

_____. *Hutterian Songs: A Collection—Songs of Christian Faith*, vols. 2–5. Decker: Decker Hutterian Colony, 2006–2024.

_____. *Good Ol' Guitar Songs and Tunes...Yesteryears*. Decker: Decker Hutterian Colony, 2017.

Wolkan, Rudolf. *Die Lieder der Wiedertäufer: Ein Beitrag zur deutschen und niederländischen Litteratur- und Kirchengeschichte*. Berlin: Behr de Graaf, 1903; MacGregor: Hutterian Brethren Book Centre, 2018.

Zieglschmid, A.J.F. "A song of the persecution of the Hutterites in Velke Levary." *Mennonite Quarterly Review* 17 (July 1943):151–164.

## Prairieleut

Numerous titles listed here are also listed in other sections of this bibliography; all titles with known Prairieleut content are re-listed to facilitate ease of use. Family histories and genealogies of the Swiss Amish and Low German Mennonites also part of the Freeman, South Dakota, history were included because there are usually also connections to the Hutterite Prairieleut.

Bengston, Ben. *History of Freeman: Dakota Territory to South Dakota*. N.p., 2015.

_____. Pictorial History of Freeman, South Dakota. N.p., 2014.

Freeman Centennial Steering Committee, comp. *Freeman Facts, Freeman Fiction: 1879–1979, Celebrating our Centennial*. Freeman: Pine Hill Press, 1979.

Gering, John J. *After Fifty Years: A Brief Discussion of the History and Activities of the Swiss-German Mennonites from Russia who settled in South Dakota in 1874*. [Freeman]: Pine Hill Printers, 1924.

Glanzer, Paul E., Marilyn Wipf, and Jeanette Hofer. *A Century of God's Blessings: A History of the Neu Hutterthaler Mennonite Church, Bridgewater, South Dakota*. N.p., [1988].

Glanzer, Reuben E., et al. *Memories of the Reuben E. Glanzer Children*. N.p.: n.d.

Gross, David, comp. *The Schmiedeleut Family Record*. High Bluff: Sommerfeld Digital Printing Centre, 2017.

Gross, Erwin R., ed. *History of the Hutterthal Mennonite Church, 1879–1968*. Freeman: Pine Hill Press, 1968.

Gross, Joe D.M., comp. *The Rev. Paul F. Gross Family Record*. Freeman, 1972.

Gross, Mrs. Paul S. [Mary Ann]. *A History of the Salem Mennonite Brethren Church, Bridgewater, South Dakota*. Freeman: Pine Hill Press, 1986.

Hofer, Arnold, and Norman Hofer. *History of the Hutterite Mennonites*. Eugene: Wipf and Stock Publishers, 2011.

———. *Hutterite Roots*. Eugene: Wipf and Stock Publishers, 2012.

Hofer, [David] M. *Die Hungersnot in Rußland und Unsere Reise um die Welt* [The Famine in Russia and our Travels Around the World]. Chicago: K.M.B. Publishing House, 1924.

Hofer, Delmer, ed. *Hutterthal Mennonite Church Cemetery Directory, 1902–2004*. [Freeman, 2004].

Hofer, E.F., and [Sam] J.R. *God's Way of Salvation in the Seven Dispensations and Building God's Kingdom as Revealed from Genesis to the End of Revelation*. Carpenter, N.d.

Hofer, George M. *My Memoirs*. [Freeman], 1990.

[Hofer, Joe P.] *History of the Neu Hutterthal Church, Bridgewater, South Dakota: 80th Anniversary, 1888–1968*. 1968.

Hofer, Joseph. *The Diaries of Joseph "Yos" Hofer*. Edited by Arnold M. Hofer. Freeman: Hutterian Centennial Committee, 1997.

Hofer, Verlyn. *A Wartime Odyssey: The Personal Story of One Teenage G.I. Wounded in Battle in World War II*. 2015.

———. *An American Independent: The Life and Times of Verlyn V. Hofer*. Bolton: Amazon.ca, 2016.

———. *The Hofer Clan*. Bolton: Amazon.ca, 2017.

———. *The Maverick Hutterite: The Journey of David Hofer*. Bolton: Amazon.ca, 2017.

———. *Ole: The Sage of a Norwegian Immigrant in America*. Bolton: Amazon.ca, 2017.

Hofer, Verlyn, and Mary Beth Hann. *Faith, Family and the Newspaper: The Story of Edward and Cora Hofer*. 2019

Hoover, Walter B. *The Hutterian Language/Di Hutrisha Shproch: An Introduction to the Language of the Hutterites of North America with a Special Emphasis Upon the Language and History of the Hutterian "Prairie People" at Langham, Saskatchewan, Canada: A Grammar and Lexicon*. Saskatoon: Self-published, 1997.

———. *Hutterian-English Dictionary: Compendium of the Common Vocabulary of the Hutterian Prairie People at Langham, Saskatchewan (1905–1997)*. Saskatoon: Self-published, 1997.

Hostetler, John. *Hutterite Society*. Baltimore: Johns Hopkins University Press, 1974.

Janzen, Rod. "Jacob D. Hofer: Evangelist, Minister and Carpenter." *California Mennonite Historical Society Newsletter*, May 1994.

———. *Paul Tschetter: The Story of a Hutterite Immigrant Leader, Pioneer, and Pastor*. Eugene: Pickwick Publications, 2009.

———. "The Prairieleut: The Forgotten Hutterite People." *Communal Studies* 14 (1994): 67–89.

———. *The Prairie People: Forgotten Anabaptists*. Hanover: University Press of New England, 1999.

Janzen, Rod, and Jean Janzen. "Paul Tschetter's 'Chicago Fire' Hymn." *Mennonite Quarterly Review* 81 (2007): 261–271.

Janzen, Rod, and Max Stanton. *The Hutterites in North America*. Baltimore: Johns Hopkins University Press, 2010.

Kleinsasser, Allen "Jack." *Memories of "Dakota Jack," 1935–1956*, 2003.

Kleinsasser, Amos J., Norma Hofer, Rachel Friesen, Colin Hofer, Delmer Hofer, and Norman Hofer. *Our Journey of Faith: a History of the Hutterthal Mennonite Church*. Sioux Falls: Pine Hill Press, 2004.

Kleinsasser Towne, Marian. *Bread of Life: Diaries and Memories of a Dakota Family, 1936–1945*. Freeman: Pine Hill Press, 1994.

———. *Jacob Hutter's Friends: Twelve Narrative Voices from Switzerland to South Dakota Over Four Centuries*. Indianapolis: M.K. Towne, 1999.

Krause, Bertha Louise Schmidt. *Tschetter-Waldner and Allied Families*. Ridgefield, WA: self-published, 1991.

*Memoirs by Members: Memories and Experiences of Members of the Senior Citizens Centres, Freeman, South Dakota*. Freeman: Freeman Senior Citizens Centre, 1994.

Mendel, J.J. *History of Freeman from 1879 to 1958*. Freeman: Pine Hill Printery, 1958.

_____. *History of the People of East Freeman, Silver Lake, and West Freeman and the History of Freeman (1958–1961) Continued*. Freeman: Pine Hill Press, 1961.

Mendel, Jacob Jr. *The Jacob Mendel [1829–1872] Family Tree, 1829–1976*. N.p., [1976].

Ortman, David E., and Maxine M. (Mueller) Ortman. *The Schrian Mueller and Anna (Schrag) Mueller Family Genealogy, 1842–2002*. Sioux Falls: Pine Hill Press, 2003.

Plett, Cornelius F. *The Story of the Krimmer Mennonite Brethren Church*. Winnipeg/Hillsboro: Kindred Press, 1985.

Preheim, Lyle, and Tim Waltner. *Reflections of a Heritage: A Musical Drama Commemorating the Volhynian Swiss and their Coming to the Plains of South Dakota in 1874*. Freeman, 1974.

*Salem Mennonite Brethren Church, Bridgewater, S.D. 1886–1966: 80th Anniversary and Dedication Program*, July 10, 1966.

Shane, Esther, comp. and ed. *Echoes of an Era, 1880–1980, Bridgewater, South Dakota*. Bridgewater: Bridgewater Tribune, 1980.

Stahl, Debbie P., and Melissa Wollman. *Sarah's Journey: The Story of a Hutterite Woman*. MacGregor: Hutterian Brethren Book Centre, 2014.

*Three Groups, One Story: The Journey that Built a South Dakota Community*. Freeman: Heritage Hall Museum and Archives, 2018. DVD.

Tschetter, Edna, Solomon Tschetter, Beverly Frankenstein, and Gary Frankenstein. *Family Records of Mr. & Mrs. John J.K. Hofer*. N.p., 1985.

Tschetter, Mrs. Joseph W. [Kathrina]. *My Life-Story, 1880–1945*. Chicago, 1945.

Tschetter, Larry and Edith, comp. *The Jacob W. Tschetter Family Record*. Freeman, 1977.

Tschetter, Paul. "The Diary of Paul Tschetter, 1873, Part I." Translated and edited by J.M. Hofer. *Mennonite Quarterly Review* 5 (April 1931): 112–127. The German manuscripts are located at the Heritage Hall Museum and Archives, Freeman, South Dakota.

_____. "The Diary of Paul Tschetter, 1873, Part II." Translated and edited by J.M. Hofer. *Mennonite Quarterly Review* 5 (July 1931): 198–220.

Unruh, John D. *The Daniel Unruh Story*. Freemann, 1970.

Unruh, John D., and Gary J. Waltner. *An Andreas Schrag Document with some Implications*. Freeman, 1982.

Voth, Frances Janzen. *The House of Jacob: The Story of Jacob Janzen (1822–1885) "Jacobs Ruhe" Freeman, South Dakota and His Descendants*. N.p., 1984.

Waldner, Marie J., and Marnetter D. Ortman Hofer. *Many Hands, Minds and Hearts: A History of Freeman Junior College and Freeman Academy, 1900–2000*. [Freeman]: Freeman Academy, 2000.

Waltner, Gary J. *The Joseph Waltner Family: Tracing the Second Son of Andreas and Kathrina Schrag Waldner of the Bruderhof Raditschewa, Russia, 1797–1960*. Freeman: Pine Hill Printery, 1962.

Waltner, Kenneth J., comp. *The Matthias M. Hofer Family Record*. Freeman, 1971.

Waltner, Tim. *The Times and Life of Smokey Joe Mendel*. Freeman: Pine Hill Press, 1992.

Waltner, Tim L. *Schmeckfest at 60: A Comprehensive look at Freeman, South Dakota's 'Festival of Tasting' on the Occasion of its 60th Anniversary*. Freeman: Second Century Publishing, 2018.

Waltner, Timothy L. "Schmeckfest: An Experience in Communal Hospitality." *Pacific Journal* 13 (2018): 137–142.

Wipf, Elenora. *The Andreas Wipf and Susanna Glanzer Family Record, 1842–1962*. Yale, [1962].

_____. *The Michael Hofer and Sarah Kleinsasser Family Record, 1842–1960*. Yale, [1960].

Wurtz, Edna, and Catherine Masuk. *Rooted and Grounded in Love: The History and Family Records of the Langham Prairie People*. Saskatoon, 2000.

## Autobiography, Biography, Travelogue, and Memoir

Baer, Mary Irwin, ed. *Ephraim & Lovina Baer Family History Book*, 6th edition. Portage la Prairie, 2015.

Baer, Rachel. *My Palmgrove Diary: November 25, 1999–November 15, 2000*. Ste. Agathe: Crystal Spring Colony, 2001.

Brednich, Rolf Wilhelm. *The Bible and the Plough: The Lives of a Hutterite Minister and a Mennonite Farmer*. Ottawa: National Museums of Canada, 1981.

'The Nine' [Sheryl Waldner, Karen Waldner, Rodney Waldner, Titus Waldner, Glenda Maendel, Cindy Waldner, Darlene Waldner, Junia Waldner and Jason Waldner]. *Hutterites: Our Story to Freedom*. [Rolla]: Risen Son Publishing, 2013.

_____. *Since we Told the Truth: Our Life can Never be the Same*. [Rolla]: Risen Son Publishing, 2014.

Friedmann, Robert. "Hutterites Revisit European Homesteads: Excerpts from the Travel Diary of David Hofer." *Mennonite Quarterly Review* 33 (1959): 305–22, 346.

Gross, Paul S. "On the Trails of our Anabaptist Forefathers, Summer 1968." *Mennonite Quarterly Review* 44 (January 1970):85–99.

Hofer, [David] M. *Die Hungersnot in Rußland und Unsere Reise um die Welt* [The Famine in Russia and our Travels Around the World]. Chicago: K.M.B. Publishing House, 1924.

Hofer, Joshua. *Japanese Hutterites: A Visit to Owa Community*. Elie: James Valley Book Centre, [1980].

Hofer, Rebecca. *Removing the Hutterite Kerchief*. Kelowna: Collegium, 2009.

Hofer, Rhoda. *A Hutterite Return: The Persecuted Visit the Land of their Ancestors (December 5–15, 2000)*. Carberry: Acadia Community, 2022. An updated edition of *Our Return Visit*.

_____. *Our Return Visit: Vertriebene Besuchen Heimat der Vorvater* [*sic*]. N.p., 2001.

Hofer Kubisewsky, Helen. *My Roots are Showing: My Hutterite Story: A Memoir of a Young ex-Hutterite Girl*. N.p., 2023.

Holzach, Michael. *The Forgotten People*. Translated by Stephan Lhotzky. Sioux Falls: Ex Machina Publishing Company, 1993.

_____. *Das vergessene Volk: Ein Jahr bei den deutschen Hutterern in Kanada*. Hamburg: Hoffmann & Campe, 1980; Munich: dtv, 1996.

Janzen, Rod A. *Terry Miller: The Pacifist Politician: From Hutterite Colony to State Capitol*. Freeman: Pine Hill Press, 1986.

_____. *Paul Tschetter: The Story of a Hutterite Immigrant Leader, Pioneer, and Pastor*. Eugene: Pickwick Publications, 2009.

Kirkby, Mary-Ann. *I am Hutterite: The Fascinating True Story of a Young Woman's Journey to Reclaim her Heritage*. Prince Albert: Polka Dot Press, 2007; Nashville: Thomas Nelson, 2011.

_____. *Ich bin eine Hutterin: Die faszinierende Geschichte meiner Herkunft*. Holzerlingen: SCM Hänssler, 2001. A German-language translation of *I am Hutterite*.

Maendel, David. *Through the Fiery Furnace*. Bloomington: AuthorHouse, 2011.

Maendel, Linda. "A Father's Stories." In *Chicken Soup for the Soul: The Spirit of Canada: 101 Stories of Love & Gratitude*. [Cos Cob]: Chicken Soup for the Soul, 2017.

_____. *Hutterite Diaries: Wisdom from my Prairie Community*. Harrisonburg: Herald Press, 2015.

Rumanicik, Jenny. *I met Jesus at the Gym*. Winnipeg: Word Alive Press, 2016.

Rhodes, Robert. *Nightwatch: An Inquiry into Solitude*. Intercourse: Good Books, 2009.

Smith, George E. "Ye shall know the truth, and the Truth shall make you Free." *Only Believe* 4, no. 3 (September/December 1991): 33–43, 46.

Stahl, Debbie P., and Melissa Wollman. *Sarah's Journey: The Story of a Hutterite Woman*. MacGregor: Hutterian Brethren Book Centre, 2014.

Stahl Taylor, Esther. *Hutterite to Independence*. Meadville: Christian Faith Publishing, 2020.

Tschetter, Peter. *Growing up Hutterite*. [Bloomington]: Trafford Publishing, 2012.

Waldner, Michael. *Reise Bericht: Ein Bericht von einer Reise nach Europa von Amerika von Zwei Diener des Worts, David Hofer und Michael Waldner, im Jahr 1937* [Travelogue: An Account of a Journey to Europe from America by Two Servants of the Word, David Hofer and Michael Waldner, 1937], Joseph J. Kleinsasser, scribe. Ryegate: Golden Valley Gemein[de], 1997.

Waldner, Mike, and Tillie Waldner. *The Story Mike & Tilly Waldner: From Hutterite Colony to World Missions*. N.p., n.d.

Waldner, Rosanna. *Gift of Life: To share my Experience with Lung Transplantation before, and with a Hopeful Heart, after…* Dugald: n.p., 1993.

Waltner, Tim. *The Times and Life of Smokey Joe Mendel*. Freeman: Pine Hill Press, 1992.

Wipf, John J. *Blight of Denominationalism*. [Victoria]: Tellwell Talent, 2021.

Wurtz, Joe, and Danny Gross. *Washington Tagebuch, January 18–24, 2010*. Published by authors, 2010.

Wurtz, Andrew A. *The Memoirs of the Rev. Andrew Wurtz*. Gibbon: Starland Hutterian Brethren, 1996.

Wurz, Joseph, John Hofer, Daniel Gross, and David Tschetter. *Pilgrimage: A Journey through Hutterite Beginnings*. [Wanham]: Shady Lane Colony and Birch Hills Colony, 2019.

Youmans, Vance Joseph. *The Plough and the Pen: Paul S. Gross and the Establishment of the Spokane Hutterian Brethren.* Boone: Parkway Publishers, 1995.

## Children's Literature

Bly, David. *The McIntyre Liar.* Rev. ed. Calgary: Mind's Eye Publications, 2001.

Buhle, Paul, ed. *Radical Jesus: A Graphic History of Faith.* Illustrated by Sabrina Jones, Gary Dumm, and Nick Thorkelson. Waterloo: Herald Press, 2013.

Harder, Geraldine and Milton. *Christmas Goose.* Illustrated by Lavonne Dyck. Newton: Faith and Life Press, 1990.

Hasselstrom, Linda M., Gaydell Collier, and Nancy Curtis, eds. *Crazy Woman Creek: Women Rewrite the American West.* Boston: Houghton Mifflin Company, 2004.

Hofer, Gilbert. *Jewell Adventure.* Illustrated by Victor Kleinsasser. MacGregor: Hutterian Brethren Book Centre, 2008.

Hostetler, John A. *Hutterite Life.* Scottdale/Kitchener: Herald Press, 1983.

Humes, Kathryn. *Ainsley and Amanda.* Illustrated by Wilma Lloyd-Davies. Neepawa: Wilma Lloyd-Davies, 1990.

———. *Sammy.* Neepawa: Wilma Lloyd-Davies, 1991.

Kirkby, Mary-Ann. *Make a Rabbit.* Illustrated by Sharon Strand Sigfuson. Prince Albert: Polka Dot Press, 2010.

Landsel, Jason, Sankah Banerjee, and Richard Mommsen. *By Water: The Felix Manz Story.* Walden: Plough Publishing House, 2022.

Maendel, Dora. *Deborah's Journey: A Story of Hope and Healing from the Life of a Hutterite Child.* Illustrated by Serena Maendel. MacGregor: Hutterian Brethren Book Centre, 2023.

Maendel, Dora. *Der frumma Jeronimus Vetter und ondra Tschichtlen.* MacGregor: Hutterian Brethren Book Centre, 2010. CD.

———. *Jakob Huter und ondra Hutterischa Tschichtlen.* MacGregor: Hutterian Brethren Book Centre, 2013. CD.

———. *Die olta Martha Basl und ondra Tschichtlen.* MacGregor: Hutterian Brethren Book Centre, 2008. CD.

Maendel, Elma. *A is for Ankela: A Hutterite Alphabet.* Illustrated by Valerie Waldner. McGregor: Hutterian Brethren Book Centre, 2023.

_____. *Marty's Adventure: A Hutterite Shape Book*. Illustrated by Cynthia Stahl. MacGregor: Hutterian Brethren Book Centre, 2008.

_____. *Marty's Colour Adventure: A Hutterite Colour Book*. Illustrated by Cynthia Stahl. MacGregor: Hutterian Brethren Book Centre, 2010.

_____. *Marty's Counting Adventure: A Hutterite Counting Book*. Illustrated by Cynthia Stahl. MacGregor: Hutterian Brethren Book Centre, 2019.

Maendel, Linda. *Lindas glücklicher Tag*. Illustrated by Sonia Maendel. MacGregor: Hutterian Brethren Book Centre, 2006.

Maendel, Linda, and Dick Mueller. *Hutterischa Bible Tschichtlen*, vol. 1. MacGregor: Hutterian Brethren Book Centre, 2008.

_____. *Hutterischa Bible Tschichtlen*, vol. 2. MacGregor: Hutterian Brethren Book Centre, 2009. Includes audio CD.

_____. *Hutterischa Bible Tschichtlen*, vol. 3. MacGregor: Hutterian Brethren Book Centre, 2009. Includes audio CD.

Maendel, Rachel. *Rachel, a Hutterite Girl*. Illustrated by Hannah Marsden. Scottdale: Herald Press, 1999.

Purslow, Frances. *Hutterites in Canada*. Calgary: Weigl, 2006.

Ross, Marilyn. *A Surprise for Anna*. Illustrated by Cindy Crompton. Souris: Hollow Tree Books, 1996.

Stahl, Cynthia. *Hannah's Hutterite Paper Dolls*. MacGregor: Hutterian Brethren Book Centre, n.d.

Stahl, Herman. *Flowing Through the Seasons*. Illustrated by Cynthia Stahl. MacGregor: Hutterian Brethren Book Centre, 2008.

Stahl, Ladonna. *A Hutterite Colouring Book/Ein hutterisches Malbuch*. MacGregor: Hutterian Brethren Book Centre, 2018.

Tschetter, George K. *Kinderreime* [Nursery rhymes]. Illustrated by D. Tschetter. [Wanham]: Birch Hills Colony, 2005.

Waldner, Karis. *Es Lauft e Meisl: Hutterischa Kinder Verslen*, 2nd ed. MacGregor: Hutterian Brethren Book Centre, 2014.

White, Jacquelinne. *Coyote Winter*. Toronto: Lester Publishing, 1991.

Zola, Meguido. *Moving*. Illustrated by Victoria Cooper. London: Julia MacRae Books, 1983.

## Fiction

Harbinger, T.H. *The Golden Triangle*. Columbia: Amazon.com, 2020.

Hofer, Samuel. *Born Hutterite*. Saskatoon: Hofer Publishers, 1991.

_____. *Dance like a Poor Man.* Winnipeg: Hofer Publishers, 1995.

Hughes, Monica. *Beyond the Dark River.* New York: Atheneum, 1981.

Kleinsasser Towne, Marian. *Bread of Life: Diaries and Memories of a Dakota Family, 1936–1945.* Freeman: Pine Hill Press, 1994.

_____. *Jacob Hutter's Friends: Twelve Narrative Voices from Switzerland to South Dakota over Four Centuries.* Freeman: Pine Hill Press, 1999.

Lofgren, Rachael. *In the Shadow of Eternity: The Life and Faith of Trindl, Jakob Hutter's Wife.* Berlin: TGS International: 2022.

Stucky, Naomi R. *Sara's Summer.* Waterloo: Herald Press, 1990.

## Devotional Literature

Ingraham, Joseph Holt. *Der Fürst aus Davids Hause: Drei Jahre in der Heiligen Stadt / Schilderung der Begebenheiten aus dem Leben Jesus von Nazareth.* Translated by Paul Langbein. Reutlingen: Enßlin & Laiblins Verlagsbuchhandlung, 1950.

_____. *The Prince of the House of David: Three Years in the Holy City. Being a Series of the Letters…and all the Scenes and Wonderful Incidents in the Life of Jesus of Nazareth.* Boston: Roberts Brothers, 1888.

Nagler, Franz L. *Allgemeines Handwörterbuch der Heiligen Schrift: Eine kurzgefaßt Beschreibung und Erklärung der in der Bibel genannten Städte, Länder, Völker, Personen, Namen, Lehren, Symbole u. s. w., Nebst einem Verzeuchniß bedeutender Männer der christlichen Kirche vom ersten Jahrhundert bis zur Gegenwart.* 3rd rev. ed. Baltic: J.A. Raber, 1936.

Walter, Elias. *Geschichte der zwölf Patriarchen Jakob und seiner Söhne mit Joseph ergangen. Ordentlich nacheinander geschrieben, sehr schön, holdselig und nützlich zu lesen* [History of the Twelve Patriarchs: How it Went with Jacob and his sons and Joseph. Diligently written in sequence, very beautiful, pleasant and useful to read]. Macleod: Elias Walter, 1925.

## Bibliographies

Fast, Heinold, Martin Rothkegel, and Gottfried Seebaß, eds. *Briefe und Schriften Oberdeutscher Täufer 1527–1555: Das "Kunstbuch" des Jörg Probst Rotenfelder Gen. Maler (Burgerbibliothek Bern, Cod. 464).* Gütersloh: Gütersloher Verlagshaus, 2007.

Friedmann, Robert. "A chronological bibliography of the writings of Robert Friedmann." *Mennonite Quarterly Review* 35 (July 1962): 243–247; corrections and additions, *Mennonite Quarterly Review* 36 (January 1962): 87.

Friedmann, Robert. "Bibliography of works in the English language dealing with the Hutterite communities." *Mennonite Quarterly Review* 32 (July 1958): 237–238; additions in *Mennonite Quarterly Review* 36 (January 1962): 87.

Friedmann, Robert. *Die Schriften der huterischen Träufergemeinschaften: Gesamtkatalog ihrer Manuskriptbücher, ihrer Schreiber und ihrer Literature, 1529–1667.* Wien: Hermann Böhlaus Nachfolger, 1965.

Hillerbrand, Hans Joachim. *A Bibliography of Anabaptism 1520–1630.* Elkhart: Institute of Mennonite Studies, 1962.

Hostetler, John A. "A Bibliography of English Language Materials on the Hutterian Brethren." *Mennonite Quarterly Review* 44 (January 1970): 106–113.

Janzen, Rod. *Hutterites and the Bruderhof.* Unpublished, https://communalstudies.org/wp-content/uploads/2021/03/3_HutteritesBruderhof_RodJanzen.pdf

Krisztinkovich, Maria H. *An Annotated Hutterite Bibliography.* Kitchener: Pandora Press, 1998.

———. "Anabaptist book confiscations in Hungary during the eighteenth century." *Mennonite Quarterly Review* 39 (April 1965): 125–146.

———. *Primary Sources Relating to the Anabaptists in Hungary.* Lectures and Papers in Hungarian Studies 40. Toronto: Hungarian Studies Association of Canada, 2003.

Miller, Michael M. *Researching the Germans from Russia: Annotated Bibliography of the Germans from Russia Heritage Collection at the North Dakota Institute for Regional Studies, North Dakota State University Library, with a listing of the library materials at the Germans from Russia Heritage Society.* Fargo: North Dakota Institute for Regional Studies, 1987.

Miller, Timothy. *American Communes 1860–1960: A Bibliography.* New York: Garland Publishing, 1990.

Penner, Glenn H. *Hutterite Documents in Russian and Ukrainian Archives.* Winnipeg: Mennonite Heritage Archives, 2019.

Rauert, Matthias H., Martin Rothkegel, and Gottfried Seebass, eds. *Katalog Der Hutterischen Handschriften Und Der Drucke Aus Hutterischem Besitz in Europa.* 2 vols. Gütersloher Verlagshaus, 2011.

Riley, Marvin P. "The Hutterian Brethren: An Annotated Bibliography with Special Reference to South Dakota Hutterite Colonies." *Bulletin* 529. Brookings: South Dakota State University, November 1965.

Rothkegel, Martin. "The Hutterian Brethren and the printed book: a contribution to Anabaptist bibliography." *Mennonite Quarterly Review* 74 (January 2000): 51–85.

Smucker, Donovan E. *The Sociology of Mennonites, Hutterites and Amish: A Bibliography with Annotations*, 2 vols. Waterloo: Wilfrid Laurier University Press, 1977–1990.

## Literature Referring to Hutterites

Coates, John W. *Catcut, Crocuses and Cows: A Prairie Veterinarian's Journey into Practice.* Abbotsford: Helejameon Publishing, 2002.

Ingalls Wilder, Laura. *On the Way Home: The Diary of a Trip from South Dakota to Mansfield Missouri, in 1894.* New York: Harper Collins Publishers, 1999. "German Russians" are mentioned on July 21–22, pp. 23–28.

Manfred, Frederick. *The Chokecherry Tree.* Albuquerque: University of New Mexico Press, 1975. First published in 1943 or 1948. Hutterites are mentioned pp. 194–202.

_____. *Sons of Adam.* New York: Crown Publishers, 1980.

Mitchell, Ormond and Barbara Mitchell, editors. *The Devil is a Travelling Man: Two Plays by W.O. Mitchell.* Don Mills: Oxford University Press, 2009.

Rasmussen, Beryl. *The Leaves are Silver.* Saskatoon: Modern Press, 1969.

Tenuto, Jim. *Blood Atonement: A Dahlgren Wallace Mystery.* Guilford: The Lyons Press, 2005. See Chapter 15.

Wanner, Irene. *Sailing to Corinth: Stories.* Owl Creek Press, 1977.

## Cookbooks

Hofer, Samuel. *A Feast of Perogies & Dumplings and other Scrumptions Pockets and Pasteries Filled with all Sorts of Cultural Tastes.* Saskatoon: Hofer Publishers, 1998.

_____. *The Hutterite Community Cookbook.* Saskatoon: Hofer Publishers, 1992. 3rd expanded ed., 2002.

_____. *Hutterite Cooking.* Melville: Hofer Publications, 1984.

_____. *The Hutterite Treasury of Recipes.* Saskatoon, 1986.

_____. *True and Basic Ethnic Cooking From Around the World.* Saskatoon: Hofer Publishing (On the Prairie), 1990.

_____. *Soups and Borschts from Hutterite, Amish, Mennonite, Dutch, Ukrainian, and Russian Kitchens*. Saskatoon: Hofer Publishing, 1990.

Kant, Joanita. *The Hutterite Community Cookbook*. Intercourse: Good Books, 2013.

Kirkby, Mary-Ann. *Secrets of a Hutterite Kitchen: Unveiling the Rituals, Traditions, and Food of the Hutterite Culture*. Toronto: Penguin, 2014.

Tschetter, G[eorge] and K[athrina]. *Cookbook*. [Wanham]: Birch Hills Book Binding, 2009.

Walter, Judy. *At Home in the Kitchen: Mennonite, Hutterite, and Amish-style Cooking*. N.p., 2010.

Wurtz, Anne. *Taste and See that the Lord is Good: Hutterian Favourites*. Kearney: Morris Press Cookbooks, 2011.

## Utopian and Non-Hutterite Communal Studies

Erasmus, Charles J. *In Search of the Common Good: Utopian Experiments Past and Future*. New York: Free Press, 1977.

Hamel, Elsie W. *Utopian Communities: Survival of Old Order Hutterite, Amish and Mennonite Groups*. CreateSpace, 2011.

Miller, Timothy. *Communes in America, 1975–2000*. Syracuse: Syracuse University Press, 2019.

_____. *The Quest for Utopia in Twentieth-Century America, 1900–1960*, vol. 1. Syracuse: Syracuse University Press, 1998.

Sutton, Robert P. *Heartland Utopias*. Dekalb: Northern Illinois University Press, 2009.

## Linguistics

Bräutigam, Dorothea. *Die deutsche Sprachinsel Kanada: Die religiösen Gemeinden der Mennoniten und Hutterer*. Norderstedt: Grin Verlag, 2003.

Hoover, Walter B. *The Hutterian Language = Di hutrisha Shproch: An Introduction to the Language of the Hutterites of North America with a Special Emphasis Upon the Language and History of the Hutterian "Prairie People" at Langham, Saskatchewan, Canada: A Grammar and Lexicon*. Saskatoon: Self-published, 1997.

_____. *Hutterian-English Dictionary: Compendium of the Common Vocabulary of the Hutterian Prairie People at Langham, Saskatchewan (1905–1997)*. Saskatoon: Self-published, 1997.

Maendel, Dora. *Der frumma Jeronimus Vetter und ondra Tschichtlen*. MacGregor: Hutterian Brethren Book Centre, 2010. CD.

_____. *Die olta Martha Basl und ondra Tschichtlen*. MacGregor: Hutterian Brethren Book Centre, 2008. CD.

_____. *Jakob Huter und ondra Hutterischa Tschichtlen*. MacGregor: Hutterian Brethren Book Centre, 2013. CD.

Maendel, Linda. *Lindas glücklicher Tag*. Illustrated by Sonia Maendel. MacGregor: Hutterian Brethren Book Centre, 2006.

Maendel, Linda, and Dick Mueller. *Hutterischa Bible Tschichtlen*, vol. 1. MacGregor: Hutterian Brethren Book Centre, 2008.

_____. *Hutterischa Bible Tschichtlen*, vol. 2. MacGregor: Hutterian Brethren Book Centre, 2009. Includes audio CD.

_____. *Hutterischa Bible Tschichtlen*, vol. 3. MacGregor: Hutterian Brethren Book Centre, 2009. Includes audio CD.

Scheer, Herfried. "Research on the Hutterian German Dialect." *Canadian Ethnic Studies* 1, no. 2 (1969): 13–20.

_____. "The Linguistic Heritage of the Hutterian Brethren." *German Canadian Yearbook* 1 (1973): 91–94.

_____. "Die Mundart der Hutterischen Brüder: Ein Sprachgeschichtliches Denkmal aus dem 16. und 18. Jahrhundert." In *Deutsch Als Muttersprache in Kanada*, edited by Leopold Auburger and Heinz Kloss. Wiesbaden: Steiner, 1977: 133–137.

_____. *Die Deutsche Mundart der Hutterischen Brüder in Nordamerika Beiträge Zur Sprachinselforschung*, Bd. 5. Wien: VWGÖ, 1987.

Wipf, Butch. *Wörterbüchlein für die Lehren des Hutterer Gottesdienstes*. Decker: Decker Hutterian Colony, 2014.

Wirth, Hartmann O. *Tiroler Mundart-Wörterbuch*. Brixen: Suedmedia, 2023

## The Bruderhof and Plough Publishing

The Hutterite-Bruderhof relationship is a significant component in the Hutterite story of the twentieth century. In addition to being a source of renewal and tension, it also produced a considerable corpus of publications, especially small pamphlets. These are typically transcriptions of community gatherings and include both Hutterites and Bruderhof members. (It is important to note that at numerous points in history Bruderhof members were formally Hutterite.) These publications were intended for devotional reading by members. The list here cannot be considered complete, but rather representative, and is limited to the sources available in the Hutterian Brethren Book Centre Archive collection.

Allain, Roger. *The Community That Failed: An Account of Twenty-Two Years in Bruderhof Communes in Europe and South America*. San Francisco: Carrier Pigeon Press, 1992.

Arnold, Eberhard, ed. *Am Anfang war die Liebe: Dokumente, Briefe und Texts der Urchristen* [In the Beginning was Love: Documents, Letters, and Writings of the Early Christians]. Wiesbaden: coprint Verlag, 1986.

_____. *Brothers Unite*. Rifton: Plough Publishing House, 1988.

_____. *The Early Anabaptists*. Rifton: Plough Publishing House, 1984.

_____. *Inner Land: A Guide into the Heart and Soul of the Bible*. Rifton: Plough Publishing House, 1976.

_____. *Inner Land: A Guide into the Heart of the Gospel*. Rifton: Plough Publishing House, 1935.

_____. "History of the Baptizers [Anabaptist] Movement in Reformation Times." *Mennonite Quarterly Review* 43 (July 1969): 213-233.

_____. *Salz und Licht: Über die Bergpredigt* [Salt and Light: Concerning the Sermon on the Mount]. Moers: Brendow Verlag, 1982.

_____. *Salt and Light*. Rifton, NY: Plough, 1977.

_____. *Selected Writings*. Edited by Johann Christoph Arnold. Maryknoll: Orbis Books, 2000.

_____. *Lebensbeweise lebendiger Gemeinden: die Liebe zu Christus und die Liebe zu den Brüdern* [Signs of Life of Living Community: Love toward Christ and Love toward Brothers]. Rifton: Plough Publishing House, 1973.

Arnold, Eberhard, et al. *Else von Hollander, January 1932*. Rifton: Plough Publishing, 1973.

Arnold, Eberhard. *Why We Live in Community*. Rifton: Plough Publishing House, 1976.

Arnold, Eberhard and Emmy. *Seeking for the Kingdom of God: Origins of the Bruderhof Community*. Rifton: Plough Publishing House, 1974.

Arnold, Emmy. *Torches Together: The Story of the Bruderhof Communities—their life together, sharing all things in common*. Rifton: Plough Publishing House, 1964.

Arnold, Heini. *Gemeinsames Leben: ein Weg zu wahrer Bruederlichkeit* [Living Together: A Way to True Brotherhood]. Rifton: Plough Publishing House, 1977.

Arnold, Heini, and Annemarie Arnold. *Living in Community: A Way to True Brotherhood: A Letter from The Society of Brothers also called the Bruderhof united with the Brothers called Hutterians*. Rifton: Plough Publishing House, 1974.

Arnold, Heinrich. *Discipleship: Following Christ in the Daily Grind.* Rifton: Plough, 1994; new expanded edition with subtitle altered to "Living for Christ in the Daily Grind," 2011.

_____. *Freedom from Sinful Thoughts: Christ alone breaks the Curse*. Rifton: Plough Publishing House, 1973. A translation of *Freiheit von Gedankensünden: Nur Christus bricht den Fluch*.

_____. *Freiheit von Gedankensünden: Nur Christus bricht den Fluch*. Rifton: Plough Publishing House, 1973.

_____. *In the Image of God*. Rifton: Plough Publishing, 1977.

_____. *May Thy Light Shine: Prayers*. 7 vols. Rifton: Plough Publishing House, 1985.

_____. *A Printed Sendbrief to the Elders of the Schmiedegemeinden, of the Lehrergemeinden, and of the Dariusgemeinden, and to all Brothers and Sisters called Hutterians in Manitoba, Alberta, and Saskatchewan, and in South and North Dakota, Minnesota, Montana, and Washington, March 1974*. Rifton: Plough Publishing House, 1974.

_____. *A Second Printed Sendbrief, […] March 1974*. Rifton: Plough Publishing House, 1974.

Arnold, Johann Christoph. *Hope for a Dying Church: Brotherhood Meeting, Woodcrest, April 10, 1995*. Farmington: Plough Publishing House, 1995.

_____. *A Guideline for our Young People who seek a Marriage Partner*. Ulster Park, Plough Publishing House, 1987.

_____. "An Open Letter from the Bruderhof." *The Plough* 41 (Winter 1995): 2–6.

_____. *Palmgrove Diary, February 1994*. Rifton: Plough Publishing House, 1994.

_____. *Prayer*. Rifton: Plough Publishing House, 1992.

Arnold, Johann Christoph, and Jacob Kleinsasser. *Palmgrove Diary / The Present Struggle of the Church*. Farmington: Plough Publishing House, 1993.

*Baptism Meetings at Darvel, March 6 and 13, 1994*. Farmington: Plough Publishing House, 1994.

*Baptism Preparation Meetings: Accounts of January 7, 1974*. Rifton: Plough Publishing, 1986.

*Baptism: The Covenant of a Clear Conscience with God: Baptism Meetings at Elm River held Jointly by Reuben Hofer Vetter and Christoph Arnold Vetter, Palm Sunday, March 24, 1991*. Farmington: Plough Publishing House, 1991.

Barnett, Michael Cole. "The Bruderhof and the Hutterites in Historical Context." PhD diss., Southwestern Baptist Theological Seminary, 1995.

Barth, Emmy. *An Embassy Besieged: The Story of a Christian Community in Nazi Germany*. Eugene: Cascade Books; Rifton: Plough Publishing House, 2010.

_____. *Botschaftsbelagerung: Die Geschichte einer christlichen Gemeinschaft im Nationalsozialismus* [An Embassy Besieged: The Story of a Christian Community in Nazi Germany]. Walden: Plough Publishing House, 2015.

_____. *No Lasting Home: A Year in the Paraguayan Wilderness*. Rifton: Plough Publishing House, 2009.

Barth, Karl, and Christoph Blumhardt. *Action in Waiting / Joy in the Lord*. Rifton: Plough Publishing House, 1979.

Barth, Emmy. *A Fire Kindled*. Rifton: Plough Publishing House, 2006.

Baum, Marcus. *Against the Wind*. Rifton: Plough Publishing House, 1998.

Bohlken-Zumpe, Elizabeth. *Torches Extinguished: Memories of a Communal Bruderhof Childhood in Paraguay, Europe and the USA*. San Francisco: Carrier Pigeon Press, 1993.

*Bought the Whole Field: The Life Experience of John and Sarah Maendel*. Bruderhof Historical Archives, 2014.

*The Bruderhof: A Christian Community*. Rifton: Plough Publishing House, 1984.

The Bruderhof. *Foundations of our Faith and Calling*. Rifton: Plough Publishing House, 2012.

Burns, Maurenn, ed. *Outcast, but not Forsaken: True Stories from a Paraguayan Leper Colony*. Rifton: Plough Publishing House, 1986.

Ciponte, Andrea Grosso, and Dacia Palmerino. *Renegade: Martin Luther, The Graphic Biography*. Translated by Michael G. Parker. Walden: Plough Publishing House, 2017.

Clement, Jane T. *The Sparrow and Other Stories*. Farmington: Plough Publishing House, 1968

Domer, Richard E., Winifred Hidel, and John Hinde. *May They all be One: The Life of Heini Arnold*. Farmington: Plough Publishing House, 1992.

*Do to others what you would have them do to you (Matthew 7:12): Meetings at Woodcrest, November 8, 1993*. Farmington: Plough Publishing, 1993.

Dreher, Trautel. *The Stars Shall Light your Journey: The Life of Felix Markus Dreher, October 25, 1940–October 14, 1941*. Rifton: Plough Publishing House, 1985.

Eggers, Ulrich. *Community for Life: A Visitor from Abroad tells the Fascinating Story of Life Inside a New York Colony of the Hutterian Brethren*. Scottdale, PA: Herald, 1988.

Eggers, Ulrich. *Gemeinschaft—Lebenslänglich: Erfahrungen bei den Hutterern* [Community for Life: Experiences with the Hutterites]. Wuppertal/Zürich: R. Brockhaus Verlag, 1992. A German-language edition of *Community for Life*.

*The Forest River Story, 1954–1957: Extracts from Letters Written by Heini and Annemarie Arnold and Emmy Arnold*. Farmington: Plough Publishing House, 1999.

Fros, Melchior, ed. *Primavera: Springtime of our Youth*. Self-published, 2018.

*"God is the Unity": Another Important Visit from the West: Crystal Spring, Woodland, Huron, Milltown, and Decker Colonies, June 24–July 10, 1977*. Rifton: Plough Publishing House, 1997.

Horsch, Volker. "Michael Horsch und die Auflösung des Rhönbruderhofs 1937: Ein anderer Blick [Michael Horsch and the Dissolution of the Rhön Bruderhof in 1937: Another Perspective]." In *Mennoniten in der NS-Zeit: Stimmen, Lebenssituationen, Erfahrungen*, edited by Marion Kobelt-Groch and Astrid von Schlachta. Bolanden-Weierhof: Mennonitischer Geschichtsverein, 2017: 214–216.

Hutterian Brethren, eds. *Brothers Unite: An Account of the Uniting of Eberhard Arnold and the Rhön Bruderhof with the Hutterian Church*. Ulster Park: Plough Publishing House, 1988.

———. *God's Revolution: The Witness of Eberhard Arnold*. New York: Paulist Press, 1984.

Hutterian Brethren, Woodcrest Bruderhof, eds. *Youth Movement to Bruderhof: Letters and Diaries of Annemarie Arnold, née Wächter*. Rifton: Plough Publishing House, 1986.

*Jacob Hutter Writes with a Burning Finger into our Hearts.* Rifton: Plough Publishing House, 1979.

Janzen, Rod. "The Hutterites and the Bruderhof: The Relationship Between an Old Older Religious Society and a Twentieth-Century Communal Group." *Mennonite Quarterly Review* 79, no. 4 (2005): 505–544.

[Kleinsasser, Jacob]. *Jake Vetter's Diary of his Trip to Darvel & Woodcrest, October 1983.* No publication data.

———. *Parables About the Kingdom of God: Gemeindestunde held by our Elder Jake Kleinsasser, December 2, 1990.* Farmington: Plough Publishing House, 1991.

Kleinsasser, Jacob et al. *For the Sake of Divine Truth: Report on a Journey to Europe in the Summer of 1974.* Rifton: Plough Publishing House, 1974.

Landsel, Jason, Sankah Banerjee, and Richard Mommsen. *By Water: The Felix Manz Story.* Walden: Plough Publishing House, 2022.

Löber, Sophie, and Rose Kaiser. *Early Memories of Sannerz and the Rhön Bruderhof*, vol. 1. Rifton: Plough Publishing House, 1977.

Manley, Belinda. *Through Streets Broad and Narrow: A Woman's Ongoing Search to Find a Christian Pacifist Lifestyle, including a 17-year Sojourn in the Bruderhof Communities.* San Francisco: Carrier Pigeon Press, 1996.

Mathis-Rimes, Christine. *Cruel Sanctuary: A Young Woman's Battle to Escape from a Fanatical Religious Sect.* Self-published, 2018.

*The Meaning of the Church and the Service of the Word: Joint Brotherhood Meeting at Darvell [England], February 8, 1993.* Farmington: Plough Publishing House, 1993.

Meier, Hans. *Solange das Licht brennt: Lebensbericht eines Mitgliedes der neuhutterischen Bruderhof-Gemeinschaft* [As Long as the Light is Burning: The Biography of a Member of the New Hutterian Bruderhof Community]. Klosters, Switzerland: Brassel, 1990.

Mommsen, Peter. *Homage to a Broken Man: The Life of J. Heinrich Arnold.* Rifton: Plough Publishing House, 2004; 2015.

———. *Radikal barmherzig: Das Leben von Johann Heinrich Arnold eine Geschichte von Glauben und Vergebung, Hingabe und Gemeinschaft* [Radical Mercy: The Life of Johann Heinrich Arnold—A Story of Faith and Forgiveness, Devotion, and Community]. [Cuxhaven]: Neufeld Verlag, 2017.

Moore, Charles E., ed. *Called to Community: The Life Jesus Wants for his People*. Walden: Plough Publishing House, 2016.

Moore, Charles E., and Timothy Keiderling, eds. *Bearing Witness: Stories of Martyrdom and Costly Discipleship*. Walden: Plough Publishing House, 2016.

Mow, Merrill. *Torches Rekindles: The Bruderhof's Struggle for Renewal*. Ulster Park: Plough Publishing House, 1989.

Nauerth, Thomas. "Bergpredigt und Widerstand: Die Bruderhofgemeinschaft 1933–1937 [The Sermon on the Mount and Resistance: The Bruderhof Community 1933-1937]," Presentation at *"Bergpredigt leben" anlässlich des 80. Todestages von Eberhard Arnold, 1883–1935* ["Living the Sermon on the Mount" on the occasion of the 80th anniversary of the death of Eberhard Arnold (1883–1935)]. Fulda, November 21, 2015.

_____. "Hutterer und Mennoniten in Europa: Begegnungen und 'Vergegnungen' 1933–1937 [Hutterites and Mennonites in Europe: encounters and 'misencounters' 1933-1937]." In *Mennoniten in der NS-Zeit: Stimmen, Lebenssituationen, Erfahrungen*, edited by Marion Kobelt-Groch and Astrid von Schlachta. Bolanden-Weierhof: Mennonitischer Geschichtsverein, 2017: 198–213.

_____. *Zeugnis, Liebe und Wiederstand: Der Rhönbruderhof 1933–1937* [Witness, Love, and Resistance: The Rhönbruderhof 1933–1937]. Leiden: Verlag Ferdinand Schöningh, 2018.

Oved, Yaacov. *Distant Brothers: History of the Relations between the Bruderhof and the Kibbutz*. Ramat Efal: Yad Tabenkin, 1993.

_____. *The Witness of the Brothers: A History of the Bruderhof*. London: Transaction Press, 1996.

Pleil, Nadine Monje. *Behütet und Betrogen: Nach vierzig Jahren in Bruderhofgemeinschaft in drei Kontinenten* [Sheltered and Betrayed: After Forty Years in Bruderhof Communities on Three Continents]. Translated by Renatus Klüver. Indianapolis: Dog Ear Publishing, 2011.

_____. *Free from Bondage: After Forty Years in Bruderhof Communities on Three Continents*. San Fransisco: Carrier Pigeon Press, 1994.

Randall, Ian M. *A Christian Peace Experiment: The Bruderhof Community in Britain, 1933–1942*. Eugene: Cascade Books, 2018.

*Rejoice in the Lord Always! Reacceptance of Nineteen Brothers and Sisters at Oakwood, Woodcrest, October 24, 1993*. Farmington: Plough Publishing House, 1993.

Rubin, Julius H. *The Other Side of Joy: Religious Melancholy among the Bruderhof.* New York: Oxford University Press, 2000.

Sabin, Edward, and Amy Woods Butler. *Searching for Life's Purpose: Still Working on it.* Kansas City: Story Scribe Books, 2022.

_____. *A Wider Horizon: The Primavera Journals of Ray Sabin.* [Kansas City]: Story Scribe Books, 2021.

*South Dakota Journey, February 3–13, 1986: Lovemeal at Woodcrest, February 14, 1986.* Rifton: Plough Publishing House, 1986.

Thomson, Watson. *Pioneer in Community: Henri Lasserre's Contribution to the Fully Cooperative Society.* Toronto: Ryerson Press, 1949.

Tolstoy, Leo. *Walk in the Light While There is Light.* Rifton: Plough Publishing, n.d.

*Up, Join the Battle Now: In Memory of our Beloved Brother Hardy Arnold: Selected from Meetings, November 2–13, 1987.* Ulster Park: Plough Publishing House, 1988.

Waggerl, Karl Heinrich. *The Dance of Robber Horrificus.* Illustrated by Martin Horning. Rifton: Plough Publishing House, 2010.

Wagoner, Bob and Shirley. *Community in Paraguay: A Visit to the Bruderhof.* Rifton: Plough Publishing House, 1991.

Wipf, Harry, and Tim Wipf. *Oakwood Hutterian Brethren: Letters and Documents, 1985–1995.* Rifton: Plough Publishing House, 1996.

Yousif, Jacoub. *I Put my Sword Away: An Iraqi Soldier's Journey from Battlefield to Brotherhood.* Rifton: Bruderhof, 2015.

Zablocki, Benjamin. *The Joyful Community: An Account of the Bruderhof—a communal movement now in its third generation.* Baltimore: Pelican Books, 1971.

Zündel, Friedrich. *Pastor Johann Christoph Blumhardt: An Account of his Life.* Blumhardt Series. Eugene: Cascade Books, 2010; Rifton: Plough Publishing House, 2010.

## Folk Art, Pottery, and Architecture

Bird, Michael, and Terry Kobayashi. *A Splendid Harvest: Germanic Folk and Decorative Arts in Canada.* Toronto: Van Nostrand Reinhold, 1981.

Goa, David J. "For the Eyes of God Alone: The Meaning of the Hutterian Brethren Aesthetic." In *Just for Nice: German-Canadian Folk Art*, edited by Macnús Einarsson and Helga Benndorf Taylor. Hull: Canadian Museum of Civilization, 1993.

Fleming, John, and Michael Rowan. *Folk Furniture of Canada's Doukhobors, Hutterites, Mennonites and Ukrainians.* Edmonton: University of Alberta Press, 2004.

Horvath, J. Eugene, and Maria H. Krisztinkovich. *A History of Haban Ceramics: A Private View.* Vancouver, 2005.

Kalinová, Alena, Brigitte Fassinder-Brückler, and Theodor Brückler. *Täufer-Hutterer-Habaner: Geschichte, Siedlung, Keramik in Südmähren, Westslowakei und Niederösterreich* [Anabaptists-Hutterites-Habaner: History, Settlement, Ceramics in Southern Moravia, Western Slovakia, and Lower Austria]. Horn/Wien: Verlag Berger, 2004.

Mayer, Carol E. *A Discerning Eye: The Walter C. Koerner Collection of European Ceramics.* Vancouver: Museum of Anthropology at the University of British Columbia, 2014.

_____., ed. *The Potter's Art: Contributions to the Study of the Koerner Collection of European Ceramics.* Vancouver: University of British Columbia Museum of Anthropology, 1997.

Pajer, Jiří. *Anabaptist Faience from Moravia, 1593–1620: Catalogue of Documents from Institutional and Private Collections.* Strážnice: Etnos Publishing, 2011.

Waldner, Karen. *Janker Notebook: A Step-by-Step Photo Tutorial on Tailoring a Men's Dress Jacket.* [Elkton]: Newdale H.B., 2018.

Wollmann, Kenny. *Hutterisches Hondwerk* [Hutterite Handcrafts]. MacGregor: Hutterian Brethren Book Centre, 2009.

## Pictorials, Photo Essays, and Books

Allard, William Albert. "The Hutterites, Plain People of the West." *National Geographic* 138 (July 1970): 98–125.

_____. "Solace at Surprise Creek." *National Geographic* 209, no. 6 (June 2006): 120–147.

Butet-Rock, Laurence. "Slowing Down to Listen Better: Tim Smith's Nuances Look at the Deerboine Hutterite Colony." *Photolife* 41, no. 5 (2016): 20–22.

Capp, Kristin. *Hutterite: A World of Grace.* Schaffhausen: Edition Stemmle, 1998.

Cary, Brian, and Louise Guay. *Kryn Taconis: Photojournalist.* Ottawa: National Archives of Canada, 1989.

Hennel, Leah. *Along the Western Front.* Calgary: Rocky Mountain Books, 2020.

Hofer, Elaine. *Walking Home: A Memoir and Photographs*. Mixbook Photo, n.d.

Hofer, Elie. *Rocklake Colony: 1940s–1950s*. Britt Hofer, ed. Published by author, 2014.

Hofer, Kelly. *Hutterite: The Things I saw Growing up as a Hutterite Teen*. [Calgary], 2016.

Hofer, Samuel. *Hutterites: Lives and Images of a Communal People*. Saskatoon: Hofer Publishers, 1998.

Kant, Joanita. *Hutterites of South Dakota: The Schmiedeleut*. Coral Springs: Llumina Press, 2006.

Koga, Mary. *Mary Koga: Photographs*. Edited by Ellen Ushioka, [1998].

Parlato, Gabriella Nessi, and Gianni Berengo Gardin. *Die Hutterer: Tiroler in Amerika*. Bozen: Edition Rætia, 1996.

Rautert, Timm. *No Photographing: The Amish: The Hutterites*. Göttingen: Steidl, 2011.

Smith, Tim. "Hazy Summer Days: A Photographer Documents the Diversity of Rural Life in Western Manitoba." *Maclean's* 132, no. 8 (September 2019): 54–59.

Smith, Tim et al. *Rogue: A Canadian Photo Collective: Honest Stories by Honest Rogues*. N.d.: 2–5.

Spiteri, [Edward], and Hugh Dempsey. *Hutterites / Spiteri: The Hutterite Diamond Jubilee*. Calgary: Glenbow-Alberta Institute, 1978.

Webber, George. *A World Within: An intimate Portrait of the Little Bow Hutterite Colony*. Markham: Fifth House, 2005.

Wilson, Laura. *Hutterites of Montana*. New Haven: Yale University Press, 2000.

## International Hutterite Communities

### I. Owa, Japan

Buckton, Mark. "Japan's Hutterites Hold on to a Dream for Community." *The Japan Times*. April 7, 2014. Accessed May 19, 2019. https://www.japantimes.co.jp/community/2014/04/07/issues/japans-hutterites-hold-on-to-a-dream-for-community/#.XOHHwKZ7ngE.

"Friedmann-Sakakibara Library to be Established." *Gospel Herald*, September 22, 1970: 801.

Hofer, Joshua. *Japanese Hutterites: A Visit to Owa Community*. Elie: James Valley Book Centre, [1980].

Lehr, John C. "Owa: A Dariusleut Hutterite Colony in Japan." In *Prairie Perspectives: Geographical Essays* 13 (2010): 30–38.

Sakakibara, Gan. *Junkyo to Romei Hataraito nv Yon-hykaku-go-ju-Nen* [Four Hundred and Fifty Years of Hutterite Martyrdom and Exile]. Tokyo, 1967.

Shimazaki, Hiroshi Tanaka. "The Emergence of Japanese Hutterites," *Japan Review* 12 (2000): 145–164.

Stanton, Max E. "Getting Lost in Translation and Finding Tranquillity: A Traveller's Diary Entry, August 12, 1987." Unpublished field notes.

Tanaka, Hiroshi. "Albertan Gift to Asia: Hutterites in Japan." *Canadian Geographic* 98 (1979): 70–73.

———. "Emergence of the New Hutterian Brethren in Japan." *The Bellingham Collection of Geographical Studies* 27, Vancouver: Tantalus Research Limited, 1979: 73–80.

## II. Palmgrove, Nigeria

Arnold, Johann Christoph. *Palmgrove Diary, February 1994*. Rifton: Plough Publishing House, 1994.

Arnold, Johann Christoph, and Jacob Kleinsasser. *Palmgrove Diary/The Present Struggle of the Church*. Farmington: Plough Publishing House, 1993.

Baer, Rachel. *My Palmgrove Diary: November 25, 1999–November 15, 2000*. Ste. Agathe: Crystal Spring Colony, 2001.

Idiong, Inno. *A Brief History of Mission Struggles in Africa: The Experience of a Christian in Nigeria*. Gibbon: Starland Hutterian Brethren, 2000.

———. *How to Live Wisely in the Midst of Acute Poverty*. Farmington: Plough Publishing House, 1992.

———. *The Genesis of the Hutterian Brethren in Nigeria*. Farmington: Plough Publishing House, 1992.

———. *We Failed More than Once but God's Love Lingers On*. [Rifton]: Woodcrest Bruderhof, 1994.

Kleinsasser, Jacob. *A Visit to Palmgrove Community, November 23–December 15, 1995*. Ste. Agathe: Crystal Spring Colony, [1996].

———. *The Journey to Nigeria: The Report of our Visit to Palmgrove Community, May 1995*. Ste. Agathe: Crystal Spring Colony, [1995].

## Film

Alleway, Lynn, dir. *How to get to Heaven with the Hutterites*. Cymru Wales: BBC, 2013.

Buller, Burton, dir. *The Hutterites: To Care or Not to Care*. Gateway Video/Vision Video, 1984.

Canell, Marrin, dir. *God's Dominion: By the Word of God*. Montreal: National Film Board Of Canada, 1993.

Collins, Jeff, prod. *American Colony: Meet the Hutterites.* National Geographic Channel, 2012. The first season included 10 episodes: 1. Harvest Party Scandal; 2. The Shunning; 3. Rockin' Road Trip; 4. Battle of the Sexes; 5. Shoot to Kill; 6. ER Bound; 7. Show Me the Money!; 8. Breaking the Law; 9. We're Not a Cult; 10. Barnburners.

Flinn-White, Rebecca, dir. *Hutterite*. 2017

Holzer, Louis, dir. *Jakob Hutter und die Hutterer: Märtyrer des Glaubens*. Lienz: TAURA Film, 2004.

Kasseroler, Marianne, prod. *Land & Leben: Das Leben und Wirtschaften der Hutterer in Amerika*. Raiffeisenverband Südtirol, 2015.

Low, Colin, dir. *The Hutterites*. National Film Board of Canada, 1991.

"In Community: A Hutterite Experience." *Manitoba Moments*, CTV News/JAR Communications, 2006.

Marshall, Peter D., dir. *Eli's Lesson*. Astral Video, 1993. Starring Robbie Bowen, Kenneth Welsh, and Jack Palance.

Nimoy, Leonard, dir. *Holy Matrimony*. Burbank: Buena Vista Pictures, 1994.

Potter, Chris, dir. *Heartland*. Season 8, episode 7, "Walk a Mile." Toronto: Canadian Broadcasting Corporation, 2014.

Powell, Michael, dir. *49th Parallel*. Culver City: Columbia Pictures, 1941.

Smith, Bryan, dir. *Born Hutterite*. Black Hat Productions, National Film Board, 1996.

Stanjek, Klaus, dir. *Kinder der Utopie/Children of Utopia*. Berlin: Ventana, 1999.

_____. *Kommune der Seligen/Commune of Bliss*. Werder: Cinetarium, 2004.

Treays, Jane, prod. *How to get to Heaven in Montana*. London: British Broadcasting Corporation, 1992.

www.ingramcontent.com/pod-product-compliance
Lightning Source LLC
Chambersburg PA
CBHW061753070526
44586CB00023B/2601